First Print Edition [1.0] -1432 H. (2011 C.E.)

http://taalib.com
Learn Islaam, Live Islaam.SM

Taalib al-Ilm Education Resources products are made available through distributors worldwide. To view a list of current distributors in your region, or information about our distributor/referral program please visit our website. Discounts on bulk quantities of our products are available to community groups, religious institutions, and other not-for-profit entities, inshAllaah. For details and discount information, contact the special sales department by e-mail:
service@taalib.com.

The publisher requests that any corrections regarding translations or knowledge based issues, be sent to us at:
service@taalib.com. Readers should note that internet web sites offered as citations and/or sources for further information may have changed or no longer be available between the time this was written and when it is read.

We publish a variety of full text and free preview edition electronic ebook formats. Some content that appears in print may not be available in electronic book versions.

ISBN: 1-4538-7721-5 [Print Edition]
EAN-13: 978-1-453-87721-0 [Print Edition]

From the Publisher

Golden Words Upon Golden Words...For Every Muslim.

"Imaam Al-Barbahaaree, may Allaah have mercy upon him said:

May Allaah have mercy upon you! Examine carefully the speech of everyone you hear from in your time particularly. So do not act in haste and do not enter into anything from it until you ask and see: Did any of the Companions of the Prophet, may Allaah's praise and salutations be upon him, speak about it, or did any of the scholars? So if you find a narration from them about it, cling to it, do not go beyond it for anything and do not give precedence to anything over it and thus fall into the Fire.

Explanation by Sheikh Saaleh al-Fauzaan, may Allaah preserve him:

'Do not be hasty in accepting as correct what you may hear from the people especially in these later times. As now there are many who speak about so many various matters, issuing rulings and ascribing to themselves both knowledge and the right to speak. This is especially the case after the emergence and spread of new modern day media technologies. Such that everyone now can speak and bring forth that which is in truth worthless; by this meaning words of no true value - speaking about whatever they wish in the name of knowledge and in the name of the religion of Islaam. It has even reached the point that you find the people of misguidance and the members of the various groups of misguidance and deviance from the religion speaking as well. Such individuals have now become those who speak in the name of the religion of Islaam through means such as the various satellite television channels. Therefore be very cautious!

It is upon you oh Muslim, and upon you oh student of knowledge individually, to verify matters and not rush to embrace everything and anything you may hear. It is upon you to verify the truth of what you hear, asking, 'Who else also makes this same statement or claim?', 'Where did this thought or concept originate or come from?', 'Who is its reference or source authority?'. Asking what are the evidences which support it from within the Book and the Sunnah? And inquiring where has the individual who is putting this forth studied and taken his knowledge from? From who has he studied the knowledge of Islaam?

Each of these matters requires verification through inquiry and investigation, especially in the present age and time. As it is not every speaker who should rightly be considered a source of knowledge, even if he is well spoken and eloquent, and can manipulate words captivating his listeners. Do not be taken in and accept him until you are aware of the degree and scope of what he possesses of knowledge and understanding. As perhaps someone's words may be few, but possess true understanding, and perhaps another will have a great deal of speech yet he is actually ignorant to such a degree that he doesn't actually possess anything of true understanding. Rather he only has the ability to enchant with his speech so that the people are deceived. Yet he puts forth the perception that he is a scholar, that he is someone of true understanding and comprehension, that he is a capable thinker, and so forth. Through such means and ways he is able to deceive and beguile the people, taking them away from the way of truth.

Therefore what is to be given true consideration is not the amount of the speech put forth or that one can extensively discuss a subject. Rather the criterion that is to be given consideration is what that speech contains within it of sound authentic knowledge, what it contains of the established and transmitted principles of Islaam. As perhaps a short or brief statement which is connected to or has a foundation in the established principles can be of greater benefit than a great deal of speech which simply rambles on, and through hearing you don't actually receive very much benefit from.

This is the reality which is present in our time; one sees a tremendous amount of speech which only possesses within it a small amount of actual knowledge. We see the presence of many speakers yet few people of true understanding and comprehension.' "

[The eminent major scholar Sheikh Saaleh al-Fauzaan, may Allaah preserve him- 'A Valued Gift for the Reader Of Comments Upon the Book Sharh as-Sunnah', page 102-103]

﴾ ***Is not He better than your so-called gods, He Who originates creation and shall then repeat it, and Who provides for you from heaven and earth? Is there any god with Allaah? Say: 'Bring forth your proofs, if you are truthful.'*** ﴿-(Surah an-Naml: 64)

Explanation: ﴾ ***Say: "Bring forth your proofs...*** ﴿ This is a command for the Prophet, may Allaah's praise and salutations be upon him, to rebuke them immediately after they had put forward their own rebuke. Meaning: '*Say to them: bring your proof, whether it is an intellectual proof or a proof from transmitted knowledge, that would stand as evidence that there is another with Allaah, the Most Glorified and the Most Exalted*'. Additionally, it has been said that it means: '*Bring your proof that there is anyone other than Allaah, the Most High, who is capable of doing that which has been mentioned from His actions, the Most Glorified and the Most Exalted.*' ﴾***...if you are truthful.***﴿ meaning, in this claim. From this it is derived that a claim is not accepted unless clearly indicated by evidences."

[Tafseer al-'Aloosee, vol. 15, page 14]

Sheikh Rabee'a Ibn Hadee Umair al-Madkhalee, may Allaah preserve him said,

'It is possible for someone to simply say, "*So and so said such and such.*" However we should say, "*Produce your proof.*" So why did you not ask them for their proof by saying to them: "*Where was this said?*" Ask them questions such as this, as from your weapons are such questions as: "*Where is this from? From which book? From which cassette?...*" '

[The Overwhelming Falsehoods of 'Abdul-Lateef Bashmeel' page 14]

The guiding scholar Imaam Sheikh 'Abdul-'Azeez Ibn Abdullah Ibn Baaz, may Allaah have mercy upon him, said,

'It is not proper that any intelligent individual be mislead or deceived by the great numbers from among people from the various countries who engage in such a practice. As the truth is not determined by the numerous people who engage in a matter, rather the truth is known by the Sharee'ah evidences. Just as Allaah the Most High says in Surah Al-Baqarah, ﴾ ***And they say, "None shall enter Paradise unless he be a Jew or a Christian." These are only their own desires. Say "Produce your proof if you are truthful."*** ﴿-(Surah Al-Baqarah: 111) And Allaah the Most High says ﴾ ***And if you obey most of those on the earth, they will mislead you far away from Allaah's path. They follow nothing but conjectures, and they do nothing but lie.*** ﴿-(Surah Al-'Ana'an: 116)'

[Collection of Rulings and Various Statements of Sheikh Ibn Baaz -Vol. 1 page 85]

Sheikh Muhammad Ibn 'Abdul-Wahaab, may Allaah have mercy upon him, said,

'Additionally verify that knowledge held regarding your beliefs, distinguishing between what is correct and false within it, coming to understand the various areas of knowledge of faith in Allaah alone and the required disbelief in all other objects of worship. You will certainly see various different matters which are called towards and enjoined; so if you see that a matter is in fact one coming from Allaah and His Messenger, then this is what is intended and is desired that you possess. Otherwise, Allaah has certainly given you that which enables you to distinguish between truth and falsehood, if Allaah so wills.

Moreover, this writing of mine- do not conceal it from the author of that work; rather present it to him. He may repent and affirm its truthfulness and then return to Allaah, or perhaps if he says that he has a proof for his claims, even if that is only a single statement or if he claims that within my statements there is something unsupported, then request his evidence for that assertion. After this if there is something which continues to cause uncertainty or is a problem for you, then refer it back to me, so that then you are aware of both his statement and mine in that issue. We ask Allaah to guide us, you, and all the Muslims to that which He loves and is pleased with.'

[Personal Letters of Sheikh Muhammad Ibn 'Abdul-Wahaab- Conclusion to Letter 20]

Sheikh 'Abdullah Ibn 'Abdur-Rahman Abu Bateen, may Allaah have mercy upon him, said,

'And for an individual, if it becomes clear to him that something is the truth, he should not turn away from it or be discouraged simply due to the few people who agree with him and the many who oppose him in that, especially in these latter days of this present age.

If the ignorant one says: "*If this was the truth so and so and so and so would have been aware of it!*" However this is the very claim of the disbelievers, in their statement found in the Qur'an ﴿ ***If it had truly been good, they would not have preceded us to it!*** "﴾-(Surah al-Ahqaaf: 11) and in their statement ﴿ ***Is it these whom Allaah has favored from amongst us?*** "﴾-(Surah al-Ana'am: 53). Yet certainly as Alee Ibn Abee Taalib, may Allaah be pleased with him, stated "*Know the truth and then you will know it's people.*" But for the one who generally stands upon confusion and uncertainty, then every doubt swirls around him. And if the majority of the people were in fact upon the truth today, then Islaam would not be considered strange, yet by Allaah it is today seen as the most strange of affairs!"

[Durrur As-Sunneeyyah -vol. 10, page 400]

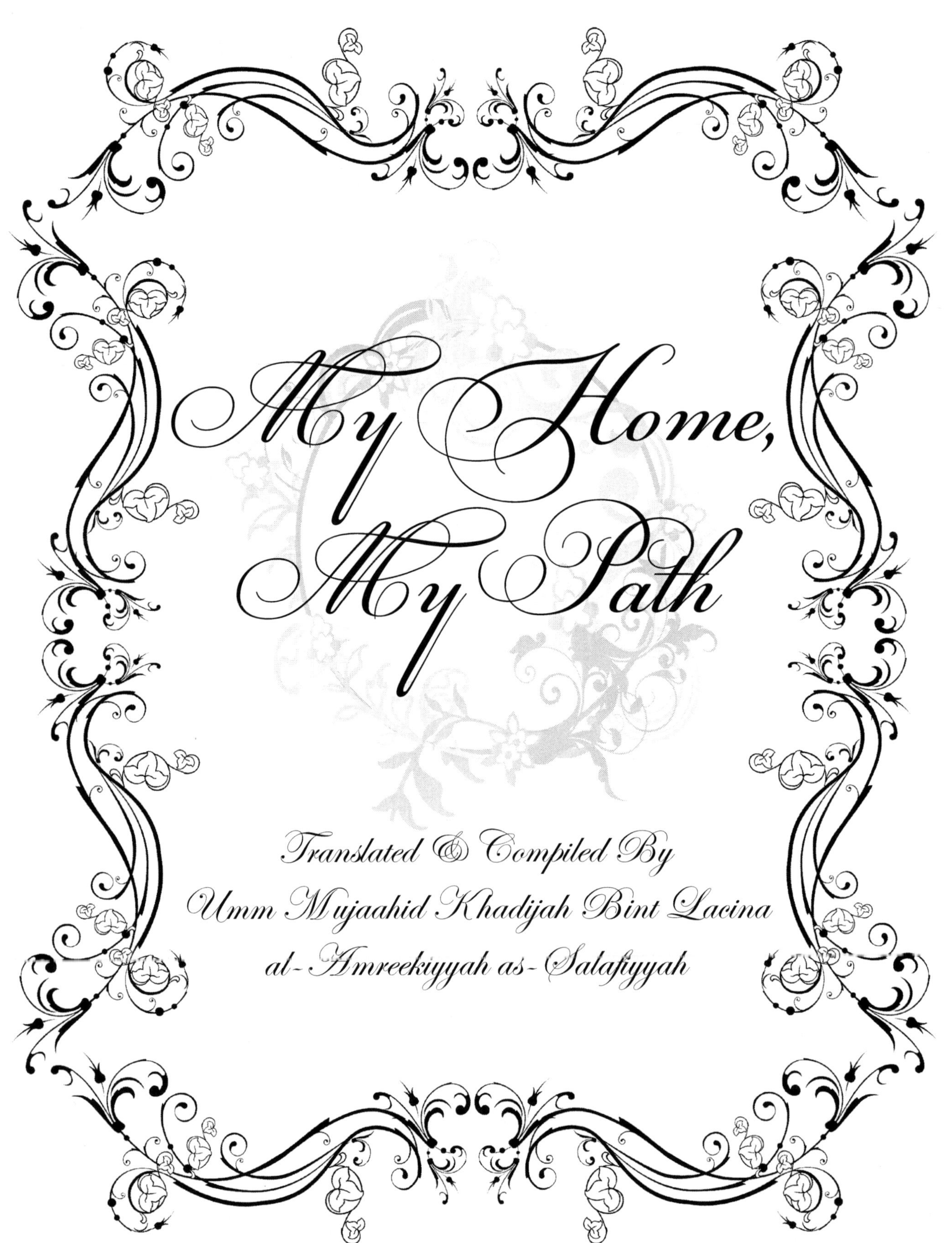

My Home, My Path

Translated & Compiled By
Umm Mujaahid Khadijah Bint Lacina
al-Amreekiyyah as-Salafiyyah

Table of Contents

Publisher's Introduction

All praise is due to Allaah, Lord of the Worlds, peace and salutations be upon the Messenger of Allaah, his household, his Companions, and all those who follow his guidance until the day of Judgment. To proceed:

The place of the Muslim woman and her essential contribution and fundamental influence in increasing the spread of the light Islaam through our world is undeniable. Yet the problem often faced today by many Muslim women is not fully understanding the true alternative which the perfect religion of Islaam opens up and offers to them to use their many blessings and abilities to please Allaah and strengthen Islaam. What are the priorities, goals, and foundations of her essential role? How can she be a successful Muslimah in today's world? Who should we turn to in order to understand these crucial issues? Should this be undertaken upon the western model of working women first and foremost, and educators and caretakers of their children secondarily? In looking at this issue the guiding scholar Imaam ash-Shanqeetee, may Allaah have mercy upon him stated in his explanation of the Qur'an, "*Adhuaa' Al-Bayaan*" vol. 4 page 381-383

"A complete and definitive investigation of the issue indicates that modern western civilization, as has been mentioned, encompasses aspects of both benefit and harm. As for that which is of benefit, it is by way of material development, and its preeminence in every such area of technical development is more apparent than my having to elucidate it, and what it encompasses of potential usefulness to humanity is greater than what can be covered in a limited description. Their service to humanity from the direction of approaching him as a living animal has been tremendous.

But as for that which is harmful is its comprehensive negligence and disregard of that aspect of human life which is the head of every good, without which there cannot truly be any benefit and good in the world of this life without its presence- the spiritual cultivation of humanity and its moral education. This cannot be achieved except through the light of heavenly revelation which clarifies for humanity the path of contentment and lays out a wise plan and structure for every area of human life in this world and the next world, and so connecting them to their Lord at every moment.

Therefore modern western civilization abounds with benefit in the first aspect or area, while being tremendously deficient and nearly bankrupt from the second aspect or area. Additionally, it is acknowledged and well known that the domination of materialism over the concern for spiritual wellbeing has ruined much of the world, as is witnessed in the numerous dangers and decimating forms of social ruin which have suddenly collected around us. Yet the desired goal of freeing ourselves from these dilemmas will never be possible unless humanity is illuminated by the guiding light of heavenly revelation which has been legislated by the Creator of both the heavens and the earth. Because the one whose material existence completely rules and commands him such that he rebels against the One who created him and sustains him - will never be successful. Therefore the correct division of the possible positions one might take in their relationship to western civilization falls into four options, all which are based upon an intelligent division about which there is no doubt.

Firstly, the complete abandonment of western civilization, both what it contains of benefit and what it contains of harm.

Secondly, the total embrace of western civilization completely, including what it contains of benefit and what it contains of harm.

Thirdly, taking what it contains of harm while leaving what it contains of true benefit.

Fourthly, taking what it contains of true benefit while leaving what it contains of harm.

The correctness of the fourth category is what invariably becomes clear through a sound examination and division of affairs. That being to take what is beneficial and to abandon that which is harmful. And this is the way that the Messenger of Allaah, may Allaah's praise and salutations be upon him, proceeded. Indeed, he benefited and made use of the defensive trench during the Battle of the Parties despite that fact that as a military tactic its origin was from the Persians. Yet when Salman al-Farsi informed him of it, the fact that its origin came from the disbelievers did not prevent him from utilizing it for defense...

...Consequently it becomes apparent from these evidences that the natural position to be adopted by Islaam and the Muslims in relation to modern western society is to strive to benefit from it from the direction of material and technological progress, and to still be warned away from what they have plunged into from rebellion against the Creator of everything, High and Exalted is He. This enables the successful rectification of their worldly affairs and the affair of their success in the next life."

May Allaah reward our scholars for such explanations which clarify both our perspective and the straight path. Indeed the inheritors of our prophet are the ones we must turn to in order to understand these significant issues that affect all Muslims. Yet for the enemies of Islaam, this balanced position stated by Imaam Shanqeetee, may Allaah have mercy upon him, which many Muslims choose to adopt with foresight, freedom, and the responsibility of self determination -is not acceptable. What they consider necessary is a wholesale abandonment of the sources and practices of Islaam and an indiscriminate embracing of the western way of life and ideals, with Muslims merely being permitted to maintain a shallow outward cultural connection to certain aspects, or a token ritual attachment to what in reality is a rich, comprehensive path of Islamic guidance and, as history bears witness to, a culture and civilization. But for those threatened by Islaam to accomplish this long term objective the scholars state that it is necessary that the Muslims be distanced -through various means both apparent and subtle- from the guidance of the Book of Allaah and the Sunnah of our beloved Prophet, may Allaah's praise and salutations be upon him. The Messenger of Allaah, may Allaah's praise and salutations be upon him, clearly said during his farewell pilgrimage, as found in "*Al-Mustadrak*" of Imaam Haakim, narrated in an authentic hadeeth from Abu Hurairah, ***{ Certainly, I am leaving with you two things which if you hold fast to them, you will not go astray; the Book of Allaah and my Sunnah ... }*** Sheikh Rabee'a al-Madhkhalee describes this assault to separate us from these two anchors of guidance and the proper response towards it by saying:

"Indeed the enemies of Islaam understand perfectly the effect of the Qur'an and Sunnah upon the lives of the Muslims, so they artfully and ingeniously attempt to bring about a separation between the Muslims and the Eternal Book and the pure Sunnah of the Prophet; these two sources which, in both the past and present times, came forward to bring forth and produce the true life of sincere faith, and which have brought forth among the Muslims the spirit of jihaad, thus enabling them to achieve victory over their enemies. As when they adhere firmly to the Book of their Lord and the Sunnah of their Prophet then Allaah is with them, aids them, and grants them victory over their enemies.

As such, it is clearly seen that underneath the slogan of "scholastic research", and "freedom of thought", the advocates of western thought, the colonizers, the crusaders, the Zionists, and the socialists all attempt to confront and attack the Qur'an, with an evil assault and variety of true hostility.

In the name of "civilization" and "culture" they struggle to uproot what Islaam contains of true legislative guidance and proper worship.

In the name of "freedom of thought" they promote supposed "freedom" from the "shackles" of the fundamental and essential beliefs of Islaam, and by these different means they shake and loosen the foundations of the religion of Islaam within those individuals who are unsteady in their practice.

In the name of "scholastic research" they claim that the Qur'an is in fact valued and held in esteem solely by individuals who are weak and lack any true strength of understanding. And these forms of attack are more severe and harmful upon Islaam and the Muslims than any of the military wars which are launched against them!

But there is no true response nor any sound defense against their strategy and their abominable efforts, except that we fortify our youth through education upon the Book of Allaah and the Sunnah, that we arm and equip them with decisive proofs and evidences that eliminate deceptions such as this assault of falsehood and these false claims coming from the enemies of Islaam. Otherwise we will not be able to produce within our societies the truly Muslim soldier, and the Muslim doctor, and the Muslim engineer, as well as producing the insightful Muslim scholar of hadeeth, and the discerning Muslim scholar who understands how to apply the guidance of the source texts.

Yet all of these mentioned objectives can be realized through that methodology of education which we have explained clearly and discussed, if Allaah so wills."

[The Book and the Sunnah and their Effect, Position, and Necessity in Establishing the Educational Methodology Within our Schools - Sheikh Rabee'a Ibn Haadee 'Umair al-Madkhalee- Magazine of the Islamic University of Medinah: vol. 67]

A further clarification of this false call of indiscriminate abandonment of Islamic guidance regarding the precious women of this Ummah, and its supposed replacement by the western social model -as well as describing those Muslims who have wrongly embraced it- is found in the words of the guiding scholar Sheikh Muhammad Ibn Saaleh al-'Utheimeen, may Allaah have mercy upon him, when explaining the hadeeth of Umm Salamah as narrated in Saheeh al-Bukharee (no. 870) which states:

{ Whenever Allah's Apostle completed the prayer with taslim, the women used to get up immediately, and Allah's Apostle would remain at his place for some time before getting up.} The sub-narrator, Az-Zuhri, said, "We believe, and Allah knows best, that he did so, so that the women might leave before any of the men would encounter them."

He, may Allaah have mercy upon him, stated,

"Within this there is very clear evidence that from among the goals and objectives of Islaam is restricting the interaction of women with men. That the standard and principle of Islaam is the public separation of men from women as opposed to the Western disbelieving standard which aims to encourage the unrestricted mixing of women among men. It is a practice which many Muslims have been beguiled and fooled into accepting today, such that they have no concern or consideration about the free interaction of a woman with any unrelated man. Rather they see this as an aspect of democracy, development, and progress!

Whereas in reality it is an indication of backwardness and regression. Because the unrestricted mixing of women among men is simply for the satisfaction of the desires of men at the cost and detriment of women. So where in this is the liberating democracy that they claim?!

In fact, this is oppression and injustice; as for what is truly justice then that is found within the woman remaining safeguarded and protected, not being sported and toyed with by men, neither by their lustful gazes, nor through their speech nor through physical contact, nor through any matter which inevitably leads to and requires that their harm and tribulation come from it. However, due to a weakness of faith and being distant from the teachings of Islaam, those deceived Muslims have been beguiled by the practices found among the disbelieving societies.

We assuredly know, holding this as something we have continually affirmed, that the disbelieving nations slowly suffer from a chronic condition of illness under the pressure of this established practice, and would like to free themselves from the consequences of this custom of unrestricted mixing- however they are not able to do so. As such the damage to the fabric of their society has only continued to increase.

Yet that which also causes our regret are those from amongst the Muslims who have also attached themselves to the movement of those who were calling to what they have entitled "freedom", while in reality it is simply the freedom of unchecked or unrestricted desires, not a guided freedom. Just as was mentioned by Ibn Qayyim, may Allaah mercy on him,

They flee from that servitude for which they were created

only to be captured and afflicted by servitude to individual desires and to Shaytaan.

As "that servitude for which they were created" is servitude and submission to Allaah, the Most Glorified and the Most Exalted, such that they stand as a true worshiper of Allaah. However these individuals from among the Muslims flee from and fight this true submission, only end up entrapped by another form of servitude to individual desires and Shaytaan. They end up being those who continually call others and devise plans for the sake of bringing forth a situation in which men and women are upon an equal level of participation in the office workplace, in commercial shops, and in every social institution.

Certainly I bear witness by Allaah that these individuals are individuals who are defrauding and swindling their religion and the Muslims in general. As it is an obligation that the Muslim takes his beliefs and teachings from the Book of Allaah and from the Sunnah of the Messenger of Allaah, may Allaah's praise and salutations be upon him, and from the guidance of the first three righteous generations of Muslims. And we if we look at the wise teaching of the Sharee'ah, we find that it strives in every possible way it is able to prevent the unrestricted mixing of men and women.

For this reason the Messenger of Allaah , may Allaah's praise and salutations be upon him, would remain sitting after saying the tasleem at the completion of his prayer in order that those women who were praying would be able to leave without them having to mix with those men who prayed. This is despite the clear fact that the people in that time and age were purer and better than the people in our present time, and stronger in their faith as was mentioned by the Prophet, may Allaah's praise and salutations be upon him, ***{ The best of people are my generation, then those that come after them, then those that come after them...}***

[Sharh Al-Mumta'a Alaa Zaad Al-Mustagna' vol. 4 page 307]

And specifically related to the call to denigrate the place and position of the Muslim home which Islaam makes the primary sphere of societal contribution for striving Muslim women, Sheikh al-'Utheimeen, may Allaah have mercy upon him, was asked,

"Esteemed Sheikh do you have a word of guidance for those women who say staying in the home is like being in a prison?"

He responded,

"Yes, that which I have to say to that Muslim woman who holds her house to be a prison, if this expression can be considered correct, is that this way is from Allaah, the Most Glorified and the Most Exalted. As Allaah the Most High says, ﴿ ***And remain within your homes*** ﴾ *and as it is found in the narration of the Prophet, may Allaah's praise and salutations be upon him, regarding women,* **{... And their homes are better for them.}** *A women within her house is free to go to any area of the house, and take care of any needs within her home, and work for herself, so where is the confinement and where is the prison? Yes, it could be considered a prison by the one who wishes to needlessly go out and be like men. But what is well known is that Allaah, the Most High, gave men specific characteristics, and women specific characteristics, and distinguished between men and women in His creation of them in terms of physical traits, intellectual traits, character traits, and aspects of the religion, according to what was required by the boundaries and guidelines of Allaah, the Most Glorified and the Most Exalted....*

....So it is upon women to fear Allaah and to refer back to whatever was stated by their Lord and their Creator, and refer back to whatever was directed by the Messenger of the Lord of all the worlds to them and to other women. And that they be aware and know that they will meet Allah, the Most Glorified and the Most Exalted, and that He will ask them what was their response and stance towards the Messenger sent to them and his guidance. And indeed no one knows when an individual will return back to Allaah and be questioned. Certainly a woman might start the morning within her home, her fortress, and when the evening arrives she would have entered her grave. Or she may spend the evening in her house, by when the morning arrives she has entered her grave. Therefore these Muslim women must fear Allaah, and turn away from the corrupt Western callers. As these western callers are those who, after they consumed that corruption, they threw its remaining bones and gristle to us. And some of us snatched up that remaining bone and gristle after these western nations have already consumed whatever benefit it had!

Rather, a woman should be like that Muslim woman who resides in her house, living her proper life, being distant from all places of trials and societal corruption. However they, as women, are now confronted by these issues; and they are being assaulted as women from a far off location. So we must build a wall for ourselves, as we are Muslims; we have our own religion, we have our own unique nature, we have our own manners, and we have our own character. Yet we still are hurrying along behind the disbelievers gasping and out of breath due to our efforts to follow them into corruption. How free is Allah, the Powerful from any imperfection or shortcoming, indeed there is no change nor power except in Allaah!"

[From the Radio Program Nur Alaa Dharb]

There remains no question today that one of the greatest dangers facing the Muslim woman who wishes to reflect and practice Islaam within her life, are those deceived and misguided Muslims whose propaganda she must confront as mentioned by our guiding scholars. It is very important to be aware, as has been stated clearly by Sheikh al-Fauzaan and others within the texts of this book, that the carriers of the banners of this corrupt call to change Islaam and its guidance regarding gender based roles for the well being of society, are those who state that they are Muslim and that they are doing this for the benefit of Islaam, as he states, *"this is the amazing thing, that these enemies are from amongst us ... "*. So consider, dear reader, in detail, the exposure by Sheikh Muhammad al-Imaam of the false claims which such individuals around the world bring forward in struggling to get us to understand, "why the Muslims must change", as well as some of the undeniable realities of those Muslims who have accepted and chosen to promote this false call to Muslims from outside Islaam. He poses the following questions in his extraordinary work '*The Immense Plot Again the Muslim Woman' (page 496)* for every striving Muslim and Muslimah when faced with this issue to carefully consider:

"Questions for the reader.

1. Could it ever be possible that the true beneficial rights of women be given to them through the ways of the Judeo-Christian societies, which have disbelieved in Allaah, and rejected the truth of His creating them, providing for them, and blessing them with so many varied types of blessings?

2. Could it ever be possible that Judeo-Christian societies be more merciful to the woman than her Lord who created her?? Those very societies who hold that Islaam is only an oppression upon her and that which dissolves her rights, advancing this claim like no others have?

3. Is it possible that they, these societies, are more knowledgeable than Allaah about what is beneficial for His worshippers, and from within those matters is knowledge of what is needed by the woman?

4. Is it conceivable that all of the Muslims through history from the time of the Messenger of Allaah, may Allaah's praise and salutations be upon him, up until our present time have consistently neglected the true rights of women, such that now disbelieving Judeo-Christian societies which are ignorant of Allah's guidance could come forward today to properly give women their rights?

5. Could it be considered as making sense that Judeo-Christian societies which have been historically guilty of injustice all across the world could now step forward as being more merciful to the Muslim woman than her own father, mother, and close relations?

6. Has there ever occurred historically any instance where the enemies of the Muslims have brought forth anything that truly secured and ensured well being for the Muslims, even to the smallest degree? Then how then could our enemies now suddenly become those who secure for us our honor and rights?!

7. Has there come about any actual elevation of Muslim women through the way of turning to and raising complaints to the Jews and then to the Christians and requesting from them these alleged rights? Or rather have these nations in fact regularly approached Muslim women deceptively and disguised, using every subterfuge and deception in their affairs?

8. Who has authorized and granted permission to Judeo-Christian societies to undertake this war as soldiers in these issues which are specific to our societies, such as the role and position of Muslim women?

9. Is it possible or conceivable that these individuals from among the corrupted ones from within Muslim societies who now stand forward with this call (such as those proponents of the western definition of "rights") who in fact are people who have only been cultivated and educated by our enemies, could they be sensibly believed to truly be those who are serving us and our religion??

10. Is it possible that those corrupted proponents of establishing western "rights" from among those who have come out from of our Muslim societies could realistically bring about their claim of true rights for women, while they stand as those who contradict the guidance of the Noble Qur'an and Pure Sunnah and that goodness which the people of knowledge and rectification have always been established upon from the time of the Messenger of Allaah, may Allaah's praise and salutations be upon him, up until our present age!?!

11. Is it something more beneficial for us that these tainted individuals who have come forth from our Muslim societies who have accepted the corruption of Europe and the West, and who have then proceeded to deceive the Muslims regarding it under the title of "modern civilization" and "rights"? Such that they have betrayed and sold out the Muslims with the worst form of treachery: that being that they have facilitated the path for Muslims to apostate and eventually disbelieve in their religion?!? Where is their faith and their attachment to their religion, to their Ummah, and to their Muslim societies?

12. Do those corrupted individuals who are proponents of establishing western "rights" within our Muslim societies have as a basis independently striving to establish such "rights" internally and in cooperation with the people of their own lands? Or is the very basis of their efforts that they are standing upon the "shoulders" of -meaning supported by- those who are from among our enemies?

13. Is it possible that these proponents of establishing western "rights" truly have sound intentions and goals when they clearly act as tools for the plans and designs of those from among the nations of the Christians and Jews??

14. Do those corrupted individuals from among the proponents of establishing western "rights" within our Muslim societies stand as those who struggle against the ones who curse Allaah and the Messenger of Allaah, may Allaah's praise and salutations be upon him, and fight against his religion, and have targeted him Ummah? Or do they in fact stand with them?

15. Is it acceptable that we embrace this call which comes from those who have come forth from our own Muslim societies as proponents of establishing western "rights" while they have sold away their honor to our enemies by receiving significant amounts of compensation and money for their efforts to spread this ideology?

16. Is it acceptable to us that those who act with treachery towards their land, their Ummah, and their society, and those who have embraced this lowly servile call, is it acceptable to us that whenever their foreign backers say anything they reply, "Indeed, how true how true!" And whenever their foreign backers do anything they say "How excellent!"?

17. Is it possible that those who have come forth as proponents of establishing western "rights" from our own Muslim societies understand and are more knowledgeable of what will benefit the Ummah than those well grounded guiding scholars, and those knowledgeable callers to rectification and a return to Islaam?

18. Have those individuals who claim to advocate the "rights" of Muslim women ever called for struggling against the oppressions of Jewish and Christian societies against us? Or have such individuals who raise this call from our own Muslim societies established any efforts to call the young men and women of our society towards establishing the rights of their mothers and fathers, brothers and sisters, and neighbors upon them? Or in fact is it the case that we have come to see that those who stand forth with such efforts to gain "rights" in those Muslim societies- how severely they struggle against the way of morality and virtue, and how severely they rebel against establishing these rights of others and similar matters from Islaam.

19. Are those individuals from among those proponents of establishing western "rights" for Muslim women who have come forth from our Muslim societies- are they individuals who the people out of their own self determination have chosen and invested them with authority regarding advocating for the daughters of Muslim Societies, or are they those who have imposed themselves upon them forcibly without the people's choice? And why?"

So dear Muslims take heed and examine everything you read or listen to on this crucial subject, and beware of those who only serve as corrupted intermediaries by calling to and facilitating the abandonment of various aspects of the Islamic path and way of guidance. And remember, as our scholars continually remind us:

"... What is obligatory upon the Muslims is that they protect and preserve the honor given to their women. That they do not turn their faces toward misguided callers, and that they carefully consider the harmful results which have already befallen women in those societies who accepted this call and the claims of such misguided callers and were so deceived by them. Indeed, the content and happy one is the one who takes a lesson from that misfortune which has happened to someone else."

[Rulings by Permanent Committee for Scholastic Research & Issuing of Islamic Rulings: vol. 17 page 377]

Yet this is not only for the Muslim women in Muslim countries, it also applies for the Muslim woman who is a convert within a society whose general direction, model, and focus for women opposes Islaam. So the following guidance from the eminent guiding scholar Muhammad Naasiruddeen al-Albaanee, may Allaah have mercy upon him, applies to many misguided callers among Muslim communities in Western countries as well as to those within the Muslim countries themselves:

"But indeed, it is upon this Muslim woman who truly and properly adheres to her religion, whenever she is put to trial and tested by any matter relating to her role and social interaction with her present day society, that she strive to save and protect herself from being affected by and harmed from those ways of deviation and separation from the truth that many women have fallen into. The causes of which we have mentioned, such as corrupt and deficient educating and upbringing, as well as the corruption of society. And this is only a reminder, as indeed the reminder benefits the believers. "

[From the tape series "Gatherings of Guidance & Light": From tape number 19]

In the Muslim countries such callers strive to make it easy for a Muslim woman to become a so-called "modern Muslimah" based upon the western social ideal. In the case of the convert the objective may be to ensure that the striving Muslim woman never really challenges and questions the western ideal and model, for fear that she might turn away from that ideal and the partial and limited reflection of Islaam that is compatible with it, and freely choose to fully step into the light of Islaam and the Sunnah, inviting that light into every area of her life.

But in either situation, for the sincere Muslim and Muslimah anywhere in the world who thoughtfully examines what our scholars have indicated and then recognizes the falseness of this false call which claims to be the key to success of Muslims in the modern world, a new question inevitably comes forward: "*Then what is the real way to our success as believing men and women in today's world? What is the foundation of our success if not this? How can we be successful as Muslims and rectify the problems we see all around us? How can we change the present Muslim situation in which other countries have dominated us?*" Sheikh Muhammad al-Imaam in that same work regarding the effort to corrupt Muslim women states,

"The path to the rectification of all our various conditions.

The path of general rectification is given precedence over the way of openly confronting our enemies, because the path of general rectification is the first primary foundation and confronting them a secondary foundation.

There can be no confronting them except by first giving precedence to general rectification, as it is the true foundation. Furthermore, general rectification is an individual obligation in every circumstance and every age and location. But as for the way of openly confronting our enemies, then it is not required in all situations; rather its ruling differs according to the differing circumstances. Additionally, general rectification in its comprehensive meaning encompasses aspects of confrontation, while open confrontation is more restricted and does not necessarily include or encompass the general rectification of our affairs.

That rectification that we want and that which we call to is the rectification of beliefs, such that the beliefs of the Muslims become sound and authentic- free from any blemishes and significant deficiencies. Likewise the rectification of our performance of ritual acts of worship from any significant shortcoming or errors. And the rectification of our characters, such that they be high excellent characters far from any type of failings and flaws. As well as the rectification of our acts of mutual dealings and interactions such that they stand far and distant from any type of wrongdoing, whether regarding the right of Allaah upon us or regarding the right of the creation upon us. And the rectification of our affairs of general governance, such that they are free from the flaws of the deceptions and deceivers, forgery and hypocrisy. And rectification of our economic affairs, such that they are free from the deficiencies of doubtful and clearly forbidden transactions, starting with the most important of them, interest in economic transactions.

Through these the rectification which Allaah decreed and desires will be realized, As Allaah, the Most High has stated. ﴾ **Allaah has promised those among you who believe, and do righteous good deeds, that He will certainly grant them succession to the present rulers in the earth, as He granted it to those before them, and that He will grant them the authority to practice their religion, that which He has chosen for them (i.e. Islaam). And He will surely give them in exchange a safe security after their fear provided the believers worship Me and do not associate anything in worship with Me.** ﴿ *-(Surah An-Nur: 55)*

This is the rectification which we are seeking and striving to achieve, and it is facilitated for the one whom Allaah makes it easy for. And what is intended by us regarding this rectification is that we clarify and make clear to the people the path to reaching a state of goodness. And those who accept that path will find acceptance with Allaah, and the ones who reject that path gain only distance and remoteness from Allaah. Yet we could never be unaware that the people that oppose this way of rectification are numerous, and those who turn away from it are not only a few. However, that will not turn us away from stating the truth and inviting to it. And Allaah's assistance is sought, and upon him we place our trust.

The foundations of rectification.

I consider it suitable to mention some of the foundations upon which true rectification is based, and to direct you an explanation of them.

The first foundation is that the rectification of our own selves is the starting point of every form of goodness.

The second foundation is that you know your Lord who has given you your various rights.

The third foundation is that it is obligatory on every male and female Muslim, whether the ruler or the one ruled by another, to know with certainty that it is an obligation to content oneself with the rule of Allaah, with a complete satisfaction, without any doubts or misgivings, and without any contradictions.

The fourth foundation, it that it is obligatory upon everyone who believes in Allah as his Lord, and in Islaam as his religion, that he have a firm unwavering belief in the perfection of the Sharee'ah of Allaah, the way of guidance of Muhammad Ibn 'Abdullah, may Allaah's praise and salutations be upon him.

The fifth foundation is that it is obligatory for every Muslim to have an unwavering faith that the Sharee'ah of Islaam has been perfectly preserved in its entirety, from the first day that Muhammad, may Allaah's praise and salutations be upon him, was raised as a messenger, up until this very day, and that it will remain preserved up until the Day of Judgment.

The sixth foundation is that you should know, oh Muslim, that if you desire to acquire and obtain your safeguarded preserved right, by this meaning this true religion, from Allaah, Al-Wadood, and your compassionate Prophet, then it is upon you to take it from those well grounded guiding scholars.

The seventh foundation is that if you fall short in fulfilling the rights indicated by the Sharee'ah, then those others who do indeed fulfill them are indeed many, and certainly the one who is oppressed in this world can only seek for his right and achieve justice through ways which are acceptable to the Sharee'ah.

Indeed Allaah created us to worship him, and that is His right upon us. And from those forms of worship which are required by right from us are:

Purifying our worship for Him alone, not with any association, nor doing any matter to be seen by others. Being sincere in our worship without any hypocrisy, and that our completely and properly loving him means that love which is greater than our love of any created thing from what He has created, that we fear His punishment which occurs in this world or that punishment which occurs in the next. We are not secure except through trusting in Him, so we do not rely upon anyone else. We should desire that which He possesses, not seeking anything from other than Him. We must also give tremendous importance to His lofty names and attributes, and actions -understanding them in accordance with that which is suitable and required by His perfection and transcendence. That we call upon Him alone, not supplicating nor submitting, nor yielding to anyone other than Allaah. And the worship of Him, glorified is He from any fault or shortcomings, is reflected within three matters:

a. the correctness of your belief

b. the soundness and validity of your methodology and path

c. the sincerity of your aim and goal

These three cannot be achieved except by returning back to the Book of Allaah and the Sunnah according to the understanding of the Salaf, the first generations of Muslims. And perhaps one could also say that through establishing and affirming three other matters you are struggling and fighting against another three which are their opposites.

-worshiping Allaah along with fighting against the association of others in worship with Him.

-the obedience of Allaah along with opposing engaging in acts that he has prohibited.

-adhering to the Sunnah of His Messenger, may Allaah's praise and salutations be upon him, along with fighting against any innovation and changing of this religion.

As the one who establishes these three matters in the specific manner found in the Noble Qur'an and the Pure Sunnah, with a sound understanding and an upright implementation, is indeed guided to the straight path.

['The Immense Plot Again the Muslim Woman' page 523-531]

It is important to note that this work is intended to clarify and address many of the general doubts and specific misunderstandings circulating regarding the essential role of Muslim women in today's world. As has been shown, many from outside the Muslim Ummah, and many of those within it, have calls or aspects of their calls which stand in conflict with the true guidance of its prophet and messenger and those believers in every century who have always followed him in goodness. From among the Muslims who stand in conflict with some aspects of guidance are many who identify themselves as callers, and who have committed themselves to Islaam and seek to learn and convey this religion but who still may have misplaced priorities and understandings. And among these misunderstandings is the confusion among Muslim women regarding this issue of how practically to seek knowledge and still fulfill one's obligatory familial responsibilities; as what is needed is neither negligence nor excessiveness either in priorities or practice. At times there is often subtly put forward an unspoken claim that seeking non–obligatory knowledge or teaching takes precedence over the priority of the individual obligation of educating, maintaining, and raising one's family for both the caller and the student. Yet this misconception can easily be removed by the one who sincerely turns to the sources of Islaam, the tremendous incredible examples of the first believing women, and to the clarifying words of the scholars in our age. The Eminent Guiding Scholar Muqbil Ibn Haadee Al-Waadiee, may Allaah have mercy upon him- definitively clarified this when he was asked,

Question: A woman studies within her home and she prefers to remain in her home- not even going out to the masjid to study. Is she better or the woman who seeks knowledge outside and visits? His full answer was,

"The woman who stays within her home and learns within her home is better, because the Prophet, may Allaah's praise and salutation be upon him and his family, said: ***{ Do not prevent the maidservants of Allaah from attending the masjids, but their houses are better for them. }***

(A Defending Mission from Audio Lectures Upon the People of Ignorance & Sophistry: vol. 2 page 481)

In a related question regarding the difficult situation of our striving sisters in disbelieving countries, Sheikh Rabee'a is asked about the issue of women studying in the masjid as well as the proper place for women teaching,

"I have a problem as I have a sister who wishes to study the areas of knowledge of this religion in the masjid; however we have heard some of the people claim that this way is not in accordance with the path of the first generations. So what is your guidance regarding this, as we reside in this land of the disbelievers?

He responded, "If these masjids have partitions between where she is and between the men, and she then listens to the lessons, then there is no harm in this. She should not attend the lessons directly sitting along with the men. But if she is some distance from the area of men, and can listen, then this is fine. Indeed, she may have no other way to learn other than this. So she should be praised for this and encouraged upon it. And she undertakes this by not mixing with the men, nor crowding in among them shoulder to shoulder. Yes.

Questioner, "Then from this issue is the question of women teaching other women there."

Sheikh, "As for a woman teaching there in the masjid then no. She should teach within her home. As the wives of the Messenger did not used to teach in his masjid and yet they were the Mothers of all the Believers. Yet not a single one of them established a class in the masjid, may Allaah bless you, but they would teach within their homes spreading and conveying the Sunnah of the Messenger of Allaah. And this is the guidance of the righteous first generations in this matter, and every goodness is to be found in following them, as Allaah has willed. For her to be preoccupied by spending her time in the masjid, then this is a mistake. Yes. As certainly the affair of the women covers both etiquette and the issue of modesty."

Similarly the guiding scholar Sheikh al-Albaanee, may Allaah have mercy upon him, was asked,

"What is the ideal example of calling to Allaah by women?"

"I say to the women: Stay attached to their homes, as the matter of calling to Allaah (da'wah) is not for them. And I disapprove of the usage of the term "da'wah" as found between the young men, meaning by this that they are the "people of da'wah". Such that "da'wah" has become something fashionable or trendy in the present time, with every individual who learns a small amount of knowledge then becoming a "caller". In addition, this phenomenon has not stopped at the young men, but has spread to the young women, until it has even reached those women who are responsible for their households. These women then become those who turn away from much of the commitment of time needed for the responsibilities of their homes, their husbands, and their children. They turn away from these obligations, for that which is not obligatory upon them- in order that they can give "da'wah".

Yet the basic rule for the woman is that she strives within her home, and it is not legislated for her to leave except for an urgent need, due to the statement of the Prophet, may Allaah's praise and salutation be upon him, that their homes are better for them for prayer than prayer in the masjid. Despite this we see in the present age the widespread coming out of women: they may frequently go out to the masjid for general congregational prayer rather than simply going to Friday congregational prayer, while their remaining in their houses is actually better for them…":

[From the magazine Al-Isaalah, Dhul-Qaedah 1419 H., Issue 19- page 74]

Indeed we see that Allaah has blessed some of those believing women who have gained knowledge with the correct understanding of seeking the right goals through the right means, meaning that by which a knowledgeable Muslim woman can best spread knowledge and to stand firmly upon this. This is seen clearly in the affirmation of some of our senior scholars of the correctness of one sister's reply to the call by others that she come teach outside her home.

Question: A Muslim woman is asked by others to come out of her house to teach fiqh, the principles of recitation, and the various sciences of the Qur'aan in the masjid. But she responded, "Certainly calling to the religion and teaching to a small number of people is better and has precedence over going out to the masjid and engaging in calling to a larger number of people. And the clear proof of that is that this practice of studying in the masjid was not practiced by the Muslim women of the first generations. Moreover, they were never commanded to do this by the Messenger of Allaah, may Allaah's praise and salutations be upon him, despite the need of Muslim women for such teaching and learning. Rather they left this practice of teaching in the masjid to men, as the men where the ones who had the greater ability to do so, and their coming out of their homes was not associated with trials." Is this explanation correct? Which one of these two is better a woman teaching within the home with a smaller number of people or going out to the masjid to teach?

Answer: Your establishing your efforts of teaching within your house is better. Because it is safer and farther away from trials, and what is more fitting and suitable is what the first generations practiced. And the success is from Allaah, May Allaah's praise and salutations be upon our prophet Muhammad, his household, and the Companions.

Council Head- 'Abdullaah Ibn 'Abdul-'Azeez Ibn Baaz / Vice Head - "Adul-Razzaaq Al-Afeefee / Member -'Abdulluh Ghudyaan

[7th Question from Ruling number 9881 issued by the Permanent Committee for Scholastic Research & Issuing of Islamic Rulings)

So we say to our sisters assaulted by those enemies from outside of Islaam, with their call to leave the home entirely, but also confused by those of her well-intentioned sisters who claim that their way of focusing on calling others and teaching and non-obligatory study first, and to put the responsibilities of family second is best- to reject the first false call as well as the second false call, and to stand firm upon the way of the believing women of the first generations and their excellent examples which helped carry Islaam around the world! Without question it may be the case that some people or communities may have circumstances which do not allow them to implement this preferred way of our knowledgeable sisters teaching within their homes, may Allaah rectify our affairs. Yet this does not change what should be recognized as the ideal and true model called to by the Pure Sunnah and the believers' way, and our taking steps to ensure that the next generation of children understand and can follow that original blessed model which Islaam has established upon revelation. It is important to note that this book is intended not just for our Muslim sisters; rather it is also for us as Muslim fathers who strive to raise our daughters upon clear guidance in order to fully understand what we are guiding our daughters to and what we are aspiring them to be upon. But regarding the responsibility that our Lord has placed in our hands regarding educating, protecting, and safeguarding our precious families how often we fall short! Our Sheikh al-'Utheimeen, may Allaah have mercy upon him reminded us,

> "... *We have been commanded to guard our families from the Hellfire. This means that we provide them with an education which will preserve them from the Fire. But with regret, we see that many men are not truly men. Rather they are something close to being men or imitating men, but not true men.*"

[Statements of the Guiding Scholars of our Age Regarding Books & Their Advice To the Beginner Seeker of Knowledge Q. 63]

The New Review and Discussion Format & Our Expanding Online Efforts.

With the publication of this work we introduce a new book format that we hope will benefit the striving Muslims in their efforts to learn Islaam through our publications, by facilitating both the assessment of your individual understanding as well as permissible beneficial discussion about related benefits and consideration of the possible areas or ways of implementation in our daily lives as Muslims. This new format is a "review and discussion" format, and it differs from the more structured question and definition testing format, as found in our course based publications such as "*Al-Waajibaat*" (and the upcoming publication of "*Thalathatu al-Usool*"). This new format does not have any formal testing exercises; rather, it is made up of general self assessment review exercises and then discussion and consideration points at the end of each specific section. What is intended is that after the completion of each section the reader can then answer the review questions to the best of his or her ability in spoken or written format and if they find that they do not recall every answer they can use the text indicated in brackets which shows which page and page section that issue or subject was discussed. In addition, they then can also use our newly expanded website to benefit from the discussion sections with contributions from others.

The three main purposes of this format are as follows:

1. To enable a simple and easy review and checking of your overall comprehension of the text by quickly referring back to the original text, rather than to separate answers as in our other format. It does not replace the other format but is for a different purpose and for a different kind of book.
2. To facilitate and enable the opportunity for individual or shared review of the general subject matter with other students studying the same book through structured discussion at our website. This also enables other brothers and sisters to bring forth further relevant information on the same topic of discussion from the source texts and the people of knowledge about that issue or subject.
3. To make possible clarifications of those topics found within the book in which there are common

misunderstandings or misconceptions, either due to the present day lack of knowledge or due to false understanding promoted by people of misguidance of this age and the past, especially in relation to the many prevailing yet incorrect understandings and conceptions of how to implement different areas of Islaam which are put forward in our time and age. Also relevant questions can then be directed -in the appropriate time and manner -to the people of knowledge in an effort to better strive to correct that implementation. We hope this new format will be an additional tool that we Muslims can use in our studies and efforts of clarification of what is Islaam and true education and cultivation upon it.

About the Compiler & Translator

In closing I offer some background regarding the compiler and translator. So often those who attempt to explain and encourage the efforts of Muslim women to openly and wholeheartedly commit themselves to the religion of Islaam and to the tremendous role that it offers women are labeled as backwards and ignorant- in an effort to try to weaken their effect and the truth of their call. Their western detractors explain away a caller's "ignorant" attachment to Islaam as only due to their not knowing anything else nor any other way of life- that they "don't understand the freedom of the enlightened western way!" The compiler of this work, Umm Mujaahid Khadijah Bint-Lacina, was raised in a small town in the heartland of middle America. She graduated with honors from the University of Wisconsin only a short time after embracing Islaam and starting to live her life as a committed Muslim. She has been blessed with eight Muslim children she is committed to raising, and is regularly involved in various endeavors to benefit herself, fulfill her responsibility to her household, as well as her community and this blessed Ummah. Additionally, she has, in the years before traveling overseas to seek knowledge of this religion, previously run two successful small business enterprises from home - despite her main occupation as a Muslim mother and wife.

By Allaah's mercy she has been studying Islaam and the Arabic language generally since the time she embraced Islaam almost twenty years ago, and both of these subjects intensively for the past nine years from scholars and students of knowledge in the various centers of learning in Yemen and through the books and recorded lectures of the scholars of the Sunnah from throughout the world. Related to her studies in Arabic, she successfully completed two independent study seminars from the Islamic University of Medina while in the United States before having been blessed with the opportunity to study in Yemen. After beginning her language studies in Yemen with the well-known University of Medina Arabic language series through a private tutor, she then built upon this with the study of related classical works of Arabic Grammar when she started studying at Dar Al-Hadeeth in Mab'ar as well as other recommended works with a focus on works related to the fundamental beliefs of Islaam.

She later was blessed to continue her studies of this deen for three years in Dar Al-Hadeeth in Damaaj where she benefited from several excellent teachers. Among them was her daily class with Umm Salamah, may Allaah preserve her, previously the wife of Sheikh Muqbil, with whom in daily study she completed the work Bulugh al-Maram with the exception of two individual chapters due to illness. There she also benefited from the weekly class of the daughter of Sheikh Muqbil, Umm 'Abdullah, and from the lectures of well-known scholars of Ahlis Sunnah throughout Yemen who would come to address the students at the center. She has always striven to benefit from the people of knowledge in every city where her family resided in Yemen, while always making her home the center of her efforts to both study and teach this perfect religion.

May Allaah forgive us, her, and all the Muslims their errors and shortcomings, and guide us to every matter of belief, statement, and action that pleases Him alone.

Abu Sukhailah Khalil Ibn-Abelahyi
Taalib al-Ilm Educational Resources

Compilers Introduction

All praise is due to Allaah Alone. We praise Him, seek His help, and ask His forgiveness. We seek refuge in Allaah from the evil of our souls, and the adverse consequences of our deeds. Whomsoever Allaah guides, there is none who can misguide him, and whoever He misguides, there is none who can guide him.

I bear witness that there is nothing worthy of worship except for Allaah; He is alone and has no partners. I bear witness and testify that Muhammad, may Allaah's praise and salutations be upon him and his family, is His perfect worshipper, and messenger.

﴾ ***Oh you who believe! Fear Allaah, as He deserves, and die not except as Muslims.*** ﴿ -(Surat al-'Imraan, Ayat 102)
﴾ ***Oh mankind! Fear your Lord, Who created you from a single soul, and from him, He created his wife, and from these two, He created multitudes of men and women. Fear Allaah, from Whom you demand your mutual rights, and do not cut off the ties of kinship. Verily, Allaah is Ever-Watcher over you.*** ﴿ -(Surat an-Nisaa', Ayat 1)
﴾ ***Oh you who believe! Fear Allaah, and say righteous speech. He will direct you to do righteous deeds, and He will forgive you your sins. And whoever obeys Allaah and His Messenger has indeed achieved the ultimate success.*** ﴿-(Surat al-Ahzaab, Ayat 70-71)

As to what follows: then the best of speech is the speech of Allaah, and the best guidance is the guidance of Muhammad, may Allaah's praise and salutations be upon him and his family. And the worst of affairs are newly invented matters (in the religion), and every newly invented matter is a misguidance, and every misguidance is in the Hellfire.

To Proceed:
Alhamdulillah, the position of the woman in Islaam is undoubtedly one of honor. The woman who is strong in her religion and who follows the teachings of the Qur'aan and Sunnah is respected and a great trust and responsibility is laid upon her shoulders. She is the one who is primarily responsible for raising and educating her children with an Islamic education. She is responsible for their physical health as well as their emotional and spiritual well-being. She is responsible for the organization and running of her household- and this includes budgeting, decorating, planning and preparing meals, caring for sick children, serving her husband and being his companion and helper, and so much more. While it is not forbidden that the woman work outside the home, her primary role in life is found within the comfort and security of her own home, as we shall see in the pages that follow- and this is a very great position, and a most elevated role, as we will see as we read the words of the scholars on the pages that follow, insh'Allaah. Concerning this, Sheikh Saalih al-Fauzaan, may Allaah preserve him, says,

> *"Additionally, there remains to be stated that it should be understood that it is not forbidden for the woman to leave her house without exception, as texts have been narrated which are proofs that it is permissible for the woman to go out, as well as for her to work outside the home. However, this situation is not the general case; rather, it is the exception, and is done out of necessity."*
>
> *("My Home, My Path")*

The one who has taken on the illness of the Western world, who claims that a woman cannot be happy in her home and that she is oppressed, mistreated and ignorant, is clearly ignorant of her true position and situation, and does not understand all that is entailed in the care of the house and family. Here is a list of some of the duties that girls where taught in a girls' secondary school course on household management in the Muslim land of Ottoman Turkey in 1858:

"What is a home? What things are necessary for a house to be called a home? How can it be set up, protected, heated, aired and lighted? The characteristics of a good home; arranging furniture, inner divisions, sanitary conditions…cleaning copper, bronze, marble and jewelry, solutions for getting rid of bugs, bedbugs, fleas and lice; the characteristics of summer and winter homes, information about fuel…protecting clothing in different seasons, sewing, weaving underwear, weaving carpets and rugs, information about looms, cleaning clothes…starching and ironing, removing stains, embroidery, needlework…making bread, yeast, preserving food in different seasons…pantries, determining minimum weekly consumption of basic foods according to the number of family members, home pharmacy, making tooth powder and water and creams for chapped hands and lips, natural and artificial toothbrushes, bath luffas, wash cloths and bath robes, introduction to natural herbs and home medicines, information on bleeding, poisoning and so on, home medical information, regarding wounds, bruises, sprains, broken bones and burns, caring for people who have just recovered from illness, conditions for choosing a family doctor, clothing and food for every season, arranging meal times, daily nutrition for children, middle aged persons and the elderly, sleeping times according to age, daily and weekly cleaning, information on keeping the sitting room for guests…rules of etiquette, customs regarding speaking, serving, respect and love…"

("Ottoman Women: Myth and Reality", Pages 56-58)

In addition to just this one course, the girls were also taught in alphabet and verbal studies, Qur'aan and recitation rules, religious studies, reading, writing, literature, Ottoman grammar, Arabic, Persian, calligraphy, general information about life, ethics, health, arithmetic and geometry, geography, history and handcrafts. *("Ottoman Women: Myth and Reality", Page 55)*

Is it even conceivable that one who studied all of these things diligently and put that which they learned into practice could be considered uneducated or ignorant?? And that they were a backwards nation?!?

Sheikh Saalih al-Fauzaan, may Allaah preserve him, says,

"Indeed the work of the woman in her home, even if some people believe it to be insignificant- in fact it is significant, joining together many specific roles, and it requires that which the country requires- it calls for knowledge and understanding. It necessitates strictness. It requires administration as well as economic management. It calls for gentleness and mercy and compassion, and necessitates lofty principles.

Indeed the woman who regards the work in the home with scorn, belittling it- this is an evidence that she does not properly understand this as it should be understood; therefore she is not someone who establishes it properly. Likewise, those who believe that she is inactive and unproductive in her house- either they do not understand this work, or they in fact understand it but have a disease in their hearts."

("My Home, My Path")

The woman has the responsibility of taking care of her house and raising and educating her children. We have all seen the results of both a good upbringing and a bad upbringing in children- and what we see of them as children is a great indicator of what they will be when they grow up! This is not a small thing, nor an unimportant one. Rather, it is of utmost importance for the health of the family and Muslim society that the children be brought up with good character and a sound Islamic education.

Sheikh Husain ibn 'Abdul-'Aziz aal-Sheikh, may Allaah preserve him, says,

> *"The family in Islaam is truly priceless in itself, with lofty goals and objectives. And from the roles of the family which devotes its attention to Islaam through making it a reality, is that it is the natural incubator which watches over and manages the younger generation and takes care of them- the development of their bodies, their intellects, and their souls. In its shadow they receive feelings of love, mercy, and solidarity. Upon the bright light of the family's righteousness and piety the youth become upright and virtuous, and on the basis of the family's corruption its members will be corrupted. Moreover, it has been proven by experience that any institution other than the family cannot replace the family, and cannot stand in its place."*

("My Home, My Path")

Another of the greatest and most important roles a woman will have in her life is that of being a righteous, loving wife to her husband. Allaah, the Most High, says,

﴾ ***And among His Signs is that He created for you wives from among yourselves, that you may find repose in them, and He has put between you affection and mercy. Verily, in that are indeed signs for a people who reflect.*** ﴿ -(Surat ar-Room, Ayat 21)

Both the husband and the wife have rights and obligations concerning the other. It is upon them, if they want a happy and beneficial life, to diligently strive to fulfill these, as they have been put in place by Allaah, the Most High, who knows what is in the hearts of mankind, and that which they need for contentment and success.

Sheikh Jamaal al-Haarithi, may Allaah preserve him, said,

> *"So when you understand and have certainty, oh Muslim woman, in respect to the obligations which you have concerning your husband, then it is an upon you to seek various ways to please him- so if one path is exhausted, then pursue another newly created path, such that he will experience joy and contentment and then this will be returned back to you because of what he is experiencing of rest and peace of mind in his house after the difficulty and fatigue which he meets outside of the home."*

("My Home, My Path")

And beyond the house the Muslim woman has obligations towards her extended family, her husband's family, her friends, neighbors, students, teachers…the list goes on, as the role of the Muslim woman in her society is broad one. So it is essential that we work hard to obtain correct Islamic knowledge, then to implement that knowledge in our everyday lives- and our rights and obligations to our family and society are a large part of that knowledge.

The Goal of this Book

My goal in compiling this work is to show my sister Muslimah how vital her role on this earth is, and to present her with firm knowledge and guidelines for fulfilling this role to the best of her ability, so that with the Grace of Allaah she will be granted success in this life and the next. I have used the words of many of the people of knowledge of our time to present this knowledge, as the scholars are the inheritors of the Prophets, and they are the ones best suited to deliver, explain and clarify that which Allaah sent to mankind in the Qur'aan and upon the tongue of His Prophet, may Allaah's praise and salutations be upon him. They stress again and again that each right and obligation that the woman has, has its basis in this revelation, and that we have great examples to follow in the lives of the wives, daughters, and female companions of the Prophet, and those who follow them in righteousness.

The first section of the book contains translations of various lessons, lectures and *khutbahs* concerning the role of the woman in the Islamic society, and then more specifically in marriage and family life, especially the upbringing and education of the children. I would recommend that as you read each section, you use a highlighter or take notes on the lines provided in the margins concerning important points. Then, take the time to write out this information in a journal or notebook, along with three things that you can do to implement this knowledge which you have been granted, insh'Allaah.

The next section contains a compilation of religious rulings concerning the many different facets of the life of the righteous Muslimah: her religion, her general role in Islaam, education, employment, household, marriage, children- these rulings are intended to provide insight concerning these matters, as we see how the scholars guide the questioners to the correct understanding and implementation of Islaam in their lives. As anyone can read a verse of Qur'aan, or a *hadeeth* of the Messenger of Allaah, may Allaah's praise and salutations be upon him, but it is the scholars who can put the verses and *ahaadeeth* together and show us the way to the correct ruling on any given matter. I have tried to choose rulings that address some general matters, as well as some that address matters that I have heard and seen to be ones that the Muslims in the West are in need of understanding. In some of these rulings there are differences of opinion amongst the scholars, so if you have further questions concerning an issue I urge you to take the many opportunities which are available to us to contact a person of knowledge for clarification and an answer to your specific question. Again, use a highlighter and the lines provided in the margins to accent important points, as this will assist you in remembering and implementing the information you find in these rulings.

As for the third section, I am indebted to our sister Umm 'Amr bint Ibraaheem Badawi and her compilation, "*Waajibaat al-Mar'at al-Muslimah*", which has an introduction by Sheikh Muqbil ibn Haadi al-Waadi'ee, may Allaah have mercy upon him, and may Allaah preserve her. Her book is a compilation of the obligations of the Muslim woman, along with evidences from the Qur'aan and Sunnah. I have found it to be immensely beneficial, may Allaah reward her for her efforts, as it is simply written and well researched, and it is the inspiration for this section of the book.

I have attempted here to bring together a listing of many of the obligations of the Muslimah in various aspects of her life, along with their proofs from the Qur'aan and Sunnah and explanations from the scholars for clarification and explanation. I have tried to organize this information in a useful, easy to use fashion, so that this section of obligations can be a "field guide" as it were, for us to use as we navigate through the various situations that Allaah has decreed for us in this life. It is not a complete listing of all the obligations, nor did I include every proof for each point. Rather, I tried to be as comprehensive as possible, and attempted to provide a foundation for the reader to build her actions upon. For the section on *'aqeedah*, I borrowed some quotes from the book "*al-Waajibaat: The Obligatory Matters*", which is available at our website, for some of the sections, as it is comprehensive and simple, and the information within it is pertinent here as well, alhamdulillah.

Here, again, not only the highlighter and note taking lines are important- I would suggest you use a journal or notebook to write down these obligations and how you will strive to implement them- and then go a step beyond this to check up on yourself and take a reckoning on how you are proceeding along this path- if not daily, then weekly. List ideas that you can implement to assist you in reaching these goals, insh'Allaah, as this makes it much easier to go forward and actually make progress towards our goals. May Allaah make it easy for us and rectify our affairs.

The first appendix is a compilation I put together concerning the woman and seeking knowledge, the programs offered at some of the centers of learning here in Yemen, as well as a listing of some of the female students who have studied at the *markaz* in Damaaj. This is the first time it has been in print, though some of you may have read it from the internet in the past. My intention in putting this appendix in the book is to encourage my sisters to strive to seek religious knowledge in any way they are able, and to show them how some of their sisters are doing this very thing.

The second appendix concerns the specific rulings regarding the mixing of the sexes. I felt that this issue is a very important one for the Muslimah to understand, as she so often enters into situations that concern this, and she must be aware of the rulings and how she should conduct herself in these situations.

The third appendix was taken from an article in "*al-Asaalah*" magazine. In it the author lists several suggestions, based upon evidences from the Qur'aan and Sunnah, which, if we implement them in our family lives, our lives will become happier and richer, by the Grace and Mercy of Allaah. I chose to include this, as it is a very simplified listing, which brings everything down to clear and basic suggestions in a form that is easy to refer to and understand, insh'Allaah. Listed here are suggestions for BOTH the husband and the wife, Alhamdulillah, to take note of and try to implement, insh'Allaah.

I have tried, in this work, to define all of the Arabic words clearly the first time that they are mentioned, and then to use the transliteration of the word subsequently in order for the reader to become familiar with certain important Arabic terms. Most Arabic terms are italicized, with the exception of some that are common and understood by the majority of Muslims, insh'Allaah. In many instances I put in the original Arabic word for those who can read the Arabic, as transliteration is an inexact science at best, and the Arabic is best for proper pronunciation and better comprehension. I have done my best to transliterate each word clearly and precisely, and to be consistent in these transliterations. For Qur'aan, I relied mostly upon "*The Noble Qur'aan: English Translation of the Meanings and Commentary*", translated by Dr. Taqi ad-Din al-Hilali and Dr. Muhammad Muhsin Khan, may Allaah reward them. Concerning sources of *ahaadeeth*, I have in general relied on the scholars presenting them concerning their authenticity, though in many cases I had to additional research, as their sources were not always listed in the original work or transcription. Abu Sukhailah assisted me in this, may Allaah reward him for his efforts. To the best of our knowledge, all those quoted herein are people of good standing, and Allaah knows best.

Also, since the source texts I used were in Arabic, there may be some discrepancies between the names of people which are not originally Arab, and their translated forms, as well as between my translation and quotes that were originally in languages other than Arabic. I simply translated their meanings to the best of my ability, as it was not possible for me to find the original quote in the original language.

In order to make this compilation as beneficial as possible, I ask my brothers and sisters to please send any knowledge based comments, suggestions, and corrections to us at ***kitaabtakreem@taalib.com***. For supplementary information, study guides, and related classes and courses, please check ***www.taalib.com*** frequently for updates and new listings. Alhamdulillah, the site has been completely updated, with many new features such as articles with self administered quizzes to assist us in testing our understanding of the subjects. I would also like to extend an invitation to you to join the community in our online "learning circles". These learning circles are divided by gender, alhamdulillah, and in them we will discuss points brought forth in our publications and strive to bring forth information which will be beneficial as we travel down this path together, insh'Allaah. One circle, From the Tayyibaat, will be devoted specifically to the health- of the mind, body, and heart- of the Muslimah and her family. Please join us, insh'Allaah, and help benefit yourself and others as part of our online community within the larger worldwide Ummah.

Lastly, I would like to thank Umm Usaama, Sukhailah Bint Khalil, for all of her work assisting me in the publication of this book, from transcribing and translating two of the selections, to editing, and to holding the baby while I typed one last paragraph here or there. Also, Abu Hamzah, Hudhaifah ibn Khalil, who assisted in finding pertinent rulings and in research and translation for some of the rulings. I would like to thank, as always, Abu Sukhailah for his assistance, encouragement, support and technical and religious knowledge- he has been beneficial in the production of this book every step of the way. Also, my deepest gratitude and love goes out to those scholars who are guiding lights to the rest of us, who assist us and encourage us to live Islaam, and to be firm and strong in our religion. May Allaah preserve those who are amongst us today such as Sheikh Saalih al-Fauzaan, and Sheikh Rabee'a ibn Haadee al-Madkhalee, Sheikh Muhammad al-Imaam, and may he have mercy upon those who have passed, such as Sheikh 'Abdul-'Aziz Ibn Baaz, Sheikh Muhammad ibn Saalih al-'Utheimeen, Sheikh Al-Albani, and Sheikh Muqbil.

I ask that Allaah correct my mistakes, preserve my intentions, and accept this work from me, and I pray that the Muslim *ummah* in general, and my Muslim sisters specifically, benefit through it. Any good in this work is from Allaah alone, who has no partners, and any evil is from myself and the accursed *Shaytaan*. All praise is for Allaah alone, through whom all good deeds are completed.

Umm Mujaahid Khadijah Bint Lacina
al-Amreekiyyah as-Salafiyyah
Shawwal 19, 1431 - Shihr, Yemen

Short Treatises on the Woman in Islaam by Some of the Leading Scholars

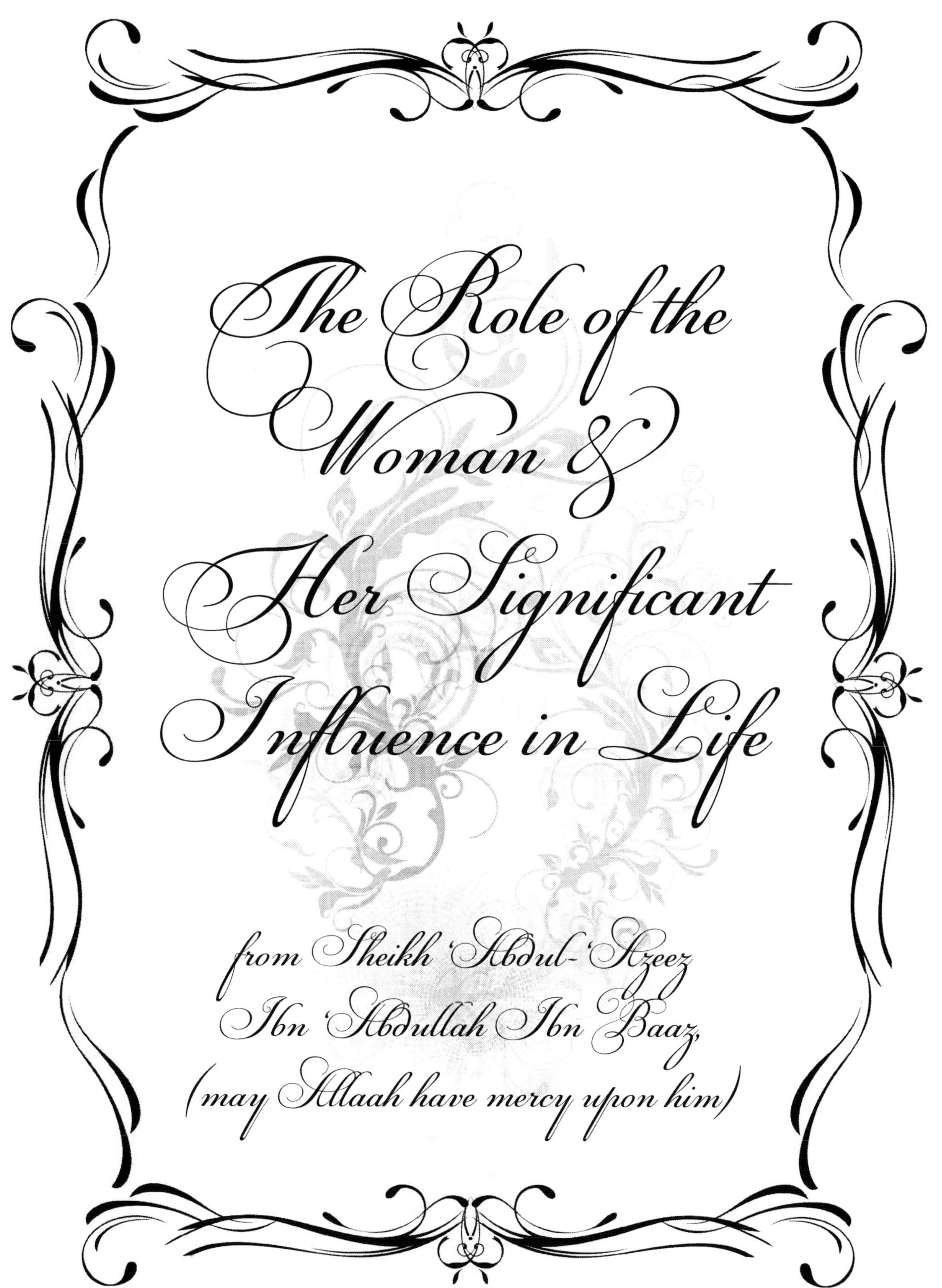

The Role of the Woman & Her Significant Influence in Life

from Sheikh 'Abdul-'Azeez Ibn 'Abdullah Ibn Baaz, (may Allaah have mercy upon him)

All praise is due to Allaah, the Lord of the Worlds, and may His praise and salutations be upon the most noble of the prophets and messengers, and upon his family and his companions and those who walk upon their path until the Last Day. To proceed:

Indeed the Muslim woman has a highly esteemed place in Islaam, and a great effect upon the life of every Muslim, as she is the first teacher in the efforts towards establishing of a righteous society. And this is when this woman adheres to the guidance of the Book of Allaah and the Sunnah of His Prophet, may Allaah's praise and salutations be upon him; as firm adherence to these two keeps every Muslim and Muslimah far from going astray in every matter.

The various nations going astray and deviating doesn't occur except through their removing themselves from the path and way of Allaah, Glorified is He, Most High, and that way which His prophets and messengers came with, may Allaah's praise and salutations be upon all of them. The Messenger of Allaah, may Allaah's praise and salutations be upon him, said,

{ I am leaving with you two matters, those who hold onto them will not go astray: the Book of Allaah and my Sunnah }

(The compiler of "*at-Tuhfat al-Baaziyyah al-Fataawa an-Nisaaiyyah*" says: Its chain is continuous: it is narrated by Maalik in "*al-Muwatta*" 2/70 Number 1874. Maalik said, "It has reached us that the Messenger of Allaah, may Allaah's praise and salutations be upon him, said..." and he mentioned the hadeeth. And this hadeeth is from that which is narrated from Maalik, and it is corroborated by the hadeeth in al-Haakim (1/931) narrated on Ibn 'Abaas, may Allaah be pleased with him, and it has been determined to be authentic from other than the narration of Maalik in "*al-Muwatta*" from another hadeeth. The meaning of the hadeeth is correct, through the joining of the various source texts which are well known and numerous concerning this subject from the Book and the Sunnah. And Allaah knows best. Look at the hadeeth in "*al-Muntaqa 'ala Sharh al-Muwatta*" (9/270, No. 1606) and other than it in the explanations of "*al-Muwatta*")

The importance of the woman as a mother, wife, sister, and daughter has also been brought forth and shown in the Noble Qur'aan, which also makes clear that which she has of rights and that which is upon her of obligations. The pure Sunnah thereafter brings that which explains and clarifies those verses.

This prominence and significance of her position is due to those burdens imposed upon her, as well as the hardships which she endures, some of which are more difficult than those which the men are charged with. Thus, from the most important obligations is gratefulness to one's mother, and being loyal and dutiful to her and having good relations with her- and she comes before one's father in this. Allaah, the Most High, says,

> ***﴾ And We have enjoined on man to be dutiful and good to his parents. His mother bore him in weakness and hardship upon weakness and hardship, and his weaning is in two years – Give thanks to Me and to your parents. To Me is the final destination. ﴿*** -(Surah Luqmaan, Ayat 14)

And He, the Most High, says, ***﴾ And We have enjoined on man to be dutiful and kind to his parents. His mother bears him with hardship. And***

she brings him forth with hardship, and the bearing of him, and the weaning of him is thirty months... ﴾ -(Surat al-Ahqaaf, From Ayat 15)

A man came to the Messenger of Allaah, may Allaah's praise and salutations be upon him, and said, "Oh Messenger of Allaah, who of the people has the most right upon me of good treatment and companionship?" He said, ***{Your mother }***. The man said, "Then who?" He replied, ***{Your mother}***. The man said, "Then who?" He replied, ***{Your mother }***. He asked, "Then who?" He said, ***{Your father }***. ("*Saheeh al-Bukhaari*" and "*Saheeh Muslim*", from the hadeeth of Abi Hurairah, may Allaah be pleased with him)

This makes it necessary that the mother be given three instances of dutifulness, compared to the one that is granted to the father.

Similarly, the place of the wife and her influence upon the tranquility of the spirit is made clear in the noble verse in which Allaah, the Most High says,

﴿ ***And among His Signs is that He created for you wives from among yourselves, that you may find repose in them, and He has put between you affection and mercy.*** ﴾ Surat ar-Room, From Ayat 21)

al-Haafidh ibn Katheer, may Allaah have mercy upon him, said, in his explanation of the saying of the Most High, (...***affection and mercy***.): *al-muadda*: love or affection, and *ar-rahmah* is mercy- as the man holds on to the woman out of his love for her, or out of being merciful to her, or because she has borne for him children.

An example of the unique position which Khadijah, may Allaah be pleased with her, was placed in, is the great effect she had in calming the fear of the Messenger of Allaah, may Allaah's praise and salutations be upon him, when Jibreel, Allaah's salutations be upon him, came to him with the revelation in the cave of Hiraa for the first time. The Prophet, may Allaah's praise and salutations be upon him, came to her, trembling from what had happened. He said, ***{ Cover me! Cover me! I am afraid that something may happen to me!} She replied, may Allaah be pleased with her, "Never! By Allaah, Allaah will never disgrace you. You keep good relations -maintaining your family ties, help the poor and the destitute, serve your guests generously and assist the deserving ones who are afflicted with calamity.}*** (This is authentic, and is found in al-Bukhaari, 1/21-26, from the hadeeth of 'Aishah, may Allaah be pleased with her, and it is from a longer hadeeth)

We must also not forget the effect of 'Aishah, may Allaah be pleased with her, since the major companions and many of the women took both the narrations of the Sunnah and the rulings which were related to these ahaadeeth from her. And from the near past, in the time of Imaam Muhammad ibn Sa'ud, may Allaah have mercy upon him- when his wife advised him to accept and endorse the call of Imaam Muhammad ibn 'Abdul Wahaab, may Allaah have mercy upon him, when he had presented his call to him. As indeed her counsel to him had the greatest influence in their agreeing to take part in renewing this call to Allaah's worship alone and to spread it, until even today we are aware of the effect of that in the steadfastness of the correct system of beliefs found in the establishment of this peninsula.

There is no doubt that the house which the woman governs by affection, love and mercy, as well as with the Islamic upbringing and education, will have an effect upon the man- as he will become, by the permission of Allaah, successful in his affairs, and be granted success in any action he attempts from seeking knowledge, earning money in trade or agriculture or other than that from the different occupations.

And I ask Allaah that He grant success to the people in that which He loves and is pleased with, and may Allaah's praise and salutations be upon our prophet, Muhammad, his family and his companions.

(From "at-Tuhfat al-Baaziyyah al-Fataawa an-Nisaaiyyah" Volume 1, Page 22. This was originally published as the Sheikh's answer to a question in the magazine, "al-Jayl" based in Riyaadh, concerning the place of the woman in Islaam)

Review and Discussion Questions

Questions for The Role of the Woman & her Significant Influence in Life by Sheikh Bin Baaz

Review:

1. What condition does Sheikh Bin Baaz, may Allaah have mercy upon him, stress is necessary for the woman to be the foundation of the building of the righteous society? (Page 30, Top half of page)
2. List three proofs for the elevated position of the mother from the Qur'aan and Sunnah. (Page 30, Bottom half of page, Page 31, Top half of page)
3. What is one of the signs which Allaah has given us, in regards to marriage? (Page 31, Top half of page)

Discussion and Consideration:

4. How can a woman influence both her family and the society towards righteousness and goodness?
5. How are some of the hardships which the woman endures greater than those which the man endures?
6. Choose one of the righteous women mentioned in this treatise, or whom you have read or studied about, and explain how they are a good example for the modern woman to follow today.

After each numbered review question you will find an indication of the page number and page area where that specific answer should be found. For example the first review question:

1. **What condition does Sheikh Bin Baaz, may Allaah have mercy upon him, stress is necessary for the woman to be the foundation of the building of the righteous society?** ***(Page 30, Top half of page)***

The text "***(Page 30, Top half of page)***" indicates that the correct section and page number needed to review or find an answer for that specific question or point is somewhere within the top half of the text on page 30. These should be completed immediately after reading a section to strengthen your understanding.

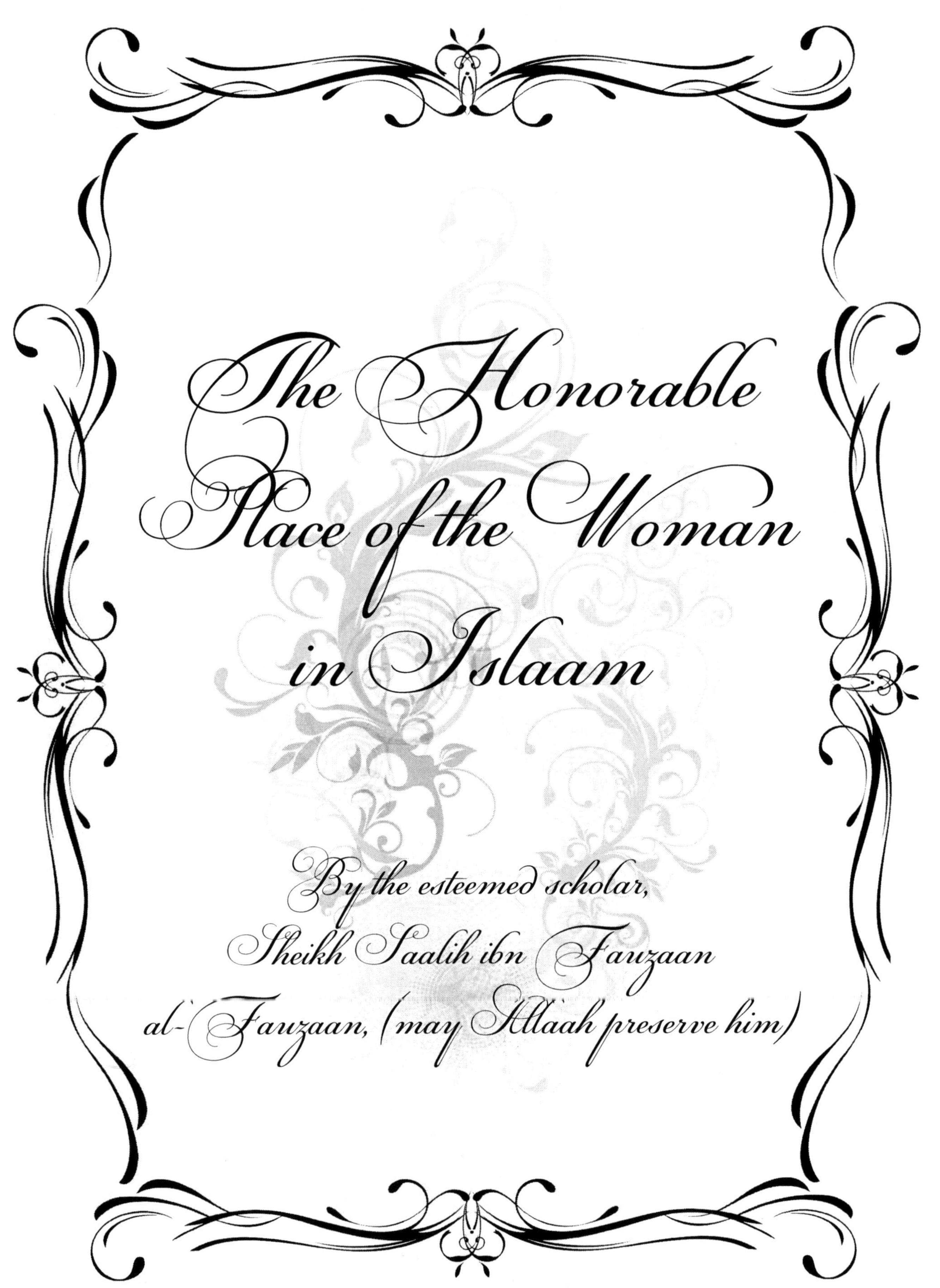

The Honorable Place of the Woman in Islaam

By the esteemed scholar,
Sheikh Saalih ibn Fauzaan
al-Fauzaan, (may Allaah preserve him)

In the name of Allaah, the Most Beneficent, the Most Merciful

The First Part of the Khutbah

All praise is due to Allaah, Who predetermines everything, as He has guided His creation, both the male and the female, and has differentiated between them in their innate characters, attributes, and their actions; ﴾ ***And the male is not like the female*** ﴿-(Surat Aal-Imraan, Ayat 36)

I testify that there is no god worthy of worship except for Allaah, alone, and that He has no partners or equals; for Him are all the good names (which He has ascribed to Himself in His book, or on the tongue of His Messenger, may Allaah's praise and salutations be upon him). I bear witness that Muhammad is His slave and His Messenger, the Prophet, al-Mustafa, may Allaah's praise and salutations be upon him, his family, his companions, and all those who follow upon his way and example- may many praises be upon them.

To proceed, oh people: Fear Allaah, the Most High, and know that Allaah, Glorified is He, and Most High, created mankind from a state of non-being, and has made that which was created by Him differ in their attributes, actions, and in that which they are entrusted with. He has made the males and the females differ- as He has created for the males those attributes, innate characteristics, and actions which are appropriate for them, and He has created for the women innate characteristics, attributes, and actions which are likewise appropriate for them.

And if all of the people from the two sexes were to perform the undertakings which they are entrusted with, then life would be well-organized, and the religion would be firmly established, and the common interest and well-being of society would be achieved. As for when this divinely prescribed system is disrupted- with the men beginning to take on the attributes and undertakings of the women, and likewise, the women beginning to take on the attributes and the undertakings of the men- then society becomes disordered and confused, families separated and dispersed, and its well-being is lost. This is what our enemies from the disbelievers, and those who associate others with Allaah, desire for us. They are not pleased with anything for us, except for that we leave our religion. Allaah, the Most High, says,

﴾ ***Never will the Jews nor the Christians be pleased with till you follow their religion.*** ﴿ -(Surat al-Baqara, Ayat 120) and He says,

"***And they say,*** ﴾ ***Be Jews or Christians, then you will be guided.*** ﴿-(Surat al-Baqara, Ayat 135)

﴾ ***They wish that you reject Faith, as they have rejected Faith, and thus that you all become equal*** ﴿-(Surat an-Nisaa', 89)

﴾***And they will never cease fighting you until they turn you back from your religion if they can.*** ﴿-(Surat al-Baqara, Ayat 217).

Allaah has clarified this issue for us, that this is from the behavior of the disbelievers, and they are always and forever upon this- they do not ever change their approach, until the very Hour is established- except for the one from among them who embraces Islaam or submits to Islaam. However, what is stunning about this call which has been established to change the natural order of things-meaning to change the men so that they take on the attributes, behavior, and actions of women, and to change the women so that they perform the actions of men, and take on the attributes of men- is that a group from amongst us, from our own men and women, also calls to this, from those individuals who are in fact hypocrites, both male and female, who command the evil, and forbid that which is good; this is the amazing thing, that our enemies are from amongst us, and from amongst our children.

Just as the Messenger of Allaah, may Allaah's praise and salutations be upon him, mentioned, that there were callers to the doors of Hellfire. It was said, "Describe them to us, Oh Messenger of Allaah!" He said, ***{ ...They are a people with an appearance like ours, and who speak with our tongue. (i.e. in the same language }***(Bukharee 3430, Muslim 3523)

Indeed, they want to exchange everything from the sexes from one to the other, in order to destroy the society, with the intention that we adhere to the societal formula and pattern of the disbelievers, and no longer be distinguishable from them, and that we be deprived of this great blessing of guidance. Indeed, this way is only a great disaster, as he, may Allaah's praise and salutations be upon him, has cursed the men who resemble the women, and has cursed the women who resemble men. This is in order to preserve each upon those attributes which are particular to them, and upon that which is natural for them and the actions which are specific to them, in order to perfect the building of the society as well as to make complete that which benefits society and safeguards honor. (The hadeeth in which the Messenger of Allaah, may Allaah's praise and salutations be upon him, cursed them is found in al-Bukhaari, Abu Daawud, at-Tirmidhi, who declared it *hasan saheeh*, and Ibn Majaah, Ahmad, ad-Daarimee, and an-Nasaa'ee in "*'Ashrat an-Nisaa*")

Their goal is to ruin the Muslim woman, and to cause her to leave the work and endeavors which are specific for her and by which she is characterized, as well as to remove from her those attributes which are the attributes of femininity, modesty, and virtue; to alter them towards the attributes of the men and towards a lack of modesty and virtue. They want to incite her to leave her house and her family, and to force her into jobs for which she is not best suited. And so when they see that the Islamic legislation has put in place restraints and limits for her to proceed upon as a Muslimah, certainly they wish to remove these limits and restraints and change the limits placed by Allaah, Exalted is He, Most High.

When they see that Islaam commands the woman to wear the *hijaab*, they say, "*Hijaab* is an old tradition and behavior, and from the outdated practices, so a woman should free herself from it, and go out uncovered. Why are these shackles placed upon her, when she is a person, with human rights? Why does the woman wear this *hijaab*, instead of going out uncovered??" They say these things until it affects some of those women who are of weak faith, or those who are deceived, and so they then adopt this becoming swords of this evil call. This becomes their call- to remove the *hijaab*- towards nudity, degeneracy and degradation- until the effects are seen upon them, because they are weak women; weak in their intellects and their religion, just as the Prophet, may Allaah's praise and salutations be upon him, said. Such individuals effect a portion of the Muslim women, until they make them followers of their desires.

When they saw that the general work of the woman in the house is to raise and educate the children, to organize the affairs of her house, and to safeguard her husband's affairs and his belongings in his absence- when they saw that, they wished to debase this position and status of hers, and to cause her to abandon it for difficult positions which she is not suited for, and to take upon herself men's work; to do the jobs of the men in offices, and to do the jobs of the men in the markets and places where things are sold and bought, as well as adopting the practice of attending seminars and conferences where they mix freely with men.

When they saw that the Wise Legislator has commanded the women with staying away from being in the company of men who are not *mahram* (meaning, from those men which it is forbidden for her to marry) for her, and has forbidden the free mixing between the sexes, they said, "Mixing is necessary, so why has the woman been restrained, why put a barrier between her and men?!?" Until they took the matter upon themselves and then demanded that the woman lecture in front of the men, and deliver the *khutbah* at the *Jumu'ah* and *Eid* prayers, and lead the men- lead them in the prayer, while the Prophet, may Allaah's praise and salutations be upon him, said ***{ Do not prevent the female worshippers of Allaah from attending the masjid, yet their homes are better for them. }***(Abu Daawud, Vol. 1, No. 567, and Sheikh al-Albaani has declared it to be authentic in "*Saheeh Abu Daawud*") It, meaning their homes, are better for them than going out, even in relation to the *masjid*, which is a house from the houses of Allaah, and is a place dedicated to worship! So how about when she goes out to other than the *masjid*? Indeed, this issue is a significant matter. They say, "No. The woman is human; the woman is able to go out without any restraint put upon her. She should be able to abandon any obedience of her husband, father, or guardian. Likewise, she should be able to use her car by herself at any time, in the night or day, and go and meet with whomever she likes, and whoever wants to can stop her in the street in order to speak to her, and whoever wishes can ride along with her in a vehicle without any guidelines or anyone accompanying her."- meaning without having any fear of Allaah, Glorified is He, the Most High.

They also demanded that the woman be able to have her photograph taken. They sought to have her photo taken for personal identity cards, resulting in various men then being able to become familiar with her picture, such that her photo is demeaned and becomes a means of calling to evil, and her photo causes the people to discuss her appearance and attractiveness amongst themselves. Likewise they say, "There is no prohibition or restraint upon the woman who travels without a *mahram*." Yet the Prophet, may Allaah's praise and salutations be upon him, said, ***{ It is not permissible for the woman who believes in Allaah and the Last Day to travel except that she is with a mahram }*** ("*Saheeh Muslim*", "*Musnad Ahmad*", "*Saheeh al-Bukhaari*", at-Tirmidhi and Abu Daawud)

When they saw that marriage "hindered" her in their view, since marriage results in her staying in the house of her marriage, becoming pregnant, giving birth, and raising her children- and that this hinders her from those objectives which they want to achieve; they said, "Choose *"urfee"* marriage. This Egyptian *"urfee"* unofficial marriage is a marriage in which the one who marries her passes an occasional night or day with her, and sometimes the people around her do not even know that he is her husband! So they might falsely accuse her, and accuse him of wrongdoing. As he occasionally visits her in order to gratify their desires, and that is all. But as for safeguarding her, and as for the husband safeguarding his children by her, and as for his supervising where she goes- all of this is eliminated with this Egyptian *"urfee"* type of marriage."

So she is "free", and her husband has no true connection to her except when he comes to satisfy his desires, just like an animal- just like the wild animals! And we seek refuge with Allaah from that. They want the situation to become like this, and this is what they in fact aim to accomplish. However, we ask Allaah, Glorified and Exalted is He, to prevent their evil from reaching the Muslims.

Additionally, they wanted for the Muslim woman to establish specific markets for trade and commerce. Such that they say, "Indeed, only women should sell to other women." In this way, they come by way of the religion, by saying only women should sell to other women. Yet this naturally leads to the necessity of the woman being active in the commercial markets, that she travels for her trade, and presents her merchandise to buyers, and she does not simply buy from the general sellers, so consequently there is no one watching over her, and no one to interfere with whatever she does. So they wanted to establish for Muslim women here such markets using this argument that this is more modest for her. In this way, they approached their goal in a deceptive roundabout manner. But the reality is that women- if they establish such independent stores- then this eventually is a cause for them to throw aside modesty and honor, and to spend day and night in this market. So she is becoming similar the man- as she likewise has to oversee her trade, her store, and her clients. Therefore she does not generally remain in her house; and this is exactly what they want to achieve. This is that which they want for her, and this is what they aim for from behind their call for women's markets, which they present to the naive people, claiming that in it is good for us as Muslims. And because women would be with women, and the women tend the stores for other women- superficially, this appears good. However, they do not desire that apparent benefit. Rather, overall what they want is to remove from the woman her endowed femininity and her inherent nature, so that she eventually becomes like the man completely. This is the overall goal.

Yet the women from the time of the Messenger, may Allaah's praise and salutations be upon him, up until our time have all lived and gone out (for their needs); yet they have never established markets solely for the women. The commands which she must generally conform to are that she takes that which she in reality has need of from the market, along with her properly covering, and being modest when doing so. And there is no problem if she buys from men, and men sell to her, while those men themselves behave chastely and modestly, or that her husband or guardian or one from her household is entrusted with bringing that which she needs to her from the market. Therefore, it is not necessary for the Muslims to establish markets which are specific for the use of women.

Furthermore, from their deceptions and schemes is that they wish make it obligatory upon the businesses and institutions to employ women. If they do not, then the authorities would not grant them a license for business. So they would not grant a license to the one who owns an institute, business, or venue except with the condition that they hire a certain number of women. This is also from the doorways of deception for the Muslims, and from the entrances by which they coerce and force the Muslims to conform to their evil beliefs and way.

Likewise, they say: "The woman is a person, so why are all these restraints and controls placed upon her- why do you not give her her freedom?" In reply it can be asked, Is there freedom in allowing her to step outside of the Islamically legislated standards of behavior? This is in fact slavery; it is not freedom. Freedom is her remaining in compliance with her virtue and femininity, and that she performs those duties which she is best suited for. This is freedom, as for when she is forced into the maze of general employment, and into men's jobs, and she is naturally a vulnerable woman- then this is from the causes of her destruction, and from that which damages the very pillars of the society.

So it is upon the Muslims to take heed of the plots of their enemies, as, by Allaah, they continue to be vigorous in their attempts to destroy the Muslims as much as they are able by leading them towards that path, and they do not find any easier route than using the Muslim women to try to destroy our society. They have made her into a form of propaganda, as she then goes out in front of the men, and appears on the television and film screen unveiled and beautified. They have caused her to freely mix within the sphere of media announcers, such that first the man begins speaking on a subject, then the woman speaks concerning it, and so on. Why is all of this brought forth in our Muslim societies? For no other reason except that it is the deliberate scheme against Islaam and the Muslims. Is it proper for the woman to be a public news announcer? Is it fitting for the woman to go out on the television screens in front of the people? Rather, this stands as one of the doorways of the deception of the Muslims. As is society without the men able to fulfill this role??

Now the situation has come about that in some cases the men have been removed from their positions, and removed from the government posts in order for women to replace them- yet the men are supposed to be the caretakers of the women! So when the men are granted the jobs, and they are given compensation and salary, then they spend it upon the women, upon their children, and their house. As for when they are left without adequate work, then they become stingy. And yet these individuals, as we have mentioned, put forward the call towards the necessity of hiring women in the workplace. However, we will not heed the one who calls to employ women in the workplace because this is clearly from the plots which are directed at the Muslims- for this reason it is upon the Muslims to be aware of that and to be cautious of it concerning their wives and daughters because they are guardians over them in front of Allaah, Glorified is He and Most High. Indeed the woman must adhere to modesty, virtue, and remaining in the house, and she must marry the one whose religion and trustworthiness pleases her. He, may Allaah's praise and salutations be upon him, said, ***{ If one comes to you, whom you are pleased with his religion and his trustworthiness, then marry him; if this is not done, there will be trial on the earth, and great corruption.}***

(at-Tirmidhi, 1084, Ibn Maajah ,1967, and the wording is his- and that chain is weak. However, the meaning is correct, and Sheikh al-Albaani has declared it to be *hasan* due to that which supports it, in "*as-Saheehah*" 1066 and "*al-Irwaa*" 1868)

It is necessary concerning the husband in the household, that he be one who possesses religion and is trustworthy, so that he shelters and safeguards the woman. As for if his religion is weak or he does not have a firm practice of the religion or is not trustworthy and honorable, then this is from deception- as the one who marries with this lack of religion and trustworthiness, this is a forfeiture of the trust and places the woman in other than that position which is suitable for her. So it is upon the Muslim men to realize and understand this matter, and that they be aware that the enemies of Islaam plot against them day and night, with the false argument that the woman is presently paralyzed, or not fully functioning in society. Glorified is Allaah, how are the women paralyzed, when they are performing essential duties

within household!? The duties of the household are greater in number than the work which the men perform outside of the houses. Do they claim that the woman should leave, while the man sits in the house? Yes, this is what at times occurs now, as a woman may go out from the house in order to teach or to study, or she travels some distance to her place of work- and this is also related to their schemes, that she has an office in a city which is far away from her own city- so she travels back and forth every day, while the husband remains in the house caring for the children. And if the man does not stay in the house, then the children are placed in a nursery school or day-care, as occurs with the disbelievers.

The Muslims, we have proceeded and been developed upon the religion of Islaam, upon honor and chastity, and upon the religion and trust, and good character (and when the mother of the good character does not stay, then the good character itself also leaves).

So it is obligatory upon the Muslims to recognize and understand the plots of their enemies, and to know that they are the ones who feign sorrow for the Muslim woman, and claim that she is oppressed- yet they are the true oppressors. They hope for the ruin of the Muslim woman, and have no mercy for the woman. The Muslim woman, and Allaah deserves all praise, in the lands of the Muslims and under the Islamic governance, is not oppressed. Rather, she is treated justly, and her rights are granted to her. And if it comes about that man oppresses a woman, then there are recognized authorities to oppose his forbidden tyranny and oppression upon her. As Allaah, Exalted is He, Most High, has created the Islamic judicial system and authorities for the purpose of removing those who oppress the people under their responsibility. As such the one who wishes to tyrannize a woman and to abuse or even abandon his guardianship, then the Islamic courts exist to stop this tyranny and oppression.

And it is not opposing oppression when the woman is being pushed toward a veritable bottomless pit, and towards that which is not suitable for her- while they announce that this is from "freeing" the Muslim woman! Worshippers of Allaah, fear Allaah, and distinguish your enemies from your friends, and do not be deceived by this dishonest, insincere call. Do not be deceived by that speech which in fact has a deadly poison well hidden inside, while its outer appearance is that of goodness and advice, and a claimed desire for the good of Muslim society. Do not be deceived in this matter, as the hypocrites among us are many, not to mention the disbelievers who are quietly whispering behind them- and all of them are doing battle against you.

So fear Allaah, worshippers of Allaah, and safeguard your wives and the women of your household, and repent to Allaah, all of you, oh Believers, in order that you all be successful.

I have spoken that which I have spoken, and I ask Allaah to forgive me, all of you and the totality of the Muslim society of every sin, as He is the One who can forgive them, He is the Oft-Forgiving, the Most Merciful.

The Second Part of the Khutbah

All praise is due to Allaah for His favors and beneficence, and gratefulness is due to Him for the success He has granted and thankfulness is to Him. I bear witness that there is no god worthy of worship except Allaah, alone, without any being associated with Him, as nothing is comparable to Him in His standing. I bear witness that Muhammad is His slave and His Messenger, may Allaah's praise and salutations be upon him, and upon his family and companions much praise.

To Proceed: Oh people, fear Allaah, the Most High. The Commander of the Faithful, 'Umar ibn al-Khattaab, may Allaah be pleased with him, said, "Indeed the ties of Islaam are broken one by one, when those who do not know about the conditions of the times of ignorance are raised in Islaam." The matter is the same concerning the issue of the woman; during the time of ignorance she was considered to be a loss or burden, since society disliked her. When a daughter was born to a man, then it was if a tragedy had befallen him. Allaah, the Most High, says, ﴿ ***And when the news of the birth of a female child is brought to any of them, his face becomes dark, and he is filled with inward grief! He hides himself from the people because of the evil of that whereof he has been informed. Shall he keep her with dishonor or bury her in the earth? Certainly, evil is their decision.*** ﴾-(Surat an-Nahl, Ayat 59)

As from them- the ignorant ones- are the ones who took buried the girl alive, so that she was buried alive and died underneath the dirt. And from them are those who kept her alive though they viewed her as an insult or disgrace; he kept her while feeling outraged, meaning that she was a degradation to him.

This was her place in the time of ignorance- and it was a time when the man was able to marry numerous wives, without any limits. Then Islaam came, and the woman became someone who was valued greatly, and honored. The Muslim who has daughters born to him, and he raises them upon good and is patient with them, has been promised Paradise; Paradise has been promised to him.

This state has been exchanged with that which came previously- meaning that they disliked the woman and were discontented with her before; as within her is good, and she is the mother of society- she is the pillar of the houses- so how can the man dislike her? How can he dislike her, when she gave birth to him?

They were able to marry numerous wives, without any limits, and to then neglect the women. Then Islaam came, and limited the man to four, or to one. If he is able to be just between them, then he is allowed up to four, and if he is not able to be just, then he is limited to one. Allaah, the Most High, says, ﴾ ***... then marry (other) women of your choice, two or three, or four; but if you fear that you shall not be able to deal justly (with them), then only one or (slaves) that your right hands possess.*** ﴿ - (Surat an-Nisaa', from Ayat 3)

In the times of ignorance the woman was not able to inherit, even if her relatives had a lot of wealth and she was poor- she could not inherit from them, and the money always went to the men while the women were deprived of any inheritance. Islaam came, and treated the women with justice. Allaah, the Most High says, ﴾ ***There is a share for men and a share for women from what is left by parents and those nearest related, whether, the property be small or large – a legal share.*** ﴿- (Surat an-Nisaa', Ayat 7) In the times of ignorance they were bored or weary with the presence of the woman, and looked down upon that which women said. They considered her mention to be from that which was an insult, when the people mentioned her or he mentioned the woman in his speech.

Yet Islaam gave her a position of honor, safeguarded her, raised her in importance, and created rights for her from honor and justice- whether she be a daughter, sister, wife, or relative. Islaam gave to her rights upon the man.

Likewise, in the time of ignorance they did not choose well-suited husbands for the women; rather, they often married them to the men who could give the most money. As if he could not give a lot of wealth, then he was often rejected and not permitted to marry her- this is hindering men in a way which Allaah has prohibited.

Allaah has forbidden the man to hinder or obstruct the woman, with the meaning that he forbids her from marrying someone whose qualities she is pleased with. He does not have the right to continually forbid her, and if he perpetually forbids her from marrying, then the judge enters into the situation and marries her to the one whom she is pleased with, and whom is suitable to her- because the judge is the guardian for the one who has no guardian or no suitable guardian.

These are all from the ways in which Islaam has honored the woman, and given her her rights- how can there now come men and women who claim Islaam, and yet they also say that Islaam oppresses woman? This is disbelief in Allaah, Glorified and Exalted is He. This is an accusation against Allaah, the Glorified and Exalted, as well as a censure of the Islamic legislation. It is obligatory upon them to repent to Allaah, Glorified and Exalted is He, and it is obligatory upon the scholars and students of knowledge and the people of honor to refute these sayings until the ones who say them are restrained from their statements. As the Muslim society, and to Allaah is due all praise, is a firmly interconnected society, a clean society, and pure society- as such the Muslims do not permit this false ideology to enter into it.

This is the meaning of the saying of the Commander of the Faithful, 'Umar, may Allaah be pleased with him, that the young people in Islaam are ones who do not know the reality of the time of ignorance, therefore they now are the ones who drone on about the woman being oppressed in Islaam- they do not refer to her history in the times of ignorance, and they know how Islaam brought her from oppression to justice, mercy, kindness, and to being protected.

Allaah, the Most High, says, ﴾ ***Men are the protectors and maintainers of women*** ﴿- (Surat an-Nisaa', Ayat 34).

The man takes on the burden and is entrusted with protecting and caring for the woman, through spending his wealth on a house and provisions, as well as through keeping her from that which is not suitable for her- he is the protector and caretaker over her, and he is responsible for her.

So how can someone come and say that the woman is oppressed in the Muslim society, except that it is apparent that this speaker is ignorant, and does not look at the woman in the society of the disbelievers and at how she lives now, and then compare her place to the position of the Muslim woman to understand the difference between the two, and to comprehend the state of ignorance, until he would not utter that which he stated, and that which is then heard by others and repeated without any chain of narration, and without any comprehension at all. Fear Allaah, oh worshippers of Allaah, and know that the best speech is the Book of Allaah, and the best guidance is the guidance of Muhammad, may Allaah's praise and salutations be upon him; and the most evil of matters are the newly invented matters in the religion, and every newly invented matter is a going astray, and it is upon you to adhere to the *jamaa'a*, as the Hand of Allaah is upon the *jamaa'a*, and whoever leaves them, leaves them for the Hellfire.

﴾ ***Allaah sends His salaat (Graces, Honours, Blessings, Mercy) on the Prophet (Muhammad [may Allaah's praise and salutations be upn him]), and also His angels (ask Allaah to bless and forgive him). Oh you who believe! Send your salaat on (ask Allaah to bless) him (Muhammad [may Allaah's praise and salutations be upon him]), and (you should) greet (salute) him with the Islamic way of greeting (salutation, i.e. asSalaamu 'alaikum).*** ﴿- (Surat al-Ahzaab, Ayat 56)

Oh Allaah, may Your praise and salutations be upon Your servant and messenger, our Prophet, Muhammad, and Your pleasure, Oh Allaah, upon his rightly guided *Khaleefahs*, the rightly guided leaders Abu Bakr, 'Umar, 'Uthmaan, and 'Ali, and upon all of the Companions, and upon those who followed them, and those who followed them in goodness until the Day of Judgment.

Oh Allaah, fortify and support Islaam and the Muslims, and humiliate and debase the association of others along with Allaah and those who do so, and destroy the enemies of the religion. Make this country safe and comfortable, as well as the general lands of the Muslims, oh Lord of All the Worlds.

Oh Allaah, assist Your religion, Your book, the Sunnah of Your Prophet, and Your worshippers, the Believers.

Oh Allaah, the one who desires good for Islaam and the Muslims, assist and guide him, and bless him in his efforts.

Oh Allaah, the one who desires evil for Islaam and the Muslims, cause him hardship and frustrate him, and turn his plots of destruction back upon himself, and cause his destruction to be his ruin, as truly You have power over all things.

Oh Allaah, destroy your enemies, the enemies of the religion from the Jews and the Christians, and the rest of the disbelievers and those who associate others with You in worship.

Oh Allaah, separate their cohesion, and cause differences between their statements, and weaken their strength and divide their groups.

Oh Allaah, create discord between them, and turn their plots back upon them. You have power over all things.

Oh Allaah, rectify our scholars and those leaders who are responsible over us. Oh Allaah, rectify our scholars and whose who are responsible over us.

Oh Allaah, cause them to be from those who guide the guided ones, not from those who are astray and who lead others astray.

Oh Allaah, rectify that which is inside of them, those who are with them, and their advisors, and make them far from hidden evil and those who are corrupt. Oh Lord of the Worlds, our Lord, accept from us. You are the All Hearer, the All Knower.

Worshipper of Allaah, ﴾ ***Verily, Allaah enjoins al-'adl (i.e. justice and worshipping none but Allaah Alone – Islamic Monotheism) and al-ihsaan [i.e. to be patient in performing your duties to Allaah, totally for Allaah's sake and in accordance with the sunnah (legal ways) of the Prophet in a perfect manner], and giving (help) to kith and kin (i.e. all that Allaah has ordered you to give them, e.g., wealth, visiting, looking after them, or any other kind of help), and forbids al-fahshaa' (i.e. all evil deeds, e.g. illegal sexual acts, disobedience of parents, polytheism, to tell lies, to give false witness, to kill a life without right), and al-munkar (i.e. all that is prohibited by Islamic law: polytheism of every kind, disbelief and every kind of evil deeds), and al-baghy (i.e. all kinds of oppression). He admonishes you, that you may take heed.*** ﴿-(Surat an-Nahl, Ayat 90)

So remember Allaah, and He will remember you, and be grateful to Him for His blessings which He has bestowed upon you, ***and*** ﴾ ***the remembering (praising) of (you by) Allaah (in front of the angels) is greater indeed [than your remembering (praising) of Allaah in prayers]. And Allaah knows what you do.*** ﴿-(Surah Al-Ankaboot, 45)

(A Khutbah Taken from Arabic original at his website)

Review and Discussion Questions

Questions for The Honorable Place of the Woman in Islaam by Sheikh Fauzaan

Review:

1. What is the Qur'anic proof that the men and women are not alike in all aspects? (Page 35, top half of page)
2. What three areas of difference does the Sheikh, may Allaah preserve him, mention? (Page 35, top half of page)
3. What do the people who oppose Islaam want for the Muslims and the Muslim society? (Page 35, bottom half ofpage)
4. What proof does the Sheikh bring that, while it is permissible for the woman to leave her house, her house is the best place for her? (Page 31, top half of page)
5. Is it permissible for a man to oppress a woman? What exists in Islaam to stop this from happening? (Page 40, bottom half of page)

Discussion & Consideration:

6. List five specific ways in which the enemies of Islaam want to change the Muslim woman in particular, and the Muslim society in general.
7. What are some of the benefits of choosing a righteous spouse, rather than marrying for money or some other worldly benefit?
8. Compare the state of the woman in the times of ignorance before Islaam with her state after the advent of Islaam.
9. How would you respond to one who says that Islaam makes the woman a prisoner or oppresses her?

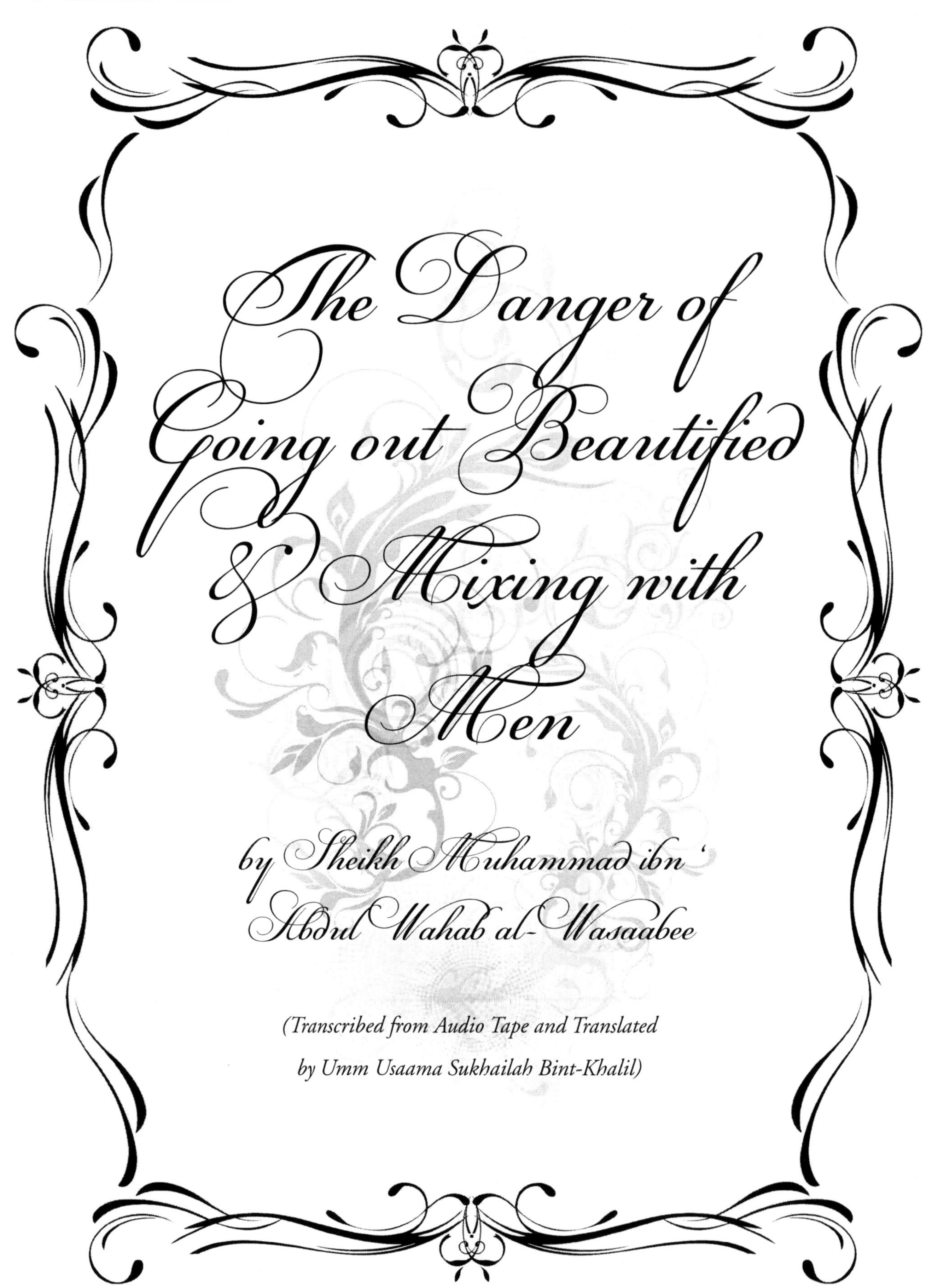

The Danger of Going out Beautified & Mixing with Men

by Sheikh Muhammad ibn 'Abdul Wahab al-Wasaabee

(Transcribed from Audio Tape and Translated by Umm Usaama Sukhailah Bint-Khalil)

All praise is due to Allaah, we praise him and ask for His help and forgiveness, and we seek refuge with Allaah from the evil of our own selves and the evil of our deeds. Whosoever Allaah guides then there is no misguidance for him and whosoever Allaah misguides than there is no guidance for him. I bear witness that there is no god worthy of worship except Allaah alone with no partners, and I bear witness that Muhammad is His slave and His Messenger, May Allah's praise and salutations be upon him and his family and companions until the day of resurrection.

To proceed:

Oh people, indeed the enemies of Islaam- from the Jews, and the Christians and the atheists- are placing a heavy load and burden upon the Muslim woman. They desire her to do as the disbelieving woman has done and become a toy in their hands. The Jewish woman, as well as the one who is Christian or an atheist, is already a toy in the hands of the disbelievers. The Muslim woman is the only one remaining, so they desire her to become like a toy as well. They carry out heavy campaigns, may Allaah fight them, and they invest a great deal of money, devote all of their energy, and they waste all their time, using every known technique towards this end.

As you know, the evil person is evil, and the criminal is criminal; he does not fear Allaah regarding his own affairs, so how would he fear Allaah regarding the affairs of others? He does not fear Allaah regarding his own women, so how would he fear Allaah regarding the women of others?

So this will be my subject tonight, for perhaps Allaah will benefit by it those who are attending, and also benefit those who hear it on the tape; for tapes can go where I cannot, and reach those whom I cannot reach.

Religion is advice, as the Messenger of Allaah said, ***{The religion is advice...}*** The companions said, "For whom, Oh Messenger of Allaah?" He replied, ***{...To Allaah, His messenger, the Muslim leaders, and the common people..}*** (Narrated by Muslim in his "*Saheeh*") And Imaam Ahmad narrated in his *"Musnad*", and others (have narrated it as well) with a sound chain of narrators, on the authority of Abu Bakr As-Siddiq, who said, The Messenger of Allaah, may Allaah's praise and salutations be upon him said, ***{ If the people see wrongdoing and do not change it, it is feared that Allaah will make them share in the punishment...}***

Also narrated by Imaam Ahmad in his *"Musnad*", and other than him, with a sound chain of narrators on the authority of Abu Bakr As-Siddiq that the Messenger of Allaah said, ***{ If the people see a tyrant yet they do not restrain his hand it is feared that Allaah will make them share in his punishment. }***

So the women going out uncovered and beautified is wrongdoing, and calling to that is also wrongdoing, and whoever calls for the women to go out uncovered and beautified and mix with the men is a tyrant; and religion is advice, before Allaah makes us share in their punishment.

Alhamdulillah, the texts pertaining to women and *hijaab* are many, and from them is the saying of Allaah the Most High,

﴾ ***...and when you ask (the wives of the prophet) for anything you want then ask them from behind a screen, that is purer for your hearts and theirs*** ﴿- (Surat al-Ahzaab, From Ayat 53)

This honorable verse sticks in the throats of those who call to immorality and the free mixing of the sexes and to evilness and afflictions. We are Muslims, we are not Jews, or Christians, or atheists, or disbelievers, or hypocrites, or communists. We are Muslims, ruling according to the Book and the Sunnah in everything. Allaah says,

﴾ ***But no, by your Lord, they can have no Faith, until they make you (Oh Muhammad) judge in all disputes between them, and find in themselves no resistance against your decisions, and accept (them) with full submission*** ﴿- (Surat an-Nisaa, Ayat 65)

A man cannot be a believer and a Muslim until he submits to the book of Allaah and the Sunnah of His Messenger. Likewise a woman cannot be a believer until she submits to the Book of Allaah and the Sunnah of his Messenger. Allaah, Glorified is He, Most High, negated the faith of the one who does not submit, and He swore by His Exalted Self, as He said, ﴾ ***But no, by your Lord, they can have no faith*** ﴿, an oath and a denial, the first denial is ﴾ ***But no*** ﴿ while the second denial is, ﴾ ***they can have no faith*** ﴿ and the oath is between them. Then He says, ﴾ ***until they make you (Oh Muhammad) judge in all disputes between them, and find in themselves no resistance against your decisions*** ﴿ . He makes total submission, inward and outward, a condition when He says, ﴾ ***and accept (them) with full submission.*** ﴿ And he asserts it with, the noun, submission, which indicates assertion.

So from this we see that a man who is a believer as well as a woman who is a believer- if they submit entirely to Allaah and His Messenger, outwardly and inwardly, then we do not disagree with, nor turn away from the command of Allaah. Rather, we say, "We hear and we obey" and follow that with action.

﴾ ***and when you ask (the wives of the prophet) for anything you want then ask them from behind a screen*** ﴿ What is our stance in relation to this verse, as it says, ﴾***from behind a screen***﴿? It does not say for men and women to mix with each other, it does not say for them to dance together, it does not say shake hands and hug each other, it does not say for the woman to uncover herself and the man to look at her. We must fear Allaah, we must be aware of Allaah. Today is this worldly life and tomorrow is the Hereafter; today is work and tomorrow is accounting and recompense, and one will not be safe from the punishment of Allaah unless he is a believer. If he is a hypocrite, showing Islaam outwardly but inwardly hiding disbelief and misguidance, then Allaah says, ﴾ ***Verily, the hypocrites will be in the lowest depth (grade) of the Fire; no helper will you find for them.*** ﴿ (Surat Aan-Nisaa, Ayat 145)

So where is the submission to the book of Allaah and the Sunnah of His Messenger? A believer searches for the truth and follows it, while a hypocrite flees from the truth and rejects it. This hypocrite is one who claims Islaam- if he does not claim Islaam then he is a disbeliever. But if he is a person who claims Islaam then we say to him that the way of a Muslim is that he searches for the truth and pursues and follows it because of his love for his religion, while the hypocrite flees from the truth and if it catches up to him he rejects it. Claiming Islaam without acting upon it brings no benefit. People claimed it in the time of Allaah's Messenger, and they used to pray with him and fast with him and make *hajj* with him and fight with him- and yet Allaah revealed in their case,

﴾ ***And of mankind, there are some (hypocrites) who say: "We believe in Allaah and the Last Day," while in fact they believe not. They think to deceive Allaah and those who believe, while they only deceive themselves, and perceive it not! In their hearts is a disease of doubt and hypocrisy and Allaah has increased their disease. A painful torment is theirs because they used to tell lies.*** ﴿- (Surat al-Baqara, Ayats 8-10)

Those people lied when they said, ﴾***We believe in Allaah and in the Last Day***﴿. They outwardly displayed belief while they did not truly carry out the commands of Allaah. So be careful, Oh servant of Allaah! Be careful in regards to yourself, for indeed belief has its pillars, and its conditions, and its obligations. This matter is not a matter of simply claiming belief, as Allaah says, ﴾ ***It will not be in accordance with your desires (Muslims), nor those of the people of the Scripture (Jews and Christians), whosoever works evil, will have the recompense thereof, and he will not find any protector or helper besides Allaah.***﴿- (Surat An-Nisaa', Ayat 123)

This matter is not a matter of claims and desires. Someone stands forward as a Muslim, but where is his Islaam? A believer, but where is his belief? The hypocrites used to stand up and speak in front of the Messenger of Allaah, and bear witness. Allaah says,

﴾ ***When the hypocrites come to you (Oh Muhammad), they say: "We bear witness that you are indeed the Messenger of Allaah." Allaah knows that you are indeed His Messenger, and Allaah bears witness that the hypocrites are liars indeed.*** ﴿-(Surat Al-Munaafiqun, Ayat 1)

They, the hypocrites, spoke in front of him, they prayed along with him, they fasted along with him, they fought against the disbelievers along with him, they performed *hajj* along with him. By Allaah, then can you feel yourself to be immune to hypocrisy after realizing this? For by Allaah, no one feels himself to be immune to hypocrisy except a hypocrite, and no one fears hypocrisy for himself except a believer. 'Umar Al-Farooq, after the death of the Prophet, when he became the *khaleefah* (leader of the Muslim *Ummah*), if a deceased was brought to be prayed over what did he do? Look at this *khaleefah*, this truthful, righteous, god-fearing man, who was nicknamed *al-Farooq* because truth and falsehood was distinguished by him when he entered Islaam- what did he do? He would look to Hudhaifah Ibn Al-Yamaan, may Allaah be pleased with him, the keeper of the secret of the Messenger of Allaah, the one whom Allaah's Messenger told the names of the hypocrites, meaning "So and so is a hypocrite, and so and so is a hypocrite...", with the names of their fathers and their towns. So 'Umar would look to him and if Hudhaifah stood up to pray, 'Umar stood up and led the prayer, and if he saw that Hudhaifah did not stand up then he knew that the one who had died was one of the people on that black list, who were hypocrites. This hypocrite would live among them upon the appearance that he was a Muslim, and 'Umar did not know the truth about him; he did not find out until after the person's death. And Hudhaifah was a trustworthy companion, the Messenger of Allaah confided to him the names of the hypocrites and he did not reveal the secret. Yet 'Umar Ibn Al-Khattaab, the leader of the believers, may Allaah be pleased with him and the rest of the companions, came to Hudhaifah and asked him, by Allaah, "Did the Messenger of Allaah name me as one of the hypocrites?"

From this I tell you that no one feels himself to be immune to hypocrisy except a hypocrite and no one fears it for himself except a believer. So Hudhaifah said, *"By Allaah, By Allaah, he did not name you as one of them, and I will not tell anyone else after you."* For it was a secret. 'Umar feared for himself while we feel safe? How many of the Muslims commit sins, crimes, and evil acts, yet they claim that they are believers and that their hearts pure!? Certainly, we seek refuge in Allaah from this ignorance, and from hypocrisy and deception. So be careful, Oh slaves of Allaah! Beware of these affairs, and watch out for your family. Watch out for your daughters and sisters and wives. Our Lord, Most Exalted is He, says,

﴿ ***Oh you who believe! Ward off yourselves and your families against a Fire (Hell) whose fuel is men and stones, over which are appointed angels stern and severe, who disobey not, from executing the commands they receive from Allaah, but do that which they are commanded.*** ﴾- (Surat at-Tahreem, Ayat16)

And the Messenger of Allaah, praise and salutations be upon him, said, ***{ A man is a caretaker in his household and will be questioned about that over which he was given supervision, and a woman is a caretaker in her husband's house and she will be questioned about that over which she was given supervision, and the leader is a caretaker, and he will be asked about that over which he was given supervision....}*** until he said, ***{ All of you are caretakers and you will all be asked about that over which you were given supervision. }*** The hadeeth was recorded by Bukhaari and Muslim narrated on 'Abdullaah Ibn 'Umar. You will be questioned on the Day of Judgment about your wives, your daughters, and your sisters.

You will be questioned about those whom you were given supervision over. The woman is deficient in intellect and religion, as the Messenger of Allaah, praise and salutations be upon him, said, ***{ Indeed I have seen that the women make up most of the people of the Fire. The women said, "And why is that, Oh Messenger of Allaah?" He replied, You are ungrateful.They asked, "We are ungrateful to Allaah?" He said, You are ungrateful to your husbands and you curse excessively. I have never seen anyone with deficient intellect and religion, who can lead astray a serious man, other than one of you. They said, "And what is the deficiency of our intellect?" He replied, Isn't it true that the witness of two women equals the witness of one man? They said, "Yes." He said, Then that is the deficiency of your intellect. Then he said, Isn't it true that if one of you menstruates she doesn't pray or fast? They said, "Yes." He said, Then that is the deficiency of her religion.}*** (Authentic, found in al-Bukhaari, 3/384, Muslim, 2/694, 695, 1000, and other than them, in both this form and shortened form)

She is deficient in her intellect and her religion, so we should not open the doors for her to go wherever she simply wants. So be careful, oh slaves of Allaah! You are not in the times of the companions of the Prophet; you are not in the times of the companions of the Prophet, may Allaah be pleased with them! You are in the times of secularism and Free Masonry, the times of Christianity and Judaism. There has been nothing like these times of yours previously, there has been nothing comparable to them ever before, in evilness, in trials, in deception, in treachery! Deceptions against Islaam and the Muslims, treachery towards Islaam and the Muslims, scheming against the dignity of Islaam and the Muslims!

If in the times of the Companions, and the Messenger of Allaah, Allaah says, ﴾ ***and when you ask (the wives of the prophet) for anything you want then ask them from behind a screen, that is purer for your hearts and theirs*** ﴿- (Surat al-Ahzaab, Ayat 53).

Allaah says, and His saying is the truth, ﴾ ***from behind a screen*** ﴿. And these hypocrites say, "What is this extremism? What is this harshness? What is this severity?" *Hijaab* to them is extremism! Hypocrites, immoral hypocrites! They do not fear Allaah concerning themselves, nor their families nor the Muslim nation. They do not accept Allaah's legislation with submissiveness and acceptance. They are blind in regards to the Book and the Sunnah. They say, "Strictness! Narrow-mindedness! What is this *abaaya*? What is this *hijaab*?" We say, Allaah says, ﴾ ***and when you ask (the wives of the prophet) for anything you want then ask them from behind a screen, that is purer for your hearts and theirs*** ﴿- (Surat al-Ahzaab, Ayat 53)

Allaah wants purity and chastity for His slaves, Allaah wants purity and chastity for the believing men and the believing women, and the Muslim men and the Muslim women. He wants chastity, modesty, shyness, belief and religion, while those who follow their own desires want the believers to deviate from their path, those who follow their desires want you to turn totally away from your religion and the truth. So will you not fear Allaah, Oh slaves of Allaah?

And it is also upon the Muslim women to fear Allaah! By Allaah, all these deceptive calls directed towards the Muslim woman, by Allaah, if a woman answers them then she harms no one except herself and she will come to regret it at a time when her regret is of no use. The enemies of Islaam only desire to have the Muslim women for their own pleasure, so they bring forth the call for women's emancipation. What is this emancipation? Rather you should say the women's torture! They are nothing but liars. They are deceivers! They are not advisors, they are deceivers! What is this women's emancipation? Are the women being punished by us?!? The woman in Islaam is supported and honored. The woman in Islaam is a leader, a leader in her house and a caretaker.

The Prophet, may Allaah's praise and salutations be upon him said, { ***A woman is a caretaker in her husband's house and she will be questioned about that over which she was given supervision.*** } This means that she is a leader. Her sons, her daughters, her household- all this she takes care of and oversees. The man must go out and work and have a job, and bring in the money, and carry out his role outside of his house with great exertion, while the woman must carry out her work with great exertion inside the house. By this, married life will go on smoothly with the cooperation of both husband and wife. Her duties in the house are many- raising the children, caring for them, nursing them, overseeing their health, cleaning the house, learning, teaching her sons and daughters, taking care that her husband meets with an excellent reception when he enters the house, preparing food, honoring her guests. A woman's duties are many. But these people want to make her carry out other work as well, outside of her home, and call it emancipation! Is this emancipation or punishment, Oh oppressors! Oh evil ones! The woman is to be pitied, for she has heavy duties upon her already, so that she sometimes exerts herself more than the man does.

From the mercy and equality of Islaam is that the Messenger, may Allaah's praise and salutations be upon him, gave her three allotments of rights. Are these three rights only for play, or are they to show courtesy and appreciation? They are nothing but compensation for the hard work she carries out in her house. A man came to the Messenger of Allaah, may Allaah's praise and salutations be upon him, and said, ***{ Oh Messenger of Allaah, who has the most right to good treatment and companionship from me?" He replied, Your mother. The man said, "Then who?" He said, Then your mother. The man said, "Then who?" He said, Then your mother.}*** (Agreed upon)

Three rights to compensate for all that she goes through in each pregnancy. How much time does she spend during each pregnancy, enduring sickness and cravings and carrying the child in her womb? How much time does she spend in hardship during childbirth? How much does she spend taking care of her children? Years! Years and years! She does not get enough sleep or rest; she is always tired. And yet these people, instead of calling for the man to help the woman, are calling for the woman to help the man! They call themselves merciful, but, By Allaah, they are liars. By Allaah they are liars! By Allaah, they are calling to corruption and immorality. As Allaah says, ***﴾ And when it is said to them: "Make not mischief on earth." they say: "We are only peacemakers" Verily! They are the ones who make mischief, but they perceive not. ﴿***-(Surat al-Baqara, Ayats 11-12)

They are so stupid, that they do not say to the man, "Fear Allaah regarding your wife and help her with putting the household in order and raising the children." 'Aishah, may Allaah be pleased with her, was asked how the Messenger of Allaah used to occupy himself in his home. She replied, ***{ He would serve his family, and if he heard the call to prayer he would leave. }*** (Bukhaaree 655) He used to serve his family, and his wives did not have any children; he did not have any children except from Khadijah, may Allaah be pleased with her, and he did not marry again until after she died, and also he had Ibraaheem by Maariyah al-Qibtiyyah. As for his wives after Khadijah, then he did not have any children by them at all, there were no pregnancies, none of the illnesses and cravings that result from pregnancy, no caring for babies, no cleaning of their excrement, none of these tiring jobs. And yet he used to serve them and assist them.

These people want the woman to go out and work, and become tired and exhausted, and taste bitterness- and they call this equality. And afterwards she returns to her home, and also exhausts herself there. They only desire to destroy her life, and destroy the family, and destroy the society. Destroy the entire society! The children will become delinquents, the home will be destroyed, and where is the woman when this is occurring? Outside the home. The children become like delinquents, they are even run over by cars in the street, and smashed into the ground. Then the mother and father die from sorrow. By Allaah, these people have no mercy! They have no mercy for the family, nor for the society, nor the woman, nor the man, nor the children. They are oppressors, they do not fear Allaah in their lives, so beware of this, may Allaah grant you good.

The woman in Islaam has a high position that is not found in any of the other nations. Ask about the women of America, Britain, France, or any of the lands of disbelief, and you will find that she is in evil and hardship. In America and France the woman is simply like a piece of merchandise, displayed to everyone who passes. In Islaam she is a leader; she is honored, respected, and loved. She is a mother, a wife, a daughter, an aunt, a grandmother, a sister, and other than that. She is surrounded by honor and respect. The family is always visiting, giving gifts, and keeping ties. The parents are gentle with their children and the children respect their fathers and mothers. Respect is exchanged between brothers and sisters, and between the sisters and themselves, and between a woman and her aunt and a woman and her grandmother, and the entire family.

When the disbelievers saw that the woman had become ruined in their societies, and the mother had become ruined, and the entire family was ruined, what did they do? They called one day in every year "Mother's Day"- for their mothers are forgotten- the mother does not know where her daughters are, or where her sons are. They are all scattered in the streets and other places. The mother stays all alone, and her husband, also, is nothing but someone neglectful always fleeing, so what does she have left? She has nothing except her companion, the dog. Her dog to her is more dutiful than her son. Her son has deserted her, her son has left with his girlfriend, her daughter has left with her boyfriend, and her husband has left with his girlfriend. So all she has is her dog. So when they saw that the American family, the British family and the French family have been destroyed, they made one day a year for the mother. Look at this hardheartedness, only one day a year! Her son comes, and greets her and gives her a gift, then says goodbye and leaves. And it is the same from year after year. If he ever meets her at all, he will meet her next year. And if she died in her apartment, then it would only be discovered when the offensive smell came out from under her door.

We have no need for a Mother's Day because we are constantly in contact with our families. They eat breakfast together, and dinner together, and they ask after their mother, and ask after their father, and there is mutual respect between them. They call each other, and the son is always in front of his father and on his right and his left, and the same with his mother, and everyone asks after the others. Yet they want to destroy the Muslim family as they have destroyed the Western family and the European family.

Beware, may Allaah grant you good, beware of the free mixing of the sexes. The best of the people after the prophets and messengers are the Companions, may Allaah be pleased with them, as the Messenger of Allaah said, ***{ The best of the people are my generation. }*** (see "*as-Saheeh al-Musnad*" of Sheikh Muqbil, may Allaah have mercy upon him) They are the best of people other than the prophets and the messengers, and even so Allaah revealed, ﴿ ***and when you ask (the wives of the prophet) for anything you want then ask them from behind a***

screen, that is purer for your hearts and theirs ﴾ (Surat al-Ahzaab, Ayat 53)

The time of the Companions was the time of prophethood, the time of purity, chastity, and security, and even so Allaah says, ﴿ ***And stay in your houses, and do not display yourselves like that of the times of ignorance*** ﴾- (Surat Al-Ahzaab, Ayat 33)

The woman is commanded to be tranquil, calm, and peaceful, and to stay in her house in order to take care of the household affairs in an excellent manner, and to bring into the world a new generation; a generation with good manners, a generation of pious men and pious women and men and women who fear Allaah. She should raise them, and read supplications over them and supplicate for them, and feed them, and mediate between them with advice, teaching, and guidance, and other than that.

Allaah says, ﴿ ***And stay in your houses, and do not display yourselves like that of the times of ignorance*** ﴾ The woman should not go out of her house except for her needs, and even then there are conditions which must be fulfilled, such as that she seek her husband's permission, that she is not perfumed or scented, and that she is not displaying her beauty. Nothing of her body should show, she must cover her entire body, and she must go to safe places, such as to visit her mother, sister, daughter, aunt, or father. Or she goes to visit her neighbors to console them after a death, or to congratulate them on the birth of a child, or a marriage. She must have modesty and good manners, and not be gone for too long, for she is a leader and supervisor of her house, and she must take care of the house and its furnishings, and of the sons and daughters of the household, and she must take care of her husband, the overall supervisor and caretaker; she must give him his rights. She must ask his permission before leaving the house, or ask permission of her guardian. As we said, there are conditions for her leaving the house and from them is that she ask her husband's or her guardian's permission. Allaah says,

﴿ ***Men are the protectors and maintainers of women, because Allaah has made one of them to excel the other, and because they spend to support them from their means. Therefore the righteous women are devoutly obedient to Allaah and to their husbands, and guard in the husband's absence what Allaah orders them to guard (e.g. their chastity and their husband's property*** ﴾- (Surat?, Ayat?) To the end of the verse.

And our holy Prophet, May peace and salutations be upon, who is the best of mankind, the best of the prophets and messengers, and the best of the creation, said, ***{ I do not shake hands with women.}*** (Imaam Ahmad in his "*Musnad*", Vol. 6, No. 357, and it is found in "*as-Saheeh al-Musnad*" of Sheikh Muqbil, Vol. 2, No. 1557) Meaning unrelated women, who are not from those of his relatives whom he is unable to marry, nor from his wives.

Come and look at those who follow their own desires, like those about whom Allaah said, ﴿ ***But if they answer you not (i.e. do not bring the Book nor believe in your doctrine of Islamic Monotheism), then know that they only follow their own lusts. And who is more astray than one who follows his own lusts, without guidance from Allaah? Verily, Allaah guides not the people who are wrong doers, disobedient to Allaah***, ﴾-(Surat al-Qasas, Ayat 50)

These people shake hands with everyone, everyone, and they say, "My heart is clean", while they are lying. Have you opened your heart and seen that it is clean? Rather, you are speaking about that which you have no knowledge of. Allaah says, ﴾ ***And follow not (Oh man, i.e., say not or do not or witness not) that of which you have no knowledge. Verily, the hearing, and the sight, and the heart of each of those ones will be questioned (by Allaah).*** ﴿-(Surat al-Israa', Ayat 36) Yet they lie to the people, and say, "My heart is clean."

Allaah says, ﴾ ***And of mankind, there are some (hypocrites) who say: 'We believe in Allaah and the Last Day,'*** ﴿ Then Allaah says, ﴾ ***while in fact they believe not.*** ﴿ (Surat Al-Baqara, Ayat 8)

The hypocrites, out of ulterior motives, claim for themselves belief, Islaam, righteousness, chastity, purity of heart, and other than that, while in fact they are lying. Your heart is clean? Your heart only becomes clean if you obey Allaah; if you disobey Allaah, your heart is not clean; rather it becomes covered in black, Oh heedless one! Stupid one! You are unaware of the Book of Allaah, and the Sunnah of His messenger! You commit evil deeds and then claim cleanliness of the heart! We are not ignorant! We judge according to the Book and the Sunnah. Allaah says, ﴾ ***and when you ask (the wives of the prophet) for anything you want then ask them from behind a screen, that is purer for your hearts and theirs*** ﴿- (Surat al-Ahzaab, Ayat 53) This is purity! From behind a screen, without shaking hands, without mixing, without a man and woman being alone together.

It has also been narrated in Al-Bukhaari and Muslim, on the authority of 'Uqbah Ibn Aamir, that he said, the Messenger of Allaah, may Allaah's praise and salutations be upon him, said, { ***Beware of entering in among women.*** } This saying was directed towards the Companions, and the remainder of the *Ummah* follows in their footsteps. The Companions are the best of humanity other than the prophets and messengers. The Messenger of Allaah said to them, { ***Beware of entering in among women.*** } Meaning, beware of entering in upon strange women. A man from the Ansaar said, "Oh Messenger of Allaah, what about our in-laws?" Meaning, can we enter among them? The husband's relatives, his brother, his uncle, his cousin, can they enter upon his wife? What do you say about them? What was the Messenger's reply? The Messenger, who does not say anything out of his own desires, rather, his words are revelation sent down. The Messenger of Allaah, may praise and salutations be upon him, said, { ***The in-laws are like death.*** } (Agreed upon)

They are like death! Destruction! Devastation! Even the in-law is not allowed to enter in among his brother's wife, his brother's son's wife, his sister's son's wife, etc. But some of us just hide the texts behind our backs and follow our customs and traditions. Let us see if these customs benefit you on the Day of Judgment! When you are brought to account before Allaah say, "The customs, the traditions, the ways of our lands forefathers, the heritage of our country!" This, by Allaah, will not help you at all. If you say about democracy, "We lived in the time of democracy." Will this help you at all on the Day of Resurrection? Will that save you from the punishment of Allaah? Can you make the excuse of democracy, communism, secular ideology of Baathism, or that of the followers of Nasser? By Allaah it will not increase you in anything but misery.

So beware, may Allaah reward you with good. Religion is advice, and whoever deceives us is not from us. The Messenger of Allaah said, ***{ A man is not alone with a woman except that the Shaytaan is the third of them.}*** (Narrated by Imaam Ahmad in his "*Musnad*", and Tirmidhi in his "*Jami*", on the authority of Umar Ibn Al-Khattaab with a sound chain of narration) The meaning of 'woman' here is a unrelated woman. A man is not alone with an unrelated woman except that the *Shaytaan* is the third of them. He goes back and forth from the man to the woman and from the woman to the man. The accursed *Shaytaan* desires the forbidden to occur between them. This means that it is not permissible for an unrelated man to be alone with an unrelated woman, even if they are in a car. An unrelated driver, and there is no one else in the car- this is forbidden. She cannot ride alone with him like that, as it is not permissible for her to ride alone with an unrelated driver. Similarly, also that which occurs in the doctor's office- there is no one present except for her and the unrelated doctor, or her and the unrelated male nurse. This is forbidden and impermissible. A man is not alone with a strange woman except that the *Shaytaan* is the third of them.

Oh worshippers of Allaah, indeed we will be brought to account. We have in front of us accounting, and the Day of Judgment, the day of reward or punishment. We have in front of us a bridge, and the bridge is thinner than a strand of hair and sharper than a sword, and the people must pass over it. If we took a board of wood the length of which is, for example, eight meters, and placed it between two tall buildings, and the board is only eight meters long. Then if you are told to walk across the board, would you be able to do it? The two buildings are only six stories high, and there is nothing between them except that board. You might fall, and become nothing but small pieces. This is even though the distance is only maybe six, seven, or eight meters. What is that? It is nothing but to cross from this end to that. So we ask Allaah to make us firm. The people are careless and heedless! The people are careless except those whom Allaah has mercy upon. Also, the width of the board we mentioned would be perhaps a handspan, while the bridge on the Day of Judgment will be thinner than a strand of hair, and sharper than a sword, while it is also very long. And what is under the bridge is the expanse of Hellfire, and this is only six stories high. Six stories, and yet one could easily become dizzy, and fall and die. How can you not guard yourselves?

May Allaah grant you good, speak to the hypocrites, the communists, the Baathees, the secularists, and tell them, "Beware! Watch out for yourselves, for you only follow your own desires, and you think that you will be secure in the Day of Judgment from the punishment of Allaah. ﴿ ***So, your Lord poured on them different kinds of severe torment.***﴾- ***(Surat Al-Fajr***, Ayat 13)" They must fear Allaah in their own actions before Allaah takes them in a great punishment. You constantly and forever are calling to the woman's going out beautified and uncovered, to misguidance, to ascribing partners to Allaah, to going astray and fleeing from the religion and all righteousness. To them, religion is old-fashioned, not in keeping with the modern times, and harsh, while disbelief and misguidance is what they themselves love, and we ask Allaah for peace and wellbeing.

There is also the saying of the Prophet, may praise and salutations be upon him, ***{ For one of you to be stabbed in the head with a needle would be better than for him to touch a woman who is not lawful for him. }*** (Collected by at-Tabarani in "*al-Kabeer*", narrated on Mi'qal Ibn Yasaar, may Allaah be pleased with him with a good chain of narration) Tell this to those who shake hands with women, and the one who places his hand in that of his female friend's, and they dance together and sport together. Fear Allaah, Oh worshippers of Allaah! Oh Allaah, indeed we declare ourselves free from what those people do, we declare ourselves free from what those people do, those who do not fear Allaah in the affairs of their religion, the nation, their way of life, the Book and the Sunnah, or in anything at all! By following their desires, they wish to turn away from the truth a significant turning, and they want the *Ummah* and the society to turn away from the truth a significant turning. So, Oh Allaah, we declare ourselves free from their actions.

This is, by Allaah, a misfortune; this is a misfortune. Indeed Allaah, Exalted is He, decreed that Iraq be filled with secular Baathism, communism, revolts, calamity, disasters, misfortunes, and fleeing from the truth. Then you have seen and witnessed what Allaah has done to them now, and what He has done with Saddam, who fought against the truth and the religion. Allaah has destroyed him, and put him under the power of some of the most evil of His creation, put Saddam under the power of one who is even more evil than him or equaling him in evil. The punishment came to him from all around, from in front of him, behind him, on his right, and on his left, from above him and below him, and he could do anything but wait for his destruction- and his country, his political party, and his army were all destroyed as well.

Allaah says, ﴾ ***So when they angered Us, We punished them,*** ﴿ (Surat Az-Zukhruf, Ayat 56)

The Messenger of Allaah says, ﴾ ***Indeed Allaah prolongs the reign of an oppressor, until when He takes him He does not spare him.*** ﴿ (Agreed Upon, and Narrated on the authority of Abu Musa Al-Ash'aree, May Allaah be pleased with him) Where is Yaasir Arafat? Where is his disassociation with the secularists? Where is his call to *tawheed*? Isn't it necessary for him to worship Allaah alone and call to the religion of Islaam? Secularism has entered into the heads of some of the people and changed them into Masons and secularists, all except for those upon whom Allaah has mercy. Where is Yaasir Arafat now? Did falsehood and evil help him at all? They did not help him. Everyone should fear Allaah in his affairs. A president and those he rules over, a king and his subjects, a shepherd and his flock, rich and poor, educated and ignorant common people, everyone must fear Allaah. Indeed Allaah is All-Hearing, All-Seeing, All-Knowing, All-Powerful, and He has the most severe punishment, the punishment that is unbearable.

﴾ ***And your Lord comes with the angels in rows. And Hell will be brought near that Day. On that Day will man remember, but how will that remembrance (then) avail him? He will say: "Alas! Would that I had sent forth (good deeds) for (this) my life!" So on that Day none will punish as He will***

punish. And none will bind (the wicked, disbelievers and polytheists) as He will bind. ﴾- (Surat al-Fajr, Ayats 22-26)

There is no punishment like the punishment of Allaah and no prison like the prison of Allaah for those who go against His commands, disobey Him, those who have called to wrongdoing, and warned away from good actions! For those who call for the women to go out, uncovered and beautified! A severe punishment, a punishment that, by Allaah, is great! An unbearable punishment! So watch out for your daughter. Beware of the mixing between men and women in the universities. Do not allow your daughter to study in these mixed universities, but rather let her stay in her home honorably, and learn the Qur'aan and the Sunnah. Let her learn modesty and shyness, belief, tranquility, and certainty. Do not allow her to enter mixed schools, not elementary, not high school, not college. Say to her, "My daughter, this life is only temporary. I will die, and you also, everyone will die. ﴿ ***Whatsoever is on it (the earth) will perish. And the Face of your Lord full of Majesty and Honor will remain forever.*** ﴾- (Surat Ar-Rahmaan, Ayat 27) Stay in your home, and that will bring you honor. Allaah says, ﴿ ***And stay in your houses, and do not display yourselves like that of the times of ignorance.*** ﴾.

They gather them in the schools, as they have schemes in store for them. They say, "We are having a celebration, we are having a fair for the young women to attend, meet, dance, and do this and that." So you prepared your daughter for this, you brought her to it. Rather let her stay in her home, May Allaah grant you good. Allaah will make her independent of employment, Allaah will make her independent of needing to become a doctor, Allaah will make her independent of this world and what is in it. Whoever leaves something for Allaah's sake, then Allaah gives him something better than it. The people of today are wolves, except those upon whom Allaah has mercy. It is not only the teachers, except those upon whom Allaah has mercy, it is not only the doctors, except those upon whom Allaah has mercy, but it is the common people in the streets as well, who have become nothing but human wolves, except those upon whom Allaah has mercy.

Your daughter should stay with you, honored, respected, and held dear, being taught in her home to read and write and do math, to memorize Qur'aan, and learn ahaadeeth and the explanation of the Qur'aan. And if there is a *masjid* close by that holds classes for the women, with no biased partisanship to some group, organization, or sect, or the like of it, which has classes on the Book and the Sunnah, then that is good. Let her pray the obligatory prayers, fast the month of *Ramadhaan*, and learn the book of her Lord, and the Sunnah of her messenger, Muhammad, praise and salutations be upon him, and your reward for that will be great, for teaching your wife, or your daughter, or your sister. This is from the good actions, ﴿ ***And whatever good you send before you for yourselves (i.e. nawaafil – non-obligatory acts of worship: prayers, charity, fasting, hajj and 'umrah), you will certainly find it with Allaah, better and greater in reward.*** ﴾- (Surat Al-Muzammil, Ayat 20)

My brothers, if a girl becomes accustomed to going out every day to school, then it ingrains itself in her head, and if you attempt to prevent her, she says, "I will go out, I will go," repeatedly, and she then leaves. Yet it is her father who let her become accustomed to that. She meets her girlfriend so and so, and so and so, and she meets Professor so and so, and Professor so and so; therefore beware. Do not let them get accustomed to going out like this. ***﴾ And stay in your houses, and do not display yourselves like that of the times of ignorance. ﴿*** Her provisions are already written for her, Allaah has already ordained this, and no person dies without having received their share.

Perhaps Allaah will provide her with a righteous husband, who will assist her in righteousness and fear of Allaah, and will make it easy for her to study the legislated knowledge, and the Sunnah. It is, By Allaah, an honor for her in this world and the Hereafter. How many now, from among the male university students say, "We do not want the female university students as wives." They do not want them, and say that the female university students are looked at and viewed by whoever wishes to do so! Rather, they say that they want a female student of knowledge, who is chaste, well-protected, a pearl, a beautiful jewel in her family's house, and her mother is the best of mothers, helping her daughter to fear Allaah, and gain knowledge and understand the religion. And her father is the best of fathers, helping her to fear Allaah, and gain knowledge and understand the religion. As for these people related to this university, this doctor and that doctor, this professor and that professor, then we already know about these types of people. He is a doctor, but he does not pray. What kind of doctor is this? And a professor, but he does not pray. What kind of professor is this? Where is the righteous professor, who lowers his gaze, does not shave his beard, no smoking, no qat, with no secular Nasserism ideas in his head, nor communism, nor democracy, nor Baathism, no hypocrisy in his heart, where is this type? They are not found there, except for those whom Allaah has mercy on.

I ask Allaah for firmness, soundness, and assistance, for me, and all of you, and all of the Muslims, Oh Allaah, take on the enemies of Islaam, Oh Allaah, take on the enemies of Islaam, Oh Allaah, take on the enemies of Islaam, Oh Allaah, whoever fights against Islaam then fight him, Oh Allaah, whoever plots against Islaam then plot against him, and whoever betrays Islaam then cause him to be betrayed, Oh Lord of the universe. Oh Allaah, whoever desires evil for Islaam and the Muslims than stick his plot in his neck, and busy him with his own self, and make his organizing into a disaster for him, Oh Lord of the Universe. And much praise and salutations be upon our prophet Muhammad, and his family, and companions.

[Transcribed and translated from audio cassette]

Review and Discussion Questions

Questions for The Danger of Going out Beautified and Mixing with the Men

Review:

1. What are three proofs that we must advise and urge one another to that which is good, and away from that which is bad? (Page 47, Top half of page)
2. How does the Sheikh, may Allaah preserve him, compare the hypocrite to the Believer? List two verses concerning the hypocrites. (Page 48, Bottom half of page
3. List two proofs (one verse and one hadeeth) that we are responsible to Allaah for those under our care. (Page 50, Top half of page)
4. What is the proof that one cannot mix freely with her in-laws? How does the Sheikh explain this? (Page 55, Bottom half of page)
5. List some more proofs that free mixing of the sexes is unlawful. (Page 56, Bottom half of page, to Page 57, Top half of page)

Discussion & Consideration:

6. Explain how submission is a condition for true belief.
7. In the time of the Prophet, the women were commanded to guard their modesty and chastity. Explain why this is even more important for us today.
8. List five ways that a woman is a leader and has a place of honor in her home and her community.
9. In what ways does the Western call to "liberate" the woman actually call for her to be a slave?
10. Is it true that Islaam does not allow girls to be educated? List some ways in which we can ensure that our children are educated in that which is beneficial without overstepping the bounds of Islaam.

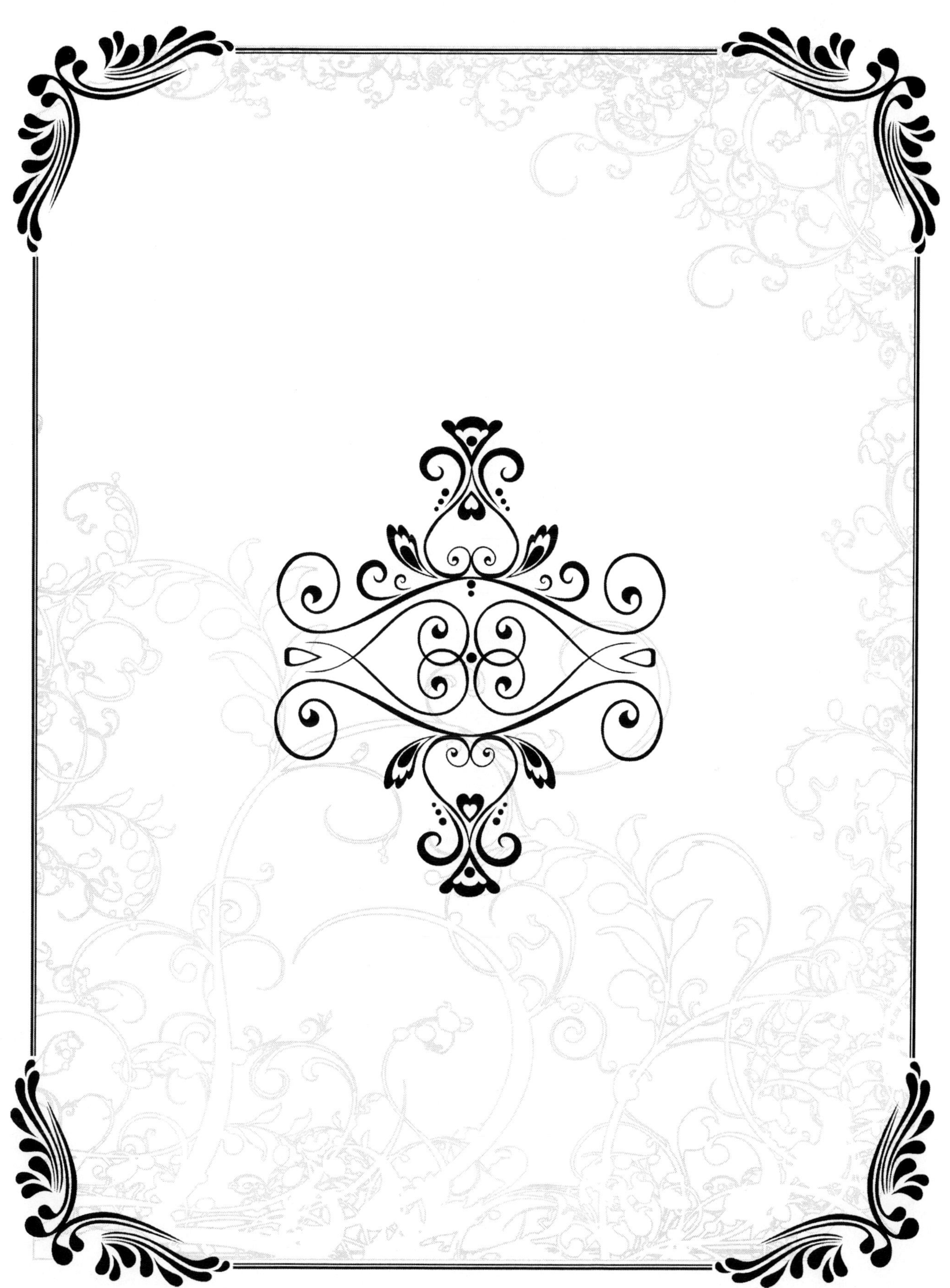

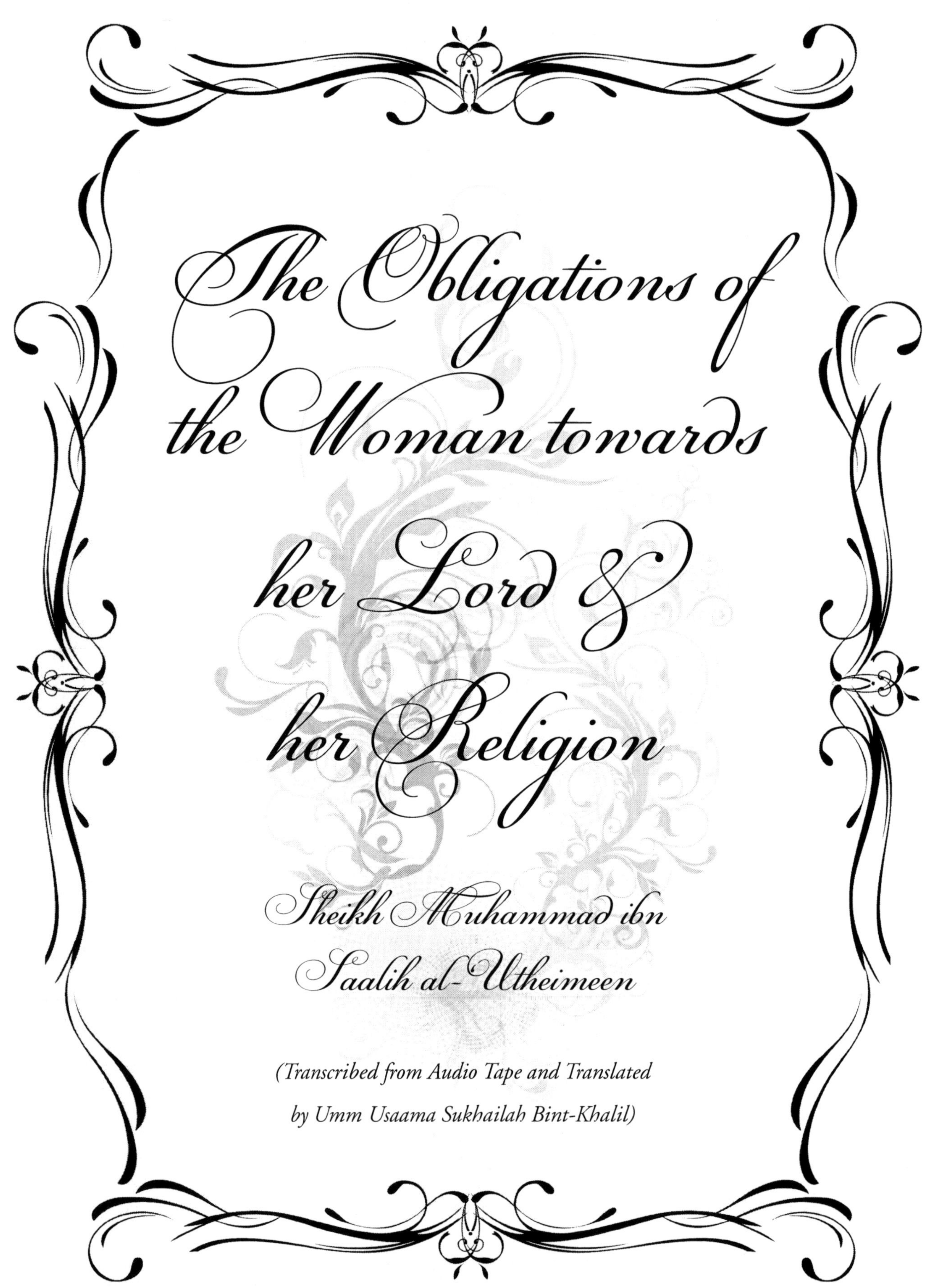

The Obligations of the Woman towards her Lord & her Religion

Sheikh Muhammad ibn Saalih al-'Utheimeen

(Transcribed from Audio Tape and Translated by Umm Usaama Sukhailah Bint-Khalil)

All praise is to Allaah, Lord of the worlds, and praise and salutations be upon Muhammad, the Seal of the Prophets, and the Imaam of the pious, and upon his family and companions and those who follow them in good until the Day of Judgment. To proceed:

It pleases me this day, Tuesday, the thirtieth of Jumada al-Akhirah, the month after Jumada al-Ula, in the year 1413, to attend the college for training women teachers, in order that Allaah might make it easy for us to give some advice or answer questions, as much as He wills.

This is because it is narrated on the Prophet, May praise and salutations be upon him, that he said, ***{A believer to a believer is like a building, some of it holds the other parts up.}*** (Muslim, No. 6257) And he said, ***{ The example of the believers in their love and mercy and gentleness with each other is like one body, if one part of the body ails, the rest follows it in tiredness and fever. }*** (Muslim No. 6,258)

And just as a man has rights upon another man, a woman has rights upon the man as well; as Allaah says,﴿ ***And they women have rights (over their husbands as regards living expenses) similar to those of their husbands over them (as regards obedience and respect) to what is reasonable*** ﴾- (Surat al-Baqara, Ayat 228)

And if it is obligatory upon the people of knowledge to get together with the men in order to advise them and admonish them, then it is also obligatory upon them to get together with the women and advise and admonish them. In relation to this, the women came to the Messenger of Allaah, may Allaah's praise and salutations be upon him, and said to him, "Indeed the men have taken over your time, so appoint a day in which you come to us." So the Messenger of Allaah promised them a day in which they then gathered, and he would admonish them. This is the precedent for the fact that it is obligatory upon the people of knowledge from among the men to share their knowledge with the women as they share it with the men.

However, it is from the mercy of Allaah that in these times, it is possible for any woman who desires to seek knowledge to derive benefit from Islamic tapes- for tapes are available, and all praise is due to Allaah, and they are extremely easy to obtain, and this makes it possible for a woman to listen to that which a man says amongst other men, from beginning to end, and to hear the questions which are put to him and the answers he gives. However, hearing about something is not the same as seeing it yourself, and sometimes a woman may have problems which need to be directly addressed by the people of knowledge. Because of this, I saw that it was obligatory upon me to accept the invitation put forth by this college to come to this place, for the purpose of exploring that which is obligatory upon the woman in regards to her religion and society.

The foundational ruling in this is that the woman is like the man concerning that which is obligatory upon her and what is forbidden to her, and what is recommended for her, and generally in all of the rulings of the religion, both in theory and in action. And it is the same for the men, for they are similar to the women in that which is obligatory, or forbidden, or recommended, because the basic ruling is that the men and the women are the same in the rulings of Allaah, except in that which the Islamic law has specified a matter for one or for the other. In these cases, then it is necessary for the men to fulfill that which is specific to them, and for the women to fulfill that which is specific to them.

There is no doubt that there are some things which are specific to women and not men. The woman has obligations to Allaah in her religion, and has obligations to Allaah in her society. As for her obligations towards her religion, then it is upon her to fear Allaah, in private and in public, and fear of Allaah is righteousness in the heart combined with righteousness in the body, as the Prophet, may Allaah's praise and salutations be upon him, said, ***{ Indeed there is a piece of flesh in the body, and if it becomes righteous, then the entire body also becomes righteous, and if it becomes evil, then the entire body also becomes evil, indeed, it is the heart. }*** (Bukharee 53, Muslim 3081, Ibn Maajah 3982)

And fear of Allaah is acted upon by performing the prayer, giving the obligatory charity, fasting, *Hajj,* good treatment of parents, fulfilling the ties of kinship, having good relations with neighbors, taking good care of ones affairs, and other than that from that which is well-known from the religion of Allaah. Likewise, it is also upon her to stay away from all that which Allaah has forbidden, from evil actions and greater sins, as well as smaller sins. Also from that, meaning, from that which it is necessary upon her to shun and avoid, is going out uncovered and beautified, as occurs with some of the women, who go out beautified in their clothing, countenance, or scent. It is not permissible for her to leave her house beautified by her clothing, or scented so that her fragrance spreads, or walking in a beautified manner, leaning forward (walking in a provocative way), because all of these are reasons for corruption and matters which call to evil. Because of this, we see that Allaah says in His book,

﴾ ***And come not near to unlawful sex.*** ﴿- (Surat Al Israa', Ayat 32), ﴾ ***Come not near to al-fawaahish (great sins and illegal sexual intercourse) whether committed openly or secretly*** ﴿- (Surat Al-An'aam, Ayat 151)

So the forbiddance of coming near to fornication and evil deeds also includes everything that leads to these things; and there is no doubt that going out beautified and scented is a reason for eventually committing evil and forbidden actions. Because of this, it is obligatory upon every woman, if it is necessary for her to leave the house, that she go out in the manner that is requested of her, and that manner is that which the Prophet, may Allaah's praise and salutations be upon him, said in one (Arabic) word, ***{ the women go out without having any fragrant smell apparent from of their body }*** (Musannaf Abdur-Razzaq 4964) Meaning, staying very far away from causing corruption by their clothing, appearance, or by any fragrance.

And from that which it is necessary to avoid is a woman being alone with a man who is not her *mahram*, except if her *mahram* is also present. This is because the Prophet, may Allaah's praise and salutations be upon, said, ***{ A man should not be alone with a woman except with her mahram. }*** (al-Bukhaari, Vol. 9, No. 233, and Muslim, Vol. 2, No. 1341) If a woman is alone with a man, no matter how righteous he is, the *Shaytaan* is the third of them, and what do you think about two people, and the *Shaytaan* is the third of them? They are in great danger; it is as though they were standing on the edge of a pit full of fire or boiling water. The women now have become accustomed to an evil custom, which is that the woman goes out alone with a driver who is not her *mahram*, and he takes her to the market, or *masjid*, with the excuse that she is safe with him. How can someone be safe who has the *Shaytaan* as her third companion along with the driver? And whoever tells herself that this is safe, than she is only telling himself meaningless excuses, with nothing substantial to support them.

The Messenger of Allaah, may Allaah's praise and salutations be upon him, is the most knowledgeable about his *Ummah*, and what their characteristics are, and how to guide them; so if it were not the case that the matter is very dangerous, then he would not have forbidden it, may Allaah's praise and salutations be upon him. For in forbiddance there is a type of restraint and suppression, and it is not possible that the Prophet, may Allaah's praise and salutations be upon him, would restrain and suppress his *Ummah* from something which had no danger in it. Rather it is obvious that there is true, real, great danger in it. And if this person thinks that he is safe, than it is indeed a false safety. We have all heard of the dangers of the man and woman being alone together, and it makes no difference whether the driver is one of the household servants, or he is a stranger who has no connection with the woman, for example a taxi driver, or a relative who is not her *mahram*, such as her paternal or maternal cousin, or other than that, for the danger is still great. Because of this, it is necessary for one to beware of such things.

And from those things which are obligatory upon the woman, and which is from fear of Allaah, is taking good care of the household, as she is the one responsible for this. She should manage it in a manner that agrees with the Islamic legislation as much as is possible. ﴾ ***And those who, when they spend, are neither extravagant nor stingy, but hold a medium way between those extremes.*** ﴿- (Surat al-Furqaan, Ayat 67)

She should neither be excessive in food, drink, dishes, furnishing, and cleaning, nor be stingy with her children. Rather, she should take a path between these two things. Neither excessive, nor stingy, for she will be asked about how she took care of this household, as the Messenger of Allaah, may Allaah's praise and salutations be upon him, said,***{ A woman is a caretaker in her husband's house and she will be questioned about that over which she was given supervision. }*** (Recorded by Bukhaari and Muslim, narrated on Abdullaah Ibn Umar)

And from that which is obligatory on the woman is that she raises her children in a good way according to the Islamic legislation, as the Islamic legislation leaves no need for any additional guidance. There is no need for us to go, or for the woman to go and study this book or that book from among those books that we know their information was not taken from the Book of Allaah, nor the Sunnah of His Messenger, may Allaah's praise and salutations be upon him. Rather these are only observed customs and practices that the people were upon, and then they extracted from that their principles of psychology, and they wrote that which they wrote concerning "good" psychological upbringing. Sometimes this manner of upbringing is far from the Islamic upbringing, and because of this it is necessary that one stay away from reading books of psychology, if they are not taken from Islamic sources, and we know that the authors are righteous men from the scholars of Islamic law. There is no problem if we take benefit from that which has been written by other than the Muslims, because it is necessary to accept all that is beneficial, no matter where it comes from. However, if the source is not known to be beneficial then it is necessary to be on our guard against what was written, for there is no benefit in evil, and it may be harmful in a way that we cannot recognize.

And from that which is obligatory upon the woman is that she learn the rulings of her religion in that which is specific to her, such as the ruling on not praying when there is a legislated excuse, as well as the legislated excuse that the rulings are based upon. Many women do not understand some of the rulings on menstruation, so she might fall into a mistake, and keep upon that, or she might find herself in a problem that she does not understand, and stay in ignorance, doing things which have no basis in the religion. And from the causes of that, meaning, the causes of the complications in the matter of menstruation, is that some women use medications that prevent menstruation or pregnancy. These medications not only harm the body, especially the womb, they also cause the woman to fall into complications. Sometimes it (her menses) comes late and other times early, and sometimes becomes irregular, and so the woman has no peace. So I warn against these medications because of their harmful effects on the emotions and the body, as well as their harmful effects upon efforts to practice the Islamic guidelines.

And from that which is obligatory upon the woman in regards to the society, is that she treat others the way she likes to be treated. The Prophet, may Allaah's praise and salutations be upon him, said, ***{ Whoever likes to be freed from the hellfire and entered into Paradise, then he should bring forth his faith and believe in Allaah and the Last Day, and he should treat the people as he wishes to be treated. }*** (Muslim 3520, Ibn Maajah 3954) So if one proceeds on this foundation in his interaction with others, great good will come to him and many people will be benefited by him.

It is obligatory upon the woman that she treat others in a good way, with gentleness, advice, guidance, and counsel. Because of this, I suggest that women callers be sent out from this college, callers to Allaah and His Messenger, callers to the truth, who make clear to the people that which was sent down to Muhammad. The woman should not confine herself to correcting her own personal practice of this religion; rather, she should take the utmost care to spread that which she has learned, so that she will be from the callers to the truth and the helpers of the truth. Allaah said to His messenger,

﴿ ***Invite (mankind, Oh Muhammad to the way of your Lord (i.e. Islaam) with wisdom (i.e. with the Divine Revelation and the Qur'aan) and fair preaching, and argue with them in a way that is better.*** ﴾- (Surat an-Nahl, Ayat 125)

And The Most High says, directing His speech to the *Ummah*, ﴿ ***Let there arise out of you a group of people inviting to all that is good (Islaam), enjoining al-ma'roof (i.e. Islamic Monotheism and all that Islaam orders one to do) and forbidding al-munkar (polytheism and disbelief and all that Islaam has forbidden). And it is they who are the successful. And be not as those who divided and differed among themselves after the clear proofs had come to them. It is they for whom there is an awful torment.*** ﴾- (Surat aal-Imraan,

Ayats 104-105)

However, it is obligatory on the caller to Allaah that she be the first to carry out that which she is calling to of righteousness and rectification; for indeed, whoever wishes to be obeyed must be the first to obey. If one is not carrying out that which he is commanding others with, then the people will have doubts about the truth of his call. One would say, 'If he was truthful in his call then he would be the first to act upon this thing that he is calling to, and if he does not, then how can he call to something that he does not himself act upon?' Because of this we say: indeed it is obligatory upon the caller to Allaah that she be the first person to act upon that which she is calling to, and the first to shun that which she is warning against. Otherwise she will be from those whom Allaah said about them,

﴾ ***Oh you who believe! Why do you say that which you do not do? Most hateful it is with Allaah that you say that which you do not do.*** ﴿- (Surat as-Saff, Ayats 2-3)

Or she will be like those Jews about whom Allaah said, ﴾ ***Enjoin you al-birr (piety and righteousness and every act of obedience to Allaah) on the people and you forget (to practice it) yourselves, while you recite the Scripture [the Tauraat]! Have you then no sense?*** ﴿- (Surat al-Baqara, Ayat 44)

And it is obligatory upon the caller to Allaah that she make clear to the people the merits and goals of Islaam, in a confident manner, without causing regret, or scolding and cursing the people. This is because some of the callers, both men and women, clash with the people, and mention their defects, and scold, and criticize, without mentioning the merits of Islaam in these actions. If he considered the merits of Islaam, then he would find that the religion of Islaam is the religion of the *fitrah* (natural disposition), and it is natural for the people to accept it and turn to it rather than rebuff it. As for clashing with the people and bringing up their wrongdoings, and mentioning their evil rather than their good, then this causes the people to flee from the acceptance of his call. Because of this, I advise the callers to Allaah to shun this way of clashing and mentioning defects. Rather, you should mention the merits of Islaam.

We were once told by a man who came here from Russia after the breakup of the Soviet Union, when some of the people began to go to the Muslim countries that had been forced into communism, until Allaah freed them from it and all praise is to Allaah, that some of the people met for a reminder of Allaah and warning. It was attended by men and women, and the women came uncovered and beautified. So some of the callers to Allaah who had come to these places said to each other, "Do not directly criticize the women, or criticize the free mixing of men and women, and going beautified, but rather, mention the merits of Islaam, and the goodness of what it enjoins from shunning the mixing of men and women, and dressing modestly and not going out beautified. Then see what happens." So they did this and did not criticize anything the women were doing. Instead, they spoke about how it is obligatory in Islaam for the men and women to stay separate, and to wear modest clothing and *hijaab*. He (the brother) said, "So we waited for three days, and after those three days, the women began to come wearing long clothing, and covering their hair, some with a handkerchief and others with a scarf. Then two weeks had not passed before they were wearing the legislated clothing of complete *hijaab*."

So look at this excellent manner of calling to Allaah, which achieves its purpose without any struggle.

It is also necessary that if a committee of female callers to Allaah is organized, that they have a leader, a director, who will instruct them and organize their actions. Without this it will be total chaos, as each woman will call to Allaah in a separate manner, and perhaps this way could be one which conflicts with the efforts of the others, so that disagreement arises between the callers and doubt will then take the place of trust previously between them. However, if they have a leader and director, then she can direct them, and tell them what the call to Allaah must consist of, starting with the most important. And if she directs all of the callers in this manner then their stance will become one, and they will agree. Also, Allaah blesses whom He wishes with eloquence, clarity, and strength in calling to Allaah and giving rulings. There is no way to make these characteristics equal in everyone, as people differ greatly in these aspects, but their methodology and path can and should be made one- but this cannot be accomplished unless a woman from the best of them is appointed as their director and leader, to make the call to Allaah (*da'wah*) go smoothly.

It is also necessary not to accept any woman who desires to be included in the committee, until it is known by interacting with her how she is qualified to call to Allaah, and what thoughts she maintains, and what her methodology is. This is because there are some women who have a strong desire to call to Allaah, but they are not qualified for this. Or she could also be ignorant of some of the matters of legislation, so because of this we say that every woman who desires to be a member of this committee or to the *da'wah* organization (not be accepted into it), except until they interact with her to determine her qualifications, or if she is already known to them, in order that she does not fall into error. For indeed, it should be understood that if an individual from a group of people falls into error, then the enemies of the *da'wah* will use this mistake and ascribe it to them all collectively, and place barriers in the path of the *da'wah*, and its ideology. And by this we will lose the people's inclination towards the religion of Allaah, and we will lose the acceptance of the people for what we are calling to.

It is very important that the spirit of affection be cultivated amongst the women, without divisions, because if division and dislike is bred among them, then it is impossible to rectify and make the society more righteous. Allaah, glorified and exalted is He, said about the believers, ﴾ ***and remember Allaah's Favor on you, for you were enemies one to another but He joined your hearts together, so that, by His Grace, you became brethren (in Islamic Faith), and you were on the brink of a pit of Fire, and He saved you from it.*** ﴿- (Surat Aal-Imraan, 105)

And this love and harmony should be weighed in the scales of the Book of Allaah and the Sunnah of his Messenger, may Allaah's praise and salutations be upon him, as the woman should not carry this love into excessiveness. Some of the women are excessive in their love for their teacher, for example, or their friend or companion, until this becomes the sole occupation of their hearts, and sometimes love of this person overcomes their love for Allaah and His Messenger. So their love for this friend of theirs, or teacher or companion, becomes everything to them, and many women fall into this error, for the *Shaytaan* beautifies this to their emotional hearts, and says that this love is for the sake of Allaah, when in reality it is love for someone along with Allaah, rather than for the sake of Allaah.

And loving someone along with Allaah is *shirk*: ﴿ ***And of mankind are some who take for worship others besides Allaah as rivals to Allaah. They love them as they love Allaah. But those who believe, love Allaah more than anything else*** ﴾- (Surat Al-Baqara, Ayat 165). So loving someone along with Allaah is a kind of *shirk*, but loving for the sake of Allaah is a type of brotherhood, and it is one of the most bonding of covenants, and it has been said: Love your beloved with some reserve, as he may be your enemy some day, and hate your enemy with some reserve, as he may be your beloved some day.

And this is wise, as a person should always walk between excessiveness and negligence, with neither one nor the other becoming prominent, and by this he will live in a moderate way without turning to excessiveness or negligence.

And because of the many questions which I foresee will be asked, I will confine my words to only that which I have already mentioned, and I ask Allaah to grant goodness and blessing in it, as well as great benefit, as indeed he is Most Generous.

And all praise is to Allah, Lord of mankind, and praise and salutations be upon our Messenger Muhammad, and his family and companions.

[Transcribed and translated from audio cassette]

Review and Discussion Questions

Questions for The Obligations of the Woman towards her Lord and her Religion by Sheikh al-'Utheimeen

Review:

1. List two proofs for the interdependence of the Muslims upon each other. (Page 63, Top half)
2. What part of the body influences the rest of the body towards good or evil? (Page 64, Top half)
3. What are some of the actions that the Sheikh, may Allaah have mercy upon him, lists as demonstrating fear of Allaah. (Page 64, Middle of page)
4. What is the proof that a woman should not be excessive in her spending, nor should she be miserly? (Page 65, Top half of page)
5. List two verses that mention giving da'wah, or calling to Allaah? (Page 66, Bottom half of page)

Discussion & Consideration:

6. Explain how it is relatively easy for the Muslim woman today to learn about her religion.
7. How do men and women differ in regards to rights and obligations? In general, are they equal or do they differ?
8. What are some of the ways that we can cut off the path to evil actions through our own deeds?
9. What are some of the actions that the Sheikh, may Allaah have mercy upon him, brings as obligations upon the woman in regards to her self, her home and her family?
10. In what ways can the woman who is calling to Allaah help to ensure that her call will be effective? What are some of her obligations in regards to this tremendous task?

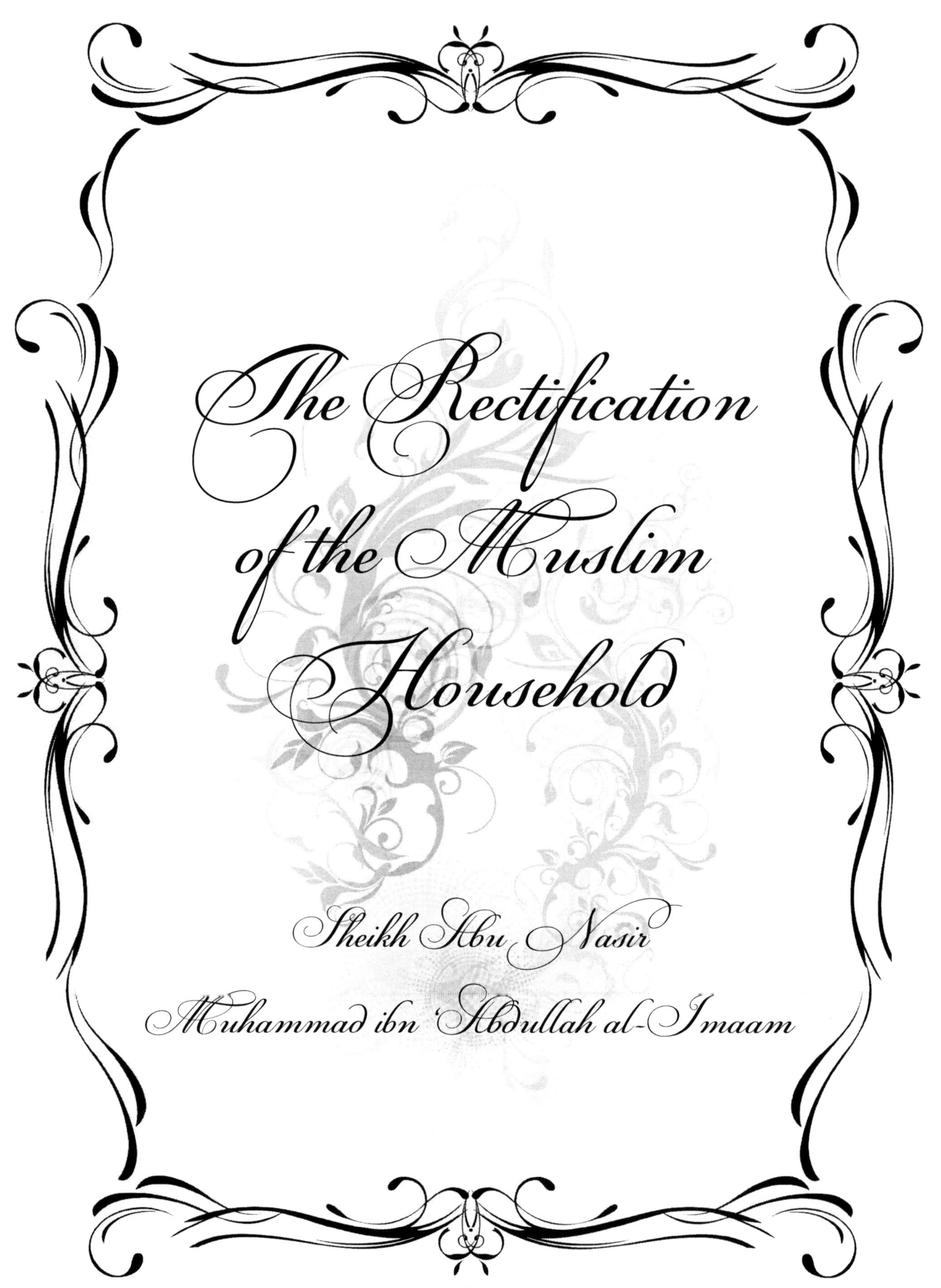

The Rectification of the Muslim Household

Sheikh Abu Nasir
Muhammad ibn 'Abdullah al-Imaam

The First Part of the Khutbah

All praise is due to Allaah Alone. We praise Him, seek His help, and ask His forgiveness. We seek refuge in Allaah from the evil of our souls, and the adverse consequences of our deeds. Whomsoever Allaah guides, there is none who can misguide him, and whoever He misguides, there is none who can guide him.

I bear witness that there is nothing worthy of worship except for Allaah; He is alone and has no partners. I bear witness and testify that Muhammad, may Allaah's praise and salutations be upon him and his family, is His perfect worshipper, and messenger.

﴾ ***Oh you who believe! Fear Allaah, as He deserves, and die not except as Muslims.*** ﴿ -(Surat aal 'Imraan, Ayat 102)

﴾ ***Oh mankind! Fear your Lord, Who created you from a single soul, and from him, He created his wife, and from these two, He created multitudes of men and women. Fear Allaah, from Whom you demand your mutual rights, and do not cut off the ties of kinship. Verily, Allaah is Ever-Watcher over you.*** ﴿-(Surat an-Nisaa', Ayat 1)

﴾ ***Oh you who believe! Fear Allaah, and say righteous speech. He will direct you to do righteous deeds, and He will forgive you your sins. And whoever obeys Allaah and His Messenger has indeed achieved the ultimate success.*** ﴿- (Surat al-Ahzaab, Ayats 70-71)

As to what follows:

Indeed from the greatness of Islaam and its comprehensiveness is the attention and consideration which it gives to rectification of the households; as the houses of the Muslims must establish Islaam upon the way of the Prophet. How could Islaam not give attention to it, when it is the foundation of good within the society, the nation and the land- when this is due to the state of the household? So Islaam has given great attention and consideration to educating the Muslims in how they must establish their households and act within them. Allaah says in His Noble Book,

﴾ ***And remember (Oh you the members of the Prophet's family, the Graces of your Lord), that which is recited in your houses of the Verses of Allaah and al-hikmah. Verily, Allaah is Ever Most Courteous, Well-Acquainted (with all things).*** ﴿- (Surat al-Ahzaab, Ayat 34)

Remember that which is recited in your houses from the verses of Allaah, meaning the Qur'aan, and from *al-hikmah*, meaning, the purified Sunnah. So it is necessary, oh Muslim, that your house be a source of good; and if you want for it to indeed be like that, then adhere to the practice if teaching and educating within your house. Adhere, as well, to commanding the good and forbidding the evil in your house, and hold fast to the advice and counsel concerning that which is related to you and your family in your house. The husband and wife are both included in the meaning of rectification of the households, as they are both foundations of the Muslim household, anchors in its support, and that which establishes and holds its pillars firm; as it is through them that the family is rectified or perishes and fails.

The husband succeeds in that which there can be success, and attains proper goals in a beneficial and correct manner when he joins together two matters- having fear of Allaah and strictness in the house. The Lord of the Worlds has said in His Noble Book,

﴾ ***Oh you who believe! Verily, among your wives and your children there are enemies for you (who may stop you from the obedience of Allaah); therefore beware of them!*** ﴿- (Surat at-Taghaabun, from Ayat 14)

The "enemies" here are not malicious enemies, in hatred and enmity; rather they are, in truth, enemies because of love. As the man will often incline one way or another due to love of his family and children, until he disregards and excuses their deviations from the correct way, as well as their mistakes- and anything that is mentioned to him concerning the faults or defects of his family or children causes him to defend or attempt to vindicate them. This type of person must know that there is no medicine for the people of his household better than judging and deciding according to the Islamic legislation- as utilizing other than the Islamically legislated rulings causes him to deviate, whether due to excessiveness or negligence, or in the way of strictness and severity or its opposite weakness and lack of firmness.

And the woman, likewise, is called upon to carry out the matters necessary for the rectification of the household. Concerning this, al-Bukhaari and Muslim have narrated from the hadeeth of 'Abdullah ibn 'Umar, may Allaah be pleased with both of them, in which the Messenger of Allaah, may Allaah's praise and salutations be upon him, said,

{...and the woman is a guardian in her husband's house...} (al-Bukhaari, No. 853, Muslim, No. 1829)

So the importance of the woman, and that which she undertakes in order to rectify the household, is not any less than the importance of the man in this issue.

That house is a righteous one when there occurs cooperation from both the man and from his wife; as when the husband and wife establish a household upon the directions of the prophetic methodology, there will result from this a rectification of both the house and the family, and the light will spread and goodness and blessings will come to the family- and the family will be one of virtue, chasteness and piety.

There is nothing for which there is a greater need than that we rectify the households, as the households are being brought to ruin; meaning, the Muslims are being torn from their foundations. Rectification of the houses preserves the true wealth of goodness of the household. In regard to this, it is most important for the person, when he seeks to marry, that he searches for a righteous woman. This is because he wants to build a family, and this family is itself a cause for the establishment of the Muslim nation. Likewise, the righteous woman, when she seeks to marry- it is necessary for her family and guardians to find for her a righteous, pious man- as the issue is in fact that of establishing the religion of Allaah, the Lord of the Worlds, Glorified is He, Most High.

When many of those in charge of the family are ignorant of the importance of rectifying the household, and are negligent concerning this duty, many of the households of the Muslims become filled with that which opposes and conflicts with the legislation decreed by Allaah. Their degree of ignorance may be lesser or greater; but in either case, it brings about the eventual destruction of the household from its very foundations.

From the mistakes and destroyers of the houses and the family is a great deal of quarrelling and disagreement between the husband and wife. This leads to acting hurriedly concerning getting divorced. The wife says, "Divorce me!" and the husband sets out to do that, whether she demands it of him or not. This is what the *Shaytaan* wants, as the Messenger of Allaah, may Allaah's praise and salutations be upon him, made clear with his saying,

{Iblees places his throne upon water; he then sends detachments out for creating dissension; the nearest to him in rank are those who are most notorious in creating dissension. One of them comes and says, 'I did so and so'. And he says, 'You have done nothing'. Then one amongst them comes and says, 'I did not spare so and so until I sowed the seed of discord between a husband and a wife. So Iblees approaches him and says, 'Yes, you '.} (Narrated in Muslim, No. 2813, on the authority of Jaabir ibn 'Abdullah, may Allaah be pleased with him) Meaning (by, *'Yes, you'*): ' You are the one who deserves my reward and praise, because you have succeeded in performing your duty to me.'

Look, oh Worshipper of Allaah, how *Shaytaan* views the dissension between a husband and wife as being greater than drinking alcohol, knowing that this, drinking alcohol, is the mother of the great sins- why is this!? And this is what often occurs. As for separation between the husband and the wife, then it destroys that which the heads of the family have built up for a time that seemed like forever, over a lifetime, as well as a separation and discord of that which has been brought together for the purpose of that establishment of the household; as it is necessary for each one of them, the husband and the wife, to build this life from new- especially the woman. And if causing separation between the spouses is from the duties of the *Shayaateen* of the *jinn*, then it is also from the tasks of the *Shayaateen* amongst mankind, such as the ones who perform magic, and other than them. And that which the *Shayaateen* of the *Shayaateen* perform of separation and disruption in relation to the married couple undertake- then the *Shayaateen* of mankind likewise follow them in this. Allaah, the Most High, has said, clarifying that which the *Shayaateen* of mankind do with the husband and wife,

﴿ ***...people learn that by which they cause separation between man and his wife...*** ﴾- (Surat al-Baqara, from Ayat 102)

And this spreading of differing which is caused by the *Shayaateen* from the men is that which the married people engage in most often; particularly the wives upon their husbands and close family members, in taking revenge upon others.

Connected to this, is the group which seeks to sow dissension between the husband and wife by way of setting one of them against the other using any possible method from the different methods of doing this. It is related in Abu Daawud, al-Haakim, and other than them from the hadeeth of Abi Hurairah, may Allaah be pleased with him, that he said, that the Messenger of Allaah, may Allaah's praise and salutations be upon him, said,

{He is not of us, who causes mischief between the woman and her husband}

(Abu Daawud, No. 2175, al-Haakim, 2/196, and Ahmad, 2/397 and Sheikh al-Albaani, may Allaah have mercy upon him, has declared it to be authentic in "*as-Saheehah*" Number 324)

Meaning by "causes mischief", that he causes her to turn against her husband, or be in disagreement with him.

This foolishness reaches a point with some of the married couples, that divorce is pronounced quickly from the tip of their tongues. But these people should fear Allaah, and safeguard the rulings and wisdom of Allaah concerning marriage.

So, worshipper of Allaah, guard your tongue! As how many from the people are taken by surprise when he asks the scholars concerning this issue of divorcing his wife, while he has actually previously divorced her with the final permissible divorce years ago without realizing he has done so- and so he has unknowingly lived with her in a way that is forbidden and immoral, believing that she was still his wife; and this has all occurred simply because he was excessive or hasty in his speech!?

So, oh worshipper of Allaah, it is often the case that divorce is pronounced and demanded without attempting those other means to solve their differences, such as solving the marriage difficulties by finding a remedy for them and getting advice, or separating from the woman for a certain time, or admonishing her by striking her in a manner which is not excessive or severe, and warning, exhortation and counsel.

Also from the calamities which occur in many of the houses, is that which comes about from the spouses- and particularly from the women- of calling upon the *jinn* and invoking them against the children and the animals, such as saying to them: "Oh *jinn* of the tribe of so and so, take this person or that person!" (Translator's note: This is often done by the mothers merely to frighten the children- they do not necessarily believe that the *jinn* called upon will actually come and harm the child. A corollary in the West would be warning the child to be good or the "bogey man" will come and get you. Of course, it does occur also that the mother does intend this evil thing- may Allaah protect us from both of these things.) Many children have suffered because of this, and they have not done anything wrong. And the *jinn* are thus informed about them and harm them, and yet this harm comes about because of the supplication of the mother, as she has called upon the *jinn*, or *ifreet*, or the strong *jinn*, or the *Shayaateen*; and we ask Allaah to protect us from that! Indeed, some of the women call the *jinn* upon themselves, and this is due to profound ignorance concerning the intervention and preservation (from that) which is available for the Muslim. So that we must all join together in accepting this and supplicate against the attacks of the *Shayaateen*, and seek Allaah's protection against them, and return to utilizing legislated supplications and remembrance of Allaah, in order that Allaah preserve us from their plots and evil. But, where are they, those who call in this way upon the *Shayaateen*, in relation to utilizing these legislated fortifications, and these divinely proscribed defenses? How shameful is the ignorance of the Muslims!

Likewise, from among other things is that which occurs in some of the houses from the grave matter of cursing; indeed, it is common amongst some of them. Even one curse is a great sin- so how about if the curses are increased, so that from the spouses is the one who says, "Upon you be sixteen curses"; and some of them say one hundred! And a great many of the curses are from the women upon their children, their neighbors, and their livestock.

It is related in "*Saheeh Muslim*" (Number 79) from the hadeeth of Ibn 'Umar, may Allaah be pleased with both him and his father, that the Messenger, may Allaah's praise and salutations be upon him, said,

{Oh women! Give a good deal of charity, as I have seen that you are prevalent amongst the people of the Hellfire!} They said, "Oh Messenger of Allaah, what is the matter with us, that we make up the majority of the people of the Hellfire?" He replied, {Because you curse much, and are ungrateful to your husbands.}

Cursing, in this narration, has increased their entrance to the Hellfire; as the one who does not repent to Allaah is not safe from the punishment of Allaah which is mentioned in this hadeeth. And from that which is necessary is they are made to know that the curse returns upon the one who states it if the one who is originally cursed does not deserve it. It has been related in the hadeeth of Ibn 'Abaas, may Allaah be pleased with both him and his father, and other than him, that the Messenger of Allaah, may Allaah's praise and salutations be upon him, said, ***{The one who curses something which is undeserving of the curse , then the curse returns upon him.}*** (Abu Daawud, No. 4908, and at-Tirmidhi, No. 2016, and Sheikh al-Albaani has stated that it is authentic)

Also from that which many of the households enter into from those things which hinder their rectification is when the spouses engage in a lot of insulting, swearing and using abusive language, and lying; whether from one of them concerning that which is due to the another; or from the children- do they know that the Messenger, may Allaah's praise and salutations be upon him, said, ***{Insulting the Muslim is wrongdoing, and killing him is disbelief.}*** This hadeeth is agreed upon from the hadeeth of 'Abdullaah ibn Mas'ood, may Allaah be pleased with him. (al- Bukhaari, No. 48, Muslim, No.24)

It is also brought forth in the hadeeth of Abi Dardaa', may Allaah be pleased with him, which is found in Muslim, that the Messenger of Allaah, may Allaah's praise and salutations be upon him, said, ***{The ones who invoke curses will not have intercession, nor will they be able to intercede for others, on the Day of Judgment.}*** (Number 2598)

So, oh Muslims, purify your tongue from shameful and indecent speech, from those things which we have already mentioned as well as those which we have not mentioned. And if you raise the children upon insults, curses and lies because they are following the example of their parents- then how damaging and harmful this is to both the children and the parents! So the fathers and mothers must resolve to curb and control their language when one of them becomes angry at the other, or becomes angry at the children.

Also from the disasters which occur in many of the houses of the Muslims is belittling and playing around with the obligatory prayers- how sorrowful this is! How is this to be belittled, and it is the greatest pillar after the *shahaadah*, and the greatest of acts, and also that which Allaah has made to be that which differentiates the Muslim and the disbeliever, between the one who worships Allaah alone and the one who associates others along with Him in worship?! So there are fathers and mothers who neglect their sons and daughters, leaving them free to do as they wish- they pray when they like, so their religion becomes a trifling thing to them, something to play with- except those who hear the saying of Allaah, Glorified and Exalted is He, to His prophet,

(***And enjoin the prayers on your family, and be patient in offering them (i.e. the prayers). We ask not of you a provision: We provide for you. And the good end (i.e. Paradise) is for the pious.***) (Surah Taa Haa, Ayat 132)

As well as the saying of the Prophet, may Allaah's praise and salutations be upon him, ***{Command your children to perform the prayer when they are at the age of seven, and beat them (if they are negligent of it) when they reach the age of ten, and separate their beds.}*** (Abu Daawud, No. 490 and Ahmad, 2/187, from the hadeeth of 'Abdullaah Ibn 'Amr, may Allaah be pleased with him; and Sheikh al-Albaani has declared it to be authentic, may Allaah have mercy upon him)

So it is obligatory upon the fathers and mothers to persist in enjoining the prayers on their children, both male and female. As perhaps a girl reaches the age of maturity and reason, and yet does not pray, or does not make the preservation of the prayer a habit because of the heedlessness of her father and mother. So fear Allaah, oh Worshippers of Allaah! We have been commanded to teach them the prayer from the age of seven, and to beat them ***(if they are negligent of it)*** when they are ten- so if they put it off or are playing or they lie by saying that they have prayed when they have not- then they should be educated concerning this lying before they are mature.

Likewise, Islaam teaches the Muslims what the family should be like, as well as how to make their houses places of worship of Allaah, the Lord of the Worlds, Glorified is He.

As the pious people have been commanded to preserve their people and their children from the punishment and displeasure of Allaah, Glorified is He, as Allaah, the Most High, says,

﴿ ***Oh you who believe! Ward off yourselves and your families against a Fire whose fuel is men and stones, over which are (appointed) angels stern (and) severe, who disobey not, (from executing) the commands they receive from Allaah, but do that which they are commanded.*** ﴾-(Surat at-Tahreem, Ayat 6)

Likewise, from that which occurs often in the houses of the Muslims- except for those who are protected by Allaah's mercy- is the presence of singing and musical instruments- as they contain many evils. As one of the scholars has said, "Music brings forth hypocrisy, immorality, stubbornness, and heedlessness in a people." And it is sufficient to clarify the great danger of it, and the vast amount of evil it contains, to mention the saying of the Prophet, may Allaah's praise and salutations be upon him, ***{Two voices are cursed, in this life and in the next: the pipes at the time of blessing, and the shrieking at the time of calamity.}*** (Narrated by al-Bazaar as found in "*al-Kashf*", 1/377, No. 795, and Abu Bakr ash-Shaafi'ee has narrated it in "*ar-Rubaa'yaat*", 2/1:22, and al-Maqdasee in, "*al-Ahaadeeth al-Mukhtaara*", 6/188, 2200,2201 from Anas, may Allaah be pleased with him, as the scholar of ahaadeeth in our time, Sheikh al-Albaani, may Allaah have mercy upon him, has mentioned in his book "*Tahreem Aalaatal-Lahu wa at-Tarb*", page 51, and he has declared it to be authentic.) And the "voice of the pipes" includes music.

Along with this is another well known means of corruption which has appeared in many of the homes- the television and the satellite television channels. As how many of these show immorality and vice, and call to them!? These cause the same effect in the ones who watch and listen to them as poisons cause in their bodies. So how contemptible is it that the Muslims allow these evils to enter their homes, which cause their intellects to become corrupt, contaminate their thoughts and ideas, defile their inherent natures, destroy their values, and cause the breakdown of their characters? Do you not have any intellect, oh Muslims, that you do not show any care or concern for long-possessed honor, and praiseworthy distinction? As it has come about that the condition of some of the Muslims has reached the point about which the poet said:

You would be heard if you called one of the living

But there is no life in the one whom you call

If you blow on fire it will light up

But you are blowing on ashes

From that which has also afflicted the homes is the presence of pictures of those things which contain souls for which there is no overriding necessity, and for which there is no legislated reason for them to be present. And from these pictures of which there is no doubt concerning their impermissibility and which cause harm to the people of the house, are those photos simply kept for memories. They fill up the walls of the rooms and the sitting places as they are hung up there! And it is related in al-Bukhaari and Muslim from the hadeeth of 'Aishah, as well as the hadeeth of Abi Talhah, may Allaah be pleased with them both, that the Messenger of Allaah, may Allaah's praise and salutations be upon him, said,

{Indeed, the angels do not enter a house in which there is a dog or a picture.} (al-Bukhaari, No. 2150, and Muslim, No. 2107)

The angels which are mentioned in the hadeeth are those by whom Allaah sends His mercy to you, and they are appointed specifically to you, and they safeguard you, your children and your family from the general *Shayaateen* and the *ifreet -meaning the powerful jinn*, as well as the sorcerers, the soothsayers, the trespassers or assailants, and diseases. With this these angels are driven away from entering the houses- this possessing of pictures! As if these angels are evicted, and the houses are empty of them, and the family is deprived of them- then look out for the *jinn* and the *Shayaateen* to pour into such houses, and so beware of their harming the family and their corruption of it. Glorified be Allaah!

How often the heedless Muslim fights himself, with his own self, and how many causes of harm to his family, children, and near relatives come about without him being aware of them? So it is upon them to get the aforementioned pictures out of their houses, and from their places of trade and administration; as even though they do not blind the physical sight, they do blind the hearts which are in the chests.

I ask Allaah's forgiveness, indeed He is the One who Forgives, the Most Merciful

Second Part of the Khutbah

All praise is due to Allaah, alone, and may His praise and salutations be upon the one whom there is no prophet after him, and upon his family and his companions.

To proceed:

My noble brothers, Allaah, the Most High, has said, in Surat an-Noor,

﴾ ***This is a surah which We have sent down and which We have enjoined; and in it We have revealed manifest ayaat (proofs, evidences, verses, lessons, signs, revelations – lawful and unlawful things, and set boundaries of Islamic religion) that you may remember.*** ﴿- (Surat an-Noor, Ayat 1)

What is meant by "*faradnaahaa*" is 'We have made obligatory its rulings'. And this chapter contains in it many rulings; and from these rulings are those which are related to the households. More than one scholar has said, "These rulings have been made obligatory upon the Muslims." And from the proofs of that is that Allaah has concluded this chapter with His, the Most High, saying,

﴾ ***And let those who oppose the Messenger's (Muhammad's) commandment (i.e. his sunnah) beware, lest some fitnah (disbelief, trials, afflictions, earthquakes, killing, overpowered by a tyrant) should befall them or a painful torment be inflicted on them***. ﴿- (Surat an-Noor, From Ayat 63)

From those things related to rectification of the houses which many of the Muslims have become heedless concerning is preserving the legislated *hijaab*. It is seen that they are very lenient, especially in rural areas, where there is more than just one family in the house. They abandon having separate places for the men and the women, and they mix with one another, and look at one another, and there is seclusion between the sexes which is a set up for their ruin- and this happens with them all being pleased with it. It is claimed that they are all relatives, and merely a single family- and this is a false claim. This is because it is only those who it is permanently unlawful to marry that are rightfully considered in this, and this does not include all the relatives and the entire family.

Along with this, they are not concerned with the matter of the *hijaab* even in the situation where outside people come to the houses, whether they be guests, workers, visitors, or other than them. Rather, it occurs with some of the Bedouin that the woman meets the guests and welcomes them, and lets them into the house of her husband even if they are strangers- and this is done through the claim of honoring the guest!!! The people regard the lack of doing this as a deficiency in the right of the woman and her husband, as (they claim) she does not perform her obligations in regard to the guest. This is from the evil understandings towards that which is contained in the Islamic legislation concerning that which is affirmed and authentic in regard to generosity to the guest. As the guest is not allowed to enter a house in which there are women who do not have a *mahram* with them, and it is not permissible for the women to enter into their presence without the presence of a *mahram*.

And we must not forget that which the *Shaytaan* possesses of ways to inspire the people, and of rousing one against another, and of making the forbidden thing attractive until one falls into wrongdoing. Indeed, the *Shaytaan* can overwhelm a man who is considered to be chaste, and a woman who is considered chaste. As the *Shaytaan* beautifies the woman in the sight of the ones who pass by her, as the Messenger of Allaah, may Allaah's praise and salutations be upon him, has said,

{The woman comes in the form of a Shaytaan, and she leaves in the form of a Shaytaan....} (Muslim, No. 1403, From a longer hadeeth narrated on Jaabir Ibn 'Abdullaah, may Allaah be pleased with him)

First, *Shaytaan* beautifies her when one is alone with her, and is sitting with her, and the lack of a *mahram* is more serious even than this. So, oh people, leave off this foolishness and ignorance concerning the plots of the self and its arousal towards desires, and the effect of the *Shaytaan* on humanity in regards to desiring the women. So read the Qur'aan in order that you understand that which this enemy of the worshippers of Allaah does to test them and lead them astray in the matter of the women, and other than that.

So what do you have, oh Muslims, of the Prophetic stringency and the praiseworthy jealousy; as it has been narrated in al-Bukhaari and Muslim from the hadeeth of Sahl ibn Sa'd, may Allaah be pleased with him, that the Messenger of Allaah, may Allaah's praise and salutations be upon him said to the man who he suspected had looked at his family within their house from outside,

{If I knew with certainty that you had looked, I would have poked you - meaning, with steel- in your eyes.} (Muslim, No. 2156, and al-Bukhaari, No. 5924)

And what do you have in answer to the Qur'anic verse,

﴾***And when you ask (his wives) for anything you want, ask them from behind a screen, that is purer for your hearts and for their hearts.***﴿- (Surat al-Ahzaab, From Ayat 53)

So, by Allaah, you must safeguard the household, and rectify and preserve it, and defend it from everything which corrupts it in regard to the worship of those within, as well as their *aqeedah* (Islamic beliefs), modesty and honor, in order that we will be pleased with all that is pleasant, and spare no effort in that which we are capable of doing; with the goal that our houses become filled with the light of guidance and a refuge of piety, and a sign of obedience to Allaah. And this will not be difficult, as it is easy upon the one for whom Allaah makes it easy, and the one who is pleased with being connected to the correct path. So beware, beware of extremism in the mentioned rectification, as it is an indication of disappointment and a cause of destruction.

[From "Khutub Fadeelatul ash-Sheikh Muhammad Abu Nasir Muhammad ibn 'Abdullah al-Imaam" Pages 228-241 Published by Maktabat al-Imaam al-Wadi'ee, Sana'a, Yemen]

Review and Discussion Questions

Questions for The Rectification of the Muslim Household by Sheikh Muhammad al-Imaam

Review:

1. What is the verse in which Allaah warns us that our families may be a source of fitnah for us? How does the Sheikh, may Allaah preserve him, explain this?? (Tope half of page 74)
2. What action does the Shaytaan praise the most in the hadeeth which begins, "Iblees placed his throne upon the water…". What does the Sheikh, may Allaah preserve him, say concerning this? (Bottom half of page 75)
3. What are some of the steps that should be taken before divorce is resorted to? (Middle of page 76)
4. List two proofs (one verse and one hadeeth) that indicate the importance of establishing the prayer amongst the family members. (Top half of page 78)
5. List one proof for the forbiddance of music, and one for the forbiddance of pictures of things with souls. (Bottom half of page 78, Top half of Page 79)

Discussion & Consideration:

6. Why must the Muslim take great care to ensure that his household is a righteous one?
7. Why is it crucial that we look for righteous spouses, instead of marrying just for worldly advantages?
8. Why is it important that the husband and wife refrain from a lot of cursing and insulting each other?
9. Explain how the television is a source of evil and corruption in the household
10. Why is it important that we familiarize ourselves with the deceptions and tricks of the Shayateen?

Advice Concerning Marriage

Sheikh Muqbil ibn Haadee al-Wadi'ee
(may Allaah have mercy upon him)

All praise is due to Allaah Alone. We praise Him, seek His help, we ask His forgiveness, and we ask for His guidance. We seek refuge in Allaah from the evil of our souls, and the adverse consequences of our deeds. Whomsoever Allaah guides, there is none who can misguide him, and whoever He misguides, there is none who can guide him.

I bear witness that there is nothing worthy of worship except for Allaah; He is alone and has no partners. I bear witness and testify that Muhammad, may Allaah's praise and salutations be upon him and his family, is His perfect worshipper, and messenger.

﴾ ***Oh you who believe! Fear Allaah, as He deserves, and die not except as Muslims.*** ﴿- (Surat aal 'Imraan, Ayat 102)

﴾ ***Oh you who believe! Keep your duty to Allaah and fear Him, and speak (always) the truth. He will direct you to do righteous good deeds and will forgive you your sins. And whosoever obeys Allaah and His Messenger, he has indeed achieved a great achievement (i.e. he will be saved from the Hellfire and will be admitted to Paradise).*** ﴿-(Surat al-Ahzaab, Ayats 70-71)

To Proceed: Allaah, Glorified is He and Most High, says in His Noble Book:

﴾ ***It is He Who has created you from a single person (Aadam), and (then) He has created from him his wife [Hawaa'], in order that he might enjoy the pleasure of living with her. When he (a polytheist from Adam's offspring – as stated by Ibn Katheer in his tafseer) had sexual relations with her (the polytheist's wife), she became pregnant and she carried it about lightly. Then when it became heavy, they both invoked Allaah, their Lord (saying): "If You give us a Saalih (good in every aspect) child, we shall indeed be among the grateful." But when He gave them (the polytheist and his wife) a Saalih (good in every aspect) child, they ascribed partners to Him (Allaah) in that which He has given to them. High is Allaah, Exalted above all that they ascribe as partners to Him.*** ﴿- (Surat al-A'raaf, Ayats 189-190)

In this blessed verse Allaah, Glorified is He, Most High, informs us that He created mankind from a single soul. We believe in this, as mankind is created, and their father is Aadam. This differs from the sayings of some of the philosophers which we address in our sittings. As Allaah, Glorified is He, Most High, created them from a single soul, and he was Aadam. It is found narrated in "*Saheeh al-Bukhaari*" that which clarifies this, as it is related in al-Bukhaari and Muslim in their two Saheehs, from Abi Hurairah, may Allaah, the Most High, be pleased with him, who said that the Messenger of Allaah, may Allaah's praise and salutations be upon him and his family, said,

{And I command you to take care of the women in a good manner, for they are created from the rib, and the most curved part of the rib is its upper part; if you try to straighten it you will break it, and if you leave it, then it will remain as it was.} (al-Bukhaari, 3331, Muslim 1428)

In this hadeeth is proof that the woman was created from the bent rib. Allaah, Glorified and Most High, desired for Aadam that He make for him a wife in order that he live with and find repose in her; so He created from him his wife, Hawaa'. We believe this.

There is also in these blessed verses which you have heard, mention of that which Allaah, Glorified and Exalted, has bestowed (upon mankind); as He created for mankind spouses from themselves, so that there will occur between them love, companionship, and goodness- a sign from the signs of Allaah. He, Glorified is He, Most High, says in His Noble Book,

﴾ ***And among His Signs is that He created for you wives from among yourselves, that you may find repose in them, and He has put between you affection and mercy. Verily, in that are indeed signs for a people who reflect.*** ﴿- (Surat ar-Room, Ayat 21)

This is a sign from the signs of Allaah- that a foreigner marries an Arab, or a dark man marries a light woman, or perhaps the woman is from the East and her husband is from the West, or she is from Yemen and her husband is from Syria, along with other examples similar to these. Allaah, Glorified and Most High, unites their hearts, and it does not require charms or spells. Allaah unites them, as she follows him and travels throughout the Earth, travelling with him- and she loves him as she loves her own family; indeed, more strongly than her love of her own family. This is a sign from the signs of Allaah.

And for this reason the Prophet, may Allaah's praise and salutations be upon him and his family, desired and encouraged marriage- indeed, marriage is a Sunnah from the Sunan of the Prophets. Allaah, Glorified is He, Most High, says in His Noble Book,

﴾ ***And indeed We sent Messengers before you (Oh Muhammad), and made for them wives and offspring.*** ﴿- (Surat ar-Ra'd, From Ayat 38)

The Prophet, may Allaah's praise and salutations be upon him and his family, said, ***{Beloved to me in this world of yours is beautiful fragrance or and women, and that which cools my eyes is the prayer.}*** (Al-Haakim 2608, Sunan As-Sughrah 3899)

He encouraged his *Ummah* to marry, and indeed marriage is obligatory if one fears that he will fall into that which has been forbidden, and that he may commit the act of fornication. Marriage then becomes obligatory according to that which was narrated by al-Bukhaari and Muslim in their two Saheehs, from Ibn Mas'ood, may Allaah, the Most High, be pleased with him, that he said, "The Messenger of Allaah, may Allaah's praise and salutations be upon him and his family, said,

{Oh young people! Whoever amongst you is able to marry, should marry, as it assists him in lowering his gaze and protecting his private parts (from illegal acts). And whoever is not able to marry, he should fast, as fasting will lessen the sexual desire.} (al-Bukhaari, 5066, 1905, and Muslim 1/1400 in the Book of Marriage)

The one who does not have wealth, or a house, or does not have that which could be used to properly clothe or dress himself and a wife- then it is upon him to fast since marriage is not possible for him at that time. It is from the medicine of the Prophet that he fast. Some of the people of knowledge have taken from this hadeeth that masturbation is prohibited, because the Prophet, may Allaah's praise and salutations be upon him and his family, directed the people to fast (to control their desires).

It has been narrated in al-Bukhaari and Muslim in their two Saheehs, from Anas, may Allaah, the Most High, be pleased with him, that he reported, "Three people came" or, in another narration, ***{A group of three people came to the houses of the wives of the Prophet, may Allaah's praise and salutations be upon him and his family, asking about the worship of the Messenger of Allaah, may Allaah's praise and salutations be upon him and his family. When they were informed of the extent of his worship, they considered their own worship insufficient, and said, "Indeed the Messenger of Allaah, may Allaah's praise and salutations be upon him and his family, has had all of his sins which have come before, and all that will come after, forgiven. One of them said, "As for me, I will stand all night in prayer and not sleep." The second one said, "As for me, I will fast, and will not break the fast." And the third one said, "As for me, I will not marry women." The Prophet, may Allaah's praise and salutations be upon him and his family, was informed of what they said, and he said to them, Are you the ones who said such and such?} They replied, "Yes." He said,***

{By Allaah, I have more fear of Allaah than you, and am more conscious of Him than you; however, I stand in prayer, and I sleep, and I fast, and I break my fast, and I marry from the women. So whoever does not follow my Sunnah is not from me.} (al-Bukhaari, 5063, Muslim, 1401)

It is narrated in "*Saheeh al-Bukhaari*" from 'Uthmaan ibn Madh'oon and a group of the Companions that they wanted to devote themselves solely to *jihaad*, and so sought from the Messenger of Allaah, may Allaah's praise and salutations be upon him and his family, permission to be castrated. But the Prophet, may Allaah's praise and salutations be upon him did not give them permission to do this, and Allaah, Glorified is He, Most High, revealed in His Noble Book,

﴾ ***Oh you who believe! Make not unlawful the tayyibaat (all that is good as regards foods, things, deeds, beliefs, persons) which Allaah has made lawful to you, and transgress not. Verily, Allaah does not like the transgressors.*** ﴿- (Surat al-Maa'idah, Ayat 87) (al-Bukhaari, 5073, Muslim 1402)

It is narrated in "*Saheeh al-Bukhaari*" also, that Abu Hurairah, may Allaah be pleased with him, went to the Prophet, may Allaah's praise and salutations be upon him and his family, and asked for permission to be castrated. He turned away in refusal, then said to him, ***{... so it does not matter if you get yourself castrated or not.}*** (al-Bukhaari, 5076) (Translator's note: The full text of the reply of the Prophet, may Allaah's praise and salutations be upon him and his family, is, ***{Oh Aba Hurairah, the pen has dried after writing that which you are going to confront. (Meaning, your fate has already been decreed for you and written down) So it does not matter whether you get yourself castrated or not.}***)

The incitement and encouragement to marry is found in these *ahaadeeth* which you have heard, because of that which marriage contains of repose and peace. This differs with this time in which we live, when marriage has become a problem from the problems of life. And Islaam is free from this problem (meaning, it is not responsible for it). There are from the Muslims those who do not comply with that which is in the Book of Allaah, nor with the Sunnah of the Messenger, may Allaah's praise and salutations be upon him and his family. And this is in regard to many matters related to marriage, and from them is greed or avariciousness.

The Prophet, may Allaah's praise and salutations be upon him and his family, when 'Ali wanted to marry Fatimah, said, ***{Oh 'Ali, what do you have to offer as a dowry? He replied, "I have nothing, oh Messenger of Allaah, except my Hatamee armor." He, may Allaah's praise and salutations be upon him and his family, said, Give it to her as her dowry.}*** (Abu Daawud, 6/162, and it is in "*al-Jaami' as-Saheeh*" of Sheikh Muqbil, may Allaah have mercy upon him, 3/68, from ibn 'Abaas, may Allaah be pleased with him)

It is narrated in the two Saheehs from the hadeeth of Sahl ibn Sa'd, may Allaah, the Most High, have mercy upon him, that ***{A woman came to the Messenger of Allaah, may Allaah's praise and salutations be upon him, and said, "Oh Messenger of Allaah! I have come to offer myself in marriage to you." So the Prophet, may Allaah's praise and salutations be upon him, looked at her, meaning, he gazed at her, then the Prophet, may Allaah's praise and salutations be upon him, was silent. A man stood up and said, "Oh Messenger of Allaah, if you are not in need of this woman, then marry her to me." So the Messenger of Allaah, may Allaah's praise and salutations be upon him and his family, said to him, What do you have to offer as a dowry? He replied, "Oh Messenger of Allaah, I have nothing except my waist wrapper." He, may Allaah's praise and salutations be upon him, said, What would she do with your waist wrapper? If she takes it, you will be without it. Go and seek something, even if it is an iron ring. The man went to his house and looked, then returned to the Prophet, may Allaah's praise and salutations be upon him and his family, and the woman was still standing, and he said, "Oh Messenger of Allaah, I didn't see anything, not even an iron ring." The Prophet, may Allaah's praise and salutations be upon him and his family, was quiet, and so the man left. Then he said, Bring him back.The Prophet, may Allaah's praise and salutations be upon him and his family, said to him, What have you memorized from the Qur'aan? He said, "Surat such and such." He said, may Allaah's praise and salutations be upon him, I have married her to you for that which you know of the Qur'aan.}*** So he, the Prophet, informed her of the marriage. (al- Bukhaari, 5135, Muslim, 1425, by meaning)

So this is the Sunnah of the Messenger of Allaah, may Allaah's praise and salutations be upon him and his family. And the Prophet did not exceed twelve *awqiah* (a measure of weight) and one *nash* (a smaller measurement of weight) (as his dowry) to his wives. 'Aishah, may Allaah, the Most High, be pleased with her, said, "Do you know what *an-nash* is? It is one half of an *awqiah*." (Muslim, 1426) And this is like less than 1000 Yemeni riyals. And this is how marriage was with them the Companions, meaning that they did not pay huge dowries as is a common practice today.

Indeed, he, may Allaah's praise and salutations be upon him, saw 'Abdur Rahmaan ibn 'Awf and he was wearing a garment like that which one would wear to get married in. He said, ***{What is with you? Have you married? He replied, "Yes." He said, Hold the wedding anouncement celebration, even if it is with only one sheep.}*** (al-Bukhaari, 2049, 5155, and Muslim 1427)

Yet we, oh Muslims- the amount of the dowry has become oppressive to us, while the Sunnah of the Messenger of Allaah, may Allaah's praise and salutations be upon him- in this matter, it has become so it is not turned to. So this is one problem, that being expensive dowries.

The second problem in which the fathers transgress, and it is one which results from the first, is that the man does not look for a suitable match. What does he look for? He looks for money. The Messenger, may Allaah's praise and salutations be upon him and his family, said, as is found in "*as-Saheeh*", ***{A woman is married for four things: her wealth, her family, her beauty, and her religion. So you should marry the religious woman, or you will be the loser}*** (al-Bukhaari, 5090, Muslim 1466, from the hadeeth of Abi Hurairah, may Allaah the Most High be pleased with him)

And likewise, concerning the husband. ***{A woman, and she was Fatimah Bint Qais, may Allaah, the Most High, be pleased with her, came to the Prophet, may Allaah's praise and salutations be upon him and his family, seeking his opinion. She said, "Oh Messenger of Allaah, Mu'aawiyyah and Abu Jahm have asked me to marry them." The Prophet, may Allaah's praise and salutations be upon him and his family, said to her, As for Mu'aawiyyah, he is a poor man, having no wealth. As for Abu Jahm, then he does not drop his staff down off of his shoulder....}*** (Sheikh Muqbil then states in an aside that this either indicates that he travels often, or that he beats his women) ***{...Marry Usaama.}*** (Muslim 1480) Usaama was his *mawlaa*, and she was of the tribe of the Quraish (meaning, they were of unequal social status- she had greater status than he did). So she obeyed the Messenger of Allaah, may Allaah's praise and salutations be upon him and his family, and Allaah brought to her goodness and blessings through it.

And in *Saheeh Muslim*, (This story is narrated by Ahmad, with an authentic chain of narration) that the Prophet, may Allaah's praise and salutations be upon him and his family, said to a man, ***{I have come to ask for your daughter in marriage. The man replied, "Yes, Oh Messenger of Allaah". The Prophet, may Allaah's praise and salutations be upon him and his family, said, It is not for me, but rather it is for Julaybeeb. The man and his wife belittled Julaybeeb, and said, "For Julaybeeb? For Julaybeeb?" The daughter heard this, and she was in her tent. So she said, "Do not refuse the command of the Messenger of Allaah, may Allaah's praise and salutations be upon him and his family, as I am pleased with that which the Messenger of Allaah, may Allaah's praise and salutations be upon him and his family, is pleased with for me.}*** And she was married to Julaybeeb.

Likewise, oh Muslims, choose the suitable, righteous man- choose him for your daughter. Also, beware of forcing your daughter to marry a man she does not want to marry, even if you like the man, and he is righteous; as the righteous are many. Perhaps she may choose other than him because the women desire good looks, just as the man does. The Prophet, may Allaah's praise and salutations be upon him and his family, said, ***{The permission of the virgin must be sought, and the previously married woman must be consulted. They said, "Oh Messenger of Allaah, indeed she is shy (i.e. the virgin is shy to answer aloud when asked)." He, may Allaah's praise and salutations be upon him and his family, replied, Her silence is her consent.}*** Meaning, the silence of the virgin. (Muslim, 1420,1421,1422)

So you go to her, and you should not have a stick behind your back, and say, "We wish to marry you to so and so." Such that if she declines, you then beat her with the stick- this way is certainly a problem! And the essential thing is that you choose for your daughter a suitable, righteous man.

Beware also of the man who does not perform the prayers, as it is not permissible for you to marry your daughter to one who does not perform the prayers. Allaah, Glorified and Exalted, has said in His Noble Book:

﴾ ***Oh you who believe! When believing women come to you as emigrants, examine them; Allaah knows best as to their faith, then if you ascertain that they are true believers send them not back to the disbelievers. They are not lawful wives for the disbelievers nor are the disbelievers lawful husbands for them.*** ﴿- (Surat al-Mumtahanah, From Ayat 10)

And He says, ﴾ ***Likewise hold not the disbelieving women as wives*** ﴿-(Surat al-Mumtahanah, From Ayat 10)

As the woman who does not pray is not permissible, oh you who do pray, to marry, as she is considered a disbelieving woman and it is not permissible for you to marry your daughter to a man who does not pray. And the women are affected and influenced by the men, and similarly the men are affected and influenced by the women.

'Imraan ibn Hataan was a righteous man from the people of the Sunnah. He wanted to marry his cousin because she had been affected by the school of thought of the *Khawaarij* and he wanted to bring her back to the truth. Instead, he was affected by her, and became from the *Khawaarij*, those who declare the Muslims to be disbelievers due to sins.

It is narrated in the two Saheehs from Abi Musa al-Ash'aree, may Allaah, the Most High, be pleased with him, that he said, "The Messenger of Allaah, may Allaah's praise and salutations be upon him, said, ***{The example of a good righteous companion and an evil one is that of a person carrying musk and another blowing a pair of bellows (a blacksmith). The one who is carrying musk will either give you some musk, or you will buy some from him, or you will at least get a good scent from him. As for the blacksmith, he will either burn your clothes, or you will get a bad scent from him.}*** (al-Bukhaari, 3534, Muslim, 2628)

It is narrated that the Prophet, may Allaah's praise and salutations be upon him and his family, said, ***{A man is on the religion of his close friend- so each of you must look to who your close friends are.}*** (Ahmad, 2/334, and other than him, from Abi Hurairah, may Allaah be pleased with him, and it is in "*al-Mishkaat*", 5019) So what do you think about the woman, who the Prophet, may Allaah's praise and salutations be upon him, characterized as being deficient in intellect and religion? (al-Bukhaari, 304, Muslim, 80, on Abi Sa'eed, may Allaah be pleased with him. See Sheikh Bin Baaz's explanation of this hadeeth in the *Rulings* section of this book, insh'Allaah, for a more complete discussion and clarification of the meaning of the hadeeth) The Lord, who is Most Glorious, says in His Noble Book,

﴾ ***Oh you who believe! Ward off yourselves and your families against a Fire (Hell) whose fuel is men and stones*** ﴿- (Surat at-Tahreem, From Ayat 6)

And He, Glorified is He, Most High, says in His Noble Book, ﴾ ***And enjoin as-salaat (the prayers) on your family, and be patient in offering them. We ask not of you a provision (i.e. to give Us something): We provide for you. And the good end (i.e. Paradise) is for the Muttaqoon*** ﴿- (Surah Taa Haa, Ayat 132)

And in the two Saheehs, from the hadeeth of 'Abdullah ibn Umar, may Allaah the Most High be pleased with them both, in which he said, The

Messenger of Allaah, may Allaah's praise and salutations be upon him and his family, said, ***{All of you are guardians, and are responsible for your wards.}*** And in it, ***{The man is the guardian of his family.}*** (al-Bukhaari, 5200, Muslim 1829)

Also in the two Saheehs, from the hadeeth of Ma'qal ibn Yasaar, may Allaah, the Most High, be pleased with him, it is narrated that he said, The Messenger of Allaah, may Allaah's praise and salutations be upon him and his family, said- the Prophet, may Allaah's praise and salutations be upon him and his family, said, concerning the condition of the one who is not just-

(Here the Sheikh asks for one of the students to recite the hadeeth, and asks him to raise his voice so it will be heard by the other students. The text of the hadeeth he then mentions is as follows, that the Prophet, may Allaah's praise and salutations be upon him and his family, said, ***{Anyone who Allaah has given authority to rule over others, and he does not look after them in an honest, just way, will never have even the smell of paradise.***} (al-Bukhaari, 7150, Muslim 142, and this is the wording of al-Bukhaari)

This is a matter which I must chastise you concerning. A man marries a Bedouin woman who does not know anything except for her sheep. This is better than for him marry a woman who will intermingle with the men in the places of business, and who goes in and out of the places of business as a manager or a secretary, or she graduates from the university, or likewise that she is out working in the hospital. Their natural dispositions are effaced or destroyed, and many of them do not believe in the saying of Allaah, Glorified and Exalted is He,

﴾Men are the protectors and maintainers of women, because Allaah has made one of them to excel the other, and because they spend (to support them) from their means. Therefore the righteous women are devoutly obedient (to Allaah and to their husbands), and guard in the husband's absence what Allaah orders them to guard (e.g. their chastity and their husband's property). As to those women on whose part you see ill conduct, admonish them (first), (next) refuse to share their beds, (and last) beat them (lightly, if it is useful); but if they obey you, seek not against them means (of annoyance ﴿-" (Surat an-Nisaa, From Ayat 34)

It is also related in "*as-Saheeh*" that the Prophet, may Allaah's praise and salutations be upon him, said, in clarification of the measure the man has over the woman, ***{If a man calls his wife to the bed and she refuses or turns away, the angers curse her.}*** (al-Bukhaari, 1593, Muslim, 1436, 122, 120 on the authority of Abu Hurairah, may Allaah the Most High be pleased with him) And in another narration, ***{...except that the One Who is in the heavens is displeased with her.}*** (Muslim 1436, 121)

However the call to false freedom which makes the women miserable, and causes them to be unhappy- the call to "freedom" insists on the woman leaving her happy home, with her honorable position within it. In it she has children to work for her, and family members who love her. Is that which is contained in that call to "freedom" understood? In severing the family connections, and severing the foster relationships, and cutting the societal connections in the name of "freedom" and by calling it this or that. As the religion of

Islaam raises the position and stature of the woman, making her the mistress of the house, the one in charge of the family, while the enemies of Islaam make the woman miserable. And by Allaah, by Allaah, by Allaah, I have seen young women going forth carrying their bags, this one heading for her work at the company, and another going to her school to study or teach, and another heading for the streets, and indeed they are miserable and at a loss, they are miserable, and at a loss.

The Prophet, may Allaah's praise and salutations be upon him and his family, said, ***{The woman is 'awrah (something to be concealed) as if she goes out the Shaytaan elevates her (makes her desirable to the eyes of the people).}*** (at-Tirmidhi, 4/337, from Ibn Mas'ood, may Allaah, the Most High, be pleased with him, and it is in "*al-Jaami' as-Saheeh*" of Sheikh Muqbil, may Allaah have mercy upon him).

And the Prophet, may Allaah's praise and salutations be upon him and his family, said, ***{I have not seen one who is deficient in intellect and religion more able to affect the intellect of a reasonable man than one of you (women).}*** (al-Bukhaari, 304, Muslim, 80, on Abi Sa'eed, may Allaah be pleased with him)

And he said, may Allaah's praise and salutations be upon him and his family, as found in "*as-Saheeh*" from the hadeeth of Usaama, ***{There will not be a trial after me more difficult upon them men, than the women.}*** (al-Bukhaari, 5097, and Muslim, 1740)

As the woman is a trial, and the woman is deficient in her intellect and her religion; and her religion cannot be safeguarded, and our religion cannot be safeguarded, except with returning to the Book of Allaah and to the Sunnah of the Messenger of Allaah. We must place every ignorant call under our feet if we are Muslims (meaning deny and turn away from it), because the Prophet, may Allaah's praise and salutations be upon him and his family, said, ***{Every matter of the time of ignorance has been placed under my feet. (i.e. it has been abolished)}*** (Muslim, 1218, from the hadeeth of Jaabir, may Allaah the Most High be pleased with him)

Do you know the point which their condition has reached? If we wished to visit America, Russia, or other than them, they have reached the point where it is permitted that a man marry a man! And we are Muslims- Allaah has fortified us with Islaam, and has honored us with Islaam, and Allaah has made us the best nation to come out of mankind, if we live according to the Book of Allaah, and live according to the Sunnah of the Messenger of Allaah, may Allaah's praise and salutations be upon him and his family, and we praise Allaah, Glorified is He, the Most High.

We have seen the goodness and divine blessings manifested in some of our brothers from the people of the Sunnah, from Allaah, Glorified and Exalted is He. One of them marries his daughter to a man with something easy or small, or without anything except the dowry; then what comes about? Love and harmony between them. I haven't heard of any who have run away from their husbands. Rather, she is patient with him in a state of poverty, and is patient with him in her situation which Allaah knows how difficult it is. And the people, and all praise is due to Allaah, when they see these good results, we will only hear then that the students of knowledge will be married in large numbers, until the women of the Sunnah will be afraid and say, "The other women are marrying without anything, we are afraid that the men will leave us and marry others."

Likewise, the Sunnah of the Messenger of Allaah, may Allaah's praise and salutations be upon him and his family; as the good- every good- is in that which he was upon, may Allaah's praise and salutations be upon him and his family. And know- know with certainty- that nothing is as comprehensive for us as the Book of Allaah and the Sunnah of the Messenger of Allaah, may Allaah's praise and salutations be upon him and his family. The lowest of the dowries is thirty thousand *riyaals*, or twenty thousand *riyaals*, and they get it through means which you know are not necessarily good- perhaps through swearing a false oath and immoral means. However, the religion should restrain them from doing this.

A person should know the worth of his daughter. I read in a magazine or newspaper from Riyaadh that a man gave his daughter in marriage for fifty Saudi *riyaals* and built an apartment for her husband and her. He was asked about that, and he said, "My daughter is worth more to me than gold and silver and paper money." Yes! The man's daughter was worth more to him than gold. So as you see, those who make their daughters into a commodity have done evil to the society and to the young men, and evil to the religion. And it may come about that some of the people join different organizations for the purpose of marrying- as with the *takfeeris* (those who declare the Muslims to be disbelievers without going to the proper authorities) it is their condition that they have a low dowry of three hundred, and such as that- so some may join them in order to get married (i.e. they will join a deviant group because the women's dowries are cheaper with them)

It is obligatory upon us to have fear of Allaah, Glorified is He, and Most High, and that we return to the Sunnah of the Messenger of Allaah, may Allaah's praise and salutations be upon him and his family, just as it is necessary to choose a righteous woman, as she will assist him in raising and educating his children, and in goodness to his parents. So 'Umar, may Allaah the Most High be pleased with him, went to the Prophet, may Allaah's praise and salutations be upon him and his family, and he said, ***{ Oh Messenger of Allaah, I have ordered 'Abdullah to divorce his wife." However, 'Abdullah refused. So the Prophet, may Allaah's praise and salutations be upon him and his family, called 'Abdullah to him, and compelled him to divorce her.}*** (at-Tirmidhi, 4/368, Abu Daawud, 5/350, and it is in Sheikh Muqbil's "*al-Jaami' as-Saheeh*", 6/107)

As the woman- perhaps the woman is a cause of trial, and perhaps she, and Allaah's protection is sought from this, is a barrier from good. If he wants to keep good relations with his parents, his neighbors, or his family, her face becomes dark with displeasure. And likewise she will raise her voice and other than that.

And the woman who is supportive and helps is the one who desires that which is with Allaah. I do not say to you that she is one who studies in the university, and I do not say to you that she is the one who studies in the schools, and I do not say to you that she is a Bedouin; rather, she is the one who desires that which is with Allaah, as the Prophet, may Allaah's praise and salutations be upon him and his family said, ***{A woman, if she guards her private parts,***

obeys her husband, prays her five prayers, and fasts her month (Ramadhaan)}* *or something with this meaning, {her Lord will enter her into Paradise.} (Ibn Hibaan has narrated this from Abu Hurairah, may Allaah be pleased with him)

So the women- the Prophet, may Allaah's praise and salutations be upon him and his family, when the women requested that he make a day for them- the Prophet, may Allaah's praise and salutations be upon him, said, ***{Oh women, give charity. Indeed I have seen that you are the majority of the people of the Fire.} It was said, "And why is that, oh Messenger of Allaah?" He said, {You curse often, and are ungrateful.} It was said, "Ungrateful to Allaah?" He replied, {You are ungrateful to your husbands. If he is always good to you, and then you see something evil from him, you say, 'I have never seen any good from you'.}*** (al-Bukhaari 304, Muslim 80, from Abi Sa'eed, may Allaah be pleased with him)

This is the nature of the women. Then the Prophet, may Allaah's praise and salutations be upon him and his family, said, ***{There is not one of you from amongst the women who raises three children, except that they will be a covering for her from the Fire.} A woman said, "And two, oh Messenger of Allaah?" He replied, {And two.}*** (al-Bukhaari, 101, 73133, Muslim 2633 from Abi Sa'eed, may Allaah be pleased with him)

And we say to our brothers, this is the nature of the woman- imprudence, except for the one upon whom Allaah has mercy. Due to this Allaah has placed divorce in the hand of the man, as if the divorce was in the hand of the woman, perhaps she would divorce her husband twenty times a day, then return, crying, after she divorces him- she returns and cries, and Allaah knows best. Oh our brothers! So Allaah, Glorified is He, has made the divorce by the hand of the man, as he has patience and he understands the ramifications. He knows that *Shaytaan* is pleased if a man divorces his wife.

Likewise, the women are deficient in their intellect and religion, and it is for us to fear Allaah regarding them. Beware; beware, lest we corrupt the woman with tools of entertainment and singing (such as the television or radio). It has been heard of, may Allaah bless you. Maybe the woman is righteous, and her rebellious husband corrupts her; and perhaps the man is righteous and the wife corrupts him- and it is the same if he is her husband or not her husband. As the Glorified Lord says in His Noble Book,

﴿***And when you ask (his wives) for anything you want, ask them from behind a screen, that is purer for your hearts and for their hearts***﴾- (Surat al-Ahzaab, From Ayat 53)

Allaah says this in regards to the woman of the Prophet, the ones who were the best of our woman. As Allaah said this concerning the Companions, who were the best from amongst us. As the woman is a trial, so beware, beware, of being overconfident in this matter of the women. Beware, beware, of being overconfident concerning seclusion with the woman who is not *mahram* for you, or the matter of going in with the women who are not *mahram* to you- as indeed, they are a trial.

The Prophet, may Allaah's praise and salutations be upon him and his family, said, as found in the two Saheehs, from the hadeeth of Abi Hurairah, may Allaah the Most High be pleased with him, ***{A portion of zeenah (fornication, adultery) has been written for the sons of Aadam, there is***

no escape for him from that which will reach him. The zeenah of the eyes is the looking at that which it is unlawful to look at, and the zeenah of the ears is listening to that which It is unlawful to listen to, and the zeenah of the hand is oppression, and the zeenah of the leg is to walk to do that which is unlawful and the heart desires and yearns for that which is impermissible and the private parts make that a reality or refrain from it} (al-Bukhaari, 11/6612, Muslim 3/2657)

Listen, oh gathering of tribes, and do not deceive yourselves and say that our hearts are in a good state; fear for yourselves that your hearts have died, as the dead one is the one that is not aware of the pain…so the woman is a trial, and what is better than the one who said,

Brothers cannot trust each other with women

No man with women is trustworthy

Indeed the trustworthy might preserve his trust once

but there is no doubt that with a glance he will betray

And another says, *Every accident springs from a glance*

and the great torment of the fire is from belittling evil

How many glances have wrought in the heart of their master

The evil of an arrow without bow or string

It pleases his eye yet harms his heart

There is no welcome for pleasure that brings harm

Do not be alone with a woman, even if you are teaching her Qur'aan, as Sa'eed ibn al-Musayyib, may Allaah have mercy upon him, said, "I have reached the age of eighty years, and if I were to be entrusted with this and that amount of gold, I would find myself trustworthy, but if I were to be entrusted with a black slave girl, I would not find myself trustworthy."

And there is nothing better to be found than that which one said, clarifying the condition of the woman being a trial for the man, as he says,

Tell the beautiful one in the black khimaar

what have you done to the worshippers

He was preparing his clothes for salaat

Until you appeared to him at the door of the masjid

Return to him his prayer and fasting

Do not be a trial to him by the right of the Lord of Muhammad

So we, my brothers in Allaah- it is not permissible for us to deceive ourselves. The Prophet, may Allaah's praise and salutations be upon him and his family, said, ***{The woman is awrah (something which is not to be seen by those who are not mahram for her).}*** (Narrated by at-Tirmidhi, from the hadeeth of Ibn Mas'ood)

The Prophet, may Allaah's praise and salutations be upon him and his family, the one who Allaah, Glorified is He, and Most High, has preserved, saw a woman passing by, as is found in "*Saheeh Muslim*"; so he went into his house and had intercourse with his wife, and he went out, and the water dripped from his head (from *ghusl*), and the Prophet, may Allaah's praise and salutations be upon him and his family, said, ***{If one of you sees a woman and she fascinates him, he should go to his wife and have intercourse with her, as indeed she has what the other one has.}*** (Muslim, 10/9, from Jaabir, may Allaah be pleased with him). Or that which has this meaning. This is the Prophetic cure, oh Muslims.

Yes, the women circumambulate the house of Allaah- now we are mentioning some of the doubts; we are mentioning some of the doubts (brought by the enemies of Islaam)- (they circumambulate) mixing with the men. However, the truth is that they do not go out, may Allaah be pleased with you, amongst you beautifully adorned (at this time). The women also may go out in company with their husbands, they go out to *jihaad* in the cause of Allaah; *jihaad*. 'Aishah said in "*Saheeh al-Bukhaari*": ***{ Oh Messenger of Allaah, we see that jihaad is the best of deeds, so why do we not go out in jihaad?" He answered, Upon you is the jihaad in which there is no combat.}*** (al-Bukhaari, 1520, 1861, from 'Aishah, may Allaah be pleased with her) But perhaps he takes his wife out of fear that he will desire women, or so she can serve him, or tend the wounded, or give water to the sick- maybe they take the women. They go out for these reasons, not to carry his weapon, or to stand before the enemy.

However, if it is necessary that she protect herself, and she is in her country, or in a war along with her husband, then there is no harm. ***{Abu Talhah went to the Prophet, may Allaah's praise and salutations be upon him and his family, and he was laughing , and he said, "Oh Messenger of Allaah, ask Umm Sulaim about this, as she is carrying a dagger." So the Prophet, may Allaah's praise and salutations be upon him and his family, said to her, {Umm Sulaim, why do you carry this dagger?} And this was during the battle of Hunayn. She said, "Oh Messenger of Allaah, I have taken it up so I can tear open the stomach of any mushrik who comes near me." So the Prophet, may Allaah's praise and salutations be upon him and his family, laughed.}*** (Muslim, Book of *Jihaad*, 134, from Anas, may Allaah be pleased with him)

So it is for her to protect herself, and to give water to the wounded; as for her going out and she has two stars (i.e. like the rank of a general) or she is his *effendi* and above him in rank, or she is in a position of authority like this...then the Messenger of Allaah, may Allaah's praise and salutations be upon him and his family, said, ***{A people will not be successful if they are lead by a woman.}*** (al-Bukhaari, 4425, on Rabee', may Allaah be pleased with him)

The woman should not cry out to be in the sittings of consultation, or to be a judge, or to be a president; she should call out to be the head of her house. And there is no problem if she is a doctor, as long as the men do not mix with her except due to necessity. There is no problem when this is a necessity- as if a man cannot find a male doctor, but there is a female doctor, and you are sick- to go to her and she treats you when you cannot find other than her. And likewise also the woman, if she can only find a male doctor- there is no problem, according to the hadeeth which has been heard, and it is, ***{The women go out and treat the wounded and give water to the sick.}*** (al-Bukhaari, 5679, on Abi Bakrah) There is no problem for you with that. We do not want to make something unlawful for the people that Allaah has made permissible for them; but we and our women do want to always return to the Book of Allaah.

And the last part of this *Ummah* will not be rectified except through that which rectified the first of it, and how excellent that would be! Indeed I advise our brothers of the people of the Sunnah to be the strongest of those who comply and are obedient. We are in a Muslim society, and all praise is due to Allaah. We do not say that the Muslims are disbelievers; however we do say that we are in a society which does not comply with the Book and the Sunnah- or it complies with the Book and the Sunnah when it agrees with its desires.

Then after that if Allaah makes easy for you to obtain a wife...so beware, beware of meeting the blessing with disbelief, as is the state of many of the people. As Allaah, Glorified is He and Exalted, has provided for him a wife, and then who knows except that in the wedding feast they invent and bring forth some new thing which is not legislated. And the Supreme Lord has stated in His Noble Book to His Prophet, Muhammad, may Allaah's praise and salutations be upon him,

"***...nor am I one of the mutakallifoon (those who pretend and fabricate things which do not exist)"*** (Surat Saad, From Ayat 86)

And 'Umar, may Allaah the Most High be pleased with him, said, ***{We were forbidden from inventing or fabricating things (which were not legislated Islamically.}*** (al-Bukhaari, 7693, from Anas, may Allaah be pleased with him) And it was heard that the Messenger, may Allaah's praise and salutations be upon him and his family said to 'AbdurRahman ibn 'Awf. He said to him, ***{Have a waleemah (wedding feast even if it is with one sheep.}*** (al-Bukhaari, 2049, 5167, Muslim 1427, from Anas, may Allaah the Most High be pleased with him) This is one matter.

There is another matter which is considered uglier and more offensive, and it is paying women to come and sing. This is found in many of the Islamic countries; as for us in our area, which is the area of Sa'da, then I do not know if it has reached us or not. It has definitely reached Sana'a and Ta'iz, as they think- some of those people think- that progress lies in resembling the enemies of Islaam. They think this; however the Prophet, may Allaah's praise and salutations be upon him and his family, said, ***{He who resembles a people is one of them.}*** (Ahmad, from Ibn 'Umar, may Allaah be pleased with both him and his father) As the Prophet, may Allaah's praise and salutations be upon him and his family, prohibited wasting money (Agreed upon, on al-Mugheerah ibn Shu'bah); this is one matter.

The second matter: the music at these events mentions the attributes of the cheek and the figure and in it there are lyrics which stir the sexual impulses- so perhaps it happens that an old man listens to it and hears these lyrics, and perhaps he is affected, my Brothers in Allaah. As we hear these lyrics on the broadcasts, and we hear from the television, and we hear from many of the instruments of amusement and singing (such as the television or radio). Our legislation has forbidden it.

Perhaps we will mention and speak about the ruling of music, as we do not wish to make anything forbidden for the people which Allaah has made permissible. In the "*Saheeh*" from Abi Maalik or Abi 'Aamir al-Ash'aree, the Messenger of Allaah, may Allaah's praise and salutations be upon him and his family, said, ***{There will be a people of my Ummah who will make permissible the wearing of silk for the men, alcohol, and musical instruments.}*** As for that which is permissible in the wedding entertainment, then the Prophet, may Allaah's praise and salutations be upon him, said, ***{Make public the wedding, and beat upon the duff (an instrument similar to a skin drum).}*** (Ibn Maajah, 1895, at- Tirmidhi, 1089, and Sheikh al-Albaani has declared it hasan due to gathering its different paths of transmission, but has said that the mention of the *duff* is not authentic.)

There is no problem if the women take something like a sieve and beat upon it. There is no problem if they sing like the women sing at the weddings. And she (one of the woman singers mentioned in the hadeeth the Sheikh is going to quote from) said, ***{ He has chosen a sheep for her, and it is confined." (from the lyrics of the wedding song) and one of them said, "Amongst us is a Prophet, who knows what will happen tomorrow." Then the Prophet, may Allaah's praise and salutations be upon him and his family, said, "{No one knows the future except Allaah, return to (singing) that which you had been saying before.}*** (al-Bukhaari, 5147, on ar-Rabee', may Allaah be pleased with her)

Meaning, "He has chosen a sheep for her, and it is confined." This problem in this matter is not that she says, "He has chosen a sheep for her, he has appointed it for her." (As the Prophet allowed the singing to continue) But as for the songs and the singer which are hired for this and that, then indeed it is from the squandering of wealth which will be asked about. And there is none from amongst us except that he will be asked about his wealth- where he earned it and in what did he spend it.

Another abominable matter attached to marriage which we must draw attention to is the matter of some of the people; when they make the contract, they go to a soothsayer and he asks, "What is her name, and the name of her mother?" He says, her name is Zainab, and her mother is Fatimah." He (the soothsayer) says, "No, it is necessary that her name be Jameelah, or some other name. This Zainab is a dangerous name, and she will never stay with you." And this is a slanderous, fabricated claim, there is no doubt about it! If Allaah unites them, Allaah, Glorified is He and Most High, has decreed this regardless of whether her name is Zainab or Saalihah.

Yet there is no problem with changing a name which is not a righteous one, as the Prophet, may Allaah's praise and salutations be upon him and his family, changed the name 'Aasiyyah to Zainab (Note: He changed 'Aasiyyah to Jameelah, as found in Muslim, 14 and 15, narrated on Ibn 'Umar) and he also changed Burah to Zainab. (Muslim, 12 and 17, on Zainab Bint Umm Salamah and Abi Hurairah, respectively) So he changed a name which meant disobedient ('Aasiyyah) to obedient. So there is no problem with changing some of the names which are not good. As for changing them due to the soothsayers, then no, no to this matter- and what matter is this? Changing the name due to such a false claim (as that it is unlucky, etc).

The second matter is one that the people torture themselves with on the night of the marriage- as the husband is allowed to leave with their wife soon after *'Isha*, or something like that. The problem is when instead they intentionally stay and do not go to the husband's house until such and such a star rises, as if they go before that star rises, then it is claimed that this or this will happen, and they will not be happy in their marriage…until the end of such false statements.

And all praise is due to Allaah, the Lord of the Worlds.

[Collected in the book, "Fataawa al-Mar'at al-Muslimah", a collection of advices and rulings from Sheikh Muqbil, may Allaah have mercy upon him. Pages 406-423 Published by Maktabatu Sana'a al-Athariyyah, Sana'a, Yemen

Review and Discussion Questions

Questions for Advice Concerning Marriage by Imaam al-Wadi'ee

Review:

1. List two proofs that Hawaa' was created from Aadam, aleihi as-salaam. (Page 85)
2. List some of the proofs that marriage is encouraged or even obligatory in Islaam. (Page 85, Bottom half, Page 86 Top half)
3. List two ahaadeeth which mention the importance of having good companions. (Bottom half of page 90)
4. What is necessary for us to hold firmly onto if we want to safeguard ourselves and our religion? (Middle of page 92)
5. Is it necessary for the wedding feast to be extravagant? Explain using at least one of the proofs. (Page 97, Bottom half)
6. What proof does the Sheikh, may Allaah have mercy upon him, bring concerning the impermissibility of music in general? (Top half of page 98) List one of the proofs he brings concerning the use of the duff or singing at the wedding feast. (Top half of Page 98)

Discussion & Consideration:

7. How is a successful marriage from the signs of Allaah?
8. Why is it important that we not make the dowries large or extravagant, or focus on wealth when looking for a spouse? Mention any proofs from the Sunnah that you can think of to support this.
9. Why is it crucial that we seek out righteous people to be our spouses, or spouses for our children?
10. What are some ways in which Islaam safeguards the health of the family and the society in general?
11. Is it permissible for the woman to be alone with the man if they are both pious people? Explain your answer.
12. Explain the Sheikh's, may Allaah have mercy upon him) statement, "And the last part of this Ummah will not be rectified except through that which rectified the first of it, and how excellent that would be!"

T.Saead

The Righteous Raising & Educating of Children

by Sheikh Husain ibn 'Abdul-'Aziz Aal-Sheikh

(may Allaah preserve him)

The First Khutbah:

All praise is due to the One who Supports and Protects the righteous ones, and I bear witness that there is no god worthy of worship except for Allaah, alone, without associating any partners along with him from the creation, and I bear witness that our leader and prophet, Muhammad, is His worshipper and His messenger, the foremost of the prophets and messengers, may all be praise and salutations and blessings be upon him, his family, and all of his companions. To proceed:

Oh Muslims:

I advise you and myself with having fear of Allaah, Exalted and Glorified is He; as piety brings great happiness, and obedience to Him brings great reward.

Oh Muslims:

The Muslims must devote themselves to the establishment of the family in accordance with the proper division of rights and laying down the obligatory matters, surrounding it with those boundaries from the principles and rulings which are responsible for its well being and for a radiant future; and to preserve it from the violent agitations of the desires and the factors which bring about destruction and devastation.

The family in Islaam is truly priceless in itself, with lofty goals and objectives. And from the roles of the family which devotes its attention to Islaam through making it a reality, is that it is the natural incubator which watches over and manages the younger generation and takes care of them- the development of their bodies, their intellects, and their souls. In its shadow they receive feelings of love, mercy, and solidarity. Upon the bright light of the family's righteousness and piety the youth become upright and virtuous, and on the basis of the family's corruption its members will be corrupted. Moreover, it has been proven by experience that any institution other than the family cannot replace the family, and cannot stand in its place.

And from this is the starting point. As from those great obligations and significant duties in Islaam is: Making the education of the children an Islamic education, and raising them in a righteous manner- guiding them to the praiseworthy behavior and the Islamic character, as well as progressing with them towards superior heights and elevations. Our Lord, Glorified and Exalted is He, has said, ﴾ ***Oh you who believe! Ward off yourselves and your families against a Fire...*** ﴿- (Surat at-Tahreem, From Ayat 6) The scholars who specialize in explanation of Qur'aan say: That is to say, that the Muslim educates his children and his family in an upright manner, and commands them with good and forbids them from evil.

From the important matters which this trust has placed upon one's shoulders is directing the children towards the exemplary accomplishments, and guiding them to exalted character, as well as giving significant attention to them in regards to a comprehensive material education, which includes the body, the soul, the spirit, the intellect, the behavior, and the society. This is so that the child has a proper early start in all aspects which a good and happy life require; so that the children can lead a life which is distinguished by good reputation and which occupies a high standing.

It has been narrated from Ahmad, at-Tirmidhi, and al-Haakim from the Prophet, may Allaah's praise and salutations be upon him, that he said, ***{A parent cannot give a gift to his children better than good manners.}***

Muslim brothers:

Indeed from the rights of the children which the command of Allaah, Exalted and High is He, makes obligatory, as well as that which He sent His Messenger, may Allaah's praise and salutations be upon him, with, is: That the parents safeguard and look after their children by teaching them the rulings of Allaah, Exalted and High is He, and guiding them to the teachings of Islaam and its mannerisms- as our Lord, Exalted and High is He, has said to His Prophet, commanding his people, ﴾ ***And enjoin the prayers on your family, and be patient in offering them...*** ﴿- (Surat Ta Ha from Ayat 132)

The Prophet, may Allaah's praise and salutations be upon him, said, ***{Command your children with the prayer when they are seven years old, and beat them (to assure they make it) when they are ten years old, and separate them in their sleeping places.}*** (Collected by Ahmad and Abu Daawud, with an authentic chain of narration) And he, may Allaah's praise and salutations be upon him, said, concerning this aspect, ***{The best of you is the one who learns Qur'aan and teaches it to others.}*** (al-Bukhaari)

And 'Ali, may Allaah be pleased with him, and he was the first student in the school of the Prophet, may Allaah's praise and salutations be upon him, said, "*Educate your children upon three characteristics: Love of your Prophet, Muhammad, may Allaah's praise and salutations be upon him, and love for the people of his house, and reading the Qur'aan.*"

Concerning taking our Messenger, may Allaah's praise and salutations be upon him, as a model- this was directed towards the son of his paternal uncle, Ibn 'Abaas, may Allaah be pleased with him, and he was a young man- as he, may Allaah's praise and salutations be upon him, said, ***{Oh young man! Let me inform you: Remember Allaah and He will remember you. Remember Allaah and you will find Him beside you...}*** To the end of the hadeeth (at-Tirmidhi, who stated that the hadeeth is *hasan saheeh*)

So it is upon the parents to train their children to love of Allaah, Exalted and Most High, and love of His Messenger, may Allaah's praise and salutations be upon him; as well as upon the correct worship, moral excellence and meritorious behavior, and respect for and reverence of the legislated commands, as well as refraining from those things which have been forbidden by the Qur'aan. This is because good upbringing and education brings about the good early life, and the evil or incorrect upbringing and education brings about various types of deviation.

The parents must beware of raising the children upon evil, deviant or aberrant behavior, and abominable habits, as our Messenger, may Allaah's praise and salutations be upon him, has said, ***{No child is born except that he is upon the fitrah, or the natural state (Islaam). And his parents turn him into a Jew, Christian, or fire worshipper. }*** (Agreed upon)

Oh gathering of Muslims:

Kindness in the raising of girls, and striving in regards to their education, discipline, and teaching them the Islamic moral system, as well as teaching and learning Qur'aan, is from the greatest causes of one entering Paradise, and success in gaining the pleasure of the Most Merciful. He, may Allaah's praise and salutations be upon him, said, ***{The one who suffers anything from these daughters then be kind to them, as they are for him a covering from the Fire.}*** (Agreed upon, and this is the wording of Muslim) And in one narration: ***{The one who has three daughters, or three sisters, or two daughters, or two sisters, and has the best association with them, and fears Allaah in regard to them, then Paradise is for him.}*** (Ahmad, at-Tirmidhi, and Ibn Hibaan)

Oh Muslims:

The parents earn ripened fruits and generous returns in the righteous upbringing of the children. Our Messenger, may Allaah's praise and salutations be upon him, has said, ***{When one of mankind dies, his actions cease, except for three...}*** And he, may Allaah's praise and salutations be upon him, mentioned from these: ***{...or a righteous child who supplicates for him...}*** (Agreed upon)

Indeed, when the Islamic upbringing and education is absent, and the parents are neglectful in regards to rectification and education, and omit or neglect the counsel and guidance of the children- that returns back to the parents before the child, with every misery and each thing endured. And our Prophet, may Allaah's praise and salutations be upon him, has mentioned that which means this when he said, ***{Indeed from the greatest of the grave sins is that a man curses his parents.}*** It was said, "Oh Messenger of Allaah! How can a man curse his parents?" He, may Allaah's praise and salutations be upon him, replied, ***{He abuses a man's father, so the man abuses his father, and he abuses a man's mother, and the man abuses his mother.}*** (Agreed upon)

Muslim brothers:

Beware, as neglect concerning raising the children, and leniency in regards to their care, keeping, and protection in the matters of both their religion and their worldly affairs is a grave offense and wrongdoing, and a great betrayal. Our Lord, Exalted and Most High is He, says, ﴿ ***Oh you who believe! Betray not Allaah and His Messenger, nor betray knowingly your amaanaat (the things entrusted to you, and all the duties which Allaah has ordained for you).*** ﴾- (Surat al-Anfaal, Ayat 27).

And our Messenger, may Allaah's praise and salutations be upon him, has declared it to be an immense ruling, which continues until the Day of Judgment, as he says, ***{All of you are shepherds and are responsible for your flocks; the leader who is over the people is a shepherd over them and is responsible for them, and the man is the shepherd over the people of his household, and he is responsible for them, and the women is the shepherd over her husband's house and his children, and she is responsible for them...}*** (This hadeeth is agreed upon)

The orphan is not just the one whose parents have left the concerns of this worldly life (due to their deaths) and left him behind.

Rather, the orphan is also the one who has been given a mother who has virtually abandoned him, or a father who is busy.

Brothers in Islaam:

From the responsibilities which are neglected: The mother entrusts the guardianship of her children to other than herself, from hired workers and other than them. Indeed there is evil in that, and dangers which reality bears witness to, and which have been proven through experience. As the mother is the trustee and mistress over the kingdom of those who are under her guardianship- both the sons and the daughters, and the affectionate husband. So she must be a good teacher, and the best of educators, in the shade of obedience to Allaah, Exalted and Most High. Also, it is upon her to direct all of her attention, thought, and time to her loved ones. As behind her (supporting her) are her sincerity and faithfulness and attachment to her maternal instincts-and it is not possible for someone other than her to have these things to any profound degree in the performance of the obligatory acts. Our Messenger, may Allaah's praise and salutations be upon him, has stated, ***{...and the woman is the shepherd over her husband's house and his children, and she is responsible for those under her care...}*** And it has been said,

"The mother is a teacher, so if you prepare her then you have produced a righteous people in those who come after."

Oh virtuous people:

From the responsibilities of the parents: To educate the children with worldly knowledge, which will allow them to establish their lives upon a good state, and from that which will prepare for them a pleasant, happy life. 'Umar al-Farooq, may Allaah be pleased with him, said, addressing the Muslims: "*Teach your children swimming, archery, and horseback riding.*"

Oh virtuous people:

From the responsibilities of the parents: Training the children in that which will give them success in their lives and their religion, and to make an effort to develop their intellectual abilities and capabilities. As our Lord, Exalted and Most High is He, says, ﴿ ***And test the orphans (as regards their intelligence) until they reach the age of marriage; if then you find sound judgment in them, release their property to them...*** ﴾- (Surat an-Nisaa', from Ayat 6)

Oh Gathering of Muslims:

From the pillars of the righteous upbringing: to accustom the children to the performance of good actions, and being adorned with that which signifies good character, until this becomes a habit with them in all phases of life.

Instilling good manners and correct morals will be of benefit to the children in youth, but it will not be successful to teach them these things afterward (when they are older).

Also from its pillars: The beneficial exhortation, and beautiful advice concerning that which will instruct them as to the reality of things, and by which they will be incited to obey the exalted commands. Our Lord,

Exalted and Most High is He, says, ﴾ ***And (remember) when Luqmaan said to his son when he was advising him: "Oh my son! Join not in worship others with Allaah. Verily, joining others in worship with Allaah is a great wrong indeed...*** ﴿- (Surah Luqmaan, Ayat 13) To the end of the verse.

From the greatest pillars of education and upbringing, and the most correct means of rectification: That the parent set a good example for the children; so the parents should perform beneficial acts, and beautify their speech, and build their lives upon the pleasing guidance and the exalted and superior path which pleases Allaah, Exalted and Most High, and they should be the best of examples for their children in correct behavior and manners. Our Messenger, may Allaah's praise and salutations be upon him, has said, ***{The one who says to a young person: 'Come here, and I will give you something', and then he does not give it to him, then he has lied to him.}*** (Collected by Imaam Ahmad) As the good example has profound significance upon the process of education and upbringing of children- such as that which the evidences of Islamic legislation establish, and from that which is brought in the Sunnah. And it has been said before,

"The result of that which is produced by the youth amongst us can be traced back to his father."

As the saying goes: "Every young girl admires her father."

Along with this it is obligatory upon the father and mother to be the favorable example for her in goodness and virtue, as well as being a teacher through action and behavior for their children in fulfilling the principles and rulings of the Islamic legislation, and to behave in every praiseworthy manner. Our Lord, Exalted is He, and Most High, says, ﴾ ***And those who believe and whose offspring follow them in faith, – to them shall We join their offspring, and We shall not decrease the reward of their deeds in anything...*** ﴿- (Surat at-Toor, From Ayat 21)

And from the well-known sayings: "The goodness of the fathers is perceived in the sons."

And our Lord, Exalted is He, and Most High, says, ﴾***...and their father was a righteous man...*** ﴿- (Surat al-Kahf, From Ayat 82)

From those things which are most important from that which is obligatory upon the parents: Choosing the righteous companions for their children- the people of the religion who are pious, so as not to let go of the hold one has upon the child, such that the child alone chooses to befriend whomsoever he chooses, and certainly the companion is the greatest influence upon him, whether he be righteous or corrupt. Our Messenger, may Allaah's praise and salutations be upon him, has said, ***{The man is on the religion of his close friend, so each one of you must look at the one you befriend.}*** (Collected by Ahmad, Abu Daawud, and at-Tirmidhi). And in the two Saheehs (Muslim and al-Bukhaari), he, upon him be Allaah's praise and salutations, says, ***{The examples of the righteous sitting and the evil sitting are like the one who sells musk, and the blacksmith.}***

And 'Adee ibn Zaid said, "It is upon the person to question the connection with his associates, as every person emulates his companion."

It is also upon the parents to keep company with their children in the very best manner, and upon their individual capacity, and to have great compassion in forgiving mistakes or false steps, and overlooking the offenses in which there is no sin or evildoing. It is upon them to understand the children and that path or way which they are upon, and that which they enter into, and that which they leave.

May Allaah bless me and you with the Qur'aan, and benefit us with that which is in it from signs, verses, guidance, and clarification. I have said that which has been said, and I ask Allaah for forgiveness for myself and for all of you and the rest of Muslims for all of our sins, and I seek forgiveness from him, as He is the All-Forgiving, Most Merciful.

The Second Khutbah:

All praise is due to Allaah, Lord of all the Worlds, the Most Beneficent, the Most Merciful, the Master of the Day of Judgment, and I bear witness that there is no god worthy of worship other than He, alone, without partners- He is the First and the Last which is worshipped, and I bear witness that our leader and our prophet, Muhammad, is His slave and Messenger, the best of those who are pious. Allaah, give praise and salutations and blessings upon him, and upon his family and all of his companions. To Proceed:

Oh Muslims:

I advise you and myself with the fear of Allaah, Exalted is He, Most High, as He preserves and shelters the one who has fear of Him, and he is pleased, and is not unhappy.

Oh Muslims:

Indeed the necessary education and upbringing is that which instills in the children virtue, and fashions them in a way which is in accordance with the way of Muhammad and the prophetic guidance. It has been narrated from al-Baraa', may Allaah be pleased with him, that he said, "I saw the Messenger of Allaah, may Allaah's praise and salutations be upon him, and upon his shoulders was al-Hassan (one of his grandsons from Faatimah and 'Ali, may Allaah be pleased with all of them). And the Messenger of Allaah, may Allaah's praise and salutations be upon him, said, ***{Oh Allaah, indeed I love him, so You love him.}*** (Agreed upon)

Indeed it, that necessary education, is an education of kindness and leniency, and the rulings and good teachings maintain a balance between admonition and exhortation. It should be neither a weak nor a rough upbringing, nor one that is too easy or is exceptionally severe. Rather, it should be a righteous and virtuous upbringing, not one full of admonishments, great fear, or violence. As Allaah, Exalted is He, Most High, has said, addressing the Messenger of Allaah, may Allaah's praise and salutations be upon him, ﴿ ***And had you been severe and harsh-hearted, they would have broken away from about you...*** ﴾- (Surat aal-'Imraan, From Ayat 159)

And our Messenger, may Allaah's praise and salutations be upon him, has said, ***{Indeed Allaah is merciful, and He loves mercy.}*** (Bukharee

6544, Muslim 4803, Abu Daawud, 4194, Ibn Maajah 3686, Musnad 887) So it is obligatory that the guidance which is directed towards the children be comparatively compassionate and affectionate. The Prophet, may Allaah's praise and salutations be upon him, said, ***{The best of the women who ride the camels are the women of the tribe of Qur'aish; as they have compassion for the child when he is young, and pay attention to their husbands concerning that which is in his hand.}*** (Agreed upon)

Indeed the education and upbringing which it is obligatory that the children obtain- it is required that it be an upbringing which springs forth from the mercy and compassion which the honorable Islamic legislation commands us with. It is reported in the two Saheehs from 'Aishah, may Allaah be pleased with her, that she said, "The Messenger of Allaah, may Allaah's praise and salutations be upon him, kissed al-Hassan and al-Hussein (his grandsons), and with him was al-Aqra' ibn Haabis. al-Aqra' said, 'Indeed I have ten children, and I have not kissed even one of them.' The Messenger of Allaah, may Allaah's praise and salutations be upon him, looked at him, then said, ***{The one who is not merciful, will not be shown mercy.'}***

Allaah, Exalted is He, Most High, has commanded us with a great matter, and it is: Asking for Allaah's praise and salutations upon the Noble Prophet-

Oh Allaah, may your praise, salutations and blessings be upon our prophet and leader, Muhammad, and oh Allaah, your pleasure be upon the rightly guided *khaleefahs*, and the leaders of those who are guided: Abu Bakr, 'Umar, 'Uthmaan, 'Ali, and upon all the rest of the companions, and upon the generation which followed them, and those who follow them in righteousness to the Day of Judgment.

Oh Allaah, advance and fortify Islaam and the Muslims. Oh Allaah, advance and fortify Islaam and the Muslims. Oh Allaah, advance and fortify Islaam and the Muslims. Oh Allaah, destroy our enemies and the enemies of the Muslims. Oh Allaah, deal with the enemies of the Muslims, as indeed they are unable to harm You. Oh Allaah, deal with the enemies of the Muslims, as indeed they are unable to harm You. Oh Allaah, deal with them, as indeed they are unable to harm You. Oh Allaah, bring your punishment down upon them, as you are the One worthy of worship. Oh Allaah, bring your punishment down upon them, as you are the One worthy of worship. Oh Allaah, show them the wonder of Your ability. Oh Allaah, show them the wonder of Your ability. Oh Allaah, show them the wonder of Your ability.

Oh Allaah, guide the one who is in charge of our affairs to that which You love and are pleased with. Oh Allaah, guide him to that which You love and are pleased with, oh the One who has the Exaltedness and the Honor. Oh Allaah, rectify the judges of the Muslims. Oh Allaah, rectify the judges of the Muslims. Oh Allaah, rectify the judges of the Muslims.

Oh Allaah, grant the leadership to those who have fear and awareness of You. Oh Allaah, grant the leadership of the Muslims to those who have fear and awareness of You. Oh Allaah, grant the leadership of the Muslims to those who have fear and awareness of You. Oh Allaah, grant their leadership to the best of them. Oh Allaah, grant their leadership to the best of them.

Oh Allaah, grant their leadership to the best of them, and strengthen them, Oh the One who has the Exaltedness and Honor. Oh Allaah, protect them from the evil ones among them, Oh Allaah, protect them from the evil ones among them, Oh the One who has the Exaltedness and Honor.

Oh Allaah, forgive the Believing men and the Believing women, and the Muslim men and the Muslim women, the living from amongst them and the dead. Oh Allaah, prepare for us clear guidance in our affairs. Oh Allaah, prepare for us clear guidance in our affairs. Oh Allaah, protect us and our offspring with Islaam. Oh Allaah, protect us and our offspring with Islaam. Oh Allaah, protect us and our offspring with Islaam.

Oh Allaah, grant us good in this life, and good in the Hereafter, and protect us from the punishment of the Fire.

Oh Allaah, bring to our souls piety, and increase it, as You are the best of the ones who increase, you are its guardian and protector.

Oh Allaah, You are al-Ghanee, al-Hameed, oh Allaah You are al-Ghanee, al-Hameed. Oh Allaah, help us, oh Allaah, help us. Oh Allaah, bring water to our country and the countries of the Muslims. Oh Allaah, bring water to our country and the countries of the Muslims. Oh Allaah, bring water to our country and the countries of the Muslims.

Oh worshippers of Allaah:

Remember Allaah, remember Him often, and Glorify Him morning and night.

(From a khutbah given at the Prophet's Masjid, 2/18/1430)

Review and Discussion Questions

Questions for The Righteous Raising and Educating of Children

Review:

1. What are some of the general responsibilities of the parent to the child does the Sheikh list? (Bottom half of page 103)
2. What three characteristics did 'Ali, may Allaah be pleased with him, mention we should raise our children upon? (Middle of page 104)
3. List two proofs from the Sunnah that the daughters must treated kindly and raised well. (Top of page 105)
4. List two proofs (one verse and one hadeeth) that the one who neglects her responsibility towards her family has committed a grave offense. (Bottom half of page 105)
5. What are some of the proofs that we must be merciful when dealing with the children? (Page 108, Bottom Half)

Discussion & Consideration:

6. How does the family and household environment affect the children, for good or evil?
7. In what ways do the parents reap rewards for raising their children well, and conversely, how do they suffer when they do not raise them well?
8. Explain the Sheikh's, may Allaah preserve him, saying, "The orphan is not just the one whose parents have left the concerns of life (due to their deaths) and left him behind. Rather, the orphan is also the one who has been given a mother who has virtually abandoned him, or a father who is busy."
9. The parents are responsible for making sure the children are educated in religions matters as well as worldly matters which will lead them to success in this life and the next. Explain this.
10. Why is it so important that a parent set a good example for the children in every aspect of life?

The Role of
the Woman in
the Raising &
Education of
the Family
Sheikh Saalih al-Fauzaan,
(may Allaah preserve him)

All praise is due to Allaah, we praise Him, and ask for His help and His forgiveness, and we seek Allaah's protection from the evil of our own selves and from the evil of our deeds. The one whom Allaah guides, none can lead astray, and the one whom Allaah misguides, then there is no guidance for him. I bear witness that there is no god worthy of worship except for Allaah alone, with no partners associated with Him, and I bear witness that Muhammad is His slave and messenger, may Allaah's praise and salutations be upon him, and upon his family and his companions.

To proceed: Our lecture is related to the Muslim woman; and discussion concerning this subject is something which is considered to be very important in our time. The reason for this is that the woman in our society is aggressively attacked by the enemies of this religion; such that they put forth that which are called "issues" or "women's issues"- intending by this to take the Muslim woman out of that position which Allaah wishes and wants for her...

We do not know of any true "issue" for the Muslim woman other than the issues connected to the state of her *Ummah*, the Muslim *Ummah*. As indeed the ignorance of the Muslim people of their religion, and their weakness in adhering to it- these are the issues that concern the Muslim *Ummah* as well as her as a Muslim woman. And we are endeavoring to clarify matters concerning this in this lecture, which is entitled, "The Role of the Woman in the Upbringing and Education of the Family". As for what is found in the title of this lecture, we have the following observations to make:

Firstly: In respect to understanding the term, "*at-tarbiyyah*" (upbringing and education); we intend by it the broad meaning concerning the establishment of the family, and the related requirements of caring for the family and focusing on it. This is in order that some of the people do not think that *at-tarbiyyah* is merely teaching good manners and rectifying them- as indeed this is from that which is included in *at-tarbiyyah*. However, *at-tarbiyyah* of the family encompasses a much broader scope than just this.

Secondly: It might be understood from the title that the woman has a place in the education and upbringing of the family, but that it is something secondary. However, the truth of the matter is that the efforts of the woman in educating and raising the family should be her chief effort and concern, and anything that infringes upon that is the exception. Therefore if the title of the lecture were to be "The Role of the Woman *is* Educating and Raising the Family" that would be more suitable.

The Position of the Woman:

This subject requires both clarification and elaboration. So we say: Truly, the natural place for the woman is the home; and it is the general realm of her work- this is the general case and the foundation. This is that which the evidences of Islamic law support, and logically according to the woman's nature, this is her innate orientation.

As for the proofs from the Islamic law concerning this, then the texts and realities which bear witness to it are many. From them:

1. Allaah, the Most High, says, addressing the Mothers of the Believers, ﴾ ﴿... ***and stay in your houses...*** ﴿- (Surat al-Ahzaab, From Ayat 33)

2. And He, the Most High, says, ﴾ ***And turn them not out of their (husband's) homes nor shall they (themselves) leave...***﴿- (Surat at-Talaaq, From Ayat 1)

And this is for the one who is in her waiting period after divorce. And the scholars have said that indeed the ruling is not specific to her- rather, it extends beyond the woman in this specific case. The additional proof is *"bayootikunna"* -your houses, and *"bayootihinna"* is their houses; so that even though usually the houses are actually owned by their husbands, the command is connected to the home itself, not to the ownership of it- indicating that the basic principle for her is staying in her residence.

3. There are also lessons and examples in the lives of the prophets. Such a the story of Musa with the two women: ﴾ ***And when he arrived at the water (a well of Madyan), he found there a group of men watering their flocks, and besides them he found two women who were keeping back their flocks. He said: "What is the matter with you?" They said: "We cannot water our flocks until the shepherds take their flocks. And our father is a very old man...*** ﴿ (Surat al-Qasas, Ayat 23) To His saying, ﴾ ***And said one of them (the two women): "Oh my father! Hire him! Verily, the best of men for you to hire is the strong, the trustworthy." He said: "I intend to wed one of these two daughters of mine to you...*** ﴿- (Surat al-Qasas Ayats 26 -27)

Let us carefully consider the lessons in these verses. This is Musa coming across the shepherds near the water, and apart from them there are two women holding back their cattle so that the other people's cattle do not mix with them. He asks them, "What's wrong? Why do you not water your cattle with the people?"

The answer comes: "We cannot water our flock until the shepherds take theirs away." Truly, they are pious, fearing Allaah, and this prevents them from intermingling with the men. Then, it is as if he advanced another unspoken question which is, "What is it that causes you to come out from your home?" Then the answer comes immediately after this, "And our father is a very old man." So necessity and need caused them to do that, yet when they were compelled to go out, they maintained good character and behavior, as they did not mix with the men.

Then there comes another lesson, when one of the two women reflects that the time has come that the matters be returned to their natural state: ﴾ ***And said one of them (the two women): "Oh my father! Hire him! Verily, the best of men for you to hire is the strong, the trustworthy.*** ﴿ And Shu'ayb was satisfied with the solution, as he proposed to Musa, "I intend to wed one of these two daughters of mine to you on condition that you serve me for eight years..." So Musa accepted the proposition, and matters were returned to their natural, original state, as Musa worked with the flocks and the woman he married took to working within her home. Other narrations similar to this are related to us in the Qur'aan, and in their stories are worthy examples for us.

4. The congregational prayers in the *masjid* are Islamically legislated as the realm of the men, and from the best of their actions, and how much better if it is in the *masjid* of Allaah's Messenger, praying with him, may Allaah's praise and salutations be upon him. And yet, in spite of all this, he used to encourage the women to pray in their houses.

It is narrated from the wife of Abi Humaid as-Saa'idee, that she went to the Messenger of Allaah, may Allaah's praise and salutations be upon him, and said, "Oh Messenger of Allaah, truly I love praying with you." So he replied, ***{I know that you love to pray with me, and your prayer in (an inner room in) your house is better than your prayer in your outer room, and your prayer in your outer room is better than your prayer in your residence and your prayer in your residence is better than your prayer in the masjid of your people, and your prayer in the masjid of your people is better than your prayer in my masjid.}*** So she ordered a *masjid* to be built for her in the darkest and most private part of her house, and she prayed in it until she met her Lord, Glorified and Exalted is He. (The hadeeth is found in Ahmad 6/371, and Ibn Khuzaimah in his "*Saheeh*" 3/95 and it is *hasan*. Look in "*Saheeh Ibn Khuzaimah*")

So the suggestion of the hadeeth is clear, in that the fundamental situation is that the woman stays in her home, so much so that the benefit of the prayer in her house is greater than the benefit of the prayer in his *masjid* with the Messenger of Allaah, may Allaah's praise and salutations be upon him- yet in spite of that he did allow the woman to go out to the *masjid*.

5. The state of the woman in the favored first generations- who hold the position of being a model for us- advocates this, such that we find that her leaving the home and establishing work outside of the home was considered a cause of calamity for her, and that which brought disaster to her. Indeed, this is the understanding of the Companions of the Messenger of Allaah, may Allaah be pleased with them all. It is narrated concerning Ibn Mas'ood, that his wife asked of him that he allow her to wear a *jilbaab* (loose outer garment worn by Muslim women). He said, "*I am afraid that you will forsake the outer garment of Allaah, which He has dressed you with." So she said, "What is it?" He said, "Your home.*"

6. That which is Islamically legislated is that which agrees with one's natural disposition. Allaah says, ﴿ ***Should not He Who has created know? And He is the Most Kind and Courteous (to His slaves), the Well-Acquainted (with everything).*** ﴾- (Surat al-Mulk, Ayat 14) Indeed, the woman generally staying in her home is that which is rational according to the natural disposition which is suitable for her position and her nature, and it protects her from that which is incompatible with it- that which divides and dissipates her efforts. This has been supported and established through both scientific and psychological studies; as some of the impartial researchers in the West have put forth conclusions concerning avoiding the danger of the woman engaging in that which differs from her natural disposition and innate nature. However, the people of desires are deaf to every call to recognize this. Rather, they put forth the accusation that this model is a call to return the woman to the age of narrow minded intolerance and slavery- this is what they claim! More will be said in clarification of this during the present discussion of this subject.

The Correct Position Concerning the Woman Leaving the House

Additionally, it remains to be stated that it should be understood that it is not forbidden for the woman to leave her house without exception, as texts have been narrated which are proofs that it is permissible for the woman to go out, as well as for her to work outside the home. However, this situation is not the general case; rather, it is the exception, and is done out of necessity.

From them is that which has been narrated concerning the permission of the Messenger of Allaah, may Allaah's praise and salutations be upon him, given to the woman to perform the obligatory prayer in the *masjid*, keeping in mind the fact that he indicated the greater merit of her choosing to pray within her home. Also from them is that which has been narrated concerning the early Muslim women's participation in some of the battles, engaged in carrying water and tending the wounded.

And the callers to so-called "women's liberation" cling to only this- rather, truly it is the callers to her corruption from the people of desires. Just as some of the well intentioned people who have unfortunately been defeated by the recent cultural pressures and forces directed towards Muslims use it as proof, believing that they are defending Islaam.

In answer to this we say: Indeed the woman leaving her home and her working outside the house is not absolutely forbidden. Rather, necessity may cause this to occur, such as is shown by the daughters of Shu'ayb having to leave their father's house. And it may be necessary to the Muslim nation, such as the woman teaching the women of her people, and providing them with medical care; and evidence supports the woman going out for this, yet it is the exceptional circumstance rather than the general rule.

We find that Imaam Ibn Hajr says concerning this, "Perhaps the woman going out with the army has been abrogated, as in the biography of Umm Kabshah al-Qadaa' narrated in "*al-Isaabah*" it says, Abu Bakr ibn Abi Shaybah and at-Tabaraani and other than them have brought forth her hadeeth by way of al-Aswad ibn Qays, from Sa'eed ibn 'Amr al-Qurshee, that Umm Kabshah, a woman from Qadaa'at, said, "Oh Messenger of Allaah, allow me to go out in the army such and such" He, may Allaah's praise and salutations be upon him, said, ***{No.}*** She said, "Oh Messenger of Allaah, I do not want to go out and fight; rather, I want to treat the wounded and the sick and to carry water." He, may Allaah's praise and salutations be upon him, said, ***{I would have given you permission, except that it would be considered a Sunnah, and it would be said, 'A woman went out', because of the permission to you; so remain.}***

And Ibn Sa'd narrates it, and in the end it states, ***{Remain. As it will not be said by the people that Muhammad fights his wars using women.}***

Then he (Ibn Hajr) said, "Perhaps the reconciliation between this and that which came before in the biography of Umm Sinaan al-Islaamee is that this abrogates that- because that one was for Khaybar, and this one was after the opening of Makkah." ("*al-Isaabah*" 4/463)

In any case, the proof is established concerning some of the women going out and participating by treating the wounded and bringing water; however they were restricted situations, limited to what was required, and not taking precedence over that which was the basic foundation. And from that which is important to clarify is the difference between the state of the woman's working outside the house being the fundamental rule or general case, and its being the exception.

As if the exception is for a specific circumstance, then we do not anticipate that negative consequences are likely or expected to occur due to that going out. Furthermore, this doesn't indicate that it is her normal domain to enter into. As for the idea that working outside the home is the basic rule, as some of those with strange ideas believe- such that it is thought that the woman is going to be left behind and dysfunctional if she works in the home, and that this paralyzes half of society, and so on. Then I say: If we proceed in this direction, those negative consequences which result from women leaving their homes to enter the workplace will inevitably occur, along with everything which results from this, such as that which has already come about in the Western societies.

The society will fall into the general evil of unrestricted free mixing between the sexes and the evil of the households generally being without their mother's presence. In any case, we must take measures to prevent this and sincerely undertake them, even if some of the people attempt to conceal the reality of this evil goal with deceptive slogans such as: "Going out in the shade of the teachings of our Islamic legislation, and to the extent of our traditions."

Furthermore, it is necessary that we understand that it has been determined that the fundamental principal or general case is that the woman works within her home, and that her work outside of the home is the exception, and that this is in accordance with the proofs of the Islamic legislation. Then it is not for us, after that, to have any free choice between adherence to this or leaving it, if we are, in truth, Muslims. As Allaah has said,

﴾***It is not for a believer, man or woman, when Allaah and His Messenger have decreed a matter that they should have any option in their decision. And whoever disobeys Allaah and His Messenger, he has indeed strayed into a plain error.***﴿- (Surat al-Ahzaab, , Ayat 36)

As this *ayat*- even though it was revealed concerning a specific issue- its meaning is general. Moreover it comes after the revelation of the verses which command the women of the Prophet, may Allaah's praise and salutations be upon him, (and more generally the believing women) with the practice of staying in their homes.

Indeed, Allaah has made it clear that to leave His revealed way and legislation, and turn away from it, is a definite cause- without any doubt- of the wretchedness like the state of most of the nations on Earth today: ﴾***But whosoever turns away from My Reminder, then verily, for him is a life of hardship...***﴿- (Surat Taa Haa from Ayat 124) And verily the state of the nation which has the correct methodology then abandons it, choosing instead to search in the scraps and garbage of the opinions of men, is like the saying of the poet,

Like the dweller in the desert who strikes down into the earth due to his thirst

Yet the water is already there running openly above its surface

What is the family?

The third observation concerning the title is regarding the word "family". What is the family which is the domain of the woman, and what is its significance?

The family is unequaled in its position as the permanent, developmental foundation, which is never separated from, as we cannot conceive of a society without the family.

Indeed, its existence, permanence, and stability are from the goals of the Islamic legislation: ***﴾Oh mankind! Be dutiful to your Lord, Who created you from a single person, and from him He created his wife, and from them both He created many men and women...﴿*** - (Surat an-Nisaa, from Ayat 1)

The verse reveals that the foundation of mankind was one family ***("...a single soul, and from him He created his wife...")*** and from this couple, He created many families. And He, the Most High, says, ***﴾And it is He Who has created man from water, and has appointed for him kindred by blood, and kindred by marriage. And your Lord is Ever All-Powerful to do what He wills.﴿*** - (Surat al-Furqaan, , Ayat 54) Descending from the lineage of the male, and joined with the lineage of the female.

Islaam encourages us to establish a family when one has the ability to do so. He, may Allaah's praise and salutations be upon him, said, ***{Oh young men, whoever among you who is able to marry, should marry.}*** (al-Bukhaari, from "*Kitaab an-Nikaah,* Chapter: The saying of the Prophet, may Allaah's praise and salutations be upon him, ***{The one who is able to marry, should marry}***; and Muslim, in "*Kitaab an-Nikaah*, Chapter: Marriage is Obligatory for the one who Desires it, and who Obtains Provisions.")

And he, may Allaah's praise and salutations be upon him, said, ***{Marry the one who is affectionate and able to have many children.}*** " (Abu Daawud, from "*Kitaab an-Nikaah*, Chapter: The Forbiddance of Marrying the One who cannot have Children from amongst the Women", and in an-Nasaa'ee in "*Kitaab an-Nikaah*, Chapter: The Dislike of Marrying the Barren Woman"; and the hadeeth is authentic- refer to "*Saheeh Abu Daawud*" , Hadeeth Number 1805, and "*Saheeh an-Nasaa'ee*" Hadeeth Number 3026)

Islaam makes clear that the position of the family and its influence is tremendous, as it is that which directs and determines the path of one's life and religion. He, may Allaah's praise and salutations be upon him, said, ***{Every child is born on the fitrah (natural state of Islaam), and it is his parents who turn him to Judaism, Christianity, or Magianism.}*** (al-Bukhaari, in the "Book of the Funerals, Chapter: What is Said about the Children of those who Associate Others with Allaah in Worship, and Chapter: If a Youth Embraces Islaam and Dies- Does one Pray over him?"; and Muslim in "*Kitaab al-Qadr*, Chapter: The Meaning of Every Child is Born upon the *Fitrah*")

The legislative guidelines of Islaam in their entirety have come to give order to and organize the family, as well as to safeguard it from disintegration. From that are the rulings of marriage, divorce, polygyny, and the rights of the fathers and mothers, and many others than these. All of which are evidence of that prominent position which Islaam has given to the family, because it is the place from which the generations are born, and whatever state the family is found in, reflects the future of this Muslim *Ummah*.

And the woman, she is the backbone of the family, as it is said, "Behind every great man, there is a woman who raised him under her guardianship."

Does not the family deserve the devotion of the woman, and is the work of the woman for her family considered wasted effort?!?! Indeed from the overall mission of the woman is motherhood, with all that it encompasses, and it is more wide-ranging than simply procreation; rather, it is the raising and nurturing which transcends the matter of one righteous person.

Certainly the work of the woman in her home, even if some people believe it to be insignificant- in fact it *is* significant, joining together many specific roles, and it requires that which the administration of a country requires. Thus, it calls for knowledge and understanding. It necessitates strictness. It requires general administration as well as economic management. It calls for gentleness and mercy and compassion, and requires lofty principles.

Indeed the woman who regards the work in the home with scorn, belittling it- this is an evidence that she does not properly understand this as it should be understood; therefore she is not someone who truly establishes it properly. Likewise, those who believe that she is inactive and unproductive in her house- either they do not understand this work, or they in fact understand it but the cause for their assertion is a disease in their hearts.

Is it correct that we could possibly say: "Indeed the woman, if she devotes herself to the care of the family, she remains paralyzed and inactive, and society loses half of its capability?!"

Rather, from that which it is necessary is that the woman understands this great position in light of our *aqeedah*, or Islamic beliefs. As Allaah, the Most High, says, ﴿ ***Say (Oh Muhammad): ﴿Verily, my prayer, my sacrifice, my living, and my dying are for Allaah, the Lord of the 'aalameen (mankind, jinn and all that exists)*** ﴾- (Surat al-An'aam, Ayat 162).

Indeed, this work is an act of worship; it is not an act of coercion, nor is it a monotonous act. Rather, it is an act in which there is peace of mind and tranquility for the one who realizes the goals of life and the mystery of the existence of mankind. The Prophet, may Allaah's praise and salutations be upon him, said, ***{If a woman fasts her five daily prayers, and fasts her month of Ramadhaan, and protects her private parts, and obeys her husband, she may enter Paradise from any door she chooses.}*** (Ahmad, 1/191, and the hadeeth is found in "*Majmu' az-Zawaa'id*" 4/306. And he said, And in it is Ibn Luhay'a, and his hadeeth are *hasan*, and the rest of the men in the chain of narration are *saheeh*." And Sheikh Ahmad Shaakir said, "Its chain of narration is severed, in my opinion." "*al-Musnad*" 3/128)

And following these observations, our discussion will concern the woman's work inside her home, as well as bringing forth its example of her principle position in this life being to participate in the building of the Islamic nation. It will become clear to us that these are immense and great undertakings if they are given their true position and rights, as indeed they are noble ways to spend time. These undertakings include:

The work of the woman inside her home:

First: Worship of Allaah:

Because that is the purpose of humankind's existence, all of it. Allaah, the Most High, says, ﴾***And I created not the jinn and mankind except that they should worship Me (Alone).***﴿- (Surat adh-Dhaariyaat, Ayat 56)

The divine guidance directed towards the Mothers of the Believers, may Allaah be pleased with them, assists us in understanding this, when they are commanded to stay in the houses. Allaah, the Most High, says, ﴾***And stay in your houses, and do not display yourselves like that of the times of ignorance, and perform the prayers, and give obligatory charity and obey Allaah and His Messenger...***﴿- (Surat al-Ahzaab, from Ayat 33)

The concept of "worship" is broader than the performance of the ritual acts of worship, though they are a large part of worship. And performing such acts of worship is from the greatest of acts appointed to the woman of the deeds required of her in performing her role with excellence within her home.

As the righteous woman is the one who performs her role in the desired manner. Likewise, that is the foundation of the righteous upbringing of children by example. Such that when the woman establishes the acts of worship with piety and tranquility, this has a tremendous effect upon the ones who are in the home- from the children and others. When the woman perfects the *wudoo* (ritual purification for prayer), and then stands before her Lord with humility and submission, this will be cultivated within the children. This is the meaning of setting an example, along with her efforts at clarification and guidance through speech.

This aspect of her efforts is known; however it is necessary that its aim, purpose, and effects be clarified, and it should be understood to be something distinct, far from that which is merely done as routine, as that stifles the high ideals related to it.

Second: The woman is a source of peace and stability to the husband and the home.

Allaah, the Most High, says, ﴾***And among His Signs is that He created for you wives from among yourselves, that you may find repose in them, and He has put between you affection and mercy. Verily, in that are indeed signs for a people who reflect.***﴿- (Surat ar-Room, Ayat 21)

The Use of the Expression "sakan" and that which it Carries in Meaning

The word "*sakan*" carries a tremendous meaning, including stability, relaxation, and peace of mind in the home- and if we attempt to find an expression which articulates all that which it encompasses, we cannot, and we never will be able to. That is the word of the Lord of the Worlds which cannot be attacked by falsehood from in front of His hands, nor from behind them. As the woman provides peace and stability to the husband, and so peace and stability to the home. Then Allaah characterizes the relationship as one of ﴾***...affection and mercy...***﴿

He also says, ﴾*It is He Who has created you from a single person (Aadam), and then He has created from him his wife (Hawwaa), in order that he might enjoy the pleasure of living with her.*﴿- (Surat al-A'araaf, from Ayat 189)

That is to say, he is kind and gentle to her, and turns to her as a refuge and shelter for him. And we understand the secret of the expression "*ilayha*" (with her) in the two verses, where the pleasure refers back to the woman, as she is his place and his home- as the husband lives with her, and turns to her. And the home, along with the ones in it, takes pleasure in living with her. As such the woman is not a pleasure for her husband until she understands his rights and his position, then establishes his rights upon her, in joyful and content obedience to her Lord.

In regard to that, Islaam affirms this position of the husband, because it is the foundation. The Messenger, may Allaah's praise and salutations be upon him, said, ***{If I were to command anyone to prostrate to another, I would have commanded the woman to prostrate to her husband.}*** (at-Tirmidhi, in the chapters of nursing- Chapter Concerning the Right of the Husband over his Wife; and Ibn Maajah in his book of marriage, Chapter: The Right of the Husband over the Wife"; and the hadeeth is authentic. Look to "*Saheeh at-Tirmidhi*", hadeeth number 926)

Rather, the reminder of his position even continues until after his death. ***{It is not permissible for a woman who believes in Allaah and the last day to mourn over the dead for over three days, except for over her husband- as she mourns for him four months and ten days.}*** (al-Bukhaari, in the Book of Funerals, Chapter: The Woman's Mourning over other than her Husband"; and Muslim, in the Book of Divorce, Chapter: The Obligation of Mourning in the Time of Waiting after Death")

It is understood that the mourning period is in addition to the waiting period, so in it is a declaration of the right of the husband over the wife. In Islaam guidelines have been legislated about the conferring of obligatory marital rights, through which the home is a refuge and becomes a righteous environment.

Yet these rulings and legislated acts are not specific to the woman; rather they are upon both the husband and the wife. However, the position of the woman concerning them is greater because she is the backbone and pillar, as we have mentioned, considering the specific domain we discussed of the woman and her position in raising and educating the family.

It is necessary that we indicate of some of the responsibilities and required means by which she makes her home the refuge that Allaah desires. From them:

1. Complete obedience to the husband in that which does not contain disobedience to Allaah.

This obedience is the foundation of the stability and peace, because the maintenance and protection are delegated to the men. Allaah says, ﴾***Men are the protectors and maintainers of women...***﴿- (Surat an-Nisaa', From Ayat 34) So how can we imagine the role of protecting and maintaining her without her obedience to him? The home is a school, or administrative center. So if the director of the school or establishment has employees and they do not obey him, is it possible for the work to be easy? And the home is similar to this. Indeed the obedience to the husband is a legislated obligation, for which the woman is rewarded for fulfilling. Indeed, we find that the obedience to the husband comes before superogatory acts of worship. The Messenger of Allaah, may Allaah's praise and salutations be upon him, said, ***{If her husband is present a woman cannot fast -other than the obligatory fast of Ramadhaan- except by his permission.}*** (Agreed upon- al-Bukhaari in The Book of Marriage, Chapter: The Voluntary Fast of the Woman is with the Permission of her Husband; and Muslim, in The Book of Charity, Chapter: The Slave does not Spend from the Wealth of his Master) And in this is an indication of the importance of obedience to the husband, that it is even given precedence to the worship of voluntary fasting.

2. Performance of the housework, by which she is the caretaker of the family life, including cooking, cleaning, washing, and other than that.

In order for the performance of these acts to bear fruit, it is necessary that they be done with efficiency, self-contentment, pleasure, and the awareness that indeed they are worship.

And for you, oh Sister, is a model from the life of the pious predecessors of this nation. Imaam Ahmad has related, with its chain of narration on Ibn A'bad, that he said, 'Ali ibn Abi Taalib, may Allaah be pleased with him, said, "Should I not narrate to you concerning me and Faatimah, may Allaah be pleased with her, who was the daughter of the Messenger of Allaah, may Allaah's praise and salutations be upon him, and who was the most precious of his family to him, and who was my wife? As she pulled with the handmill until the impression of the handmill was upon her hand, and she carried water in the waterskin until the impression of the waterskin was evident on her upper chest, and she lit the fire under the cooking pot until it dirtied her dress, so she was afflicted with harm from that. So some slaves had come to Allaah's Messenger, may Allaah's praise and salutations be upon him. I ('Ali) said, so I said to her, "Go quickly to the Messenger of Allaah, may Allaah's praise and salutations be upon him, and ask him for a servant who will preserve what freedom you have. So she went quickly to the Messenger of Allaah, may Allaah's praise and salutations be upon him, and found that he had with him servants, or a servant. She returned, and had not asked him, as he mentioned the hadeeth in which he said, ***{Should I not inform you of that which is better for you than a servant? When you retire to your bed, say "subhanAllaah" thirty three times, and say "alhamdulillah" thirty three times, and say Allaahu akbar thirty four times.}*** So she put the request out of her head, and said, "I am content with Allaah and His Messenger once again." (According the Sheikh Al-Albaani this version from "*Musnad*" of Imaam Ahmad 1/153 is not authentic, but authentic versions are found in "*Saheeh al-Bukhaari*" which summarized from this, in "The Book of the Obligation of the One Fifth, Chapter: Proof of the One Fifth to the Representative of the Messenger of Allaah" may Allaah's praise and salutations be upon him, and in Muslim, in "The Book of Remembrance of Allaah and Supplication, Chapter: Saying *Subhaanallaah* in the First of the Day, and when one Sleeps", and in Abu Daawud, in the chapters of sleep, "Chapter: Saying *Subhaanallaah* when one Sleeps", and in at-Tirmidhi, in the chapters of supplications, "Chapter: Concerning Saying *Subhaanallaah*, and *Allaahu Akbar*, and *Alhamdulillah* when one Sleeps") So he, the Messenger of Allaah, did not deny her having to perform this hard work; and this is despite her position of merit and honor! Rather, he was content with that and guided her to worship to assist her in that, and that was better for her than a servant.

It is narrated by Ibn Ishaaq, with its chain of narration to Asmaa' Bint 'Umays, that she said, "When Ja'far and his companions were killed, Allaah's Messenger, may Allaah's praise and salutations be upon him, visited me. I had just finished tanning forty of our hides, kneaded my loaves of bread, washed my sons, put oil on them, and cleaned them." She said, "So the Messenger of Allaah, may Allaah's praise and salutations be upon him, said, ***{Bring me to the sons of Ja'far.}*** She said, "So I brought him to them, and he smelled them (their cleanliness) and his eyes shed tears, so I said, "Oh Messenger of Allaah, my father and mother for you, what causes you to weep? Have you been informed of something concerning Ja'far and his people?" He said, ***{Yes, they were killed today.}*** to the end of the hadeeth ("*Seerat Ibn Hishaam*", 3/380)

3. Compliance to her husband in that which Allaah has made permissible for him of physical enjoyment.

He, may Allaah's praise and salutations be upon him, said, ***{If a man calls his wife to his bed and she refuses, and he spends the night angry with her, the angels curse her until the morning comes.}*** (al-Bukhaari, "The Book of the Beginning of Creation, Chapter: If one of you says, "*Ameen*", and Muslim, "The Book of Marriage, Chapter: The Forbiddance of her Abstaining from the Bed of her Husband") Rather, the best fulfillment of such rights is to approach him without his demanding it, and to be prepared and beautified for that. And it is from the regrettable things that some of the women beautify themselves to go out- while they have been forbidden from that- more than they beautify themselves for their husbands- and that is something they have in fact been commanded with. And all of that is a proof of either ignorance concerning the responsibilities which they have, or the failure to follow Allaah's legislation.

Indeed, for the woman to perform this command, and receive it well, has a great effect upon the stability and peace of the home, including the virtue of the husband, and his pleasure with that which he has, and the lack of feeling frustration and deprivation, and consequently there will come peace of mind as well.

How many of the men live a life that is not settled and peaceful, by reason of their feeling deprived because the woman does not give attention to this aspect of marriage, or does not understand how to fulfill his right in establishing it? So the woman should understand her position concerning that, and then consider and seek ways to perform it.

4. Safeguarding his secrets and his honor

She does not engage in that which may cause a trial, or *at-tabaruj* (going out unnecessarily, without the proper covering). She is not lax or careless in regard to being exposed to the men in the doorway of the house or through the windows, or when she is outside her home- and when she does go out, she does so modestly.

He, may Allaah's praise and salutations be upon him, said, ***{As for your rights upon your women- that they not invite those whom you dislike to visit and rest upon your furnishings, nor do they give permission to the one you dislike to enter your houses.}*** (With this wording, it is found in at-Tirmidhi, in the chapters of nursing, "Chapter: That which has come Concerning the Right of the Woman upon her Husband". And it is a *hasan* hadeeth. Look to *"Saheeh Sunan at-Tirmidhi"*, 1/341. It is also found in Muslim from the hadeeth of Jaabir concerning the attributes of the pilgrimage of the Prophet, may Allaah's praise and salutations be upon him, in "The Book of *Hajj*, Chapter: The Pilgrimage of the Prophet, may Allaah's praise and salutations be upon him", without his saying, ***{And they do not give permission to the one you dislike to enter your houses.})***

This contributes to maintaining the moral character of the home, and confidence of one's husband, and educating the children concerning chastity. The home in which there occurs something from laxness in any matter from these matters is not secure, peaceful, and comfortable, and it is not a stable environment.

5. Preservation of Wealth

He, may Allaah's praise and salutations be upon him, said, ***{And the woman is a shepherd in the house of her husband, and is responsible for her flock.}*** (al-Bukhaari, in "The Book of *al-Jumaa'*, Chapter: *al-Jumaa'* in the Villages and Towns", and in Muslim, in "The Book of *al-Imaara*, Chapter: The Merit of the Just Imaam") And he, may Allaah's praise and salutations be upon him, said, ***{The best of the women are those who ride camels, the righteous women of Quraish. They are the most compassionate towards their children when they are young, and the most careful in guarding their husband's wealth.}*** (al-Bukhaari, in "The Book of Marriage, Chapter: The One whom should be Married, and the Women which are Good", and Muslim in "The Book of the Merits of the Companions, Chapter: Merits of the Women of the Quraish")

And the matter of wealth is a significant issue, with other matters attached to it. From them:

a. Rectification the affairs of the home through preserving that which is in it

b. The absence of waste and extravagance

c. Undertaking it properly will prevent the husband from having to bear that which he cannot endure of expenses

And the monetary matters today have become a system and matters of proper management and accounting- as how many means and ways abound for the family to live comfortably without economic troubles? And these techniques have been studied. So does the wife understand her position concerning accomplishing that?

6. Good behavior

- The husband is in the position of being the caretaker and guardian; so it is necessary that the treatment of the husband proceed from this, and from a display of good conduct.

- She should tolerate his mistakes if he errs

- She should seek to placate him when he is angry

- She should let him know that she loves and appreciates him

-The beautiful speech and the sincere smile. The Messenger of Allaah, may Allaah's praise and salutations be upon him, said, ***{Your smile in the face of your brother is charity.}*** (at-Tirmidhi, in the chapters of charity and gifts, "Chapter: That which has come Concerning Kindness" And the hadeeth is authentic. Look at "*Saheeh Sunan at-Tirmidhi*" 2/186)

So how much more is this the case, if it is from the wife towards her husband?

- She should pay attention to his personal affairs, specifically in regard to food, drink, and clothing, from the aspect of its types, and the time related to it being ready for him. And the woman must know that there is not any transgression or encroachment on her personally or individually in her having to establish of these matters, nor a lowering in her position. Rather, this is the path to happiness and well-being. And there is no contentment except in the shade of a husband who is treated well, and that is the estimation of The Most Great, The Most High, ***﴾Men are the protectors and maintainers of women...﴿*** (Surat an-Nisaa, From Ayat 34).

The Prophet, may Allaah's praise and salutations be upon him, said, ***{If I were to command any one of you to prostrate to another, I would have commanded the wife to prostrate to her husband.}*** (Abu Daawud, in "The Book of Marriage, Chapter: Concerning the Right of the Woman on her Husband", and in at-Tirmidhi, in the chapters concerning nursing, "Chapter: Concerning the Right of the Husband on the Wife". And the hadeeth is authentic. Look at "*Saheeh Sunan Abi Daawud*", 2/402)

So understand the purpose and objectives of the Islamic legislation, and do not be misled by the deceiving callers, and then make your slogan, "We hear, and we obey."

﴾Then if there comes to you guidance from Me, then whoever follows My guidance he shall neither go astray nor shall be distressed.﴿- (Surah Taa Haa, From Ayat 123)

7. Organization of Time

Persist in continually organizing your time, so that your work will be a pleasure, and make the house always like a clean and well-ordered garden. As the house is the evidence of the one who is in charge of it, and with cleanliness and order the house will have the most beautiful aspect, even if the furnishings are humble and not so beautiful.

Indeed the husband and the children, when they return from their work and studies, they are tired, so when they find the house to be well organized and clean, their troubles and exhaustion are lightened. Correspondingly, the opposite is true as well. As cleanliness of the home and its organization are from the most important reasons for it to be stable and restful.

8. Supporting your husband-

Meaning support him during events and emergencies- and what occurs more than these in this life?! Assist him with patience and advice, so that when emergencies occur, he escapes to his home, and to his wife, to give him shelter and peace- he does not flee from her. That is from the greatest reasons for harmony, and with this the home is stable and peaceful.

9. Truthfulness with him

Be a truthful person with him in everything, in particular concerning that which occurs when he is outside of the house, and remove yourself from deceit and concealment. As concerning this matter, just because perhaps he was deceived on one occasion, then it should certainly not continue as the normal state, as then trust is lost- and if trust is lost, then the home cannot be one of stability and ease, nor is it a place for the righteous upbringing.

10. How do you behave when differences occur?

And, finally, know that we are just human beings, and inevitably there is weakness, and assuredly differences will occur in regard to some matters. However, the important thing is how the differences are dealt with and treated. And even if it is natural for some differences to occur, it is not natural that every difference changes into a problem, leading the structure of the home to approach collapse. Therefore, here are some recommendations for you to pay attention to when differences occur.

1. Avoid continuing to dispute while in a state of anger and alienation and disaffection; rather, wait until your nerves calm down.

2. Utilize the technique of conversation, not argument, and the identification of exactly what the problem is, and its cause.

3. Stay away from interrupting and cutting him off when he is talking, and listen well.

4. It is necessary to show affection, and to make it clear that every side loves the other; and that certainly you sincerely desire a solution to the problem.

5. It is necessary to be willing to make concessions and be accommodating, as if each side persists upon that which he or she is upon it leads to a worsening of the situation, and may end in divorce.

These are some of ways which it is proper for the woman to behave in her home, so that she is a partner in bringing about true peacefulness and stability. The home which is a calm, peaceful abode for the husband is a result of its mother, and the children are raised in it with a sound upbringing within it. As the Muslim nation is rectified through rectification of the generations, and the husband and wife are the foundation of the family; if the relationship between them is bad, then there is no stability in the home.

Thirdly: Having harmony within the extended family

From the things that the woman must carry out to fulfill her duties in raising her family is paying attention to establishing harmony and stability within the environment of the extended family. In the preceding passages we were speaking about the family in a limited manner: husband, wife, and children. However the structure of the family is broader than that and includes the mother, father, brothers and sisters; and each of them have rights, whether they are residing in the same house or not. It is necessary that their larger family group be joined and rectified, and that she improves the relationships between them, since many principles depend upon that. From them are being dutiful to the parents and keeping the ties of kinship.

The woman has a considerable role in that, as how many of the women, by giving attention to this aspect, and by their fear of Allaah, have enabled a good relationship between their husbands and the husbands' mothers and fathers and brothers and relatives, so they become beneficial instruments in uniting the family upon good? And how many of the women are ignorant of their obligations in this aspect, or they understand but lack fear of Allaah, and they are a cause of differences in the family? Then there is disobedience to the fathers and mothers, and the ties of kinship are severed- all of that because of the ignorance of the woman of her position in this aspect of life, and her failing to perform it?

Fourth: Raising and educating the children

From the domains of raising and educating the family in which the position of the woman is manifested, is that of raising and educating the child. This is from the most important fields, and its most weighty, from two aspects:

The First: Because it concerns the overall guidance of the child, and the Muslim nation is formed from the child. Whatever position the child is found in, and his upbringing today, the situation of the Muslim nation in the future will be likewise. From here we understand that every member of the Muslim nation will pass through the schooling of his mother.

The Second: Because a child is full of unperceived things, which are sometimes clear, sometimes obscure, sometimes easy, sometimes hard. And so because of this, his care and upbringing require hard work- as it is not easy. This is what we are going to clarify in that which follows.

The upbringing of the children is the responsibility of both of the parents, He (the Messenger of Allaah), may Allaah's praise and salutations be upon him, said, ***{All of you are shepherds, and all of you are responsible for your flocks. The man is the shepherd in his house and is responsible for his flock, and the woman is a shepherd in the house of her husband, and is responsible for her flock.}*** (al-Bukhaari, in "The Book of *Juma'ah*, Chapter: *Juma'ah* in the Village and City", and Muslim, in "The Book of *al-Imaara*, Chapter: The Virtue of the Just Imaam")

And He, the Most High, says, ﴾***Oh you who believe! Ward off yourselves and your families against a Fire (Hell) whose fuel is men and stones***﴿- (Surat at-Tahreem, From Ayat 6)

However, if we look into the reality of the matter, we find that the man can spend only a limited part of his time in his home and with his children- and this is in respect to quantity- and as for its manner then in this time he may be weary from work, and he seeks to rest, and he does not have the ability at that time to think fully about the affairs of his children. Because of this, it is made clear to us that the greatest position in this is the position of the woman, and her responsibilities.

al-Bukhaari collected from Jaabir ibn 'Abdullaah, may Allaah be pleased with him, that he said, "My father died, and left seven daughters, or nine daughters, so I married a mature, previously married woman. So the Messenger of Allaah, may Allaah's praise and salutations be upon him, said to me, ***{You married, oh Jaabir?}*** And I replied, "Yes." So he, may Allaah's praise and salutations be upon him, said, ***{A virgin or a previously married woman?}*** I replied, "Rather, a previously married woman." He, may Allaah's praise and salutations be upon him, said, ***{Why did you not marry a young virgin, as you could play with her, and she with you, and you could joke with her, and she could joke with you?}*** He (Jaabir) said, So I said to him, " 'Abdullaah (Jaabir's father) died, and he left daughters, and I did not like to bring another like them, to them- so I married a woman who can instruct and rectify them." He, may Allaah's praise and salutations be upon him, said, ***{Allaah's blessings to you.}***, or he said, ***{This is good.}*** (al-Bukhaari, "Book of Expenditures, Chapter: The Woman Assisting her Husband Concerning his Children") The hadeeth is proof of the partnership of the woman with her husband concerning the upbringing and education of the children. Indeed, her role is the primary one, (as Jaabir said), "...instruct and rectify them."

Oh Muslim Sisters:

Indeed your fulfilling of this important and great role requires your complete understanding of it, so that you are able to perform any of its required aspects. Caring for and raising and educating the child in a good manner requires one who understands some of the different facets which are related to the child, and to be able to avoid some negative ones. From them are:

First: The aspect of physical health: The child who is ill or handicapped is not an individual who is entirely beneficial to the Muslim nation.

Because of this, the first matter which the woman should perform and give attention to is the physical health of her child. There are numerous books written concerning this subject. From them is the book "Care of the Healthy Child" by Doctor Nabeeh al-Ghabrah. It presents the care of the healthy child with simple, easy to obtain methods, which every woman who has even a little ability to read and comprehend can understand. From the observations which pertain to health and the child (mentioned in the book):

1. The issues related to the pregnant woman and her caring for her health, since her health is the health of the unborn baby. And it is essential that the necessary steps are taken (to ensure their health).

2. The phases which the child goes through after birth; and every phase is a specific situation, and has health care which is specific to it. We will summarize them in that which follows.

- The Newborn in the First Month: Because of his delicacy and susceptibility at this age, it is necessary for the mother to understand: What are the indications of health and illness in this stage, how one cares for and treats the baby, the suitable place or position for him to sleep, proper nursing techniques, how he should be dressed... along with other than that.

- The Second Phase: This comes after the newborn stage, and it is the nursing baby. In this phase the baby eventually begins to walk and speak, and the mother must know what is necessary to keep the baby healthy. As when the child attempts to walk, he should not be forced beyond his capacity, and he should not be given a walker or other aid to hold on to. Rather, it should be left to his own steps towards development and capability.

A note about speech: Don't you know that sometimes the speech impediments are caused only by the family claiming that they are there (in other words, the child does not have one, but is simply developing at his own pace, and the family says it is a problem with his speech)? Meaning their saying that they are present, and taking some means to try remedy them (which ultimately cause harm to the child and his development).

-The Third Phase: The years before the child attends school, and in them his preparation for school occurs, taking into consideration the ability of the child, so that attending school and reading becomes that which he desires.

-Then after that comes the stage of middle childhood and adolescence. And the striving and efforts towards their education at these levels is indeed difficult.

Then there is the mention of some of the health issues which it is necessary that you have knowledge of.

1. Childhood vaccinations: What are they, and when they are given

2. The normal growth and development of the child

3. Development of special abilities or talent in the child

4. Issues related to children's games and toys

The importance of playthings in the life of the child is not merely for amusement; rather, they are a means of educating the child and developing his talents and natural abilities.

Every age of the child has specific toys and games connected with it, so that if he is given a toy which is below his mental level, then he does not have any interest in it, and if he is given a toy or game above his level, it requires effort which is beyond his ability, and may impair it. Additionally, there are toys and games which are harmful, that one must be wary of.

5. Bedwetting or urinating at night- its causes, and the correct manner of curing it

6. Issues related to the left-handed child- Environment and Guidance: these two things have a great role or position concerning this.

7. Accidents: Falling down, ingesting that which may be harmful, poisoning, burns, or being run over or hit by a car... and other similar accidents. For every age there are dangerous accidents which may occur- how does the mother protect the child from them? (see the book, "Care of the Healthy Child" by Doctor Nabeeh al-Ghabrah)

This is only one aspect of the different aspects involved in the care of the child. Do you have adequate experience and know-how concerning it? The purpose of that which has been mentioned is not to give details and particulars, or to explain the healthy way of living, as this is not the subject of this talk. In fact, it is merely offering some indication that these matters are not as simple as one might expect them to be.

We move on to another aspect, and it is the aspect of educating the child concerning morals and ethics, and in providing him with a correct foundation and planting good habits, as well as keeping him away from forming evil habits, until a righteous child is produced, who is the delight of his parents' eyes. Indeed, this aspect requires a significant number of discussions as it is an issue with many branches and ramifications. In fact, it is necessary that the one who attends to the education and upbringing of the child understands the characteristics of the child, so that he deals with him in a fully informed manner, and thus, what is the best and most effective means of educating and raising the child.

It is necessary, oh sister, to understand that every age in the life of the child has natural characteristics, and each has educational tools specific to it; and the books concerning this are many. When you comprehend that this is an important part of your great role in raising and educating the family, then it is necessary that you have knowledge concerning it, which makes it possible to establish your great mission. From that which I advise you with concerning this aspect, is to listen to the lesson which has been transcribed by Doctor 'Abdul 'Aziz an-Nagheemshee, entitled, "The Reality of the Muslim Child". I will mention some general statements concerning this:

Characteristics of the child:

It is necessary for the one who wishes to raise the child on an educational and sound methodology to understand these general characteristics. From them:

1. Their state of acceptance and adaptability: as the child is a white page; he has not studied any behavior or way of thinking. He is naturally accepting of change and guidance. This is like the supple branch, which accepts being shaped into any form which is needed; therefore, it is necessary that the woman fully understand her position in this matter.

2. That the child generally only understands concrete matters, not that which is abstract: The mother should not worry if the child does not understand some matters, as he is attached to that which is in front of him by concrete thinking. So if you say to him, three plus three, then he does not understand this; however, if one puts three pens in front of him, and another three, then he says, six- and other situations like this.

For that reason, the person is not required to perform certain acts until after maturity. And his being brought up with praiseworthy characteristics is undoubtedly connected to the influence of activity which is concrete and real to him, not that which is abstract.

3. Individuality and self-centeredness: meaning that the child feels that everything should be directly related to him. The role of the educator is to remove this so that he develops a regard and respect for others.

4. The child has various needs, and undoubtedly from them are those which, if if not fulfilled, then his growth and development are hampered, or else

he will come to have bad behavior. From them are:

A. Love and security from his parents

B. Appreciation and confidence; as if he is not appreciated and entrusted with matters, it may come about that he has no self esteem and confidence in himself.

C. Companionship: it is necessary that he have friends. It is necessary that one chooses companions whose upbringing has been given attention to so that contradiction and opposition to your child's upbringing does not occur.

How do we raise and educate a child?

Everything that we use from the devices and mediums of raising and educating the child return to one of the following paths:

1. Instruction wherein the student merely repeats what the teacher says, without necessarily understanding that which is taught. And this is often solely relied upon concerning the matter- and as such it is not very beneficial. It is regrettable that it is that which is used by many of the people.

2. Combining other matters along with this type of instruction, such as sound advice and counsel, and the encouragement in the good and discouragement from the bad. And this is more beneficial than what was first mentioned.

3. By way of observation and imitation- and this is the most important of them and the most advisable. And here is the role of the examples and behavior which are seen in the home. And the behavior of the mother determines the state of the child; as how can she teach him truthfulness and forbid lying when she lies in front of him?

After this, there are some general statements concerning raising and educating the child, and from them:

- Physical punishment and it being used in a harmful, as opposed to beneficial, way: As there is no doubt that hitting is a means of teaching the child; however how and when is it used? This is an important matter.

- Frightening the child with stories or statements of nonsense and falsehood, and the effects of it upon the child's personality

- Raising them in a manner between pampering them and being severe with them

- Keeping the child away from children who are ill-mannered or have bad character

- Keeping track of the child in regards to his studies

- Raising girls upon modesty

- Raising the child upon compassion and mercy, and making him accustomed to that

- Avoiding disagreement between the husband and wife concerning orders or guidance to the child, such as when this one commands an action, while the other one forbids it.

- There should be no contradictions between one's sayings and one's actions

- Supervising the children in the house without this being perceived by the children themselves

- There should be no name calling, swearing or cursing

There is no doubt that every item which has proceeded is in need of further explanation and elaboration, yet it is not within the scope of this talk to explain all the means and ways of raising and educating the children. In fact, I merely mentioned them in order to clarify that the work of the woman in raising and educating the child is not simple work; rather, it is an act that requires knowledge, and necessitates hard work and serious efforts in carrying it out.

The Fifth: Other actions

These four preceding areas are the most important fields of the woman's work in her home, and they are based upon her participation in raising and directing the family in a correct manner. However, there are other actions which contain concrete, tangible benefits to the family and its education, if the woman has enough time remaining- after her establishment of the primary actions which have already been mentioned. Additionally, these other actions are many; there is no limit to them, and they evolve in accordance to the material circumstances. There are limitless examples of them, such as:

- Sewing clothing. How much does the family's wealth is spent on this need (for clothing), and what other negative things occur due to buying their clothes rather than making them? Such as that the woman passes long periods of time in front of this strange tailor, attempting to explain to him what she wants- and he is usually foreign, he understands some of the language and does not easily comprehend a good portion of it. Added to that is that which enters the home from the styles and fashions which differ from the Islamically legislated clothing, and oppose moral character and tastes of the society.

Indeed it is from the strange things that the woman goes out to work outside of the home to earn some of the money, then spends some of this salary on the tailor, and on the nanny who takes care of the children. Just think if the woman devoted her time to raising and educating her children, and that which remains of her time in making her clothes- how much the people would save. Not just saving that which is spent from wealth, but also "saving" in regards to preserving the generation of the Muslim nation and safeguarding its character.

And there are exceptions to this, as it has occurred among us that the Muslim *Ummah* is in need of the female worker in some of the areas which cannot be established by other than her (such as female doctors and midwives, etc.); however the difference is that this is the exception, not the general condition.

- From the occupations which the woman can perhaps participate in inside of her home is to create some works of art and beautiful pictures. In fact, the seeking of that which is beautiful is a matter which is embedded in the natural disposition, as is shown by mankind's love for beautiful landscapes. Well-made pictures are a lawful matter if they do not have in them any wastefulness or extravagance, and do not have anything in them which differs from the Islamic legislation, such as the presence of beings with souls. Indeed, many of these pictures are made by women. Some of the people are passionately attached to these works of art, and spend much of their wealth in acquiring them, so what is wrong if the woman utilizes some of her time and makes something from these works of art and saves some of this money? This aspect of work does not have any great importance; however, I mention it in order to clarify that the woman has available to her areas to consider in relation to beneficial ways of spending her time in that which be advantageous both to her and to her family.

Now, after we have discussed these important occupations which the woman can perform in her home and participate in while at the same time raising and educating the family, could it possibly be true that which is said: Indeed the woman, if she stays in her home and occupies herself with these jobs, that she remains paralyzed and inactive in society? And is the statement which they say true, that: "The woman staying in her home causes half of society to be idle or unemployed"?

The true question is, what is the true gauge of measuring unemployment or idleness? The woman goes out in order to abandon a sanctified position within her home, and she is advised to perform the job of taking dictation or transcribing , or using a typewriter, which any young man from the unemployed men can use!! And the woman, by her going out, surrenders the care of her children, as well as their education and upbringing, to the servant and the babysitter! Then she becomes accustomed to spending this wealth which she takes from her principle employment by way of spending this wealth on this servant, and on the driver, and on the dressmakers! However, the soul is sickened, and the natural disposition deteriorates and declines.

Indeed clearly mankind deteriorates when they deviate from the way of Allaah. ***But whosoever turns away from My Reminder (i.e. neither believes in this Qur'aan nor acts on its teachings), verily, for him is a life of hardship, and We shall raise him up blind on the Day of Resurrection.*** - (Surat Taa Haa, Ayat 124) Some of those, when all aspects of reality are imposed upon them, they feel pressured by it, and it comes about that they do not consider anything except by way of how it is considered or judged by a particular society. They claim: "This emotional speech is far from the reality of the world."

Examples of the reality of the woman in the West:

I say to the likes of such people, come and listen to the calls of some of the Western people whose condition is a result of the women in their societies going out and abandoning the home. Indeed the West has progressed materially; however it is socially and ethically backward and its society is becoming increasingly prone to breakdown or general deterioration. And the Western intellectuals have themselves begun warning of the dangerous consequences of the present condition which the family in their society has reached, and the condition of the woman after her introduction into the workplace outside of the home. August Kante, the founder of the science of sociology says, "It is necessary that the man provides for the woman; this is the natural human principle. This is the law which is appropriate for the fundamental life of the woman within her household. And this principle is the same as the principle which compels the working class of people to feed the intellectual class, so that the intellectual class may carry out their duties in a complete manner, except that the duties of the men in regards to providing for the women is more sacred than that, because the employment of the women concerns the household life."

And this well-known female Western writer says in an article published in the journal, "The Eastern Mail" from the tenth of May 1901. She says, "For our girls to work in the home as servants or like servants is better and less trying than for them to work in the factories, which remove the beauty of their lives forever. How I wish our country was like the country of the Muslims, in which the clothing is modest, honorable and pure. The maid and the servant live in comfort with a pleasant existence, and they work with the children of the home, and their honor is not touched with evil. Yes- indeed it is a disgrace on the English country that its daughters have become examples of vice and depravity due to the great amount of their mixing with the men. As what is the matter with us that we do not look beyond, to the girl working in that which agrees with her natural disposition from staying in the home and leaving the work of men, to the men, as befits her honor. (Quoted from "*al-Mara't bayna al Fiqh wa al-Qaanoon*" page 178 -from the magazine "*Al-Manaar*")

Look at the speech of this woman in the first part of this (last) century- and the condition of the Western woman became more evil after that. So where is the sense in the claimed call to freedom or to allow the sickness of low desires to overcome her?

And Joel Simon said, "The woman who works outside of her home perhaps performs the tasks of the simplest worker; however she does not perform the true undertaking of the woman." ("*al-Mara't bayna al-Fiqh wa al-Qaanoon*", Page 179)

And this woman, known as Kathleen Lind, the wife of the American astronaut Doctor Don Leslie Lind- and they do not have an ignorant family, rather it is a western family at the peak of scientific progress- this woman says, "I am simply a housewife, as I spend the majority of my time in the home. And like a woman should, as I understand that the woman is obligated to give all of her time to her home and her husband and her children... And I must mention the story of one religious man who said, in answer to the question: If the woman's destiny is to simply remain in the home, then why is it permitted for her to be educated? By answering -'If you educate a man, then you teach one person; but if you educate a woman, then you have taught a generation and a nation.'"

Then she says, "And I am very happy to remain in the home, at the side of my husband and my children. Even in times of difficulty-I mean those times when we needed money, my husband did not want me to work. His philosophy was that we could meet our most basic requirements with what we had, but that we could never succeed in raising our children if we once lost control over them." ("A Letter to Eve" 2/61, as quoted in a Kuwaiti newspaper, 'The Sons of Kuwait')

Indeed these texts are clear, and there is no need to add onto them. Rather, it is actually unnecessary to even turn towards these statements, as we believe that that which Allaah chose for mankind is the most suitable and correct, and it is what came within the religion of Islaam. Allaah says, ﴾***It is not for a believer, man or woman, when Allaah and His Messenger have decreed a matter that they should have any option in their decision. And whoever disobeys Allaah and His Messenger, he has indeed strayed into a plain error.***﴿- (Surat al-Ahzaab, Ayat 36)

The Last Question:

After this comes the last question, and it is very important. Is it possible for women to fulfill this great service and undertaking, and is the woman merely sitting in her home sufficient to achieve this service?

We say, in answer to this question, that the fundamental condition and qualification concerning the woman who is able to perform this important task, is that she is a righteous woman, like that which the Prophet, may Allaah's praise and salutations be upon him, guided to with his saying, ***{Marry the woman for four things: For her wealth, for her honorable lineage, for her beauty, and for her religion; so you should marry a religious woman or you will be the losers.}*** (Saheeh al-Bukhaari, from the hadeeth of Abi Hurairah narrated in the "Book of Marriage", and in Muslim)

The Prophet, may Allaah's praise and salutations be upon him, made clear the criteria by which man would establish a life partner, then he gave a command by placing the religion as the first criterion. In fact, some of the people have placed the greatest importance upon beauty, and man is diverse in his description of beauty, and some of them have put wealth first, making it the important criteria whether it is endowed and inherited or earned.

And some of them have made honorable lineage and her family attachments the main criterion; however the most significant criterion according to the *Sharee'ah*, the Islamic legislation, is her religion. The righteous woman- she is the one who can be entrusted to establish this great, vital service. Indeed, the one who chooses the religious woman has saved himself from a tremendous struggle and effort.

If a woman is to fulfill the condition of being righteous, then it is necessary that she has some amount of knowledge which makes her qualified to perform her tasks in a good manner. She must know what is obligatory upon her, and she must be heedful and aware of her mission in life. And with this we know that what is intended by knowledge here is not a diploma or certificate; rather it is the knowledge of her duties which it is desired and beloved that she establish, and knowledge of those matters which are the means for her to accomplish that objective.

It is necessary that after learning her religion she learns all other matters that are necessary for her from that which enables her to establish her undertaking and work in the home. She must continue to pursue all that which is considered beneficial from that which has been written about the subjects related to the child, whether or not that concerns his health or his education, subjects related to the home and housekeeping, subjects related to some of the societal issues, and issues which have been written concerning the woman and other than her from that which is important for the woman. Indeed it is the presence of beneficial knowledge in the righteous woman which makes it possible for her to perform her duties.

And certainly the ignorance of the woman, and the lack of her righteousness, is a reason for loss or failure, even if the woman is devoted but is not knowledgeable- as she will waste time with senseless visiting, and "he said this and she said that", and following the latest fashions, and the likes of this. As such there is little hope from her, the one lacking knowledge, that she will establish this important undertaking and position, or produce a righteous generation after herself. And Allaah knows best. May the praise and salutations of Allaah be upon our Prophet Muhammad, and upon his family and his Companions.

(The source of this lecture is a lecture entitled, "The Role of the Woman in the Upbringing and Education of the Family", which was delivered on the night of Monday, corresponding with the date 6/11/1411 hijra, and it was a part of a symposium of knowledge entitled, "Fiqh of the Woman", which was held by the Center of Calling to Islaam and Guidance in Riyaadh, at the congregational Masjid adh-Dhiyaab in the neighborhood of an-Naseem)

Review and Discussion Questions

Questions from The Role of the Woman in Raising...

Review:

1. What does Sheikh Fauzaan, may Allaah preserve him, mean by the word "tarbiyyah" in this lecture? (Page 113, Middle of page)
2. List and briefly discuss three of the six proofs the Sheikh, may Allaah preserve him, brings concerning the place of the woman primarily being in the home. (Page 114, Top of page)
3. If Allaah has decreed for something to be, is it our place to turn away or disagree with it? What verse refers to this? (Page 117, Bottom of Page)
4. What is the proof that the family has a crucial role in the guidance of the child upon the fitrah? (Page 118, Bottom of page)
5. List some of the example the Sheikh brings of good behavior toward the husband. (Page 125, Top of page)

6. What recommendations did the Sheikh, may Allaah preserve him, give in regards to dealing with disputes when they occur? (Page 126, Top of page)
7. The raising of the children is from the most important fields in the woman's domain. What two aspects does the Sheikh bring in regards to this? (Page 127, Middle of page)
8. What are the three mediums the Sheikh mentions for teaching the child? Which is the most beneficial and why? (Page 131, Top of page)
9. What is the fundamental qualification that a woman must have in order to have a righteous household? (Page 135, Middle of page)

Discussion & Consideration:

10. Is it forbidden for the woman to leave her house? Explain your answer.
11. Explain the saying of the Sheikh, may Allaah preserve him, "And verily the state of the nation which has the correct methodology then abandons it, choosing instead to search in the scraps and garbage of the opinions of men, is like the saying of the poet, 'Like the dweller in the desert who strikes down into the earth due to his thirst/Yet the water is there running above its surface'".
12. How would you reply to the ones who belittle and deride the work a woman does in her house, and say that a women who stays in the house is being wasted or kept from her true role in society?
13. Explain how there can be peace and stability in the home, and the benefits of that. Choose at least two of the ten responsibilities that the Sheikh mentions that will make the home a refuge for the family, and give example of them from real life.
14. Why is the position of the woman so great in regards to the raising of the children, such that the Sheikh says that her role in this is greater than that of her husband?
15. What are some of the matters involved in caring for the physical health of the child? How can a woman prepare herself to deal with these matters?
16. Sheikh Fauzaan, may Allaah preserve him, brings many suggestions for raising the child in a righteous manner. Can you think of anything to add to his list, or could you elaborate on any of those aspects he has mentioned?
17. What are some other beneficial occupations that a woman can do in her home while still taking care of her family and household responsibilities ?
18. What are some of the areas that a woman must have knowledge in, in order to run her household well and raise her children righteously?

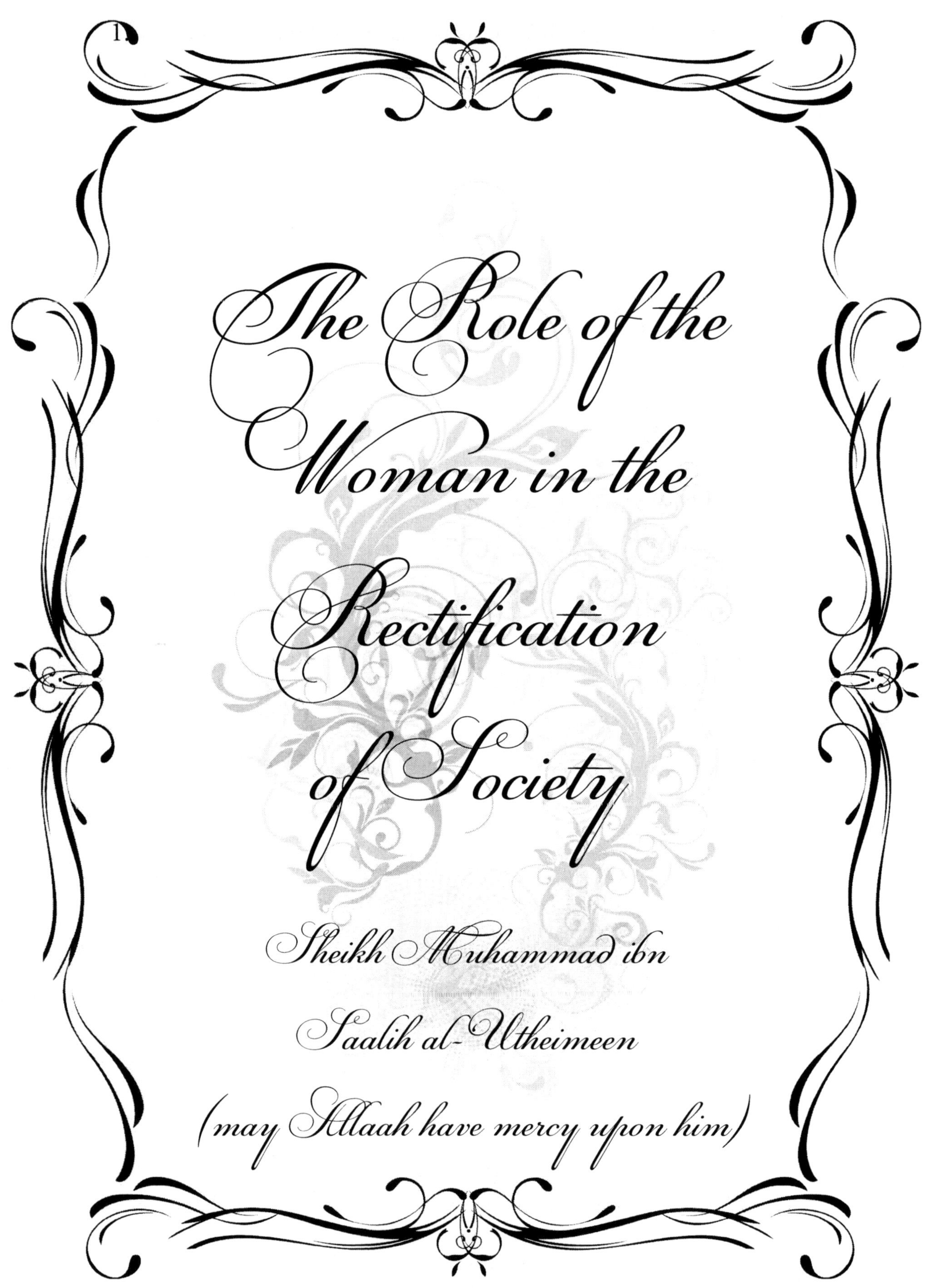

1.

The Role of the Woman in the Rectification of Society

Sheikh Muhammad ibn Saalih al-Utheimeen

(may Allaah have mercy upon him)

All praise is due to Allaah. We praise Him, we seek His assistance, and we ask for His forgiveness. We ask for His protection from the evil of our own selves, and from the evil of our actions. The one whom Allaah guides, then none can lead him astray, and the one who Allaah causes to be misguided, then there is no guidance for him. I bear witness that there is no god worthy of worship except for Allaah, alone, without any partners, and I bear witness that Muhammad is His slave and messenger. Allaah, the Most High, sent him with guidance, and the true religion, and he delivered the message, fulfilled the trust, advised the Muslim nation, and strived in the way of Allaah with the correct and true striving, may Allaah's praise and salutations be upon him, and upon his family, his Companions, and those who follow them in righteousness until the Day of Judgment.

To proceed:

Indeed it gives me pleasure to present a speech on my position concerning this important subject- and that subject is the position of the woman in the rectification of the society. I speak seeking assistance from Allaah, Glorified and Exalted is He, seeking from Him success in making it sound and correct.

Indeed the position of the woman in the rectification of society is a position of the greatest significance. That is because the rectification of the society is of two types.

The First Type: Outward rectification:

This is that which occurs in the marketplaces, *masaajid*, and other than them from the apparent, outward matters. This is, in general, from the role of the men, as they are the ones who are outside the home and exposed to this aspect of society.

The Second Type: The rectification of society concerning that which is behind the walls:

It is that which occurs in the houses, and usually this important matter is entrusted to the women, because the woman is the mistress of the house. As Allaah, Glorified is He, Most High, said, guiding, speaking to and commanding the women of the Prophet, may Allaah's praise and salutations be upon him, in His saying,

﴾***And stay in your houses, and do not display yourselves like that of the times of ignorance, and perform as-salaat (the prayers), and give zakaat (obligatory charity) and obey Allaah and His Messenger. Allaah wishes only to remove evil deeds and sins from you, Oh members of the family (of the Prophet), and to purify you with a thorough purification.***﴿- (Surat al-Ahzaab, Ayat 33)

The Significance of the Position of the Woman in the Rectification of the Society

I believe after that, there is no harm upon us if we say: Verily, the woman is entrusted with half of the rectification of the society, or more than that.

The first reason for this: The women are like the men in number, if not greater than them in number; meaning, that the majority of the descendents of Aadam are women, as the Prophetic Sunnah gives evidence for. However, this differs from land to land, and from time to time, as it may be that the women of a certain land are not more numerous than the men, and the opposite may be true in another land; just as the women may be more than the men in one time, and the opposite may be the case in another time. Whatever the case may be, the woman has a significant position in the rectification of the society.

The second reason: Indeed, the first of that which is established in the young of every generation occurs at the breast of the women; and by this fact the importance of that which is obligatory upon the woman in the rectification of the society is made clear.

The Foundations by which the Woman can Rectify Society

In order that the significance of the woman in the rectification of the society be made a reality, it is necessary that the woman be suited for her important role in that rectification. And these aspects of these foundations are upon you to establish:

The First Foundation: That the woman is righteous: The woman herself must be righteous, in order that she set a good example and model for the girls of her family as well as other people; but how does the woman attain righteousness? Every woman must know that she will not attain righteousness except with knowledge. What is meant by this is Islamic knowledge, which she must study- whether this be from reading books, if that is possible, or if it be from the mouths of the scholars- whether these scholars be men or women. In our time this is very easy- that the woman learn the knowledge from the mouths of the scholars- and that is by utilizing recorded tapes. As these tapes, and to Allaah is all praise, have a great role in guiding the society to that which is in them of goodness and righteousness, if they are used for that. So, knowledge is necessary for the woman to be upright- as there is no way for this to come about except through knowledge.

The Second Foundation: Eloquence and correct speech: That is to say, that Allaah has blessed her- the woman- with eloquence and correct speech, in order that she have fluency in speech and express herself clearly, so that she expresses that which she intends in a correct manner which gives voice to the meaning of what is in her heart and herself. This is something which many of the people have- meaning the correct knowledge- but they fall short in conveying it, or they convey it but with speech which is not clear nor well-spoken, so that then that which is intended by the speaker is not presented in the correct manner.

From that we then ask: What is it that leads to this? Meaning, that leads to having eloquence and correct speech, and expressing that which is inside oneself with truthful, clear speech concerning that which is in the heart? We say: The path to this is that the woman acquire something from the sciences of the Arabic language- its grammar, morphology, and rhetoric. In order for that to occur, it is necessary for the woman to have lessons in that, even if just a few, in order that she is able to express herself with correct speech, which enables her to convey the meaning to the hearts of the other women.

The Third Foundation: Wisdom: Meaning, that the woman has wisdom in calling to Allaah, and in conveying the knowledge to the one who is listening, as well as wisdom concerning placing something in its correct place, such as the people of knowledge have stated. This is from the blessings of Allaah, Glorified is He, and Most High, upon the worshipper- that Allaah grants him wisdom. Allaah, Exalted is He, Most High, says,

﴾ ***He grants hikmah (wisdom) to whom He wills, and he, to whom hikmah is granted, is indeed granted abundant good.*** ﴿- (Surat al-Baqara, From Ayat 269)

And it occurs very often that the intended meaning of the speech is lost, while the shortcomings are brought forth, if wisdom is not present.

And from wisdom in calling to Allaah, Exalted is He, Most High, is that the one who is being spoken to is addressed on a level which is suitable for him. As if he is ignorant, then he must be dealt with in a manner suited to his condition. And if he has knowledge, but he has something within him of negligence, carelessness, and heedlessness, then he is dealt with using that which his condition calls for. And if he has knowledge but has something in him of pride and rejecting the truth, then he is dealt with using that which his specific condition requires.

So consequently the people are of three levels: The one who is ignorant, the one who has knowledge but is lazy or heedless, and the one who has knowledge but is obstinate- so there is no way that each of the women is like another. Rather, it is necessary that we place each person in his correct place, as the Prophet, may Allaah's praise and salutations be upon him, did, when he sent Mu'aadh to Yemen. He said, ***{Indeed you are going to a people of the Book...}*** (Bukharee 1436, Muslim 53, Abu Daawud 1364, Ibn Maajah 1779) The Prophet, may Allaah's praise and salutations be upon him, said that to him in order that Mu'aadh understand their condition so that he could appeal to them with that which this condition required, and speak to them in the manner suited to this condition as well.

Examples of using wisdom in calling to Allaah: The evidence exists for using wisdom in calling to Allaah- from the one who was the most wise of the creation in calling to Allaah- and that is the Prophet, may Allaah's praise and salutations be upon him. We will now bring examples of that.

The First Example of Wisdom: The Bedouin who urinated in the *masjid*: It has been related by al-Bukhaari and Muslim and other than them from the hadeeth of Anas Ibn Maalik, that a Bedouin entered the *masjid*, then went and urinated. The Companions became very agitated, and wanted to prevent him from finishing, and chastise him; however, the Prophet, may Allaah's praise and salutations be upon him, the one on whom Allaah bestowed wisdom in calling to Allaah, Exalted is He, Most High, said, ***{Do not restrain him.}***; meaning, do not stop him from urinating. Then when the Bedouin finished urinating, the Prophet, may Allaah's praise and salutations be upon him, commanded him to pour a container of water on the urine, then called the Bedouin and said to him, ***{This is the masjid, and it is not proper that anything harmful (or from that which is unclean) be in it. Indeed, it is for praying, and reading the Qur'aan, and remembering Allaah, Glorified and Exalted is***

He...} Or words to that meaning. Imaam Ahmad, may Allaah have mercy upon him, has related that this Bedouin said, "Allaah have mercy upon me and Muhammad, and do not have mercy on anyone along with us."

We take from this story the following lessons:

The First Lesson: The Companions, may Allaah be pleased with them, became agitated and very concerned and called out to this Bedouin. And we take from that that it is not permissible to sanction or permit wrongdoing. Rather, that which is obligatory is that one take action to prevent the person from committing the wrongdoing. However, if this action leads to a greater evil, then that which becomes obligatory is that one be patient until this greater evil is eliminated. Because of this the Prophet, may Allaah's praise and salutations be upon him, prohibited them from acting; indeed, he restrained them from stopping the Bedouin and chastising him.

The Second Lesson: The Prophet, may Allaah's praise and salutations be upon him, allowed the evil act in order to stave off that which was a greater evil than it. As the evil act which he assented to was the Bedouin continuing to urinate, and the evil which he staved off by this consent, was that one of these two matters was the case if the Bedouin was standing:

1. Whether he was standing with his *'awrah* uncovered in order that his clothing not become soiled with urine- then the *masjid* would become soiled from it to a greater degree, and the man's *'awrah* would be revealed to the people - and these are two evils.

2. Whether he was not standing in this way, and he was covering his *'awrah*- however his garment would become soiled by any urine which fell upon it.

On account of these evils, the Prophet, may Allaah's praise and salutations be upon him, allowed him to finish urinating, as perhaps also these potential evils would reach a degree above the matter as it already was; as if he stood, then these evils which occurred would not be concealed.

So we take a lesson from this narration, and it is that the evil, if it cannot be removed except by that which is a greater evil, then it is obligatory to refrain from the attempt. This is in order to prevent the greater evil by allowing the lesser.

Concerning this, the foundation is found in the Book of Allaah, as Allaah, the Most High, says, ***{And insult not those whom they (the disbelievers) worship besides Allaah, lest they insult Allaah wrongfully without knowledge.}***- (Surat al-An'aam, From Ayat 108)

We all know that insulting the gods of those who associate others with Allaah is from those matters which are beloved to Allaah, Exalted is He, Most High. However, when insulting these false gods leads to insulting the One who is not one of these gods, and He is Allaah the Lord, Exalted is He, Most High, then Allaah, Glorified is He, Most High, has forbidden insulting their gods in the preceding verse.

The Third Lesson: The Prophet, may Allaah's praise and salutations be upon him, hastened to remove the filth because leaving it until later could cause harm. Perhaps if the Prophet, may Allaah's praise and salutations be upon him, may have put off cleaning this spot of the *masjid* until the time when the people had to pray in it. So it was cleansed immediately for that purpose. However, first of all, one must hasten to remove the impurity so that one not be afflicted by inability or forgetfulness.

This point is very important, and it is to hasten to remove the impurity out of fear that one may not be able to remove it in the future, or will forget to. For example: If the garment has some impurity attached to it, and it is the garment in which one prays, or even not the one in which he prays... so the first thing is to hasten to wash this impurity, and to not put it off, because perhaps one will forget to do so in the future, or be unable to remove it, whether that is due to an absence of water or some other reason.

And concerning this, when it happened that the Prophet, may Allaah's praise and salutations be upon him, had the young boy sitting in his lap, and the child urinated in the lap of the Prophet, may Allaah's praise and salutations be upon him- he, may Allaah's praise and salutations be upon him, commanded that water be brought to him, and he washed the urine off immediately. He did not put off washing his garment until the time of the prayer, as we have mentioned previously.

The Fourth Lesson: The Prophet, may Allaah's praise and salutations be upon him, informed the Bedouin of the affairs of this *masjid*, and that was to establish the prayer, and read the Qur'aan, and to remember Allaah, and it is as if he said, "It is not correct that there be in it anything of harm or filth." So, from the affairs of the *masjid*: That it be treated with honor, cleaned, and purified, and that nothing is done in it except that which pleases Allaah, the Most High, including prayer, reading the Qur'aan, and remembering Allaah, Glorified is He, Most High, and that which resembles these things.

The Fifth Lesson: That if the people call others with wisdom, kindness, and gentleness, that which is sought after will come about to a greater degree than if one wants to deal with the matter harshly. As this Bedouin was persuaded by and satisfied completely with that which the Prophet, may Allaah's praise and salutations be upon him, taught him, so that he said these well-known words, "Oh Allaah have mercy upon me and Muhammad, and do not have mercy on anyone along with us."

So we find here that the Prophet, may Allaah's praise and salutations be upon him, used the aspects of gentleness and kindness with this man because he was undoubtedly ignorant, as it was not possible for one who had knowledge concerning the sanctity of the *masjid*, and the obligation of treating it with respect, to stand in front of the people and urinate from any way you look at the matter.

The Second Example of Wisdom: The Companion who had intercourse with his wife during the day in the month of *Ramadhaan*: It is narrated in al-Bukhaari from the hadeeth of Abi Hurairah, may Allaah be pleased with him, that a man came to the Prophet, may Allaah's praise and salutations be upon him, and said to him, "Oh Messenger of Allaah, I am ruined!" The Messenger of Allaah, may Allaah's praise and salutations be upon him, said, ***{What has ruined you?}*** He answered, "I have had sexual relations with my wife in *Ramadhaan*, and I am fasting!" And this is a great forbidden matter, that a person purposely have intercourse with his wife and he is fasting during *Ramadhaan*. However, let us look at how the Prophet, may Allaah's praise and salutations be upon him, taught him... Did he drive him away? Did he speak about him? Did he rebuke him? No. Because the man came to him, repentant and remorseful. He did not appear, taking it lightly or not heeding that which he had done. So the Prophet, may Allaah's praise and salutations be upon him, asked him, ***{Do you have a slave whom you can free, as an expiation for that which has occurred?}*** He answered, "No." So he, may Allaah's praise and salutations be upon him, asked him, ***{Are you able to fast two months, one right after the other?}*** He answered, "No." So he, may Allaah's praise and salutations be upon him, asked, ***{Are you able to feed sixty poor people?}*** He said, "No." Then the man sat down, and the Prophet, may Allaah's praise and salutations be upon him, gave him some dates. He, may Allaah's praise and salutations be upon him, said, ***{Take this, and give it as charity.}*** Meaning, it was the expiation. So he said, "To one poorer than me, oh Messenger of Allaah?! In between the two sides of the valley there is no family poorer than us!" So the Prophet, may Allaah's praise and salutations be upon him, laughed until his molar teeth showed, then said, ***{Feed your family.}***

We find in this story many lessons. From them:

That he did not treat the man harshly, nor did he drive him away or rebuke him, because he came in a repentant, regretful manner. And there is a difference between a man who is obstinate, and a submissive man who comes to us for assistance and seeks from us that we help free him from that which he has fallen into. Because of that, the Prophet, may Allaah's praise and salutations be upon him, dealt with him in this manner so that he returned to his family, taking with him that which the Messenger of Allaah, may Allaah's praise and salutations be upon him, gave to him- and it was these dates which it was enjoined upon him to feed to sixty poor people, if he had not been poor himself.

The Third Example of Wisdom: The man who sneezed during the prayer: We take this example from the hadeeth of Mu'aawiyyah ibn al-Hukum, may Allaah be pleased with him, when he went in with the Prophet, may Allaah's praise and salutations be upon him, and prayed, and a man from the people sneezed. So he said, "*alhamdulillah*." Mu'aawiyyah said to him, "*Yarhamaka Allaah*." Then the people looked at him accusingly; that is to say, in condemnation of that which he said. So he said, "Woe upon me (why are they staring at me?)." So they struck their hands upon their thighs, in order to silence him; so he was quiet. So when the Prophet, may Allaah's praise and salutations be upon him, finished the prayer, he called him and said to him, ***{Indeed, this is the prayer- it is not correct that there be anything in it of the speech of the people, as it is only the takbeer and the recitation of the Qur'aan.}***- or words to this effect. Mu'aawiyyah said, "I would ransom my father and my mother, I never saw a teacher who taught better than him, as he did not scold, beat or revile me." ("*Saheeh Muslim*", No. 537)

The Fourth Example of Wisdom: The man who wore a gold ring: We take this example from the story of the man who was wearing a ring made of gold, and the Prophet, may Allaah's praise and salutations be upon him, has made it clear that gold is forbidden to the men of this nation. As the Prophet, may Allaah's praise and salutations be upon him, said, ***{One of***

you takes to himself a live ember from the Hellfire, and places it in his hand.}* *Then the Prophet, may Allaah's praise and salutations be upon him, removed the ring himself, and threw it away. When the Prophet, may Allaah's praise and salutations be upon him, left, it was said to the man, "Take your ring and benefit from it." He replied, "By Allaah, I will not take a ring which the Prophet, may Allaah's praise and salutations be upon him, threw away." (Muslim 3990, Al-Mu'jam Al-Kabeer 11966)

We see something from harshness in the manner in which the Prophet, may Allaah's praise and salutations be upon him, dealt with this man, as it is apparent that the fact that gold is forbidden to the males of this nation had been previously related to him- so because of this, the Prophet, may Allaah's praise and salutations be upon him, dealt with him in this way which was harsher than the treatments which we mentioned earlier.

Therefore, it is necessary that the one who is calling to Allaah places every person in their proper place, according to that which is required by their specific condition. As certainly there is the ignorant one who does not have knowledge, and there is the one who has knowledge but he is heedless or lazy, and there is the one who has knowledge but is obstinate and proud- so it is obligatory that each one of them be placed in the category of approach for which he is suited.

The Fourth Foundation: Good upbringing and education: Meaning, that the woman raises and educates her children in a good way, because her children are the men and the women of the future. And the mother is the one who has the first contact and care of them. So if the mother deals with them with good character and correct behavior, and they are raised and educated at her hands, then they will have a great affect in rectifying the society.

Towards that, it is obligatory upon the woman who has children to devote her attention to caring for her children, and to place great importance on their upbringing and education, and to ask their father or the one who is in charge of their affairs for assistance if she is unable to correct them- if they do not have a father, then from brothers, uncles, or sisters' sons, or other than that. It is not proper for the woman to surrender to the "modern times", and say, "The people are upon this, and I am not able to change it"; because if we remain like that, surrendering to "modern times", then rectification cannot be achieved.

Therefore, it is necessary that the rectification change that which is corrupt to that which is good, and it is necessary that it changes that which is good for that which is better than it, until the matters are truly correct. Also, submitting to "modern times" is a matter which is not mentioned in the Islamic legislation- as we see concerning this that when the Prophet, may Allaah's praise and salutations be upon him, was sent to his nation, which associated others with Allaah, who worshipped one from many idols, who cut the ties of kinship and oppressed others, and who were unjust to the people with no right to do this- he did not submit to the ways of their time! Rather, Allaah forbade him from submitting to that which was considered the "norm". Indeed, Allah, Glorified is He, and Most High, said to him,

{Therefore proclaim openly that which you are commanded (Allaah's Message), and turn away from al-mushrikoon (those who associate others

with Allaah) - (Surat al-Hijr, From Ayat 94)

So He, Glorified is He, Most High, commanded him to proclaim the truth openly, and to turn away from those who associate others with Allaah, and to ignore their associating of others with Allaah, and to make them enemies until the matter was brought to completion- and this is that which occurred- yes- and one may say, "It is from wisdom that we change, but not necessarily as quickly as we would wish. This is because society as a whole differs significantly from that rectification which we desire."

So then, it is necessary for the people to move towards the rectification of mankind, beginning with that which is most important and going to that which is below it. That is to say, begin with the most important correction, or the most urgent, then move the people little by little until the matter (of rectification) is completed.

The Fifth Foundation: Being active in calling to Allaah: Meaning, the woman has a role in the education of the women of her community, and that is in any meeting of women, whether that be in the school, university, or in a phase which comes after the university such as the schools of higher education, and also during the gatherings which take place amongst the women, including visits which contain beneficial speech. It has reached us, and to Allaah is due all praise, that some of the women have a great role in this matter, and that they organize sittings for the women of their communities in the sciences of Islamic legislation and the Arabic language- and this, no doubt, is a good thing for which the woman should be praised, and its reward will continue after her death, as the Prophet, may Allaah's praise and salutations be upon him, said, ***{When one of the sons of Aadam dies, his deeds are cut off except for three: The continuing charity, or the knowledge which is benefitted by, or the righteous child who supplicates for him.}*** (Muslim, from the hadeeth of Abi Hurairah, may Allaah be pleased with him, No. 1631)

As such when the woman is active in her community in spreading the call to Allaah- during her visits, during meetings at school or other than it- then she has a great affect and a wide role in the rectification of the society.

This is that which comes to my mind now concerning the position of the woman in the rectification of society, and mentioning the foundations of this rectification.

This, and Allaah is Most Glorified. I ask Allaah to make us of the ones who are guided, and from those who are righteous, and to grant us His mercy. Indeed, He is the One Who Provides all Things.

All praise is due to Allaah, the Lord of the Worlds, and may His praise and salutations be upon our Prophet, Muhammad, and upon his family, his companions, and those who follow them in righteousness until the Day of Judgment.

Review and Discussion Questions

Questions for The Role of the Woman in the Rectification of Society by Sheikh al-'Utheimeen

Review:

1. What are the two types of societal rectification, and who is most responsible for each? (Page 139, Top half of page)
2. What two reasons did the Sheikh, may Allaah have mercy upon him, give for his statement that the woman is entrusted with half of the rectification or more than that? (Page 139, Bottom of page, and Page 140, Top half of page)
3. What are the three levels of the people who are being called to Islaam? Which category does each of the four ahaadeeth the Sheikh brings fall under? (Pages 141-end of section with the four hadeeth)
4. What five lessons are learned from the hadeeth of the Bedouin urinating in the masjid? (Pages 142-143)
5. What is the role of the woman in calling to Allaah? (Page 140, Bottom half of Page)

Discussion & Consideration:

6. The first condition of the woman rectifying society, is that she be righteous. What are some ways that a woman can become righteous?
7. Why is it crucial that the woman be eloquent and correct in her speech?
8. How would you deal with a person who is simply ignorant about Islaam, as compared to how you would treat the one who has knowledge, but is obstinate or proud and so does not practice it? Give a clear example of this.
9. Why must the Muslim woman stand firm in the face of "westernizing" her behavior and character? What are some ways for her to do this?
10. Why must we be patient concerning the rectification of society, when we are eager for this rectification to spread quickly?

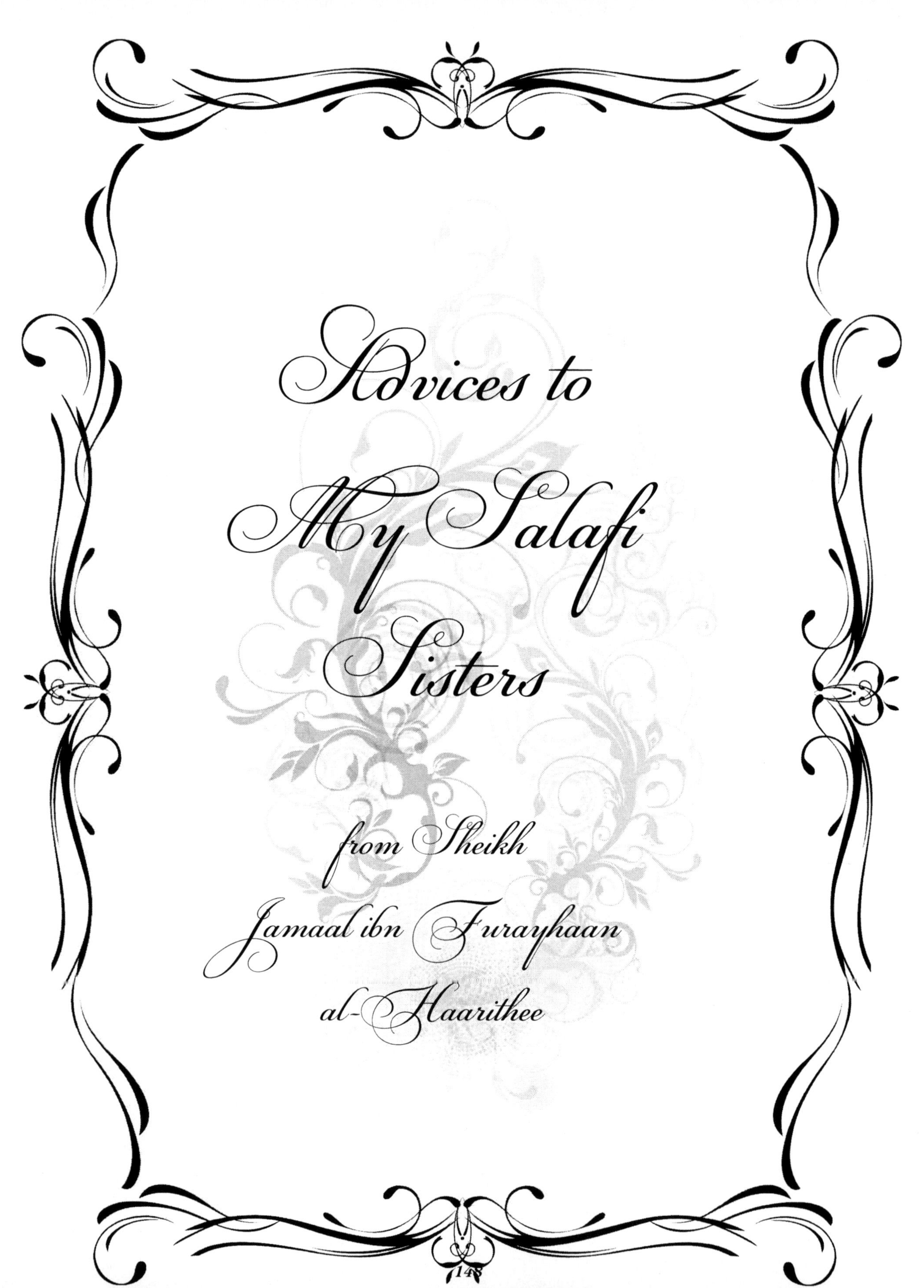

Advices to My Salafi Sisters

from Sheikh Jamaal ibn Furayhaan al-Haarithee

All praise is due to Allaah, Alone, and may His praise and salutations be upon the one who there is no Prophet after him.

To Proceed:

This summarized statement is directed toward the Muslim women in every place through means of the internet- especially as this global network has become the quickest and most useful means by which to spread the call which is drawn from the Book and the Sunnah upon the way of the Pious Predecessors, may Allaah have mercy upon them all. I have presented its content in points or summarized points. And surely the best speech is the speech of Allaah, and the best guidance is the guidance of Muhammad, may Allaah's praise and salutations be upon him. This comes as an indication from me that I am going to suffice in some places with simply listing some of the verses which clarify that which is intended.

From the Treatise, "Advice to every Muslim Woman"

I say, and the success is only with Allaah:

I advise every Muslim woman, whether she is married or single, young or old, an elderly woman or a young woman- to fear Allaah concerning herself, and keep her duty to Him, as Allaah, the Most High, says to His Prophet, may Allaah's praise and salutations be upon him,

﴾***Oh Prophet ! Keep your duty to Allaah...***﴿- (Surat al-Ahzaab, From Ayat 1)

So indeed those other than the Prophet, may Allaah's praise and salutations be upon him, are more in need of this guidance and counsel (than he is).

Beware of looking at men outside your family (those who are not *mahram* for you), whether they are in the street, in the market, on the television programs, in pictures and in magazines and newspapers, or on the internet- because this is only a means which leads to falling into that which is more significant (in wrongdoing).

Allaah, the Most High, says,

﴾***And tell the believing women to lower their gaze (from looking at forbidden things), and protect their private parts (from illegal sexual acts) and not to show off their adornment except that which is apparent (like both eyes for necessity to see the way, or outer palms of hands or one eye or dress like veil, gloves, headcover), and to draw their veils all over juyoobihinna (i.e. their bodies, faces, necks and bosoms) and not to reveal their adornment except to their husbands, or their fathers, or their husband's fathers, or their sons, or their husband's sons, or their brothers or their brother's sons, or their sister's sons, or their women, or the (female) slaves whom their right hands possess, or old male servants who lack vigor, or small children who have no sense of feminine sex. And let them not stamp their feet so as to reveal what they hide of their adornment. And all of you beg Allaah to forgive you all, Oh believers, that you may be successful.***﴿- (Surat an-Noor, Ayat 31)

Furthermore, a woman should not soften her voice in front of the man who is a stranger to her- who is not *mahram* for her- whether that be in direct speech, such as selling and purchasing items in the markets, or like the one who speaks with the brothers of her husband, or one of his close family, or from her family members who are not *mahram* for her- such as occurs in some societies. Also, if the speech is from behind the *hijaab*, or it is speech which occurs over the phone, or via PalTalk or Instant Messenger, as Allaah, the Most High says,

﴾Oh wives of the Prophet! You are not like any other women. If you keep your duty (to Allaah), then be not soft in speech, lest he in whose heart is a disease (of hypocrisy, or evil desire for adultery) should be moved with desire, but speak in an honorable manner.﴿ - (Surat al-Ahzaab, Ayat 32)

And this, in reality, was in reference to the virtuous, chaste, Mothers of the Believers, and concerning the pure, clean society which Allaah, the Most High, chose for the company of the Prophet of Allaah, may Allaah's praise and salutations be upon him- so the women of our time, today, are certainly more in need of this Divine guidance and counsel.

It is upon the Muslim woman to generally remain in her house, and to not go out to the markets except for the utmost necessity; and then at such times (as she does go out) she must not do so adorned or improperly covered. Additionally, if one can be found who can purchase that which she requires from the market for her, then she should praise Allaah and allow them to do this. And it is upon her to beware of going out to the gardens and parks and the places of mixing with the men, regardless of whether those men are young or not. Allaah, the Most High, says,

﴾And stay in your houses, and do not display yourselves like that of the times of ignorance, and perform the prayers, and give obligatory charity and obey Allaah and His Messenger. Allaah wishes only to remove evil deeds and sins from you, Oh members of the family (of the Prophet), and to purify you with a thorough purification.﴿ - (Surat al-Ahzaab, Ayat 33)

It is upon every Muslim woman who loves Allaah and His Messenger, may Allaah's praise and salutations be upon him, truthfully, not just claiming to do so, to adhere to the Islamically legislated *hijaab*- and that includes covering her face, and wearing the loose, long garments, those which are not narrow, short, or transparent- when she desires to leave the house for her needs. Allaah, the Most High, says,

﴾Oh Prophet! Tell your wives and your daughters and the women of the believers to draw their cloaks (veils) all over their bodies (i.e. screen themselves completely except the eyes or one eye to see the way). That will be better that they should be known (as free respectable women) so as not to be annoyed. And Allaah is Ever Oft-Forgiving, Most Merciful.﴿ - (Surat al-Ahzaab, Ayat 59)

Umar, may Allaah be pleased with him, said, "The Muslim woman is not prohibited from going out for her needs, in her unadorned, plain clothing, or that of her neighbor, such that she is concealed and no one will recognize her until she returns to her home."

All of this- I mean staying in the houses, and adhering to the *hijaab*- comes as a result of acquiring legislated knowledge obtained from the Book and the Sunnah. Allaah, the Most High, says,

﴾*And remember (Oh you the members of the Prophet's family, the Graces of your Lord), that which is recited in your houses of the Verses of Allaah and al-hikmah (i.e. Prophet's Sunnah – legal ways, so give your thanks to Allaah and glorify His Praises for this Qur'aan and the Sunnah). Verily, Allaah is Ever Most Courteous, Well-Acquainted (with all things).*﴿- (Surat al-Ahzaab, Ayat 34)

And this speech was directed towards the Mothers of the Believers; however the example, by the generality of the expression, is not specific to this sole purpose- as other than the Mothers of the Believers are undoubtedly in more need of knowledge and being taught that which establishes her religion (than they are).

With that which it is most obligatory amongst those matters that it is necessary for the male and female Muslim to understand is *tawheed* Allaah (knowing that Allaah, alone, is the only god worthy of worship, and singling Him out alone for all acts of worship, and affirming and calling upon Him with His names and attributes which He has identified Himself with in the Qur'aan and on the tongue of His final Messenger, may Allaah's praise and salutations be upon him), the Most High and His uniqueness. Also, that the Muslim woman guards and preserves herself and her honor. Allaah, the Most High, says,

﴾***Oh Prophet! When believing women come to you to give you the bai'ah (pledge), that they will not associate anything in worship with Allaah, that they will not steal, that they will not commit illegal sexual intercourse, that they will not kill their children, that they will not utter slander, intentionally forging falsehood (i.e. by making illegal children belonging to their husbands), and that they will not disobey you in Ma'roof (Islamic Monotheism and all that which Islaam ordains), then accept their bai'ah (pledge), and ask Allaah to forgive them. Verily, Allaah is Oft-Forgiving, Most Merciful.***﴿- (Surat al-Mumtahanah, Ayat 12)

So know, oh Muslim Sisters, that this (following) verse is comprehensive, complete, and definitive, containing all that is necessary for the who one contemplates it, understands it thoroughly, and acts upon it. And it is His, the Most High, saying,

﴾***Verily, the Muslims, men and women, the believers men and women, the men and the women who are obedient (to Allaah), the men and women who are truthful (in their speech and deeds), the men and the women who are patient (in performing all the duties which Allaah has ordered and in abstaining from all that Allaah has forbidden), the men and the women who are humble (before their Lord – Allaah), the men and the women who give charity, the men and the women who observe the (fast) (the obligatory fasting during the month of Ramadhaan, and the optional fasting), the men and the women who guard their chastity (from illegal sexual acts) and the men and the women who remember Allaah much with their hearts and tongues – Allaah has prepared for them forgiveness and a great reward (i.e. Paradise).***﴿- (Surat al-Ahzaab, Ayat 35)

I advise the Muslim sisters to devote their attention to religious knowledge, which is reached through the evidences of the Book and the Sunnah- that knowledge which, without it, it is impossible to establish those required matters from acts of worship. Yet I do not mean that she master and delve deeply into the secondary issues at the expense of fulfilling those obligatory matters which it is required upon her to perform from deeds and work, such as her attention to her husband, children, and managing the household- as these are more obligatory upon her than delving into secondary matters from the matters of the religion.

Indeed, it is upon her to begin with the proper foundation. This is by understanding *at-tawheed* and that which opposes it from *ash-shirk* (associating others with Allaah in worship) which is from that which nullifies the religion. Then, to proceed onward to the related matters such as that which makes her prayer correct, and likewise issues of purification specifically related to women. It is required for her to learn when it is obligatory upon her to pray and fast, and when it is obligatory upon her to refrain from prayer and fasting, for example. Likewise, she must learn that which enlightens her about raising and educating her children, and likewise the pathways to beautifying her marriage to her husband.

The result of all this is that the Muslim woman learns that which is obligatory upon her- those matters of obligation without which her general worship cannot be properly established. She must also avoid issues of differing to the best of her ability- indeed, she must make every effort within herself to adhere to that.

Likewise, I advise the Muslim women to refrain from disputing and arguing about the religion, as well as those refutations which some of those who claim to be seeking knowledge busy themselves with. As indeed it is known that the students of knowledge and scholars at times may compete in the matter of the refutation of the one who opposes a matter of guidance- so this one writes a refutation of this one, and this one writes a refutation of that one. It is forbidden that one of you falls into preoccupation this, such that you wrongly become absorbed in this and are occupied with other than those obligatory matters which you will be asked about.

Wahb ibn Munabbih, may Allaah have mercy upon him, said, "Leave arguing and disputing, as truly you will not fail to encounter one of two men: The man who is more knowledgeable than you- and how can you argue and debate with the one who is more knowledgeable than you? Or the man who you are more knowledgeable than him- and how can you argue and debate with one whom you are more knowledgeable than? And yet he does not submit to what you direct him towards. So cut yourself off from this."

'Abdullaah al-Basree, may Allaah have mercy upon him, said, "It is not from the Sunnah according to us that you refute the people of desires. However, it is from the Sunnah according to us that you do not speak to anyone from them."

al-Abaas ibn Ghaalib al-Waraaq, may Allaah have mercy upon him, said, "I said to Ahmad ibn Hanbal, 'Oh, Abu 'Abdullaah, I am in a sitting in which contains no one who understands the Sunnah other than me- so when someone from the innovators speaks should I refute him?' He said, "Do not put yourself out to engage in this. Relate the Sunnah and do not dispute." So I repeated my question to him. So he said, "I only see that you are person bent upon engaging in arguing and disputing."

Oh my sisters, likewise leave off from "he said" and "he said" between yourselves, and do not pass judgment upon someone from amongst you in anything in which there is differing until you have established and confirmed the matter and asked one of the people of knowledge or the scholars. Or, if necessary, ask a student of knowledge- one who is known for integrity and steadfastness upon the way of the Salaf, and who is from the people of composure and sound judgment. But do not ask one of the students from those who are hasty and conceited- even when they are Salafis- concerning that issue which it is believed one of you differs in, such hopefully that you all can in fact be united upon one position and not divided with your hearts falling into conflict and disagreement.

Additionally, to the one amongst you who identifies herself as a caller to Islaam- she must fear Allaah, the Most High, concerning her efforts of calling, and distinguish herself with the expected high character of the callers to Allaah. She should be characterized by patience with the one who differs with her as well as the one who is ignorant, both in the same way. And even before that, it is upon her to be properly armed with the weapon of knowledge of that which she needs to say and that which she calls towards.

And from what reflects the knowledge and understanding of Imaam al-Bukhaari, may Allaah have mercy upon him, and his correct and sound comprehension of the Book and the Sunnah, is his custom of placing of titles upon the various sections of his work "*al-Jaami' as-Saheeh*" is the section which he entitled:

"Chapter: Knowledge comes Before Speech and Action." And Allaah, the Most High, says, ***﴾So know (Oh Muhammad) that La ilaaha illallaah (none has the right to be worshipped but Allaah), and ask forgiveness for your sin...﴿*** - (Surah Muhammad, From Ayat 19)"

To every woman who has a husband- and the engaged one who is upon the path preparing to enter the house of marriage- I say to you that you must understand the rights of your husband as well as the rights of your parents, and do not become confused between the two obligations- as both are obligatory; yet the right of the husband is foremost.

The truthful one, the trustworthy one, may Allaah's praise and salutations be upon him, said,

{If I were to command anyone to prostrate before anyone else, I would have commanded the woman to prostrate before her husband. And the woman has not fulfilled all the rights of Allaah, Glorified and Exalted is He, until she has fulfilled all of the rights of her husband over her- until if he were to ask her for herself (to gratify his desire) and she is on the birthing chair, she would obey and give herself to him sexually.} (Ahmad, and other than him, with similar wording- and Sheikh al-Albaani has declared it to be authentic in "*as-Saheehah*" Number 1203)

And he, may Allaah's praise and salutations be upon him, said concerning it,

{If blood, pus, and infected matter were to pour out of his nostrils, and she licked it up with her tongue, she would not have fulfilled his right. If it was proper for a person to prostrate to another person, I would have commanded the woman to prostrate to her husband if he came into the house, due to that which Allaah has given him, over her... } (al-Haakim and other than him, and he said "Its chain of narration is authentic and it was from those authentic hadeeth of their level but not included by al-Bukhaari and Muslim in their collections")

So when you understand and have certainty, oh Muslim woman, in respect to the obligations which you have concerning your husband, then it is proper for you to seek various ways to please him- so if one path is exhausted, then pursue another newly opened path, such that he will experience joy and contentment and then this will be returned back to you because of what he is experiencing of rest and peace of mind in his house after the difficulty and fatigue which he meets outside of the home.

Act towards him like that righteous woman who pampered her husband and who tried to alleviate that which he encountered of the harshness of life, the one who strove for his hopes and wishes and assisted him in making them a reality, who placed attention to those things that were difficult for him before concern for herself- and this is none other than the Mother of the Believers, Khadijah Bint Khuwayled, may Allaah be pleased with her. She was a blessed wife to the Prophet, may Allaah's praise and salutations be upon him, before the revelation, and set aside for him the days in which he devoted himself to worship in the Cave of Hiraa. Then, she comforted him and eased his fear when the revelation came to him. As the Prophet, may Allaah's praise and salutations be upon him, returned that day when the saying of Allaah, the Most High, was revealed to him, ***﴾Read, in the name of your Lord who has created...﴿*** His heart trembled until he went in to where Khadijah was, and he said, ***{Cover me! Cover me! }*** So she covered him until the fear left him. He said to her, ***{Oh Khadijah! What is happening to me? I am afraid for myself. }*** And he told her what had happened. And Khadijah replied, “”Never! By Allaah, Allaah will never disgrace you. You keep good relations with your family ties, help the poor and the destitute, serve your guests generously and assist the deserving ones who have been afflicted with calamity.” (Narrated by both al-Bukhaari and Muslim)

Look at this beautiful speech which came from this lamp of righteousness, purity, honor and piety! It had a great effect in easing the fear in the heart of the leader of the children of Aadam, may Allaah's praise and salutations be upon him. So indeed Khadijah and the rest of the Mothers of the Believers are examples and models for you.

And fashion yourselves, oh female servants of Allaah, to be like this woman- Zainab bint Jareer, one of the women of the tribe of Handhalah, from the tribe of Tameem-

As it is related from al-Haytham ibn 'Ada at-Taa'ee, that he said, it was related to us from Mujaalid from ash-Sha'bee that he said: Shurayh said to me, “Oh Sha'bee! “Adhere to the women of the tribe of Tameem, as I perceive them to be sensible and intelligent.” He said, “And what have you seen of their intelligence?” He said, “I once approached a funeral procession from behind, and came to stop alongside their houses. So then I found myself with an old woman at a door of a house, and next to her a young woman whose beauty I have never seen the like of from the young women. So I turned away from her. Then I asked for a drink as I was very thirsty. So she, the older woman, said, “What drink would you like the most?” So I said to the girl, “May Allaah have mercy upon you, oh girl, whatever is available.” She said, “May Allaah have mercy upon you, oh girl, bring him milk, as I believe that he is a stranger.”So she left and I said to the older woman, “Who is this young woman?” She said, “This is Zainab ibnatu Jareer, one of the women of Handhalah.” I said, “Is she unoccupied, or is she busy?” (This is a polite way of asking if she is a single or married woman) She said, “Rather, she is unoccupied.” (meaning, she is not married) I said, “Marry her to me.” She said, “If you are well suited to her, otherwise you might come to say to her “Enough of you!”.” (And this was from the language of Tameem.) So afterwards I went to the house to take a nap, but I could not sleep. Then when I prayed *Dhuhr*, I took my brothers from the noble reciters, 'Alqamah, al-Aswad, al-Musayyib, and Musa ibn 'Ariftah by their hands and we went to see her uncle. He came out from his house and said, “Oh Aba Umayyah, what do you need?” I said, “Zainab the daughter of your brother.” He said, “It seems that she doesn't dislike you.” So, he married her to me. But when it was all concluded, I regretted it. I said, “What have I entered into with the women of Bani Tameem?!?!” as then I remembered the hardness of their hearts. So I said to myself, “I will divorce her.” Then I said, “No first I will go be with her, and if I see that which I like I will stay married to her, and if not then I will divorce her.” If only you had seen me, oh Sha'bee, and their women were approaching with her, until she came close to me. So I said, “Indeed, it is from the Sunnah that when the woman comes to live with her husband, that he stands and prays two *raka'at*, and he asks Allaah to grant him good from her, and he asks Allaah's protection from her evil.” So I prayed, and said the *tasleem* to finish the prayer, and she was behind me, praying along with me. So when I finished my prayer her slave girls came and took my *thobe* and dressed me in a loose garment which was dyed with safflower.

When the house was empty of others I approached her and reached my hand out to her. She said, to me, “Slow down, Aba Umayyah- please stay as you are!” Then she said, “All praise is for Allaah, I praise Him, and ask for His help, and I ask Allaah's praise to be upon Muhammad and his family. I am a woman from those who is a stranger to you, so I have no knowledge of your specific character. Therefore make clear to me what you like, that I may do it, as well as that which you dislike so I may stay away from it.” And then she said, “Indeed there were others within your family whom you could have married, and there were the same for me in my family, but if Allaah has decreed something it comes to be, and you have been put in authority over me so do that which Allaah has ordered you to do: stay with me in marriage with kindness or let me go with kindness, I offer you this statement of mine and ask Allaah's forgiveness for me and you.”

(He said) In this way she compelled me, By Allaah, Oh Sha'bee, to also give a speech in return on that subject, so I said, “ All praise is for Allaah, I praise Him, and ask for His help, and I ask Allaah's praise to be upon Muhammad and his family, to proceed: Indeed you have said words that if you stay firm upon them then you will be fortunate and successful, and if you turn away from them then they will stand as something against you. I like such and such, and I dislike such and such. And now we are together so do not separate between us, and whatever you see of good then speak of it, and whatever you see of evil then hide it.” Then she said something which I had not thought of before, “ How would you like for my family to visit us?” I said, “I do not want to be influenced by my in-laws.” She said, “So who do you like of your neighbors to enter your house so that I may give them permission, and whoever you dislike I also dislike.” I said, “The tribe of so-and-so are righteous and the tribe of so-and-so are bad people.”

Then he said, So I spent, Oh Sha'bee, the most blessed night, and she lived with me for an entire year, and I did not see from her anything except that which I was pleased with. Then at the beginning of the next year once I came back from the court of law, and I found that there was an old lady giving commands in our house. So I said, "Who is this?" They said, "It is so-and-so, your mother-in-law." So the surprise and unhappiness I had initially felt then left me and when I sat down the old lady approached me and said, "*Assalaamu alayka Aba Umayyah*" I said: "*Wa alayki as-salaam*, and who are you?" She said, "I am so-and-so, your mother-in-law." I said, "May Allaah bring you near." She said, "How have you found your wife?" I replied, "As the best wife." So she said to me, "Abu Umayyah! Indeed a woman is never worse than in two situations: If she gives birth to a son or if she is spoiled by her husband; so if you see something questionable in her then you must hit her, for by Allaah, men never bring anything more evil to their houses then a spoiled woman."

I said, "As for this then by Allaah, you have disciplined her well so she has good manners, and you have taught well so she is indeed well-raised." She said, "Would you like for your in-laws to visit you?" So I replied, "Whenever they like." Then he said, Thereafter she used to come at the beginning of every year, and advise me with that same advice.

My wife lived with me for twenty years I did not blame her for anything except for once, and that time I was unjust to her. Once the *mu'adhin* was calling the *iqaama*, after I had prayed the two Sunnah *raka'at* of Fajr prayer, and I was the *Imaam* of the neighborhood *masjid,* when suddenly there was a scorpion crawling in the house. I took a container and caught it, then I said, "Zainab, do not move that container until I come back" If only you had seen me Oh Sha'bee, after I had prayed and returned, and I saw that the scorpion had gotten out had stung her, so I called for water and salt and I began soaking her fingers and reading al-Faatiha and Surat an-Naas and Surat al-Falaq." (Ibn 'Abdu Rabbah al-Andaloosee relates this story in his book, "*Tabaa'i an-Nisaa*" and Abu al-Fath al-Ibsheehee mentions it in his book, "*al-Mustatrif*")

Oh Muslim women, take an example from the following story, as it is a mother speaking to and advising her intelligent daughter, just as it should be spoken to every married woman.

A well known expression or phrase of example from the phrases of examples of the Arabs originated due to this story. And it is the phrase:

"What have you left behind you, oh 'Aasim?" It is related by Abu al-Fadl an-Naysaabooree in his book, "*Majmu' al-Amthaal*". He says about this phrase, "What have you left behind you, oh 'Aasim?":

al-Mufadil said "The first to say that was al-Haarith ibn 'Amr, the King of Kindah. When he was told of the beauty of the daughter of 'Awf ibn Muhallam ash-Shaybaanee, and her perfection and the strength of her intellect, he called for a woman from his people of Kindah to come to him. She was called 'Aasim, and she was a woman of intellect, good speech, manners and clarity of mind.

He said to her, "Go to them, so that you can inform me about the daughter of 'Awf." So she left and went until she reached the other woman's mother, Umaamah Bint al-Haarith. She then informed her of what she had come for. So Umaamah called for her daughter, and she said, "Oh my dear daughter, this is a woman like one of your aunts. She has come to look at you, so do not cover yourself with anything, as she wants to look at you from the front and back. And respond to her if she asks you anything."

So the daughter came in, and 'Aasim had never seen the like of her before. Then she left the young woman, saying, "The one who leaves off deception is the one who removes disguises." She gave this as an example, then she returned to al-Haarith.

When he saw her coming, he said to her, "What is behind you, oh 'Aasim?" She said, "The cover of the churn has been lifted revealing pleasing butter..." (The Sheikh then goes on to relate a section of the narration in which the woman's great beauty is described with very eloquent, descriptive language and specific Arab idioms, then goes on to the next part of the story, which is as follows):

Accordingly, the King then sent for her father, was engaged to her, and then the father married her to him. He sent her dowry to her, and she prepared to go to his home to live.

At the time, when her family wanted to take her to her husband, her mother said to her, "Oh my daughter, if one did not need to be advised due to their good character, then you would not need to be advised- but a reminder is both for the heedless, as well as an aid to the intelligent one. If any woman was not in need of a husband because of the richness of her parents and their great need for her, then you would be of those people who are the least in need of one. However, women are created for men, and men are created for women.

Oh daughter, you have left the situation that you were born in, and you have left behind the life that you grew up in to move to a place that you do not know, and to a companion which you are not familiar with. So bend to his dominance over you as he has become your ruler and king, as if you are towards him like a slave, then he will be like a slave and captive for you. Oh my daughter, take from me ten characteristics which will be for you both a provision and reminder. Have contented companionship, and intimacy which is achieved through the excellence in hearing and obeying. Be watchful about that which his eye falls upon, and be aware of that smell which reaches his nose, so that his eye does not fall upon anything from you which is ugly, and he does not smell from you anything except for the best of fragrances. Indeed, *kohl* is the most excellent of those things which beautify, and water is the most pleasant of pleasant smells, which has been forgotten. Guard the time intended for his eating his meals, and ensure quiet when he is sleeping- as intense hunger will ignite anger, and disturbed sleep will infuriate him. Guard his house and his wealth, and care for and protect him, his honor, and his children. As for guarding his wealth- this is being proficient in spending discreetly- and the caring for the children and his honor, is through superior and excellent management. And do not betray his secrets, nor disobey his commands, as if you betray his secrets you will not be safe from his betrayal, and if you disobey his commands you will wound his heart. Avoid along with that being happy when he is sad and sadness when he is happy; because the first thing is falling short, and the second is from that which causes annoyance. The greater your esteem for him, the greater his kindness will be for you, and the more agreeable you are to him, the longer you will be his companion in marriage. Know that you will not attain that which you desire until you place his pleasure over your own, and his wishes over yours- in that which you like, and that which you hate. May Allaah bestow His favor on you."

Thereafter, she was taken and given to him and her position with him was tremendous, and she gave birth to seven kings who ruled over Yemen after him." (End of narration)

It is upon every Muslim woman who desires that which Allaah has of reward to guard her tongue from backbiting and slander, and from "he said" and "she said", as well as from asking many questions, and being ungrateful to her husband. As more often than not the time spent in the sittings of the women is spent in these prohibited matters. It is as if these actions were in their eyes the example of salt on food, such that the sitting could not be pleasant except with it!

It is narrated by Hakeem ibn Hizaam, that he said that the Prophet, may Allaah's praise and salutations be upon him, spoke to the women one day, and he admonished them and commanded them to have fear of Allaah and obey their husbands. He said, ***{Indeed from among you are the ones who will enter Paradise.}*** And he put his fingers together.

{And from you are the ones who will be wood for the fire of Hell.} And he separated his fingers. So one of them said, "The reason oh Messenger of Allaah! Why is this?" He, may Allaah's praise and salutations be upon him, said, ***{You are ungrateful to your husbands, and curse often, and put off the doing of good.}*** (Narrated by Ibn Hibaan, in his "*Saheehah*")

It is upon every Muslim woman to avoid resembling the disbelieving women and those women who are immoral in all items of their clothing and outward appearance. She is forbidden from wearing tight clothing, and that which exposes her- be it from any direction and from any side. She is forbidden from the clothing which is transparent or short, pants, and high heels. She must avoid following the latest fashion trends- as is said- in both clothing and hairstyles.

As he, may Allaah's praise and salutations be upon him, said, ***{The one who resembles a people is of them.}*** (Narrated in Sunan Abu Daawud)

And describing a group from the women, he, may Allaah's praise and salutations be upon him, said,

{There are two types of the people of the fire who I did not see: A people having whips like oxtails with them, with which they beat the people, and women who would be dressed yet appear naked, who would be inclined to evil and incite others towards it. Their heads are like the bumps of camels, inclined to one side. They will not enter Paradise, nor smell its fragrance, though its fragrance be detectable from such and such a far distance.} (Narrated in *Saheeh Muslim* and other collections)

an-Nawawi said, in his explanation of Muslim:

"This hadeeth is from the miracles of the Prophethood, as that which he has informed us of has come to be, may Allaah's praise and salutations be upon him. As for the one who is dressed, then this has different aspects:

One of them is that its meaning is that they are clothed or adorned in blessings from the beneficence of Allaah, yet stripped of or lacking gratitude for these blessings of His.

The second, is that they are dressed in clothing, yet they are stripped of good actions- failing to engage in good deeds- and they have no concern for their Hereafter, or consideration for obedience.

The third is that she uncovers only some aspects or parts of her body, in order to make her beauty apparent, so she is dressed and yet naked.

The fourth is that she wears thin clothing which generally describes all that is under it, so is dressed, yet is naked in actuality.

As for ***{inclined to evil and incite others towards it}***, then it is said they have strayed from obedience to Allaah, the Most High, and do not hold firmly to the safeguarding of their private parts and similar matters. And "inclining others towards it" means they teach other than themselves by the example of their actions. And it is said, she combs her hair in an attractive fashion and it is the style of the prostitute, which they are known for, thus this fashion attracts others to them. And it is said they are attracted to men, and so they attract men to them with that which they display of their beauty, and similar matters.

As for their heads being like the humps of camels, then it means that they make them larger and grander, wrapping it (their hair) into a turban or head cloth or that which resembles them, until it looks like the hump of the camel. This is that which is well-known from its explanation. al-Maaziree said, "And it is possible that its meaning is that they desire men and do not cast their eyes down away from them, and do not generally turn their heads away." And al-Qaadee preferred the explanation that their "inclining" is their combing their hair in an attractive style. He said, "And the hair is braided in braids which are drawn tight above and gathered to the middle of the head so it appears like the camel's hump." He said, "And this is an indication that what is meant by resembling the camel's hump is that it is from the height of the braids above their heads, and the gathering of them there, and making it abundant due to the braiding, until it inclines to one side of the head." (End of quote from Imaam an-Nawawi, may Allaah have mercy upon him)

And Ibn al-'Arabee, may Allaah have mercy upon him, said, "They are dressed because they are wearing clothes; and they are described as being naked because the nature of the drcss is actually thin and so describes them and makes their beauty apparent, and this is prohibited."

al-Qurtubee, may Allaah have mercy upon him, said, "I say: This is one of the explanations of the scholars concerning this meaning. The second: That they are wearing clothes, but they are not wearing the clothing of piety, about which Allaah, Most High, says, ﴾***...and the raiment of righteousness, that is better...***﴿ (Surat al-A'raaf, from Ayat 26) And they recite in poetry:

If the person never wears the raiment of piety

He changes to being someone naked, even if he is physically clothed

As best clothing for man is obedience to his Lord

And there is no good in the one who disobeys Allaah

And in a hadeeth of Dahyah ibn Khaleefah al-Kalbee, may Allaah be pleased with him, that he was sent to Hercule, and when he returned the Messenger of Allaah, may Allaah's praise and salutations be upon him, gave him a Qubitee garment. So he said, ***{Use half of it as a shirt for yourself, and give half of it to your wife as a khimaar.}*** So then when I turned to leave, he, may Allaah's praise and salutations be upon him, said, ***{But command her to wear something under it, so that it does not describe her body.}*** (Narrated by al-Haakim; and he said, "This hadeeth has an authentic chain of narration on their standards but was not narrated by al-Bukhaari and Muslim")

Abu Hurairah mentioned the thinness of the garments of the women. He said, "The ones who are dressed yet appear naked are those wearing clothing which is delicate and split with openings."

And the women of the Tribe of Tameem came to 'Aishah, may Allaah be pleased with her, and they were wearing garments which were transparent. So 'Aishah, may Allaah be pleased with her, said, "If you are truly believers, then this is not the clothing of the believers. And if you are not believers, then enjoy them."

And a bride came to 'Aishah, may Allaah be pleased with her, and she was wearing a *Qubtee* head covering dyed with safflower. When 'Aishah, may Allaah be pleased with her, saw her, she said, "The woman who wears this does not believe in Surat an-Noor."

This concludes what was written, and I ask Allaah, the Most High, the Almighty, to make my action righteous, and to that it be done purely for seeking His face, Glorified and Exalted is He, and to not make anything from it be for anything along with Him, and to accept me as one of the Righteous. Ameen.

And may Allaah's praise and salutations be upon our Prophet, Muhammad, and upon his family, and all of his companions.

Written by:

Abu Furayhaan, Jamaal ibn Furayhaan al-Haarithee

7/20/1426

Review and Discussion Questions

Questions for My Advices to the Salafi Sisters by Sheikh Jamaal

Review:

1. List two of the verses of the hijaab mentioned by the Sheikh, may Allaah preserve him. (Bottom half of page 150)
2. What is tawheed? (Top half of page 151)
3. What should be our position regarding arguing and disputing? Give one saying of the Salaf concerning this matter. (Bottom half of page 152, Top half of page 153)
4. List two ahaadeeth which are evidences for the great position of the husband? (Bottom half of page 153)
5. Make a numbered list of possible beneficial points from the mother's advice to her daughter in the narration "What have you left behind you, oh 'Aasim?" (Bottom half of page 157, Top half of page 158)
6. How does Imaam an-Nawaawi, may Allaah have mercy upon him, explain the people who are "dressed yet appear naked" in the hadeeth of the two types of people of the hellfire. (Top half of page 159)

Discussion & Consideration:

7. In light of Verse 31 of Surat an-Noor ﴾ ***And tell the believing women to lower their gaze...*** ﴿ and Verse 32 of Surat al-Ahzaab ﴾ ***Oh Wives of the Prophet...*** ﴿ how should a Muslimah deal with men who are not mahram to her if the need arises?
8. What are some of those things included in the knowledge which the Muslim woman must obtain? Why are these things important?
9. Why must the one who calls to Allaah set higher ideals and aspirations for herself than the common person?
10. What are some lessons we can learn from the narration of Zainab bint Jareer that the Sheikh mentions in his treatise?
11. How should we sisters conduct ourselves around other sisters, at meetings and gatherings, in order to protect ourselves from falling into that behavior or speech which is disliked or forbidden?

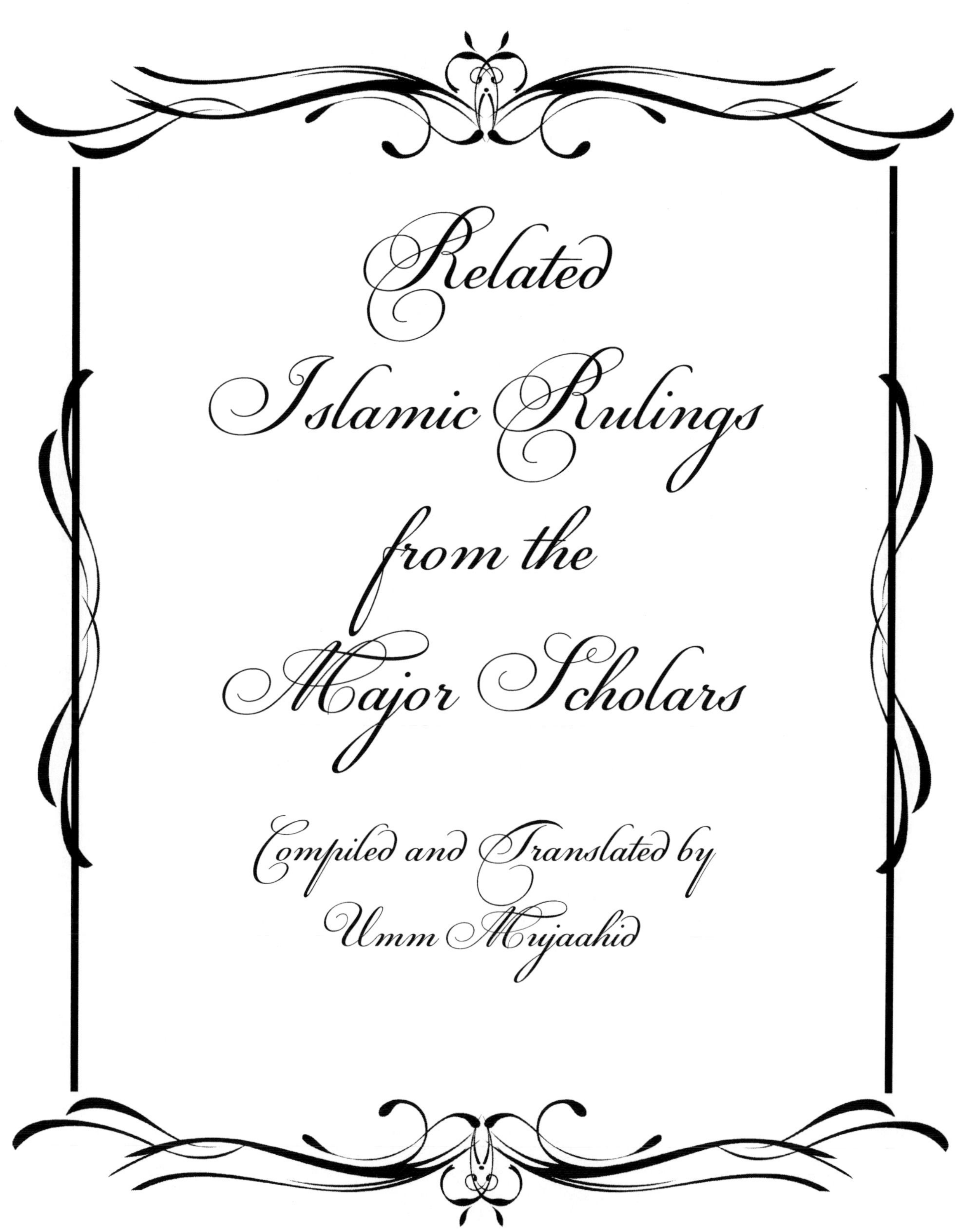

Related Islamic Rulings from the Major Scholars

Compiled and Translated by

Umm Mujaahid

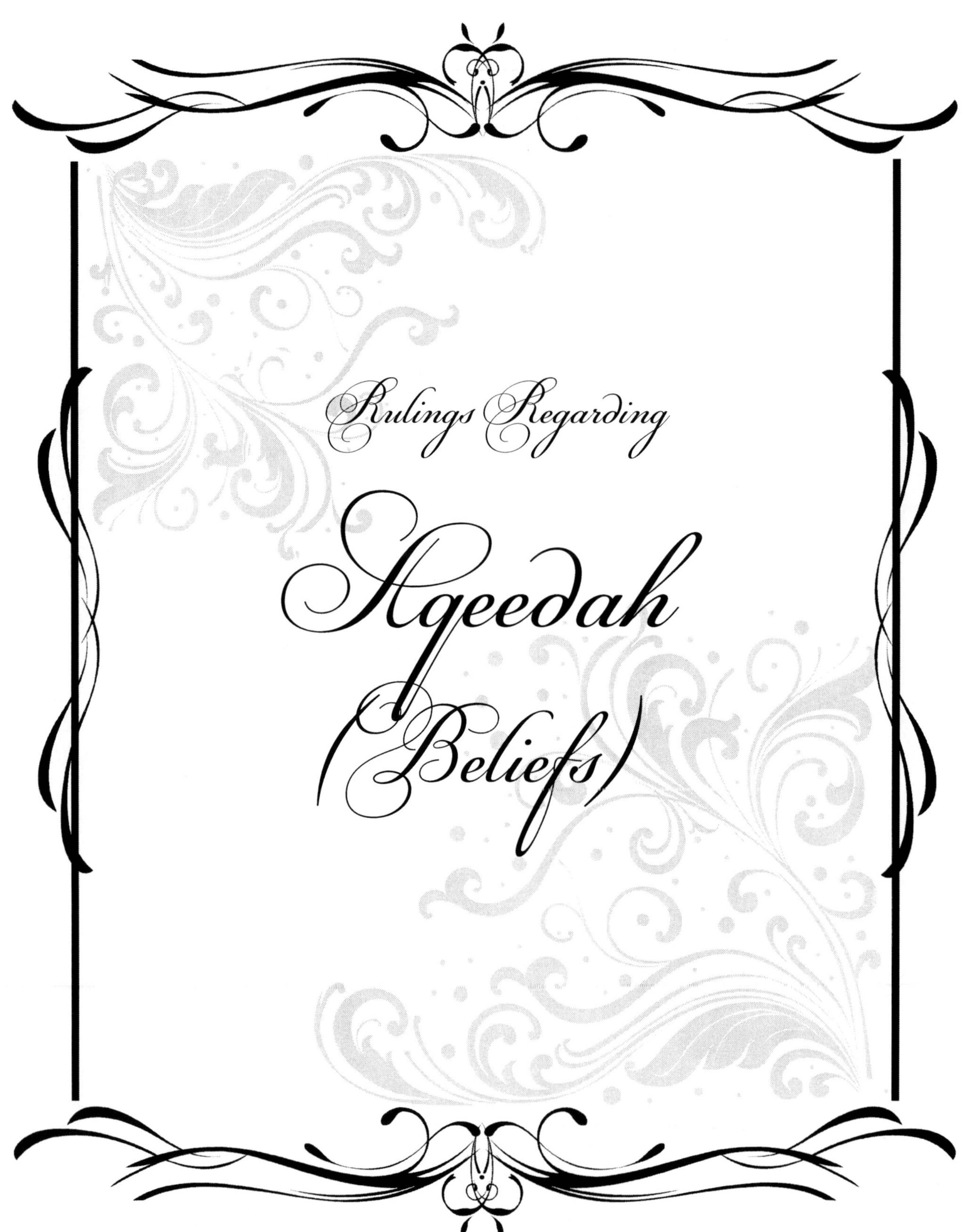

Rulings Regarding Aqeedah (Beliefs)

The Conditions of Islaam

Question: What are the conditions of Islaam?

Answer from Sheikh 'Abdul 'Aziz ibn Baaz, may Allaah have mercy upon him: The conditions of Islaam are two:

The First Condition: Sincerity of intention for Allaah alone (الإخلاص , *al-ikhlaas*); and that you desire by your Islaam and entering into the religion of Allaah and by your actions, the face of Allaah, Glorified and Exalted is He. There is no doubt but that this is from it. This is because every action that is performed and it is not done seeking the face Allaah- whether it be the prayer, charity, fasting, or other than these- there is no benefit in it, and it is not accepted. This includes *ash-shahadatain* (testifying that there is no god worthy of worship except Allaah, and that Muhammad is His Messenger) if it is done to impress the people or hypocritically; it is not accepted and it will not benefit you, and you will be of the hypocrites.

It is necessary that your saying, "I testify that there is no god worthy of worship except Allaah, and I testify that Muhammad is the Messenger of Allaah in truth, and that he is the Messenger of Allaah sent to the *thaqaleen* (i.e. both the *jinn* and mankind), and he is the seal and last of the prophets"- if that is said by you truthfully, and with sincerity of intention for Allaah alone, then it will benefit you. Likewise, you are worshipping Allaah alone through your prayer, as well as in your charity, recitation, your saying "*La ilaha ila Allaah*", your fasting, and your pilgrimage- these are all for Allaah alone. (and the compiler of "*at-Tuhfat al-Baaziyyah*" adds a note here, as proof of this statement, the statement of Allaah, the Most High, ﴾ ***Say, "Verily, my prayer, my sacrifice, my living, and my dying are for Allaah, the Lord of the 'aalameen (mankind, jinn and all that exists).*** ﴿- (Surat al-An'aam, Ayat 162)

The Second Condition: Conformance to the Islamic legislation. It is necessary that your actions conform to the Islamic legislation, and are not from your opinion or your independent reasoning. Rather, it is necessary that you study and seek information concerning what conforms with the Islamic legislation, so that you pray as Allaah has legislated, fast as Allaah has legislated, give the obligatory charity as Allaah has legislated, make *jihaad* as Allaah has legislated, make the pilgrimage as Allaah has legislated it- so everything is approached like this.

The Prophet, may Allaah's praise and salutations be upon him, said, ***{One who performs a deed which is not in conformance to that which we have been sent with, it is rejected.}*** (This hadeeth is authentic, and is found in al-Bukhaari 2/116, Muslim 2/25,4/437, Abu Daawud 4606, Ibn Maajah 14, ad-Daaraqutanee pages 52 and 521, Ahmad 6/`46, 180,240,256, and 270 and other than them)

Allaah says in His Noble Book, ﴾***Or have they partners (with Allaah – false gods) who have instituted for them a religion which Allaah has not ordained?***﴿- (Surat ash-Shooraa, From Ayat 21) Allaah, Glorified is He, reproaches them for this action.

And He, Glorified is He, says, "***Then We have put you (Oh Muhammad) on a (plain) way of (Our) commandment [ike the one which We commanded Our Messengers before you. So follow you that (Islamic monotheism and its laws), and follow not the desires of those who know not. Verily, they can avail you nothing against Allaah (if He wants to punish you).***﴿- (Surat al-Jaathiyah, From Ayats 18-19)

So it is obligatory to follow the Islamic legislation, which Allaah has legislated through the hand of His Messenger, Muhammad, may Allaah's praise and salutations be upon him, and to avoid leaving it in all of the acts of worship through which one becomes close to Allaah, Glorified is He, Most High.

These are the conditions of Islaam, and they are two conditions: The first is purity of intention for Allaah in action (including belief, speech and the action of the limbs) and the second is conformance to the Islamic legislation. This is that which will bring you benefit in your acts of worship, and through which Allaah will accept your worship from you, if you are Muslim.

("at-Tuhfat al-Baaziyyah fee al-Fataawa an-Nisaa'iyyah" Pages 56-57; originally from Fataawa min Noor 'ala ad-Darb)

The Fundamental Beliefs in Regard to Creed

Question: What are the fundamental beliefs of ahl-as-sunnah wa ahl-al-jama'ah' concerning matters of creed and other matters related to the religion?

Answer from Sheikh Muhammad ibn Saalih al-'Utheimeen, may Allaah have mercy upon him: The fundamental principle of *ahl-as-sunnah wa ahl-al-jama'ah'* in regard to creed and other matters related to the religion is complete adherence to the Book of Allaah and the Sunnah of His Messenger, may Allaah's praise and salutations be upon him, as well as the guidance and Sunnah which the righteous *khalifas* (Abu Bakr, 'Umar, 'Uthmaan, and 'Ali, may Allaah be pleased with all of them) followed, in accordance with the words of Allaah, the Most High,

﴾***Say (Oh Muhammad): "If you (really) love Allaah, then follow me (i.e. accept Islamic monotheism, follow the Qur'aan and the Sunnah), Allaah will love you...***﴿- (Surat aal-'Imraan, From Ayat 31) Also, the statement of Allaah, the Most High,

﴾***He who obeys the Messenger (Muhammad), has indeed obeyed Allaah, but he who turns away, then We have not sent you (Oh Muhammad) as a watcher over them.***﴿- (Surat an-Nisaa', Ayat 80)

And the saying of Him, the Most High, ﴾***And whatsoever the Messenger (Muhammad) gives you, take it; and whatsoever he forbids you, abstain (from it).***﴿- (Surat al-Hashr, From Ayat 7)

And though this chapter was revealed regarding the distribution of the spoils of war, it is even more fitting in matters pertaining to the Islamic legislation. The Prophet, may Allaah's praise and salutations be upon him, used to address the people on the day of *Jumu'ah*, saying,

{To proceed: Truly, the best speech is the Book of Allaah, and the best

guidance is the guidance of Muhammad, may Allaah's praise and salutations be upon him. And the worst of matters (in the religion) are the newly invented matters, for indeed every newly invented matter is an innovation, and every innovation is a misguidance, and every misguidance is in the Fire.} (Muslim, 867)

And the Prophet, may Allaah's praise and salutations be upon him said, ***{Adhere to my Sunnah and the Sunnah of the rightly guided khalifahs who came after me. Hold firm to it and cling to it with your molar teeth. And beware of newly invented matters, for indeed every newly invented matter is an innovation, and every innovation is misguidance.}*** (Abu Daawud, 4607)

The proofs of this are many; so the way of *ahl-as-sunnah wa ahl-al-jama'ah* and their methodology is complete, in compliance with the Book of Allaah, the Sunnah of His Messenger, may Allaah's praise and salutations be upon him, and the Sunnah of the rightly guided *khalifahs* who followed him. In this way they established the religion, and they did not differ in it, in obedience to the words of Allaah, the Most High,

﴾He (Allaah) has ordained for you the same religion (Islamic Monotheism) which He ordained for Nuh, and that which We have revealed to you (Oh Muhammad), and that which We ordained for Ibraaheem, Moosa and 'Eesa saying you should establish religion (i.e. to do what it orders you to do practically) and make no divisions in it (religion) (i.e. various sects in religion).﴿ - (Surat ash-Shura, From Ayat 13)

Even though differences did occur between them in matters in which it is permissible to utilize *ijtihaad* (utilizing independent judgment by the scholars, based upon the established texts), this differing did not then lead to a differing in their hearts. Instead, one finds that there was mutual affection and love between them in spite of this differing which did occur between them due to this *ijtihaad*.

("Fataawa Arkan al-Islaam", Vol. 1, No. 3)

How to Increase Faith

Question: How can a person increase his faith, putting into effect the commands of Allaah, and fearing His punishment?

Answer from the Permanent Committee of Scholars in Saudi Arabia: That comes about by reading the Book of Allaah, and studying it, and contemplating its meanings as well as its rulings. Also, by studying the Sunnah of the Prophet, may Allaah's praise and salutations be upon him, and understanding the details of legislation which come from it, and the actions which are required by that. One must conform to the correct Islamic beliefs, both in action and speech, be mindful of Allaah, and the heart must take heed of His magnificence. He must remember the Last Day, and that which it contains of the reckoning, of rewards and punishments, of severity and that which will cause terror. Also he must take as companions those who are known to be righteous, and must shun and turn away the people of evil and wrongdoing.

("Qatf al-Azhaar al-Mutanaathara min Fataawa al-Mar'at al-Muslimah", Page 67)

Extremism and Negligence

***Question:** What are the limits that, if mankind exceeds them in the religion, they are considered extremism (غلو ghuloo), and what is the definition of al-ghuloo? Likewise, what are the limits of negligence (التفريط at-tafreet) in regards to the religion?*

Answer from the Permanent Committee of Scholars in Saudi Arabia: The boundary in the religion which, if it is exceeded it is considered extremism, is to surpass or go beyond that which has been legislated.

الغلو: it is entering too deeply into a matter, going beyond its proper limits or being excessive concerning it. The Prophet, may Allaah's praise and salutations be upon him, prohibited excessiveness, when he, may Allaah's praise and salutations be upon him, said, ***{Beware of extremism in the religion, as verily people which came before you were destroyed through extremism in the religion.}*** (Ahmad and other than him, and its chain of narration is authentic; see "*as-Silsilat as-Saheehah*" of Sheikh al-Albaani, may Allaah have mercy upon him, No. 1283)

As for negligence (التفريط *at-tafreet*), then it is falling short in establishing that which Allaah has made obligatory, performing some acts of wrongdoing, such as fornication, backbiting, or carrying tales, as well as leaving off some of the other obligatory acts, such as respect for the parents, keeping the ties of kinship, returning the Islamic greeting and that which is similar to these. And with Allaah is the success, and may Allaah's praise and salutations be upon our Prophet, Muhammad, his family, and his companions.

What will the Women have in Paradise?

***Question:** It has been stated that the men will have al-hoor al-'ain (beautiful maidens) in Jennah (Paradise). What will there be for the women?*

Answer from Sheikh Muhammad ibn Saalih al-'Utheimeen, may Allaah have mercy upon him: Allaah, Glorified is He, the Most High, states, regarding the blessings of Paradise:

﴾***Therein you shall have (all) that your inner selves desire, and therein you shall have (all) for which you ask. "An entertainment from (Allaah), the Oft-Forgiving, Most Merciful."***﴿- (Surat al-Fussilat, From Ayats 31-32)

And He, the Most High, says, ﴾***...(there will be) therein all that inner selves could desire, and all that eyes could delight in and you will abide therein forever.***﴿- (Surat az-Zukhruf, From Ayat 71)

It is well known that marriage is one of the things which the souls desire most, and so it will be found in Paradise for the people of Paradise, whether they be men or women. So Allaah, Glorified is He, the Most High, will marry the woman in Paradise to the man who was her husband in the life of this world, as He, Glorified is He, the Most High, says,

"﴾*Our Lord! And make them enter the 'Adn (Eden) Paradise (everlasting Gardens) which you have promised them – and to the righteous among their fathers, their wives, and their offspring! Verily, You are the All-Mighty, the All-Wise."*﴿- (Surat Ghafir, Ayat 8)

If she did not marry in the life of this world, then Allaah, the Most High, will marry her to one whom she is pleased with in Paradise.

("Fataawa Arkaan al-Islaam" Vol. 1, No. 58)

The Majority of the People of the Hellfire

Question: Is it true, as has been said, that most of the people of the Hellfire will be women, and why?

Answer from Sheikh Muhammad ibn Saalih al-'Utheimeen, may Allaah have mercy upon him: This is true, as the Prophet, may Allaah's praise and salutations be upon him, said, while delivering a speech to them, ***{Oh gathering of women! Give charity, as I have seen that you are the majority of the people of the Hellfire.}*** This doubt raised by the questioner was expressed to the Prophet, may Allaah's praise and salutations be upon him, as they said, "For what reason, oh Messenger of Allaah?" He, may Allaah's praise and salutations be upon him, replied, ***{You curse frequently and are ungrateful to your husbands.}*** (Agreed upon)

Thus, the Prophet, may Allaah's praise and salutations be upon him, made clear the reasons why they are the majority of the inhabitants of the Hellfire; because they malign, curse, and revile others frequently, and they are ungrateful to their husbands. Due to these reasons, they are the majority of the people of the Hellfire. ("*Fataawa Arkaan al-Islaam*" Vol. 1, No. 59)

Question: What is the ruling concerning visiting the disbelievers, accepting gifts from them, attending their funerals, and wishing them well on their holidays?

Answer from Sheikh Saalih al-Fauzaan, may Allaah preserve him: There is no problem with visiting the disbelievers for the purpose of calling them to Islaam. As the Prophet, may Allaah's praise and salutations be upon him, visited his uncle Abu Taalib, and was present there, and he called him to Islaam (see "*Saheeh al-Bukhaari*", 2/98, from the hadeeth of Sa'eed ibn al-Museeb, on his father). He also visited the Jews, and called them to Islaam (see "*Saheeh al-Bukhaari*",2/97, from the hadeeth of Anas ibn Maalik). As for visiting the disbelievers just for pleasure or comfort, then this is not permissible, because that which is obligatory is hatred of them and separating from them.

It is permissible to accept gifts from them, because the Prophet, may Allaah's praise and salutations be upon him, accepted gifts from some of the disbelievers- for example the gift of al-Maqooqs, the king of Egypt (see "*Nasb ar-Raayah*" 4/421, "*Zaad al-Ma'aad*" 3/691-692)

It is not permissible to congratulate them on their holidays, because that is showing attachment and support of them, and acceptance of their wrongdoing. ("*al-Muntaqa min Fadeelatu ash-Sheikh Saalih al-Fauzaan*" 1/255, as quoted in "*Fataawaal-'Aqeedah*" of Sheikh Saalih al-Fauzaan, Page 31)

Review and Discussion Questions

Questions for 'Aqeedah rulings

Review:

1. What are the conditions of Islaam, as stated by Sheikh Bin Baaz, may Allaah have mercy upon him? (Top of page 165)
2. List some of the proofs that we must adhere to the Qur'aan and the Sunnah as understood and practiced by the salaf as-saalih. (Bottom half of page 166)
3. Define ghuloo and tafreet, and give an example of each in the religion. (Top half of page 168)

Discussion & Consideration:

4. If you ask almost any Muslim if he follows the Qur'aan and the Sunnah, he will say, "Yes." What is the difference between this and that which ahl-as-sunnah wa ahl-al-jama'ah believe in regards to creed and religious matters?
5. What would you say to a person who said to you, "The men in Islaam get beautiful women in Paradise- what do the women get?"
6. How do we deal with the disbelievers in regards to visiting them and congratulation them on their holidays?

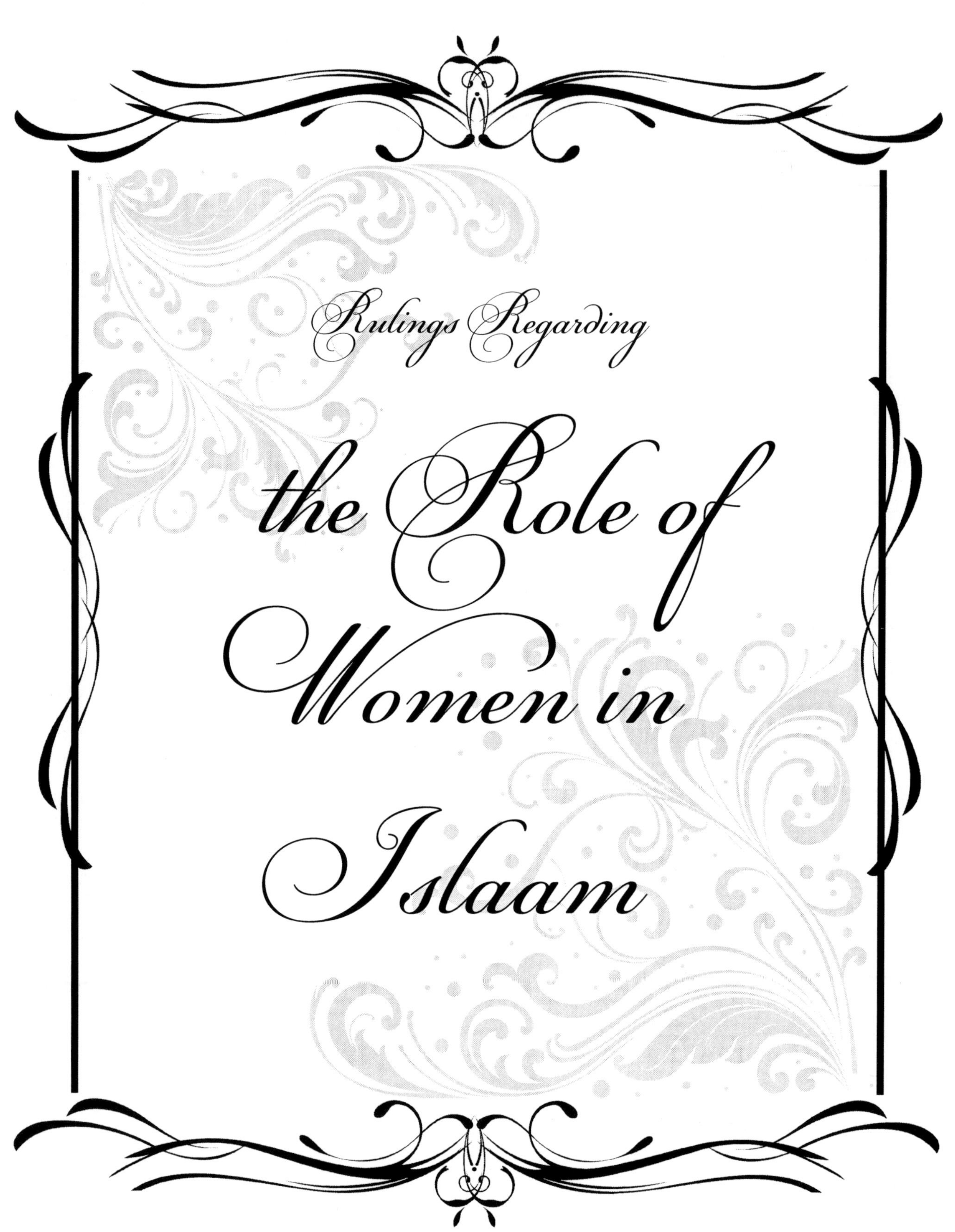

Rulings Regarding the Role of Women in Islaam

The Exalted Position of the Woman in Islaam

Question: Some of the people say that the women are deficient in intellect, religion, inheritance, and giving testimony. And some say, "Allaah has made them equal (to the men) in reward and punishment." What is your opinion? Are they deficient in regards to the legislation of Muhammad, or not?

Answer from the Permanent Committee of Scholars in Saudi Arabia, may Allaah preserve them all: The Islamic legislation has come with honor and respect for the woman, raising her status, putting her in the position for which she is best suited, safeguarding her and preserving her honor and dignity. As it is made obligatory upon the one who is responsible for her or her husband to spend upon her, to support her monetarily and otherwise in a good way, to take charge of her affairs, and to treat her well. Allaah, the Most High, says,

﴾ ***...and live with them honorably...*** ﴿- (Surat an-Nisaa, From Ayat 19)

And it is verified that the Prophet, may Allaah's praise and salutations be upon him, said, ***{The best of you are those who are best to your family, and I am the best to my family.}*** (Authentic, see "*as-Silsalat as-Saheehah*")

Islaam has given the woman everything which is fitting for her from rights and Islamically legislated freedoms. Allaah, the Most High, says,

﴾***And they (women) have rights (over their husbands as regards living expenses) similar (to those of their husbands) over them (as regards obedience and respect) to what is reasonable, but men have a degree (of responsibility) over them. And Allaah is All-Mighty, All-Wise.***﴿- (Surat al-Baqara, From Ayat 228) And this includes all the various types of deeds and actions, such as buying, selling, rectification, responsibility, loans, trusts, and other than these.

And it has been made obligatory upon her that which is fitting for her, from acts of worship in obligatory matters. These are like those of the men in regard to purification, prayer, obligatory charity, fasting, pilgrimage, and that which is similar to them from the Islamically legislated acts of worship.

However, the ruling of the Islamic legislation concerning inheritance is that the woman gets half of that which the man receives, as she is not responsible for providing for herself or spending upon her house and children- as indeed the one who is responsible for that is the man.

Just as it falls to the man to be the one charged with care of the guests, the overall decision making and determination of affairs, preserving the wealth, and that which is similar to that.

Just as the testimony of two women is equivalent to the testimony of only one man in some circumstances. This is because the woman is prone to forgetfulness more often (than the man) due to that which is related to the way in which she is fashioned, from that which befalls her due to her menses, pregnancy, childbirth, and raising the children; her mind is busy with all of these things and may cause her to forget.

Concerning this, the evidences of the Islamic legislation are proof that her sister supports her testimony, as that adds to her own accuracy, and strengthens her performance of the act. And there are other matters which are specific to the women, in which the testimony of one woman is sufficient, such as matters of nursing, marital problems and that which is similar.

The woman is equal to the man in regards to the recompense, and rewards for faith, righteous action, and with pleasure in the good life of this world, as well as the great rewards of the life of the Hereafter. Allaah, the Most High, says,

﴾***Whoever works righteousness – whether male or female – while he (or she) is a true believer verily, to him We will give a good life (in this world with respect, contentment and lawful provision), and We shall pay them certainly a reward in proportion to the best of what they used to do (i.e. Paradise in the Hereafter).***﴿- (Surat an-Nahl, Ayat 97)

Along with that, it is known that the woman has rights, and that also upon her are obligations, just as the man has rights and obligations. There are matters for which the men are suited, which Allaah has entrusted to the men, just as there are matters for which the woman is suited which Allaah has entrusted to the women. And with Allaah is the success, and may His praise and salutations be upon our Prophet, Muhammad, his family, and his companions. ("*Qatf al-Azhaar al-MutanaQathara min al-Fatawaa al-Mar'at al-Muslimah*", Volume 1, Page 21-22)

Explanation of the Woman being Deficient in Intellect and Religion

Question: We always hear the noble hadeeth which states that the women are deficient in intellect and religion. Some of the men take from this that they can oppress or abuse the women. We would like for you to clarify the meaning of this hadeeth.

Answer from Sheikh 'Abdul 'Aziz Bin Baaz, may Allaah have mercy upon him: It is clear that the hadeeth of the Messenger of Allaah, may Allaah's praise and salutations be upon him, is that he said, ***{I have not seen one who is deficient in intellect and religion more able to affect the intellect of a reasonable man than one of you women.}*** So it was said to him, "Oh Messenger of Allaah, what is deficient in her intellect? He, may Allaah's praise and salutations be upon him, said, ***{Is it not true that the testimony of two women is equal to that of one man?}*** It was then said, "What is deficient in her religion?" He replied, ***{Is it not the case that the one who is on her menses does not pray, nor does she fast?}*** (Authentic, found in al-Bukhaari, 3/384, Muslim, 2/694, 695, 1000, and other than them, in both this form and shortened form)

So he, may Allaah's and salutations be upon him, clarified that her deficiency in intellect is due to her weakness in recollection, and so her testimony is to be supported by another woman; and that is to give accuracy to her testimony due to the reasons that she may forget, or add something in her testimony.

As for the deficiency in her religion, then it is in the case of the menses and post childbirth bleeding, when she leaves off praying, and does not fast, and she does not perform the prayers; so this is from her being deficient in the religion. However, there is no blame upon her for this deficiency, and this deficiency is a result of Allaah's legislation, Glorified and Exalted is He. He, Glorified is He, Most High, is the One who has legislated it as a mercy for her, and to make things easy for her. As if she fasts when she has her menses and the post childbirth bleeding, she is harmed by that- so from the Mercy of Allaah is that He has legislated for her that she leave the fast. As for the prayer, due to her having her menses there issues forth from her that which negates the purification- so from Allaah's mercy, Glorified and Exalted is He, is that He legislated that she temporarily leave off the prayer. This is also the case during the post childbirth bleeding; then He has legislated for her that she not perform the prayer because there is great hardship in performing it due to its being repeated five times in the day and the night. And the menses can be for many days, as it may continue for seven or eight days, and the post childbirth bleeding for forty days. So it is from Allaah's mercy upon her, and His benevolence, that He has removed from her the prayer, both its obligation and performance (i.e. it is not obligatory for her to make up the missed prayers).

And this does not make it necessary that her intellect is considered deficient in every area, or that her religion is deficient in every matter. As indeed, the Messenger, may Allaah's praise and salutations be upon him, explained that the deficiency in her intellect was in the aspect of that which occurs from a lack of accuracy, and the deficiency in her religion is from the aspect of what occurs from the leaving of the prayer and fasting when she is on her menses or post childbirth bleeding. Yet one should not necessarily conclude from this that she is lesser than the man in everything, and that the man is better than her in everything.

Yes, the form of the men is better than the form of the women in general, due to many reasons, as Allaah, Glorifed is He, and Most High, as Allaah says,

﴾***Men are the protectors and maintainers of women, because Allaah has made one of them to excel the other, and because they spend (to support them) from their means.***﴿- (Surat an-Nisaa, From Ayat 34)

However, she may be raised above him in some instances in many matters- as how many of the women are superior to many of the men in intellect, religion, and reliability? And this is along with it being related from the Prophet, may Allaah's praise and salutations be upon him, that the form of the women is inferior to the form of the men in intellect and religion from these two aspects which he has explained.

She may put forth many righteous acts, which raise her above many of the men, due to those righteous acts and her fear of Allaah, Glorified and Exalted is He, as well as in her position in the Hereafter. She may have consideration in some of the matters in which she has significant reliability, and so she is more reliable than some of the men concerning them. And this is in many matters in which she works, and strives hard in her memorization and accuracy. So she could be an expert in Islamic history, or in many other matters. This is clear to anyone who examines closely the state of the women in the time of the Prophet, may Allaah's praise and salutations be upon him, as well as after that. By this it is known that this deficiency does not prevent relying upon her in narration, and likewise in testimony if it is supported by another woman, and it also does not prevent her having fear of Allaah, and being from among the best from among both the male worshippers of Allaah and the female worshippers of Allaah if she stands firm upon her religion. And this is despite her not having to fast during the time of her menses or post childbirth bleeding- being relieved of its immediate performance, but not its general obligation (meaning, she is responsible for making it up at a later date), and with her not having to pray, being relieved of both its performance and its obligation.

Therefore this does not require that she be deficient in everything, from the aspect of fear of Allaah, or from the aspect of her establishing His commands, or from the aspect of her reliability in that which she is an expert from other knowledge based areas. As it is a specific deficiency in the intellect and religion, as the Prophet, may Allaah's praise and salutations be upon him, made clear.

So it is not proper that a Believer accuse her of being deficient in everything, and weak in her religion in every matter. As indeed it is a specific weakness in her religion, and a specific weakness in her intellect, due to what is connected to the weakness of the testimony and such as is related to that. It is necessary that one be just and fair to her, and take the Prophet's, may Allaah's praise and salutations be upon him, words upon the best and most perfect of meanings. And Allaah knows best. ("*Fataawa al-Mar'at*" Pages 189-191, "*Majmoo' al-Fataawa wa Maqaalaat Mutanawa*" 4/292-294, as quoted in, "*at-Tuhfat al-Baaziyyah fee al-Fataawa an-Nisaaiyyah*", Volume 3, Pages 152-154)

General Advice to the Righteous Muslimah

Question: Is there a comprehensive statement of advice for that Muslim woman whose priority has become a preoccupation with running around to different stores, thereby falling short in many obligations due to her persistence in that behavior?

Answer from Sheikh Saalih ibn Fauzaan ibn 'Abdullah al-Fauzaan, may Allaah preserve him: A comprehensive statement of advice directed toward the Muslim woman is that she fear Allaah concerning herself, her husband and her children. So she must perform her household duties, raise and educate her children, and fulfill the rights of her husband. She must learn the affairs of her religion and be diligent in performing those things which Allaah has made obligatory. She should also perform many of recommended acts and give a good deal of charity, as much as these matters are within her capabilities. She should not leave her house except out of necessity, and when she does go out she must be completely covered (with the Islamically legislated *hijaab*), without perfume or beautification while she is out. She must also avoid riding alone with a driver who is not *mahram* for her.

She must not crowd together with the men outside or unnecessarily mix with them, or go to the male doctor alone, without a *mahram* with her. Likewise she must not travel without a *mahram*. She should seek medical care from female doctors, and not from the male doctors, except under these two conditions:

The First: There is no female doctor to be found

The Second: It must be necessary for her to go to him in order to be cured

The Muslim woman should stay far away from resembling the men or the female disbelievers in her hairstyle, clothing, and methods of beautification. She should hasten to marry if she is not married, and should not remain without a husband, and should be willing to abandon some of her other goals when she finds a righteous husband.

Concerning this, it is upon the Muslim woman to not pay heed to those senseless callers who desire to strip the woman of her honor and chastity, as they call her to leave the bounds of the legislated behavior of Islaam and to disobey the one who is in charge of her affairs who looks after her well-being.

Similarly, it is upon her to be dutiful to her parents, and to keep the ties of kinship, and to respect her neighbors and to refrain from doing them harm. And Allaah is the One who grants success, and may His praise and salutations be upon our Prophet, Muhammad, and upon his family and Companions. ("*Naseehah wa Fataawa Khaasat bil-Mara'at al-Muslimah*", a collection of rulings and advices from Sheikh Fauzaan, Pages 29-30)

Concerning Calling to Allaah

Question: Is it the domain of the woman to call to Islaam outside of her house, and how so?

Answer from the Permanent Committee of Scholars in Saudi Arabia, may Allaah preserve them: The place for women to call to Islaam first is in home, to her family, including her husband, the women, and those men who are *mahram* to her (those whom she is permanently forbidden to marry). And there is for her a place in Islamic *da'wah* outside of her home as well, addressing the women- as long as this does not include travelling without her husband or a *mahram*, and there is no fear of *fitnah*. And this must be with the permission of her husband if she is married, and she is motivated to do this through its necessity- and this must not cause her to leave off of that which is a greater obligation upon her from the rights of her family. And success is from Allah, and may His praise and salutations be upon our Messenger, Muhammad, his family, and his Companions. ("*Fataawa al-Lejnatu ad-Daa'ima*" 12/249, as quoted in "*Qatf al-Azhaar al-Mutanaathirah min Fataawa al-Mar'at al-Muslimah*" Page 860)

Question: How should we call the general people to as-salafiyyah (adhering the to Book of Allaah, and the Sunnah of His Messenger, may Allaah's praise and salutations be upon him, according to the understanding and practice of the Pious Predecessors), the way of the Pious Predecessors- especially since the people have a strong attachment to those who only invite to evil and wickedness?

Answer from Sheikh Rabee'a al-Madkhalee, may Allaah preserve him: Allah has made clear to us the correct manner of calling to Him. Allaah says to His Prophet,

﴾Invite (mankind, Oh Muhammad) to the way of your Lord with wisdom (i.e. with the Divine Revelation and the Qur'aan) and fair preaching, and argue with them in a way that is better.﴿ - (Surat an-Nahl, From Ayat 125)

Calling to Allaah with wisdom- and wisdom is knowledge, clarification and establishment of the proof. So call with knowledge, good manners, kindness and gentleness- and this is in regards to the common person as well as those who are not common people. However, most of those who will receive the message are general people, who may accept the truth without arguing or disputing. And if it is necessary to resort to argument or debate, such as if someone has within him something from stubbornness, or something from adhering to deviation, then argue with him with that which is best. Allaah, the Most High, says,

﴾The good deed and the evil deed cannot be equal. Repel (the evil) with one which is better (i.e. Allaah orders the faithful believers to be patient at the time of anger, and to excuse those who treat them badly) then verily he, between whom and you there was enmity, (will become) as though he was a close friend. But none is granted it (the above quality) except those who are patient – and none is granted it except the owner of the great portion (of happiness in the Hereafter, i.e., Paradise, and of a high moral character) in this world.﴿ - (Surat al-Fussilat, Ayats 34-35)

As someone does not possess such wisdom, except that he is the owner of the something tremendous. (From "*at-Tahdheer min ash-Shar*" as quoted in, "*Qatf al-Azhaar al-Mutanaathirah min Fataawa al-Mar'at al-Muslimah*" Page 67)

Review and Discussion Questions

Questions for Rulings concerning the Role of women in Islaam

Review:

1. List two proofs (one verse and one hadeeth) showing that the man must treat his wife well. (Top half of page 173)
2. What conditions does Sheikh Fauzaan, may Allaah preserve him, list for the person to go to a doctor of the opposite sex? (Top half of page 177)
3. Is it permissible for a woman to give da'wah outside her home? If so, what conditions must be met before she does so? (Bottom half of page 177)

Discussion & Consideration:

4. What are some matters in which the women and the men are equal in Islamic legislation? What are some matters in which they differ?
5. In the light of Sheikh Bin Baaz's, may Allaah have mercy upon him, explanation of the hadeeth of the woman being deficient in her intellect and her religion, what would you say to one who said to you, "Islaam says that women are stupid and weak"?
6. How should we begin calling the general people to Islaam?

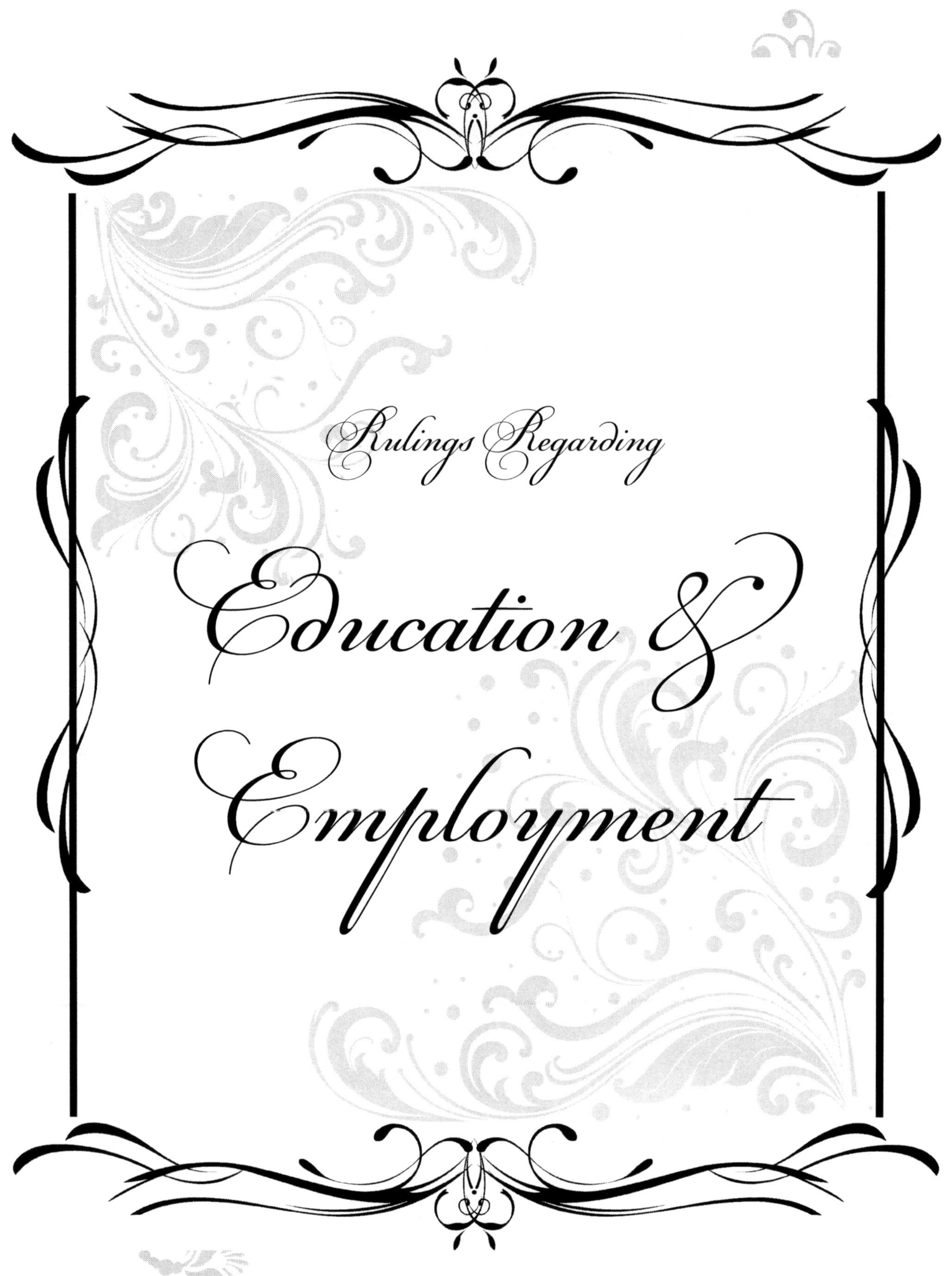

Rulings Regarding Education & Employment

The Muslim Woman Attending Islamic Lectures or Going to the Masjid

Question: Is it allowed for the Muslim woman to go to the masaajid and Islamic lectures?

Answer by Sheikh Saalih Fauzaan, may Allaah preserve him: Yes, it is definitely allowed for the Muslim women to go to the *masaajid* and Islamic lectures, as long as they are screened by being behind the men; as the Prophet, may Allaah's praise and salutations be upon him, said, in the hadeeth of Ibn Masood, ***{Put them back where Allaah put them back.}*** (Saheeh Ibn Khuzaymah 1596, Musannaf Abdu-Razzaq 4960, Al-Mu'jam Al-Kabeer 9330) And he said in the hadeeth of Abu Hurairah, ***{The best of the men's rows is the first and the worst of them is the last, and the best of the women's rows is the last and the worst of them is the first.}*** (Muslim 693, Ibn Khuzaymah 1469, Saheeh Ibn Hibban 403, Abu Daawud 586, Ibn Maajah 996, At-Tirmidhi 213) So if they go to the *masaajid* and attend Islamic lectures then this is a good thing.

And the caller to Islaam should give the women a separate lecture, as the Prophet, may Allaah's praise and salutations be upon him, gave them a separate lecture specific to them.

In Saheeh Al- Bukhaari Jaabir bin Abdullah narrated, ***{The Prophet, may Allaah's praise and salutations be upon him, stood up on the day of Eid and started with the prayer ,and after that he delivered the khutbah (for the men). When the Prophet of Allaah, may Allaah's praise and salutations be upon him, had finished he went to the women and preached to them.}*** And this is a proof that the women need a *khutbah* specifically for themselves.

The problem can be solved if a curtain is set up between the women and the men, so that they can hear the teacher's words and can send up questions, and the teacher can answer their questions with a divider and screen being present. ("*Naseehah wa Fatawaa Khaasat bi al-Mar'at al-Muslimah*" Page 42-43)

Notes

Advice to Women, to Remain in their Homes, to Pray, Study and Recite within Them

In the name of Allaah, the Most Gracious, the Most Merciful

Assalaamu Aleikum wa Rahmatullaahi wa Barakatuhu

Sheikh Saalih al-Fauzaan, may Allaah preserve him, was asked, "Esteemed Sheikh, may Allaah guide you and grant you success, this questioner from Libya asks, 'What is the ruling of the group reading for the women in the *masjid* for the purpose of learning and reviewing; and if it is not permitted, do the women leave the *masjid* for this matter?"

He, may Allaah have mercy upon him, answered, saying,

By Allaah, there is no doubt that the women staying in their houses- whether for prayer, or learning Qur'aan- their being in their houses- there is no doubt that this is the foundation. And if they make it a habit to go out to learn Qur'aan, and I do not know what else they undertake- then this distances them from remaining in the houses.

So it is my opinion that the women studying in the houses, and their prayer in their houses- this is the foundation, and it is the best for safeguarding her.

Now it is the case that the women get up and leave their houses in cars, and they are those who consistently go out. And women love and desire this getting up and leaving and going out. Yet you men opened up this possibility now. It has become the case that they are not accustomed to the houses, and they do not establish the household. And they make the excuse that they are studying and I don't know what else.

So it is my opinion that the best thing is to abandon it, and that the women stay in the houses, and the knowledge they have is enough, insh'Allaah; there is no need to delve beyond necessity into outside places of education...yes.

This transcribed from a voice recording.

From the website *Sahaab as-Salafiyyah*

Reconciling between Seeking Knowledge and the Family in Regard to Time

Question: How does a person reconcile between seeking knowledge and the family in regard to time- which of them is most important concerning that?

Answer from Sheikh Saalih Aal ash-Sheikh, may Allaah, the Most High, preserve him: There is no doubt that that which is obligatory is given preference over that which is superogatory. Some of the knowledge is obligatory; that which rectifies and perfects your belief is a personal obligation upon every Muslim. And it is those answers to the three questions- the three fundamental principles- Who is your Lord? What is your religion? Who is your prophet? Learn that, with its evidences- this is a personal obligation upon every Muslim, it is necessary that he learn it, even if he neglects some of the rights of the family in order to do so.

Likewise, if he is ignorant of *fiqh*, the intended guidance of the source texts, his worship will not be correct, and his prayer will not be correct. If he is a person with wealth, how does he give charity and what is its proper place, and other than that. It is obligatory that he learn these things.

So if the knowledge is obligatory, then it is given priority over that which is superogatory. If the knowledge is not obligatory, and there are obligatory matters which are in opposition to the non-obligatory matters, then the obligatory matter is given preference. For example, the right of his parents, or the right of his family and his wife and children- as he cannot neglect this obligatory right over him for the purpose of accomplishing a superogatory matter from the acknowledged superogatory matters.

The people differ in their situations; from them are those who are busy, and from them are those whose family relies upon him, and from them are the ones who are only moderately relied upon- they differ. And that which is obligatory is that the person puts the obligatory matters first, and the superogatory matters after the obligatory ones.

And you cannot get closer to Allaah, Glorified and Exalted is He, by anything which is more beloved to Him, than that which Allaah, Glorified and most High, has enjoined upon him, as comes forth in the authentic hadeeth, ***{My slave does not draw near to me with anything dearer to me than that which I have enjoined upon him, and my slave continues to draw near to me through those acts which are preferred but not obligatory until I love him.}*** (Bukhaare 6147, Ibn Hibaan 348) Meaning, after those things which are obligatory.

So it is necessary- from deeds- to give precedence to the obligatory matters over the superogatory matters. The Prophet, may Allaah's praise and salutations be upon him, said, ***{Indeed your family has rights over you, and your soul has rights over you, and your Lord has rights over you. So give to each one who has rights upon you, his right.}*** (Narrated with this wording on Ibn Masood in Hilyat al-Awliyaa 14877, and authentically on the Prophet with similar meaning in Sunan Abu Dawood 1175, and Sunan at-Tirmidhe 2395) The obligatory matters are many, so perform that which is obligatory, and the obligatory matters are given preference over the superogatory matters, and the application of that is not understood except with the practice- and give priority to the legislated obligatory matters over personal pleasure.

The farthest away from that is that some of the people go to the superogatory acts, and not to the obligatory ones. Or rather, focus on that which is permissible, but neither rewarded nor punished (*mubaahaat*)- while neglecting the obligatory matters. He stays up all night engaging in various activities, and he leaves his family, and in this way he leaves the obligatory matters whose performance is demanded of him. His father may be elderly, and it would be difficult for him to take care of the household affairs, and the son goes off to gossip, "he said and he said", or does whatever he wants- and by his actions he is neither performing an obligatory nor a superogatory act- and in addition to that, he also neglects that which is obligatory..

There is no doubt that many of the people's problems and their opposition to that which is legislated - many of the problems and complaints which occur from the family concerning the children, and the fathers concerning the children, and from the wife concerning the husband, and the husband concerning the wife- they are from the failure to perform the obligatory duties, and failure to give priority to the obligatory matters over those which are recommended but not obligatory, and to give priority to these over those acts which are merely permissible, but are not rewarded or punished.

The true system which Allaah sent His Prophet, may Allaah's praise and salutations be upon him, with is proceeding in the call from the foundational principle. And the firm pillar is only worshipping Allaah alone, free from and devoid of the murky blemish and flaw of associating others with Allaah, and innovating in the religion, and wrongdoing. And any call which is built upon other than this foundation, then it is destined to rapid failure and there is no place of acceptance for it. (From the tape, "*Qawaa'id al-Qawaa'id*", the fifth question on the first side)

Becoming Firm in Knowledge

Question: I desire to seek knowledge in my house through reading the books of Islamic jurisprudence and memorizing some of the ahaadeeth- however, I quickly forget that which I have memorized. How can I become firm in the knowledge I have?

Answer from Sheikh Muqbil ibn Haadee al-Wadi'ee, may Allaah have mercy upon him: That which I advise every male and female Muslim with is to stay far away from any blameworthy actions and wrongdoing and to fear Allaah, Glorified and Most High. As blameworthy actions and wrongdoing weaken the understanding, and cause that which is memorized to leave. Likewise, also Allaah has said in His Noble Book,

﴾Oh you who believe! If you obey and fear Allaah, He will grant you furqaan [(a criterion to judge between right and wrong)﴿ - (Surat al-Anfaal, from Ayat 29)

As if we fear Allaah, Glorified and Most High, Allaah will bring light to our hearts, while wrongdoing darkens the heart, as is found in "*Saheeh Muslim*" from the hadeeth of Hudhaifah, may Allaah be pleased with him. in which the Messenger of Allaah, may Allaah's praise and salutations be upon him and his family, said, ***{Turmoil and trials will be presented to the hearts as a reed mat is woven stick by stick, and any heart which accepts them will be marked with a black mark, while any heart which rejects them will have a white mark placed upon it. The result is that there will become two types of hearts: one like a white stone which will not be harmed by any turmoil or trial, as long as the heavens and the earth endure; and the other black and dust covered like an upset vessel, not recognizing that which is good, nor rejecting that which is hated, drinking in from that which is from its desires.}*** (Muslim, 144)

Also, from "*Jaami' at-Tirmidhi*", from Abi Hurairah, may Allaah be pleased with him, that the Prophet, may Allaah's praise and salutations be upon him and his family, said, ***{When a worshipper of Allaah commits a sin, a black mark is made within his heart. If he repents, this is polished away, and if he commits a sin again (repeatedly), then a black mark is made within his heart, until the heart is covered by ar-raan.}*** (at-Tirmidhi, 9/253, and it is found in "*al-Jaami*", 6/232)

Meaning, it is eventually enveloped by the black marks of their sins. Then the Prophet, may Allaah's praise and salutations be upon him and his family, recited the saying of Allaah, the Most High,

﴾***Nay! But on their hearts is the raan (covering of sins and evil deeds) which they used to earn.***﴿- (Surat al-Mutafifeen, Ayat 14)

So it is necessary that we fear Allaah, Glorified is He, Most High Also, one must act according to any hadeeth (which one has memorized), as this will establish it more firmly in the mind, as will mentioning it amongst the sisters. As az-Zuhri sat with his paternal aunt, and said a hadeeth to her, and she said, "By Allaah, I do not know what was said." So he said, "Be quiet, oh foolish one, when I am relating my information."

So when you call your sister to you, you mention that which you have learned to her, or to your husband- you tell him about it- then, Allaah willing, it will become more firmly established, and then, also, you will be upon good- a good that is better than becoming busy with "he said, she said", or being occupied with means of amusement and pleasure.

I advise you to not be rushed, but rather to persist upon this seeking of knowledge and acting upon it, as you do not know but that by the permission of Allaah, the Most High, an abundant yield may be produced from that- and knowledge is light, and Allaah, Glorified is He, Most High, puts it into the heart of whom He desires to from His worshippers. He, the Most High, says,

﴾***Allaah burdens not a person beyond his scope.***﴿- (Surat al-Baqara, From Ayat 286), and,

﴾***Allaah puts no burden on any person beyond what He has given him.***﴿- (Surat at-Talaaq, From Ayat 7)

So if you are not able to memorize a whole page, then memorize half a page- do not then attempt to memorize a full page or an entire sheet. If you are able to memorize a short hadeeth, then do not try to memorize a long hadeeth that takes up half a page or a whole page. That which is important to note is that memorization is a gift from Allaah, Glorified is He, Most High, and it is like a heavy load someone carries- there comes a person who is able to carry a heavy rock and lift it up to his head, while another person is not able to even lift it up off the ground. So as for yourself, do not be in a hurry, as you are upon that which is something good, may Allaah bless you. (From "*Asilat al-Hadeedah*", as found in "*Fataawa al-Mar'at al-Muslimah*", a collection of rulings and advices from Sheikh Muqbil, may Allaah have mercy upon him, Pages 67-68)

Review and Discussion Questions

Questions for Rulings regarding education and employment

Review:

1. Is it permissible for the woman to go out to the masaajid and attend Islamic lectures? Is it better for them to remain in their homes? Explain. (Top half of page 181)
2. Make a numbered list summarizing Sheikh Muqbil's, may Allaah have mercy upon him, advice for making our knowledge firm in our hearts and minds. (Middle of Page 184)

Discussion & Consideration:

3. What are some ways that a woman can obtain beneficial Islamic knowledge within her own home? How can she spread that knowledge to others in a permissible way?
4. Sheikh Saalih aal-Sheikh, may Allaah preserve him, explains that it is necessary to put the obligatory matters before the superogatory matters. Give two examples of this.

Rulings Pertaining to Work

Question: What is the ruling concerning the woman working when she is married?

Answer from the Permanent Committee of Scholars in Saudi Arabia: It is not permissible for the woman to work in a situation in which there is mixing with the men, and this is regardless of whether she is married or unmarried. This is because Allaah, Glorified is He, created the men to incline toward and be attracted to the women, and He created the women to incline toward and be attracted to the men, along with there being present a weakness within them. As if there is mixing between the men and the women, then societal trials will occur, and it becomes a cause of corruption, because the soul is naturally inclined towards evil. However, it is permissible for her to work in a venue in which there is no mixing with the men, if she has the permission of her husband.

And Allaah grants all success, and may Allaah's praise and salutations be upon our prophet Muhammad, and his family and companions. ("*Fataawa al-Lajnatu ad-Daa'imah*" 17/234, as quoted in "*Qatf al-Azhaar al-Mutanaathirah min Fataawa al-Mar'at al-Muslimah*" Volume 2, Volume 2, Page 522)

Question: What is the ruling on the woman taking on jobs which it is possible for men to undertake instead of her, and this is done specifically - the creation of job openings intended for women?

Answer From the Permanent Committee of Scholars in Saudi Arabia: The foundational principle in the Islamic legislation is for the woman to stay in her home which Allaah honored her with, and remain there, and stay away from the places of trials and questionable things, and not expose herself to harm, while taking care of her children's Islamic upbringing, and undertaking the serving of her husband and the matters of her household.

However, if she is forced to work then it is necessary for her to choose those jobs which are suitable for her religion and her worldly affairs, which will not interfere with taking care of her husband and children, if her husband consents to this. As for her competing with the men for the jobs which are in the men's field, then that is not permissible, because of the negative effects, harm, and evil which will come about because of that; for in giving her this opportunity there is the ruin of the men, and the suppression of the available opportunities for men's employment. Also her employment in these jobs exposes her to mixing with the men and temptations, and things will occur that will not have praiseworthy consequences. Added to that is the fact that this will interfere with her fulfillment of her obligations towards her husband, and the affairs of her household and children, which will make it necessary to pay others or hire servants, and that brings about more harm and causes problems in the upbringing of the children, as well as in the religion, as is not hidden from anyone.

And Allaah grants all success, and may Allaah's praise and salutations be upon our prophet Muhammad, and his family and companions. ("*Fataawa al-Lajnatu ad-Daa'imah lil Bohooth al-'Ilmiyyah wa al-Iftaa*" 18/236)

Question: Is it permissible for the husband to command his wife to work at a job if he is a person who is incapable of procuring the basic matters of living such as clothing and a place to live?

Answer from Sheikh al-Albaani, may Allaah have mercy upon him: It is not permissible. It is upon him to leave her in her house, and that he work in a job which will provide a living for them. As for causing her to leave his house to work in a workplace, and to mix with the men, then this is not permissible. ("*al-Haawee min al-Fatawaa ash-Sheikh al-Albaani*" Collected by Abu Yusuf Muhammad ibn Ibraaheem, Page 462)

Question: Afwaan; is it permissible for the husband to command the wife to work?

Answer from Sheikh al-Albaani, may Allaah have mercy upon him: If there is a legitimate excuse, then it is obligatory if it is a necessity; because it is obligatory upon the wife to obey her husband in that which he commands her with within the limits of the Islamic legislation. ("*al-Haawee min al-Fatawaa ash-Sheikh al-Albaani*" Collected by Abu Yusuf Muhammad ibn Ibraaheem, Page 462)

Question: If a woman works, with the permission of her husband, to whom belong the wages of her work?

Answer from Sheikh al-Albaani, may Allaah have mercy upon him: This differs; the affair differs per situation:

If a contract exists between the spouses, and the woman works and earns money through this work, and no condition has been made in the contract that the money is for her husband, or half is for her and half is for her husband, or this, or that, then the money remains with her. And the opposite is completely true if the contract does state this as a condition.

That which occurs today, wherein a man marries a woman, and she is, for example, a teacher and has a salary- then there may arise between them differing after that as to whom this salary of hers belongs.

We say, so long as the husband is content with the situation of the woman before he makes a contract with her, then it is not for him to share in her earnings or provisions. However, we have observed that her working takes from her time with her husband, as well as his comfort and her serving him in his house, as well as concerning the upbringing of children. So it is his prerogative to give her the option of staying in her work, and he shares in some of her wealth, or that she stay in her house and leaves her work. And I believe that there is no differing amongst the scholars that the husband, if he commands his wife with a command that does not differ from the Islamic legislation, then it is obligatory upon the woman to obey him, especially if it is due to the reason that she is so busy with her job that she falls short in managing the matters of her house and serving her husband. (From the audio series, "*Silsilat al-Hudaa wa an-Nur*", Tape Number 791, as quoted in, "*Qatf al-Azhaar al-Mutanaathirah min Fataawa al-Mar'at al-Muslimah*" Volume 2, Volume 2, Page 527)

Review and Discussion Questions

Questions for rulings pertaining to work

Review:

1. What reasons does the Permanent Committee of Scholars give for the impermissibility of the women working in jobs for which they compete with the men? (Bottom half of Page 189)

Discussion & Consideration:

2. It is permissible for the woman to work outside of the home. Is this statement correct or incorrect? Explain your answer.

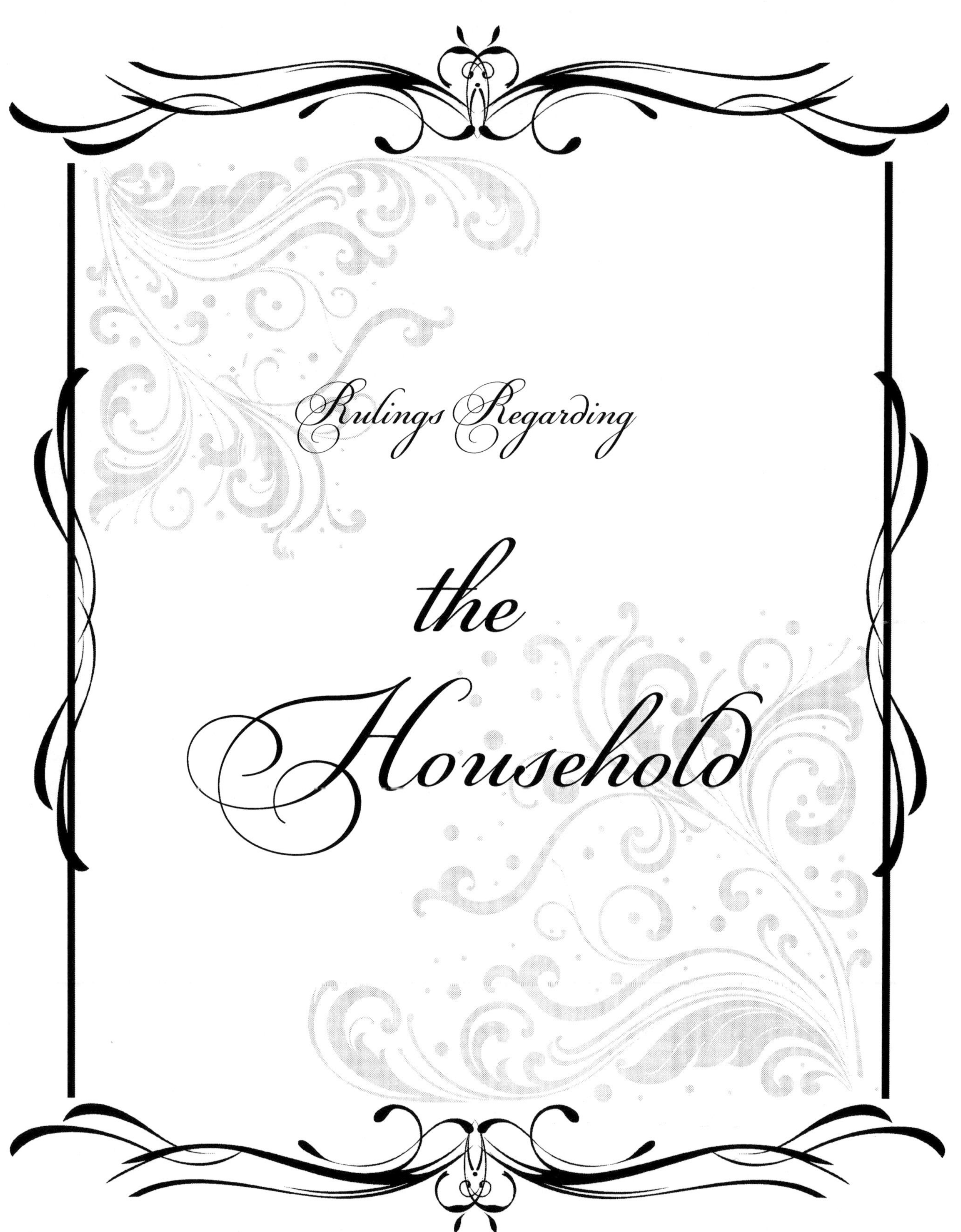

Rulings Regarding the Household

The Salafi House

Question: What are the physical attributes which should be found in the Salafi house?

Answer from Sheikh al-Albaani, may Allaah have mercy upon him: It is not possible to restrict the answer; as this differs from one person to another. As it is sufficient for the illiterate man to have a cupboard to keep his food, for example, while the scholar will additionally need a cupboard or shelf in which to keep books in. So each case is relative, and every person is aware of that which is necessary for him, or is not necessary for him. For example, the prayer rug; is it something which must be present in the Salafi household? The answer is no- it is sufficient to have an ordinary rug, one that is not adorned or of exceptional quality. Even this rug differs from one place to another. In a cold country, the rug is necessary; indeed it needs to be made of wool (for warmth). As for the hot country, if one sits upon the ground, a large room rug is itself not necessary, let alone a prayer rug as well. So in relation to that, the case is relative, as it differs from place to place- for example an air conditioner is necessary in hot countries, to assist one in seeking knowledge, whereas in Syria there is no necessity for it, as a small fan will take care of the heat. So the case cannot be specified in regard to every person in every place. ("*al-Haawee min al-Fatawaa ash-Sheikh al-Albaani*" Collected by Abu Yusuf Muhammad ibn Ibraaheem, Pages 462-463)

Spending of Wealth

Question: There is textual evidence that Allaah loves to see the sign of His blessings upon His worshipper; and some of the women spend a lot of money on their clothing and matters concerning beautification. What do you say in regard to this?

Answer from Sheikh Saalih ibn Fauzaan ibn 'Abdullah al-Fauzaan, may Allaah preserve him: The one whom Allaah blesses bestows permissible wealth, Allaah has blessed him with this favor, and it is obligatory upon him to be grateful for it. This is through giving charity with it, and purchasing food and clothing- but this is without extravagance or that which is doubtful. And the action of some of the women, spending extravagantly or excessively when purchasing clothing, or buying a lot of things without necessity, is only out of pride or a desire to show off and keep up with the latest fashions advertised- all of that is from the wastefulness and extravagance which is prohibited, and wasting money.

It is obligatory upon the Muslim woman to be moderate in regards to that, and to stay far away from *at-tabarruj (*going out dressed or beautified in an improper manner) and exaggeration concerning matters of beautification- especially when leaving the house.

Allaah, the Most High, says, ***﴾and do not display yourselves like that of the times of ignorance﴿***- (Surat al-Ahzaab, From Ayat 33)

And He, the Most High, says, ***﴾And tell the believing women to lower their gaze (from looking at forbidden things), and protect their private parts (from illegal sexual acts) and not to show off their adornment except***

that which is apparent to His, the Most High, saying, ***And let them not stamp their feet so as to reveal what they hide of their adornment.***- (Surat an-Noor, From Ayat 31)

And we will be asked concerning this wealth on the Day of Judgment, as to where we acquired it, and how we spent it. ("*Naseehah wa Fatawaa Khaasat bil-Mara'at al-Muslimah*", a collection of rulings and advices from Sheikh Fauzaan, Page 71)

Question: If a Muslim woman makes a lot of different food, and makes it attractive in order to make her husband happy, is this from the vanity in the world and worldly things which we are responsible for from wealth and luxury?

Answer from Sheikh Muqbil ibn Haadee al-Wadi'ee, may Allaah have mercy upon him: There is no problem with this, insh'Allaah- however *az-zuhd* (abstinence, simplicity) is better. Allaah, Glorified is He, and Most High, says, ***Oh Children of Adam! Take your adornment (by wearing your clean clothes) while praying [and going round the Ka'bah], and eat and drink but waste not by extravagance, certainly He (Allaah) likes not al-Musrifoon (those who waste by extravagance).***- (Surat al-A'raaf, Ayat 31)

So if there is anything left from the food, do not throw it away. Rather, it is necessary that it goes out to the poor and destitute. The matter is simple, insh'Allaah- it is not necessary to restrict or oppress ourselves, but *az-zuhd* is better, and the state upon which the Prophet, may Allaah's praise and salutations be upon him and his family, was upon is best. It has been narrated from 'Umar, may Allaah be pleased with him, and look at its truthfulness, "*Prepare yourself for a rough life, as indeed the blessings do not endure.*" (Narrated by Ibn Abi Shaybah in "*Kitaab al-Aadaab*", No. 80. Its chain of narrations is weak, however it has other narrations which support and strengthen it)

It is necessary that we prepare for rough times, and prepare for hunger, so that when the matter occurs we do not remain as though we are young chickens- it is necessary that we become accustomed to deprivation. And Allaah knows best. ("*Fataawa al-Mar'at al-Muslimah*" Pages 368-369. Originally found in "Questions from the Young Algerian Women")

Listening to the Qur'aan while Working in the House

Question: I spend a good portion of time- long hours- in the kitchen in order to prepare food for my husband. I wish to benefit from my time, so I listen to the Noble Qur'aan, either on the radio, or a recording. Is my action in this correct, or is it not proper for me to do this, as Allaah, the Most High, says, "So, when the Qur'aan is recited, listen to it, and be silent that you may receive mercy.*﴾- (Surat *al-A'araaf, From Ayat 204)

Answer from Sheikh Saalih al-Fauzaan, may Allaah preserve him: There is no problem with listening to the Noble Qur'aan on the radio or from a recording while people are working, and there is no contradiction between this and His saying, "...listen to it, and be silent..." because the silence is required in accordance to that which is possible- so the one who is working is quiet and listens to the amount that he is able. ("*Fataawa al-Mar'at al-Muslimah*", a collection of rulings concerning women from various scholars, Page 578)

Review and Discussion Questions

Questions for Rulings regarding the household

Review:

1. What verse does Sheikh Muqbil bring concerning the encouragement to az-zuhd? (Top half of Page 194)

Discussion & Consideration:

2. How can we find balance in our households between being miserly and spending extravagantly?
3. What are some possible examples of how we can fulfill our obligations to the household but still benefit in a secondary way at the same time?

Rulings Regarding Marriage

Regarding Living with the Wives Honorably

***Q**uestion: Some of the young men, may Allaah guide them, are generally concerned with adhering to the religion, yet they do not live with their wives honorably, as they busy themselves working a great deal, or spending their time studying and working- but they leave their wives alone or with their children in the house for long periods of time, due to their needing to work or study. What do you, Esteemed Sheikhs, say, concerning that, and are work and seeking of knowledge to be done at the expense of the time for the wife? Benefit me, and may Allaah benefit you.*

Answer from Sheikh 'Abdul 'Aziz ibn Baaz, may Allaah have mercy upon him: There is no doubt that it is obligatory upon the husbands to live with their wives in an honorable fashion, as Allaah, Glorified and Exalted, says,

﴾***...and live with them honorably.***﴿- (Surat an-Nisaa, From Ayat 19)

As well as His, Glorified is He, saying, ﴾***And they (women) have rights (over their husbands as regards living expenses) similar (to those of their husbands) over them (as regards obedience and respect) to what is reasonable, but men have a degree (of responsibility) over them. And Allaah is All-Mighty, All-Wise.***﴿- (Surat al-Baqara, From Ayat 228)

Also, the saying of the Prophet, may Allaah's praise and salutations be upon him, to 'Abdullah ibn 'Amr ibn al-'Aas, may Allaah be pleased with them both, to the one who busied himself with standing in the night prayer, and fasting during the day, ***{Fast, and break the fast. Sleep, and stand in prayer. Fast from each month three days, as every good deed is worth ten like it. As you have a right upon yourself, and your wife has a right upon you, and your guest has a right upon you- so give to each one his rights.}*** (Authentic, narrated in al-Bukhaari, 1153,1976,1977,1978,1979,3418,3419,5052, and Muslim 2/812, 1159, at-Tirmidhi, 3/550, Abu Daawud, 1/739, 2427, and others)

As well as other *ahaadeeth* which have been reported concerning this. So that which is legislated for the young men and other than them is that they live with their wives honorably, and to beautify this living, and if it is possible for them to do their research or some of their other jobs in their home, whenever it is possible, then that is best for the family and children. So in any case, it is legislated for the husband to set aside a time for his wife, in order to make her happy, and treat her well. Especially if she is alone in the house and does not have anyone else with her except her children, or she does not have anyone to spend time with. As he, may Allaah's praise and salutations be upon him, said, ***{The best of you is the one who is best to his family, and I am the best of you to my family.}*** (Authentic, narrated by at-Tirmidhi, 10/363, 3904, Ibn Hibaan, 9/484, 4177, and ad-Daaramee, 2/159 by way of Hishaam ibn 'Urwah from his father, from 'Aishah) And his, may Allaah's praise and salutations be upon him, saying, ***{The believers who have the most perfect faith are those with excellent character, and the best of you are the ones who are best to their wives.}*** (*Hasan*, from the hadeeth of Abi Hurairah, may Allaah be pleased with him)

It is legislated for the wife that she cooperate with her husband in that which he must perform from studying or work, and to be patient concerning that which occurs of the shortening of time with her which cannot be avoided, so that there comes about cooperation between them, thus acting upon the saying of Allaah, Glorified and Exalted,

﴾***Help you one another in al-birr and at-taqwa (virtue, righteousness and piety)***﴿- (Surat al-Ma'idah, From Ayat 2) as well as the generality of his (the Messenger of Allaah's) saying, may Allaah's praise and salutations be upon him, ***{The one who is concerned with the needs of his brother, Allaah is concerned with his needs.}*** (Authentic) And his, may Allaah's praise and salutations be upon him, saying, ***{And Allaah assists the worshipper, as the worshipper assists his brother.}*** *(*Authentic*)* (From "*Fatawaa Islaamiyyah*", 3/213, 214, as quoted in "*at-Tuhfat al-Baaziyyah fee al-Fataawa an-Nisaaiyyah*", Volume 2, Pages 185-186)

Question: What is the Islamic ruling in your opinion concerning the one who beats his wife and takes from her wealth, and does these with severity, and he treats her in an evil manner?

Answer from Sheikh al-'Utheimeen, may Allaah have mercy upon him: This person who beats his wife, takes from her wealth, and treats her in an evil manner is a wrongdoer, disobedient to Allaah; as Allaah, the Most High, says,

﴾***...and live with them honorably.***﴿- (Surat an-Nisaa, From Ayat 19)

And His, the Most High, saying, ﴾***And they (women) have rights (over their husbands as regards living expenses) similar (to those of their husbands) over them (as regards obedience and respect) to what is reasonable***﴿- (Surat al-Baqara, From Ayat 229)

And it is not permissible for him to treat his wife in this evil manner and then to go and demand from her that she treat him in a good manner, as this is from the oppression or injustice which falls under His, the Most High, saying,

﴾***Woe to al-mutaffifoon (those who give less in measure and weight). Those who, when they have to receive by measure from men, demand full measure, And when they have to give by measure or weight to (other) men, give less than due.***﴿- (Surat al-Mutafiffeen, Ayats 1-3)

So every person who takes his full right from the people, then does not give the people their full right, then he is included under these noble verses.

And that which I advise this person, and those like him, with, is: To fear Allaah concerning the women, as the Prophet, may Allaah's praise and salutations be upon him, commanded in his *khutbah* at 'Arafaat the year of the Farewell Pilgrimage, when he said, ***{Fear Allaah concerning the women, as you have taken them as a trust from Allaah and they have been made permissible for you by the Word of Allaah.}*** (Muslim 2212, Ibn Maajah 3072, Ibn Hibaan 1473, Sunan Ad-Daaramee 1842)

And I say to him, and the likes of him: It is not possible for you to have a happy life until the spouses treat each other with justice, goodness, and overlooking that which offends and taking notice of and acknowledging that which is good.

The Prophet, may Allaah's praise and salutations be upon him, said, ***{The believing man should not dislike a believing women, as if he dislikes one aspect of her character, there is another aspect which he will be pleased with.}*** (Muslim 2750, Musnah Ahmad 8179) (Collected in "*al-Fataawa al-Qayyimah lil-Usrat al-Muslimah*" Collected by Sa'eed 'Abdul-Ghafaar 'Ali, Pages 105-106)

Rights and Obligations of the Wife

Question: What are the rights of the wife, and those things which are obligatory upon her?

Answer from Sheikh Muhammad ibn Saalih al-'Utheimeen, may Allaah have mercy upon him: The rights and obligations of the wife and those matters which are upon her, are not necessarily specifically itemized in the legislation. Rather, they also refer back to that which is customary among people, as Allaah, the Most High, says, ***﴿...and live with them honorably﴾***- (Surat an-Nisaa, From Ayat 19), and His saying, ***﴿And they (women) have rights (over their husbands as regards living expenses) similar (to those of their husbands) over them (as regards obedience and respect) to what is reasonable﴾***- (Surat al-Baqara, From Ayat 228)

So that which is held to be customary among people concerning rights, then that is obligatory, and that which is not held to be customary, then it is not obligatory, except for those things which differ from that which is clearly Islamically legislated. So if it is the custom of the people that the man not command his family to perform the prayer, or to beautify their characters, then this is a false, wrong custom and is considered null and void. As for when the custom of the people does not differ from the Islamic legislation, then Allaah has referred to this in the preceding verses.

It is obligatory upon the ones responsible for the household to fear Allaah concerning that which Allaah has made them responsible for- and this is from both the men and the women- and that they not neglect these things. As it occurs that the man may neglect his children, both the boys and the girls, as he does not ask about which ones are absent, or present, and he does not sit with them. And a month or two may go by and he does not spend time with his children or wife. This is a tremendous error. Indeed, we advise our brothers to gather together with the family and to not be isolated, and that lunch and dinner be eaten with the family together- however without the wife sitting with men who are not *mahram* for her, as this is from those things which occur among the people from the evil customs which differ from the Islamic legislation, that they men and women all gather together to eat, even if they are not *mahram* for one another. ("*Fataawa al-Mar'at al-Muslimah*", a collection of rulings concerning women from various scholars, Page 279)

Notes

Question: I am a woman who obeys her husband and follows the commands of Allaah, but I cannot meet my husband with joy and a clear face, because he does not fulfill that which is obligatory for him in the matter of providing me with clothing, and I shunned and turned away from him in my bed- so is there any sin upon me?

Answer from Sheikh Saalih ibn Fauzaan ibn 'Abdullah al-Fauzaan, may Allaah preserve him: Allaah, Glorified and Most High, has made it obligatory to have good relations between the husband and the wife, and that both of them give to the other his or her rights, so that they bring benefit to the marriage. And it is upon the husband and wife to be patient concerning the shortcomings of the other spouse, and with problems in their relationship, and to fulfill their obligations, as this is from the reasons which bring about a lasting marriage, its working well together and the endurance of the marriage. So my advice to you is to be patient with your husband's shortcomings, and to give your husband his rights. That way, by the grace of Allaah, your ending will, insh'Allaah, be good. And through giving him his rights, it may come about that he would be encouraged to give you your rights as well. ("*Naseehah wa Fatawaa Khaasat bil-Mara'at al-Muslimah*", a collection of rulings and advices from Sheikh Fauzaan, Page 57)

Question: A wife falls short in fulfilling her obligations to her husband, her children, and her house, and she wishes to have a servant. Should she get a servant?

Answer from Sheikh Muhammad ibn Saalih al-Utheimeen, may Allaah have mercy upon him: The matter of having a servant has become one of pride and vanity if one does not truly have a need for one. And much of what comes about due to that is only a great trial; for example adultery or fornication between the owner of the house or his teenage sons and the servant, and such as occurs from the men who are servants entering the house, and what occurs from trials to the women of the house. Due to that, it is required that you do not bring servants into the house except if there is an extreme need to do so, and the servant must have a *mahram* with her.

As for the woman who desires a servant due to having a lot of housework, then it is necessary that her husband say to her," I am going to marry another Muslim woman, to assist you in the housework!" Then this wife will cease to ask for this thing.

In reality, this beneficial remedy is of advantage to the man, as all that increases marriages is best, and marrying more than one wife, if the man is able to fulfill his obligations, is better than restricting it. And the Prophet, may Allaah's praise and salutations be upon him, said, ***{Marry the ones who are loving and bear many children, as I hope my ummah will be expanded through you.}*** (Collected by Ahmad, at-Tabaraanee, and Abi Daawud by meaning) If the people are afraid due to the matters which occur between the two wives, then we say to him: Bring in a third, as this eases the disputes between the first two, as has been seen. Concerning this, they say that the one with three has it easier than the one with two. And if disputes occur between the three, then bring in a fourth. ("*Fataawa al-Mar'at al-Muslimah*", a collection of rulings concerning women from various scholars, Page 278)

Q*uestion: Is it permissible for the husband to take pleasure in the whole of his wife's body, front and back, including between her buttocks, while not entering her anus?*

Answer from the Permanent Committee of Scholars in Saudi Arabia, may Allaah preserve them all: It is permissible for the man to take pleasure with his wife from any aspect of her body, excluding only the anus, intercourse during her menses or post childbirth bleeding, during *ihraam* for *Hajj* or *Umrah* until they have totally completed the rites.

And Allaah grants all success, and may Allaah's praise and salutations be upon our prophet Muhammad, and his family and companions. ("*Fataawa al-Lajnatu ad-Daa'imah*" 19/251, as quoted in "*Qatf al-Azhaar al-Mutanaathirah min Fataawa al-Mar'at al-Muslimah*" Volume 2, Page 607)

Concerning the Woman Raising her Voice to her Husband

Q*uestion: What is the ruling concerning the woman raising her voice to her husband during conversation or argument?*

Answer from the Permanent Committee of Scholars in Saudi Arabia, may Allaah preserve them all: That which is permissible is that the husband and wife speak to each other in a manner which brings about love and affection, and which strengthens the marriage bonds, and that they both avoid raising their voices to their companion, or speaking in a manner which is disliked. Allaah, Glorified and Exalted is He, says, ﴾***...and live with them honorably...***﴿- (Surat an-Nisaa'a, From Ayat 19) It is not proper for her to raise her voice to him, as Allaah, Glorified is He, says, "***And they (women) have rights (over their husbands as regards living expenses) similar (to those of their husbands) over them (as regards obedience and respect) to what is reasonable, but men have a degree (of responsibility) over them.***﴿- (Surat al-Baqara, From Ayat 228)

However, it is necessary that the husband remedy any problem with that which is most suitable, in order that the strong emotion not be further intensified. And with Allaah is the success, and may Allaah's praise be upon our Prophet, Muhammad, his family, and his companions, and Allaah's salutations. ("*Fataawa al-Lejnatu ad-Daa'imah*" 19/247 as found in the book, "*Qatf al-Azhaar al-Mutanaathirah min Fataawa al-Mar'at al-Muslimah*" Page 623)

Review and Discussion Questions

Questions regarding rulings regarding marriage

Review:

1. What evidences does Sheikh Bin Baaz, may Allaah have mercy upon him, cite as proof that men must live with their wives honorably?? (Top half of Page 199)
2. What are three things that Sheikh Fauzaan, may Allaah preserve him, recommends for a successful, lasting marriage? (Top half of Page 202)

Discussion & Consideration:

3. After studying this section, list some of the proofs given that the husband and wife should do their best to give each other their rights, and support and encourage each other in their individual undertakings? List five ways you can implement this in your own married life.
4. What advice would you give to the woman who desires that her husband hire a servant?

Rulings Regarding

Polygeny

***Question:** A noble verse is mentioned in the Noble Qur'aan in regard to the place of polygeny (the practice of the man being permitted to marry up to four wives at one time) which says,*

﴾*...but if you fear that you shall not be able to deal justly (with them), then only one...*﴿- (Surat *an-Nisaa, From Ayat 3)*

And in another place, He, the Most High, says, "You will never be able to do perfect justice between wives even if it is your ardent desire﴿- (Surat *an-Nisaa, From Ayat 129)*

So in the first, justice to the spouses if there is more than one is made a condition, while in the second it is made clear that the condition of justice is not possible to attain. Does this mean that the first verse is abrogated, and the marrying of more than one wife is not allowed because the condition of justice is impossible to achieve?

Answer from Sheikh 'Abdul 'Aziz ibn Baaz, may Allaah have mercy upon him: There is no contradiction between the two verses, nor is this a case wherein the first of the two is abrogated by the second. Indeed the justice which is commanded is that which is possible, and that is justice concerning the division of time and the giving of provisions. As for justice in love, the desire for intercourse, and such as these, then this is not possible. And this is what is meant in the saying of the Most High,

﴾***You will never be able to do perfect justice between wives even if it is your ardent desire***﴿- (Surat an-Nisaa, From Ayat 129)

Concerning this it has been established from the Prophet, may Allaah's praise and salutations be upon him, from the hadeeth of 'Aishah, may Allaah be pleased with her, in which she said, "The Messenger of Allaah, may Allaah's praise and salutations be upon him, divided between his wives and was fair, and he said, ***{Oh Allaah, this is my division in that which I am capable; so do not blame me for that which you are in possession of and which I do not possess.}*** (Abu Daawud, at-Tirmidhi, an-Nasaa'ee, Ibn Maajah, and Ibn Hibaan and al-Haakim have declared it to be authentic. This hadeeth comes through various chains, and is either *hasan* or *saheeh*, Allaah knows best) And with Allaah is the Success. ("*Fataawa al-Mar'at*", Pages 108-109) as quoted in "*at-Tuhfat al-Baaziyyah fee al-Fataawa an-Nisaa'iyyah*" Vol. 2, Page 228)

***Question:** A married man travelled from his country to another country, then married in the country in which he was staying without the knowledge of his first wife. Is this permissible according to the Islamic legislation?*

Answer from the Permanent Committee of Scholars in Saudi Arabia, may Allaah preserve them: It is permissible for him to marry a second wife without the permission of the first- indeed, even without her knowledge, as long as he sees a benefit in that, and he is able to support the wives and deal justly between the two wives or all of the wives in that which he is capable of, as Allaah, the Most High, says,

﴾***And if you fear that you shall not be able to deal justly with the orphan girls then marry (other) women of your choice, two or three, or four; but if***

you fear that you shall not be able to deal justly (with them), then only one or (slaves) that your right hands possess. That is nearer to prevent you from doing injustice.﴿- (Surat an-Nisaa', Ayat 3)

And from Allaah is the success, and may His praise and salutations be upon our Prophet, his family, and his Companions. ("*Fataawa al-Lejnatu ad-Daa'imah*", 19/79, as quoted in "*Qatf al-Azhaar al-Mutanaathirah min Fataawa al-Mar'at al-Muslimah*" Vol. 2, Page 634-635)

Question: Some of the women object to the matter of polygeny, or they object to their husbands entering into it- does this matter enter into some aspect of hypocrisy?

Answer from Sheikh 'Abdul 'Aziz bin Baaz, may Allaah have mercy upon him: It is upon her to be content with the ruling of Allaah; however, her being pleased with having a companion co-wife- then this is not required. However, it is upon her to be content with the general ruling of Allaah concerning polygeny, and Allaah's wisdom is great and far-reaching. It is not permissible for her to dislike that or to deny it- but as regards to her being personally pleased, then some people cannot bear it; but it is upon her to listen to and obey her husband if she is able. And if she is not able due to circumstances, and she seeks a divorce, then this is due to her, and it is not required that her husband comply with her in this. However, if due to polygeny he sees from her that which he does not like, and that which is harmful, then it is better if he separates from her, as some of the women cannot endure this. ("*Fatawaa Kitaab ad-Da'wah*", 4/216, as quoted in "*at-Tuhfat al-Baaziyyah fee al-Fataawa an-Nisaa'iyyah*" Vol. 2, Page 229)

Review and Discussion Questions

Questions Regarding Rulings regarding Polygeny

Review:

1. What does the "justice" referred to in the verses concerning polygeny refer to? (Top half of Page 207)
2. Is it necessary that the first wife be informed that the husband is going to marry another? Explain. (Bottom half of Page 207, Top half of Page 208)

Discussion & Consideration:

3. If a woman dislikes that her husband marry a second wife, does this make her a hypocrite? Explain.
4. What practical advice can you come up with for yourself and others concerning dealing with the fact of polygeny? What are some things that might help to ensure that your marriage is a strong, successful one, and that you have retain a good relationship with your husband?

Rulings Regarding Children

An Exhortation to have many Children

Question: A young man married and has three children, and he says, "My wife and I decided to prevent further pregnancies so that we may be able to raise our children with a correct Islamic upbringing, and to attempt to keep distant the many temptations that surround them. What is your opinion of this, may Allaah reward you?

Answer from Sheikh Muhammad ibn Saalih al-'Utheimeen, may Allaah have mercy upon him, said,

All praise is due to Allaah, Lord of the worlds, and I ask that His praise and salutations be upon our Prophet Muhammad, his family, his companions, and all those who follow them in righteousness until the Day of Judgment.

To Proceed:

This solution is not correct- I mean, the prevention of procreation, as this differs from that which the Prophet, may Allaah's praise and salutations be upon him and his family, guided to, since he said, ***{Marry the ones who are loving and fruitful, as I desire to have the most followers from the prophets on the Day of Judgment.}*** (Collected by Ahmad in his "*Musnad*" (13569) and at-Tabaraanee in ("*al-Awsat*", 5099, from the hadeeth of Anas, may Allaah be pleased with him, and Sheikh al-Albaani has declared it to be authentic due to a supporting hadeeth collected by Abi Daawud)

Because a person does not know if perhaps those children which he already has may die and he will be left with no progeny. The explanation that it (not having more children) is for the sake of having control over their upbringing and perhaps fulfilling the act of providing for them, is in reality an unsound justification. This is because righteousness is only by the Hand of Allaah, Glorified and Exalted is He. And education and upbringing is undoubtedly a cause as well- and how many of the people do not have but one child and fail in regards to his education and upbringing; and how many of the people have ten children and Allaah makes it possible to carry out their education and make them righteous by His Hand?

There is no doubt that the one who says, "If there are many children, it is not possible to control them"- this is having the bad suspicion of Allaah, Glorified and Exalted is He. And perhaps he will be punished for this suspicion. Rather, the steadfast believer performs those things which are legislated which are causes for success in undertaking education and upbringing and asks Allaah for assistance and success. And when Allaah knows from him that he is truthful and correct in his intention, Allaah will rectify his affairs for him.

So I say to the brother who asked the question: Do not do this- do not stop having children, do not stop having children. Have as many children as you are able, as their sustenance is upon Allaah, and their piety is upon Allaah. And the more you increase in educating and bringing them up, the more you will increase in reward. As if you have three and you teach them good character and educate and raise them well, you only have the reward for three. But if you have ten, then you are rewarded for ten- and you do not know if perhaps Allaah will make from those ten scholars and fighters in the way of Allaah who will benefit the Islamic *Ummah*, and that will be from the signs of your performance of good deeds. Have many children, and Allaah will increase your wealth, and make your provisions plentiful. (End of Sheikh al-'Utheimeen's exhortation)

(From "Fataawa Noor 'ala ad-Darb") as quoted in, "Tarbiyat al-Abnaa': Sawaal wa Jawaab", Pages 10-11)

Rulings Regarding Birth Control

Question: What is the ruling on the woman taking birth control pills, or using an I.U.D or diaphragm (meaning, a barrier method of some sort) for contraception, particularly when it is a method which is specifically utilized by the woman?

Answer from Sheikh Muqbil ibn Haadee al-Wadi'ee, may Allaah have mercy upon him: That which I advise you with is *al-'azl* (العزل) (this is what is known in the West as "withdrawal", wherein the man removes his private parts from inside the woman before ejaculation occurs), as this is what has been mentioned (in the Sunnah). As for the birth control pill, then in it there is harm, as well as blind following of the enemies of Islaam. From its harms is that it may cause inflammation or infection of the womb, which requires medical treatment- and this treatment may cure it, or it may not. Likewise the issue of using the barrier method- it, itself may break, or cause damage, or perhaps the sperm will come out, or it may cause irritation to the male organ, or the device may come out with the intimate relations. So that which I advise you with is the *al-'azl*, as it is that which has been mentioned and the Prophet, may Allaah's praise and salutations be upon him and his family, has permitted it.

("Fataawa al-Mar'at al-Muslimah", Pages 242-243)

Question: The questioner asks concerning the one who uses the birth control pill, or the injection, or al-'azl (withdrawal) to prevent contraception...

Answer from Sheikh Muqbil ibn Haadee al-Wadi'ee, may Allaah have mercy upon him:

As for the pill and the injection, then I do not know of them that they are established in the source texts. It is not proper to use them, because Allaah, Glorified is He, the Most High, says in His Noble Book, ﴾***And kill not your children for fear of poverty.***﴿- (Surat al-Israa, from Ayat 31)

And the Prophet, may Allaah's praise and salutations be upon him and his family, said, ***{Marry and have children, because I will compete with you against the other nations on the Day of Judgment.}*** (Abu Daawud and other than him, from Ma'qil ibn Yasaar, may Allaah be pleased with him, and it has many supporting narrations and Sheikh al-Albaani has declared it authentic in "*as-Sunan*" and Sheikh Muqbil, may Allaah have mercy upon him, in his collection, "*Kitaab an-Nikaah*") And the Prophet, may Allaah's praise and salutations be upon him and his family, has informed man that Allaah will increase his wealth and children. (al-Bukhaari, 6378 and Muslim 268 and 141)

As for *al-'azl*, then it is permissible, and some of the people say that is permissible, but is disliked. It is permissible because Jaabir Ibn 'Abdullah, may Allaah be pleased with him, said, "*We practiced al-'azl during the period in which the Qur'aan was being revealed.*" (al-Bukhaari, 5208, and Muslim, 1440) And it has been reported that the Prophet, may Allaah's praise and salutations be upon him and his family, said when asked concerning *al-'azl*, ***{It is the lesser burying alive.}*** (Muslim, 141 from 'Aishah, may Allaah be pleased with her) And the Prophet, may Allaah's praise and salutations be upon him, said, ***{There are none from the souls but that if Allaah decrees its creation, then it is created.}*** (Muslim, 30-31) So using the withdrawal method of birth control is permissible. As for using the birth control pill or likewise the injection to prevent pregnancy, then this is not permissible due to that which is known regarding it. And this is that Allaah, Glorified is He, the Most High, said, ***﴾And kill not your children for fear of poverty.﴿*** - (Surat al-Israa, from Ayat 31). And in another verse, ***﴾kill not your children because of poverty﴿*** - (Surat al-An'aam, From Ayat 151)

So it is proper to know that Allaah, Glorified is He, the Most High, is more merciful to His worshippers than any person could be; He is the Most Merciful to the woman, and the Most Merciful to the child, and he is the Most Merciful to the married one; however, *al-'azl* is permitted.

("Fataawa al-Mar'at al-Muslimah" Pages 243-244)

Question: A woman has a small, ill child, and she is pregnant again. So she finds it difficult to care for her present children, and she finds the pregnancy difficult as well. Is it all right for her, after she gives birth this time, to use birth control pills?

Answer from Sheikh Muqbil ibn Haadee al-Wadi'ee, may Allaah have mercy upon him:

I advise her to entrust her affair with Allaah. And if she fears harm for herself, and if a Muslim doctor who is a specialist in this area has said that damage may come to her, and she may die due to pregnancy, then it is permissible for her to use that (the birth control pill).

("Fataawa al-Mar'at al-Muslimah", Page 245)

Regarding Naming of Children

Question: Allaah, Glorified is He, the Most High, has blessed me with a daughter, and I would like to give her one name, and my wife wants to name her something else. I proposed to her that we draw lots on paper with the two names, and name her according to the outcome of this drawing of lots- so is this from those things which are appropriate? And if it is not so, then how do we resolve this difference? And is the naming the right of the father, only? Benefit us, may Allaah give you good.

Answer from Sheikh 'Abdul 'Aziz ibn Baaz, may Allaah have mercy upon him: In this situation, drawing lots is from the accepted legislated matters, according to that which it contains for remedying the situation and pleasing the people involved. The Prophet, may Allaah's praise and salutations be upon him, used it in many matters, and it has been narrated from him that he, may Allaah's praise and salutations be upon him, drew lots between his wives when he had to travel, and the one whom the marked lot indicated went with him. (The hadeeth concerning this is found in al-Bukhaari, 2593, and Muslim, 8196). Also, when he advised the man to free some slaves, and he had six, and he did not have other than them, the Prophet, may Allaah's praise and salutations be upon him, drew lots between them, and he freed two, and kept four. (Muslim, 4425)

The naming of the child is from the rights of the father; however it is recommended that he consult the mother concerning this, in order to reconcile the two of them, and join their hearts. It is legislated for both of them that they choose good names, and avoid the disliked names. And it is not permissible to name them as the worshipper of other than Allaah, such as 'Abd an-Nabee (worshipper of the Prophet), 'Abd al-Ka'bah (worshipper of the Ka'bah), 'Abd al-Husayn, or similar to these. This is because all of worship is for Allaah, Glorified is He, and it is not permissible to worship other than Him.

And it has been related from the famous scholar Abu Muhammad ibn Hazm, that there is consensus among the scholars that this forbiddance of naming one as a worshipper of other than Allaah does not include 'Abd al-Mutalib, because the Prophet, may Allaah's praise and salutations be upon him, allowed this name for some of his companions, may Allaah be pleased with all of them. (He is 'Abd al-Mutalib, ibn Rabi'ah, ibn al-Haarith, ibn 'Abd al- Mutalib, ibn Haashim, al-Qursh al-Haashimee, and he is the son of the paternal uncle of the Prophet, may Allaah's praise and salutations be upon him.) And with Allaah is the success.

(From "Fatawaa Islaamiyyah lil-Musnad", 3/221, as found in the book, "Qatf al-Azhaar al-Mutanaathirah min Fataawa al Mar'at al Muslimah" Volume 2, Pages 491-492)

Question: Is it permissible to name my son Jibreel or Meekaa'eel? (These are the names of two of Allaah's angels)

Answer from Sheikh Rabee'a al-Madkhalee, may Allaah preserve him: It is not forbidden- one is not forbidden from that. There is no prohibition concerning naming with the names of the companions, the generation after them, the scholars, and the prophets. As for naming with Jibreel, then there is no harm in that.

(From the tape called, "Inna Allaah la Yanza' al-Ilm Antazaa'an" as quoted in the book, "Qatf al-Azhaar al-Mutanaathirah min Fataawa al-Mar'at al-Muslimah" Volume 2, Page 494)

Nursing of Children

Question: Concerning the woman who "nurses" her child with formula, and not her own milk- is this considered nursing from the viewpoint of Islaam?

Answer from Sheikh al-Albaani, may Allaah have mercy upon him: Unquestionably, there are no texts upon this matter, so that it is from those matters whose answer must come from independent reasoning based upon evidence (الإجتهاد). That which is most apparent to me, and Allaah knows best, is that it is not considered nursing, because in the case of her "nursing" her child with the formula, then she does not exert herself and does not use her own body's nourishment as nourishment for her child. As for reserving all of her nourishment for herself, then this is like not nursing.

("al-Haawee min al-Fatawaa ash-Sheikh al-Albaani" Collected by Abu Yusuf Muhammad ibn Ibraaheem, Page 458)

Toys for Children and Teaching Children through the use of Pictures

Question: Here there are many types of dolls; from them are some that are made of cotton, and they are constructed of a sack or bag connected to a head, two hands and two legs. From them are some which resemble a human completely, and from them are those that talk or cry or walk. What is the ruling concerning making or buying the likes of these types for small girls in order to educate them and for their amusement?

Answer from Sheikh al-'Utheimeen, may Allaah have mercy upon him: As for those which are not found to be a complete or perfect image of a human being, in which there are limbs and a head but their resemblance to creation is not obvious or plain, then there is no doubt as to their permissibility, and that they are in the form of the dolls which 'Aishah, may Allaah be pleased with her, played with. As for those that completely resemble creation as though one were seeing a person, especially those which move or have a voice, then I find in myself that which causes me to dislike them and doubt their permissibility because they imitate Allaah's creation. That which is evident is that the dolls which 'Aishah, may Allaah be pleased with her, played with did not have these attributes and so it is best to avoid them. However, I do not place upon them the definite ruling of being forbidden, as the small children have that which is allowed to them, which is not allowed to adults in matters similar to this. As the children are naturally disposed to play and amusement and are not responsible for anything from the acts of worship, so that we say, "His time is wasted upon play and frivolity." And when the people desire to be cautious concerning this type of thing, then remove the head, or heat it so that it becomes soft, then squeeze or compress it until its features are removed.

("Majmoo' al-Fatawaa", 2/277, as quoted in "Qatf al-Azhaar al-Mutanaathirah min Fataawa al-Mar'at al-Muslimah", Pages 817-818)

Question: There are statements and rulings about children's toys which have become numerous. So what is the ruling concerning the dolls and animals and three dimensional toys with human form? There are some who have allowed keeping them with the condition that they are debased and that they are not given much importance; and there are some who have completely prohibited them. So what is the correct ruling? And what is the ruling of using the flash cards which have upon them pictures for teaching the children letters and numbers or the manner of performing wudhoo and salaat?

Answer from Sheikh Saalih al-Fauzaan, may Allaah preserve him: It is not correct to keep the pictures of things with souls except for necessary pictures like the pictures on the driver's license, that which is needed protect oneself, and the identity card. And pictures other than these are not allowed to be kept for children's toys or for teaching them because of the generality of the prohibition of picture making and their use. And there are many children's toys without pictures and there are other methods of teaching them without pictures. And whoever allowed the pictures for children's toys, then his saying is not sound because he is depending upon the hadeeth of 'Aishah the day when she was small. And it is said that the hadeeth of 'Aishah is abrogated by the narrations which prohibit the pictures. And it is said that the forms (dolls) were mentioned in it were not like the forms (dolls) of today. They were only made from pieces of cloth and sticks as was known in their time; they did not resemble animals in the same way as those toy animals which are known now. And this latter statement is the most correct saying. And Allaah knows best. And the pictures which we have now look exactly like animals, and some of them even move like animals.

("al-Fataawa al-Qayyimah lil-Usrat al-Muslimah", Pages 169-170)

Question: What is the ruling upon making dolls out of clay and then kneading it back into a formless lump?

Answer from Sheikh al-'Utheimeen, may Allaah have mercy upon him: Whoever makes something which competes with the creation of Allaah, then he is included in the meaning of the hadeeth, ***{The Prophet, may Allaah's praise and salutations be upon him, cursed those who make pictures.}*** (Bukharee 5038) And the hadeeth, ***{The most severely punished people on the Day of Judgment are those who made pictures.}*** (Bukhaaree 5613, Muslim 4030, Al-Haakim: 5235, at-Tirmidhi 335) However, if it is as you said, it is not a clear picture- meaning, it does not have eyes or nose or mouth or fingers- then this is not a complete picture and is not competing with the creation of Allaah.

("al-Fataawa al-Qayyimah lil-Usrat al-Muslimah", Page 206)

Question: Many toys have hand-drawn pictures of living things with souls (such as animals and people); and the reason for this is usually teaching them, as in the speaking books (these are computerized toys which teach small children supplications or the like of that, and Allaah knows best).

Answer from Sheikh Muhammad ibn Saalih al-'Utheimeen, may Allaah have mercy upon him: If it is for entertaining the small children, then this is from that which is allowed for the children's toys- that which is similar to these pictures. And this is not prohibited because the figures in these pictures are not similar to that which Allaah created, as that which is in front of me makes clear (he was give an example of what the questioner was asking about). And this matter with this is some ease concerning the children.

If this is so, Esteemed Sheikh, if it is for the children then there is no problem, then why do we not say about the music which is in these toys, like the speaking book, which are aimed at the small children- is this also a case of ease because they are small?

The Sheikh went on to say, We cannot be easy concerning this aspect of music because there is no precedent from the Sunnah and because musical instruments have been prohibited in general- which is not the case with pictures. And if the child gets used to music, it will become something natural to him.

("Majmoo'at Asilah Tuhim al-Usra al-Muslimah" quoted in, "Tarbiyat al-Abnaa': Sawaal wa Jawaab" Pages 106-107)

Question: What is the ruling on teaching the children with pictures and stories about animals and other things which have souls? And these stories are in books specifically for teaching the children, which have pictures in them of things which have souls.

Answer from Sheikh al-Albaani, may Allaah have mercy upon him: Making this generalization that it is permissible is not something praised, nor is it legislated.

("Silsilat al-Huda wa an-Noor", as quoted in "Tarbiyat al-Abnaa': Sawaal wa Jawaab" Page107)

Question: What is the ruling on educating children with cartoons for the purpose of benefiting them and teaching them good manners?

Answer from Sheikh Fauzaan, may Allaah preserve him: Allaah made pictures of those things with souls forbidden, and it is forbidden to acquire them- so how can we teach our children upon them?? How can we educate them based upon something that is prohibited, upon pictures that are forbidden and drawings that move and speak and are similar to human beings? This is an evil picture and it is unlawful to educate children using it.

This is what the disbelievers want. They want us to oppose what the Messenger of Allaah, may Allaah's praise and salutations be upon him, prohibited us from. And the Messenger, may Allaah's praise and salutations be upon him, prohibited us from pictures, and using them, and acquiring them. And those who spread cartoons amongst the youth and the Muslims, claiming that it is from teaching the children then this is an immoral education. And the correct education is to teach them what will benefit them in their religion and worldly affairs.

(Translated from transcription from the web site: Ajurry.com)

***Question:** What is the ruling on watching and buying "Islamic" animated-cartoon movies, given that these movies present purposeful and beneficial stories for children which promote good character, dutifulness to parents, honesty, offering the prayer regularly and the like. These animated movies are intended as good substitutes for television which has become widespread. However, the problem we face is related to the fact that such movies present hand-drawn pictures of humans and animals. Is it permissible to watch these animated cartoons? Please advise us. May Allah reward you with the best!*

Answer from the Permanent Committee of Scholars in Saudi Arabia: It is not permissible to buy, sell or use cartoon movies, because they include pictures which are forbidden. Raising children should be done in ways that are Islamically acceptable with regard to teaching, disciplining, encouraging them to offer the prayer and taking good care of them. May Allah grant us success and may His praise and salutations be upon our Prophet Muhammad, his family and Companions

***Question:** In the curriculum of teaching in some of the schools the child is told to draw a picture of something with a soul or is given, for example, a picture of half a chicken and told to complete the rest, and he is sometimes asked to cut this picture into pieces and to put it back together again on a piece of paper, or he is given a picture and told to color it- so what is your opinion of this?*

Answer from Sheikh Muhammad ibn Saalih al-'Utheimeen, may Allaah have mercy upon him: It is my opinion that this is not permissible (*haraam*) and should be prohibited. It is necessary that the ones who are in positions of authority in educational matters fulfill their trusts in this area by prohibiting these things. If they wanted to prove the intelligence of the student, they could say, "Draw a car or a tree" or something similar to that from that which is familiar to him. By this one can discover the extent of his intelligence and ability in various matters.

This is from that which the people have been tried with which comes from *Shaytaan*. As indeed, there is no difference to the child whether he draws a car or a tree or a castle, or a person. I believe that those in positions of authority should forbid these things. If they are compelled, they should draw an animal without a head.

***Question:** These pictures which are in books- is it necessary to erase them or otherwise obliterate them, and can the head be removed by drawing a line between it and the body, and does this change the prohibition?*

Answer from Sheikh Muhammad ibn Saalih al-'Utheimeen, may Allaah have mercy upon him: I am of the opinion that it is not necessary to erase it completely because this is very difficult; and also the purpose of the book is not the picture itself- rather, it is to convey knowledge. And drawing a line between the neck and the body does not change the picture (so it is not sufficient to change it from being a forbidden picture) .

Question: *The student may fail in school if he does not draw this picture in school. That is, he may not get a grade for the picture and then he will fail.*

Answer from Sheikh Muhammad ibn Saalih al-'Utheimeen, may Allaah have mercy upon him: If it is like this, then the student is compelled to do this, and the sin is upon the one who ordered him and compelled him to do that thing. However I hope that the authorities will not reach such a state and force the servants of Allaah to disobey Allaah.

("Majmoo'at Asilah Tuhim al-Usra al-Muslimah" quoted in, "Tarbiyat al-Abnaa': Sawaal wa Jawaab" Pages 107-108)

The Use of Fictional Stories to Teach the Children

Question: Is it permissible for a person or individual to write stories from the imagination and everything that is in these stories is, in reality, just fabrications? However, they give them as stories to the children to read and to take lessons from.

Answer from The Permanent Committee of Scholars in Saudi Arabia: It is not allowed for the Muslim to write these lying stories. And the stories of the Qur'aan and the stories of the prophets and other than these from true events and that which narrate real happenings are sufficient for taking examples and morals from. And with Allaah is the success, and may Allaah's praise and salutations be upon our Prophet Muhammad, his family, and his companions.

("al- Fataawa al-Qayyimah lil-Usrat al-Muslimah", Pages 187-188)

Giving to One Child and not the Others

Question: Is it permissible for me to give one of my children that which I do not give another of them, because the other one is rich?

Answer from Sheikh 'Abdul 'Aziz bin Baaz, may Allaah have mercy upon him: It is not permissible for you to single out any of your children, whether male or female, with something while leaving out the other. Rather, it is obligatory upon you to have justice and fairness between them in regards to inheritance, or to avoid giving anything to any of them. The Prophet, may Allaah's praise and salutations be upon him, said, ***{Fear Allaah, and be just between your children.}*** (Its authenticity is agreed upon, and it is found in al-Bukhaari, 5/250, 2586, Muslim, 3/1242, 1623 and other than them)

However, if they are content with you singling out one of them with something, then there is no problem, as long as the ones who are content with this are mature and knowledgeable. Likewise, if there is from your children one who is unable to earn wages, due to illness or some sort of medical issue which does not allow him earn a salary, and he perhaps has no father or older brother who provides him, and there is no governmental stipend which allows him to fulfill his needs, then it is required that you provide for him enough to take care of his needs until Allaah causes him to be out of that situation.

("at-Tuhfat al-Baaziyyah fee al-Fataawa an-Nisaa'iyyah", Vol. 3, Page 227)

Question: If a parent has sons who live far from their parent and have less money than him, and other sons are living with their father, serving him, and under his command- is it allowed for their father to give the ones serving him some money during his lifetime or after his death due to their serving and staying with him? And, similarly, if he has more than one wife, and there is similar case to the above situation?

Answer from The Permanent Committee of Scholars in Saudi Arabia: It is permissible for the father to give to his children who have been at his service and attending to his affairs due to this service, as long as this is not showing preference to them over the other brothers. This is with the condition that that which he gives to them is similar to wages; whether that is daily, monthly or yearly. And the success is from Allaah, and may Allaah's praise and salutations be upon our Prophet, Muhammad, his family, and his companions.

("al-Fataawa al-Qayyimah lil-Usrat al-Muslimah", Pages 161-162)

Teaching the Children the Religion

Question: When should we begin teaching our children the religion?

Answer from Sheikh Fauzaan, may Allaah preserve him: Begin teaching the children when they reach the age of discernment; as beginning their learning in Islamic education is in accordance with the saying of the Prophet, may Allaah's praise and salutations be upon him, saying, ***{Command your children with the prayer at the age of seven, and beat them concerning it when they are ten, and separate between them in their beds.}*** (Hasan, Narrated in Ahmad, 2/180, 187, 6689,6756, and Abu Daawud, 490,496, from the hadeeth of 'Abdullah ibn 'Amr ibn al-'Aas by way of 'Amr ibn Shu'ayb from his father. It has been declared *saheeh* in "*al-'Irwah al-Ghaleel*", Number 2109).

As when the child has reached the age of discernment, then this is when his parents must teach him and educate him upon the good, by teaching him the Qur'aan, and that which is easy from the *ahaadeeth*, as well as teaching him the legislated rulings which are relevant to the age of this child, such as teaching him how to make *wudhoo* and *salaat*. And teach him the supplications for going to sleep, waking up, and eating and drinking, as when he has reached the age of discernment, then he understands that which he is commanded with and that which he is forbidden from. Likewise, forbid him from the matters which are not suitable or proper, making it clear to him that these matters are not permissible for him to perform- such as lying, backbiting, and other than that- so that he will be educated and raised upon the good, and upon staying away from evil from the time he is small. This is a very important matter, which some of the people are heedless of concerning their children.

Indeed, many of the people do not place importance upon the affairs of their children, do not steer them on the sound, correct course, but abandon them, neglected. They do not command them with the ritual prayer or guide them to that which is good. Instead, they bring them up upon ignorance and upon deeds which are not beneficial or good, and the those children associate with evil and badly behaved associates in the streets and neglect their lessons, and do other than that from the things which many of the young Muslims desire but which are from those things that are harmful. This is due to the negligence and heedlessness of their parents, who are guardians over them, as Allaah has charged them with taking care of their children. The Prophet, may Allaah's praise and salutations be upon him, said, ***{Command your children with the prayer at the age of seven, and beat them concerning it when they are ten, and separate between them in their beds.}*** This is a command and an injunction to the parents, so the one who does not command his children with the prayer has disobeyed the Prophet, may Allaah's praise and salutations be upon him, and has committed that which is forbidden, and abandoned that which he has been commanded with, that which the Messenger of Allaah, may Allaah's praise and salutations be upon him, has enjoined upon him.

And he, may Allaah's praise and salutations be upon him, said, ***{You are all shepherds, and are guardians over your charges.}*** (al-Bukhaari 893, and Muslim, 4828) Some of the parents, and this is regrettable, are busy with worldly matters, and this is a great danger which is widespread in the Muslim lands- these Muslim societies deteriorate due to the lack of proper education and raising of their children, and so the result it that these societies are neither rectified or correct in the religion nor successful in worldly matters. And there is no power to change, nor strength except through Allaah, the Most High, the Most Great.

("al-Muntaqa" 5/297, as quoted in, "Qatf al-Azhaar al-Mutanaathirah min Fataawa al-Mar'at al-Muslimah", Page 816)

Question: How does a father teach his children at-tawheed (the singling out Allaah alone for worship)?

Answer from Sheikh al-'Utheimeen, may Allaah have mercy upon him: One teaches them *at-tawheed* just as one teaches them other than that from the matters of the religion. And from that which is the best in this category is the book "*Thalaathatu ul-Usool*" by Sheikh Muhammad ibn 'Abdul Wahaab; if they memorize it by heart and its meaning is explained to them in a way which is suitable for their understanding and intellects, much good will come of this. This is because it is built upon questions and answers and with clear, easy language- there is nothing complex in it.

Then show them things from the signs of Allaah which reinforce or demonstrate that which is mentioned in this small book; for example the sun- say, "Who is it who created it?" Refer to the moon, the stars, the night, the day, and say to them, "The sun- who is it who created it? Allaah. The moon? Allaah. The night? Allaah. The day? Allaah. Allaah, Glorified and Exalted is He, created all of them"- so that the tree of their natural disposition of Islaam is watered and nourished by that. Because mankind by itself is naturally disposed to singling out Allaah alone for worship, as the Prophet, may Allaah's praise and salutations be upon him, said, ***{Every newborn is born upon the fitrah (the natural disposition***

towards Islaam) and his parents make him become a Jew, Christian, or Magian.} (al-Bukhaari and Muslim)

Likewise, they must be taught *al-wudhoo* (purification for prayer): how one makes *al-wudhoo*, through action. One says, "*al-wudhoo* is done in this manner..." And he makes *al-wudhoo* in front of him. Likewise with the prayer- along with asking Allaah, the Most High, for assistance, and asking him, Glorified and Exalted is He, for guidance for them. And one must avoid all speech in front of them which differs from good Islamic manners, and every forbidden act, so that they do not become habituated to lying, deception, and bad behavior- even if one is afflicted with it. So that even if one wrongly smokes tobacco, he does not smoke it in front of his child; because they will become used to that behavior, and it will become easy for them to fall into it.

And one must know that everyone who is in charge of the house is responsible for the people who live inside, as He, Blessed is He, the Most High, says, ***﴾Oh you who believe! Ward off yourselves and your families against a fire (Hell)...﴿***- (Surat at-Tahreem, From Ayat 6)

And it is not possible for us to ward the members of a household away from the Fire, except through accustoming them to good actions, and leaving off evil actions. The Messenger of Allaah, may Allaah's praise and salutations be upon him, affirmed this when he said, ***{The man is the guardian over his family, and is responsible for his charges.}*** (al-Bukhaari 893, and Muslim, 4828)

The father must know that his rectifying them is also a benefit for him himself in this world as well as the Hereafter, as the ones who are the closest to their fathers and mothers are the righteous people from both the males and the females: ***{When one of the children of Aadam dies, his works are cut off except for one of three: the continuing charity, the beneficial knowledge, or a righteous child who supplicates for him}*** (Muslim, from the hadeeth of Abi Hurairah, may Allaah be pleased with him, No. 1631)

We ask Allaah, the Most High, to assist us all concerning that which we carry of trust and responsibility.

(From "al-Fataawa al-Qayyimah lil-Usrat al-Muslimah", Pages 152-153)

Question: Some of the fathers have complained about their inability to raise their children. So what is the correct methodology in raising them?

Answer from Sheikh Muqbil ibn Haadee al-Waadi'ee, may Allaah have mercy upon him: The methodology of raising the children in the Sunnah starts from the very beginning. It is related in al-Bukhaari and Muslim, on Abi Hurairah, that the Prophet, may Allaah's praise and salutations be upon him, said, ***{Every newborn is born upon the fitrah (the natural disposition towards Islaam) and his parents make him become a Jew, Christian, or Magian.}***

And in Saheeh Muslim, from the Prophet, may Allaah's praise and salutations be upon him, from that which he narrated from his Lord, ***{Verily, I created my servants hunafaa' (upon tawheed) and then the Shaytaan caused them***

to stray.}

Once the Prophet, may Allaah's praise and salutations be upon him, saw al-Hasan eating a date. So he took it from his mouth with his fingers and removed it from his mouth and said, ***{Ukh. Ukh. Verily, I fear that it might be from the dates of sadaqa (charity).}*** (al-Bukhaari and Muslim)

And in the two *saheeh*s, from the hadeeth of 'Umar ibn Abi Salamah, may Allaah be pleased with him, who said that he began to eat with the Messenger of Allaah, may Allaah's praise and salutations be upon him, and his hand heedlessly roamed about the dish. So the Prophet, may Allaah's praise and salutations be upon him, said, ***{Oh young man, say "Bismillaah" and eat with your right hand, and eat from that which is closest to you.}***

In the *Sunnan* the Prophet, may Allaah's praise and salutations be upon him, said, ***{Command your sons to pray when they are seven, and beat them concerning it when they are ten.}*** Or a narration with that meaning. And it has two chains of narration which can be used for evidence for this matter.

And after that, also, you must be diligent in accustoming him to worship. But perhaps you might take your son to the *masjid* to accustom to worship and then we hear our elder brothers there saying only that they cause trouble or mischief by yelling- so they turn them out of and forbid them from the *masjid* using a weak hadeeth as a proof, which is narrated from Ibn Maajah from the narration Haarith ibn Nabhan, ***{Keep your children and insane people away from your masaajid.}*** Or a similar meaning- and this hadeeth is weak, as it has in its chain of narration Haarith ibn Nabhan, and his weakness is agreed upon.

As the Prophet, may Allaah's praise and salutations be upon him, would bring children with him, and would not forbid them from being in the *masjid*. And in the *Saheeh* (al-Bukhaari), that the Prophet, may Allaah's praise and salutations be upon him, was praying, and his granddaughter Umaama was with him, and when he stood he held her, and when he wanted to make prostration, he put her down. And in the *Saheeh* also, that the Prophet, may Allaah's praise and salutations be upon him, said, ***{I sometimes enter into salat and I would like to lengthen it, but I shorten it because I hear the crying of the child, out of mercy for its mother.}***

And in that which is *saheeh* also, and I mean here, in an authentic hadeeth, but this one is in the *Musnad* of Ahmad, that the Prophet, may Allaah's praise and salutations be upon him, was giving a *khutbah* on the *minbar*, and he saw al-Hasan and al-Husain entering and tripping on their new garments. So the Prophet, may Allaah's praise and salutations be upon him, left off his khutbah and picked them up and said, ***{I saw my two grandsons and I was impatient because of them, and Allaah is Most Truthful when He says, "Your wealth and your children are only a trial…".}***

And in the *Saheeh* that Anas said, "I prayed when I was a young man, behind the Prophet, may Allaah's praise and salutations be upon him, and the old woman was behind us."

Ash-Shawkaani said that there is a proof in this that the child took a place in the row.

And the Prophet, may Allaah's praise and salutations be upon him, said, ***{When the time for prayer comes, then the one of you who is most knowledgeable in Qur'aan should lead you in prayer.}*** And 'Amr ibn Salamah said, "They found out that I knew the most Qur'aan among them, so I lead them in prayer when I was seven." (Bukharee 4062) So if his prayer is correct and he is seven, then he is allowed to pray in the row (with the men).

And yet the people treat the children in a repulsive manner. A child may have memorized a third of the Qur'aan, or half of the Qur'aan, or five parts of the Qur'aan, and then an ignorant old man comes and pulls him out of the row and makes him leave it!

My brothers, we must be established upon the Book of Allaah and the Sunnah of His Messenger, may Allaah's praise and salutations be upon him. And as for the hadeeth that the Prophet, may Allaah's praise and salutations be upon him and his family, would put the men in front, then the children, then the women- it is a weak hadeeth, as in its chain there is Shahr ibn Hawshab and there is a difference over whether the hadeeth of Shahr ibn Hawshab can be used as a proof. And the strongest opinion is that it is weak.

(From "al-Fataawa al-Qayyimah lil-Usrat al-Muslimah", Pages 150-152)

Physically Disciplining A Child

Question: Esteemed Sheikh, it is permissible to strike the child if he makes a mistake when he is small? And is there some affect of this striking upon the child's psyche? And how is one to guide the child in this stage?

Answer from Sheikh Muhammad ibn Saalih al-'Utheimeen, may Allaah have mercy upon him: If the child is taught or corrected through this striking, and there is no other choice (nothing else will correct him) then there is no harm in this. And this has become the custom of the people in regard to this.

If he is not going to be taught or corrected with this method, such as the child in the cradle yelling or crying and the mother hits him, for example – then this is not permissible. It is blameworthy, as in it there is no benefit.

The pivotal point concerning all of it is: Will the child be taught or corrected through this hitting, or will he not be taught or corrected?

And if it is the case that he will be corrected through it, then even then it is not a severe beating; for example, do not strike him in the face, or in a place which could kill him- he should be hit upon the back or shoulder or that which resembles them, from those parts which would not cause any damage.

Hitting the face is dangerous, because the face is the greatest area of honor and esteem from that which belongs to a person and the most precious thing upon the person, and if one is stricken upon it, he is humiliated and disgraced more so than when he is hit upon the back. Thus, it is forbidden to hit in the face. (From the hadeeth narrated from Abu Hurairah, may Allaah be pleased with him, in "*Saheeh Muslim*", No.6212)

(From, "Tarbiyat al-Abnaa': Sawaal wa Jawaab", Pages 39- 40. Originally from "al-Fataawa Noor 'ala ad-Darb")

Being Merciful towards the Children

Question: Concerning the meaning of hadeeth: It is related from Abi Hurairah, may Allaah be pleased with him, that the Prophet, may Allaah's praise and salutations be upon him, kissed al-Hassan ibn 'Ali, may Allaah be pleased with them both , and al-'Aqra ibn Haabis said to him, "I have ten children and I have never kissed any of them!" So the Messenger of Allaah, may Allaah's praise and salutations be upon him, said, {Whoever does not have mercy on the people, Allaah will not be merciful to him.} And this was related by the two Sheikhs (al-Bukhaari and Muslim)

Answer from Sheikh Muhammad ibn Saalih al-'Utheimeen, may Allaah have mercy upon him, who said,

{Whoever does not have mercy on the people, Allaah will not be merciful to him.} This means that the one who is not merciful to the people, Allaah, Glorified and Exalted, will not show mercy to him- and may Allaah protect us from that- and he will not be favored with mercy.

That is proof of the permissibility of kissing the small children due to mercy and kindness- and this is whether the child is from your own offspring, or the children of your sons and daughters, or from those who are not related to you because this requires mercy, and that you have a heart which has mercy for the little ones. And the more mercy mankind shows to the servants of Allaah, the closer he is to Allaah's mercy. So much so that Allaah, Glorified and Exalted is He, forgave the woman who committed fornication; and He forgave her when she was merciful to a dog which was eating mud out of thirst. She went down a well and gave it water in her shoe and he drank it. She was merciful to the dog. However, if Allaah places in a person's heart mercy to these weak ones, than this is a proof that he will be forgiven or shown mercy to, if Allaah wills it. We ask Allaah to have mercy on us and you all.

The Prophet, may Allaah's praise and salutations be upon him, said, ***{Whoever does not have mercy on the people, Allaah will not be merciful to him.}*** This proves that it is necessary for a person to make his heart compassionate and merciful- and this is in opposition to what some of the fools amongst the people do. This is so much so that if a person's young son comes in when the man is in the coffee shop he scolds him and shoves him back- and this is a mistake!

And there is the Prophet, may Allaah's praise and salutations be upon him, who is the best of the people in manners, and the greatest of them in regards to character. There was a day when he was praying and while he was prostrating al-Hasan ibn 'Ali ibn Abi Taalib entered and climbed on his back while he was in prostration- like children do- and so he spent a long time in prostration. The companions were surprised and he said, ***{My grandson made me into a riding animal, and I didn't want to stand up until his desire to do so was finished.}*** ("*Musnad*" al Imaam Ahmad, Vol. 2, Page 513 and Haakim, Vol. 3, Page 127) And this was from mercy.

Another day, Umaama bint Zainab, the daughter of the daughter of the Messenger of Allaah, may Allaah's praise and salutations be upon him, who was small- the Messenger of Allaah, may Allaah's praise and salutations be upon him, took her to the *masjid.* He came forward and led the people in prayer while he was carrying the little girl. When he prostrated he put her down and when he stood up, he held her. All of this was from mercy and kindness for her. Otherwise, he could have said to 'Aishah or any of his other wives, "Take this girl!" But he felt merciful towards her because she wanted her grandfather- and he wanted her to be happy. ("*Saheeh al-Bukhaari*", Vol. 1, Page 131, from the hadeeth of Abi Qatadah al-Ansaaree)

And another day, he was giving the *Jumu'ah khutbah* and Hasan and Husayn were wearing new clothing which were too long. They kept walking on them and tripping, so he came down from the *minbar* and carried them both in front of him and said, ***{Allaah told the truth when He said, ﴾Verily your wealth and children are a trial﴿*** - (Surat at-Taghaabun, Ayat 15)***}*** (Saheeh al-Bukhaari) And he, may Allaah's praise and salutations be upon him, also said that he saw then tripping and he was not happy until he came down and carried them.

And that which is important is that we have to make ourselves love the children and be merciful towards them, and to be merciful towards anyone who needs mercy from the orphans, the poor people, the old people and others. Also, that we make our hearts merciful so that Allaah will forgive us and be merciful towards us- because we also need mercy and our mercy towards the servants of Allaah is a reason for Allaah's mercy towards us.

We ask Allaah to open His mercy for all of us.

("Sharh Riyaadh as-Saaliheen", under hadeeth number 893, From "Tarbiyat al-Abnaa': Sawaal wa Jawaab", Pages 28-29)

The Woman taking her Children to the Masjid

Question: What is the ruling concerning the woman taking her children to the masjid?

Answer from Sheikh Saalih ibn Fauzaan ibn 'Abdullah al-Fauzaan, may Allaah preserve him: Taking the children to the *masjid* is a matter which requires explanation and clarification. If the children are of the age of discernment, seven years old, then they should be taken to the *masjid* for the purpose of practicing the prayer, being educated in it, and their establishment of that which is obligatory. If they are less than seven years old, then they do not need to be taken to the *masjid*, in order that they not disturb the people who are praying, do harm to the *masjid* or dirty it. If it is possible to keep them under control, and it is necessary to take them, such as one fearing for them if they remain in the house, then it is permissible to do so.

("Naseehah wa Fatawaa Khaasat bil-Mara'at al-Muslimah", a collection of rulings and advices from Sheikh Fauzaan, Pages 41-42)

The Covering of the Parent from the Hellfire

Question: The Messenger of Allaah, may Allaah's praise and salutations be upon him, said, {The one who has three daughters with whom he is patient, and whom he gives them to drink and clothes them, they will be for him a covering from the Hellfire.} (al-Bukhaari, 3/332, 1418, 2/136, 8/8, Muslim, 40/2027, 2630, and other than them with similar wording) Is the covering from the Hellfire for their father only, or is the woman included in that? As I, may Allaah be praised, have three daughters.

Answer from Sheikh 'Abdul 'Aziz bin Baaz, may Allaah have mercy upon him: The hadeeth is general, including the father and the mother, with his, may Allaah's praise and salutations be upon him, saying, ***{The one who has two daughters and treats them well, they will be for him a covering from the Hellfire.}*** (see above). Likewise, if he has sisters, paternal or maternal aunts, or the like of these, and he is good to them, we hope for him by that he attains Paradise; as when he is good to them, then he has the right to a great reward due to that, he will be protected from the Hellfire- there will be a covering between him and the Hellfire due to his good actions. This is specific to the Muslims, as the Muslim, if he performs this good deed seeking the Face of Allaah, then that will be a cause for him to be saved from the Hellfire. And there are many reasons for protection from the Fire and entering Paradise, and it is necessary that the Believer perform as many of these actions as often as possible.

Islaam itself is the only foundation, and it is the principle reason for entering Paradise and being saved from the Hellfire. And there are actions that if the Muslim performs them, he will enter Paradise and be saved from the Hellfire. An example of this is providing for daughters or sisters, as treating them well is for him a covering from the Hellfire. Likewise, the one who has three young children (who have not reached puberty) die- this will be for him a protection from the Hellfire. It was said, "Oh Messenger of Allaah, and two?" And he answered, may Allaah's praise and salutations be upon him, ***{And two.}*** And he was not asked about one. (al-Bukhaari, 1248, and other than him, and it is an authentic hadeeth) Also, it has been authentically narrated that he, may Allaah's praise and salutations be upon him, said, ***{Allaah, Glorified is He and Exalted, says, "None of my believing servants, if one who is beloved to him dies in this life, there is no reward for him except Paradise."}*** (al-Bukhaari, 6424, and other than him, and it is authentic)

So He, Glorified and Exalted is He, has made clear that the true reward for the believing servant if one of his companions- meaning, his loved ones- from the people of this life dies and he is patient and satisfied with that, is the reward of Paradise. So a single young child falls under this hadeeth, if Allaah takes him, and causes him to die, and his mother and father are both patient and satisfied with this- then the reward for them is Paradise. This is a great favor from Allaah. Likewise the husband and wife, and the rest of the family and friends- if they are patient and content this will be a cause for them to be included in this hadeeth, along with their not having been affected by that which would prevent them from this, such as dying upon something from the major sins. We ask Allaah for security and righteousness.

("Majmoo' al-Fatawa wa Maqaalaat Mutanawa'" 4/375-376, and "Majalat al-Bahooth al-Islaamiyyah" 29/ 106-107, as quoted in "at-Tuhfat al-Baaziyyah fee al-Fataawa an-Nisaa'iyyah", Vol. 3, Pages 159- 161)

Question: What is the meaning of treating (the daughters) well as mentioned in the hadeeth (above)?

Answer from Sheikh 'Abdul 'Aziz bin Baaz, may Allaah have mercy upon him: *al-ihsaan* (goodness, good treatment) of the daughters and those who are like them, is through raising them and educating them with an Islamic upbringing, teaching them and bringing them up upon the truth, as well as adherence to and concern with their virtue and chastity, and keeping them far away from that which Allaah has forbidden of *at-tabaruj* (going out amongst strangers improperly covered or beautified) and other than it. Likewise, raising the sisters and the male children and other than them upon the manifestation of *al-ihsaan*, so that they are raised upon the way of obedience to Allaah and His Messenger, may Allaah's praise and salutations be upon him, and shunning that which Allaah has forbidden, and adhering to the truth of Allaah, Glorified and Exalted is He. And along with that, he must know that that which is intended is not goodness concerning food, drink and clothing only; rather, what is intended is more general than that from treating them well in the matters of the religion and the worldly matters.

("Majmoo' al-Fataawa wa Maqaalaat Mutanawa'" 4/375-376, and "Majalat al-Bahooth al-Islaamiyyah" 29/ 106-107, as quoted in "at-Tuhfat al-Baaziyyah fee al-Fataawa an-Nisaa'iyyah", Vol. 3, Page 161)

Regarding the Child who does not Pray

Question: The questioner, who is a widow, states that she has a son who does not pray. She has advised and threatened him, but he does not care. He is sixteen years old. She says that she advises him, and he mocks her. Sometimes he does return and pray, and he says that ash-Shaytaan whispers above his head, and he says the like of this repeatedly. She says, indeed I seek refuge with Allaah, and I ask for you to assist me concerning that which is in him, and to guide me to that which is correct and what action this widow should take, and there is no power nor change except with Allaah, and she desires your help.

Answer from Sheikh 'Abdul 'Aziz ibn Baaz, may Allaah have mercy upon him: This young man who does not make his *salaat* consistently- it is obligatory that he be advised and directed towards that which is good, and that he be exhorted and warned away from Allaah's anger. Allaah, Exalted is He, the Most High, says, concerning the reality of the Hellfire,

﴾ ***"What has caused you to enter Hell?" They will say: "We were not of those who used to offer the salaat (prayers),"*** ﴿- (Surat al-Mudaththir, Ayats 42-43)

As abandoning the prayer is from the greatest causes for which one enters the Hellfire, as abandoning it is from the greater disbelief. The Prophet, may Allaah's praise and salutations be upon him, said, ***{The covenant which is between us and them is the prayer, and the one who abandons it has committed disbelief.}*** (Ibn Hibaan 1470, Al-Mustradrak 11, Ibn Maajah 1075, Tirmidhee 2612) And he, may Allaah's praise and salutations be upon him, also said, ***{Between a man and associating others with Allaah and disbelief, is leaving off the prayer.}*** (Muslim)

So the prayer is a very significant matter, and it is a pillar of Islaam, and it is from those things which distinguish the believer from the disbeliever. It is obligatory upon every responsible person, from the men and the women, to offer the prayers in their allotted times- and the child is commanded with it before he reaches puberty, so that he becomes accustomed to it and it becomes a habit with him. As the Prophet, may Allaah's praise and salutations be upon him, said, ***{Command your children to make the salaat when they are seven years old, and beat them (if they do not make it) when they are ten, and separate them in their beds.}*** (Hasan, Narrated in Ahmad, 2/180, 187, 6689,6756, and Abu Daawud, 490,496, from the hadeeth of 'Abdullah ibn 'Amr ibn al-'Aas by way of 'Amr ibn Shu'ayb from his father. It has been declared saheeh in "*al-'Irwah al-Ghaleel*", Number 2109)

So also the young people. As for the one who has reached maturity, then it is obligatory upon him that he pray, and if he is late in performing his prayer, or falls behind in them, then it is obligatory that he repents. If he does not repent, then it is upon the governmental authorities who are in charge of such affairs to try him in a court and then, if this is called for, to issue an order or his execution, as the matter of the prayer is very significant, and it is the second pillar from the pillars of Islaam.

So it is upon you, sister in Islaam, to advise your son, and to strive persistently to guide him to that which is good, as well as warning him from the consequences of his evil action. If he persists in this, then disassociate yourself from him and ask him to leave you and stay away from you so that his affair does not cause damage or harm to you, and so that the punishment does not come to him while he is with you. It is obligatory upon him to obey your command, and to fear Allaah, Glorified is He, and Exalted, and to obey His command, Glorified is He, and the command of His Messenger, may Allaah's praise and salutations be upon him, concerning the performance of the prayer. So if he does not perform it, and persists upon his obstinacy and disbelief, then it is obligatory upon you to separate from him, and to dislike meeting with him, and to make clear this dislike and anger for him to his face, and to bring his affair to the one who is in charge of affairs from the governmental authorities.

And it is also upon you to tell those who are important to him from your close family, such as your father, older brother, or his uncles from his father's and mother's sides, to guide him and give him advice and punish him if they are able- as Allaah may eventually guide him through you efforts, in supplicating for him in your prayers and other than them, that he be rectified and guided, that Allaah guide him, and that he be inspired to that which is correct, and that he seeks refuge from the evil of his own self, and the evil of the *Shaytaan*, and from evil companionship, and that Allaah rectify him, and may

Allaah grant him good…and from Allaah comes success.

(Originally from "Noor 'ala ad-Darb", Tape number 842, as collected in "at-Tuhfat al-Baaziyyah fee al-Fataawa an-Nisaa'iyyah", Vol. 1, Pages 306-307)

Question: What are the reasons for many of the young people turning away from the religion, and their alienation from it?

Answer from Sheikh Bin Baaz, may Allaah have mercy upon him: There are many reasons for that which you have mentioned of the turning away of the youth and their alienation from anything that is related to the religion.

The most important is their paucity of knowledge, and their ignorance of the true reality of Islaam and its goodness, and giving no attention or concern to the Qur'aan. Also, there are few educators who have the knowledge and the ability to explain the truth of Islaam to the youth, making clear its goodness and clarifying its goals. There are other reasons as well, such as the general environment, radio and television programs, travels to outside the Kingdom of Saudi Arabia, mixing with the people from outside who have come here with corrupt beliefs, bad character and many levels of ignorance- and other than these, from the causes which are alienating them from Islaam and turning the towards godlessness and immorality.

For many of the youth, the emptiness of their hearts of beneficial knowledge and the correct beliefs, the coming of the flood of doubts and misconceptions, the misguiding calls, and the deceptive desires all come together and bring about that which you mention in the question- the turning away and alienation of many of the youth from all that is connected to Islaam.

And how good is that which has been mentioned with this meaning:

Desire for her came to me before I had any experience

It met with an empty heart and was able to fill it

And that which is more eloquent, truthful, and better is that which Allaah, the Most High, says,

﴾***Have you (Oh Muhammad) seen him who has taken as his ilaah (god) his own vain desire? Would you then be a wakeel (a disposer of his affairs or a watcher) over him? Or do you think that most of them hear or understand? They are only like cattle – nay, they are even farther astray from the Path (i.e. even worse than cattle).***﴿- (Surat al-Furqaan, Ayats 43-44)

I believe that the type of cure varies according to the type of specific illness they have. Yet the most important of these are:

- the concern and attention to the Qur'aan and the life of the Prophet, may Allaah's praise and salutations be upon him

  -a righteous teacher, director and inspector

  -the correct methodology (*minhaj*)

-rectification of the learning institutions in the Muslim countries and purifying them of that which they contain from the call to immorality and other types of godlessness and evil. And this will happen if the people who are responsible for them are truthful in calling to Islaam and sincerely desiring to guide the people and the youth to it.

-And from that (the cure): the concern with rectifying the environment and purifying it from that which has entered into it from disease.

-And also from the cure is not travelling outside (the Kingdom) except if there is a necessity for them to do so

- paying attention to the pure Islamic education through the educational system, the teachers, the callers to Islaam and the ones who deliver speeches

I ask Allaah for this, and that He rectify the leaders of the Muslims and make it easier for them to have knowledge of the religion and a strong connection to it, and to fight that which opposes it with truthfulness, sincerity, and ongoing effort. Verily, He is All Hearing and Close through His Knowledge.

(From "al-Fataawa al-Qayyimah lil-Usrat al-Muslimah", Pages 153-155)

Review and Discussion Questions

Questions for rulings regarding the children

Review:

1. Why did the Prophet, may Allaah's praise and salutations be upon him, command us to have many children? Write the hadeeth which mentions this reason. (Top half of Page 211)
2. To whom does the ultimate right of naming the child belong, the father or the mother? Why is it best that they agree on the name? (Top half of page 214)
3. Why is it not the same to feed the child formula instead of nursing her, according to Sheikh al-Albaani, may Allaah have mercy upon him. (Top of page 215)
4. What are two ahaadeeth which indicate that images of things with souls are forbidden? (Bottom half of page 216)
5. When is it permissible to give to one child without giving to the others? (Page 219, Bottom Half)
6. What are some of the proofs that the parent is responsible for teaching the children the religion? (Middle of Page 222)
7. What are some ahaadeeth Sheikh Muqbil, may Allaah have mercy upon him, brings that deal directly with the raising and educating of the children from a young age? (Page 222, Bottom Half, and Page 223, Top Half)
8. Bring examples from the Sunnah of the mercy showed to the children by the Messenger of Allaah, may Allaah's praise and salutations be upon him. (Bottom half of Page 225, Top half of Page 226)
9. What are some of the cures mentioned by Sheikh Bin Baaz, may Allaah have mercy upon him, for the illness the people turning away from Islaam? (Page 230, Bottom Half, Page 231, Top Half)

Discussion & Consideration:

10. What are some of the benefits, in this life and the next, of having many children, in contrast to one or two?
11. What sort of birth control was practiced at the time of the Messenger of Allaah, may Allaah's praise and salutations be upon him? Why is the encouraged more than the modern methods such as the birth control pill?
12. What two things does Sheikh al-'Utheimeen mention can be done to children's dolls to make them acceptable? Can you think of any other alternatives to these that you could suggest? (Hint: for some more ideas, look at Sheikh Fauzaan's ruling concerning this) Is it permissible for adults to collect dolls or keep toys like this? Why or why not?
13. How does educating our children with cartoons and the like fall under those things which please the disbelievers?
14. We should be easy on the children and not worry about teaching them Islaam until they are older. Is this statement true or false? Why?
15. How can we teach children about tawheed and other Islamic beliefs through example?
16. Is it permissible to hit a small child? How about an older one? Are there conditions ruling this? If so, what are they?
17. What are the benefits of treating the daughters well? What are some of the things that this entails?
18. How should we deal with a child that does not pray? Does this differ between the one who does not believe it is obligatory to pray and the one who is simply lazy? Explain.

Rulings Regarding Other Relationships

Question: Is the right of the mother greater than the right of the father?

Answer from Sheikh 'Abdul 'Aziz bin Baaz, may Allaah have mercy upon him: There is no doubt that the right of the mother is greater than the right of the father from many aspects. It is authentically narrated from the Messenger of Allaah, may Allaah's praise and salutations be upon him, that a questioner said, "Oh Messenger of Allaah, who of the people has the greatest right that I should treat them well?" He said, ***{Your mother.}*** He then asked, "Then who?", and he replied, ***{Your mother.}*** He asked, "Then who?" He replied, ***{Your mother.}*** He said, "Then who?" He said, ***{Your father.}*** (Muslim, 6665) And in another wording, the questioner asked, "Oh Messenger of Allaah, to whom must one be most dutiful?" He said, ***{Your mother.}*** He then asked, "Then who?", and he replied, ***{Your mother.}*** He asked again, "Then who?" He replied, ***{Your mother.}*** He said, "Then who?" He replied, ***{Your father, then the closest relatives, then those next closest}*** (Authentic, "*Saheeh Abi Daawud*", 5139)

("Majmoo' al-Fataawa", 8/309, as found in "Qatf al-Azhaar al-Mutanaathirah min Fataawa al-Mar'at al-Muslimah" Page 807)

Question: Who are the ones with whom one has ties of kinship and family relationship, as some of the people say that the husband's family are not from those to whom one has ties of kinship?

Answer from Sheikh 'Abdul 'Aziz bin Baaz, may Allaah have mercy upon him: The family members are the relations through lineage from both your mother and your father's sides. And they are the ones meant by Allaah's, Glorified is He, most High, saying, ﴾***...and the blood relations are near to one another in the decree ordained by Allaah.***﴿- (Surat al-Anfaal, From Ayat 75 and al-Ahzaab, Ayat 6) And the closest of them are the fathers and mothers and grandparents and sons and grandchildren- this is ascending up the line or down the line. After them, the closest and then the next closest from the siblings and their children and their paternal aunts and uncles and their children, and the maternal aunts and uncles and their children.

And it is authentically narrated from the Prophet, may Allaah's praise and salutations be upon him, that he said to the one who asked, "Oh Messenger of Allaah, to whom must one be most dutiful?" He said, ***{Your mother.}*** He then asked, "Then who?", and he replied, ***{Your mother.}*** He asked again, "Then who?" He replied, ***{Your mother.}*** He said, "Then who?" He replied, ***{Your father, then the closest relatives, then those next closest}*** (Authentic, "*Saheeh Abi Daawud*", 5139)

As for the relations of the wife, then they are not the husband's relations, as they are not his relatives unless they are his blood relatives as well. However, they are the relatives of his children with her and Allaah is the Granter of Success.

("Fatawaa Islaamiyyah lil Musnad", 4/195, as quoted in "Qatf al-Azhaar al-Mutanaathirah min Fataawa al-Mar'at al-Muslimah" Pages 807-808)

Question: It is known that the wife is obligated to obey her husband, as is found in the hadeeth. She is also commanded with obedience to her parents in that which is not wrongdoing. What is the ruling when the two commands conflict- which of them is first in importance?

Answer from Sheikh Saalih ibn Fauzaan ibn 'Abdullah al-Fauzaan, may Allaah preserve him: There is no doubt that the woman is commanded to obey Allaah, Glorified is He, the Most High, as well as being commanded with obedience to her husband and her parents- and these last two are included in obedience to Allaah, Glorified and Exalted is He.

As for the obedience to the created, from the parent or husband, which contains wrongdoing to the Creator, then this is not permissible, due to his, may Allaah's praise and salutations be upon him, saying, ***{Indeed, obedience is in that which is good.}*** (Narrated by Imaam al-Bukhaari in his "*Saheeh*", 8/106, from the hadeeth of 'Ali ibn Abi Taalib, may Allaah be pleased with him)

Also his, may Allaah's praise and salutations be upon him, saying, ***{There is no obedience to the created}*** and this includes the parent or husband ***{in disobedience to the Creator.}*** (Ahmad 5/66, al-Haakim 3/123, al-Baghawi in "*Sharh as-Sunnah*", 10/44)

So if the husband is going to burden her with wrongdoing to her parents and disobedience to them, then she does not obey him in this; as the rights of the parents (in this case) are given priority over the rights of the husband. So if he seeks from her to disobey her parents, then she does not obey him in that, because disobedience is wrongdoing, from the greatest of the great sins after associating others with Allaah.

("Naseehah wa Fatawaa Khaasat bil-Mara'at al-Muslimah", a collection of rulings and advices from Sheikh Fauzaan, Page 83)

Concerning Companionship

Question: I am a young woman who dislikes backbiting and slander, and sometimes I find myself in a group of people who speak about the affairs of the people, and they enter into backbiting and slander. Inside myself I dislike and hate this, but I am very shy, and so I am not able to forbid them from that. Likewise, there is no place to get away from them. And Allaah knows that I wish to enter into discussing something else. Is there any sin upon me in sitting with them? And what is it obligatory that I do? May Allaah grant you success in that which has in it good for Islaam and the Muslims.

Answer from Sheikh 'Abdul 'Aziz bin Baaz, may Allaah have mercy upon him: There is a sin upon you in that, unless you forbid that evil. And if they accept this from you, then all praise is due to Allaah, and if they do not, then it is obligatory upon you to separate yourself from them and leave off sitting with them, as Allaah, Glorified is He, Most High, says,

﴾And when you (Muhammad) see those who engage in a false conversation about Our Verses (of the Qur'aan) by mocking at them, stay away from them till they turn to another topic. And if Shaytaan causes you to forget, then after the remembrance sit not you in the company of those people who are

the dhaalimoon (polytheists and wrong doers).- (Surat al-An'aam, Ayat 68) And His, Glorified and Exalted is He, saying,

And it has already been revealed to you in the Book (this Qur'aan) that when you hear the Verses of Allaah being denied and mocked at, then sit not with them, until they engage in a talk other than that; (but if you stayed with them) certainly in that case you would be like them. Surely, Allaah will collect the hypocrites and disbelievers all together in Hell.- (Surat an-Nisaa', Ayat 140)

Also, there is the saying of the Prophet, may Allaah's praise and salutations be upon him, ***{When one of you sees evil or wrongdoing, then he must change it with his hand. If he is unable to do this, then he must do so with his tongue. If he is not able to do that, then he must hate it in his heart, and that is the weakest of faith.}*** (Muslim, 186) Imaam Muslim has collected this in his *"Saheeh"*; and the *ahaadeeth* and verses with this meaning are many. And Allaah is One who Possesses Success.

("Majmoo' al-Fataawa", 4/440, as quoted in "Qatf al-Azhaar al-Mutanaathirah min Fataawa al-Mar'at al-Muslimah" Page 856)

Question: When should one employ leniency, and when should he resort to harshness in calling to Allaah and in dealing with the people?

Answer from Sheikh Rabee'a al-Madkhalee, may Allaah preserve him: The foundational principle in calling to Allaah is kindness, leniency, and wisdom- this is the basic foundation in it, may Allaah bless you. And if you encounter one who resists and does not accept the truth, and you establish the proofs upon him and he rejects them, then you put forth the refutation. So if you are a king, and the matter calls for it, then one must use the sword, as this calls for execution if one persists in spreading corruption. There are from the scholars those from various schools of thought who believe that this is the most severe evil, worse than highway robbery. So, one is advised, and then the proofs are established upon him. And if he turns away, then turn to a judge ruling by Islamic legislation for his punishment. This may be through putting him in prison, or through expulsion, or through execution, as it was judged that al-Jahm ibn Safwaan and other than him, and upon Bashr al-Muraysee, and upon, may Allaah bless you, other than them, that they be executed. From these are al-Ja'd ibn Durham. And this is the ruling of the scholars upon the ones who stubbornly oppose and persist in spreading their call to innovation. If there is benefit in this, and retraction (of the wrong which was put forth), then this is what is hoped for.

("Alhath 'ala al-Mawdati wa al-A'itilaaf" as quoted in, "Qatf al-Azhaar al-Mutanaathirah min Fataawa al-Mar'at al-Muslimah" page 67-68)

Question: What is your opinion concerning keeping company with the disbelievers?

Answer from Sheikh Muhammad ibn Saalih al-'Utheimeen, may Allaah have mercy upon him: If one desires through this companionship with the disbelievers that they embrace Islaam, and wishes to explain its virtues and benefits to them, then there is no problem with the people spending time in their company in order to call them to Islaam. However, if the people do not desire from these disbelievers that they embrace Islaam, then they should not keep company with them, due to that which their companionship causes, of falling into wrongdoing if the friendship brings about jealousy and affection; and perhaps it may bring about strong affection and love for these disbelievers. Allaah, Glorified is He, says,

﴾***You will not find any people who believe in Allaah and the Last Day, making friendship with those who oppose Allaah and His Messenger, even though they were their fathers or their sons or their brothers or their kindred (people). For such He has written Faith in their hearts, and strengthened them with Rooh (proofs, light and true guidance) from Himself.***﴿- (Surat al-Mujaadilah, From Ayat 22)

And having sincere affection for the enemies of Allaah, and loving and supporting them, is in opposition to that which is obligatory upon the Muslim, as Allaah, Glorified is He, Most Exalted, has forbidden that, as He states,

﴾***Oh you who believe! Take not the Jews and the Christians as auliyaa' (friends, protectors, helpers), they are but auliyaa' of each other. And if any amongst you takes them as auliyaa', then surely, he is one of them. Verily, Allaah guides not those people who are the Dhaalimoon (polytheists and wrong doers and unjust).***﴿- (Surat al-Maa'idah, Ayat 51)

And He, the Most High, says, ﴾***Oh you who believe! Take not My enemies and your enemies (i.e. disbelievers and polytheists) as friends, showing affection towards them, while they have disbelieved in what has come to you of the truth***﴿- (Surat al-Mumtahanah, From Ayat 1)

There is no doubt that every disbeliever is an enemy of Allaah and of the Believers, as He, the Most High, says, ﴾***Whoever is an enemy to Allaah, His Angels, His Messengers, Jibraaeel and Mikaaeel, then verily, Allaah is an enemy to the disbelievers.***﴿- (Surat al-Baqara, Ayat 98)

It is not proper for a Muslim to take the enemies of Allaah as companions, and to have affection and love for them, from that which is in that of great danger to his religion and his beliefs and way of life.

("Fataawa al-Mar'at al-Muslimah", a collection of rulings concerning women from various scholars, Page 595)

In Regards to the Internet Forums

Question: May Allaah grant you good; this is another question from the internet.

Esteemed Sheikh, may Allaah prolong your life upon obedience to Him. We would like from you a clarification concerning the ruling of the woman participating in the Islamic internet forums- whether by writing articles, or responding to articles which were written by men. And is it permissible for her to speak to them in her responses with some of the statements of gratitude such as jazaakum Allaah Khairan, or other than that? And we would like from you the details of this matter, because some of the young men have said that it is not permissible for the woman to participate, and some of them state the opposite of that. Jazakum Allaahu Khairan.

Answer from Sheikh 'Abdul 'Aziz ar-Raajihee: There is no problem with the participation of a woman and her responding- as this is from calling to Allaah that she responds to the liars and clarifies the truth. However, this is with the condition that she does not put out her picture- she does not put out her picture. If she responds with writing then there is no problem with it, and she does not put out her picture. If she also uses an indicator of who she is or a symbol name without her actual name, then this is more proper, and if not, then there is no wrongdoing. And if there is no suspicion, doubt, or fear of *fitnah* for her, then there is no wrongdoing. And if she does not put out her picture, then there is no problem with her using name or using this symbol, and she responds to the liars, and clarifies the truth, with the condition that she not put forth her picture on the screen in front of the people. Also, her voice must not be heard. If she writes a message replying to untrue speech, and clarifying the truth, then this is from calling to Allaah- however, with the condition that her picture is not put out, or her voice, and it is preferable that she not put out her name---*and the speech is not clear on the phone connection...*

Review and Discussion Questions

Questions for Rulings regarding other relationships

Review:

1. What hadeeth is proof that the right of the mother over the child is greater than that of the father? (Top half of Page 235)
2. What two verses are proof that we should not sit with the evil companions? (Bottom of Page 246, Top of Page 247)
3. List four verses which Sheikh al-'Utheimeen, may Allaah have mercy upon him, brings to show that we should not have great love for the disbelievers, nor should we take them as companions. (Page 238)

Discussion & Consideration:

4. What should a woman do when the command of her husband conflicts with the command of her parents? Which should come first?
5. You go to a sister's house and the other women are engaging in evil or vain talk. What steps should you take when this occurs?
6. When should you employ leniency in dealing with the people, and when should you resort to a degree of harshness?

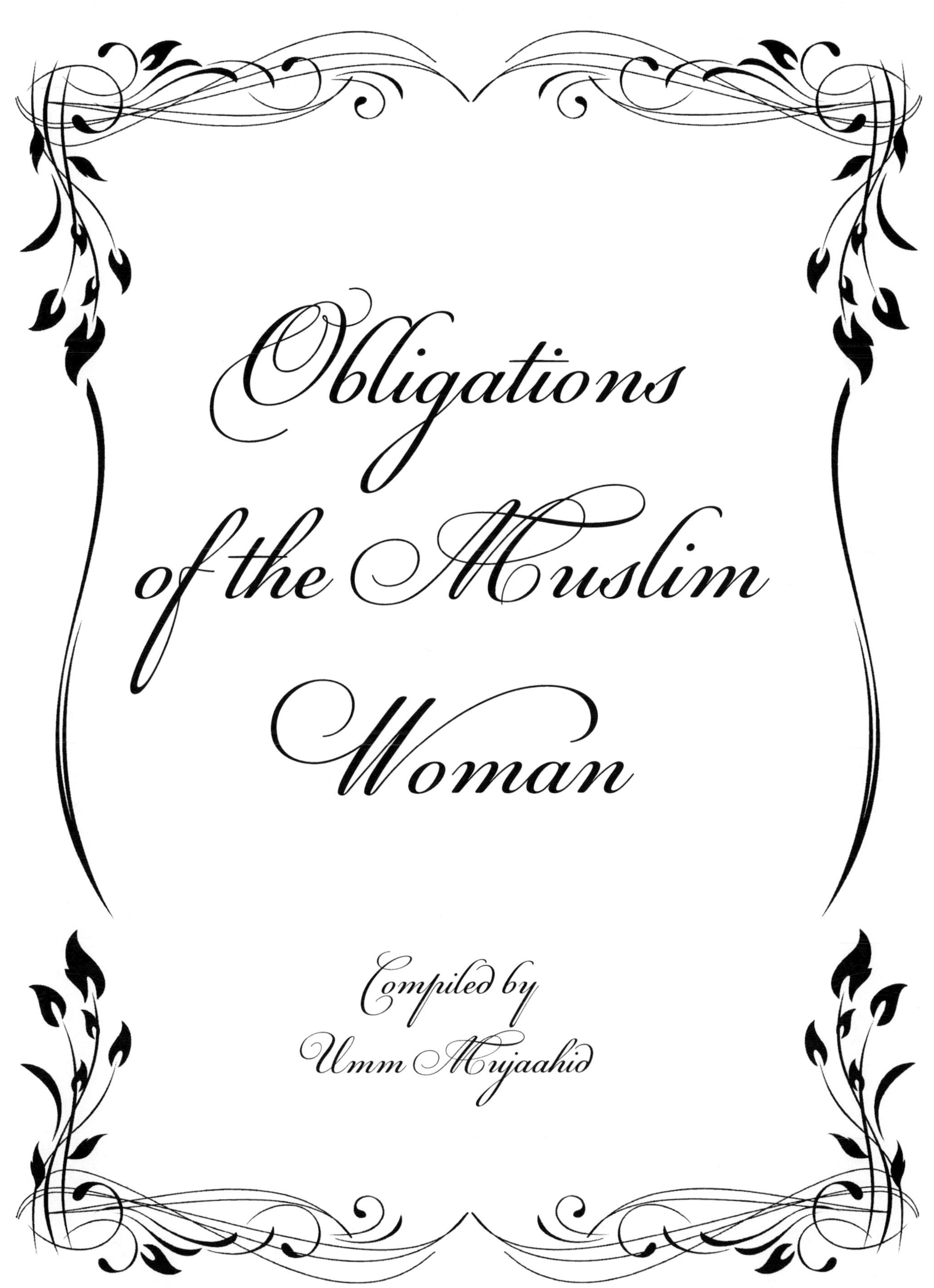

Obligations of the Muslim Woman

Compiled by
Umm Mujaahid

Obligations of the Muslim Woman in Regards to:

Her Lord & Her Religion

From among her obligations regarding her Lord & her religion are:

1. It is obligatory upon the woman to learn the correct, sound, Islamic beliefs, and to establish them as a reality in her life, basing her speech and action upon them.
2. It is obligatory upon the woman to worship Allaah alone, without associating any partners along with Him in worship.
3. Knowledge: As it is obligatory upon the Muslim woman to know and understand all that is necessary from the affairs of her religion, especially those matters which have been made obligatory upon her.
4. Righteous Action upon that knowledge
5. Calling to Allaah (الدعوة) *ad-da'wah*
6. Patience (الصبر) *as-Sabr*

Alhamdulillah, this is not intended to be a comprehensive list of those affairs which it is obligatory upon the woman to know and act upon concerning her Lord and her religion. Rather, it is meant to present an overview of many of the most crucial of those matters, with a brief description of each one mentioned. And with Allaah is the success.

The First: It is obligatory upon the woman to learn the correct, sound, Islamic beliefs, and to establish them as a reality in her life, basing her speech and action upon them.

What is *'aqeedah*?

Sheikh Fauzaan, may Allaah preserve him, said, in "*Kitaab 'Aqeedatu at-Tawheed*", pages 8-10:

The linguistic meaning of *al-'aqeedah*: That which is obtained from "*al-'aqd*" (العقد), and it is to bind or attach something, and to believe, such as, "The heart and the mind believe it.» And *al-'aqeedah* is that which the people believe. It is said, "They have a good belief." Meaning, unblemished by doubt. And *'aqeedah* is an action of the heart, and it is to believe in something with the heart, and to verify its truthfulness.

The meaning of *al-'aqeedah* in the Islamic legislation: It is faith in Allaah, His angels, His books, His messengers, and the Last Day, and faith in predestination, both its good and bad- and these are called the pillars of faith.

And the Islamic legislation is divided into two divisions: beliefs and actions.

As for the beliefs: They are those matters which are not connected to the "how" of an action; for example, belief in the Lordship of Allaah and the obligation of worshipping Him, and faith in the remainder of the pillars of Islaam which have been mentioned, and they are called principles, or roots (أصلية).

As for the actions: They are that which is connected to the "hows" of an action, such as prayer, obligatory charity, fasting, and the remaining principles of action, and they are called divisions, or branches (فريعة). This is because they are built upon the principles, whether those principles be sound or corrupt. (The Sheikh takes this from *"Sharh 'Aqeedatu as-Safaareeniyyah"*,

1/4)

As the sound *'aqeedah* is the foundation upon which the religion is built, and by which the actions are made to be correct, as Allaah, the Most High, says,

﴾***So whoever hopes for the Meeting with his Lord, let him work righteousness and associate none as a partner in the worship of his Lord.***﴿- (Surat al-Kahf, From Ayat 110)

And He, the Most High, says, ﴾***And indeed it has been revealed to you (Muhammad) as it was to those (Allaah's Messengers) before you: "If you join others in worship with Allaah, (then) surely, (all) your deeds will be in vain, and you will certainly be among the losers.***﴿- (Surat az-Zumar, Ayat 65)

And Allaah, the Most High, says, ﴾***Verily, We have sent down the Book to you (Oh Muhammad) in truth. So, worship Allaah (Alone) by doing religious deeds sincerely for Allaah's sake only. Surely, the religion (i.e. the worship and the obedience) is for Allaah only.***﴿- (Surat az-Zumar, Ayats 2-3)

These noble verses, and others which come with their many meanings, are proofs that the actions are not accepted unless they are done solely for Allaah, purified from associating others along with Him; hence, the importance which the messengers, may Allaah's praise and salutations be upon them all, placed upon *'aqeedah* first. As the first thing which they called their people to was worshipping Allaah alone, and leaving the worship of other than Him, as Allaah, the Most High, says,

﴾***And verily, We have sent among every Ummah (community, nation) a Messenger (proclaiming): "Worship Allaah (Alone), and avoid (or keep away from) taaghoot (all false deities)."***﴿- (Surat an-Nahl, From Ayat 36)

And every messenger said at the beginning of his speech to his people,

﴾***"Oh my people! Worship Allaah! You have no other Ilaah (God) but Him."***﴿- (Surat al-A'araaf, Ayats 59, 65,73, 85) Nuh said this, as did Hud, Saalih, Shu'ayb, and all of the prophets, to their people.

The Messenger of Allaah, may Allaah's praise and salutations be upon him, remained in Makkah for thirteen years after being sent, calling the people to *at-tawheed* (التوحيد), and to correct *'aqeedah*. This is because it is the foundation upon which the religion is built. And every caller and rectifier in every place emulated the prophets and messengers, beginning with calling to *at-tawheed* and the rectification of the beliefs, then turning after that to the remaining matters of the affairs of the religion. (End of quote from Sheikh Fauzaan, may Allaah preserve him)

What is the ruling concerning learning the correct 'aqeedah?

Sheikh Saalih ibn Fauzaan ibn 'Abdullah al-Fauzaan, may Allaah preserve him, was asked:

Question: What is it obligatory for the Muslim to understand about his religion, of belief and legislation?

Answer: It is obligatory upon the Muslim to understand all of the matters of his religion, both of belief and that which is legislated. With that he learns the matters of *al-'aqeedah*, and that which it makes obligatory, and that which is opposite to it, and that which completes it, and that which makes it deficient, until his *'aqeedah* is the correct, sound *'aqeedah*. And it is likewise obligatory upon him to learn the rulings of his religion concerning actions, until he performs that which Allaah has made obligatory upon him, and leaves that which Allaah has made forbidden for him, with insight and understanding.

Allaah, the Most High, says, ***﴾So know (Oh Muhammad) that La ilaaha illallaah (none has the right to be worshipped but Allaah), and ask forgiveness for your sin, and also for (the sin of) believing men and believing women.﴿*** - (Surah Muhammad, From Ayat 19)

So He begins with knowledge, before speech and action.

It is necessary that from the knowledge comes the action, as knowledge without action is not sufficient- even if the one who acts upon it dislikes it- and it is a proof upon the people. And the action without the knowledge is not correct, because it is going astray. And Allaah has commanded us to ask protection from the way of those who incur His anger, and those who are astray at the end of *Surat al-Faatihah* in every *rak'at* in our *salaat*.

("*al-Muntaqa*", from the *Fataawa* of the Esteemed Sheikh Saalih al-Fauzaan, Vol. 1, Page 310)

Sheikh Muqbil ibn Haadee al-Wadi'ee, may Allaah have mercy upon him, was asked:

Some of the women hear the word "'*aqeedah*", and they do not understand anything about *'aqeedah*. So what is "*'aqeedah*", what is its significance, and what is the ruling concerning learning it?

The Sheikh, may Allaah have mercy upon him, answered:

All praise is due to Allaah, the Lord of the Worlds, and may His praise and salutations be upon our Prophet, Muhammad, and upon his family and all of his companions. I bear witness that there is no god worthy of worship except for Allaah, alone, without associating any partners along with Him, and I bear witness that Muhammad is His slave and messenger. To Proceed:

"*'Aqeedah*" encompasses the beliefs, from *at-tawheed* (belief in the oneness of Allaah, and His uniqueness and worship of Him alone) of Allaah, Glorified is He, the Most High. This includes *tawheed ar-ruboobiyyah* (*tawheed* of Lordship), *tawheed al-uloohiyyah* (singling out Allaah alone in worship) and *tawheed al-asmaa wa as-sifaat* (*tawheed* concerning Allaah's names and attributes). Likewise it includes belief in the prophets which have come before, as well as belief in those events which will occur in the future on the Day of Judgment, *al-*

Jennah (Heaven) and *an-Naar* (the Hellfire), and the weighing of the actions in the scales, and the pathway (*as-siraat*). And the best book written concerning *'aqeedah* is the book of at-Tahaawee, may Allaah, the Most High, have mercy upon him. If possible, study it along with its explanation by Ibn Abi al-'Iz, but if that is not possible, then there is still much good in it.

Concerning the ruling of studying *al-'aqeedah*, then it is an obligatory matter, and it is contained in that which he, may Allaah's praise and salutations be upon him, said, ***{Seeking knowledge is obligatory upon every male and female Muslim.}*** (Narrated in Abu Ya'laa. No.2837, and other than him from Anas, may Allaah be pleased with him, and Sheikh al-Albaani has declared it to be authentic in "*al-Mishkaat*")

This is obligatory upon the women and the men. Yes- the matter contains that which is easy for the women, and likewise the general people. As for the student of knowledge, then it necessary that he study '*aqeedah* in its entirety and with its proofs. He must study it from the Book of Allaah, and that which is authenticated from the Sunnah of the Messenger of Allaah, may Allaah's praise and salutations be upon him and his family. There have also been books written on the subject of *'aqeedah*, such as *"Kitaab ash-Sharee'ah"* of al-Aajuree, *"as-Sunnah"* of 'Abdullah ibn Ahmad, *"at-Tawheed"* of Ibn Khuzaymah, *"as-Sunnah"* of Ibn Abi 'Aasim. Likewise, *"as-Sunnah"* of Muhammad ibn Nasr al-Maroozee, *"Sharh 'Itiqaad ahl-as-Sunnah"* of al-Laalakaa'ee, which is known to be one of the most comprehensive of the books.

So it is necessary for the student of knowledge to study the likes of these books, which encompass all of the principles of the beliefs of the people of the Sunnah- particularly the book of al-Laalakaa'ee, as it mentions predestination in it, as well as the miracles of the righteous people and other issues of belief, may Allaah grant him good. The important thing is that it is necessary for the Muslim- rather, it is obligatory upon him, to study them. And from the best of the books, is *"al-'Aqeedatu al-Waasitiyyah"* by Sheikh al- Islaam ibn Taymiyyah- and likewise its explanation, and others such as *"at-Tanbeehaat as-Sunniyyah"*, and *"Kitaab at-Tawheed"* by Sheikh Muhammad ibn 'Abdul Wahaab, and "*al-Qawlu al-Mufeed fee Adilatu at-Tawheed"* by Sheikh Muhammad ibn 'Abdul Wahaab al-'Abdulee al-Wasaabee, and also, *"Fath al-Majeed"* is from the valuable books. And perhaps the one who is able to read and write would benefit from *"al-Qawlu al-Mufeed"*, and from *"Kitaab at-Tawheed"* also, from the two Sheikhs Muhammad ibn 'Abdul Wahaab an-Najdee and the other, al-Abdulee. (Meaning the two Sheikhs named Muhammad ibn 'Abdul Wahaab- one is an-Najdee, the other is al-Wasaabee). (End of translation from *"Asilatu Nisaa li Hajj"* as collected in *"Fataawa al-Mar'at al- Muslimah"* of Imaam al-Waadi'ee, pages 18-19)

From where do we learn about 'aqeedah?

Sheikh Saalih Fauzaan, may Allaah preserve him, said, in *"Kitaab 'Aqeedatu at-Tawheed"*, pages 11-12:

'Aqeedah is established and unchanging, as it is not confirmed except through proofs from the Islamic legislation, and there is no departing from it to follow opinion or independent judgment. Consequently, its origin and source is limited to that which comes from the Book and the Sunnah. This is because there is no one who is more knowledgeable about Allaah and that which He has made obligatory, and nothing is deemed to be superior to Allaah, than Allaah. And there is no one after Allaah who is more knowledgeable concerning Allaah than the Messenger of Allaah, may Allaah's praise and salutations be upon him. This is the way of the pious predecessors and those who followed them concerning limiting obtaining one's understanding of *'aqeedah* to the Book and the Sunnah.

This is because they believed in that which is established in the Book and the Sunnah concerning the right and reality of Allaah, the Most High, they had faith in it, and acted upon it. And that which was not established in the Book of Allaah and the Sunnah of His Messenger, they denied it, as Allaah, the Most High, and rejected it. Due to this, there never occurred between them differing in beliefs. Rather, their beliefs were one, and their community was one; because Allaah guaranteed for the ones who held fast to His Book and the Sunnah of His Messenger unity of speech, and correctness of belief and a unified path. He, the Most High, says,

﴾***And hold fast, all of you together, to the Rope of Allaah (i.e. this Qur'aan), and be not divided among yourselves***﴿- (Surat aal-'Imraan, From Ayat 103)

And He, the Most High, says, ﴾***Then if there comes to you guidance from Me, then whoever follows My Guidance he shall neither go astray nor shall be distressed.***﴿- (Surat Taa Haa, From Ayat 123)

Due to that, they were labeled "The Saved Sect"; because the Prophet, may Allaah's praise and salutations be upon him, bore witness to salvation for them when he informed them of the dividing of the *Ummah* (Muslim nation) into seventy-three sects, all of them in the Hellfire except for one. And when he was questioned about this one, he said, ***{They are the ones who are upon that which I and my Companions are upon today.}***" (Narrated by Imaam Ahmad).

And confirmation of that which he spoke of has occurred, as whenever some of the people build their belief system upon other than the Book and the Sunnah- from the science of philosophical rhetoric, or rational principles transmitted from Greek philosophy- there comes about deviation and differing in beliefs due to the differing speech; and the community is divided, and a break occurs in the building of the Islamic society.
(End of quote from Sheikh Fauzaan, may Allaah preserve him)

The Second: It is obligatory upon the woman to worship Allaah alone, without associating any partners along with Him in worship.

Allaah, the Most High, says in His Noble Book, ﴿***And verily, We have sent among every ummah (community, nation) a messenger (proclaiming): "Worship Allaah (Alone), and avoid (or keep away from) taaghoot (all false deities, i.e. do not worship anything besides Allaah).***﴾- (Surat an-Nahl, From Ayat 36)

And He, Glorified and Exalted is He, says, ﴿***Verily, whosoever sets up partners (in worship) with Allaah, then Allaah has forbidden Paradise to him, and the Fire will be his abode. And for the polytheists and wrong doers there are no helpers.***﴾- (Surat al-Maa'idah, From Ayat 72)

Allaah, the Most High, says, ﴿***Verily, Allaah forgives not that partners should be set up with Him (in worship), but He forgives except that (anything else) to whom He wills; and whoever sets up partners with Allaah in worship, he has indeed invented a tremendous sin.***﴾- (Surat an-Nisaa, Ayat 48)

Sheikh Muhammad ibn 'Abdul Wahaab an-Najdee, may Allaah have mercy upon him, said,

The Principles of the Religion and its Fundamentals Consist of Two Matters:

The First: The command to worship Allaah Alone, without associating any partners with him, and being motivated by that and inciting others to it, and support and loyalty due to it, and to know that the one who leaves it has disbelieved.

The Second: Warning away from *ash-shirk* (associating others along with Allaah in worship) in the worship of Allaah, and strength upon that, and enmity due to it, and knowing that the one who engages in it has disbelieved. ("*ad-Duroor as-Suniyyah*")

The first principle the Sheikh mentions is that of *at-tawheed*. The second, *ash-shirk*.

Definition of at-Tawheed and ash-Shirk:

التوحيد *(at-tawheed)*: singling out Allaah alone as the One who creates, and the One who provides and sustains, and directing all acts of worship to Him alone, and leaving off the worship of other than Him, and confirming that which He has of beautiful names and lofty attributes, and that He is free from any fault or defect. This definition encompasses all three aspects of *at-tawheed*. (Sheikh Saalih Fauzaan, *"Kitaab 'Aqeedatu at-Tawheed"*, Page 21)

As Sheikh Muqbil, may Allaah have mercy upon him, mentioned in the preceding *fatwa*, *tawheed* is divided into three categories, according to the majority of the scholars, past and present: **توحيد الربوبية**: *tawheed ar-ruboobiyyah* (*tawheed* of Lordship), **توحيد الألوهية**: *tawheed al-uloohiyyah* (singling out Allaah alone in worship) and **توحيد الأسماء والصفات**: *tawheed al-asmaa wa as-sifaat* (*tawheed* concerning Allaah's names and attributes). It is also permissible to divide it into two categories, as has been done by many of the scholars of *ahl-as-sunnah*. The first being **توحيد في المعرفة و الإثبات**: *tawheed fee al-ma'rifatu wa al-ithbaat*, which encompasses *tawheed ar-ruboobiyyah* and *tawheed al-asmaa wa as-sifaat*, and **توحيد في الطلب والقصد**: *tawheed fee at-talab wa al-qisd*, which is *tawheed al-uloohiyyah*. This is used by Sheikh al-Islaam ibn Taymiyyah, his student, Ibn Qayyim, and others.

A Brief Description of each Category of at-Tawheed

توحيد الربوبية: *tawheed ar-ruboobiyyah* (*tawheed* of Lordship): Sheikh Sulaymaan ibn 'Abdullah ibn 'Abdul Wahaab said, "This is accepting that Allaah, the Most High, is the Lord of everything, and its Master, and the One who created it, and the One who provides for it that which it needs, and the One who gives life and causes death, the One who allows any harm, and Who brings any benefit, the Sole Possessor of the ability to answer the supplications of the one in need. The command over all things is His, and in His hand is all good, He is the One with power over all things, and there are no partners with Him in that. And faith in *al-qadr*, or the Divine Decree, falls under this category.

This branch of *tawheed* is not sufficient for the worshipper to attain Islaam. Rather, it is necessary that along with it comes the obligation of *tawheed al-uloohiyah*, or worship, because Allaah, the Most High has narrated concerning the polytheists, that they affirm this aspect of *tawheed* to Allaah alone (and it did not enter them into Islaam)." ("*Fatawaa al-Aimatu an-Najdiyyah*" Volume 1, Pages 121-122)

توحيد الألوهية: *tawheed al-uloohiyyah* (singling out Allaah alone in worship): Sheikh Sulaymaan ibn 'Abdullah ibn Muhammad ibn 'Abdul Wahaab defines this category of *at-tawheed*: "This is built upon sincerity and purity in worshipping Allaah, the Most High, alone. This includes love, fear, hope, reliance, desire, reverence, supplication to Allaah alone; and purity in that all acts of worship, the outward and the inward, are done for Allaah, alone, without any partners along with Him, as nothing can be created or put in that place other than Him- not the angels drawn near, or the sent prophets, or other than them.

And this category of *at-tawheed* is the one which is contained in the saying of Allaah, Blessed is He, and Most High, ﴾***You alone do we worship, and You alone do we ask for help***﴿- (Surat al-Faatihah, Ayat 5). And it is the first thing in the religion, and the last, the hidden and the apparent. It is the first thing that the messengers called to, and the last thing. It is the meaning of the words, *"la ilaaha ila Allaah"* (there is no god worthy of worship except Allaah). As He is the God to be worshipped with love, fear, with exaltation and glorification of Him, and with all of the aspects of worship. And the creation was created, and the messengers sent, and the books revealed, for the purpose of fulfilling this aspect of *at-tawheed*. And the people are differentiated through it into Believers and disbelievers, and the happy people of Paradise, and the unhappy people of the Fire." ("*Fataawa al-Aimatu an-Najdiyyah*" Volume 1, Pages 123-124)

توحيد الأسماء والصفات: *tawheed al-asmaa wa as-sifaat* (*tawheed* concerning Allaah's names and attributes): Sheikh al-'Utheimeen, may Allaah have mercy upon him, says in his explanation of "*Thalaathatu al-Usool*", "This is to affirm whatever names or attributes Allaah affirmed for Himself in His Book, or in the Sunnah of His Messenger, may Allaah's praise and salutations be upon him, in a manner which befits Him, without changing or distorting their wording or their meaning, without denial of them, without putting forth how they are, and without declaring them to be like the attributes of creation." (End of quote from Sheikh al-'Utheimeen, may Allaah have mercy upon him)

And the opposite of *at-tawheed* is الشرك (*ash-shirk*): to place associates with Allaah, the Most High, in His Lordship and the worship of Him. Usually this occurs in the worship of Allaah, when one supplicates to other than Allaah along with Him, or changes something from an aspect of worship to be for other than Allaah, such sacrifice, swearing, fear, hope and love. And *shirk* is the greatest of sins. (Definition of Sheikh Saalih Fauzaan, *"Kitaab 'Aqeedatu at-Tawheed"*, Page 92)

'Abdul Lateef ibn 'AbdurRahman ibn Hasan, may Allaah have mercy upon him, said concerning the principles of the religion and its fundamentals,

The foundation of Islaam and its principles are: to worship Allaah alone, and to not associate any partners along with him, and to single Him out with one's requests and intentions. And *tawheed ar-ruboobiyyah* and the belief that His actions are His, the Most High, are not sufficient for happiness and success. And it is not sufficient to make a man a Muslim until he worships Allaah alone, and disavows anything other than him from idols and false deities. (*"ad-Duroor as-Sunniyyah"*, 11/540)

He, may Allaah have mercy upon him, says elsewhere:

Ibn Qayyim said that Islaam is affirming the oneness and uniqueness of Allaah, and worshipping Him alone without any partners along with Him, and faith in His Messenger and following him in that which he came with.

The one in whom all of these are not present has not achieved the state of being Muslim, and if he is not an obstinate disbeliever, then he is still a disbeliever who is ignorant. *("ad-Duroor as-Suniyyah"*, 12/197-198)

The Correct Intention

Along with this, is the matter of the worshipper having the correct intention in all that he or she does concerning belief, speech, and action. As if one performs an action, but for the wrong reason, this action may be corrupted or not accepted from her.

Allaah, the Most High says, ***﴾And they were commanded not, but that they should worship Allaah, and worship none but Him Alone and perform as-salaat (the prayers) and give zakaat (obligatory charity), and that is the right religion.﴿*** – (Surat al-Bayyinah, Ayat 5)

It is narrated upon 'Umar ibn al-Khataab, may Allaah be pleased with him, that he said, I heard the Messenger of Allaah, may Allaah's praise and salutations be upon him, say,

{Indeed the actions are by their intentions, and indeed for each person is that which he intended. So the one whose hijrah is for Allaah and His Messenger, then his hijrah is for Allaah and His Messenger. And the one whose hijrah is for a worldly aim, or to marry a woman, then his hijrah is for that which he made hijrah.} (al-Bukhaari, No. 1, Muslim 13/53, Abu Daawud No. 2201, an-Nasaa'ee, 1/58,59, at-Tirmidhi, No. 1647, Ibn Maajah, No. 4227, Ahmad, 1/25,43, and Maalik by way of Muhammad ibn al-Hasan, No. 983)

So we must safeguard ourselves and our intentions and strive in all that we do to please Allaah, the Most High, in order that our actions not be lost. And Sheikh Muhammad ibn 'Abdul Wahaab, may Allaah have mercy upon him, says, as quoted in *"al-Waajibaat"*, concerning this purity of intention, or الإخلاص (*al-ikhlaas*) being a condition of *ash-shahaadah*, "The Third: Sincerity, which negates *ash-shirk*" as this negates the major *shirk* of worshipping other than Allaah along with Him, because we are doing our acts of worship solely for Allaah alone, without associating partners with him, and it also negates the minor *shirk* of doing an act in order to be seen by the people as again, our intention by the act is only to please Allaah, not the people. And Allaah knows best.

The Third Obligation: Knowledge

العلم: *al-'ilm*: As it is obligatory upon the Muslim woman to know and understand all that is necessary from the affairs of her religion, especially those matters which have been made obligatory upon her.

Allaah, the Most High, says, concerning knowledge, ﴾***Say: "Are those who know equal to those who know not?" It is only men of understanding who will remember (i.e. get a lesson from Allaah's Signs and Verses).***﴿- (Surat az-Zumar, From Ayat 9)

And He, the Most High, says, ﴾***So know (Oh Muhammad) that Laa ilaaha ila Allaah (none has the right to be worshipped but Allaah), and ask forgiveness for your sin, and also for (the sin of) believing men and believing women.***﴿- (Surat Muhammad, From Ayat 19)

And He, Exalted and Glorified is He, says, ﴾***And those whom they invoke instead of Him have no power of intercession – except for those who bear witness to the truth knowingly, and they know (the facts about the Oneness of Allaah).***﴿- (Surat az-Zukhruf, From Ayat 86)

It is related from Mu'aawiyah, may Allaah be pleased with him, that he said, "The Messenger of Allaah, may Allaah's praise and salutations be upon him, said, ***{The one for whom Allaah desires good, He gives him knowledge (understanding) of the religion.}*** (al-Bukhaari, 7312, Ibn Maajah, 221, Ahmad, 4/92,93,95,96,97,98,99, and ad-Daarimee, 1/73-74)

'Uthmaan, may Allaah be pleased with him, said that Allaah's Messenger, may Allaah's praise and salutations be upon him, said, ***{He who died knowing with certainty that there is none worthy of worship except Allaah, entered Paradise.}*** (Muslim, 26)

And it is known that in the time of the Prophet, may Allaah's praise and salutations be upon him, the women sought knowledge to the best of their ability. It is narrated from Abi Sa'eed al-Khudree, may Allaah be pleased with him, that, ***{A woman came to the Messenger of Allaah, may Allaah's praise and salutations be upon him, and said, "Oh Messenger of Allaah, the men are able to hear most from you, so make for us a day where we come to you and you teach us from that which Allaah has taught you." So he, may Allaah's praise and salutations be upon him, replied, "Gather together on such and such a day, at such and such a place", and he went to them and taught them that which Allaah had taught him.}*** (al-Bukhaari, 7310, Muslim 16/181 of the explanation of an-Nawawi)

These verses and ahaadeeth all bear witness to the important position knowledge has in the life of the Muslim- and the last hadeeth mentions the women in particular, as the Prophet, may Allaah's praise and salutations be upon him, set aside a time and place for addressing the women.

In addition, we know that from the best examples for us to emulate are the righteous women who have come before- and from these, the best of them are the wives of the Messenger of Allaah, may Allaah's praise and salutations be upon him. Let us look at the state of just one of his wives concerning the seeking and spreading of knowledge.

Umm al-Mumineen, 'Aishah, the daughter of Abu Bakr as-Sadeeq, learned directly from the Prophet, may Allaah's praise and salutations be upon him, and then proceeded, after his death, to teach the people of the *ummah* the matters of the religion which she herself knew and understood.

Abu ad-Dahaa narrated that they asked Masrooq, "Did 'Aishah have superior knowledge concerning that which had been enjoined upon the *ummah*?" He said, "*By Allaah, I saw the greatest of the Companions of Muhammad, may Allaah's praise and salutations be upon him, ask 'Aishah concerning those matters.*" (ad-Daarimee, 1/342,343, and al-Haakim, 4/11)

Abu Burdah narrated from Abi Musa, that he said, "*There was no hadeeth of which we, the Companions of Muhammad, may Allaah's praise and salutations be upon him, were uncertain except that when we asked 'Aishah, she had knowledge of it.*" (at-Tirmidhi, 3773)

Hishaam ibn 'Urwah narrated from his father, "*I never saw anyone more knowledgeable concerning that which was permissible and that which was forbidden, and the religious knowledge, rulings and medicine than 'Aishah, the Mother of the Believers, may Allaah be pleased with her.*" (al-Haakim in *"al-Mustadrik"* 4/11, and look in *"Seeyar 'Alaam an-Nubala"* 2/183)

'Ataa ibn Abi Rabaah, said, "*'Aishah had the most knowledge of Islamic legislation, and the most insight into the religion in general.*" (al-Haakim in *"al-Mustadrik"* 4/14, and look in *"Seeyar 'Alaam an-Nubala"* 2/185)

az-Zuhree said, "*If you gathered the knowledge of 'Aishah, may Allaah be pleased with her, and compared it to the knowledge of rest of the women combined, the knowledge of 'Aishah would be superior.*" (al-Haakim in *"al-Mustadrik"* 4/11, and look in *"Seeyar 'Alaam an-Nubala"*)

And 'Aishah, may Allaah be pleased with her, was not alone in being diligent in learning and spreading knowledge, as can be seen when one reads the lives of the women of the Prophet's household, his female Companions, and of the righteous women who have come after them through the ages. So we must take them as our examples, and strive to gain religious knowledge, and then to pass that knowledge on to our children, our families, our companions, and whoever it is within our capability to reach. And Allaah knows best.

What is meant by Knowledge:

Sheikh Saalih Fauzaan, may Allaah preserve him, says concerning knowledge in his explanation of "*Thalaathatu al-Usool*":

al-ilm: it is to know the guidance, along with the proofs; and what is intended by it is that which is an individual obligation on every person to know. And this is all knowledge which is necessary for the mature, responsible person to have concerning the matters of his religion, such as the fundamentals of faith, and the Islamic legislation, and those forbidden things which it is obligatory to stay away from, and that which is required in order to perform religious actions, and also those things which, without them, the obligatory acts cannot be completed- knowledge of these things is obligatory upon him. ("*Jaami' Sharooh al-Usool ath-Thalaathah*", Page 56)

Sheikh Muhammad ibn 'Abdul Wahaab, may Allaah have mercy upon him, says in "*Thalaathatu al-Usool*":

So if it is said to you: What are the three principles which it is obligatory upon mankind to have knowledge of? Then say: The slave must have knowledge of his Lord, his religion, and his prophet, Muhammad, may Allaah's praise and salutations be upon him. ("*Jaami' Sharooh al-Usool ath-Thalaathah*", Page 203)

Know your Lord

Sheikh Muhammad ibn 'Abdul Wahaab, may Allaah have mercy upon him, goes on to say, in the above mentioned work,

If it is said to you: Who is your Lord? Then say: My Lord is Allaah, who has nurtured me and all of creation with His blessings and beneficence. He is the only one I worship, there is nothing worthy of being worshiped other than Him (End of quote)

So how do we learn about our Lord? The first place we turn to, alhamdulillah, is the Qur'aan itself, in which Allaah tells us many of His beautiful names and perfect attributes. Secondly, we look to that which has been related from the Messenger of Allaah, may Allaah's praise and salutations be upon him, concerning Allaah's names and attributes. And, as Sheikh al-'Utheimeen said in the passage quoted earlier in the section on *at-tawheed*, we "...affirm whatever names or attributes Allaah affirmed for Himself in His Book, or in the Sunnah of His Messenger, may Allaah's praise and salutations be upon him, in a manner which befits Him, without changing or distorting their wording or their meaning, without denial of them, without putting forth how they are, and without declaring them to be like the attributes of creation." And this was the way of the Companions and those who have followed them since from the righteous people and the people of knowledge, alhamdulillah.

Sheikh Muhammad ibn 'Abdul Wahaab, may Allaah have mercy upon him, says,

If it is said to you, with what do you attain knowledge of your Lord? Then say: through His signs (آيات), and that which He has created.» ("*Jaami'*

Sharooh al-Usool ath-Thalaathah", Page 203)

Sheikh Abdullaah ibn Saaleh Fauzaan, may Allaah preserve him, says concerning this in his explanation of "*Thalaathatu al-Usool*":

This is the proof that Allaah is the one who created us, and He is the one who provides for us, and that He is the only one to be worshipped, there is nothing other than Him worthy of worship. And in the Arabic language "الآية" (*al-ayat*) has many meanings. From them are evidence and proof. And the *ayaat* of Allaah fall into two categories:

1. آيات شرعية (*ayaat shariyyah*): Legislated signs- and what is meant by them, is the revelation which the Messenger came with, as it is a sign or evidence from the signs of Allaah...
2. آيات كونية (*ayaat kawniyyah*): Universal signs- and these are those things which have been created; for example the heavens, earth, people, animals, vegetation and other than these... ("*Jaami' Sharooh al-Usool ath-Thalaathah*", Pages 240-241)

Sheikh al-'Utheimeen, may Allaah have mercy upon him, said, discussing this issue,

...so in whichever is the case, the knowledge of Allaah, the Mighty and Majestic, is arrived at through His signs in the creation, the magnificent things contained within it which are wondrous creations and clear proofs of perfect wisdom. Likewise, through the signs in His *shari'ah*, and the justice to be seen in it, and how it comprises all that is beneficial and repels all that is corrupt. ("*Jaami' Sharooh al-Usool ath-Thalaathah*", Pages 220-221)

Some of the Results of Knowing our Lord

Some of the results that can, through the Grace and Mercy of Allaah upon a person, come from knowledge of the One who created us and provides for us are as follows:

1. Increase in certainty: As by knowing about the different names and attributes of Allaah, such as His being the Most Wise, the Most Merciful, and contemplating and truly believing in them, and seeing the amazing nature of His creation, and the wisdom behind His legislation, can help to make our hearts firm upon His Straight Path.
2. Increase in purification of intention: The same is true concerning our intentions. Because if we truly see, ponder, and believe in the Greatness and Supremacy of Allaah, the Most High, it becomes even clearer that He is the only one worthy of being worshipped and asked for help and guidance.
3. Increase of faith: With an increase in knowledge, certainty, and the purification of our intentions, our faith is given a fertile garden in which to grow and prosper, alhamdulillah. And the benefits of this increase of faith can be felt in every aspect of our lives, if we make our Islaam a reality and act upon it with love, hope, fear, and all the other actions of the heart.
4. More completeness and perfection in performing acts of worship for Allaah: Again, as our knowledge and actions of the heart increase, so will

our determination to strive to worship Allaah correctly, performing all our acts of worship to the absolute best of our ability, seeking the pleasure and reward of Allaah, and protection from His anger and displeasure. This is the aspect of *tawheed al-uloohiyyah*, which has been discussed earlier.

Concerning this, Sheikh al-'Utheimeen, may Allaah have mercy upon him, said, when discussing the hadeeth, ***{Allaah has ninety nine names; whoever enumerates and believes in them, will enter Jennah.}*** (al-Bukhaari, 2736, and Muslim, 2677):

The meaning of "enumerating" them is not that they should be written down on paper until they are memorized; rather, the meaning of that is:

a. To be used by pronouncing them orally

b. To have understanding of their meanings

c. To worship Allaah by that which they necessitate. And there are two aspects of this:

1. To supplicate to Allaah with them, according to the words of Allaah, the Most High, ﴿***...so call on Him by them***﴾- (Surat al-A'raaf, From Ayat 180) making them the means to your request. So you must then choose a suitable name (from the names of Allaah) for your request, (such as) when you ask for forgiveness, say, "*Ya al-Ghafoor* (Oh, Most Forgiving)! Forgive me!" And it is not fitting that you should say, "*Ya Shadeed al-'Iqaab* (Oh, the One who is Severe in Punishment) Forgive me!" As indeed this resembles making a joke. Rather, one should say, "Grant me protection from your punishment."

2. To implement that which is required by these names into your worship. So, what is required by the name *ar-Raheem* (the Most Merciful) is mercy; thus you should perform the righteous deed through which the mercy of Allaah may be attained. This is the matter of "enumerating" them, and since this is so, it is worthy of being the price for entering *Jennah*. ("*Fataawa Arkaan al-Islaam*", Vol. 1)

Know your Prophet

Sheikh Muhammad ibn 'Abdul Wahaab, may Allaah, have mercy upon him, lists as the third principle in his book, "*Thalaathatu al-Usool*":

The Third Principle: Knowledge of your prophet, Muhammad, may Allaah's praise and salutations be upon him. (End of quote)

Sheikh 'Abdur Rahmaan ibn Qaasim an-Najdee states in his explanation of the above work:

This is a great principle, that it is obligatory upon us to know him, as he, may Allaah's praise and salutations be upon him, is the intermediary (meaning, he is the one who was sent with the message, carrying it from Allaah to the people) between us and Allaah, the Most High. And there is no success for us, and no knowledge for us, and no way for us, and we do not know that which will save us from Allaah's anger and punishment, nor that which will bring us close to Allaah's pleasure and reward- except through that which Muhammad, may Allaah's praise and salutations be upon him, brought. ("*Jaami' Sharooh al-Usool ath-Thalaathah*", Page 675)

Sheikh 'Abdul 'Aziz ibn Baaz, may Allaah have mercy upon him, said,

It is upon mankind to know his prophet who Allaah sent to him; the one who related the message, and explained to him the Islamic legislation which Allaah commanded the person with, and made clear for him the worship for which Allaah created him. . ("*Jaami' Sharooh al-Usool ath-Thalaathah*", Page 682)

Sheikh Muhammad ibn Saalih al-'Utheimeen, may Allaah have mercy upon him, lists five matters which are covered in knowledge of the Prophet, may Allaah's praise and salutations be upon him. They are, briefly:

1. His lineage: He is Muhammad ibn 'Abdullah ibn 'Abdal-Mutalab ibn Haashim; and Haashim is from the tribe of Quraish, and Quraish is from the Arabs, and the Arabs are from the descendents of Ismaa'eel ibn Ibraaheem, upon them both, and upon our Prophet the best of praise and salutations.
2. The age he attained, the place he was born, and where he migrated to. He was born in Makkah, in Saudi Arabia. His father was named 'Abdullaah and his mother was Aaminah. He lived in Makkah for fifty-three years before migrating to al-Madinah, where he completed his life. He lived to be sixty-three years old, may Allaah's praise and salutations be upon him and his family.
3. Knowledge about his life as a Prophet. This covered a period of twenty-three years, beginning when he was forty years old. We should read about the persecution and trials that he went through in the first thirteen years of his call to *at-tawheed*, as well as how he established Islaam once he migrated to al-Madinah.
4. The means by which he become a prophet and a messenger. He was given the prophethood first, with the revelation of the first verses of *Surat al-'Alaq*, and the messengership with the first verses of *al-Muddaththir*. To read more about this, read the hadeeth of 'Aishah and of Jaabir found in *"Saheeh al-Bukhaari"* and other than it, concerning the beginning of the revelation, insh'Allaah.
5. What was the message he was sent with, may Allaah's praise and salutations be upon him, and why was he sent? He was sent, as were all of the prophets and messengers before him, with the call to *at-tawheed*, worshipping Allaah alone, doing that which He orders, and leaving that which He forbids. Likewise, he was sent as a warner against *ash-shirk* (associating others with Allaah) and all that it encompasses. He was sent as a mercy to all of mankind, to show them the way to truth and eternal reward, alhamdulillah.

Sheikh al-'Utheimeen, may Allaah have mercy upon him, says concerning this,

He was sent to call to the *tawheed* of Allaah, the Most High, and His Revealed Legislation- which comprises doing whatever He ordered, and leaving off whatever He forbade. He was sent as a mercy to all creation to bring them out of the oppressive darkness of associating others with Allaah and disbelief and ignorance, and to bring them the light of knowledge, true belief, and *at-tawheed*, so that through this they could gain the forgiveness and pleasure of Allaah, and so be saved from His punishment and anger. . ("*Jaami' Sharooh al-Usool ath-Thalaathah*", Page 695)

Concerning love of Muhammad, may Allaah's praise and salutations be upon him, it is related in "*Saheeh Muslim*" that it is reported on the authority of Anas, that the Messenger of Allaah, may Allaah's praise and salutations be upon him, said, ***{No slave believes}*** and, in the hadeeth narrated by 'Abdul Warith, ***{No person believes, until I am dearer to him than the members of his household, his wealth and the whole of mankind.}*** The greatness of the matter is seen here, as the Messenger of Allaah, may Allaah's praise and salutations be upon him, linked love of him with faith itself. And Allaah knows best.

It is Obligatory to Obey the Messenger of Allaah

Sheikh Saalih Fauzaan, may Allaah preserve him, says,

It is obligatory to follow the Prophet, may Allaah's praise and salutations be upon him, by doing that which he commanded, and leaving that which he forbade, and this is from that which is required by the *shahaadah*, or testimony, that he is the Messenger of Allaah. Allaah, the Most High, has commanded that he be followed in many verses, sometimes coupled with obedience to Allaah, such as in His saying,

﴾***Oh you who believe! Obey Allaah and obey the Messenger***﴿- (Surat an-Nisaa, From Ayat 59) and sometimes He commands us with it separately, such as in His saying,

﴾***He who obeys the Messenger has indeed obeyed Allaah***﴿- (Surat n-Nisaa, From Ayat 80) and His saying,

﴾***... and obey the Messenger that you may receive mercy (from Allaah).***﴿- (Surat an-Noor, From Ayat 56)

And sometimes the one who disobeys His Messenger, may Allaah's praise and salutations be upon him, is warned or threatened, as in Allaah's, the Most High, saying,

﴾***And let those who oppose the Messenger's commandment (i.e. his Sunnah) beware, lest some fitnah (trials, afflictions) should befall them or a painful torment be inflicted on them.***﴿- (Surat an-Noor, From Ayat 63)

The Sheikh, may Allaah preserve him, goes on to say,

Allaah makes obeying him (the Messenger of Allaah, may Allaah's praise and salutations be upon him) and following him, a reason for earning the love of Allaah by the worshipper, as well as forgiveness for his sins. He, the Most High, says,

﴾***Say (Oh Muhammad to mankind): "If you love Allaah, then follow me. Allaah will love you and forgive you your sins.***﴿- (Surat Aal-'Imraan, from Ayat 31)

The Sheikh, may Allaah preserve him, says,

Allaah mentions obeying the Messenger and following him in something like forty places in the Qur'aan..." ("*Kitaab 'Aqeedatu at-Tawheed*", Pages 189-191)

Know your Religion

Sheikh Muhammad ibn 'Abdul Wahaab, may Allaah have mercy upon him, says, in "*Thalaathatu al-Usool*

The Second Principle: to know the religion of Islaam with the proofs. It is to submit to Allaah with *tawheed*, and to yield to Him in obedience, and to free and disassociate oneself from associating others with Allaah and those who do that. And it is of three levels: Islaam (submission and obedience to Allaah), *eemaan* (faith, which includes belief of the heart, speech of the tongue, and actions of the limbs) and *ihsaan* (perfection of worship). Each level has its pillars. (End of quote)These levels are taken from the hadeeth of 'Umar ibn al-Khattab, may Allaah be pleased with him, which is related by his son in "*Saheeh Muslim*", which is well known as "the hadeeth of Jibreel":

My father, Umar ibn al-Khattab, told me, "One day we were sitting in the company of the Prophet, may Allaah's praise and salutations be upon him, when there appeared before us a man dressed in pure white clothes, his hair extraordinarily black. There were no signs of travel on him. None amongst us recognized him. He sat with the Prophet, may Allaah's praise and salutations be upon him. He sat with his knees touching his knees, placed his hands on his thighs and said, 'Oh Muhammad, inform me about *al-Islaam*.' The Messenger of Allaah said, ***{To testify that there is no god worthy of worship but Allaah, and that Muhammad is the messenger of Allaah, and establishing prayer, paying obligatory charity, observing the fast of Ramadhaan, and performance of the pilgrimage to the House if you are able.}*** He (the one who was asking) said, 'You have told the truth.' He (Umar ibn al-Khattab) said, 'It amazed us that he would ask the question and then he would himself verify the truth.' He (the one who was asking the questions) said, 'Inform me about *eemaan*. He replied, ***{That you believe in Allaah, His angels, His Books, His messengers, the Day of Judgment, and you believe in the divine decree, both its good and its evil.}*** He said, 'You have told the truth.' He then said, 'Inform me about *al-ihsaan*. He, may Allaah's praise and salutations be upon him, replied, ***{That you worship Allaah as if you are seeing Him, for though you don't see Him, verily He, sees you.}*** He then said, 'Inform me about the Hour.' He, may Allaah's praise and salutations be upon him, replied, ***{The one who is asked knows no more than the one who is asking.}*** He then said, 'Tell me some of its signs.' He, may Allaah's praise and salutations be upon him, answered, ***{That the slave-girl will give birth to her master, and that you will find barefoot, destitute shepherds competing with one another in the construction of lofty buildings.}***" He (Umar) said, "Then he (the questioner) left; but I stayed with him (the Prophet, may Allaah's praise and salutations be upon him) for awhile. He then, said to me, ***{'Umar, do you know who the questioner was?}*** I replied, Allaah and His Messenger know best. He, may Allaah's praise and salutations be upon him, said, ***{He was Jibreel. He came to you in order to teach you concerning matters of your religion.}***"

الإسلام: al-Islaam:

Sheikh Muhammad ibn 'Abdul Wahaab, may Allaah have mercy upon him, defines Islaam in "*Thalaathatu al-Usool*" as,

It is submission to Allaah with *at-tawheed*, and yielding to him with obedience, and separating and disassociating oneself with the act of associating others with Allaah as well as those who do so. (End of quote)

Ibn Qayyim said that Islaam is affirming the oneness and uniqueness of Allaah, and worshipping Him alone without any partners along with Him, and faith in His Messenger and following him in that which he came with. *("ad-Duroor as-Suniyyah"*, 12/198)

Sheikh 'Abdul 'Aziz ibn Baaz, may Allaah have mercy upon him, says,

...and the first of them is Islaam, which is purity of intention directed to Allaah alone, meaning, to submit to Allaah in all aspects of worship, and to single Him out alone for them, without anything other than Him, and to free oneself from *ash-shirk* and the people who commit *ash-shirk*; and if that is done, then one has submitted in Islaam. That is to say, one must be guided by, submit to, and be obedient to Allaah alone with worship, without anyone along with Him, and free from associating others with Allaah and those who do so, as Allaah, the Most High, says,

﴾Whoever disbelieves in taaghoot (anything placed along with Allaah in worship) and believes in Allaah, then he has grasped the most trustworthy handhold that will never break.﴿ - (Surat al-Baqara, From Ayat 256) ("*Jaami' Sharooh al-Usool ath-Thalaathah*", Page 435)

The Pillars of al-Islaam

The proof for these pillars, in addition to the hadeeth of Jibreel mentioned above, is the hadeeth of Ibn 'Umar, may Allaah be pleased with both of them, who narrated that the Prophet, may Allaah's praise and salutations be upon him, said, ***{Islaam is built upon five: to testify that none has the right to be worshipped except Allaah, and that Muhammad is the Messenger of Allaah, establishment of the prayer, payment of the obligatory charity, fasting Ramadhaan, and making pilgrimage to Allaah's sacred house.}*** (al-Bukhaari and Muslim)

The Testimony that None has the Right to be Worshipped Except Allaah, and Muhammad is the Messenger of Allaah الشهادة *(ash-shahaadah)*

Sheikh 'Abdul 'Aziz ibn Baaz, may Allaah have mercy upon him, says,

'To bear witness that none has the right to be worshipped except Allaah': and by this the worshipper enters into Islaam. To testify that none has the right to be worshipped except Allaah means there is nothing worthy of worship in truth except Allaah. And this is affirmation and negation, as لا إله (*la ilaha*) is the negation, and إلا الله (ila Allaah) is affirmation. Allaah, the

Most High, says,

﴾***You Alone do we worship, and You Alone do we call on for help***﴿- (Surat al-Faatiha, Ayat 5) And He says,

﴾***And they were commanded not, but that they should worship Allaah, and worship none but Him Alone, and perform the prayers and give obligatory charity, and that is the right religion.***﴿- (Surat al-Bayyinat, Ayat 5) And the Most High says,

﴾***That is because Allaah – He is the Truth (the only True God of all that exists, Who has no partners or rivals with Him), and what they (the polytheists) invoke besides Him, it is baatil (falsehood).***﴿- (Surat al-Hajj, Ayat 62)

As for saying it without acting upon it, then there is no benefit in this…as the hypocrites say it, but they do not believe in it, and they are in the lowest level of the Hellfire…

(and the testimony that Muhammad is His Messenger): There are four matters encompassed in this:

1. Obedience to him (the Messenger of Allaah, may Allaah's praise and salutations be upon him) in that which he commands concerning the prayer, fasting, and other than them

2. Affirmation of that which he narrates concerning the Hereafter, Paradise, the Fire, and other than them

3. To leave off that which he has prohibited and spoken against, such as fornication, interest, and other than that from which Allaah and His Messenger have forbidden,.

4. To worship Allaah only with that which He has legislated, and to not invent or introduce into the religion that which Allaah has not legislated. As the Messenger of Allaah, may Allaah's praise and salutations be upon him, said, ***{He who performs an act which is not in conformity with this matter of ours, then it is rejected.}*** (al-Bukhaari and Muslim) and in a narration, ***{He who introduces something new into our affairs that are not of them, then it is rejected.}*** (Muslim)

(End of quote from "*Jaami' Sharooh al-Usool ath-Thalaathah*", Pages 464-465)

Establishment of the Prayer الصلاة *(as-Salaat)*

So know that five prayers a day have been made obligatory upon the Muslim man and the Muslim woman, and that abandoning these prayers causes one to fall outside of Islaam.

﴾***But if they repent [by rejecting shirk and accepting Islam] and perform as-salaat (the prayers), and give az-zakaat (obligatory charity), then leave their way free. Verily, Allaah is Oft-Forgiving, Most Merciful.***﴿- (Surat at-Tawbah, From Ayat 5)

Concerning the abandonment of the prayer, Sheikh al-'Utheimeen, may Allaah have mercy upon him, says,

"However if the person proposing (to the woman in marriage) does not pray at all, neither in congregation (at the *masjid*) or alone, then he is a disbeliever, and he has fallen outside of Islaam. He must be called upon to repent, and if he turns to Allaah in repentance and prays, then Allaah will turn to him with forgiveness, if his repentance is purely and sincerely for Allaah. However, if he does not repent, then he must be executed by the Muslim governmental authorities as an apostate and buried outside the burial grounds of the Muslims without being washed or shrouded or prayers being said over him. The proof of his disbelief is found in evidences from the Book of Allaah, the Most High, and the Sunnah of the Messenger of Allaah, may Allaah's praise and salutations be upon him.

Evidence from the Book is in the saying of Allaah, the Most High,

﴾***Then, there has succeeded them posterity who have given up as-salaat (the prayers) [i.e. made their prayers to be lost, either by not offering them or by not offering them perfectly or by not offering them in their proper fixed times] and have followed lusts. So, they will be thrown in Hell. Except those who repent and believe (in the Oneness of Allaah and His Messenger Muhammad), and work righteousness...***﴿- (Surat Maryam, Ayats 59-60)

His words, ﴾***Except those who repent and believe...***﴿ prove that when he abandons the prayer and follows his vain desires, he is not a believer.

And Allaah, the Most High, says,

﴾***But if they repent [by rejecting Shirk (polytheism) and accept Islamic Monotheism], perform as-salaat (the prayers) and give az-zakaat (obligatory charity), then they are your brethren in religion.***﴿- (Surat at-Tawbah, From Ayat 11)

which proves that brotherhood in the religion cannot be established except through the establishment of the prayer and giving the obligatory charity. However, the Sunnah establishes that the one who abandons the obligatory charity is not a disbeliever if he affirms that it is an obligation but is merely too stingy to pay it...

And the evidence from the Sunnah that the one who abandons the prayer is a disbeliever, is in such as the words of the Prophet, may Allaah's praise and salutations be upon him,

{Truly, between a man and shirk and disbelief is the abandonment of the prayer.} (Muslim, on the authority of Jaabir ibn 'Abdullah, may Allaah be pleased with him, who reported it from the Prophet, may Allaah's praise and salutations be upon him)

It is reported on the authority of Buraidah ibn al-Husaib, may Allaah be pleased with him, that he said, "I heard the Messenger of Allaah, may Allaah's praise and salutations be upon him, say,

{The covenant between us and them is the prayer, so whoever abandons it has committed disbelief.} This was reported by the five well known hadeeth compilers: Imaam Ahmad and the four compilers of the *Sunan*...

These are evidences from the Book of Allaah, the Most High, and the Sunnah of His Messenger, may Allaah's praise and salutations be upon him, that the one who abandons prayer is a disbeliever, whose disbelief takes him outside of Islaam..."

(End of quote from *"Fataawa Arkaan al-Islaam"*, Vol. 1)

Likewise, it is required to perform the prayers in the times in which they are commanded, as the Messenger of Allaah, may Allaah's praise and salutations be upon him, was asked, "What act is most beloved to Allaah?" He replied, ***{The prayer in its allotted time...}*** (al-Bukhaari, 527, Muslim, 2/73, an-Nasaa'ee, 1/292, at-Tirmidhi, 173, Ahmad 1/409,410, 439)

The first thing that the worshipper will be called to account for on the Day of Judgment will be the *salaat*. The Messenger of Allaah, may Allaah's praise and salutations be upon him, said, ***{The first thing that the worshipper will be held responsible for is his salaat. And the first thing that He judges between the people concerning is blood.}*** (an-Nasaa'ee, 7/83, and ibn Maajah, 2615, and the hadeeth is *hasan* due to support from other than it)

Know that *as-salaat* is a foundation of the religion. The Messenger of Allaah, may Allaah's praise and salutations be upon him said, in the hadeeth of Mu'aadh ibn Jabal, may Allaah be pleased with him, ***{Should I inform you of the head of the matter, and its pillar?}*** He said, "Yes, oh Messenger of Allaah! He, may Allaah's praise and salutations be upon him, ***{The head of the matter is Islaam, and its pillar is the salaat.}*** ('Abdur Razaaq, 20303, Ahmad, 5/231, at-Tirmidhi, 2616, and he said, it is *hasan saheeh*)

So, my sisters, guard your five daily prayers- pray them in their allotted times, and make them solely for the pleasure of Allaah alone.

Payment of the Obligatory Charity الزكاة *(az-Zakaat)*

Allaah has enjoined the *zakaat* upon the Believing men and women in almost fifty places in the Qur'aan. From them:

﴿But if they repent [by rejecting shirk and accept Islaam] and perform as-salaat and give az-zakaat then leave their way free.﴾ - (Surat at-Tawbah, From Ayat 5)

﴿Those who give not the zakaat; and they are disbelievers in the Hereafter.﴾ - (Surat al-Fussilat, Ayat 7)

﴿Those who perform as-salaat (the prayers) and give zakaat and they have faith in the Hereafter with certainty.﴾ - (Surat Luqman, Ayat 4)

﴿So, perform as-salaat, give az-zakaat and hold fast to Allaah [i.e. have confidence in Allaah, and depend upon Him in all your affairs]. He is your maulaa (Patron, Lord), what an Excellent maulaa and what an Excellent Helper!﴾ - (Surat al-Hajj, From Ayat 15)

And this obligatory charity is often linked with the obligatory prayer, as can be seen in many of the verses, showing again its importance in the religion, alhamdulillah.

Referring to the women in the family of the Messenger of Allaah, may Allaah's praise and salutations be upon him, as well as the Believing women in general, Allaah, Glorified and Exalted is He, says,

﴿And stay in your houses, and do not display yourselves like that of the times of ignorance, and perform as-salaat and give az-zakaat and obey Allaah and His Messenger﴾ - (Surat al-Ahzaab, From Ayat 33)

Giving of *az-zakaat* is linked to Allaah's mercy in many verses, as well as to a great reward. Allaah, the Most High, says,

﴾***And perform as-salaat, and give az-zakaat and obey the Messenger (Muhammad) that you may receive mercy (from Allaah).***﴿- (Surat an-Noor, Ayat 56)

﴾***That (Mercy) I shall ordain for those who are the muttaqoon (the pious) and give zakaat and those who believe in Our ayaat.***﴿- (Surat al-A'raaf, From Ayat 156)

﴾***And that which you give in gift (to others), in order that it may increase (your wealth by expecting to get a better one in return) from other people's property, has no increase with Allaah; but that which you give in zakaat seeking Allaah's Countenance, then those they shall have manifold increase.***﴿- (Surat ar-Room, Ayat 39)

And Allaah makes clear the punishment of the one who refrains from paying the obligatory charity when He, the Most High, says,

﴾***And let not those who covetously withhold of that which Allaah has bestowed on them of His bounty (wealth) think that it is good for them (and so they do not pay the obligatory zakaat). Nay, it will be worse for them; the things which they covetously withheld, shall be tied to their necks like a collar on the Day of Resurrection.***﴿- (Surat aal-'Imraan, From Ayat 180)

Abu Bakr as-Sadeeq, may Allaah be pleased with him, the Companion of the Messenger of Allaah, may Allaah's praise and salutations be upon him, who ruled the Muslims as his *khaleefah* after his death, said, concerning those people who refused to pay the *zakaat* after the death of the Prophet, may Allaah's praise and salutations be upon him, "*By Allaah, if they withhold so much as a young, female goat which they used to pay upon to the Messenger of Allaah, may Allaah's praise and salutations be upon him, we will fight with them due their withholding of it.*" (al-Bukhaari, 1400, Muslim, 1/207, Abu Daawud, 1556, an-Nasaa'ee, 7/76-77, at-Tirmidhi, 2609)

Conditions for the Obligation of az-Zakaat

Sheikh al-'Utheimeen, may Allaah have mercy upon him, was asked, "What are the conditions that must be present for the *zakaat* upon one's wealth to be obligatory?"

Answer: The conditions that make the *zakaat* obligatory are: Islaam, freedom (not being a slave), possession of the minimum amount of property upon which *zakaat* must be paid (*nisab*), its continuance during the passing of the time period after which *zakaat* becomes obligatory on the wealth except in the case of *al-mu'ashsharaat*, or the produce upon which one-tenth of its value must be paid as *zakaat*.

1. Concerning Islaam: it is due to the fact that the disbeliever is not obligated to pay *zakaat*, and it would not be accepted as *zakaat* from him if he paid it in the name of *zakaat*. This is seen in the saying of Allaah, the Most High,

﴾***And nothing prevents their contributions from being accepted from them except that they disbelieved in Allaah and in His Messenger and that they came not to as-salaat except in a lazy state, and that they offer not contributions but unwillingly.***﴿- (Surat at-Tawbah, Ayat 54)

But our saying that it is not obligatory upon the disbeliever and that it is not valid from him, does not mean that he will be pardoned for not paying it in the Hereafter. Rather, he will be punished for it, according to the words of Allaah, the Most High,

﴾***Every person is a pledge for what he has earned, Except those on the Right (i.e. the pious true believers in Islaam). In Gardens (Paradise) they will ask one another, About al-mujrimoon (polytheists, criminals, disbelievers) (and they will say to them): "What has caused you to enter Hell?" They will say: "We were not of those who used to offer the prayers, "Nor we used to feed the needy; "And we used to talk falsehood with vain talkers. And we used to deny the Day of Recompense, "Until there came to us (the death) that is certain."***﴿- (Surat al-Muddaththir, Ayats 38-47)

This is a proof that the disbelievers will be punished for their transgressions concerning acts of faith and obedience.

2. Concerning freedom: this is because the slave has no property, as his property belongs to his master, as is seen in the saying of the Prophet, may Allaah's praise and salutations be upon him, ***{Whoever sold a slave who has property, his property belongs to the seller, unless the purchaser makes it a condition (of sale).}*** (Reported by Ahmad) He (the slave) is not the owner of the property which would make the *zakaat* obligatory for him. If it happened that a slave did own something which he acquired, then his property in the end will revert to his master, because the master has the right to take that which is in his hands. Based upon this, ownership is not complete, and it is not permanent like the ownership of free men.

3. Concerning possession of the *nisab*: It means that a person has property which amounts to the minimum liable to the payment of *zakaat*, which has been determined by the Islamic legislation. This differs according to the type of property. If a person does not own the minimum amount, then there is no *zakaat* obligatory upon him because he has little wealth himself, and so it is not possible that he could help others...

4. As for the passing of the *hawl* (a period of one year): This is due to the fact that the obligation of *zakaat* in a period of less than a year would be unjust to the rich, while making it an obligation in a period greater than a year would cause harm to the people who are entitled to receive the *zakaat*. So, it is from the wisdom of the Islamic legislation that a certain period of time has been fixed for paying it, and that is a year. By making it dependent upon a year, there is a balance between the rights of the rich and the rights of those people who are entitled to receive the *zakaat*...(From *"Fataawa Arkaan al-Islaam"*, Vol. 2)

The Obligatory Fast الصوم (as-Sawm)

Allaah, the Most High, says in His Noble Book concerning the obligatory fast,

﴾***Oh you who believe! Observing as-sawm (the fasting) is prescribed for you as it was prescribed for those before you, that you may become al-Muttaqoon (the pious.) [Observing sawm] for a fixed number of days, but if any of you is ill or on a journey, the same number (should be made up) from other days. And as for those who can fast with difficulty, (e.g. an old man), they have (a choice either to fast or) to feed a needy person (for every day). But whoever does good of his own accord, it is better for him. And that you fast is better for you if only you know. The month of Ramadhaan in which was revealed the Qur'aan, a guidance for mankind and clear proofs for the guidance and the criterion (between right and wrong). So, whoever of you sights (the crescent on the first night of) the month (of Ramadhaan, i.e. is present at his home), he must observe sawm that month, and whoever is ill or on a journey, the same number [of days which one did not observe the fast must be made up] from other days. Allaah intends for you ease, and He does not want to make things difficult for you. (He wants that you) must complete the same number (of days), and that you must magnify Allah for having guided you so that you may be grateful to Him.***﴿- (Surat al-Baqara, Ayats 183-185)

And this command is general, for both the men and the women; however, if the woman is on her menses, then she does not fast, and makes up the days at a later time.

Sheikh Muqbil ibn Haadee al-Wadi'ee, may Allaah have mercy upon him, was asked,

"What is the ruling concerning the women who eats in Ramadhaan because she is pregnant and fears for her unborn baby, or the one who is nursing and fears for the health of her nursing child?"

Answer: The scholars differ concerning this; some of them say it is obligatory upon her to make up the days, others say, she must make up the days and feed the needy for each day she missed. Some say she does not have to make up the days but has to feed the needy, and some who say there is neither upon her. They (the ones who say neither are upon her) use for proof the hadeeth of Anas ibn Maalik al-Ka'bee, may Allaah be pleased with him, when he went before the Prophet, may Allaah's praise and salutations be upon him and his family, and he said to him ***{Eat.}*** He (Anas) replied, "Indeed, I am fasting." He replied, ***{Sit down and I will tell you about the fast and prayer. As Indeed Allaah has removed half of the prayer upon the traveler, and the fast from the pregnant and nursing woman.}*** (Abu Daawud, and it has been declared authentic by Sheikh Muqbil in "*al-Jaami' as-Saheeh*" 2/438 and Sheikh al-Albaani in "*Saheeh Sunan Abi Daawud*" 2107)

And that which is clear to me is that it is only upon her to make up the days she missed, as the feeding of the poor is not required from her, and it is not sufficient for her, as Allaah, the Most High, says, ﴾***(Observing the fast) for a fixed number of days, but if any of you is ill or on a journey, the same number (should be made up) from other days.***﴿- (Surat al-Baqara, from Ayat 184)

The Pilgrimage to the House of Allaah (الحج)

The Permanent Committee of Scholars in Saudi Arabia said, concerning the *hajj*,

Hajj is a pillar from the pillars of Islaam, and the one who denies it or dislikes it after this has been made clear to him is a disbeliever. He must be told to repent, and if he does so, then he is not fought (meaning, he is not considered a disbeliever). It is obligatory upon the one who is able, to hasten to perform the acts of *hajj*, as seen in Allaah's, the Most High, saying,

﴾***And hajj (pilgrimage to Makkah) to the House (Ka'bah) is a duty that mankind owes to Allaah, those who can afford the expenses (for one's conveyance, provision and residence); and whoever disbelieves [i.e. denies hajj (then he is a disbeliever], then Allaah stands not in need of any of al-'aalameen (mankind, jinn and all that exists).***﴿- (Surat aal-'Imraan, From Ayat 97) And with Allaah is success, and may Allaah's praise and salutations be upon our Prophet Muhammad, his family, and his companions.

("*Qatf al-Azhaar al-Mutanaathirah min Fataawa al-Mar'at al-Muslimah*" Vol. 1, Page 453)

And it is a condition upon the believing woman that she must have with her a *mahram* in order for her to make *hajj*. The Permanent Committee of Scholars in Saudi Arabia said concerning this,

The woman who does not have a *mahram*, then it is not obligatory upon her to make the pilgrimage. This is because in regards to her, the *mahram* is included in that which is meant by the "means" to make the pilgrimage, and having the means to do so is one of the conditions which makes the *hajj* obligatory. As Allaah, the Most High, says, ﴾***And hajj (pilgrimage to Makkah) to the House (Ka'bah) is a duty that mankind owes to Allaah, those who can afford the expenses (for one's conveyance, provision and residence)***﴿- (Surat aal-'Imraan, From Ayat 97)

It is not permissible for her to travel on *hajj* or other than it except that she has with her her husband or some other *mahram* (such as her father or brother or son), as it is related in al-Bukhaari and Muslim, from ibn 'Abaas, may Allaah be pleased with them both, that he heard the Prophet, may Allaah's praise and salutations be upon him, say, ***{A man should not be alone with a woman, except in the presence of one who is mahram for her. And a woman cannot travel except that she has with her a mahram.}*** A man stood up and said, "Oh Messenger of Allaah! My wife has gone out on *hajj*, and I am pledged in the battle of such and such!" He, may Allaah's praise and salutations be upon him, said, ***{You are released from that obligation. Go and make hajj with your wife.}*** (al-Bukhaari, 3006, and Muslim, 3336)...

And with Allaah is success, and may Allaah's praise and salutations be upon our Prophet Muhammad, his family, and his companions. ("*Qatf al-Azhaar al-Mutanaathirah min Fataawa al-Mar'at al-Muslimah*" Vol. 1, Page 456-457)

الإيمان: *al-Eeman:*

Sheikh Muhammad ibn 'Abdul Wahaab, may Allaah have mercy upon him, says, in "*Thalaathatu al-Usool*":

> The second level: *al-eemaan*; and it has seventy and some branches, the highest of which is the saying that "none has the right to be worshipped except Allaah", and the lowest of which is to remove that which is harmful from the path. And modesty is a branch of *eemaan*. Its pillars are six: to believe in Allaah, His angels, His books, His messengers, the Last Day, and to believe in *al-qadr* القدر (pre-decree) both its good and its evil (End of quote)

Sheikh Saalih ibn 'Abdul 'Aziz aal-ash-Sheikh, may Allaah preserve him, states, concerning belief:

And the foundation of "*al-eemaan*" in the language is as I have stated to you before: it is unqualified belief or affirmation, as it is affirmed and established, or definitive. As for the Islamic definition, faith is speech and action and belief, or we say, *al-eemaan* according to the Islamic definition is speech and action. This is because the speech is the speech of the tongue as well as the speech of the heart, and action is the action of the heart as well as the action of the limbs. So if it is stated by one of the people of the Sunnah who say this, "*al-eemaan* is speech and action", then what is meant by this is speech, action, and belief, because speech is divided into speech of the tongue and speech of the heart:

1. Speech of the tongue: it is pronunciation and acknowledgement made evident through its pronunciation
2. Speech of the heart: the intention

And action is divided into action of the heart and action of the limbs:

1. Action of the heart: and it has many divisions. From them are the categories of belief, and the acts of worship which take place in the heart, such as reverence, fear, and hope. As action is the category of these activities from the actions of the heart. Likewise, the various acts of worship which take place in the heart- these are actions of the heart.
2. Also, the actions of the limbs: and this (i.e these categories of speech and action) is the meaning of those who say that *al-eemaan* is speech with the tongue, and belief in the heart, and acting upon the pillars, in addition to obeying the Most Merciful and not obeying *ash-Shaytaan*. ("*Jaami' Sharooh al-Usool ath-Thalaathah*", Page 585-586)

To Believe in Allaah

Sheikh 'Abdur Rahmaan ibn Qaasim an-Najdee says, "This is the greatest of the pillars of faith, and the most fundamental of its principles. Its meaning is to have faith in the Oneness of Allaah, the Most High, and His Uniqueness concerning His Names and Attributes, as well as faith that He is the only true god, and that worship of other than Him is the most false of the falsehoods, and the most astray of all going astray." (End of quote from "*Jaami' Sharooh al-Usool ath-Thalaathah*", Page 542)

This includes understanding and affirmation of the categories of *at-tawheed* mentioned earlier.

To Believe in His Angels

Sheikh 'Abdullah ibn Saalih al-Fauzaan, may Allaah preserve him, says, in his explanation of "*Thalaathatu al-Usool*":

This is the second pillar, and it is belief in the angels. The angels are from the world of the unseen, and Allaah created them from light. They are worshippers of Allaah, the Most High, they do not disobey Allaah in anything that He commands them, and they do all that they are commanded. No one knows their number except for Allaah, Glorified is He, Most High. Allaah, the Most High, says, ***And none can know the hosts of your Lord but He.***- (Surat al-Muddaththir, From Ayat 31). And from that which is evidence of their great numbers and that only Allaah knows their numbers, Glorified is He, and Most High, is that which is narrated in the hadeeth which comes with an authentic chain of narration, concerning that which related about the *bayt al-ma'moor*. The Messenger of Allaah, may Allaah's praise and salutations be upon him, said, ***{Verily the bayt al-ma'moor in the seventh heaven in relation to the Ka'bah- seven thousand angels visit it every day and (the same ones) do not return to it.}*** (Al-Mustadrak 3677, Ahmad 12333, Sunan Al-Kubra 11084) This is proof that the number of angels is unknown except to Allaah. And belief in the angels comprises four matters: (Compiler's note: this is a summarized listing- the Sheikh goes into detail concerning each one. For more information, see his explanation of "*Thalaathatu al-Usool*")

1. Belief in their existence, and that they are created beings which worship Allaah, and who establish all that they are commanded with by Allaah
2. Belief in those angels whose names we have knowledge of, and belief in those whose names we do not know specifically
3. We believe in that which have been taught concerning their attributes and existence
4. The belief in that which we have been taught concerning their actions and that which they are charged with, which texts establish the proofs for

("*Jaami' Sharooh al-Usool ath Thalaathah*", Pages 600-601)

To Believe in His Books

Sheikh 'Abdullah ibn Saalih al-Fauzaan says, in the above quoted work, concerning belief in Allaah's books:

This is the third pillar, and it is belief in the books. And that which is intended by the books are the divine books which Allaah, the Most High, sent down to His messengers, as a guidance to mankind, and a mercy, by which one may reach happiness and well being in the two worlds (that of the present and the Hereafter). And faith in the books is not complete except with these four matters (Compiler's note: this is a summarized listing- the Sheikh goes into detail concerning each one. For more information, see his explanation of "*Thalaathatu al-Usool*"):

1. To believe that they were in truth sent down by Allaah
2. To believe in those books whose names we know, such as the Qur'aan, and that which has not been changed or distorted from previous books
3. To affirm all that is authentic from that which they relate, such as that which has been related in the Qur'aan
4. To act upon those rulings which they contain which have not been abrogated

("*Jaami' Sharooh al-Usool ath-Thalaathah*", Pages 601-602)

Belief in His Messengers

Sheikh 'Abdullah ibn Saalih al-Fauzaan, may Allaah preserve him, says in concerning this pillar of faith:

This is the fourth pillar, and it is belief in the Messengers (الرسل) *ar-rusul*. And رسل is the plural of رسول *rasool*. And رسول is: one who has been sent by Allaah to a people, and revealed to him a book, or not revealed to him a book but gave him revelation concerning rulings which were not in the previous legislation.

And as for a prophet (نبي), then he is one who has been commanded by Allaah to call to the previous divine legislation, without sending down to him a new book, or without any revelation concerning new rulings or without abrogating (the old legislation). So because of this, it can be said that every messenger is a prophet, but every prophet is not a messenger...

And belief in the Messengers contains four matters (Compiler's note: this is a summarized listing- the Sheikh goes into detail concerning each one. For more information, see his explanation of "*Thalaathatu al-Usool*"):

1. To believe that they were truly messengers, sent by Allaah, the Most High, and that they did not come with anything from themselves
2. Belief in the ones whose names we know, as well has having the general belief in all of those whose names we do not know.
3. To affirm that which is authentic from their reports
4. To act upon the legislation which was sent to us from (these messengers) and he was their seal, Muhammad, may Allaah's praise and salutations be upon him.

("*Jaami' Sharooh al-Usool ath-Thalaathah*", Pages 602-603)

Belief in the Last Day

Sheikh Fauzaan, may Allaah preserve him, states,

This is the fifth pillar, and it is belief in the Last Day, and it is the Day of Resurrection upon which Allaah will resurrect the creation in order that they face their reckoning and retribution. It is called the Last Day because there is no day after it, as the people of Jennah (heaven) will be established in Jennah, and the people of the Hellfire will be established in the Fire. And faith in the Last Day is not complete without three matters being present:

1. Belief in the resurrection
2. Belief in the reckoning and the retribution (for our deeds in this life)
3. Faith in the Jennah and the Hellfire

("*Jaami' Sharooh al-Usool ath-Thalaathah*", Page 603)

Belief in *al-qadr* القدر (pre-decree) Both its Good and its Evil

Sheikh 'Abdullah ibn Saalih al-Fauzaan, may Allaah preserve him, says,

This is the sixth pillar. And that which is meant by *al-qadr* is the decree of Allaah, the Most High, concerning that which will be or occur, in accordance with His knowledge which preceded everything, and in accordance with His wisdom. And faith in *al-qadr* is not complete except with four matters:

1. Belief in the knowledge of Allaah and that He knows what did occur, and what will occur, and how it would occur
2. Belief in the writing (in the Preserved Tablet) and that Allaah wrote all that He knows will occur up until the Day of Judgment
3. Belief that nothing can happen in the universe, except that Allaah wishes it to occur
4. Belief that Allaah, Exalted is He, Most High, created the creation and their deeds and their actions

("*Jaami' Sharooh al-Usool ath-Thalaathah*", Pages 603-204)

الإحسان: *al-Ihsaan:*

Sheikh Muhammad ibn 'Abdul Wahaab, may Allaah have mercy upon him, says, in "*Thalaathatu al-Usool*":

The third level: *al-ihsaan*; it is a single pillar, which is: that you worship Allaah as though you were seeing Him, and even though you do not see Him, then certainly He sees you. The proof is the saying of Allaah, the Most High,

﴾***Truly, Allaah is with those who fear Him (keep their duty to Him), and those who are muhsinoon (those who strive to carry out that which He has made obligatory, being heedful of His rights and consistent in obeying Him).***﴿- (Surat an-Nahl, Ayat 128)

﴾***And put your trust in the All-Mighty, the Most Merciful, Who sees you when you stand up (alone at night for tahajjud prayers). And your movements among those who fall prostrate (to Allaah in the five compulsory congregational prayers). Verily, He, only He, is the All-Hearer, the All-Knower.***﴿- (Surat ash-Shooraa, Ayats 217-220)

And His saying, ﴾***Neither you (Oh Muhammad) do any deed nor recite any portion of the Qur'aan, nor you (Oh mankind) do any deed (good or evil) but We are Witness thereof when you are doing it.***﴿- (Surat Yoonus, From Ayat 61)

(End of quote from "*Thalaathatu al-Usool*")

Sheikh 'Abdul 'Aziz ibn Baaz, may Allaah have mercy upon him, says, in his explanation of "*Thalaathatu al-Usool*":

As for *al-ihsaan*, then it is to perfect the worship, both that which is apparent and that which is hidden. "It is that you worship Allaah as though you were seeing Him, and even though you do not see Him, then certainly He sees you." As the one who worships Allaah upon his formulation, then he will reach the level of *al-ihsaan*, and will gather to himself every good, as Allaah, the Most High, says,

﴾***Truly, Allaah is with those who fear Him (keep their duty to Him), and those who are muhsinoon (those who strive to carry out that which He has made obligatory, being heedful of His rights and consistent in obeying Him).***﴿- (Surat an-Nahl, Ayat 128)

And He, Glorified and Exalted is He, says, ﴾***Surely, Allaah's Mercy is (ever) near to the good-doers.***﴿- (Surat al-A'raaf, From Ayat 56) And the ayat with this meaning are many. ("*Jaami' Sharooh al-Usool ath-Thalaathah*", Page 634)

Sheikh al-'Utheimeen, may Allaah have mercy upon him, says, concerning this level of Islaam:

al-ihsaan is the opposite of behaving wrongly. It means that a person strives to do that which is good, and to repel that which is harmful. So he strives to benefit the servants of Allaah through his wealth, position, knowledge, and his person...

As for *al-ihsaan* in the worship of Allaah, then it is that you worship Allaah as though you were seeing Him, as the Prophet, may Allaah's praise and salutations be upon him, said. So worship performed in this manner- that a person worships his Lord as if he were actually seeing Him- is worship that is accompanied by yearning and seeking, so that the person will find that his soul encourages him upon worship done in this way...

{then even though you do not see Him, then certainly He sees you}: This part shows worship done while fleeing and fearing, and is therefore the second level of *al-ihsaan*...and the people who have knowledge of these matters hold that this level is below the first level (worshipping Allaah as if you see Him). Worship of Allaah, the Most High, is, as Ibn Qayyim, may Allaah have mercy upon him, has stated, "Worship of the Most Merciful is utmost love of Him, along with the worshipper's submission and humility- they are its two pillars."... (summarized from "*Jaami' Sharooh al-Usool ath-Thalaathah*", Pages 642-644)

The Fourth Obligation: Righteous Action

As has been stated previously, along with knowledge comes the obligation of acting upon that knowledge, and performing righteous deeds with the intention of pleasing Allaah, the Most High.

Allaah, Glorified and Exalted is He, says, ***﴾Whoever works righteousness – whether male or female – while he (or she) is a true believer- verily, to him We will give a good life (in this world with respect, contentment and lawful provision), and We shall pay them certainly a reward in proportion to the best of what they used to do (i.e. Paradise in the Hereafter).﴿***- (Surat an-Nahl, Ayat 97)

And He, the Most High, says, ***﴾Whosoever believed in Allah and the Last Day, and worked righteousness, on them shall be no fear, nor shall they grieve.﴿***- (Surat al-Maa'idah, From Ayat 69)

And He, Glorified and Exalted is He, says, ***﴾And whoever does righteous good deeds, male or female, and is a (true) believer (in the Oneness of Allaah) such will enter Paradise and not the least injustice, even to the size of a naqeera (speck on the back of a date stone), will be done to them.﴿***- (Surat an-Nisaa, Ayat 124)

And righteous action has been mentioned by the Prophet, may Allaah's praise and salutations be upon him, in connection with the Muslimah entering *Jennah*, as he, may Allaah's praise and salutations be upon him, said, ***{If the woman prays her five daily prayers, fasts her month (Ramadhaan), safeguards her private parts, and is obedient to her husband, she may enter Jennah from any door she wishes.}*** (this hadeeth is authentic through gathering its different chains of narrations together)

We see from this hadeeth that some of the obligatory acts from the pillars of Islaam are mentioned, such as prayer and fasting- but that included in this are those other acts which have been enjoined upon the woman, which she must strive to perform, intending by them attaining the pleasure of Allaah, the Most High.

Let us remind ourselves what Sheikh Saalih al-Fauzaan, may Allaah preserve him, has said concerning knowledge and action, as previously quoted,

It is necessary that from the knowledge comes the action, as knowledge without action is not sufficient, even if the one who acts upon it dislikes it, and it is a proof upon the people. And the action without the knowledge is not correct, because it is going astray. And Allaah has commanded us to ask protection from the way of those who incur His anger, and those who are astray at the end of *Surat al-Faatihah* in every *rak'at* in our *salaat*. ("*al-Muntaqa*", from the *Fataawa* of the Esteemed Sheikh Saalih al-Fauzaan, Vol. 1, Page 310)

The Fifth Obligation: Calling to Allaah (الدعوة) *ad-Da'wah*

Sheikh 'Abdul 'Aziz Ibn Baaz, may Allaah have mercy upon him, said, in his explanation of "*Thalaathatu al-Usool*":

This means, calling to this religion, and advising the people to establish it and be upright upon it, and to guide them, and to command them with the good, and forbid them from that which is evil. This is calling to the religion of Islaam, and it is upon every Muslim to call to Allaah according to his ability and knowledge. Every one of them, from the men and the women, has a portion of this obligation placed upon him from conveying, calling, guidance and advising, and to call to *tawheed* concerning Allaah, and to the prayer and safeguarding it, and to the obligatory charity and fulfilling it, and to the fast of Ramadhaan, and making pilgrimage to the house if one has the means to do so, and to giving the rights to the parents, and keeping the ties of kinship, and leaving off of all wrongdoing. ("*Jaami' Sharooh al-Usool ath-Thalaathah*", Page25)

Sheikh Saalih ibn 'Abdul 'Aziz Aal-Sheikh, may Allaah preserve him, says, concerning calling to Allaah,

If one has knowledge and action, then he must call to that. And *ad-da'wah* can be through speech, or it can be through action; because making an example through one's actions is *da'wah*. If the Muslim adheres to that which he has been commanded with, then this may guide other than him through wordless guidance to (fulfill) this requirement (as well). The second is calling through the speech of the tongue, and calling through speech can be either obligatory or recommended. *ad-da'wah* with the tongue is divided into different branches of *da'wah*. From them are calling through writing with a pen through authorship (of books or articles), or in pamphlets, or in such as these. Also from them are various types of advice or counsel, exhortation, and such as that. ("*Jaami' Sharooh al-Usool ath-Thalaathah*", Pages47-48)

Concerning the one who calls to Allaah, Sheikh 'Abdullah ibn Saalih Fauzaan, may Allaah preserve him, says,

The fruits of *da'wah* will not come about, and it will not be a means of rectification and establishment (of the religion), except if the one who is calling has the attributes which may cause his call to be accepted, and through which its signs are made manifest. And from them:

1. التقوى *at-taqwa* (piety, fear of Allaah): and what is intended by this, is all of its meanings, from adherence to the commands and

leaving off that which has been forbidden and adorning oneself with the attributes of the people of faith

2. الإخلاص *al-ikhlaas* (purity and sincerity of intention): that he seeks through his *da'wah* the face of Allaah, the Most High, and His pleasure, and goodness for His creation. And he must be cautious of intending by his *da'wah* to appear better than others, or humiliating the one being called by declaring his ignorance and shortcomings

3. العلم *al-'ilm* (knowledge): It is necessary for the one calling to Allaah to have knowledge of that which he is calling to. He must have understanding of that which is brought forth in the Book of Allaah, the Most High, and the Sunnah of His Messenger, may Allaah's praise and salutations be upon him, and the way of the pious predecessors

4. Patience and restraining oneself from becoming angry; as the domain of the caller is the hearts of mankind, and the souls of the people- and these vary and differ, just as their outward appearance and form differ

5. That he begins with that which is most important; that which is most important in relation to the environment in which he is calling. And the matters of belief and the fundamentals of the religion come first. The proof of this is the saying of the Prophet, may Allaah's praise and salutations be upon him, to Mu'aadh, ***{The first matter which you must call them to is to testify that there is none worthy of worship except Allaah, and that Muhammad is His Messenger...}*** To the end of the hadeeth (Bukhaari 4099, Muslim 52)

6. To conduct himself in his calling according to the methodology which Allaah has related in His Noble Book. He, Glorified is He, says, "***Invite (mankind, Oh Muhammad) to the way of your Lord with wisdom and fair preaching, and argue with them in a way that is better.***﴾- (Surat an Nahl, From Ayat 125)

(End of quote from "*Jaami' Sharooh al-Usool ath-Thalaathah*", Pages60-61)

The fruits of calling to Islaam are many. Sheikh al-'Utheimeen, may Allaah have mercy upon him, says, in his explanation of "*Thalaathatu al-Usool*",

Calling to Allaah, the Mighty and Majestic, was the duty of the messengers, and was the path of those who followed them upon good. So when a person knows the One whom he has to worship, and he knows his Prophet, and his religion, and Allaah has favored him with that and guided him to it, then he should strive to save his brothers by calling them to Allaah, the Mighty and Majestic, and should be glad to hear of the good tidings which the Prophet, may Allaah's praise and salutations be upon him, gave to 'Ali ibn Abi Taalib, may Allaah be pleased with him, on the day of Khaybar. He, may Allaah's praise and salutations be upon him, said,

> ***{Proceed without haste until you reach their lands. Then call them to Islaam, and inform them of the rights of Allaah, the Most High, binding upon them; for, by Allaah, it is better for you that Allaah should guide a single man through you than red camels.}*** ("*Saheeh al-Bukhaari*")

And he, may Allaah's praise and salutations be upon him, said, in a narration found in Muslim, ***{Whoever calls to guidance then there is for him a reward like the rewards of those who follow him and that will take nothing away from their rewards. And whoever calls to misguidance will have sin upon him like the sins of those who follow him, and that will take nothing away from their sins.}***

Likewise, he, may Allaah's praise and salutations be upon him, said in another narration, ***{Whoever guides to some good deed, then he receives a reward like that of the one who performs it.}***("*Saheeh Muslim*") ("*Jaami' Sharooh al-Usool ath-Thalaathah*", Pages 40-41)

The Sixth Obligation: Patience (الصبر) as-Sabr

Sheikh 'Abdul 'Aziz ibn Baaz, may Allaah have mercy upon him, says concerning patience in his explanation of "*Thalaathatul Usool*"

Meaning, patiently persevering any harm which comes in any of these matters. As harm will come to mankind; he will become weary of the one he is calling or other than him, from his people or other than them. And that which is obligatory is patience, and being content with the reward which is with Allaah. So the Believer is patient upon his faith in Allaah, and patiently perseveres in acting upon that which Allaah has made obligatory for him, and leaving that which Allaah has forbidden him from. He must have patience in calling to Allaah, teaching, and commanding the good and forbidding the evil. It is necessary to have patience concerning all of these matters- as the religion in its entirety requires patience. This includes patience in calling to Allaah alone, and patience in performing the prayers, paying *az-zakaat*, fasting, making pilgrimage, commanding the good and forbidding the evil; as well as patience concerning that which is forbidden and the sins, as one must beware of coming near to them. As if mankind is not patient, he may fall into that which Allaah has forbidden him, or leave that which Allaah has obligated him with. Concerning this, Allaah, the Most High, said to His Messenger,

﴾***Therefore be patient (Oh Muhammad) as did the Messengers of strong will...***﴿- (Surat al-Ahqaaf, From Ayat 35)

And He, the Most High, says, "***So wait patiently (Oh Muhammad) for the Decision of your Lord, for verily, you are under Our Eyes...***﴿- (Surat at-Toor, From Ayat 48)

And He, the Most High, says, "***And endure you patiently (Oh Muhammad), your patience is not but from Allaah.***" (Surat an-Nahl, From Ayat 127)

And He, the Most High, says, ﴾***...Only those who are patient shall receive their reward in full, without reckoning.***﴿- (Surat az-Zamar, From Ayat 10)

And He, the Most High, says, ﴾***And obey Allaah and His Messenger, and do not dispute (with one another) lest you lose courage and your strength departs, and be patient. Surely, Allaah is with those who are as-saabiroon (the patient)***﴿- (Surat al-Anfaal, Ayat 46)

Meaning, patiently persevere in obedience to Allaah, and leaving wrongdoing, and beware of disobeying His commandments, and performing that which He has forbidden. ("*Jaami' Sharooh al-Usool ath-Thalaathah*", Page 25)

Conclusion

Allaah, the Most High, says,

﴾By al-'asr (the time) Verily man is in loss Except for those who believe, do righteous deeds, and recommend one another to the truth and recommend one another to patience.﴿ - (Surat al-'Asr, Ayats 1-3)

Ibn Qayyim, may Allaah have mercy upon him, said concerning this chapter of the Qur'aan:

And an explanation of this is that by the completion and perfection of the four levels an individual attains the upper limit of his perfection. The first is knowing the truth. The second is acting upon it. The third is teaching it to the one who is not conversant with it, and the fourth is having patience in learning it, acting upon it, and teaching it. ("*Miftaah Daar as-Sa'aadah*", 1/61)

Alhamdulillah, so much of what we have been discussing is summed up beautifully in this chapter of the Qur'aan, and made clear in the speech of Ibn Qayyim, may Allaah have mercy upon him. In this is the knowledge- and this is the beneficial knowledge of the religion, which brings success in this life and the Hereafter for the one who strives to obtain it and act upon it with purity of intention for Allaah alone. Also present is the action upon that knowledge, as we know from that which has preceded that the action cannot be correct or complete without knowledge, and knowledge is intended to be acted upon. The third is calling to Allaah and His Straight Path, and this includes enjoining the good and forbidding the evil, and this is all dependent upon the worshipper's individual ability to carry it out. The fourth, is patience in all of these things- the acquiring of knowledge, acting upon that knowledge, and spreading the knowledge, as we know that we will encounter hardships and setbacks in all of these, which will require from us patient perseverance, mash'Allaah.

Alhamdulillah, these are some of the basic obligations which Allaah has placed upon His worshippers. The reader is urged to strive with utmost diligence in these different fields, by reading the Qur'aan and studying books of ahaadeeth along with the explanations of the righteous scholars, both past and present, as well as reading other books by the noble scholars, listening to their tapes, attending their lectures, and taking classes in regards to the religion. Then, insh'Allaah, she must strive to implement her knowledge and teach it to others as best as she is able.

May Allaah grant us success in seeking knowledge of Him, His Prophet, and His religion, and making this knowledge a reality in our lives, every hour of every day.

Review and Discussion Questions

Questions for Obligations towards her Lord and her religion

Review:

1. What is the foundation upon which the religion is built? List two proofs of this. (Bottom half of page 244)
2. What is 'aqeedah, and what is the ruling on learning it? (Bottom half of page 245, Top half of page 246)
3. What is tawheed? List the well-known agreed upon categories of tawheed? (Page 248, Bottom half)
4. What are the three things which are listed as being obligatory to have knowledge of? Briefly discuss each one. (Page 253 on to end of the discussion of the point)
5. What is the meaning of al-Islaam? (Top half of page 259)
6. What are the pillars of Islaam? (Bottom half of page 259)
7. What are the pillars of Eemaan? (Bottom half of page 259)
8. What attributes should the person who is calling to Islaam have? (Bottom half of page 273, Page 274)

Discussion & Consideration:

9. Why must correct knowledge come before action?
10. Who are the "saved sect" and why are they called this?
11. Why is it insufficient for a person to only affirm one category of tawheed, to the exclusion of the other categories (for example, tawheed ar-rooboobiyyah)?
12. What would you say to someone who claimed that it was not obligatory to obey the Messenger of Allaah? Bring some proofs to support your answer.
13. Explain the saying, "Eemaan includes belief, speech, and action."
14. Is it enough for a Muslim to affirm the truth of Islaam in their hearts, or must they manifest it upon their tongues and their limbs? Explain your answer with proofs.
15. How can da'wah be through both speech and action? Give some examples of how you can perform these types of da'wah yourself

Obligations towards her Parents

From among her obligations towards her parents are:

1. To be Grateful to our Parents

2. To be Dutiful to our Parents, and Kind and Merciful to Them

The importance placed upon the relationship between the child and the parents is very great, as are that child's obligations towards the parents. Indeed, Allaah has joined being good to one's parents to singling out Allaah alone for worship and avoiding associating others along with Him in worship. He, the Most High, says, in His Noble Book,

﴾ ***Worship Allaah and join none with Him (in worship); and do good to parents…*** ﴿- (Surat an-Nisaa, From Ayat 36)

Imaam as-Sa'adee, may Allaah have mercy upon him, said concerning the *ihsaan* mentioned in this verse, "The rights of the parents are many; however, that which is stressed the most is that which Allaah mentions in His Book. He commands us to do good to them, and that includes every goodness from all of its aspects. And the meaning of that is returned (for explanation and clarification) to the custom of the people and that which is usual- as everything which is usually considered something good enters into the goodness which is commanded." ("*Noor al Basaa'ir wa al-Albaab fee Ahkaam al-Ibaadaat wa al-Mu'aamilaat wa al-Huqooq wa al-Waajibaat*" Page 67)

The major scholar, Sadeeq Hasan Khaan, may Allaah have mercy upon him, further elucidated this in his work, "*Husn al-Uswah*". He said, "And what is meant by "*ihsaan*" (goodness) is living well with the parents, and humbling oneself to them, obeying their commands, as well as anything else which Allaah has made obligatory upon the child towards his parents of rights. And from it is the *birr* concerning them, and being merciful towards them and doing everything they tell you which does not oppose the commands of Allaah and His Messenger, and bringing them everything they need, and not bothering them. If they are disbelievers then you call them to *eemaan* with softness and good manners and also if they wrongdoers then you command them with the good without being harsh or saying 'uf' (a noise which indicates disrespect and dismissal)" (Page 22)

The First Obligation: We are commanded by Allaah, Glorious is He, Most Exalted, to be grateful to our parents. He, the Most High, says,

﴾***And We have enjoined on man (to be dutiful and good) to his parents. His mother bore him in weakness and hardship upon weakness and hardship, and his weaning is in two years – give thanks to Me and to your parents.*** ﴿- (Surah Luqman, From Ayat 14)

Our parents raised us, supported us mentally and physically, cared for us, nurtured us, loved us, showed mercy to us, and so many other things- we must be grateful to them for all of these, and grateful to Allaah for granting us this immense blessing.

This thankfulness should be in our hearts, on our tongues, and demonstrated by our actions, insh'Allaah. Those of us who are parents know the joy that comes with a child saying, "Thank you" and giving us a hug. We know what it means when a grown child sends a gift just because he was thinking of us- so we should do these and other actions which show our love and appreciation for them. And this is all the time- unlike the disbelievers, we don't wait for specific days such as Mother's Day to be kind and generous to our parents!

The Second Obligation: We are commanded to be dutiful to our parents. The Prophet, may Allaah's praise and salutations be upon him, was asked, "What action is most beloved to Allaah, the Most High?" He, may Allaah's praise and salutations be upon him, answered, ***{Prayer within its allotted time.}*** The questioner said, "Then what?" He, may Allaah's praise and salutations be upon him, answered, ***{Kindness and obedience (بر birr) to parents.}*** Then the man asked, "Then what?" He, may Allaah's praise and salutations be upon him, said, ***{Fighting for the cause of Allaah.}*** (al-Bukhaari, 5970, Muslim, 2/37 of the explanation of an-Nawawi, and other than them)

This includes, among other things, assisting them in any way we are able, serving them, being kind and good to them, being merciful towards them, and obeying them in anything that does not contain wrongdoing, as we saw in the statement of Sadeeq Hasan Khaan mentioned earlier.

Allaah, the Most High, says, ***﴾And We have enjoined on man to be good and dutiful to his parents; but if they strive to make you join with Me (in worship) anything (as a partner) of which you have no knowledge, then obey them not.﴿***- (Surat al-'Ankiboot, From Ayat 8)

In addition, the Prophet, may Allaah's praise and salutations be upon him, said, ***{There is no obedience to the created in disobedience to the Creator.}*** (Musnad Ahmad, and it has been declared to be authentic by Sheikh al-Albaani, may Allaah have mercy upon him)

The meaning of بر *(birr)* includes kindness, devotion, and obedience. Both of these obligations fall under this meaning- and this *birr* does not end with the death of the parent. There are many actions which the deceased parent's children can undertake on his or her behalf, which show that this devotion to one's parents is ongoing. Some of these actions are:

Supplicating for them if they were Muslim

Abu Hurairah, may Allaah be pleased with him, reported that the Messenger of Allaah, may Allaah's praise and salutations be upon him, said, ***{Upon a person's death, his actions are cut off, except for three: ongoing charity, knowledge which continues to benefit (others), and a righteous child who supplicates for him.}*** (Muslim, 11/85 of the explanation of an-Nawawi, Abu Daawud, 2280, an-Nasaa'ee, 6/250, at-Tirmidhi, 1376, and Ahmad, 2/372)

To Fast if they have a Fast to Make Up

'Aishah, may Allaah be pleased with her, said that the Messenger of Allaah, may Allaah's praise and salutations be upon him, said, ***{One who dies and he has a fast to make up, his companion should fast for him.}*** (al-Bukhaari, 1952, and Muslim, 1147) and other than them)

We owe our parents so much, mash'Allaah, think of the blessings involved if we take on this act, and fast for them the fasts which they were unable to make up!!

The Elevated Position of the Mother

And there is clear evidence that the mother has a special position in Islaam, and that her rights over her children are very great- even greater than their father's.

It is authentically narrated from the Messenger of Allaah, may Allaah's praise and salutations be upon him, that a questioner said, "Oh Messenger of Allaah, who of the people has the greatest right that I should treat them well?" He said, ***{Your mother.}*** He then asked, "Then who?", and he replied, ***{Your mother.}*** He asked, "Then who?" He replied, ***{Your mother.}*** He said, "Then who?" He said, ***{Your father.}*** (Muslim, 6665)

And in another wording, the questioner asked, "Oh Messenger of Allaah, to whom must one be most dutiful?" He said, ***{Your mother.}*** He then asked, "Then who?", and he replied, ***{Your mother.}*** He asked again, "Then who?" He replied, ***{Your mother.}*** He said, "Then who?" He replied, ***{Your father, then the closest relatives, then those next closest}*** (Authentic, "*Saheeh Abi Daawud*", 5139)

Ibn Hajar states in "*Fath al-Baaree*": "Ibn Bataal said, 'The mother receives three examples compared to that which is for the father.' He said, 'This is due to the difficulty of pregnancy, then birth, then nursing. The mother is set apart by these, and she experiences difficulty due to them. After this she participates with the father in the raising and education (of the children) and the indication of this is included in His, the Most High, saying,

﴿ ***And We have enjoined on man (to be dutiful and good) to his parents. His mother bore him in weakness and hardship upon weakness and hardship, His mother bore him in weakness and hardship upon weakness and hardship, and his weaning is in two years – give thanks to Me and to your parents.*** ﴾- (Surah Luqman, From Ayat 14)

As it is equal between them concerning being dutiful and good, and then He singles out the mother with these three matters.' al-Qurtubi said, 'That which is intended is that the mother deserves a more abundant portion of the dutifulness and kindness.'" ("*Fath al-Baaree*", 10/402)

Concerning those of us whose parents are not Muslim, then we must still be kind and dutiful towards them in that which contains no wrongdoing- and Allaah is the One who guides the hearts- perhaps they will be led to the truth and beauty of Islaam through seeing the good character and experiencing the good treatment of their Muslim children! And Allaah knows best.

The Manner of the Child Towards his Parents who are Disobedient to Allaah

Question: My father performs actions which differ from the Islamic legislation and its behavior…what is obligatory upon me concerning my father in these circumstances?

Answer from Sheikh Bin Baaz, may Allaah have mercy upon him: We ask from Allaah guidance for your father, and to grant him success with repentance, and we advise you to be merciful towards him and advise him in a good manner, without despairing of his guidance, as Allaah, Glorified is He, says,

﴾ ***But if they (both) strive with you to make you join in worship with Me others that of which you have no knowledge, then obey them not; but behave with them in the world kindly, and follow the path of him who turns to Me in repentance and in obedience. Then to Me will be your return, and I shall tell you what you used to do.***

"Oh my son! If it be (anything) equal to the weight of a grain of mustard seed, and though it be in a rock, or in the heavens or in the earth, Allaah will bring it forth. Verily, Allaah is Subtle (in bringing out that grain), Well-Acquainted (with its place). ﴿-(Surah Luqman, Ayats 15-16)

He, Glorified is He, connects gratitude to the parents with gratitude to Him, and commands the child to behave towards them in the world with kindness even if they strive to bring him to disbelief in Allaah.

Along with this, know that that which is legislated for you is to behave kindly towards your father, and to be good to him, even if he does wrong to you, and to be diligent in calling him to the truth, in order that Allaah may guide him by way of you. And it is not permissible for you to obey him in that which is wrongdoing.

I also advise you to ask the assistance of Allaah, Glorified is He, Most Exalted, in his guidance- then ask the help of the righteous people in your family, such as your paternal uncles and other than them from those who your father honors and who are in a position with him such that he will accept their advice.

We ask Allaah for us, you and him, the guidance, and success, and for the sincere repentance. He is the One who Hears All, the Close (with His knowledge).

wa assalaamu aleikum wa rahmatullaahi wa barakatuhu (From "*al-Fataawa al-Qayyimah lil-Usrat al-Muslimah*", Page 164)

Review and Discussion Questions

Questions for Obligations towards her Parents

Review:

1. What is the meaning of ihsaan, or kindness and goodness, towards our parents? (Page 279, Middle of Page)
2. What is al-Birr? Explain it in relation to what it means concerning how we treat our parents. (Kindness and obedience (Middle of Page 280)
3. Why does the mother come ahead of the father concerning kindness, etc.? List the proof, as well as listing reasons. (Page 281, Top Half of Page)

Discussion & Consideration:

4. Why must we be thankful to our parents? What are some ways we can show this thankfulness?
5. What are some actions we can perform concerning our parents after their deaths?
6. How should we behave concerning our parents who are not Muslim? Give some examples of how this could affect them and our relationship with them for good or bad.

Obligations Towards her

Husband

From among her obligations towards her husband are:

First: It is obligatory upon her to be obedient to her husband in that which contains no wrongdoing

Second: It is obligatory upon her to safeguard his honor and his religion

Third: It is obligatory upon her to live with him, to serve him and manage the house

Fourth: It is obligatory upon her to be grateful to him for that which he does of good

Fifth: It is obligatory upon her to nurse and nurture his children, and raise and educate them

Sixth: It is obligatory upon her to safeguard his wealth

Seventh: It is obligatory upon her to seek his permission before leaving the house, as well as to not allow anyone to enter it without his permission

Eighth: It is obligatory upon her to not fast the non-obligatory fasts without his permission

Ninth: It is obligatory upon her to go to his bed when she is called to do so

One of the greatest blessings Allaah, the Most High, has granted to His servants, is that of marriage, alhamdulillah. In marriage we seek to find partners who are striving to please Allaah, and who will assist us in our own attempts to please Allaah and to attain Paradise.

Allaah, Exalted is He, says, concerning marriage,

﴾***And Allaah has made for you Aazwaaj (mates or wives) of your own kind, and has made for you, from your wives, sons and grandsons, and has bestowed on you good provision. Do they then believe in false deities and deny the Favor of Allaah (by not worshipping Allaah Alone)?***﴿- (Surat an-Nahl, Ayat 72)

He, the Most High, also says,

﴾ ***And among His Signs is that He created for you wives from among yourselves, that you may find repose in them, and He has put between you affection and mercy. Verily, in that are indeed signs for a people who reflect.***﴿- (Surat ar-Room, Ayat 21)

The affection and mercy which grows between the husband and wife is a sign, or *ayat*, from Allaah. If we reflect upon it, we see the mercy of Allaah to His creation, and we should be thankful for this great gift which we are given in a righteous husband or wife, *mash'Allaah*. As it is much easier to work for the good when we have a partner in this, one who is loving and affectionate as well as righteous, and who supports us and who we give support to.

There are many rights and obligations in marriage, and Allaah and His Messenger, may Allaah's praise and salutations be upon him, have made them clear to us, so that we may follow them and insh'Allaah attain the happiness that is possible in a marriage between righteous people. These rights and obligations provide us with guidelines to achieving the good which is sought after in marriage, and by adhering to them, insh'Allaah, the marriage will be strong and the relationship between the partners will be wholesome and satisfying to both of them. Some of the obligations of the wife towards her husband are as follows.

First: It is obligatory upon her to be obedient to her husband in that which contains no wrongdoing

Allaah, Glorified is He, the Most High, has made clear the positions of the husband and the wife in relation to each other.

Allaah, Glorified and Exalted, says,

﴾***And they (women) have rights (over their husbands as regards living expenses) similar (to those of their husbands) over them (as regards obedience and respect) to what is reasonable, but men have a degree (of responsibility) over them. And Allaah is All-Mighty, All-Wise.***﴿- (Surat al-Baqara, From Ayat 228)

And He, the Most High, says,

﴾***Men are the protectors and maintainers of women, because Allaah has made one of them to excel the other, and because they spend (to support them) from their means. Therefore the righteous women are devoutly obedient (to Allaah and to their husbands), and guard in the husband's absence what Allaah orders them to guard (e.g. their chastity and their husband's property). As to those women on whose part you see ill conduct, admonish them (first), (next) refuse to share their beds, (and last) beat them (lightly, if it is useful); but if they obey you, seek not against them means (of annoyance). Surely, Allaah is Ever Most High, Most Great.***﴿- (Surat an-Nisaa, Ayat 34)

According to the scholars, the obedience mentioned in this verse is the woman's obedience to her Lord, as well as to her husband.

Ibn 'Abaas and others have said concerning ***"qaanitaatun"***: Meaning, they are obedient to their husbands.

at-Taabari has stated, "This means, obedient to Allaah and to their husbands." ("*at-Tafseer*", Vol. 6, Page 691)

It has been related from Husain ibn Muhsin, who said, "My paternal aunt narrated to me, saying, 'I went to the Messenger of Allaah concerning some need, and he said, ***{Do you have a husband?}*** I said, 'Yes.' He said, ***{How are you concerning him?}*** I said, "I do not fail to do anything except that which I am unable to do." He said, ***{Look to where you are concerning him, as verily, he is your Paradise and your Hellfire.}*** (Haakim, 2/981, and he declared it authentic, and adh-Dhahabee agreed with him in this, an-Nasaa'ee in "*'Ashrat an-Nisaa*", 76,77,78,79,80,81,82,83 and Ahmad, 4/142 from Yazeed ibn Haarun from Yahya ibn Basheer from Husain)

Abu Hurairah, may Allaah be pleased with him, said that the Prophet, may Allaah's praise and salutations be upon him, said, ***{If I were to command one of you to prostrate to another, I would have commanded the woman to prostrate to her husband.}*** (at-Tirmidhi, Vol. 3, No. 1109, and Sheikh Muqbil, may Allaah have mercy upon him mentioned it in his "*as-Saheeh al-Musnad*" Vol.2, No. 1297)

Abu Hurairah, may Allaah be pleased with him, also narrated that the Prophet, may Allaah's praise and salutations be upon him, was asked,

"Which are the best of the women?" He, may Allaah's praise and salutations be upon him, answered, ***{The one who pleases him when he gazes at her, and obeys him when he commands (something) and the one who does not differ with him concerning that which he dislikes in regard to herself and his wealth.}*** (Imaam Ahmad in "*al-Musnad*", and Sheikh al-Albaani, may Allaah have mercy upon him, has declared it to be *hasan* in "*as-Silsalat as-Saheehah*" Vol. 4, No. 1838)

'Abdullah ibn 'Abaas, may Allaah be pleased with him, said, the Messenger of Allaah, may Allaah's praise and salutations be upon him, said, ***{Shall I not inform you about those of your women who are women of Paradise? The one who is loving and bears many children, and the one who turns back to her husband (after a disagreement), and the one who, if she harms him, or is harmed (by him) she comes and takes her husband's hand and says, "By Allaah, I will not sleep until you are pleased"}***(an-Nasaa'ee in "*as-Sunan al-Kubra*", Vol. 8, No.9094, and Sheikh al-Albaani, may Allaah have mercy upon him, has declared it *hasan* in "*as-Silsilat as-Saheehah*", Vol. 1, No. 1047)

The Prophet, may Allaah's praise and salutations be upon him, has joined obedience to the husband to the five pillars of Islaam, as he, may Allaah's praise and salutations be upon him, said, ***{If the woman prays her five obligatory prayers, fasts her month (Ramadhaan), safeguards her private parts, and obeys her husband, it will be said to her, "Enter Paradise through any gate you wish.}*** (Ibn Hibaan, 4163, al-Bizaar, 1463, and Sheikh al-Albaani, may Allaah have mercy upon him, has declared it to be authentic in "*as-Saheeh al-Jaami*", Number 673)

This hadeeth shows the great weight and position placed upon this matter, mash'Allaah, and the greatness of the reward for the woman who fulfills the conditions within it. May Allaah make us among those women, Ameen.

This obedience is in all things which do not contain wrongdoing, or that which would displease Allaah, the Most High, or go against the Islamic legislation. This is a general principle, that one cannot obey that which is created, in something which disobeys the Creator.

The Prophet, may Allaah's praise and salutations be upon him, said, ***{It is upon the Muslim to listen and to obey concerning that which I love, even if he dislikes it; except if he is commanded with wrongdoing. As for being commanded with wrongdoing, then he does not listen and obey.}*** (al-Bukhaari, 7144, Muslim, 12/226 (of the explanation of an-Nawawi) and it is his wording, and other than them)

He, may Allaah's praise and salutations be upon him, also stated, ***{There is no obedience to the created in disobedience to the Creator.}*** ("*Musnad Ahmad*", and it has been declared to be authentic by Sheikh al-Albaani, may Allaah have mercy upon him)

So, for example, if the husband tells his wife to bring him a drink, she should do so. If, however, he commands her to bring him an alcoholic drink, then in general she should not obey him, as this would be obeying him in wrongdoing.

So it is clear that the man has a degree of responsibility over the woman, and she must obey him in that which he commands which does not contain anything in it of wrongdoing. This should be understood in light of the fact that the Muslim man should treat his wives well, and live with them in a good manner. There are many evidences for this from the Qur'aan and Sunnah.

Allaah, the Most High, says, ***﴾Lodge them where you dwell, according to your means, and do not harm them so as to straiten them (that they be obliged to leave your house).﴿*** - (Surat at-Talaaq, From Ayat 6) He. Glorified and Exalted is He, also says,

﴾...and live with them honorably.﴿ - (Surat an-Nisaa, From Ayat 19)

The Messenger of Allaah,, may Allaah's praise and salutations be upon him, said, ***{The best of you is the one who is best to his family, and I am the best of you to my family.}*** (Authentic, narrated by at-Tirmidhi, 10/363, 3904, Ibn Hibaan, 9/484, 4177, and ad-Daaramee, 2/159 by way of Hishaam ibn 'Urwah from his father, from 'Aishah)

The Prophet, may Allaah's praise and salutations be upon him, also said, ***{The believers who have the most perfect faith are those with excellent character, and the best of you are the one who are best to their wives.}*** (Hasan, from the hadeeth of Abi Hurairah, may Allaah be pleased with him)

The Messenger of Allaah, may Allaah's praise and salutations be upon him, makes it clear in these two ahaadeeth the lofty position of the one who treats his wife and family well. He should not oppress her or harm her; rather he should treat her kindly and well, and insh'Allaah this, along with them both fulfilling their rights to each other, will bring love and harmony to the marriage and the household. And Allaah knows best.

Second: It is obligatory upon her to safeguard his honor and his religion

﴾Therefore the righteous women are devoutly obedient (to Allaah and to their husbands), and guard in the husband's absence what Allaah orders them to guard (e.g. their chastity and their husband's property).﴿ - (Surat an-Nisaa, Ayat 34)

Ibn Katheer, may Allaah have mercy upon him, says in his explanation of this verse,

﴾...guard in the husband's absence...﴿ "Meaning, that she guard her husband in his absence, by guarding herself and his property." ("*Tafseer Ibn Katheer*", 2/256-257)

ash-Shawkaani, may Allaah have mercy upon him, states, "So the righteous ones from amongst the women ***﴾...devoutly obedient...﴿*** who are obedient to Allaah- they obey that which has been made obligatory upon them from the rights of Allaah over them, and the rights of their husbands over them. ***﴾...guard in the husband's absence...﴿*** Meaning, his wives must guard in his absence that which it is obligatory upon them to guard, including safeguarding themselves and preserving (the family's) wealth." ("*Fath al-Qadeer*", 1/461)

An example of this from the Sunnah is found in the hadeeth of 'Aishah in which the woman is forbidden to uncover in other than her husband's house.

It has been related from 'Aishah, may Allaah be pleased with her, that the Messenger of Allaah, may Allaah's praise and salutations be upon him, said, ***{Any woman who removes her garment in other than her own house, that which is between her and between Allaah, the Most Exalted, will be closed off.}*** (Abu Daawud, 4010, at-Tirmidhi, 2703, and others, and it is in "as-*Saheeh al-Musnad*" of Sheikh Muqbil, may Allaah have mercy upon him.)

She is safeguarding herself and her chastity, and thus her husband's honor and religion.

Included in this is that the women do not go amongst the strange men without a necessity, that they wear the Islamically legislated *hijaab*, and that they deal with others in the correct manner, that which has been legislated by Allaah, in His Wisdom. (See "*My Hijaab, My Path*" for more information on this) Here is only a sampling of the guidance which we have been given concerning this matter:

Allaah, Glorified is He, says,

﴾***And tell the believing women to lower their gaze (from looking at forbidden things), and protect their private parts (from illegal sexual acts) and not to show off their adornment except that which is apparent (like both eyes for necessity to see the way, or outer palms of hands or one eye or dress like veil, gloves, headcover), and to draw their veils all over juyoobihinna (i.e. their bodies, faces, necks and bosoms) and not to reveal their adornment except to their husbands, or their fathers, or their husband's fathers, or their sons, or their husband's sons, or their brothers or their brother's sons, or their sister's sons, or their women, or the (female) slaves whom their right hands possess, or old male servants who lack vigor, or small children who have no sense of feminine sex. And let them not stamp their feet so as to reveal what they hide of their adornment. And all of you beg Allaah to forgive you all, Oh believers, that you may be successful.***﴿- (Surat an-Noor, Ayat 31)

Allaah, the Most High says,

﴾***If you keep your duty (to Allaah), then be not soft in speech, lest he in whose heart is a disease (of hypocrisy, or evil desire for adultery) should be moved with desire, but speak in an honorable manner.***﴿- (Surat al-Ahzaab, From Ayat 32)

Allaah, Glorified is He and Most High, says,

﴾***And stay in your houses, and do not display yourselves like that of the times of ignorance, and perform the prayers, and give obligatory charity and obey Allaah and His Messenger. Allaah wishes only to remove evil deeds and sins from you, Oh members of the family, and to purify you with a thorough purification.***﴿- (Surat al-Ahzaab, Ayat 33)

He, the Most High, also says,

﴾ ***And when you ask (his wives) for anything you want, ask them from behind a screen, that is purer for your hearts and for their hearts***﴿- (Surat al-Ahzaab, From Ayat 53)

An example and proof from the Sunnah is as follows:

Fadaalah ibn 'Ubayd narrated that the Messenger of Allaah, may Allaah's praise and salutations be upon him, said, ***{Three are not to be asked about.} and from them was {...a woman whose husband is away and he supplies her with all the necessary provisions, yet she goes out uncovered after he leaves.}*** (Imaam Ahmad, Vol. 6, Page 19, and al-Bukhaari in "*al-Adab al-Mufrad*", No. 603, and it is in "as-*Saheeh al-Musnad*", 2/1054, of Sheikh Muqbil, may Allaah have mercy upon him.)

Perhaps it should be mentioned here that part of safeguarding the honor of the husband is safeguarding the business of the house. It is not for the woman, when she gets angry, to go out and spread her experiences, opinions, and feelings about issues to those outside of the house, as this could cause the people to think evilly of the husband, or criticize him unjustly. As once the tales have been spread, they cannot be taken back, and the damage is done. It is best to keep the business of the house in the house, unless the couple chooses to go to a righteous person who can help them to mediate and clear up the issues. Then this is praiseworthy and something rewarded, while simply complaining and spreading ones affairs is not. In fact this carrying of tales without the proper reason falls under the prohibition of backbiting and slander as well, and Allaah knows best.

So it can be seen that when a woman is modest and chaste and safeguards her own virtue and honor, she is also obeying Allaah, the Most High, by safeguarding her husband's honor as well. And Allaah knows best.

Third: It is obligatory upon her to live with him, to serve him and manage the house

As for living with him in the same dwelling:

Allaah, the Most High, says in His Noble Book:

﴾***It is He Who has created you from a single person (Aadam), and (then) He has created from him his wife [Hawaa'], in order that he might enjoy the pleasure of living with her.***﴿- (Surat al-A'raaf, Ayats 189)

﴾***It is made lawful for you to have sexual relations with your wives on the night of as-saum (the fasts). They are libaas [i.e. body-cover, or screen, or sakan (i.e. you enjoy the pleasure of living with them – as in Verse 7:189) Tafseer at-Tabaree] for you and you are the same for them.***﴿- (Surat al-Baqara, From Ayat 187)

﴾***Lodge them where you dwell, according to your means, and do not harm them so as to straiten them (that they be obliged to leave your house).***﴿- (Surat at-Talaaq, From Ayat 6)

﴾***...and live with them honorably.***﴿- (Surat an-Nisaa, From Ayat 19)

at-Tabari, may Allaah have mercy upon him, said in "*Jaami al-Bayaan*" concerning this verse from Surat at-Talaaq,

"The meaning of ﴾***...according to your means...***﴿ is from your capacity which you are able to give." (14/145)

Allaah, Glorified is He, and Most High, has enjoined that the wife live with the husband in these noble verses, and from this comes the obligation upon her to agree to live with him whether the dwelling is grand or humble. The one who leaves this commandment from her husband is disobedient, disobeying Allaah, the Most High, and His Messenger, Muhammad, may Allaah's praise and salutations be upon him.

As for serving him and managing the house:

It has been related from Husain ibn Muhsin, who said, "My paternal Aunt narrated to me, saying, 'I went to the Messenger of Allaah concerning some need, and he said, ***{Do you have a husband?} I said, 'Yes.' He said, {How are you concerning him?}*** I said, "I do not fail to do anything except that which I am unable to do." He said, ***{Look to where you are concerning***

him, as verily, he is your Paradise and your Hellfire.}" (Haakim, 2/981, and he declared it authentic, and adh-Dhahabee agreed with him in this, an-Nasaa'ee in "*'Ashrat an-Nisaa*", 76,77,78,79,80,81,82,83 and Ahmad, 4/142 from Yazeed ibn Haarun from Yahya ibn Basheer from Husain)

The scholars have differed concerning whether or not it is obligatory for the wife to serve her husband, and the strongest opinion is that it is obligatory, due to the general nature of the obligation upon her to obey her husband in that which does not contain wrongdoing. Thus, if he commands her to serve him, this becomes obligatory for her. And Allaah knows best.

It is also for the righteous Muslimah to look for that which will bring happiness, contentment, and love to her marriage; certainly, serving the husband is a reason for this. We must also look to the examples of the righteous women in the past and present to see how they acted, so we can pattern ourselves after them, insh'Allaah.

It was known amongst the female companions of the Prophet, may Allaah's praise and salutations be upon him, that they served their husbands and took care of the house; indeed, even his daughter, Fatimah did so- and they are the best examples for us as women.

'Ali, may Allaah be pleased with him, said, Fatimah went to the Prophet complaining about the bad effect of the stone hand-mill on her hand. She heard that the Prophet had received a few slave girls. But (when she came there) she did not find him, so she mentioned her problem to 'Aishah. When the Prophet came, 'Aishah informed him about that. 'Ali added, "So the Prophet came to us when we had gone to bed. We wanted to get up (on his arrival) but he said, 'Stay where you are." Then he came and sat between me and her and I felt the coldness of his feet on my abdomen. He said, ***{Shall I direct you to something better than what you have requested? When you go to bed say 'Subhaan Allaah' thirty-three times, 'Alhamdulillah' thirty three times, and Allaahu Akbar' thirty four times, for that is better for you than a servant.}*** (al-Bukhaari, 7/274)

In another narration he said, Fatimah came to the Prophet asking for a servant. He said, ***{May I inform you of something better than that? When you go to bed, recite "Subhaan Allaah' thirty three times, 'Alhamdulillah' thirty three times, and 'Allaahu Akbar' thirty four times.}*** 'Ali added, 'I have never failed to recite it ever since." Somebody asked, "Even on the night of the battle of Siffin?" He said, "No, even on the night of the battle of Siffin." (al-Bukhaari, 7/275)

Asmaa' Bint Abi Bakr, may Allaah be pleased with her, said, "When az-Zubair married me he had nothing in the world, not money, or a slave, or anything except a water vessel, and a horse. I used find food for the horse, and carry water, mend the water vessel, and knead the bread. I was not good at baking the bread, so some of my neighbors from the Ansaar baked it for me, and they were good women. I carried date stones on my head from the land that the Messenger of Allaah granted to az-Zubair, and it was some distance from my house. One day, I was carrying the date stones on my head, when I met the Messenger of Allaah, may Allaah's praise and salutations be upon him, along with some of the Ansaar, so he called to me after saying, "Ikh, Ikh." to the camel, in order to carry me behind him on his mount. I felt shy to ride with men, and I remembered az-Zubair, and his jealousy, as he was of the most jealous of people. The Messenger of Allaah saw that I was shy, so he went on. I came to az-Zubair, and said to him, *"I met the Messenger of Allaah, and I had the date stones on my head, and he had some of his companions with him, and he called so I could ride behind him, but I felt shy, and I remembered your jealousy." He replied, "By Allaah, your carrying the date stones is harder on me than for you to ride with him." And I went on like that until Abu Bakr sent me a servant who took care of the horse for me, and it was as if he had freed me."* (al-Bukhaari, 5223 and Muslim,2182)

Narrated Abu Mulaikah that Asmaa', may Allaah be pleased with her, said, *"I used to serve az-Zubair in the house, and he had a horse which I used to take care of. Nothing was harder on me than caring for the horse, as I would bring fodder for it, and care for it." He (Abu Mulaikah) said, "That went on until she obtained a servant which had been captured by the Messenger of Allaah and then given to her. She said, "She (the servant) took care of the horse for me, and took that burden off of me. Then a man came to me and said, "Oh Umm Abdullah, I am a poor man, and I wish to sell my merchandise in the shade of your house." I said, "Indeed if I give you permission az-Zubair will refuse, so come and ask permission from me when az-Zubair is present." So the man came and said, "Oh Umm Abdullah, I am a poor man, and I wish to sell my merchandise in the shade of your house." I said to him, "Is not there any other house in Madinah for you other than mine?" So az-Zubair said, "Why would you refuse to allow a poor man to sell here?" So the man used to sell merchandise until he earned some money, and I sold him my servant. Then az-Zubair came in, and I had the money in my lap, and he said, "Give it as a gift to me." I said, "I will give it in charity."* (Muslim, 2182)

Narrated Aishah, may Allaah be pleased with her, *"Sometimes there would be fasts that I had to make up from Ramadhaan, but I would not be able to do so until Sha'baan, because I was busy with the Messenger of Allaah, or, because of the Messenger of Allaah."* (Muslim, 1146)

Sheikh al-Islaam, ibn Taymiyyah, may Allaah have mercy upon him, said concerning the verse, ﴿ ***Therefore the righteous women are devoutly obedient (to Allaah and to their husbands), and guard in the husband's absence what Allaah orders them to guard (e.g. their chastity and their husband's property).*** ﴾– (Surat an-Nisaa, Ayat 34), "(This) requires that her obedience to her husband be unconditionally obligatory: from serving, travelling with him and settling down (with him), and other than that, as the Sunnah of the Messenger of Allaah gives evidence for in the hadeeth 'the red mountain' and 'the prostration' and other than these." ("*Majmoo' al-Fataawa*", 23/260, 261)

The hadeeth of the red mountain: 'Aisha said that the Prophet, may Allaah's praise and salutations be upon him, said, ***{If I were to command anyone to prostrate to anyone else, I would command the woman to prostrate before her husband, and if a man commandhis wife to carry (stones) from a red mountain to a black mountain or from a black mountain to a red mountain it is her duty to comply with his command}*** (Ibn Maajah, 1852 and is strengthened by the hadeeeth of prostration)

The hadeeth of the prostration:

The Prophet, may Allaah's praise and salutations be upon him, said, ***{If I were to command anyone to prostrate to anyone else, I would command the woman to prostrate to her husband, due to the greatness of his right over her.}*** (at-Tirmidhi, 1079, Ibn Maajah, 1842-1843)

Ibn Qayyim, may Allaah have mercy upon him, said in "*Zaad al-Ma'aad*":

"The obligation of serving is necessary due to that which is known with the ones whom Allaah, Glorified is He, is addressing with His words. As for the wife being entertained and at ease while the husband is the one who serves- sweeping, grinding the flour, kneading the bread, washing, scrubbing, and performing the housework, then this is from wrongdoing, as Allaah, the Most High, says,

﴾And they (women) have rights (over their husbands as regards living expenses) similar (to those of their husbands) over them (as regards obedience and respect) to what is reasonable﴿- (Surat al-Baqara, From Ayat 228) And He says,

﴾ Men are the protectors and maintainers of women﴿- (Surat an-Nisaa', From Ayat 34)

As if the woman does not serve the man, or rather, he is the servant, then she has a degree over him. Also, the dowry is for the marriage. Each of the two spouses carries out that which his companion wishes. As Allaah has made it obligatory that he support and provide for her, and give her clothing, and to live with her in which he is pleased with her, and that she serve and do that which comes with the practice and custom of marriage. Also, the general contract comes from that which is known of custom, and the custom is that the woman serve and that she performs that which is necessary within the house." ("*Zaad al-Ma'aad*", 5/188-189)

So it is clear that one way to live in obedience to Allaah and His Messenger, as well as bringing about happiness and contentment in our married lives, is to live with our husbands, to take care of the household matters as well as those matters concerning him. And how often it occurs that just through such simple means as these, a greater happiness comes- as when the husband is happy with his wife, he often goes out of his way to show her he is happy, and thus she reaps benefits in both this life and the next, by pleasing her husband as well as her Lord. And Allaah knows best.

Fourth: It is obligatory upon her to be grateful to him for that which he does of good

It is related on Ibn 'Umar, may Allaah be pleased with both of them, that the Messenger of Allaah, may Allaah's praise and salutations be upon him, said, ***{Allaah will not look at a woman who is not grateful to her husband and she would not be able to do without him.}*** (Related by an-Nasaa'ee in "*Ashrat an-Nisaa*", 249, 250, 251, and al-Haakim 2/190, and Sheikh al-Albaani, may Allaah have mercy upon him, has declared it to be authentic in "*as-Saheehah*", 289)

The Prophet, may Allaah's praise and salutations be upon him, also said, ***{Oh women, give charity. Indeed I have seen that you are the majority of the people of the Fire.}*** It was said, "And why is that, oh Messenger of Allaah?" He said, ***{You curse often, and are ungrateful.}*** It was said, "Ungrateful to

Allaah?" He replied, ***{You are ungrateful to your husbands. If he Is always good to you, then you see something evil from him, you say, 'I have never seen any good from you'.}*** (al-Bukhaari 304, Muslim 80, from Abi Sa'eed, may Allaah be pleased with him)

The righteous Muslim woman must strive to be content and pleased at all times with that which Allaah has apportioned for her, and the blessings He has given her, and it is not permissible for her to disregard the blessing of her husband, and to become impatient or displeased with that which he is able to do for her and give to her from his means.

Fifth: It is obligatory upon her to nurse and nurture his children, and raise and educate them

Abu Hurairah, may Allaah be pleased with him, said that the Messenger of Allaah, may Allaah's praise and salutations be upon him said, ***{The best women among the camel riders, are the women of Quraish.}*** (Another narrator said) The Prophet said, ***{The righteous among the women of Quraish are those who are kind to their young ones and who look after their husband's property.}*** (al-Bukhaari, 7/278)

This is from the most important and greatest of the obligations of the Muslim woman, as she is her children's first teacher and one of the primary examples which they will follow throughout their lives. Her influence upon her children is incalculable, and this is for good or evil. An evil or lazy woman will provide her children with the example of evil or laziness, while a pious woman of good character who strives to do her best in the many facets of her life will be an excellent example for them to follow and emulate.

Allaah, the Most High, says in His Noble Book,

﴾***The mothers should suckle their children for two whole years, (that is) for those (parents) who desire to complete the term of suckling.***﴿- (Surat al-Baqara, From Ayat 233)

It is obligatory upon the woman to nurse her children, as it has been commanded by Allaah in the preceding verse. This obligation continues even when the parents have divorced- the mother should still nurse the child for the proscribed amount of time.

It is also upon the woman to educate and raise the children with an Islamic education- and this also applies to those children that the husband may have with him from a previous marriage. She must set a good example for them, teaching the correct Islamic behavior in all situations, as well as appropriate supplications at different times of the day.

Ibn Hazm, may Allaah have mercy upon him, said, "It is obligatory upon every mother, whether she is a free woman or a slave who is married or is under the control of a master, or if she is free from this due to the right of her son she has borne him, that she nurse her child whether she likes it or hates it, even if she is the daughter of a *khaleefah* and thinks she is too good for that."

We will discuss these matters, as well as others, more extensively under the obligations of the woman towards her children, insh'Allaah.

Sixth: It is obligatory upon her to safeguard his wealth

﴾***Therefore the righteous women are devoutly obedient (to Allaah and to their husbands), and guard in the husband's absence what Allaah orders them to guard (e.g. their chastity and their husband's property).***﴿– (Surat an-Nisaa, Ayat 34)

Abu Hurairah, may Allaah be pleased with him, said that the Messenger of Allaah, may Allaah's praise and salutations be upon him said, ***{The best women among the camel riders, are the women of Quraish.}*** (Another narrator said) The Prophet said, ***{The righteous among the women of Quraish are those who are kind to their young ones and who look after their husband's property.}*** (al-Bukhaari, 7/278)

It is not for the woman to spend any of her husband's wealth except with his permission, or without his knowledge when he provides for her, as all that the husband earns for the house is a trust for her and she is responsible for it. This is not just referring to monetary wealth; rather, it includes money, provisions and property. This is due to that which was related from Abi Umaama al-Baahalee, may Allaah be pleased with him, who said, "I heard the Messenger of Allaah, may Allaah's praise and salutations be upon him, say, in his speech the year of the Farewell Pilgrimage,

{The woman should not spend anything from the house of her husband except with the permission of her husband.} It was asked of him, "Oh Messenger of Allaah, what about food?" ***{That is of the best of his wealth.}*** (Abu Daawud, 3565, at- Tirmidhi, 670, Ibn Maajah, 2295, Ahmad 5/267, and others, and Sheikh al- Albaani, may Allaah have mercy upon him, has declared it to be *hasan* in "*Saheeh at-Targheeb wa at-Tarheeb*", 935)

It is permissible for the woman to give from the provisions of the house if she does so with good intention and there is no likely harm in it. This is due to the following hadeeth:

'Aishah, may Allaah be pleased with her, said that the Messenger of Allaah, may Allaah's praise and salutations be upon him, said, ***{If the woman gives from the food of the house and there is no harm in it, then she is rewarded for what she has given, and her husband is rewarded for that which he earned, and for the one in charge of the provisions is the like of that, and none of their rewards lessen the reward of another}*** (al-Bukhaari, 1425, 1437,1439, 1440, 1441,2065, and Muslim, 7/111 of the explanation of an-Nawawi, and others)

It is obligatory upon the husband to provide for the household and give to it that which is needed for its upkeep and the upkeep of the family. If the woman knows clearly that the family is not being provided for, then it may be permissible for her to take from her husband's earnings to supply that which is necessary.

Sheikh Bin Baaz, may Allaah have mercy upon him, was asked:

My husband does not give me spending money- neither to me nor my children- and we sometimes take from that which he has without his knowledge. Is there a sin upon us?

He, may Allaah have mercy upon him, answered,

It is permissible for the woman to take that which is needed for her and her underage children from the wealth of her husband without his knowledge from that which is reasonable, without extravagance and wastefulness, if he does not give her that which is sufficient, due to that which is related in al-Bukhaari and Muslim, from 'Aishah, may Allaah be pleased with her, that Hind, the daughter of 'Utbah, the wife of Abi Sufyan, came to Allaah's Messenger, may Allaah's praise and salutations be upon him, and said, "Oh Allaah's Messenger, Abu Sufyan does not give me and my sons enough maintenance." He replied, ***{Take from his wealth what is reasonable and enough for you and your sons.}*** And with Allaah is the success. (End of Sheikh Bin Baaz's reply, as collected in "*al-Fataawa al-Qayyimah lil-Usrat al-Muslimah*" Collected by Sa'eed 'Abdul-Ghafaar 'Ali, Page 74)

This is not the usual state of affairs, however, and is only suitable when the husband is unjust or miserly, and the needs of the family are not being met. And Allaah knows best.

Seventh: It is obligatory upon her to seek his permission before leaving the house, as well as to not allow anyone to enter it without his permission

As for leaving the house: It is obligatory upon the Muslim woman to ask her husband's permission before leaving the house, and the one who fails to do so has fallen into wrongdoing.

Ibn 'Umar, may Allaah be pleased with him and his father, reported that a woman came to the Messenger of Allaah, may Allaah's praise and salutations be upon him, and said, "What is the right of the husband over his wife?" He, may Allaah's praise and salutations be upon him, said, ***{That she not keep herself from him (when he desires her) even if she is on the back of a camel, and that she not take anything from his house except with his permission. If she does that, then upon him is the reward and upon her is the sin; and not to fast the non-obligatory prayers except with his permission. As if she does this, then the angels of anger and mercy curse her until she repents and returns (to that which is correct.}*** And it was asked, "Even if he is an oppressor?" He replied, ***{Even if he is an oppressor.}*** (at-Tayaalisee, 1901, and by another path of narration as found in "at-Tamheed" 1/231, and it has supporting narrations as well)

Sheikh al-Islaam ibn Taymiyyah, may Allaah have mercy upon him, said concerning the subject as quoted in "*Majmoo' al-Fataawa*" 32/281,

"And it is not permissible for the wife to leave her house except by his permission. It is also not permissible for someone to take her and keep her from her husband, whether she is a nursing mother, or a midwife, or other than that from types of employment. If she leaves her husband's house without his permission, then she is a disobedient woman, disobeying Allaah and His Messenger and worthy of being punished."

Imam Ahmad ibn Hanbal, may Allaah have mercy upon him, said, concerning the married woman who had a sick mother, "Obedience to her husband is more obligatory upon her than her mother (her mother's rights over her) except that he gives permission to her." (Meaning, she must have her husband's permission to visit her sick mother)

However, if the woman desires to go to the *masjid*, and there is no fear of *fitnah*, then she should be allowed to go, as is evidenced in the following hadeeth:

Ibn 'Umar, may Allaah be pleased with him, reported that the Messenger of Allaah, may Allaah's praise and salutations be upon him, said, ***{If one of your women asks permission to go to the masjid, then do not forbid them from that.}*** (al-Bukhaari (in summarized form) 865, and Muslim in the long form, 4/161 (from Imaam an-Nawawi's explanation of "*Saheeh Muslim*"), and other than them)

It is also narrated from Ibn 'Umar that Allaah's Messenger, may Allaah's praise and salutations be upon him, said, ***{Do not prevent the female servants of Allaah from the masaajid, but their houses are better for them.}*** (Abu Daawud, Vol.1, No. 567, and Sheikh al-Albaani, may Allaah have mercy upon him, has declared it to be authentic in *"Saheeh Abu Daawud"*)

These must be taken into consideration with the hadeeth from 'Abdullah ibn Mas'ood, may Allaah be pleased with him, who said that the Prophet, may Allaah's praise and salutations be upon him, said, ***{The woman's prayer in her house is better than her prayer in her courtyard, and her prayer in her private chamber of her house is more excellent than her prayer in her house.}*** (Abu Daawud, Vol.1, 570, and it is found in *"as-Saheeh Musnad"* of Sheikh Muqbil, may Allaah have mercy upon him. He said that this hadeeth is authentic according to the conditions of Muslim)

So the best place for the woman to perform her prayer is in the inner room of the house, but she should not be forbidden from the *masaajid*, if she goes out with proper dress and behavior seeking good and the pleasure of Allaah, the Most High, and there is no fear of *fitnah*. And Allaah knows best.

And indeed it is the normal state of affairs that the women stay in their homes and do not go out except for their needs. Allaah, the Most High, says,

﴾***And stay in your houses, and do not display yourselves like that of the times of ignorance, and perform as-salaat (the prayers), and give zakaat (obligatory charity) and obey Allaah and His Messenger...***﴿- (Surat al-Ahzaab, From Ayat 33)

Abu Hurairah, may Allaah be pleased with him, narrated that the Messenger of Allaah, may Allaah's praise and salutations be upon him and his family, when he made his *hajj* with his wives, said, ***{Verily, what this is, is a necessity; afterwards the period of their emerging and being out will be restricted or limited.}*** (Collected by al-Imaam Ahmad, vol. 2, page 446, with a *hasan* chain of narration)

'Aishah, may Allaah be pleased with her, said, ***{Sawdah bint Zamah went out at night for a need, and 'Umar saw her and recognized her. He said to her, "By Allaah, Oh Sawdah, you cannot hide yourself from us." She returned to the Prophet, may Allaah's praise and salutations be upon him and his family, and mentioned that to him while he was eating supper in my house. He had at that time a bone covered with meat. The Divine revelation came down upon him, and when it was finished, the Prophet may Allaah's praise and salutations be upon him and his family, was saying, "Allaah has allowed you to go out for your needs."}*** (Collected by al-Bukhaari, vol. 9, No. 5237)

Also, certain conditions must be met when she does leave the house. Sheikh Fauzaan, may Allaah preserve him, summarizes them, as quoted in "*My Hijaab, My Path*", Page 128: "It is upon the woman who fears Allaah and the Hereafter to keep away from that which many of today's women do concerning laxity in observance of *al-hijaab*, lenience in wearing adorned clothing when leaving the house, laxity in leaving the house perfumed, and in mixing with the men and kidding with them." For a more in depth discussion, see our publication "*My Hijaab, My Path*".

So it is upon the women when she leaves the house to fulfill the conditions, such as wearing the correct *hijaab* and not mixing with the men beyond what is necessary for her to undertake that which she went out to do. And Allaah knows best.

As for asking his permission before allowing anyone into the house: Then it is not permissible for the wife to allow anyone into the house without her husband's permission.

It has been related by Abi Hurairah, may Allaah be pleased with him, that the Prophet, may Allaah's praise and salutations be upon him, said, ***{It is not permissible for a woman to fast in other than Ramadhaan and her husband is present except with his permission, or to allow anyone into his house except with his permission}*** (This hadeeth is authentic, and comes by many paths, which are found in al-Bukhaari, 5195, at- Tirmidhi, 782, Ahmad, 2/464, ad-Daarimee, 2/12, Ibn Hibaan 3582, and others)

al Haafidh ibn Haajir, may Allaah have mercy upon him, said, concerning his, may Allaah's praise and salutations be upon him, saying, ***{... or to allow anyone into his house}*** "Muslim added by the way of Hamaam, on Abee Hurairah, ***{and her husband is present}***. This condition, ***{and her husband is present}***, has no real meaning; rather it is only speaking of the usual state of affairs, for the absence of her husband does not entail the permissibility of the woman allowing anyone into the house. Indeed, surely the impermissibility of that is made clear by the sound *ahaadeeth* that have been reported concerning the forbiddance of entering in upon those women whose husbands are absent. It could also be considered to have a meaning, and that is that if the husband is present it is easy to ask his permission, whereas if he is gone, and she needs to allow someone into his house, then she is excused,because of his absence, and this is all speaking about entering in upon the woman.

As for others entering into the house in general, like allowing a person to enter one of the places connected to the house, or a separate house than the one she is living in, than what is apparent is that this is also connected to the preceding ruling." ("*Fath al-Baari*", 9/296)

The Messenger of Allaah, may Allaah's praise and salutations be upon him, said, ***{I enjoin upon you good treatment of your women, for they are captives in your charge. You do not have power over them in other than in this matter. You have a right over your women, and your women have a right over you. Your right over your women is that they should not allow anyone to approach your beds and you dislike it, and should not permit to enter your houses those whom you dislike. And their right over you is that you treat them well in providing them with garments and food.}*** (at-Tirmidhi, 1423, Ibn Majah 1101, and Sheikh al-Albaani, may Allaah have mercy upon him, has declared it to be *hasan*)

These two hadeeth make it clear, alhamdulillah, that it is obligatory upon the woman to ask her husband's permission before allowing anyone into the house, and that she not allow anyone inside whom he would dislike to have enter- and this is from family and friends as well as strangers.

Along with this we should mention the spreading of the affairs of the house to those outside of the house, as this is a way of allowing others "inside" the house-but through a different door. Too often women engage in this sort of talk, complaining or spreading that which is going on in the house to others, especially her family and friends. This is not proper, mash'Allaah, and should be avoided. The exception to this is if the husband agrees, and it is done in order to remedy some problem in the household. And Allaah knows best.

Eighth: It is obligatory upon her to not fast the non-obligatory fasts without his permission

This is if she is living in the same place as her husband, and he is present. As for if he is travelling, or is not present, then it is permissible for her to fast as she likes, unless he has commanded otherwise. If he returns and she is fasting, it is permissible for him to cause her to nullify her fast, as long as it is not an obligatory fast, such as in the month of Ramadhaan.

This is due to the hadeeth of Abi Hurairah, may Allaah be pleased with him, in which he states that the Prophet, may Allaah's praise and salutations be upon him said, ***{It is not permissible for a woman to fast in other than Ramadhaan and her husband is present except with his permission or to allow anyone into his house except with his permission.}*** (This hadeeth is authentic, and comes by many paths, which are found in al-Bukhaari, 5195, at- Tirmidhi, 782, Ahmad, 2/464, ad-Daarimee, 2/12, Ibn Hibaan 3582, and others)

As for fasting the obligatory fast of Ramadhaan, then he should not command her to break it, and if he does, then she does not obey him in this call to wrongdoing, as the Prophet, may Allaah's praise and salutations be upon him, said, ***{It is upon the Muslim to listen and to obey concerning that which I love, even if he dislikes it; except if he is commanded with wrongdoing. As for being commanded with wrongdoing, then he does not listen and obey.}*** (al-Bukhaari, 7144, Muslim, 12/226 (of the explanation of an-Nawawi) and it is his wording, and other than them)

He, may Allaah's praise and salutations be upon him, also stated, ***{There is no obedience to the created in disobedience to the Creator.}*** ("*Musnad Ahmad*", and it has been declared to be authentic by Sheikh al-Albaani, may Allaah have mercy upon him)

Ninth: It is obligatory upon her to go to his bed when she is called to do so

Allaah, Glorified is He, says,

﴾***Your wives are a tilth for you, so go to your tilth, when or how you will, and send (good deeds, or ask Allaah to bestow upon you pious offspring) for your own selves beforehand.***﴿- (Surat al- Baqara, Ayat 223)

It is narrated by al-Bukhaari and Muslim in their two Saheehs, from Ibn Mas'ood, may Allaah, the Most High, be pleased with him, that he said, "The Messenger of Allaah, may Allaah's praise and salutations be upon him and his family, said,

{Oh young people! Whoever amongst you is able to marry, should marry, as it assists him in lowering his gaze and protecting his private parts (from illegal acts). And whoever is not able to marry, he should fast, as fasting will lessen the sexual desire.} (al-Bukhaari, 5066, 1905, and Muslim 1/1400 in the Book of Marriage)

The Prophet, may Allaah's praise and salutations be upon him and his family, saw a woman passing by, as is found in "*Saheeh Muslim*"; so he went into his house and had intercourse with his wife, and he went out, and then the water dripped from his head (from ghusl), and the Prophet, may Allaah's praise and salutations be upon him and his family, said, ***{If one of you sees a woman and she fascinates him, he should go to his wife and have intercourse with her, as indeed she has what the other one has.}*** (Muslim, 10/9, from Jaabir, may Allaah be pleased with him).

It is clear that one of the purposes of the marriage is that it be an outlet for the sexual desires of both spouses, thus lessening the chance of illegal sexual acts occurring. This is a clear reason for the wife to not refuse her husband when he desires her, as it assists him in staying with that which is lawful for him, and prevents evil from occurring, insh'Allaah.

Refusing the husband also brings about harm for the wife.

From the hadeeth mentioned earlier from Ibn 'Umar, may Allaah be pleased with him and his father, reported that a woman came to the Messenger of Allaah, may Allaah's praise and salutations be upon him, and said, "What is the right of the husband over his wife?" He, may Allaah's praise and salutations be upon him, said, ***{That she not keep herself from him (when he desires her) even if she is on the back of a camel... As if she does this, then the angels of anger and mercy curse her until she repents and returns (to that which is correct}*** (at-Tayaalisee, 1901, and by another path of narration as found in "*at-Tamheed*" 1/231, and it has supporting narrations as well)

The Messenger of Allaah, may Allaah's praise and salutations be upon him, said, ***{If a man calls his wife to his bed and she refuses and he is angry with her, the angels curse her until morning.}*** (al-Bukhaari, 3237) And in Muslim with the wording, ***{Except that those in the heavens are angry with her.}*** (122/1436)

Imaam an-Nawawi, may Allaah have mercy upon him, said, "This is a proof that it is prohibited for her to refuse to go to his bed without an Islamically legislated excuse. And the menses is not an excuse for prohibiting this, as he has a right concerning taking pleasure in that which is above the waist wrap. And the meaning of the hadeeth is the cursing upon her continues until the wrongdoing is cut off by the coming of Fajr and it is not necessary for them to continue, or by her repenting and returning to the bed." (*"Sharh Saheeh Muslim"*, Vol. 10, No. 249)

The Messenger of Allaah, who was most truthful in all that he said, may Allaah's praise and salutations be upon him, has informed us of these consequences of our actions- may Allaah protect us from being cursed by the angels, or incurring the wrath of those in the heavens!

An added benefit of not refusing the husband when he desires her, is the growth of love and affection, both emotional and physical, between the husband and the wife, insh'Allaah.

Question: Is it permissible for the woman to put forth any excuse when her husband calls her to his mattress- and she says she is going to pray the night prayer and glorify Allaah (saying, "*SubhanAllaah*"), and she says, "I am praying during the night, and glorifying Allaah." Is this a valid excuse?

Answer from the Permanent Committee of Scholars in Saudi Arabia: This is not an excuse, because the rights of the husband are obligatory upon her to fulfill, while praying at night is voluntary, and the *dhikr* of *tasbeeh* is a recommended Sunnah- and that which is obligatory supersedes that which is a Sunnah. The evidence for this is found in the hadeeth of Abi Hurairah, may Allaah be pleased with him, in which he says, "The Messenger of Allaah, may Allaah's praise and salutations be upon him, said, ***{If a man calls his wife to his mattress and she refuses and he goes to bed angry, the angels curse her until morning.} (Agreed upon) and in one narration he says, {Until she returns.}*** ("*Fataawa 'Ulemaa al-Balad al-Haraam*", Page 735, No. 1506)

Question: Is there a sin upon the woman if she forbids her husband (from having intercourse with her) when he seeks this due to a temporary psychological condition which has come to her, or an illness she is afflicted with?

Answer from Sheikh al-'Utheimeen, may Allaah have mercy upon him: It is obligatory upon the woman to respond to her husband when he calls her to his bed; however, if she is ill with a physical sickness which causes her to be unable to give this to him, or a psychological illness- then it is not permissible under these circumstances for the husband to seek that. This is due to the saying of the Prophet, may Allaah's praise and salutations be upon him, ***{Do not harm others, and do not be harmed (by them).}*** (Al-Haakim 2286, Ibn Maajah 2338, Muwwataa 1427)) So it is upon him to abstain temporarily or to take pleasure with her in a way which does not cause any harm. (Collected in "*al-Fataawa al-Qayyimah lil-Usrat al-Muslimah*" Collected by Sa'eed 'Abdul-Ghafaar 'Ali, Page 91)

Review and Discussion Questions

Questions for Obligations towards her Husband

Review:

1. List some of the proofs that the wife must be obedient to her husband in that which contains no wrongdoing? (Hint: use at least one verse and one hadeeth to illustrate this) (Page 286)
2. What are some of the proofs that the husband must treat his wife well and live with her in a good manner? (Top Half of Page 288)
3. Why are the women the majority of the people of the Hellfire? (Page 293, Bottom Half)
4. What are some of the proofs that, while it is permissible for the woman to go out for her needs, her home is better for her? (Bottom Half of Page 296)
5. List some of the proofs that the woman should not refuse to come to her husband's bed, in general. What are some benefits of this? (Bottom Half of Page 299, Page 300)

Discussion & Consideration:

6. How can knowing and acting upon the knowledge of the rights of the husband and the wife make for a happy marriage?
7. Explain safeguarding one's husband- his honor and his wealth. Give examples of each.
8. List some of the proofs or narrations of the salaf which show that the woman should keep the house. What are some of the obvious benefits of this?
9. Is it permissible for the woman to spend her husband's money without his knowledge or permission? Explain.
10. Why must the woman not fast the non-obligatory fasts without the permission of her husband?

Obligations towards her Children

From among her obligations towards her children are:

1. To nurse them for the allotted time

2. To raise and educate them in the proper manner

Examples of this:

a. To teach them the correct *aqeedah*

b. To teach them to pray correctly

c. To teach them Qur'aan and its memorization

d. To teach them to love the Sunnah of the Messenger of Allaah, and to adhere to it

e. To dislike the newly invented matters and innovations

f. To foster in them love of knowledge of the Islamic legislation, and its beauty, and teach them patience in learning it and spreading it to others

g. To guide them to having good character

Examples of this:

- Etiquettes of eating and drinking
- Etiquettes concerning the parents such as asking permission to enter
- Patience
- Truthfulness

h. To teach them the Arabic language

3. To treat them fairly and have justice between them

Sheikh al-'Utheimeen on Children's Rights

The rights of the children are many. From the most important of them is education, and this entails developing the religion and good character in them until there is a great importance placed upon that. Allaah, the Most High, says,

﴾***Oh you who believe! Ward off yourselves and your families against a Fire (Hell) whose fuel is men and stones…***﴿- (Surat at-Tahreem, From Ayat 6)

And the Prophet, may Allaah's praise and salutations be upon him, said, ***{You are all guardians, responsible for those under you, and the man is the guardian of his family and is responsible over those under him.}*** (al-Bukhaari, 893, Muslim, 1829, from the hadeeth of Ibn 'Umar, may Allaah be pleased with them both)

So the children are a trust with the two parents, and they will be held responsible for them on the Day of Judgment; and by educating them correctly in their religion and character the parents fulfill their responsibility over their charges, and the child becomes righteous (through this education) and is a pleasure, delighting the eye of the parents in both this world and the Hereafter.

Allaah, the Most High, says, ﴾***And those who believe and whose offspring follow them in faith, – to them shall We join their offspring, and We shall not decrease the reward of their deeds in anything. Every person is a pledge for that which he has earned.***﴿- (Surat at-Toor, Ayat 21) "التناهم" means, decrease them.

And the Prophet, may Allaah's praise and salutations be upon him, said, ***{When one of the children of Aadam dies, his works are cut off except for one of three: the continuing charity, the beneficial knowledge, or a righteous child who supplicates for him}*** (Muslim, from the hadeeth of Abi Hurairah, may Allaah be pleased with him, No. 1631) This is one of the fruits of educating the child if the education is a righteous one- that he is a benefit to his parents even up until after (their) death.

Many parents disdain, or make little of, this right, as they neglect their children and forget about them, as if they have no responsibility over them. They do not ask where they went, when they returned, who their friends and companions are. They do not direct them to that which is good, nor do they forbid them from that which is evil.

And from the strangest things is that they make every effort to guard their wealth, through saving it and amassing it, as well as being vigilant concerning its use, along with them increasing this wealth and generally benefitting other than them; as for the children, then they are not vigilant with them in anything (meaning, they do not take as good care concerning the children as they do their wealth), even though preserving them is first, and more beneficial both in this life and the next.

As it is obligatory for the father to nourish the child's body with food and drink, and to dress him in clothing, it is likewise obligatory that he nourish his heart with knowledge and faith, and to dress his soul in the garments of piety- as that is best of all.

Also from the rights of the children: That they are provided for by that which is well-known, without being extravagant nor falling short or being negligent in that. This is because that is from the obligations his child places upon him, and is from gratitude for the blessings of Allaah through what He has given him from wealth. So how can he keep the wealth from them during his life, and be stingy to them in regards to it, in order to collect it for them- as they take it by compulsion after his death? In spite of the fact that when he is stingy to them in regards to which is obligatory, then it is (permissible) for them to take from his wealth that which is sufficient for that which is known (that which is needed), as the Messenger of Allaah, may Allaah's praise and salutations be upon him, advised Hind Bint 'Utbah with. (al-Bukhaari, 2211, Muslim 1714, from the hadeeth of 'Aishah, may Allaah be pleased with her)

Also from the rights of the children: That one of them is not preferred over the others in regards to gifts and presents. As one cannot give something to some of his children and keep it from the rest, as that is from injustice and oppression and Allaah does not love oppressors, or those who are unjust. In addition, that results in the estrangement of the ones prohibited from receiving the gift and hostility occurring between them and the ones who received the gifts. Indeed, it may even result in hostility between the ones who did not receive the gifts and their fathers.

Some of the people find that one of the children stands out from the others in regards to obedience and affection to his parents, so his father singles him out for gifts and presents due to that which he shows of this obedience; however, this is not a justifiable reason for singling him out. As the singling out of one who is most obedient is not permissible, just to reward him for his obedience, because the reward for his obedience and devotion is from Allaah. In addition, singling out the one who is most obedient with gifts may make him very impressed with his own devotion, and he then believes that he has great merit; and the other is driven away and continues on his disobedience- then we do not know (what may occur), as the conditions may change, so that the one who is obedient becomes disobedient, and the one who was disobedient becomes obedient- because the hearts are in the hand of Allaah, and He turns them as He wills.

However, if I give to some of them who are in need of it, and the others are not in need- for example if one of the children needs office supplies, medicine, or to marry- then there is no problem with singling him out for that which he is in need of, because this singling out is due to necessity, and is like the providing for him.

When the father performs that which it is obligatory upon him in regards to the child from educating and providing for him, then he has opened the way so the child will establish obedience to his father and give him his rights; and when the father differs in that which is obligatory upon him from that, then he will be punished by the child denying his right, and this is a suitable punishment for him, as you will be treated as you have treated others. *("Huqooq Da'at Ilayha al-Fitrah")*

[From "Tarbiyat al-Abnaa': Sawaal wa Jawaab", a collection of advices and rulings concerning raising the children from Sheikh Muhammad Naasir ad-Deen al-Albaani and Sheikh Muhammad ibn Saalih al-'Utheimeen, may Allaah have mercy upon them both, compiled by Ahmad Haamid, Pages

12-15]

The First Obligation: To nurse them for the allotted time

Allaah has made it obligatory for the mother to nurse her children.

Allaah, Glorified and Exalted is He, says in His Noble Book,

﴾ ***The mothers should suckle their children for two whole years, (that is) for those (parents) who desire to complete the term of suckling...*** ﴿- (Surat al-Baqara, From Ayat 233)

And He, the Most High, says,

﴾***His mother bore him in weakness and hardship upon weakness and hardship, and his weaning is in two years – give thanks to Me and to your parents.***﴿- (Surat Luqmaan, From Ayat 14)

Allaah, Glorified is He, and Most High, also says,

﴾***His mother bears him with hardship. And she brings him forth with hardship, and the bearing of him, and the weaning of him is thirty months...***﴿- (Surat al-Ahqaaf, From Ayat 15)

Sheikh Sadeeq Hasan Khan, may Allaah have mercy upon him, said, in explanation of this verse, ﴾***... and the bearing of him, and the weaning of him is thirty months...***﴿: That is to say, the period is reckoned from the beginning of the pregnancy to when he is finished nursing- meaning, he is weaned from it." ("*Hasan al-Uswah*", Page 215)

Question: Is it permissible to postpone weaning a child until after the time circumscribed in the Qur'aan (two years)?

Answer from the Permanent Committee of Scholars in Saudi Arabia, may Allaah preserve them all: It is permissible if there is a reason to postpone it, just as it is permissible to wean the child before the two years is finished if there is a benefit in that. And the basic principle is that the breastfeeding is for the period of two years, and this should not be deviated from unless it is for an unexpected benefit which requires this deviation. And with Allaah is the success, and may Allaah's praise be upon our Prophet, Muhammad, his family, and his companions, and Allaah's salutations. (9/21 as found in the book, "*Qatf al-Azhaar al-Mutanaathirah min Fataawa al-Mar'at al-Muslimah*" Page 666)

The Second: To raise and educate them in the proper manner

This is the responsibility of both the parents- however it is known that the mother usually spends the most time with the children, starting from the time they are born. She is her children's first teacher and a very strong example and model for them, mash'Allaah. So they will be greatly affected by her teachings, speech, and actions, whether that be for good or bad.

Advices Concerning Raising and Educating the Children from Sheikh al-'Utheimeen

("*Alqaa' ash-Shahree*" as quoted in, "*Tarbiyat al-Abnaa': Sawaal wa Jawaab*", Pages 31-32)

Sheikh al-'Utheimeen, may Allaah have mercy upon him, said, in explanation of the verse,

﴾ ***Our Lord! Bestow on us from our wives and our offspring (dhuriyyatinaa) the comfort of our eyes…***﴿- (Surat al-Furqaan, From Ayat 74):

adh-dhuriyyah: Children, both sons and daughters

The sons and daughters need to be educated and cultivated to have good manners. And what is better than that you meet a boy who is young in the age of discernment, and you say, "Have you memorized anything from the Qur'aan?" And he says, "Yes, I recite *al-Faatihah*." And he recites it for you. The person finds his heart filled with happiness. This, and all praise is due to Allaah, is found nowadays- the people find that when they sit with their young children and teach them Qur'aan and teach them something from the principles of the religion- even if they are young- the young do not forget- they do not forget that which they hear or see. Teach your child, whether it is a boy or a girl, when he sits with you when drinking coffee, eating lunch or dinner- or upon sitting at night- teach him, and school him in good manners. Say, "Oh my son this" and "Oh my daughter" that.

Likewise, also teach him truthfulness. Do not make him a promise and then break it; because if you promise him something and then break the promise, then it makes it easy for him to lie, and also makes it easy to break promises (due to his having seen you do it yourself). If you say, "Come here, boy, I want to give you candy!" And you put your hand in your pocket as if you want to give him candy and then when he comes you grab him, whether you want to hit him or do not give him anything- what will be the repercussions of the act in him? These results will be strong and he will continue to be reinforced in lying.

Likewise, some of the people make the mistake of saying "Be quiet, be quiet, do you want candy?" when the child cries or yells. The child immediately quiets down because the candy is the most precious thing to him. When he quiets, it is said, "There isn't any candy!" And he really has this candy! Is this correct??

No, but if you do not have the candy with you to fulfill your promise, you can say, "Be quiet, yelling is not good", or speak to him with any truthful speech.

Likewise, one must also command them with the prayer. When do we command them with the prayer? When they are seven years old- before the age of seven we do not command them. If they perform the prayer, then that is from themselves, and this is desirable, so do not prevent them from doing so. However, do not command them, as you are not more perfect in judgment or wisdom than the Messenger of Allaah, may Allaah's praise and salutations be upon him and his family, and he did not order us to command them until they are seven to ten. When they reach the age of ten, then they are beaten (if they do not pray). However, this is not a severe beating, and is not like the beating of the one who has reached maturity from amongst them; rather, it is a beating meant to make them realize the importance which you place upon the prayer. And there is an appropriate saying for every time and place.

And the children differ, as some of them have a strong understanding concerning that which you prohibit him from or command him to do, and will follow your example. Others of them are obstinate and will not be increased in anything good; only that their behavior will worsen. And there is an appropriate saying for every time and place.(end of quote from Sheikh al-'Utheimeen, may Allaah have mercy upon him)

Examples of this Education:

A. Teaching them the Correct 'Aqeedah, Built upon the Qur'aan, Sunnah, and Ijma' (Consensus)

Allaah, the Most High, says, ﴾***So know that la ilaaha ila Allaah (none has the right to be worshipped but Allaah)***﴿- (Surat Muhammad, From Ayat 19)

He, Exalted is He, says, concerning the state of the newborn child, ﴾***And Allaah has brought you out from the wombs of your mothers while you know nothing. And He gave you hearing, sight, and hearts that you might give thanks (to Allaah).***﴿- (Surat an-Nahl, From Ayat 78)

He, the Most High, also says,

﴾***So, set you (Oh Muhammad) your face towards the religion (of pure Islamic Monotheism) haneef (worship none but Allaah Alone). Allaah's fitrah (i.e. Allaah's Islamic Monotheism) with which He has created mankind.***﴿- (Surat ar-Room, From Ayat30)

And the Prophet, may Allaah's praise and salutations be upon him, said, ***{Every child is born upon the fitrah, and it is his parents who turn him into a Jew, Christian or Magian .}*** (al-Bukhaari, 1358,1359,1385, 4775, 6599, and Muslim 2658, and at-Tirmidhi, 2138, and Ahmad 2/282, 346,410)

The children are born on the *fitrah*, or the true, correct nature of Islaam- it is the responsibility of the parents to educate and raise them upon that, teaching them their religion. This includes the acts of worship, as well as the belief system. This can be done with books and exercises, but perhaps the best way to teach them is by gaining beneficial knowledge ourselves, and acting upon that knowledge.

Narrated Abu Musa, may Allaah be pleased with him, "The Prophet, may Allaah's praise and salutations be upon him, said,

{The example of guidance and knowledge (the Qur'aan and the Sunnah)

with which Allaah has sent me, is like abundant rain falling on the earth, some of which was fertile soil that absorbed rain water and brought forth vegetation and grass in abundance. (And) another portion of it was hard and held the rain water and Allaah benefited the people with it and they utilized it for drinking, making their animals drink from it and irrigating the land for cultivation. (And) a portion of it was barren which could neither hold the water nor bring forth vegetation (then that land gave no benefits). The first is the example of the person who comprehends Allaah's religion and gets benefit (from the knowledge) which Allaah has revealed through me and learns and then teaches it to others. The last example is that of a person who does not care for it and does not take Allaah's Guidance revealed through me (He is like that barren land). } ("*Saheeh al-Bukhaari*", 1/79)

So we learn and follow the guidance in our own lives, and we strive to pass that guidance along to our children, using every tool we have and opportunity which is presented to us, so the child loves Islaam and lives it- and Allaah is the One who grants success.

B. Commanding the Children to Perform the Prayers

(From "*Sharh Riyaadh as-Saaliheen*", under hadeeth No. 302, as quoted in "*Tarbiyat al-Abnaa': Sawaal wa Jawaab*", Pages 48-49)

Sheikh Muhammad ibn Saalih al-'Utheimeen, may Allaah have mercy upon him, said,

From the rights of the children upon their parents is that the parents command them to perform the prayer when they reach the age of seven, and to beat them concerning it, meaning when they are negligent or remiss concerning it, when they have reached the age of ten years. However, this is with the condition that they possess intellect, as if they reach the age of seven or ten and they do not have the power of understanding or comprehension- meaning that they are mentally deficient- then they are not commanded with anything, and are not beaten concerning anything. However, they are to be prevented from corruption whether in the house or outside of it.

And his, may Allaah's praise and salutations be upon him, saying, ***{Beat them concerning it when they are children of the age of ten.}*** (Abu Daawud, 494, at-Tirmidhi, 407- and he has declared it *hasan saheeh*, ad-Daaramee, 1/333, Ibn al-Jarood, 147, Ibn Khuzaimah, 1002, al-Haakim, 1/102, and he has declared it *saheeh* on the conditions of Muslim. Sheikh al-Albaani has declared it to be raised to the level of *saheeh* through that which strengthens it from the hadeeth of Ibn 'Umar, may Allaah be pleased with both of them, in Abu Daawud, 495, Ahmad, 2/180,187, and al-Haakim, 1/197)

That which is meant by "beating" is that which brings about education and rectification without any damage. It is not permissible for the father to beat his children with a severe beating; nor is it permissible for him to beat them repeatedly when there is no necessity for it. Rather, if it is necessary to do it, for example the child does not perform the prayer except when he is beaten, then this beating is not a severe beating- instead, it is a plain (light) beating, as the Prophet, may Allaah's praise and salutations be upon him, commanded beating them, not in order to harm them or damage them, but rather to educate them and rectify them.

This hadeeth contains that which indicates that those people who came later who call themselves the people of education, who say that the youth should not be hit in the schools if they are not paying attention- this hadeeth is a refutation of them, and is a proof of the falseness of their ideology, as it is not correct. This is because some of the children are not usually benefited by speech alone, while beating them does benefit them more. So if they are left alone, without any beating, and they are remiss in that which is obligatory upon them, and neglectful in their lessons and inattentive, then it becomes necessary to beat them so that they become accustomed to the discipline and the system, and that they perform that which it is necessary for them to perform; otherwise it would become chaotic.

Except that it is as we mentioned before, that it is necessary that the beating be for educational purposes, not to cause harm or damage. So the beating must be fitting for the condition of the child, a beating which is not severe. And one must not do that which was done by some of the teachers in the past, where they beat with a great, painful beating. Nor should it cause any harm, as some of the teachers who are from those people who are farthest from correct education call to. They say that one should not say anything to the youngster because they do not understand anything, or obey or understand, but the beating will teach him. (Originally from "*Sharh Riyaadh as-Saaliheen*", under hadeeth No. 302)

C. Teaching them Qur'aan and its memorization

The greatness of the reward for doing this is found in the Sunnah of the Messenger of Allaah, may Allaah's praise and salutations be upon him, as he said, ***{The best of you is the one who learns the Qur'aan and teaches it to others.}*** (al-Bukhaari, 5027, Abu Daawud 1532, and others)

This is a very great obligation upon us, as the Qur'aan is the word of Allaah, which He gave to us to guide us through all the ups and downs of life. Through the Qur'aan we learn about Allaah, His creation, how to worship Him, and much more. The recitation of Qur'aan is a pillar of the prayer, and the prayer is not complete without the recitation of al-Faatihah. Due to this, it is perhaps best to begin teaching the child with Surat al-Faatihah, then going on to the smaller surahs at the end of the Qur'aan, such as Surat al-Ikhlaas, Surat an-Naas, and Surat al-Falaq. Teach them the meaning of the verses as you teach them the words, as the Qur'aan is meant to be understood, contemplated, and acted upon. If for some reason we are not able to teach the child these surahs, it is necessary that we find someone, such as an older sister or brother or outside teacher, who can educate them, insh'Allaah.

D. Teaching them to love the Messenger of Allaah, as well as his Sunnah, and to Adhere to it

Anas, may Allaah be pleased with him, related that the Messenger of Allaah, may Allaah's praise and salutations be upon him, said, ***{One of you does not believe until I am more beloved to him than his parents, offspring, and all of the people.}*** (al-Bukhaari, 14, Muslim 2/15 of the explanation of an-Nawawi, and others)

Alhamdulillah, this is crucial to the success of the child in both this life and the next, as the love is tied to belief itself, mash'Allaah. One of the ways in which we show our love of the Messenger of Allaah, may Allaah's praise and salutations be upon him, is by following his example from his Sunnah. Indeed, we are commanded to follow it!

Allaah mentions the obligation of following the Messenger of Allaah in the Qur'aan. He says,

﴾***He who obeys the Messenger (Muhammad) has indeed obeyed Allaah, but he who turns away...***﴿- (Surat an-Nisaa, From Ayat 80)

And He, the Most High, has said, ﴾***And whatsoever the Messenger gives you, take it; and whatsoever he forbids you, abstain (from it).***﴿- (Surat al-Hashr, From Ayat 7)

And He, Exalted is He, and Glorified, says, ﴾***Allaah has sent down to you the Book (the Qur'aan), and al-Hikmah (Islamic laws, knowledge of legal and illegal things, i.e. the Prophet's Sunnah – legal ways), and taught you that which you knew not.***﴿- (Surat an-Nisaa, From Ayat 113)

And the saying of the Prophet, may Allaah's praise and salutations be upon him, ***{I advise you to have fear of Allaah, and with hearing and obeying the ruler, even if he is an Ethiopian slave As indeed, those of you who will live after me will witness a great many differences- so keep with my Sunnah and the Sunnah of the rightly guided khaliphahs. Hold on to it and bite on to with your molar teeth.}*** (Abu Daawud 4607, at- Tirmidhi, 2676, who said it is *hasan saheeh*, ibn Maajah, 42, Ahmad 4/127,126 and others, and it has been declared to be authentic)

So we must teach them to love the Sunnah, and to follow it in all that they are able, insh'Allaah. And perhaps the best way to do this is through setting a good example, by learning the Sunnah ourselves, and implementing it in our everyday lives. When we do so, we must inform the child that this thing is from the Sunnah, so that she knows the foundation of the action, and does not think that it is merely something from our ownselves, to be taken or left.

E. Teaching them to Dislike the Newly Invented Matters and Innovations in the Religion

The religion of Islaam is a complete religion, a complete way of life. There is no need to alter it, or to add anything to it, alhamdulillah, as Allaah knows all that will happen in the future- so He gave us the religion in its entirety, all we have to know until the Day of Judgment, alhamdulillah rabbil'aalameen. And we know that the Prophet, may Allaah's praise and salutations be upon him, delivered the message and explained it to us, as Allaah willed him to do.

Allaah, the Most High, says in His Noble Book,

﴾***This day, I have perfected your religion for you, completed My favor upon you, and have chosen for you Islaam as your religion.***﴿- (Surat al-Maa'idah, From Ayat 3)

And He, Glorified and Exalted is He, says,

﴾***And whoever contradicts and opposes the Messenger (Muhammad) after the right path has been shown clearly to him, and follows other than the believers' way, We shall keep him in the path he has chosen, and burn him in Hell – what an evil destination!***﴿- (Surat an-Nisaa, Ayat 115)

And the Prophet, may Allaah's praise and salutations be upon him, said in the hadeeth of 'Abdullah ibn Mas'ood, ***{Every newly invented matter (in the religion) is an innovation, and every innovation is a going astray, and every going astray is in the Hellfire...}*** (Abu Daawud, 2118, an-Nasaa'ee, 3/104,105, Ahmad, 1/293, 393, 'abdur-Razaaq, 10449, al Haakim, 2/182,183 and it is authentic)

It is clear from these verses, and from this great hadeeth, that the path has been completed, and all that is left is for us to walk down it- not making new paths, or changing the one which Allaah has given us, alhamdulillah. We have to understand this important point, and pass this on to our children. If they understand this foundational principle of the religion, it will, insh'Allaah, assist them in remaining steadfast upon the truth when confronted with the many deviances which exist in the world today.

F. Fostering in them Love of the Legislated Knowledge, and its Beauty, and Teaching them Patience in Learning it and Spreading it to Others

This point goes hand in hand with the one before it- as if the child knows and understands the wisdom of that which Allaah has legislated, he will not need to look outside for new ideas or different explanations.

And Islamic knowledge is the most beautiful and beneficial knowledge that one can strive to attain, alhamdulillah, and the scholars themselves are the inheritors of the prophets, mash'Allaah!

Allaah, the Most High, says,

﴾***It is only those who have knowledge among His slaves that fear Allaah.***﴿-

(Surat Faatir, From Ayat 28)

and he, the Most High, also says,

﴿***...and say: "My Lord! Increase me in knowledge.***﴾- (Surah Taa Haa, From Ayat 114)

And Zur ibn Habeesh said, "I came to Safwaan ibn 'Assaal al-Muraadee, and he said, "What have you come for?" I said, "Seeking knowledge." He said, "Indeed the angels lower their wings for the student of knowledge due to being pleased with that which he is seeking." (at-Tirmidhi, 96, 3535, an-Nasaa'ee, 1/83, and others)

We, as mothers, should encourage our children in every way possible to seek Islamic knowledge. And remember that knowledge itself is not sufficient- indeed, it must be acted upon as well.

There are many precedents for us amongst women of the Salaf. There were some women who would work so that their sons could seek knowledge. For example, Sufyaan ath-Thawree, may Allaah have mercy upon him, is the one who Zaida spoke about, saying, "ath-Thawree is the most knowledgeable person in the world." And al-Awzaa'i said of him, "Nobody remains that the general people agree upon with happiness that his hadeeth are authentic, except for one man who is in Koofah." By which he meant Sufyaan. And Sufyaan did not attain this except by the help of Allaah and the help of his pious mother. And Waqee' narrated that Umm Sufyaan said to Sufyaan, "Go and become a student of knowledge and I will support you with my spinning. And after you have written a number of tens of *ahaadeeth* see if you find yourself in a better position. And if you are, then keep following knowledge and otherwise, don't worry about it." (*"Siyyar an-Nubala"* Vol. 7, 269-270)

It is obligatory upon every male and female Muslim to seek the knowledge necessary to practice his religion- so each and every one of us must be sure that our children have this knowledge at least. Then, if we are blessed by Allaah and granted His favor, we may encourage and guide them to go further, and plant their feet firmly on the path to beneficial knowledge, that they will be benefitted and benefit others as well, insh'Allaah.

G. Guiding them to having Good Character and Correct Behavior

Question: What is the sound and correct foundation for providing the youth with the correct Islamic education (*tarbiyyah*)?

Answer from Sheikh Muhammad ibn Saalih al-'Utheimeen, may Allaah have mercy upon him: *at-Tarbiyyah* consists of two methods: the theoretical method, and the practical method.

As for the theoretical method, then this is to educate the child to have the virtuous and excellent character as well as teaching him the acts of worship through the use of writings, books and tapes. And how many of the houses are rightly guided through the use of the tapes and are brought to the correct orientation through their use?

As for the practical method, then this is that you yourself put into practice this virtuous and excellent behavior and perform the acts of worship, and to teach the children through that which is good, so that they follow you and emulate this excellent behavior and perform the acts of worship as well. To encourage this, Allaah has urged us to seek out the good sitting, and warned from the evil sitting, as it has been related that the good sitting is like being in the company of the musk seller- whether he sells it to you, or he causes you to imitate or copy it- that is to say, he gives it (the good fragrance) to you- , or whether you find that he smells pleasant. And the evil sitting is like being in the company of the blacksmith- whether your garment is burned, or you find that he has a bad smell… ("*Fataawa Noor 'ala ad-Darb*" as quoted in, "*Tarbiyat al-Abnaa': Sawaal wa Jawaab*", Pages 29-30)

Some Examples of This Correct Behavior:

A. Teaching the Children the Correct Manner of Eating

'Umar ibn Abi Salamah, may Allaah be pleased with him, who was the stepson of the Messenger of Allaah, may Allaah's praise and salutations be upon him, said, "I was a young man under the guardianship of the Messenger of Allaah, may Allaah's praise and salutations be upon him, and my hands roamed about the dish (taking food from various parts of it). So the Messenger of Allaah, may Allaah's praise and salutations be upon him, said to me, ***{Oh young man, say 'Bismillaah', the Most High, and eat with your right hand, and eat from that which is closest to you.}*** And this remained my manner of eating afterwards." (al-Bukhaari, 5376, Muslim 2022)

Sheikh Muhammad ibn Saalih al-'Utheimeen, may Allaah have mercy upon him, said, in regards to this hadeeth:

There are many points of benefit in this hadeeth:

It is obligatory upon a person to educate his children concerning the correct methods of eating and drinking, as well as that which it is necessary to say when eating and drinking, as the Prophet, may Allaah's praise and salutations be upon him, did with his stepson. This is from the good character of the Prophet, may Allaah's praise and salutations be upon him, and his methods of teaching. This is because he did not scold this young man when he let his hand roam about the dish- rather, he taught him with gentleness and invited him with kindness,***{Oh young man, say 'Bismillaah', the Most High, and eat with your right hand...}***

It is known that teaching the young ones with the like of this behavior will not be forgotten. Meaning, the child will not forget if you teach him when he is small- however, if he is older, then he may forget when you teach him. And perhaps he will disobey or rebel against you in some things when he is older. However, when he is small and you teach him there will be the most acceptance. And the one who fears Allaah concerning his children, they will fear Allaah in regards to him, and the one who neglects the rights of his children, they will neglect his rights. ("*Sharh Riyaadh as-Saaliheen*", under hadeeth number 299, From "*Tarbiyat al-Abnaa': Sawaal wa Jawaab*", Page 82)

B. Teaching the Children the Etiquette of Asking Permission

Sheikh Muhammad ibn Saalih al-'Utheimeen, may Allaah have mercy upon him, said,

Allaah, the Most High, says, ﴾***And when the chil dren among you come to puberty, then let them (also) ask for permission, as those senior to them (in age).***﴿- (Surat an-Noor, From Ayat 59)

"*idha balaghoo al-hulum*": This means, mature through having had an ejaculation. However, this is from a dream, as the usual course of events is that a man's first ejaculation of semen does not come except from a dream. and some of the men become mature without the dream- however the usual thing is that it occurs from a dream. And if a child attains puberty, then he is not to enter the house except with permission. As for before that, his matter is easy.

There are three times when everyone has to ask permission to enter:

﴾***Oh you who believe! Let your slaves and slave-girls, and those among you who have not come to the age of puberty ask your permission (before they come to your presence) on three occasions: before Fajr (morning) prayer and while you put off your clothes for the noonday (rest), and after the 'Ishaa' (night) prayer.***﴿- (Surat an-Noor, From Ayat 58)

The First: ﴾***before Fajr (morning) prayer***﴿

The Second: ﴾***while you put off your clothes for the noonday (rest)***﴿

The Third: ﴾***after the 'Ishaa' (night) prayer***﴿

During these periods everyone has to ask permission to enter, as at these times a person may be sleeping and he might be wearing clothes he would not want anyone to see. So for that reason, everyone must ask permission during these three times. As for the children being able to see the women, this is not connected to becoming mature; however it is connected to it being known from the child that he looks at the woman a look of desire. If this is known, even if he is less than ten years old, then he cannot see them and they have to be veiled from him. This is due to Allaah, the Most High, saying,

﴾***And tell the believing women to lower their gaze, and protect their private parts and not to show off their adornment except that which is apparent, and to draw their veils all over juyoobihinna (i.e. their bodies, faces, necks and bosoms) and not to reveal their adornment except to their husbands, or their fathers, or their husband's fathers, or their sons, or their husband's sons, or their brothers or their brother's sons, or their sister's sons, or their women, or the (female) slaves whom their right hands possess, or old male servants who lack vigor, or small children who have no sense of feminine sex. And let them not stamp their feet so as to reveal what they hide of their adornment.***﴿- (Surat an-Noor, From Ayat 31)

Some children, from the time they are ten years old, they look at the women with a look of desire, and this varies, as I said. This child might sit with people who talk a lot about women, and this would cause this desire to be mature from the beginning. Or, he may sit with people who do not worry about anything except studying and memorizing Qur'aan or similar things, and they don't think or speak of this. And so he would not have this desire matured in him.

In this state, if we realize that the child is aware of the woman's *'awrah*, and speaks about women, and he looks at women as the men look at them, then the women have to veil themselves from him, even if he has not reached the age of ten. Some of the scholars say that some people who are not yet ten can have children, and this is not strange. So he can have a child if he gets married, which is not a strange thing. It is said that 'Amr ibn al-'Aas was only eleven years older than his son, 'Abdullah.

ash-Shaafi'ee said, "There was a woman from amongst us who became a grandmother when she was twenty-one years old. And now, when you are twenty-one, you have not even married! And the woman can become mature at the age of nine, and get married when she is ten, and have a child during the first year of her marriage. And her child may be a daughter, and then when her daughter is nine, she gets married and then she has a child in the first year of her marriage- and now the grandmother is only twenty-one years old and she has a grandchild."

And ash-Shaafi'ee, may Allaah have mercy upon him, was very truthful, and he said that he saw a grandmother that was only twenty-one years old.

The result of this is that if a child becomes mature then he should not enter until he has asked permission. So if he becomes aware of the woman's *'awrah* and speaks about them, and looks at them with desire, then the women have to be veiled from him even if he is not yet ten. And Allaah is the One who Grants Success. ("*Sharh Riyaadh as-Saaliheen*" under hadeeth number 873, as quoted in, " *Tarbiyat al-Abnaa': Sawaal wa Jawaab*" Pages 82-84)

C. Patience

Allaah, the Most High, mentions patience many times in the Qur'aan. He, the Most High, says,

﴿***Only those who are patient shall receive their reward in full, without reckoning***﴾- (Surat az-Zumar, From Ayat 10)

And He, Glorified and Exalted is He, says,

﴿***Oh you who believe! Seek help in patience and the prayer. Truly, Allaah is with as-saabiroon (the patient).***﴾- (Surat al-Baqara, From Ayat 153)

And from the Sunnah, the hadeeth of Abi Yahya, Suhaib ibn Seenaan, may Allaah be pleased with him, who said that the Messenger of Allaah, may Allaah's praise and salutations be upon him, said, ***{The affairs of the believer are amazing, as all of his affairs are good for him. And that is not for anyone except for the believer. If good befalls him and then he is thankful, then there is good for him, and if evil befalls him and he is patient, then there is good for him.}*** (Muslim, 2999, Ahmad 4/332,333; 6/16)

Sheikh al-'Utheimeen, may Allaah have mercy upon him, says in his explanation of "*Thaalathatu al-Usool*": "Patience (*as-sabr*) is to confine oneself to obedience to Allaah, and to withhold oneself from disobedience to Allaah, and from being angry with that which Allaah has decreed." He goes on to say,

"Patience is of three kinds:

1. Patience upon obedience to Allaah
2. Patience upon avoiding that which Allaah has forbidden
3. Patience with regard to Allaah's decrees which he has put into effect- both those which the servants have no control over at all, and those pertaining to the harm and the attacks which Allaah brings about by the hands of some of the people." (Pages 46-47)

Patience is something which we must cultivate in ourselves and our children- look at the reward promised in the first verse mentioned- the ones who are patient will receive their reward without reckoning...and in the second, we are told that Allaah is with those who are patient. And again, perhaps the best way to teach our children patience, is to have patience ourselves- to not complain when things are not exactly as we wish, and to strive to be obedient to Allaah and His Messenger. This is a path to success in this life, and the next, insh'Allaah.

D. Truthfulness

Truthfulness is from those praised characteristics which we must strive to raise our children upon. Allaah, the Most High, says,

﴾***Oh you who believe! Be afraid of Allaah, and be with those who are true (in words and deeds).***﴿- (Surat at-Tawbah, Ayat 119)

And He, the Most High, says,

﴾***Verily, the Muslims- men and women, the believers men and women, the men and the women who are obedient (to Allaah), the men and women who are truthful (in their speech and deeds), the men and the women who are patient (in performing all the duties which Allaah has ordered and in abstaining from all that Allaah has forbidden), the men and the women who are humble (before their Lord – Allaah), the men and the women who give sadaqaat (i.e. zakaat and alms), the men and the women who observe Saum (fast) (the obligatory fasting during the month of Ramadhaan, and the optional fasting), the men and the women who guard their chastity (from illegal sexual acts) and the men and the women who remember Allaah much with their hearts and tongues – Allaah has prepared for them forgiveness and a great reward (i.e. Paradise).***﴿- (Surat al-Ahzaab, Ayat 35)

There are many other verses concerning this, and there are also proofs from the Sunnah. It has been narrated from Ibn Mas'ood, may Allaah be pleased with him, that the Prophet, may Allaah's praise and salutations be upon him, said, ***{Indeed truthfulness leads to righteousness, and righteousness leads to Jennah (Paradise). And indeed a man tells the truth until he is written with Allaah as truthful. And indeed, lying leads to evil and evil leads to***

the Hellfire. And indeed a man lies until he is written with Allaah as a liar.} (al-Bukhaari, 6094, and Muslim, 16/160)

If a child sees that we are untruthful in our speech and actions, then he will almost certainly pick this up and become untruthful in his speech and actions. This means we must always be on our guard against lying and deceit in ourselves and our families. As Sheikh al-'Utheimeen said in a previously quoted passage,

"Likewise, also teach him truthfulness. Do not make him a promise and then break it; because if you promise him something and then break the promise, then it makes it easy for him to lie, and also makes it easy to break promises (due to his having seen you do it yourself). If you say, "Come here, boy, I want to give you candy!" And you put your hand in your pocket as if you want to give him candy and then when he comes you grab him, whether you want to hit him or do not give him anything- what will be the repercussions of the act in him? These results will be strong and he will continue to be reinforced in lying."

These are only a few of the praiseworthy characteristics which we must teach our children and raise them upon. One of the best sources for us to use in this effort is the stories of the prophets, as well as the life story of the Prophet Muhammad, may Allaah's praise and salutations be upon him, and the stories of the Companions and righteous people throughout the ages. Children need role models, and what better role models can there be for them than these people who loved Islaam and strived to live it to its fullest?

H. Teaching them the Arabic Language

Sheikh Muhammad ibn Saalih al-'Utheimeen, may Allaah have mercy upon him, said, in explanation of the importance of learning the Arabic language,

"He, the Most High's, saying ﴿***In the clear Arabic language***﴾- (Surat ash-Shu'araa', Ayat 195)

This is a great thing for the Arabic language to be proud of- which is that the Noble book of Allaah was revealed in this Arabic language. Along with that, that Arabic language is clear (مبين); meaning, clear and distinct. As it itself is clear, and it clarifies other than it.

So this Qur'aan is plain and clear, and it makes the truth clear as well, "***In the clear Arabic language***"

It is the language of the Arabs, who are the most eloquent of the eloquent speakers.

And I say that this great pride for the Arabic language is that the Qur'aan was revealed in it and foreigners have tried to learn Arabic so that they could reach and comprehend the meanings of the Qur'aan. As even if a person understands it (from translation), if his language is not Arabic, he cannot taste or savor the Qur'aan completely. And no one can savor the Qur'aan completely except for one whom Allaah grants success and who speaks Arabic. For this reason, the nations attempted to learn Arabic due to their Islaam until their speech became that of the pure Arabs. As al-Bukhaari was by lineage a Persian from Bukhaara, which is far from the Arabs- but he learned Arabic. Similarly, al-Fayroozaabaadee, who wrote "*al-Qamoos al-Muheet*" about the Arabic language- although he was not Arab in origin- he learned Arabic because he could not understand the Book of Allaah or the Sunnah of the Messenger, may Allaah's praise and salutations be upon him, except in Arabic."

("*al-Liqaa ash-Shahree*", as quoted in, " *Tarbiyat al-Abnaa': Sawaal wa Jawaab*" Pages 90-91)

It is important for the Arabs themselves to learn and educate themselves in the Arabic language- and it is vital that the non-Arabs do so as well, insh'Allaah. The Arabic language is one of the keys to understanding the Qur'aan and Sunnah of the Messenger of Allaah, may Allaah's praise and salutations be upon him, and as such it is necessary for us to strive to learn it to the best of our ability, and to make sure our children understand it as well. Indeed, certain acts of worship, such as the prayer, must, in general, be performed in Arabic.

Also, by learning the Arabic language, we are able to hear and understand the Qur'aan as it was revealed, as well as to read the words of our Noble Messenger, may Allaah's praise and salutations be upon him, as he himself spoke them. What a great blessing that is, alhamdulillah!

The Third: Obligation To treat them fairly and have justice between them

an-Nu'man ibn Basheer, may Allaah be pleased with him, said, that the Prophet, may Allaah's praise and salutations be upon him, said, ***{Be just between your children, be just between your children, be just between your children.}*** (Abu Daawud, 2544, an-Nasaa'ee, 6/262, Ahmad, 4/275,278,375, and it is authentic)

Sheikh Muhammad ibn Saalih al-'Utheimeen, may Allaah have mercy upon him, said, concerning being just between the children,

"Then, from that which is important in educating the children is that you treat them equally in that which it is obligatory to treat them equally so that none of them will carry evil thoughts about you. And often what occurs to those who are unjust in the treatment of their children, is that the ones whom they loved most turn on them and are disobedient when they are grown- and he (the father) is not benefitted except through the rest of the children whose brothers were preferred over them. And this is a worldly punishment which is hastened.

It is obligatory upon the person to be just and fair between his children, as the Prophet, may Allaah's praise and salutations be upon him, said, ***{Fear Allaah, and be just between your children.}*** (al-Bukhaari, 2587, Muslim, 1723, from the hadeeth of an-Nu'maan ibn Basheer, may Allaah be pleased with him)

This goes so far that the pious predecessors would be fair between their children in the matter of kissing them; meaning, if they kissed one of them, they kissed the others in the same way." ("*Fataawa Noor 'ala ad-Darb*" as quoted in, "*Tarbiyat al-Abnaa': Sawaal wa Jawaab*", Page 30)

These are some of the obligations which the mother has towards her child. The influence of the mother in the life of the children cannot be overstated, mash'Allaah, and the effects of her upbringing of them will be seen on them throughout their entire lives. Children learn all the time, so we as mothers must strive to present to them good character, and to show them the correct way to understand and live in a way that will please Allaah. We must admonish and exhort them, and make every effort to instill in them righteousness and piety.

And what excellent advice was given by Luqman to his son, as stated by Allaah in the Qur'aan,

﴾And (remember) when Luqmaan said to his son when he was advising him: "Oh my son! Join not in worship others with Allah. Verily, joining others in worship with Allaah is a great wrong indeed. And We have enjoined on man (to be dutiful and good) to his parents. His mother bore him in weakness and hardship upon weakness and hardship, and his weaning is in two years – give thanks to Me and to your parents. To Me is the final destination. But if they (both) strive with you to make you join in worship with Me others that of which you have no knowledge, then obey them not; but behave with them in the world kindly, and follow the path of him who turns to Me in repentance and in obedience. Then to Me will be your return, and I shall tell you what you used to do. "Oh my son! If it be (anything) equal to the weight of a grain of mustard seed, and though it be in a rock, or in the heavens or in the earth, Allaah will bring it forth. Verily, Allaah is Subtle (in bringing out that grain), Well-Acquainted (with its place). "Oh my son! perform prayers, enjoin (on people) al-ma'roof (Islamic Monotheism and all that is good), and forbid (people) from al-munkar (i.e. disbelief in the Oneness of Allaah, polytheism of all kinds and all that is evil and bad), and bear with patience whatever befalls you. Verily, these are some of the important commandments (ordered by Allaah with no exemption). "And turn not your face away from men with pride, nor walk in insolence through the earth. Verily, Allâh likes not any arrogant boaster. "And be moderate (or show no insolence) in your walking, and lower your voice. Verily, the harshest of all voices is the braying of the asses."﴿ – (Surat Luqmaan, Ayats 13-19)

The Merits of having a Righteous Child

From, "*Tarbiyat al-Abnaa': Sawaal wa Jawaab*", a collection of advice and rulings concerning raising the children from Sheikh Muhammad Naasir ad-Deen al-Albaani and Sheikh Muhammad ibn Saalih al-'Utheimeen, may Allaah have mercy upon them both, compiled by Ahmad Haamid, Pages 11-12)

Question: What is the meaning of the noble hadeeth, ***{If one of the children of Aadam dies, his works are cut off except for one of three: the continuing charity, or the beneficial knowledge, or a righteous child who supplicates for him}*** (Muslim, from the hadeeth of Abu Hurairah, may Allaah be pleased with him, No. 1631)? Please benefit us, may Allaah's blessings be upon you.

Answer from Sheikh Muhammad ibn Saalih al-'Utheimeen, may Allaah have mercy upon him: It is known that when a person dies, his actions are cut off because he is dead, and actions are during the lifetime- except for one from these three actions- as there is a reason for it, within it: the first, is the continuing charity, the second is the beneficial knowledge, and the third is the righteous child who supplicates for him after his death, as a child is from that which man earns during his lifetime. And the Prophet, may Allaah's praise and salutations be upon him, said, ***{... or a righteous child who supplicates for him}***. This is because the child who is not righteous is not concerned for anyone but himself – he is not concerned about his father or mother.

In his, may Allaah's praise and salutations be upon him, saying, ***{...or a righteous child who supplicates for him}***: This indicates that the supplication for the father or for someone other than him from the family is the best of those acts of worship which mankind performs to worship Allaah, making the rewards of it for them (the father or other family member). This is because the Prophet, may Allaah's praise and salutations be upon him, did not say, "Or a righteous child who makes the prayer for him, or fasts for him, or gives charity for him", along with that it is connected with the action in the hadeeth:***{ his works are cut off except for one of three...}*** So the action of the person for his father after his death is from that which has been appointed for him, according to the explanation of the Prophet, may Allaah's praise and salutations be upon him.

Also, supplicating for one's parents is better than to say "*SubhanAllaah*", recite, pray or give charity while doing them so that the rewards are intended for the parents. Mankind is in need of the righteous action- so he makes the righteous action for his own self, and supplicates for his parents with that which is loved. (End of quote from Sheikh al-'Utheimeen, may Allaah have mercy upon him)

May Allaah rectify us, and assist us in raising our children in a righteous manner, one which will bring success in this life and the next.

Review and Discussion Questions

Questions regarding obligations towards the children

Review:

1. What are the proofs that the mother must nurse her child, and what is the term mentioned within this proof? (Page 308)
2. At what age do we command the children with the prayer and the other obligatory acts? At what age do we punish them if they do not perform them? Bring the proof. (Bottom Half of Page 311)
3. What are some of the proofs of the obligation to obey the Messenger of Allaah, may Allaah's praise and salutations be upon him? Why does love the Messenger, may Allaah's praise and salutations be upon him, make this easier for us? (Page 313)
4. What are the three times mentioned in which everyone must ask permission to enter a room? (Top of of Page 317)
5. What is patience? What are its categories? (Top Half of Page 319)
6. What is the proof that we must be just between our children? What does this justice include? (Page 321, Middle of Page)
7. Make a numbered list of some of the advices of Luqmaan to his son, as found in the Qur'aan. (Top Half of Page 322)

Discussion & Consideration:

8. What are some of the fruits in this life and the next, of raising and educating our children with the proper Islamic upbringing and education?
9. Why is it crucial that the parent always be diligent in being a good example and guide for the child? Why is this sometimes more effective than simply stating something and not following it with action?
10. Is it unreservedly permissible for the parent to beat the child? How does Sheikh al-'Utheimeen explain what is meant with this term?
11. Discuss the theoretical and practical methods of teaching the child mentioned by Sheikh al-'Utheimeen, may Allaah have mercy upon him. Describe instances in which each may be successful to teach the child.
12. Explain how the age when a young boy must be separated from the women differs, and why.
13. What are the best ways to teach a child truthfulness and patience? Why is this so important? Give some examples of real life situations in which we may do this.
14. What are the benefits of learning the Arabic language? Why is it crucial that we make sure our children learn Arabic?

Obligations towards her

Extended Family

From among her obligations towards her extended family are:

Good Treatment and Keeping the Ties of Kinship

Islaam exhorts us to be good to our families, whether from our own lineage, or, to a lesser extent, from our in-laws- to be compassionate and gentle with them, and to safeguard their conditions.

Allaah, the Most High, says in His Noble Book,

﴾Worship Allaah and join none with Him (in worship); and do good to parents, kinsfolk, orphans, al-masaakeen (the needy), the neighbor who is near of kin, the neighbor who is a stranger, the companion by your side, the wayfarer (you meet), and those (slaves) whom your right hands possess.﴿ - (Surat an-Nisaa, From Ayat 36)

﴾So, give to the kindred his due, and to al-miskeen (the needy) and to the wayfarer. That is best for those who seek Allaah's Countenance; and it is they who will be successful.﴿ - (Surat ar-Room, Ayat 38)

We are commanded by our Lord to keep the ties of kinship, and to be patient upon this. Keeping the ties of kinship is an obligation upon us, due to what is in that of unifying the family and establishing cooperation and helpfulness between them. Allaah, the Most High, says,

"***And those who join that which Allaah has commanded to be joined (i.e. they are good to their relatives and do not sever the bond of kinship), and fear their Lord, and dread the terrible reckoning (i.e. abstain from all kinds of sins and evil deeds which Allaah has forbidden and perform all kinds of good deeds which Allaah has ordained).***

And those who remain patient, seeking their Lord's Countenance, perform as-salaat (the prayers), and spend out of that which We have bestowed on them, secretly and openly, and repel evil with good, for such there is a good end.

'Adn Paradise (everlasting Gardens), which they shall enter and (also) those who acted righteously from among their fathers, and their wives, and their offspring. And angels shall enter to them from every gate (saying):

﴾Salaamun 'Alaikum (peace be upon you) for you persevered in patience! Excellent indeed is the final home!"﴿ - (Surat ar-Ra'd, Ayats 21-24)

﴾And fear Allaah through Whom you demand (your mutual rights), and (do not cut the relations of) the wombs (kinship).﴿ - (Surat an-Nisaa, From Ayat 1)

﴾Help you one another in al-Birr and at-Taqwa (virtue, righteousness and piety); but do not help one another in sin and transgression.﴿ - (Surat al-Maa'idah, From Ayat 2)

Abu Ayyub al-Ansaari, may Allaah be pleased with him, related that a man said, "Oh Messenger of Allaah, inform me of a deed which will make me the way to enter Paradise. The people said, "What is wrong with him? What is wrong with him?" The Messenger of Allaah, may Allaah's praise and salutations be upon him, said, ***{He has something to ask.}*** Then the Prophet, may Allah's praise and salutations be upon him, said, ***{Worship Allaah and do not associate anything along with Him, establish the prayer, give the charity, and keep the ties of kinship.}*** (al-Bukhaari, 1496, 5982,5983, and Muslim 1/172, and an-Nasaa'ee, 1/234)

Imaam an-Nawawi, may Allaah have mercy upon him, said, "The meaning of having good relations with your family with whom you have blood relations is to do that which is easy according to your situation and their situation, such as spending upon them, giving the Islamic greeting, visiting them, and obeying them, as well as other matters." (an-Nawawi's Explanation of "*Saheeh Muslim*", 1/173)

What does keeping the ties of kinship entail?

Imaam as-Sa'adee, may Allaah have mercy upon him, states concerning this, "Allaah and His Messenger, may Allaah's praise and salutations be upon him, have commanded that the ties of kinship be kept; and this is with the entire family, both those who are close, and those who are distant. He has informed us of the merit of those who keep the ties of kinship. Allaah has given them both long lives and abundance of provisions, and has opened the doors of blessing and great reward with Allaah. As for the ones who sever the ties of kinship, then the situation for them will differ from that. It is upon the people to care for their family in respect to their bodies, visiting them, attending to their needs, assisting them in their affairs, and to do what he is able concerning these things, and to give gifts to those who are wealthy, and charity to those who are poor, as well as showing affection or making himself dear to them as much as possible. And this is easy for whomever Allaah has granted success to and made it easy for him. And the one who strives to connect the ties of kinship to the one who has broken them off from him; for the true connector of the ties of kinship is the one who joins the ties with all of his relatives- whoever maintained the connection with him, and whoever severed them- and this is an example of one who has purity of intention for Allaah alone. And it is certain that the one who is persevering upon that, that Allaah will favor him and give him a great reward." ("*Noor al Basaa'ir wa al-Albaab fee Ahkaam al-Ibaadaat wa al-Mu'aamilaat wa al-Huqooq wa al-Waajibaat*" Page 69-70)

Concerning the reward of long life and abundance of provision, it is related from Abi Hurairah, may Allaah be pleased with him, that the Prophet, may Allaah's praise and salutations be upon him, said, ***{Whoever will be happy that he should abundant provision and long life should keep the ties of kinship.}*** (al- Bukhaari, 5982, Muslim, 1/172, an-Nasaa'ee 1.234)

And as we have been commanded with keeping the ties of kinship, we have also been warned of what will come of severing them, in both the Book of Allaah and the Sunnah of the Messenger of Allaah, may Allaah's praise and salutations be upon him. Allaah, the Most High, says,

﴾And those who break the Covenant of Allaah, after its ratification, and sever that which Allaah has commanded to be joined (i.e. they sever the bond of kinship and are not good to their relatives), and work mischief in the land, on them is the curse (i.e. they will be far away from Allaah's Mercy), and for them is the unhappy (evil) home (i.e. Hell).﴿ – (Surat ar-Ra'd, Ayat 25)

And from the Sunnah:

'Aishah, may Allaah be pleased with her, narrated that the Prophet, may Allaah's praise and salutations be upon him, said, ***{The word "ar-rahm" (womb) derives its root from ar-Rahman. So whoever keeps good relations with it (keeps the ties of kinship) Allaah will keep good relation with him. And whoever severs it, Allaah, too, will sever His relation with him.}*** (al-Bukhaari, 5989)

May Allaah make us of those who keep the ties of kinship, even with those who would sever themselves from us. And Allaah knows best.

Review and Discussion Questions

Questions for Obligations to the Extended Family

Review:

1. What are some of the verses that mention keeping the ties of kinship. (Page 327)
2. What is the recompense of the one who severs the ties of kinship? (Page 328, Bottom Half, and Page 329, Top Half)

Discussion & Consideration:

3. What are some of the things included in the command to keep the ties of kinship? Give some real life examples of these things.
4. Why is the one who keeps the ties of kinship even with those who have sought to sever them from him to be lauded? How does this show purity of intention?

Obligations towards her

Neighbors & Companions

From among her obligations towards her neighbors & companions are:

Treating them Well and Honoring them

Alhamdulillah, Islaam, in its beauty and perfection, has made clear for us the way to have beauty and good in this life and the next life. Allaah has shown us our responsibilities towards all the people in our lives, from the greatest scholar to the poorest beggar, and through fulfilling these responsibilities our character is strengthened, our behavior made pleasing, and our relationships with others rectified and made beneficial.

Allaah has commanded us with many specific matters concerning our neighbors and their rights upon us. Allaah, the Most High, says in His Noble Book,

﴾***Worship Allaah and join none with Him (in worship); and do good to parents, kinsfolk, orphans, al-masaakeen (the needy), the neighbor who is near of kin, the neighbor who is a stranger, the companion by your side, the wayfarer (you meet), and those (slaves) whom your right hands possess.***﴿- (Surat an-Nisaa, From Ayat 36) In a more general verse, He, Glorified and Exalted is He, says,

﴾***Help you one another in al-birr and at-taqwa (virtue, righteousness and piety); but do not help one another in sin and transgression.***﴿- (Surat al-Maa'idah, From Ayat 2)

From the Sunnah, it is related from ibn 'Umar, may Allaah be pleased with them both, that the Messenger of Allaah, may Allaah's praise and salutations be upon him, said, ***{Jibreel kept on recommending me to treat the neighbors kindly and politely so much that I thought he would order me to make them heirs.}*** (al-Bukhaari, 6015, Muslim 16/176, at-Tirmidhi, 1943)

From Abi Shurayh, may Allaah be pleased with him, that the Prophet, may Allaah's praise and salutations be upon him, said, ***{By Allaah, one does not believe, by Allaah, one does not believe, by Allaah, one does not believe.}*** It was said to him, "Who, Oh Messenger of Allaah?!" He replied, ***{The one whose neighbor is not safe from his harm.}*** (al-Bukhaari, 6016)

It is related from 'Abdullah ibn 'Amr, may Allaah be pleased with him, that he said, "The Messenger of Allaah, may Allaah's praise and salutations be upon him, said, ***{The best of the companions with Allaah is the one who is best to his companion, and the best of neighbors with Allaah is the one who is best to his neighbor.}*** (This hadeeth is *hasan*, and has been related by at-Tirmidhi, Vol. 4, no 1944, and it is found in "*as-Saheeh al-Musnad*" of Sheikh Muqbil, may Allaah have mercy upon him)

The Messenger of Allaah, may Allaah's praise and salutations be upon him, said, ***{Whoever believes in Allaah and the Last Day should honor his neighbor.}*** (By meaning, this is found several times in al-Bukhaari (6019), Muslim (No. 47), and other than them)

Imaam as-Sa'adee, may Allaah have mercy upon him, said after quoting this hadeeth, under the section title, "Chapter Concerning the Rights of the Neighbors and Companions": "And know that the friends and companions have rights which are shared with the general Muslims and, in addition to these, rights which are specific to them. And the standard by which the shared rights would be weighed is his saying, may Allaah's praise and salutations be upon him, ***{You will not believe until you love for your brother that which you love for yourself }*** (On Abu Ayub al-Ansaari, narrated by at-Tabaraani 4/124, in his "*Jaami' al-Kabeer*" and also in the "*al-Jaami al-Awat*", 8568 and other than this) The friends are included in this, and you have to help them in their religious as well as worldly matters. For example, fulfilling their needs, or watching over their homes when they leave- and any other matter in which they need you to substitute for them. And you must do as much as you are able to stay connected with them, such as asking others about their welfare. You should have trust in them more than you have in other people. So from what is required in this situation is to give them advice in everything they need it for, be it small or large, in those matters which would not be mentioned to anyone else, as well as in other matters. And there are many matters which you excuse yourself from or which would be difficult for you with other than them but they are not so because of what is between you and them from the reasons such as closeness and connectedness which make that possible.("*Noor al Basaa'ir wa al-Albaab fee Ahkaam al-Ibaadaat wa al-Mu'aamilaat wa al-Huqooq wa al-Waajibaat*" Page 70-72)

This is in respect to one's companions, and the rights of the neighbors are just as great if not greater, mash'Allaah- so one must act in the same way towards them, as can be seen by the Imaam placing both the companions and neighbors under the same heading. This builds ties of love and community between the people, and shows them that you have high regard for them, in obedience to your Lord. And Allaah knows best.

It has been related from Abi Hurairah, may Allaah be pleased with him, that a man came to the Prophet, may Allaah's praise and salutations be upon him, and he (the Prophet, may Allaah's praise and salutations be upon him, sent to his wives (to see about giving the man food). They said, "We do not have anything except for water." So the Messenger of Allaah, may Allaah's praise and salutations be upon him, said (to the people), ***{Who will take care of him?} or, {Who will entertain this man as a guest?}*** A man from the Ansaar said, "I will!" He then went with him to his wife, and said, "Honor the guest of the Messenger of Allaah, may Allaah's praise and salutations be upon him." She replied, "We do not have anything except food for our children." He said, "Prepare your food and turn down the lamp, and put the children to bed if they want supper." She acted as if she were fixing the lamp, and then put it out completely. Then they pretended as if they were eating (while the guest actually ate) and they went to sleep hungry. So when morning came he (the host) went to the Messenger of Allaah, may Allaah's praise and salutations be upon him, and he (the Prophet) said, ***{Allaah laughed last night.}*** or, ***{Allaah marveled at what the two of you did.}*** And so Allah revealed, ***﴾...and give them (emigrants) preference over themselves even though they were in need of that. And whosoever is saved from his own covetousness, such are they who will be the successful.﴿***- (Surat al-Hashr, From Ayat 9) (al-Bukhaari, No. 3798, and Muslim No. 2054)

This hadeeth shows the honor with which the Companions regarded and treated the guest- they and their children went hungry, while they fed their guest will all that they had in the house- and indeed Allaah was aware of what they did, and a verse was revealed concerning it, and Allaah knows best.

Imaam as-Sa'adee, may Allaah have mercy upon him, mentions that one must perform only that which it is within his ability to do. So, if you are only able to offer parenting advice, do so; otherwise, perhaps look after her baby once in awhile. If you are able to command them with the good or warn them away from evil, then do so, or if you are able, you may teach them about the religion. You may ask after their affairs, or supplicate for them, or give them gifts.

Concerning this giving of gifts, it may be something large or small- whatever one is able to do, and the one who receives the gift must be thankful for it in either condition, as is seen in the following hadeeth:

Abu Hurairah, may Allaah be pleased with him, said that the Prophet, may Allaah's praise and salutations be upon him, used to say, ***{Oh Muslim women, a female neighbor should not look down upon the gift of her female neighbor, even if it were the hooves of a sheep.}*** (al-Bukhaari, 6017, Muslim 3/96 of Imaam an-Nawawi's explanation, and others)

Ibn Hajar, may Allaah have mercy upon him, said, concerning this, "Meaning, she should not scorn giving something to her neighbor, even if she gives to her that which is not usually considered to be beneficial. It is probable that this falls under the section that the forbiddance of one thing commands its opposite. This is equivalent to showing mutual love and affection towards one another. It is as if he said that one shows affection to her neighbor by giving a gift, even if it is something humble or disdained- and the rich and the poor are equal in this. And the women were singled out with the prohibition due to the fact that they have strong feelings of love and hate and are quicker to act upon it ." ("*Fath al-Baaree*", 10/445)

It is related from Abu Darr, may Allaah be pleased with him, that he said, "The Messenger of Allaah, may Allaah's praise and salutations be upon him, said, ***{Oh Aba Darr! If you cook broth, then add water to it and share it with your neighbors.}*** (Muslim, No. 2625)

Sheikh al-'Utheimeen, may Allaah have mercy upon him, said, in regards to this hadeeth.

"It is upon the people, if Allaah is liberal to him in his provisions, to share something from it with his neighbor with kindness, until he, may Allaah's praise and salutations be upon him, said, ***{If you cook broth, then add water to it and share it with your neighbors.}*** Increase the water means to add water to it in order to make more of it and to share a portion of it with your neighbors. And the broth is customarily made with meat or from other than it, from that which you eat bread with. And likewise also, of you have some food other than broth, or a drink such as extra milk, for example- and that which is like these – it is proper for you to share with your neighbors from it, because they have rights upon you." ("*Sharh Riyaadh as-Saaliheen*", Vol. 1, Page 688)

One should also give to the near neighbor before the distant one. 'Aishah, may Allaah be pleased with her, had two neighbors, and she asked the Messenger of Allaah, may Allaah's praise and salutations be upon him, which one she should bestow a gift upon. He, may Allaah's praise and salutations be upon him, said, ***{To the one whose door is closest to you.}*** (al-Bukhaari, 6020, Abu Daawud, 5155)

Ibn Hajar, may Allaah have mercy upon him, said in explanation of this hadeeth, "It is said that the wisdom behind this is that the one who is closer knows what enters the house of his neighbor, as a gift or otherwise, so he may desire it, as opposed to the one who is distant. The closer neighbor hastens to answer concerning that which his neighbor obtains as provisions- especially in times of inattention or heedlessness." ("*Fath al-Baaree*", 10/337)

Who are our neighbors?

There is some difference of opinion concerning this. 'Ali, may Allaah be pleased with him, said, "Whoever hears the call (to prayer) is a neighbor." And it is said, "Whoever prays Fajr with you in the *masjid* is a neighbor."

It has been related from 'Aishah, may Allaah be pleased with her, "The limit of those who are considered neighbors is forty houses in every direction." ("*Fath al-Baaree*", 10/445)

What is clear, is that the neighbors are those who live in your area, and that it is not limited to just those people who are right next door to you. And Allaah knows best.

The Warning against Leaving off the Obligations to the Neighbors

It has been narrated from Abi Sharee', may Allaah be pleased with him, that the Prophet, may Allaah's praise and salutations be upon him, said, ***{By Allaah, one is not a believer, by Allah, one is not a believer, by Allaah one is not a believer.}*** It was said to him, "Who, oh Messenger of Allaah?" He answered, ***{The one whose neighbor is not safe from his evil.}*** (al-Bukhaari, 6016, and from another chain of narration in Muslim, 2/17 of the explanation of an-Nawawi)

In this hadeeth, the Messenger of Allaah, may Allaah's praise and salutations be upon him, has joined this matter with the act of disbelief, may Allaah protect us from that! Clearly we must strive to be good to our neighbors, and treat them well.

So, insh'Allaah, we see the great obligations and responsibilities we have towards our neighbors, to treat them well and assist them as we are able, insh'Allaah. May Allaah guide us in this and help us to create strong ties with our neighbors. And Allaah knows best.

Review and Discussion Questions

Questions for obligations towards neighbors and companions

Review:

1. List verses from the Qur'aan as well as some of the ahaadeeth which stress the important place of the neighbor. (Page 333)
2. Who is considered a neighbor? (Bottom Half of Page 336)

Discussion & Consideration:

3. What are some examples of ways that we can assist our neighbors and fulfill our obligations towards them?
4. How can we honor and treat our friends well if we have little money to spend upon them?

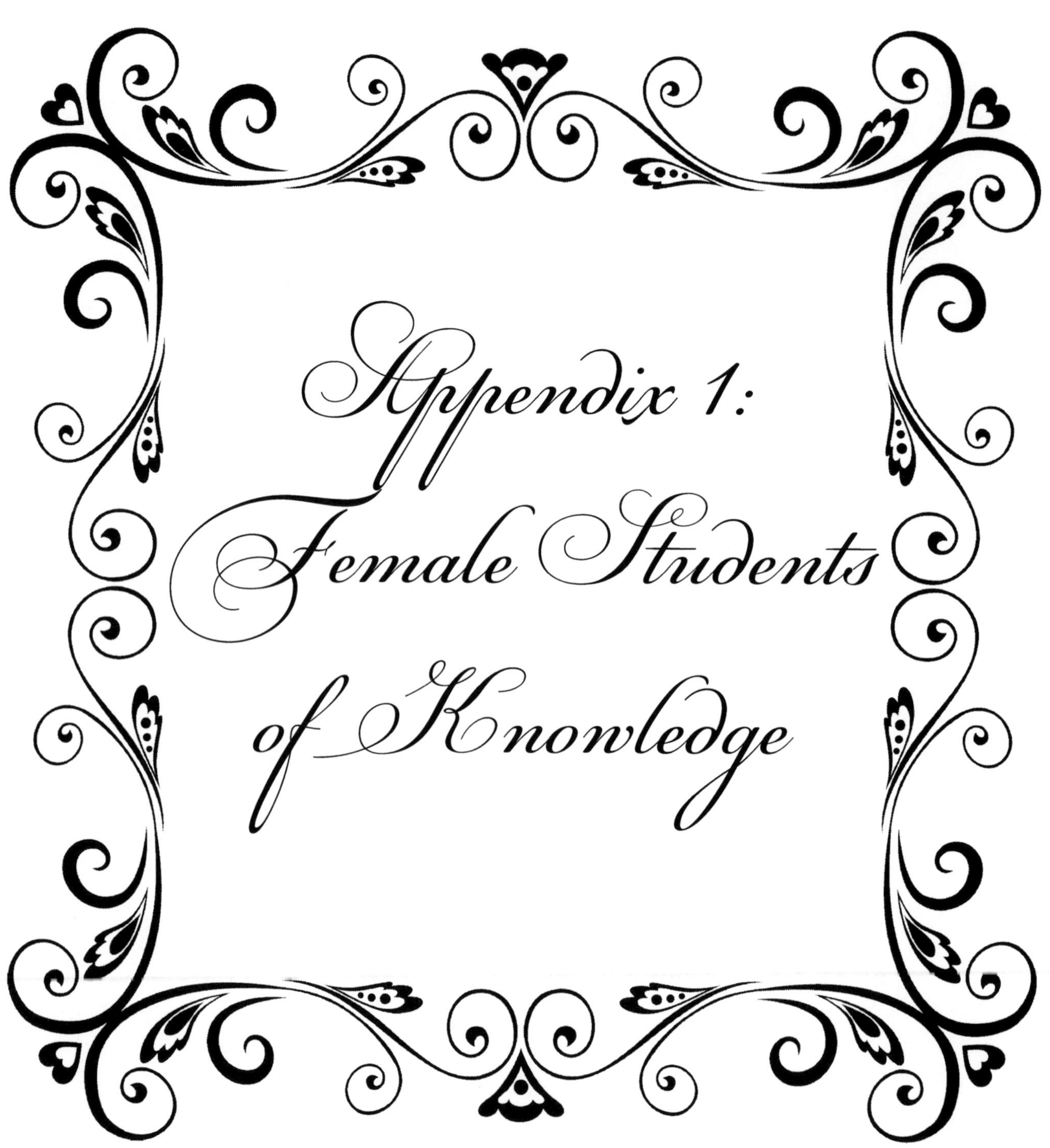

Appendix 1: Female Students of Knowledge

Part 1:

Advice on Seeking Knowledge & Clarification Regarding the Salafi Dawah

Alhamdulillah, and may His praise and salutations be upon His final Prophet and Messenger, Muhammad ibn 'Abdullaah, upon his family, his Companions, and those who follow him in righteousness until the last day. I bear witness that there is no god worthy of being worshipped in truth except Allaah Alone, He has no partners, and I bear witness that Muhammad is the Messenger of Allaah.

To Proceed:

Alhamdulillah, more and more people are coming from Western countries to Yemen all the time, seeking a place in which they can practice their *deen* fully, while learning Arabic and growing in knowledge about our beautiful and complete religion of Islaam. Some of them are able to live almost as they lived in their own countries, especially if they are in Sana'a, while others find themselves in a whole new world which includes no power or an unreliable power source, no running water, and dealing with illnesses that they only read about in books before coming here. No matter the situation, there is no doubt that the possibilities for learning and growing in the religion abound here, and that there are many centers of learning here in which one can, with the correct intention and diligence, obtain a firm foundation and build upon knowledge of the Arabic language as well as Islaam. And the success comes only from Allaah.

The importance of seeking knowledge is well established in Islaam. At the very least, we have to gain the knowledge that will allow us to live our lives as Allaah created us to live them, worshipping Him as He has legislated, staying away from those things that He has forbidden us from. And, as has been made clear by many of the scholars, once we have that knowledge, we must act upon it.

From a hadeeth from Saheeh Muslim, No. 6462:

'Abdullah b. 'Amr b. al-'As reported Allaah's Messenger, may Allaah's praise and salutations be upon him, as saying, ***{Verily, Allaah does not take away knowledge by snatching it from the people but He takes away knowledge by taking away the scholars, so that when He leaves no learned person, people turn to the ignorant as their leaders; then they are asked to deliver religious verdicts and they deliver them without knowledge, they go astray, and lead others astray}***

There is so much ignorance around us today, and so many people calling to it, that it is sometimes confusing to sort through what is correct and what is not. Alhamdulillah, we can turn to the great scholars from the distant past such as Sufyan ath-Thawree, Ibn Qayyim al-Jawzeeyah, Imaam al-Bukhaari, Imaam Muslim, Imaam Ahmad Ibn Hanbal, Imaam ash-Shaaf'ee, Imaam Maalik, Imaam ash-Shawkaanee, and so many others. In the recent past there have been Sheikh Bin Baaz, Sheikh al-Albaani, Sheikh al-Utheimeen, and Sheikh Muqbil, may Allaah have mercy upon all of these men of knowledge and others like them whom I have not mentioned. Today one can go to Saudi Arabia and sit with Sheikh Fauzaan, Sheikh Rabee'a, and literally hundreds of others, and gain knowledge. Here in Yemen, there are many centers of knowledge spread over the entire country. Some are easier to get to and live in than others, but the knowledge is here for those who are willing to work and sacrifice to get it. There are strong centers of learning in Ma'bar, Ibb, Fayoosh, Shihr, and Damaaj among others, which, though harder to reach, are so rich in knowledge from various students of knowledge that it is worth the trials one goes through to get there, and the adjustments one makes to live once they have reached it. Even in the capital city of Sana'a there are classes for men and women, as well as the weekly Friday night talk at *Jaami' al-Khair* at which scholars such as Sheikh 'Ubaid al-Jabiree, may Allaah preserve him, from Saudi Arabia, and Sheikh Muhammad al-Imaam, may Allaah preserve him, here in Yemen, have spoken. The knowledge is here, but it is not going to fall from the trees on top of your head...you have to be prepared to work, and strive, and struggle, and most likely suffer to harvest the rewards of the 'ilm. And these rewards are many, alhamdulillah.

It is important to note here that although there is a lot of confusion in the Muslim world, and has been throughout its history, there has always been a group of people that has continued upon the Straight Path of Islaam, as revealed by Allaah to his last Prophet and Messenger, Muhammad ibn 'Abdullaah, praise and salutations be upon him. The scholars that I have mentioned are only a few of those who have carried the banner of Islaam through the ages so that today we can still follow our religion as it was revealed, in all of its perfection, alhamdulillah. This group has many names, including *Ahl-as-Sunnah wa al-Jamaa'ah*, and *as-Salafiyyeen*, but the important thing is that they adhere to the Qur'aan as well as the Sunnah of Prophet Muhammad, praise and salutations be upon him, according to the understanding of the first three generations of Islaam. These were the people that were nurtured at the hand of Allaah's Messenger, praise and salutations be upon him, and, after him, at the hands of his Companions, and so on down through the generations.

al-Haafidh ibn Katheer mentions in his *tafseer*, or explanation, of the Qur'aan the explanation of the verse regarding the one who leaves the way of the first believers, which is found in Surat an-Nisaa:

﴾***And whoever contradicts and opposes the Messenger after the right path has been shown clearly to him, and follows other than the believers' way, We shall keep him in the path he has chosen, and burn him in Hell what an evil destination!***﴿- (Surah an-Nisaa, ayat 115)

﴾***And whoever contradicts and opposes the Messenger after the right path has been shown clearly to him***.﴿ This refers to whoever intentionally takes a path other than the path of the Law revealed to the Messenger, after the truth has been made clear, apparent and plain to him.

Allaah's statement, ﴾***...and follows other than the believers' way...***﴿ refers to a type of conduct that is closely related to contradicting the Messenger. This contradiction could be in the form of contradicting a text (from the Qur'aan or Sunnah) or contradicting what the *Ummah* of Muhammad has agreed on. The ummah of Muhammad is immune from error when they all agree on something, a miracle that serves to increase their honor, due to the greatness of their Prophet. There are many authentic ahadeeth on this subject.

Allaah warned against the evil of contradicting the Prophet and his *Ummah*, when He said, ﴾***We shall keep him in the path he has chosen, and burn him in Hell --- what an evil destination!***﴿ meaning, when one goes on this wicked path, We will punish him by making the evil path appear good in his heart, and will beautify it for him so that he is tempted further." (End of translation from "*Tafseer Ibn-Katheer*")

The Messenger of Allaah, praise and salutations be upon him and his family, made clear the importance of sticking to his guidance and that of the rightly guided predecessors in the following authentic hadeeth, on the authority of al-Irbaad ibn Saaryah who said: "Allaah's Messenger, may Allaah's praise and His salutations be upon him, gave us an admonition which caused our eyes to shed tears and the hearts to fear, so we said, "Oh Messenger of Allaah, may Allaah's praise and salutations be upon him, this is as if it were a farewell sermon, so with what do you counsel us"?

So he , may Allaah's praise and His salutations be upon him, said, ***{I have left you upon clear guidance, its night is like its day, no one deviates from it except one who is destroyed, and whoever lives for some time from amongst you will see great differing. So stick to what you know from my Sunnah and the Sunnah of the rightly guided caliphs. Cling to that with your molar teeth, and stick to obedience even if it is to an Abyssinian slave since the believer is like the submissive camel; wherever he is led, he follows. }***

(An authentic hadeeth found in "*Sunan Abu Daawud*" 4607, "*Sunan Ibn Maajah*" 43,44, "*Sunan at-Tirmidhi*" 2676, "*al-Musnad*" of Imaam Ahmad vol. 4/126 and other collections)

Ibn Mas'ood, may Allaah be pleased with him, said, "*The Jamaa'ah is what conforms to the truth, even if you are alone.*" (Reported by Ibn 'Asaakir in "*Taareekh Dimashq*" with a saheeh isnaad, as clarified by Sheikh al-Albaani in "*al-Mishkaat*" (1/61))

The scholar Abu Shaamah said, "The order to stick to the *Jamaa'ah* means sticking to the truth and its followers; even if those who stick to the truth are few and those who oppose it are many; since the truth is that which the first Jamaa'ah from the time of the Prophet and his Companions, may Allaah be pleased with them, were upon. No attention is given to the great number of the people of futility coming after them."*al-Baa'ith 'alaa Ahl-Bida'h wal-Huwaadith*", p.l9)

And in another authentic hadeeth: ***{My Ummah will split into seventy three sects, all of them in the Fire except one and it is al-Jamaa'ah.}*** It was said, "Who are they, Oh Messenger of Allaah?" He, praise and salutations be upon him, replied, ***{...That which I and my Companions are upon today.}***

(*Hasan* hadeeth reported by at-Tirmidhi no.2643, al-Laalikaa'ee in "*as-Sunnah*" no.147 and others)

To summarize, I would like to present a statement from Sheikh 'Ubayd al-Jaabiree, from an article, "Questions and Answers Concerning *ad-Da'watus-Salafiyyah*:"

"...*ad-Da'watus-Salafiyyah* is the pure Religion which calls to *tawheed* and sincerity of worship. It is the *da'wah* or the call to belief in Allaah, His angels, His books, His messengers, the Day of Judgment, and belief in *Qadar* (pre-decree). Therefore, *ad-Da'watus-Salafiyyah* is the *da'wah* of all of the prophets, from Nooh, who was the first messenger, all the way to Muhammad (praise and salutations be upon him) who was the last and final prophet and messenger to be sent to mankind. May praise and salutations be upon them all. Therefore, the history of *ad-Da'watus-Salafiyyah* begins with the first prophet. It can even be said that *ad-Da'watus-Salafiyyah* begins with Aadam, salutations be upon him, because it is the pure religion. And *ad-Da'watus-Salafiyyah* is understanding the Qur'aan and the Sunnah as Allaah and His Messenger, praise and salutations be upon him, have commanded us to do so. And it is doing what Allaah and His Messenger have commanded us to do desiring the reward that is with Allaah. And it is staying away from that which Allaah and His Messenger have prohibited fearing the Punishment of Allaah".

And so the way is clear for those who are willing to take heed of the words of Allaah, and those of His Messenger. And we must follow this path upon clear knowledge in order to achieve the ultimate success, which is from Allaah, Alone.

Review and Discussion Questions

Questions for Advice on seeking knowledge and clarification

Review:

1. What is the Jama'ah, and what is the meaning of adhering to it? (Page 342, Top Half)
2. What is the difference between the one who is salafi, or of ahl-as-sunnah wa al-jama'ah, and those who do not follow this methodology? (Page 341, Top Half)
3. What are some of the proofs that we must adhere to the Qur'aan and the Sunnah and the way of the pious predecessors? (Bottom Half of Page 341 to Top Half of Page 342)

Discussion & Consideration:

4. See how many righteous scholars from the past and present you can list. What do you know about them? Make it a point whenever you learn of a new scholar to find out something about him- who he has studied under, what other scholars have said about him, and some of the books he has written.
5. List some ways that you personally can strengthen your attachment to the Qur'aan and Sunnah. How can you, through your words and actions, spread the da'wah to others?
6. Make a list of Sheikh 'Ubayd al-Jaabiree's characteristics of ad-dawatus-salafiyyah.

Part 2:

First Meeting with Umm Salama in Sana'a & Class Schedule in Ma'bar

The following is from the conclusion of my previous translation of a list of the female students of Sheikh Muqbil several years ago. This occurred at Masjid Sharqain in Sana'a, approximately eight years ago, now:

"Alhamdulillah, I was blessed with the opportunity of sitting with Umm Salama for the first time, may Allaah preserve her, who was one of the wives of Sheikh Muqbil, *rahimahu' Allaah*, and who is a teacher and writer who loves the religion and strives diligently to spread knowledge to others. Alhamdulillah, there were many blessings in this, and I would like to share a few of them with you now.

The women's *musalaa* is small at this *masjid*, but mash'Allaah, it was full of sisters who had come to hear Umm Salama speak, not because it was "Umm Salama", but because she is a person with a lot of knowledge, a person who is willing to share her knowledge with others, a person who learned through sitting with one of the major scholars of our time, alhamdulillah. There was none of that sort of "celebrity" factor that seems to creep in so often in the States. And indeed, when she came in, she looked just like the rest of us, no fanfare, no huge entourage, nothing like that. She came in and quietly made her two *rak'aat*, then sat in the chair next to me and my daughter, Sukhailah.

The next thing that made an impression on me was her choice of subject matter. Often we women get caught up with the idea that we want to hear about "women's issues", like marriage, family, dealing with menstruation and child bearing, *hijaab*, etc. The fact of the matter is, all of the vast sea of knowledge that Islaam encompasses deals with women's issues. And the first and foremost of these is *aqeedah*, or beliefs. Umm Salamah spoke about *khawf*, or fear of Allaah, and *rajah*, or hope in Allaah's mercy.

She stressed that though most of us may feel that at times we are alone, and could get away with whatever we like, Allaah is always aware of what we are doing...and what is in our hearts. She also mentioned how the Jews and Christians are both astray in these matters. It reminded me of my class of the evening before, which is an explanation of *"thalaathatu al-usool"*, and made me grateful again for the interconnectedness and wholeness of this beautiful deen, alhamdulillah.

After her brief talk, sisters wrote questions down and sent them up to her. Here is another thing that was made apparent to me...no matter where we are, in what time we are living, we all are dealing with the same issues, mash'Allaah. There were questions about prayer, purification, *aqeedah*, and more. One thing that she addressed more than once was the issue of resembling the disbelievers. She stressed that this is truly dangerous, as it can weaken our *deen* and little by little take us away from Islaam. She also answered a question by a sister who was attending the university here in Sana'a, which is coeducational, with men and women in the same classroom, though in different parts of it. She said that this was *haram*, and brought her proofs, and again stressed the danger of that little by little blackening our hearts with the doubtful things, things that lead to the worse matters. The sister who asked the question was almost in tears, but she said that she was going to find another way to study, insh'Allaah.

After the talk, Sukhailah and I met Umm Salama, and she was very gracious and kind. The first thing she asked was where we are studying, and encouraged us to continue to seek knowledge however we could. She had a minute for everyone who wanted to meet her, and answered more questions from sisters as she was preparing to leave."

The following was added to the above a few months after the previous section was written. Again, this was almost eight years ago, and the program has changed and grown since then, and has continued to benefit the people immensely, alhamdulillah. May Allaah grant them continued success.

"In the months since I translated the first list of female students, I have been blessed to move with my family to Ma'bar, Yemen, the home of the largest *Salafi masjid* in the country. Here we are blessed with the presence of Sheikh Muhammad al-Imaam, who is a former student of Sheikh Muqbil. Alhamdulillah, he has written and published many beneficial works, including *"al-Mu'aamarah al-Kubraa 'ala al-Mar'a al-Muslimah."*

There are many students of knowledge here, and they have a very good program of study for both the men and the women. Since our topic today is women, and this is what I have personal knowledge of, I will share some of what I know on this subject with you, insh'Allaah.

Near the *masjid* is a large complex where the women's classes are held, known as the *musalaa*. There is usually a guard near the entrance to the courtyard, mainly to insure that only women pass through the gate.

Classes are held in the mornings from 8:00 am to 11:00 am, Saturday through Wednesday. As my daughters and I cross the street in the early morning sunshine, we are blessed with the site of sisters coming from all directions, all attired in proper *hijaab*, from the youngest to the oldest, alhamdulillah, all on their way to gain knowledge.

There are classes going on in two or three of the apartments off of the courtyard, but there is one main room where most of the sisters study. This is a large, long area, with white walls and black paint painted in each teaching area to serve as blackboards. To the left of the door is the class for those who do not read or write Arabic. It is made up of children and adult sisters, all mixed up together. You hear them reciting different letters of the alphabet and words containing them, in unison, as the teacher points to what she has written on the board. The students write down what is on the board, and their work is checked. When the teacher points to a student to say the words, and she does well, that student is allowed to stand up in front and lead her sisters for awhile by way of reward.

To the immediate right of that class is the intermediate Arabic reading and writing class. Again, it is a mix of women of all ages, alhamdulillah. They are studying from Sheikh Abu al-Fidaa Ma'mar ibn 'AbdulJaleel al-Qadisee's reading and writing book, "*al-Qaaidah fee al-Qiraa'a wal-Kitaaba*" along with "*Qaaidat al-Baghdaadiyyah*", a classic work in Arabic reading and pronunciation. This is taught similarly to the first class, with the sisters all repeating after the teacher. They also work on some of the surahs in *juz 'umma*, first reading and repeating after the teacher numerous times, and then being called upon to recite one by one.

Next to this class is an area where they begin with a class in hadeeth memorization. The teacher reads the hadeeth out to the sisters, they copy it in their notebooks, and she checks it for accuracy. This is approximately half an hour, and then the Sheikh's sister in law teaches *tajweed* from the book "*al-Mulakhas al-Mufeed fee 'Ilm at-Tajweed*", by Muhammad Ahmad Ma'bad. She writes the rule being taught, as well as many examples of it, on the board, and everyone writes in their books or notebooks as they go along.

After this is the first class taught by the wife of Sheikh Muhammad al-Imaam, Umm 'AbdurRahman, may Allaah preserve her. First is Qur'aan memorization. She reads through a page of the surah we are working on each day, and the sisters all repeat after her, ayat by ayat, with her going over trouble spots as needed, alhamdulillah. Right now we are on Surat ash-Shu'ara'. After that, we study from "*Kitaab at-Tawheed*", by Sheikh Muhammad ibn 'AbdulWahab, may Allaah have mercy upon him. She reads the Qur'aanic ayat and ahadeeth for each point, with the students repeating after her. The *daleel* for each point is memorized and the next day she calls on different students to recite it for her.

Next, she provides an explanation for the point presented that day, and asks questions to make sure the sisters understand it fully. The last portion of the class is hadeeth memorization and explanation, from "'*Umdatu al-Ahkaam*", by al-Imaam, al-Haafidh, 'Abd al-Ghani al-Maqdisee. Again, she reads it, and we repeat after her, and the next day students have to recite the hadeeth for her. Sometimes, if a hadeeth is particularly long or difficult, she will give a gift to those who recite it for her, such as a *mushaf*, alhamdulillah.

While all the above classes are going on, the last section of the room is also busy, with a class first in the grammatical work, "*at-Tuhfah as-Sunniyyah*". The teacher teaches using the book, "*al-Hulul adh-Dhahabiyyah 'ala at-Tuhfah as-Sanniyyah*", authored by a former student of Sheikh Muqbil, Muhammad as-Sagheer ibn Qaa'id al' Ibaadalee al-Maqtaari.

And while the sheikh's wife is teaching the classes mentioned above, another sister teaches another class in hadeeth, organized like the other one. This class finishes at the same time as the Sheikh's wife's class, and then she comes over to this area and all of the women from her other class join in, and for the last hour the sisters study "*Kashf ash-Shubahaat*", again with memorization of the text and a clear explanation to go along with it.

Sometimes there will be a slight change in the schedule, as was the case this last Saturday, when there was a special lecture instead of the last class. Umm 'AbdurRahman began by discussing *tawheed*, its importance and its aspects. After that, six different sisters from the classes stood up and gave individual lectures that they had prepared and memorized. Their ages ranged from around thirteen to around forty, and they each spoke on a different subject, such as the importance of patience, alhamdulillah. This gave them practice in preparing lessons, and in public speaking, and memorization.

Alhamdulillah, I would also like to add that the Sheikh's wife, Umm 'AbdurRahman, is teaching a full schedule, and this with her being eight months pregnant with her eleventh child, alhamdulillah. She is a role model for all of us, balancing study, teaching, and her family successfully. May Allaah grant her and her family success in this life and the Hereafter."

Review and Discussion Questions

Questions for First meeting with Umm Salamah…

Review:

1. Who is Umm Salamah? What are some of the things she has studied and taught? If you have biographical information from elsewhere, add it in. (Top Half of Page 345, and for more information see the listing for her under the female students list.
2. Who is Sheikh Muhammad al-Imaam? Who did he study under? What books do you know of that he has authored? If you have any other information regarding him, write it down as well. (Top half of Page 346)

Discussion & Consideration:

3. What are some of the most important issues for the Muslim woman to study, understand and implement in her life?
4. List some of the subjects that the women were studying in Ma'bar at the time this piece was written. How are these important to the Muslimah? Do you know of any other good books on the subjects mentioned? List them.

Part 3:

Importance of Seeking Knowledge & Reprint from "at-Tabaqat"...

[Note: This section was written while we were living in and studying in Daar al-Hadeeth, Damaaj, in 27 Sha'ban 1428. Again, the program has changed since that time, and the schedules will be different as well.]

Often sisters have written to me, asking me what they need to bring to Damaaj. I used to say, a couple sizes of shoes for the kids, medicines that you are comfortable with, and such as that. Now, I can only advise the people to come with firm resolution in their hearts to benefit as much as they are able from this blessed center. Too often sisters may be easily discouraged…they may complain that they feel that their houses are too small, or the bugs are too big, or the walk is too far, or the people are this way or that way…these are side issues, really. Success comes through the grace of Allaah Alone, and we need to focus on achieving that success in any permissible way that we are able. Be content with what Allaah has given us as far as worldly goods, because these are all going to be of no benefit to us in the next life. What we should be looking for is the richness of knowledge and the blessings of the beneficial sitting, all for the goal of seeking the pleasure of Allaah ta'ala.

One of the most important things to begin with is a clearly defined set of goals. Do you want to learn in order to rectify yourself? Do you want to teach your children to live as Muslims and love this deen? Do you want to give *da'wah* over the internet, or go back to your country and teach? Whatever your goals may be, keep them in mind as you seek knowledge. And be aware that they are not set in stone. Perhaps you will decide as you get further on in your studies that you want to do something different. There is no problem with that, mash'Allaah, but then be prepared to switch your plan of action along with that goal change. Remember, however, that you must have *ikhlaas* in your intention, as Ibn Qayyim and others state that the first condition for a deed to be accepted is *ikhlaas*. Make sure that your intention in all that you do is ultimately to please Allaah, not to be known by the people, or to get a job, or whatever. Again, you have to go out and seek knowledge, it will not just appear in your hands. No matter what your goal is, make sure you understand what you are learning to the fullest, to get the most benefit from it, as you do not know what tomorrow may bring. This is what 'Aishah, the wife of the Prophet, may Allaah be pleased with her, and may Allaah's peace and blessings be upon him and his family, did, as evidenced by the following hadeeth in Saheeh Muslim Volume 1, Number 103:

Narrated Ibn Abu Mulaika: Whenever 'Aishah heard anything which she did not understand, she used to ask again till she understood it completely. 'Aishah said, "Once the Prophet said, ***{Whoever will be called to account (about his deeds on the Day of Resurrection) will surely be punished.}*** I said, "Doesn't Allaah say: ***﴾He surely will receive an easy reckoning.﴿***- (Surah al-Inshiqaq, Ayat 8) The Prophet replied, ***{This means only the presentation of the accounts but whoever will be argued about his account, will certainly be ruined.}***

Alhamdulillah, we see in this hadeeth that 'Aishah, may Allaah be pleased with her, asked for clarification when she did not understand a statement of the Prophet, praise and salutations be upon him and his family. We must do the same when we are unsure of something that we are trying to learn, insh'Allaah, so that our understanding will be complete and benefit us the most.

Another important thing to remember is that Allaah has placed the woman in a unique position in regards to her husband, her family, and her society. She must have her priorities straight. The scholars throughout the ages have addressed this; for more information and insight refer to the rest of this book, as well as the previous book in this series, "*My Hijaab, My Path*".

Clearly, the woman has a distinct role to play in relation to her husband, her home, her family, and in giving *da'wah* inasmuch as she is able. She can do her part to call others to correct knowledge, once she herself has gained that knowledge, even if it is simply teaching her family and friends. The following hadeeth is taken from Saheeh al-Bukhaari, Volume 1, Number 98:

Narrated Abu Hurairah:

I said: "Oh Messenger of Allaah! Who will be the most fortunate person, who will gain your intercession on the Day of Resurrection?" The Messenger of Allaah, may Allaah's praise and salutations be upon him, said: ***{Oh Abu Hurairah! I have thought that none will ask me about it before you as I know your longing for the (learning of) ahadeeth. The most fortunate person who will have my intercession on the Day of Resurrection will be the one who said sincerely from the bottom of his heart "None has the right to be worshipped but Allaah.}***

And 'Umar bin 'Abdul'Aziz wrote to Abu Bakr bin Hazm, "Look for the knowledge of hadeeth and have it written, as I am afraid that religious knowledge will vanish and the religious learned men will pass away. Do not accept anything save the ahaadeeth of the Prophet. Circulate knowledge and teach the ignorant, for knowledge does not vanish except when it is kept secretly (to oneself)."

So we want to be generous with our knowledge, not keep it to ourselves.

Another important point mentioned in the hadeeth, is in 'Umar bin 'Abdul'Aziz's statement, "*...as I am afraid that religious knowledge will vanish and the religious learned men will pass away.*" Mash'Allaah, that is one of the largest blessings one finds in Damaaj, and in Yemen as a whole. Sheikh Muqbil, may Allaah have mercy upon him, has passed away, but his students, and their students, are going strong and working to spread the *da'wah*. In Ma'bar, there is Sheikh Muhammad al-Imaam, Sheikh Muhammad as-Sawmali in Sana'a, Sheikh al-Buraa'ee in 'Ibb, Sheikh 'Abdur Rahmaan al-'Adanee in 'Aden as well as his brother, Sheikh 'Abdullah al-Mur'ee in Shihr, Sheikh Muhammad ibn AbdulWahab al-Wasaabee, may Allaah preserve them all...the list goes on and on, alhamdulillah.

And the women are truly blessed in this area as well, as in Damaaj they can sit in the classes taught by Umm Salama as-Salafiyyah, may Allaah preserve her, who was one of the wives of Sheikh Muqbil, and who is now married to Sheikh Ahmad, the Imaam of the *masjid* in the *Maktabah* in Damaaj, as well as Umm 'Abdullaah al-Wadee'yah, may Allaah preserve her, his daughter. Alhamdulillah, Allaah has blessed them both with knowledge and wisdom, and a clear, precise manner of delivering the knowledge that benefits one in so many ways. They not only give you the knowledge, they tell you how to implement it, as well as the benefits of doing so. Just by observing them it is possible to learn good manners and characteristics of the Muslim woman. And in sitting with the people of knowledge you gain a love and respect for them that only increases with time.. The relationship between the teacher and student is one of the blessings of gaining *'ilm* from the hand of a scholar. And there are so many sisters here in Damaaj besides them who are gifted in teaching, alhamdulillah, whom one can benefit from. Some teach in the *masjid*, some in their homes, but all of them bring great benefit to the student who is willing to put forth the extra effort to truly learn and implement the knowledge that they are imparting.

One last thing I would like to mention is that people are always stressing the patience that is needed to seek knowledge here in Damaaj. Mash'Allaah, this is very, very true, as it can be difficult to seek knowledge anywhere. But the counterpart to that is gratitude. We must be grateful to be given the opportunity of seeking knowledge, here or anywhere, and increase ourselves in asking for forgiveness, in remembering Allaah, and in showing ourselves to be thankful in word and deed. There are hardships, and yes, we must be patient with them, and we must be patient with ourselves as we strive to gain the *'ilm*. But being grateful for all that Allaah has seen fit to bless us with, even in giving us this opportunity to be tested in this way, balances it out. And we know from the authentic hadeeth in Saheeh al-Bukhaari concerning the women being the majority of the people in the hellfire, that this is a problem well known amongst the women- the lack of thankfulness. Remember the Prophet Ayoob, on him be Allaah's praise and blessings, when he reminded his wife of all the good that they had experienced before the hardships. And alhamdulillah, our best examples in this and all matters are among the prophets and righteous people of this *ummah*.

Being grateful includes realizing the knowledge that we are given by making it a tangible presence in our everyday lives, part of the fabric of our existence, and in bringing up the next generation with a firm foundation in Islaam and a love for this deen and its teachings and scholars. Using our time wisely is also vitally important, here or anywhere…there are twenty four hours in a day, and we are going to be held accountable for every single one of them, mash'Allaah. It is easy to visit, and talk, and fall into idle chatter…it is not so easy to prepare for class, then attend the class, and then rewrite your notes and review after the class, and then memorize the text for the next day, then teach the children, then fix supper and beautify ourselves for our husbands…but what is going to give you the most benefit? The truth of the matter will be seen by its fruits, may Allaah make us of those who are successful in this life and in the next, and assist us in rectifying ourselves and our families, and in spreading the true Islaam in word and deed, Ameen

What follows is a republication of the list of the female students that were studying in Damaaj at the time of the publication the book, as mentioned in the text, as well as *fawaaid*, or benefits, concerning the seeking of knowledge, and some of my own experiences. I have tried to correct any mistakes I may have made in the original; I also added a few clarifying points here and there. I am reprinting it in the hopes that it will serve as a reminder to us all, and a benefit to my Muslim sisters who are treading the path of knowledge. I have also added a partial list of classes that were offered in Damaaj at the time of my writing this, as it may benefit some of you to see what your sisters were studying and help you plan your own studies as well. Know that any good in it comes from Allaah Alone, and any mistakes are from myself or the accursed *Shaytaan*.

Umm Mujaahid Khadijah bint Lacina Damaaj, Yemen

27th Sha'ban 1428

All Praise is due to Allaah, we praise Him, seek His help, and ask His forgiveness. We seek refuge in Allaah from the evil of our souls, and the adverse consequences of our deeds. Whoever Allaah guides, there is none that can misguide him, and whoever He Misguides then none can guide him. I bear witness and testify that there is no deity that is worthy of worship except for Allaah; He is Alone, having no partners. I bear witness and testify that Muhammad, praise and salutations be upon him, is His servant, slave and messenger.

﴾***Oh you who believe! Have taqwa of Allaah, as He deserves, and die not except as Muslims.***﴿-(Surat al-Imraan, Ayat 102)

﴾***Oh mankind! Have taqwa of your Lord, Who created you from a single person, and from him, He created his wife, and from these two, He created multitudes of men, and women. And have taqwa of Allaah, through whom you demand your mutual rights, and (do not cut off) the ties of kinship. Verily, Allaah is Ever Watching over you.***﴿-(Surat an-Nisaa, Ayat 1)

﴾***Oh you who believe! Have taqwa of Allaah, and say righteous speech. He will direct you to do righteous deeds and He will forgive your sins. And whoever obeys Allaah and His Messenger has indeed achieved the ultimate success.***﴿- (Surat al-Ahzaab, Ayat 70-71)

As to what follows, then the best speech is the Speech of Allaah, and the best guidance is the guidance of Muhammad (praise and salutations be upon him). And the worst of affairs are newly invented matters, and every innovation is a misguidance, and every misguidance is in the Fire.

To proceed:

Abu Umaamah, may Allaah be pleased with him, said, 'The Messenger of Allaah, praise and salutations be upon him, said:

{The excellence of the scholar over the worshipper is like my excellence over the lowermost of you. Indeed, Allaah 'aza wa jal, His angels, the inhabitants of the heavens and the earth, even the ant in its hole and the fish, supplicate for the one who teaches good to the people.} (at-Tirmidhi, 5/50, who says it is 'hasan *saheeh*'. It has also been declared *saheeh* by Sheikh al-Albaani (may Allaah have mercy upon him) in "*Saheeh at-Tirmidhi*")

Abu ad-Darda, may Allaah be pleased with him, said, 'The Messenger of Allaah, praise and salutations be upon him, said, ***{He who takes a path in search of knowledge Allaah will direct him to tread a path from the paths of Paradise. The angels lower their wings for the student of knowledge in approval of what he does. All in the heavens and the earth and the fish in the depths of the water seek forgiveness for the scholar, and the superiority of the scholar over the worshipper is like the superiority of the full moon at night over the rest of the stars. Verily, the scholars are the inheritors of the prophets. Verily, the prophets did not bequeath dinars or dirhams. All they left behind was the knowledge, so whoever takes it has indeed acquired a great fortune}*** (*al-Musnad* 5/196, Abu Daawud 3/317, at-Tirmidhi 5/49, Ibn Majah 1/81, ad-Darimi 1/98, Ibn Hibban 1/152. Declared saheeh by Sheikh al-Albaani (may Allaah have mercy upon him) in "*Saheeh al-Jaami*")

﴾***And that those who have been given knowledge may know that it (the Qur'an) is the truth from your Lord, and that they may believe therein, and that their hearts may submit to it with humility. And verily, Allaah is the Guide of those who believe, to the straight path.***﴿- (Surah al Hajj, Ayat 54)

﴾***It is only those who have knowledge amongst His slaves who fear Allaah. Verily, Allaah is All Mighty, Oft Forgiving***﴿- (Surah Faatir, Ayat 28)

﴾***But those among them who are well grounded in knowledge and the believers, believe what has been sent down to you and what was sent down before you, and those who establish prayer and give zakat and believe in Allaah and the Last Day, it is to them we shall give a great reward.***﴿- (Surah an-Nisaa, Ayat 162)

What follows is a listing of female students at *Daar al-Hadeeth*, in Damaaj, Yemen. This list is translated from the book "*at-Tabaqaat limaa Hasala ba'd Mawt Sheikhuna al-Imaam al-Wadi'ee fee ad-Dawat as-Salafiyyah bi al-Yemen min al-Mahaalat*" by Abi AbdurRahman Yahya ibn 'Ali al-Hujooree. It is a few years old now, but is the most recent list that was available to me at this time.

From it one can gain much benefit, insh'Allaah. Two of the main benefits are as follows:

First of all, when you look at this list of women, remember that each one of them has all the rights and responsibilities granted to women in Islaam, alhamdulillah. They may have children and husbands, or may be caring for parents, or perhaps are far from their homelands... and yet they have made it a priority in their lives to seek and obtain knowledge. We have to remind ourselves of the importance of knowledge to the Muslimah, as she is so often not only the first teacher of her children, but also a great influence on them throughout their lives, mash'Allaah. Within her family she is influential, as well as within her circle of friends, where she can share her knowledge and assist her Muslim sisters in the pursuit of *al-Jannah*, insh'Allaah. So, looking at this list should be an encouragement for every sister to apply herself to her studies and to make time in her life for this, and then to share her knowledge with her family and friends. It should encourage husbands to help their wives in this process of obtaining knowledge, as well as their daughters, insh'Allaah.

Secondly, look at the works that are studied by these women. By seeing what our sisters in Damaaj are studying, we can see important areas to focus on in our own studies, insh'Allaah. For example, look through the list at how many women are in the process of memorizing Qur'aan, or have already memorized it. Look at the books being taught, and see the importance of establishing a firm foundation of Islamic knowledge in our lives, insh'Allaah. The books that are mentioned here would be of benefit in the library of every Muslim who is sincerely trying to achieve success in this life and the Hereafter.

1. Umm Salama as Salafiyyah: She seeks knowledge and studies with a high amount of determination and eagerness. She memorized Qur'aan and "*Milhat al-'Iraab*" and "*Nudhum al Waraqaat*" and "*al-Bayqooniyyah*" and "*muthalathatu Qatarib*". The Sheikh, may Allaah have mercy upon him mentioned her in his biography saying, "An excellent, ascetic caller to Allaah on firm knowledge, and she has excellent character." I said, yes, and she is a strong teacher. She has taught various books, and from them are "*Mutammamah al-Ajroomiyyah*", and "*al-Baa'ith al-Hatheeth*", and "*al-Waasitiyyah*". And she teaches in "*al-Adab al-Mufrad*" by al-Imaam al-Bukhaari with her verification and commentary work in it and "*Milhaat al' Iraab*". And from what she has written are "*al-Intsaar Lil Mu'minaat*" and the refutation of az-Zandaani, and "*as-Saheeh al-Musnad fee al-Farraj ba'da ash-Shiddah*". She has verified a volume from "*Fath al-Bari*", by Ibn Hajr (may Allaah have mercy upon him). And she has not ceased to be upon the good, and learning from the beneficial knowledge.

2. Umm Shu'ayb Bint Qaaid Ibn Ahmad al-Waad'eeyyah: She seeks knowledge and studies with a high amount of determination and eagerness. She memorized Qur'aan and "*al-Arba'een an-Nawawi*", and "*Milhaat al' Iraab*" and "*Munthuumah al' Amareetee fee al-Usool*". The Sheikh, rahimahuAllaah, mentioned her in his biography, saying, "An excellent woman who fears Allaah, and who has love for the Sunnah and the people of the Sunnah. She has excellent character." I say, yes, and she is a strong teacher. She has taught various books, from them "*at-Tuhfat as-Sunniyyah*", and "*Mutammamah al-Aajroomiyyah*", and "*Sifat as-Salaat an-Nabiyy*" (A Description of the Prophet's Prayer) by ash-Sheikh al-Albaani (May Allaah have mercy upon him), and "*Fath al-Majeed*". She has written books, from among them "*as-Saheeh al-Musnad*" from al-Fadaa'il AhlBait wan-Nubuwwah, and a verification of a volume from "*al-Mahalaa*" by Ibn Hazam, and she is now working on "*as-Saheeh al-Musnad min al-Adab an-Nabawee*", and she is still continuing upon good and taking from the beneficial knowledge.

3. Umm 'Abdullah Bint ash-Sheikh al-'Allamah, Imaam of the *Salafi da'wah* in Yemen, Muqbil Ibn Haadi al-Waad'ee (may Allaah have mercy upon him):She also seeks knowledge and studies with much eagerness and determination; she memorized the Qur'aan, the "*Alfiyyah*" of Ibn Maalik, "*Bulugh al-Maraam*", and other texts (that she has knowledge of). The Sheikh, (May Allaah have mercy upon him) mentioned her in his biography, saying, "a righteous *Sheikha*, she loves the Sunnah and calls to Allaah with clear insight. She is a strong researcher and scholar who hates blind following. She strives to know the evidences and act upon them, and Allaah has made her students benefit by her, and some of them have become

callers to Allaah". I say: "Yes, and she is the head of the women's school in *Dar al-Hadeeth*, and a strong teacher who has taught various books, from them "*as-Sunnah*", by Ibn Abi 'Aasim, and "*Qatr an-Nidaa*", "*Fath al-Majeed*", and "*Sharh Ibn 'Aqeel*". She teaches "*ad-Daraaree al-Mudiyyah*" by Imaam ash-Shawkaanee. She has written many books, from them the treatise "*Naseehatee lianNisaa*" (My Advice to the Women), and "*as-Saheeh al-Musnad min ash-Shamaail al-Muhammadiyyah*", and a short booklet about the life of her father, Muqbil ibn Haadee al-Waadi'ee, and his brilliant and excellent biography. She is working on "*as-Saheeh al-Musnad fee as-Seerah an-Nabawiyyah*" and extensively gathers knowledge and she has not ceased to continue upon good and taking from the beneficial knowledge.

4. Umm 'Ammar al-Maaramiyyah al-'Adiniyyah: An outstanding woman, she memorizes Qur'aan and is a strong caller and teacher.

5. Umm 'Amr al-Waad'eeyya: She memorizes Qur'aan and is diligent in her search for knowledge

6. Asmaa' Bint Muhammad Madhashi: Memorizer of Qur'aan

7. Asmaa' Bint Yahya Ibn Ali al-Hujooriyyah: Student of knowledge. She is memorizing "*al-Usool ath-Thalathah*" and :"*Laamiyah Sheikh al Islaam*" (Ibn Taymiyyah) and "*al-Arba'een an-Nawawi*"

8 .Aasiyyah Bint Hussayn Munaa' al-Waad'eeyyah: Persevering and diligent on the lessons

9 .Aaminah Bint 'Abdul Salaam al-Pakistaaniah

10 .Eemaan Bint Hassan al-Haashidiyyah: Memorizer of Qur'aan

11 .Bilqees at-Ta'iziyyah al-Haashimiyyah: Persevering and diligent on the lessons

12 .Taqwaa Bint Muhammad Sagheer ar-Raazihee: She memorizes Qur'aan

13 .Khadijah Bint 'Ali al' Abbaasee: Persevering and diligent on the lessons

14 .Khadijah Bint 'Ali Muqawid al-Waad'eeyyah: Persevering and diligent on the lessons

15 .Khadijah Bint 'Ali Munaa' al-Waad'eeyyah: Persevering and diligent on the lessons

16 .Khadra'a Bint Muhammad al-Haashimiyyah as-Somaliyyah: Persevering and diligent on the lessons

17 .Dalaal ar-Raazihiyyah: Memorizes Qur'aan and "'*Umdatu*"

18 .Dalaal Bint Hussayn ar-Raazihee: Memorizes Qur'aan

19 .Rabaab Bint Hussayn ar-Raazihee: Memorizes Qur'aan

20 .Rahmah Bint Hameed Umm Saleem as-Sayaaghiyyah: Memorizes "'*Umdatu al-Ahkaam*" and is persevering and diligent on the lessons

21 .Rahmah Bint 'Ali al Abbaasee: Persevering and diligent on the lessons

22 .Rahmah Bint Mahmood as-Somaliyyah al-Breetanniyyah: Persevering and diligent on the lessons

23 .Saarah Bint 'Abdal'Aziz al-Adiniyyah: Memorizes Qur'aan and "'*Umdatu al-Ahkaam*"

24 .Su'aad Bint Muhammad al Haashimiyyah as Somaliyyah al Breetanniyyah: Persevering and diligent on the lessons. She teaches the foreign females students in the language (Arabic) and morphology.

25 .Sumayyah ash-Shamaaniyyah: Memorizes Qur'aan and "'*Umdatu al-Ahkaam*" and is perseverant and diligent on the lessons

26 .Sumayyah Bint Muhsin Sharqain: She is memorizing "al-*Usool ath-Thalathah*" and has the ability to teach handwriting. She is a student of knowledge.

27 .Shareefah al-Waad'eeyyah az-Zanaamiyyah: Persevering and diligent on the lessons

28 .Shaheedah Umm 'Abdullah al-Breetanniyyah al-Muhaajirah: She is a woman steadfast on her time and she works hard getting knowledge. She stays in the *masjid* most of her time, reviewing, and benefiting and teaching the foreign students.

29 .Safiyyah Bint Muhammad Bint 'Abdullah: Memorizes Qur'aan

30' .Aishah Bint 'Abd al 'Aziz Umm 'Abdullah al-'Adiniyyah: Memorizes Qur'aan and "'*Umdatu al-Ahkaam*"

31' .Abeer Bint Sa'eed al-Hamaadiyyah: Memorizes Qur'aan and is perseverant and diligent on the lessons

32 .Faatimah Bint 'Abdullah Umm Ayman as-Saaghiyyah: Memorizes Qur'aan and "*'Umdatu al-Ahkaam*" and has the ability to teach.

33 .Kareemah ar-Raazihiyyah: She has memorized the Qur'aan

34 .Marwaa al-'Adiniyyah al-Haashimiyyah: Persevering and diligent on the lessons

35 .Manaa al-Abeeneeyyah al-Lowadariyyah: Persevering and diligent on the lessons

36 .Manaa Bint 'Abdullah Umm AbdalMaalik as-Sayaaghiyyah: Memorizes Qur'aan and "'*Umdatu al-Ahkaam*", and she is a teacher.

37 .Maimoonah Bint Ahmad al-Wasaabiyyah: Memorizes Qur'aan and "'*Umdatu al-Ahkaam*"

38 .Naseem Bint 'Ali Shaa'ith al-Waad'eeyyah: Persevering and diligent on the lessons

39 .Nadhirah al-Haashimiyyah al-Baydaaniyyah: Persevering and diligent on the lessons

40 .Haajir Bint Yahya al-Haashidiyyah: She teaches

41 .Hind Bint Yahya Ibn 'Ali al-Hujooriyyah: She seeks knowledge and she is memorizing "*al-Bayqooniyyah*" and "*Laamiyah Sheikh al- Islaam*" (Ibn Taymiyyah(

42 .Hayfaa' Bint Ahmad al-Qaysee: She is memorizing Qur'aan and she has the ability to teach

43 .Umm Ibrahim at-Tarmeeyyah: She has memorized the Qur'aan and "'*Umdatu al-Ahkaam*"

44 .Umm Ibrahim as-Somaliyyah: She is a memorizer of the lessons

45 .Umm Ibrahim al-'Adiniyyah: She memorizes the Qur'aan and teaches

46 .Umm Ibrahim al-Waad'eeyyah: She memorizes Qur'aan and teaches and is a lecturer to the women

47 .Umm Ibrahim Khadijah al-Haashidiyyah: An excellent woman, she has understanding. She has memorized the Qur'aan and is perseverant and diligent on the lessons

48 .Umm Ibrahim 'Alaytah Bint al-'Aseemee al-Hudaydiyyah: She teaches, and with her is good.

49 .Umm Idrees Bushra Bint Qaa'id as-Somaawee as-Sana'niyyah: She has the ability to teach

50 .Umm Aadam al-'Adiniyyah: Persevering and diligent on the lessons

51 .Umm Usaamah as-Sana'niyyah: She memorizes Qur'aan and is one who works hard in the search of knowledge

52 .Umm Usaamah al-'Amraaniyyah: She memorizes Qur'aan and teaches

53 .Umm Usaamah al-Mahweetiyyah: She has memorized the Qur'aan

54 .Umm Ishaaq al-Indanoosiyyah

55 .Umm Ishaaq Naa'ilah Bint Rajab Joreedaani: She has memorized the Qur'aan and from "*Riyaadh as-Saaliheen*" and she teaches *tajweed* [the science of reciting the Qur'aan[

56 .Umm Asmaa' Bint 'Ali Jibreel: An outstanding, hard working woman, she has the ability to understand and know

57 .Umm Ismaa'eel al-Wasaabiyyah: Persevering and diligent

58 .Umm Ismaa'eel al-Yaafi'eeyyah: Persevering and diligent on the lessons

59 .Umm Baraa' Bint 'Ali Ibn Sa'ad al-'Abasee: She has memorized half of the Qur'aan and teaches

60 .Umm Baraa' Sa'asiyyah Bint Muhees al-Hujooriyyah: She has memorized nineteen *juz* from the Qur'aan and "*Kitaab at-Tawheed*" by Sheikh Muhammad Ibn 'AbdalWahab an-Najdee

61 .Umm Haarith al-Haydhramiyyah, wife of Sa'eed Habeeshaan: Persevering and diligent on the lessons

62 .Umm Haarith as-Sana'niyyah: A hard working woman

63 .Umm Haarith al-'Adiniyyah, wife of Saadiq al-Baytee: She has the ability to teach

64 .Umm Haarith al-'Adiniyyah: Persevering and diligent on the lessons

65 .Umm al-Hassan al-Haydhramiyyah: Persevering and diligent on the lessons

66 .Umm al-Hassan as-See'awniyyah: Persevering and diligent on the lessons

67 .Umm al-Hassan Bint 'Abdullah Shamsaani as-Salwee: She has the ability to teach

68 .Umm al-Hussayn al-'Aqdiyyah: She memorizes "'*Umdatu al-Ahkaam*" and is persevering and diligent on the lessons

69 .Umm al-Hussayn: Memorizer of "'*Umdatu al-Ahkaam*"

70 .Umm al-Khair al-Yarmeeyiah: Persevering and diligent on the lessons

71 .Umm ad-Dahdah al-Asbihiyyah al-'Atimiyyah: She memorizes the Qur'aan and teaches

72 .Umm Ruwaahah Bint Darwaysh Ibn Ibraaheem Ibn 'Ali al-Ismaa'eel: She memorizes some of the texts. She is a teacher to her sisters.

73 .Umm al-'Abbaas Asma' Bint Mahmoud ad-Daal'yyah: She has memorized the Qur'aan and teaches

74 .Umm al-'Alaa' al-'Amraniyyah: She memorizes the Qur'aan

75 .Umm al-'Alaa' Haleemah Bint Muhees al-Hujooriyyah: She has memorized nineteen *juz'* of the Qur'aan and "*al-Qowlu al-Mufeed*"

76 .Umm al-Fidaa' at-Ta'iziyyah: A beneficial woman

77 .Umm al-Fidaa' 'Aa'ishah Bint Muhees al-Hujooriyyah: She is memorizing the Qur'aan and "'*Umdatu al-Ahkaam*"

78 .Umm Fadl al-Hazamiyyah: She has memorized the Qur'aan

79 .Umm Fadl as-Sayaaghiyyah al-'Adiniyyah: Persevering and diligent on the lessons

80 .Umm Fadl as-Sana'niyyah: She is a beneficial woman and she teaches in the letters

81 .Umm Fadl Bint Hussayn Thaamir

82 .Umm Mundhir Shamiisah Bint 'Eid al-Yemaanee: She has the ability to teach in her city

83 .UmmWaleed al-Abeeneeyyah al-Lowdriyya: She is memorizing the Qur'aan and "'*Umdatu al-Ahkaam*"

84 .Umm Waleed al-Haashimiyyah al-'Adiniyyah: Persevering and diligent on the lessons

85 .Umm Anas al-Abeeneeyyah: She stands firm on the da'wah and she has the capacity to teach

86 .Umm Anas al-Haydhramiyyah: She memorizes Qur'aan and teaches

87 .Umm Anas Bint Taha Ibn Muhammad al-'Adiniyyah: She is memorizing the Qur'aan and "'*Umdatu al Ahkaam*"

88 .Umm Ameen Bint Naasir at-Taam ath-Thamaariyyah: She has memorized the Qur'aan

89 .Umm Ayyoob al-Waad'eeyyah: She memorizes Qur'aan and "*Milhatul 'Iraab*"

90 .Umm Haazim al-Hazamiyyah: She has memorized the Qur'aan and "*Riyaadh as-Saaliheen*" and other than them

91 .Umm Haazim al-Hazamiyyah: She has memorized the Qur'aan

92 .Umm Huthayfah al-'Adiniyyah: Persevering and diligent on the lessons

93 .Umm Huthayfah Bint al-Farjaanee al-Leebiyyah: For six years she has sought knowledge in *Daar al Hadeeth* and she is an excellent woman who has understanding and knowledge

94 .Umm Hafs ad-Daysiyyah: She has the ability to teach

95 .Umm Hafs: She has memorized "'*Umdatu al Ahkaam*"

96 .Umm Hamzah al-Haashidiyyah: Persevering and diligent on the lessons

97 .Umm Hamzah Bint Hussayn al-Hudaydiyyah: Persevering and diligent on the lessons

98 .Umm Hamzah Bint Muhammad Ibn Hamood al-Wasaabiyyah: She memorizes Qur'aan

99 .Umm Khaalid ar-Raaziyyah: She is memorizing the Qur'aan and "'*Umdatu al-Ahkaam*"

100 .Umm Khaalid Bint Yahyaa al-'Amraaniyyah: Persevering and diligent on the lessons

101 .Umm Khawlah ash-Shaamiyyah: Memorizer of the Qur'aan

102 .Umm Khawlah al-'Adiniyyah: Persevering and diligent on the lessons

103 .Umm Khawlah: She has the ability to teach

104 .Umm Daawud at-Tarmeeyyah: A memorizer of Qur'aan and she teaches

105 .Umm Ruqayyah: A caller in her city

106 .Umm Zakreeyah ash-Shabaswiyyah: Persevering and diligent on the lessons

107 .Umm Saalim al-Baydhaaniyyah: She has memorized nineteen *juz* of Qur'aan

108 .Umm Saalim al-Waad'eeyyah: Memorizer of Qur'aan, and she has the ability to teach

109 .Umm Sa'aad Rahmah as-Somaliyyah: Memorizer of Qur'aan

110 .Umm Sufiyaan at-Ta'iziyyah: Memorizer of Qur'aan and she benefits and she teaches

111 .Umm Salmaan al-Indunoosiyyah: Persevering and diligent on the lessons

112 .Umm Salmaan Hunaan as-Sayfaaniyyah: Memorizer of Qur'aan and she has the ability to teach

113 .Umm Salama Bint Abi 'Aadil Ibn Ahmad ar-Rumeeyyah: Memorized twenty three *juz* of Qur'aan

114 .Umm Sulaim al-'Amraaniyyah: Memorizer of Qur'aan and "*Milhatul 'Iraab*"

115 .Umm Sulaim Faa'izah Bint Qaa'id al-Waad'eeyyah: Memorizer of Qur'aan and with her is the ability to teach

116 .Umm Sulaymaan arRumeeyyah: Persevering and diligent on the lessons and she has good

117 .Umm Sulaymaan Faatimah Bint Qaa'id al-'Amraaniyyah: She has the ability to teach

118 .Umm Sulaymaan Manaal Bint Mahmood al-Wasaabiyyah: Persevering and diligent on the lessons

119 .Umm Sulaymaan Nuwaal Bint Muhammad ash-Shawkaaniyyah: An excellent woman, she has understanding and knowledge

120 .Umm Sumayyah al-Yarmiyyah: Persevering and diligent on the lessons

121 .Umm Seereen: She is qualified to teach

122 .Umm Saabir Bint al-Haamid: An excellent woman, benefiting and teaching

123 .Umm Taariq Bint 'Ali Ibn 'Ayroos al-Haashimiyyah al-laahjiyyah

124 .Umm 'Aadil as-Sana'niyyah: A righteous woman, fearing Allaah, loving the Sunnah, and calling the women to it.

125 .Umm 'Aasim at-Tareesiyyah: Persevering and diligent on the lessons

126 .Umm 'AbdurRahman al-Baydhaaniyyah as-Sultaaniyyah: Persevering and diligent on the lessons

127 .Umm 'AbdurRahman al-Baydhaaniyyah: Persevering and diligent on the lessons, and a teacher

128 .Umm 'AbdurRahman al-Hujooriyyah: a righteous woman

129 .Umm 'AbdurRahman al-Hudaa'iyyah: Persevering and diligent on the lessons

130 .Umm 'AbdurRahman al-Hadhramiyyah at-Tarmeeyyah: Persevering and diligent on the lessons

131 .Umm 'AbdurRahman al-Hadhramiyyah al-Qas'ariyyah: Persevering and diligent on the lessons

132 .Umm 'AbdurRahman as-Salafiyyah at-Ta'iziyyah: Memorizer of Qur'aan

133 .Umm 'AbdurRahman as-Soodaaniyyah: She benefits

134 .Umm 'AbdurRahman as-Say'ooniyyah al-Qarniyyah: Memorizer of Qur'aan

135 .Umm 'AbdurRahman al-'Aqaadiyyah: She has memorized twenty *juz* and with her is the ability to teach

136 .Umm 'AbdurRahman al-Haashamiyyah al-Baydhaaniyyah: She has memorized "*al-Arba'een an-Nawawi*" and she is able to give lectures to the women

137 .Umm 'AbdurRahman Bint Mathnaa al-Jawb'aee adh-Dhaal-I'iyyah: She teaches

138 .Umm 'AbdurRahman Bint Musa al-Maawee: Memorizer of Qur'aan

139 .Umm 'AbdurRahman Bint Naasir Ibn Kuroo al-'Adiniyyah: She has memorized twenty *juz* of Qur'aan

140 .Umm 'AbdurRahman Sabaah al-Abiyyah: She has memorized the Qur'aan and she teaches

141 .Umm 'AbdurRahman Safaa' Bint Qaa'id al-'Amraaniyyah: She has the ability to teach

142 .Umm 'Abdullah al-Amreekiyyah: Persevering and diligent on the lessons

143 .Umm 'Abdullah al-Indunnoosiyyah: An excellent woman, she is diligent and beneficial

144 .Umm 'Abdullah al-Ba'daaniyyah Bint 'Abdullah Ibn 'Ali al-Khayaat: She teaches her sisters in grammar, science of hadeeth and *tawheed* and she is a lecturer close to finishing the Qur'aan

145 .Umm 'Abdullah al-Haamiyyah: Memorizer of Qur'aan

146 .Umm 'Abdullah al-Hadhramiyyah as-Say'ooniyyah: Memorizer of Qur'aan and "'*Umdatu al-Ahkaam*"

147 .Umm 'Abdullah al-Hamaadiyyah al-'Adiniyyah: Memorizer of Qur'aan and persevering and diligent on her lessons

148 .Umm 'Abdullah as-Say'ooniyyah Bint 'Abdullah Baahshwaani: Memorizer of Qur'aan and "*'Umdatu al-Ahkaam*"

149 .Umm 'Abdullah al-'Adiniyyah: Persevering and diligent on the lessons

150 .Umm 'Abdullah al-'Adiniyyah: She is hard working, and she has memorized the Qur'aan and "'*Umdatu al-Ahkaam*"

151 .Umm 'Abdullah al-Qarniyyah: Persevering and diligent on the lessons

152 .Umm 'Abdullah an-Nakh'iyyah: Persevering and diligent on the lessons

153 .Umm 'Abdullah AmatuRahman Bint Qaa'id Sh'alaan al' Adiniyyah: Memorizer of Qur'aan, and she teaches

154 .Umm 'Abdullah Bint SaalIm al-Wasaabee: Memorizer of Qur'aan

155 .Umm 'Abdullah Bint 'Abdullah Ibn Ahmad as-Salwiyyah: Memorizer of Qur'aan

156 .Umm 'Abdullah Bint Yahyaa al-Haymee: She has memorized the Qur'aan

157 .Umm 'Abdul Muhaymin al-Haashidiyyah: She is memorizing the Qur'aan and "*Riyaadh as-Saaliheen*"

158 .Umm 'Abdul Muhaymin Hanaan al-Abayniyyah al-Lowdriyyah: Persevering and diligent on the lessons

159 .Umm 'Uthmaan Bint 'Ali as-Sawdee: Diligent on the search for knowledge

160 .Umm 'Ammaar Say'ooniyyah: She has memorized the Qur'aan and "'*Umdatu al-Ahkaam*"

161 .Umm 'Umaarah al-'Aqaadiyyah: She has memorized the Qur'aan and "'*Umdatu al-Ahkaam*"

162 .Umm Faatimah ad-Daysiyyah: Persevering and diligent on the lessons

163 .Umm Maalik al-'Adiniyyah: She memorizes Qur'aan and teaches

164 .Umm Maalik al-'Adiniyyah: She is a teacher

165 .Umm Maalik al-Haashimiyyah al-'Adiniyyah: Persevering and diligent on the lessons

166 .Umm Maalik Hafeedhah Bint Ahmad as-Sayaaghiyah: She memorizes Qur'aan

167 .Umm Maalik Naadiyyah Bint Muhammad al-Qaysiyyah: She has memorized the Qur'aan

168 .Umm Muhammad al-Hawtiyyah: She teaches

169 .Umm Muhammad al-Qasee'riyyah: She has memorized "'*Umdatu al-Ahkaam*"

170 .Umm Mus'ab ash-Sahriyyah: She has memorized the Qur'aan and the "'*Amdah*"

171 .Umm Mus'ab al-Adiniyyah: She memorizes Qur'aan and teaches

172 .Umm Mus'ab Mariyam al-'Adiniyyah: An excellent woman, she loves the Sunnah, and beneficial knowledge and she is a caller to Allaah with insight. May Allaah establish us and her on the Truth

173 .Umm Mu'aadh al-Ghayliyyah: She has memorized the Qur'aan

174 .Umm Mu'aadh al-Yaafi'yyah: Persevering and diligent on the lessons

175 .Umm Musa Bint 'Amr al-Hushabiyyah: She has understanding and memorizes. She memorizes Qur'aan and "*Mandhumah al-'Amreetee*"

176 .Umm Haaroon al-Baydhaaniyyah: She memorizes Qur'aan and "'*Umdatu al-Ahkaam*" and she is persevering and diligent on the lessons.

177 .Umm Haaroon Bint 'Abdul'Aziz: She has memorized the Qur'aan

178 .Umm Hamaam al-Hadhramiyyah: Persevering and diligent on the lessons

179 .Umm Hamaam al-Yarmiyyah: Persevering and diligent on the lessons

180 .Um Yaasir al-Hudaydiyyah: She teaches

181 .Umm Yahyaa al-Yaafi'yyah: Persevering and diligent on the lessons

182 .Umm Ya'qoob al-Baakistaaniyyah: Persevering and diligent on the lessons

182 .Umm Yoosuf adh-Dhaall'yyah: Persevering and diligent on the lessons

(End of the list of female students that were studying at the center here in Damaaj at the time the aforementioned book was compiled).

Review and Discussion Questions

Questions from Importance of seeking knowledge and reprint...

Review:

1. What is the proof that we must ask questions if we do not understand something that we read or are taught regarding the religion? (Page 351, Middle of page)
2. What did 'Umar ibn 'Abdul 'Aziz, may Allaah have mercy upon him, write concerning knowledge, urging the people to spread the knowledge they have? (Page 352, Top of Page)
3. Write down two ahaadeeth and two verses concerning knowledge and its people. (Page 354)
4. What are two benefits that can be gained by looking at this list of female students? (Bottom of Page 354, Top of Page 355)

Discussion & Consideration:

5. Why is it important that we be content with that which Allaah has decreed for us in this life, and grateful for any situation in which He has chosen to put us?
6. Write down some of your goals regarding knowledge, as well as your personal goals. List three steps toward realizing each goals that you can begin implement today, insh'Allaah.
7. We are blessed in this age to be able to learn from tapes, books, and articles and classes on the internet, and we should take advantage of these things. However, the ideal thing is for us to sit and gain knowledge from the people of knowledge. What are some of the benefits of sitting with a person of knowledge?
8. List some of the subjects and books that were being studied by the women in Damaaj at the time of this listing. What do they have in common with those that were being taught in Ma'bar? What does this tell us concerning the subjects we should be striving to gain knowledge in?

Part 4:

Partial Schedule of Classes in the Women's Musalaa in the Markaz in Damaaj, Summer 1428/2007

The times are approximate, and there are many more classes than these, mostly small circles and classes in the houses of knowledgeable sisters. There are also many classes held in the women's *musalaa* in the area of Damaaj known as the *Mezra'*. This is just to give a general idea of scheduling and the classes being taught. Also keep in mind that these classes are taught in the traditional manner, with the students, and very often the teachers, sitting on the floor, notebooks and pens on their laps. There are no classes as we are familiar with in the west, with desks and chairs for the students. Sometimes for the larger classes, however, the teachers may sit in a chair so the students can hear them better, and may have a table or desk in front of them to place their books and notes for teaching the class.

7:30 am: Several circles for memorization and recitation of Qur'aan taught by various sisters who have been approved for teaching by Umm Salama, may Allaah preserve her.

8:00-9:00 :Several circles divided between various levels of women and children for learning reading and writing. On Thursdays, some of the circles teach basic math, as well. Again, the teachers have all been approved for teaching their subject and level.

9:15-10:00 :Umm Salama as-Salafiyah teaches from "*Bulugh al-Maram*". Umm Salama, may Allaah preserve her, answers written questions from the sisters, and also addresses issues that are needed, such as correct behavior, bringing up the children, and keeping the *masjid* clean. When teaching the class, she brings benefits and points from many sources, and presents them in a clear, understandable way that can benefit almost everyone, on any level, alhamdulillah.

10:00-10:30 :Umm Salama teaches a smaller advanced grammar class based on the "*Alfiyah*" of Ibn Maalik

10:00-10:30 :Various circles for review and recitation of Qur'aan

Between 10:30 and 12:00 various classes that change as each one ends or a new class is announced. Some of the ones taught this summer included:

Tajweed- based on the book "*Fin at-Tajweed*"

Ilm al-Hadeeth- the one I attended was based on the book "*al-Bayquniyyah*"

Aqeedah- from the book "*al-Usool ath-Thalaathah*"

10:30" *Umdat al-Ahkaam*" This is a larger class. It was begun when Umm Salama took a break to have her first baby, and Umm Hafs, the teacher, said that it would take a year or so to complete. During this break there was also an excellent class offered in "*Usool al-Emaan*" by Sheikh Muhammad ibn Abdul Wahaab, may Allaah have mercy upon him.

After *Salaat adh-Dhuhr*: The main class for the men. It is broadcast into the women's *masjid*, as well as on the outside speakers, so that women in their homes can listen and benefit as well. It alternates according to the day of the week between "*Tafseer Ibn Katheer*" and "*al-Jaami' as-Saheeh*" compiled by our Sheikh Muqbil, may Allaah have mercy upon him. This is every day except for the day of *al-Jumu'ah*.

After *Salaat al-Asr*: The general class in "*Saheeh al-Bukhaari*". The women are encouraged to participate in all of these classes. At times questions are even sent to the women, or answers that they have sent up read aloud.

Various classes begin after the general *Asr* class, and go until *Salaat al-Maghrib*. This summer they taught "*at-Tuhfat as-Suniyyah*", a classic explanation of "*al-Ajroomiyyah*", which is itself a classical work on grammar; AbdulHakeem al-Amreekee's "*Mubada Mufeed*", a book directed at teaching non-Arab speakers Arabic; "*at-Tuhfat al-Waasabiyyah*" which is an explanation of "*al-Ajroomiyyah*" written by a teacher in Damaaj that was created to be more basic than the explanation mentioned above; "*al-Qawlu al-Mufeed*", a basic *aqeedah* book by Sheikh Muhammad ibn 'Abdul Wahaab al-Wasaabee, may Allaah preserve him; "*al-Baa'ith*", which is a more advanced hadeeth sciences course; and a class in the Prophet's prayer, may Allaah's praise and blessings be upon him.

After *Salaat al-Maghrib* there is longer class that goes until they pray *Salaat al-'Isha*. There are sometimes questions and answers from all over Yemen and the world, sometimes poetry, sometimes a lecture. "*Saheeh Muslim*" is always taught, as well as other works that vary as one is finished or a new one is added. That summer "*Sunan as-Sughra*" by Imaam al-Bayhaaqi, and "*Iqtida as-Sirat al-Mustaqim*" by Sheikh al-Islaam Ibn Taymiyyah, and others were among the books taught.

Umm 'Abdullah al-Waadiyyah, may Allaah preserve her, teaches a class every Saturday after the Sheikh's class after *Salaat al-Asr*, explaining the book, "*al-Muntaqa*". She goes beyond "*Nayl al-Awtar*", gathering benefits and points from many other scholars of our time and those preceding us. She also often answers questions written down for her by sisters in the class, or gives a lecture.

On Fridays, after the general class after *Salaat al-Asr*, they broadcast a class on "*Riyaadh as-Saaliheen*" from the brother's *masjid* into the sister's *masjid*. Many sisters attend this, as well as one on Thursdays on the character and behavior of the student of knowledge.

As I said, this is just a partial list of the offerings that summer at the center. All names of books and Arabic words and names are transliterations- for an exact pronunciation of the title, one must look to the Arabic itself. May Allaah continue to benefit the sisters in Damaaj and outside of it through the efforts of Umm Salama, Umm 'Abdullah, , and all of the other knowledgeable people who give their time and effort to spread the knowledge of this beautiful way of life, based upon the sources and correct understanding. Ameen. And Allaah knows best.

Review and Discussion Questions

Questions for Partial schedule of classes in Damaaj

Discussion & Consideration:

1. Look at this listing, taking note of the subjects being taught and the methods by which they are taught. How can you help to facilitate learning circles such as this in your own community?
2. Do you know which essential books of belief and the fundamental sources texts of Islaam have been translated into the language of the people of your land?
3. Do you know who are callers from the people of the Sunnah who teach within your land?

Part 5:

Across the Country: Learning and Living in Shihr

Fall 1430/2009

Alhamdulillah, we were blessed with the opportunity to move to Shihr, Yemen, which is a medium sized coastal town located about an hour or so from the city of al-Mukullah. Shihr is the location of another Dar al-Hadeeth, the center at which Sheikh 'Abdullah Mar'ee, may Allaah preserve him, teaches and benefits the community, alhamdulillah. The Sheikh, may Allaah preserve him, has studied with Sheikh Muqbil and Sheikh al-'Utheimeen, among many others, and has a strong tie to the people of knowledge.

We first came in the heat of summer, mash'Allaah, during the time when the school at the center is closed for a few months. There were, however, still classes at the masjid for the women after 'Asr. Soon after arriving, I found out I was pregnant with our eight baby, alhamdulillah, and due to this, I was not able to study at the *markaz* as much as I would have liked. However I was able to take two classes, and Allaah is the Best of Planners, and He made my heart content to do that which I was able to do. I also teach *'aqeedah* and Arabic classes in my home, alhamdulillah, and continued to study at the *markaz* as often as possible as suitable for someone responsible for maintaining a large family .

Alhamdulillah, the Sheikh and other teachers also give classes after the prayers, which are broadcast over the loudspeakers as well as over the *markaz* radio station. This is a real blessing for the sisters, as we can stay at home and benefit from the knowledge and the classes- and the best place for the women is in their houses. Often scholars and speakers from Saudi as well as Yemen come and give lectures and classes, and these are also broadcast over the radio. Again, the blessing of this is immense, as we can fulfill our household obligations and be in out of the heat, while simultaneously benefitting from the classes the teachers in the general *masjid* offer, alhamdulillah.

Our responsibility of seeking knowledge is immense, as is our responsibility towards our children, alhamdulillah. Due to this second responsibility, I would like to take a minute to mention my experiences having the baby here, insh'Allaah.

This is the third baby we have had in Yemen. Due to complications, I knew I would have to give birth in the hospital in al-Mukullah; however, there are midwives as well as a hospital and clinics here in Shihr. My doctor in al-Mukullah was very good, alhamdulillah. She was very knowledgeable and helped us throughout the pregnancy. When the time came to have the baby, there was also a midwife present, who was very supportive and helpful as well. I had some complications, and they responded to this very quickly and efficiently. Alhamdulillah, the character of the people working in the hospital was very nice, very helpful and good mannered.

After I had the baby, several sisters here in Shihr took turns cooking supper for us, which was a great blessing for us, as it made the first week easier for us, alhamdulillah, may Allaah reward them for their thoughtfulness and assistance. We were also given some baby items, as we had very little when we started out, mash'Allaah. These small things made such a difference, and showed again the importance of community and supporting the Muslims as much as we are able.

Insh'Allaah, I would like to take a few minutes to give you an example of what a day is like in our house, as perhaps it will help some of you who are struggling to find a balance between all the facets of Islamic womanhood some ideas for time management.

We all get up at the Fajr prayer. After Fajr it is time for recitation of the Qur'aan, both review and memorization. The children are also told to spend half an hour reading the English translation of the verses they are learning, so that they fully understand that which they are reciting, insh'Allaah. After Qur'aan, they put away their sleeping mats and straighten up their rooms while Juwairiyah, our twelve year old, makes breakfast. During this time the baby often naps, and I take the opportunity to exercise for forty-five minutes to an hour.

After breakfast Sukhailah does the dishes and the children, after doing various chores, bring in their books for homeschooling. I try to divide the subjects they study evenly between days, so that they are not overwhelmed but are not idle, either. On Saturdays they do English grammar, mathematics, science, *tafseer* (Qur'aanic explanation), Arabic grammar, reading and writing, *'aqeedah*, and *adab* (Islamic behavior). Some classes are Arabic, others English. The children are all at different levels, so I go through and plan out what they have to study each day. Some subjects, such as English grammar, history and social studies, they can read themselves and answer comprehension questions. Other subjects, such as *tafseer* and Arabic language studies, I explain to them more fully. I like to plan activities and learning experiences for them, but depending on all that is going on outside of schooling, sometimes we rely most on books and questions in several different formats. I urge everyone to speak Arabic as much as possible within the house, as this helps the smaller children become more natural in their speech and heightens their understanding. This is all done with the baby in arms, or playing on the floor on a blanket.

While the children are doing their schoolwork, I often work on translating and editing for whatever projects I am currently working on. This usually lasts for three hours or so in the morning, taking into consideration numerous "baby breaks" when the little one needs attention and care. When I am teaching classes at home, the girls watch the baby while I am teaching, so that the class will not be too disrupted. We then eat lunch and have a naptime after Dhuhr, wherein everyone is supposed to rest. Of course, with small children this is not always what happens, but mash'Allaah.

After 'Asr prayer this year I am teaching an *'aqeedah* class as well as an Arabic class three days a week. Each class is about an hour long, and starts promptly each day. During the afternoons I also like to work on sewing or crocheting projects that I have begun. Currently I am making a quilt and outfits for the girls, as well as some little gifts for the children. When I work on these sorts of projects I often listen to Islamic lectures and classes on the radio. When I am taking a class at the *masjid* or teaching, I time these activities to occur before and after the class, and usually spend extra time in the mornings and after Dhuhr reviewing and memorizing for class. Sometimes I edit, write, or translate right before dinner, if possible.

After supper the children clean up the house for the day, then we sit together and read out loud a chapter from a book. This is a nice time for the children to wind down, and to spend time together as a family. The baby does not always cooperate, so whoever is not reading, is often walking around or playing with her, and trying to listen at the same time. The children go to bed early, alhamdulillah, so that they can get up in the mornings for Fajr and Qur'aan, insh'Allaah.

In the evenings I like to write in my journal, review notes and texts for classes, and read Arabic books in order to improve my language skills and expand my vocabulary. My husband and I spend at least an hour together every evening as well, taking time out to nurture and be thankful for the blessing of marriage, alhamdulillah. I schedule any other evening activities around this time, insh'Allaah. Bedtime comes early for me as well, alhamdulillah, as long as the baby agrees!

I check my email once or twice a week, right after Fajr. I also take time to do research online for any projects that I am working on. Once in awhile I check the news, but I find that more often than not it is a waste of time. I find that it is crucial to limit internet time, as even just answering email sometimes takes much longer than it may be worth- one could be doing something much more beneficial, and it is one of the traps of Shaytaan that we do that which is permissible instead of that which is actually recommended or rewarded.

Insh'Allaah, I hope that by sharing our day with you, I have given you some ideas for how you can begin to structure your days to give the time necessary to your studies, your home, and your family, as we are all trying to follow the blessed example of the Sunnah and the first believers. Everyone's situations are different, mash'Allaah, and some days you will have to just accept that you are not going to get everything done. But by prioritizing what needs to be done, and planning ahead, insh'Allaah Allaah will reward you with the contentment of knowing that you have spent your time wisely, doing all that you could to please Him.

Epilogue

I would like to end with some words from Sheikh Muqbil, rahimahu'Allaah from his introduction to "*as-Saheeh al-Musnad min Fadaail ahl-Bayt an-Nabi*" by Umm Shuayb al-Wadi'eeya.

"To Proceed:

Allaah *subhanahu wa ta'ala* says:

﴿Let there arise out of you a group of people inviting to all that is good (Islaam), enjoining al-Maruf (Islamic monotheism and all that Islaam orders one to do) and forbidding al-Munkar (polytheism and disbelief and all that Islaam has forbidden). And it is they who are the successful.﴾- (Surah al-Imran, Ayat 104) And *Allaah subhanahu wa ta'ala* says:

﴿The believers, men and women, are Auliya' (helpers, supporters, friends, protectors) of one another; they enjoin (on the people) al-Ma'ruf (Islamic monotheism and all that Islam orders one to do) and forbid (people) from al-Munkar (polytheism and disbelief of all kinds, and all that Islaam has forbidden); they perform As-Salat (Iqaamatas-Salat), and give the Zakat, and obey Allaah and His Messenger, Allaah will have Mercy on them. Surely, Allaah is All Mighty, All Wise.﴾- (Surah at-Tawbah, Ayat 71) And Allaah *subhanahu wa ta'ala* says:

﴿There is no good in most of their secret talks save (in) him who orders Sadaqah (charity in Allaah's cause), or Ma'ruf (Islamic monotheism and all the good and righteous deeds which Allaah has ordained), or conciliation between mankind; and he who does this, seeking the good pleasure of Allaah, We shall give him a great reward.﴾-(Surat an-Nisaa, Ayat 114)

These verses include both the men and the women, as when Allaah *ta'ala* says,

﴾And perform as-Salat (Iqaamatas-Salat), and give Zakat, and obey the Messenger (Muhammad, praise and salutations be upon him) that you may receive mercy (from Allaah)﴿ - (Surah an-Nur, Ayat 56)

He includes the men and the women.

And Allaah *subhanahu wa ta'ala* gave success to a good group of women who have striven for the beneficial knowledge, and the practice of it, and who call to Allaah. And from them are the teachers, and from them are the authors, and from them are the callers to Allaah on clear, correct knowledge.

And Allaah benefits us with them, and with them is the best example in 'Aishah and Umm Salama and Hafsa, and the rest of the Prophet's women, and a large group of the female sahabah and from the tabaa'ieen (those who followed them), such as Hafsah Bint Sireen, 'Amarah Bint AbdurRahman and Umm Darda as-Saghra, and they have spread by their examples, may Allah be pleased with them, much good. And truly the women they are the twin halves of the men, except in situations which are made clear through evidence".

Review and Discussion Questions

Questions for Across the Country

Review:

1. Who are some of the women Sheikh Muqbil, may Allaah have mercy upon him, mentions whom we should take as example in our own lives, to help each other and others? What are some ways in which we can assist our Muslim sisters in the community? (Bottom of Page 371, Top of Page 372)

Discussion & Consideration:

2. The Muslim woman must benefit and seek knowledge as much as she is able, in any situation. How can a sister who stays at home benefit herself, and benefit others, from her home?

Appendix 2:

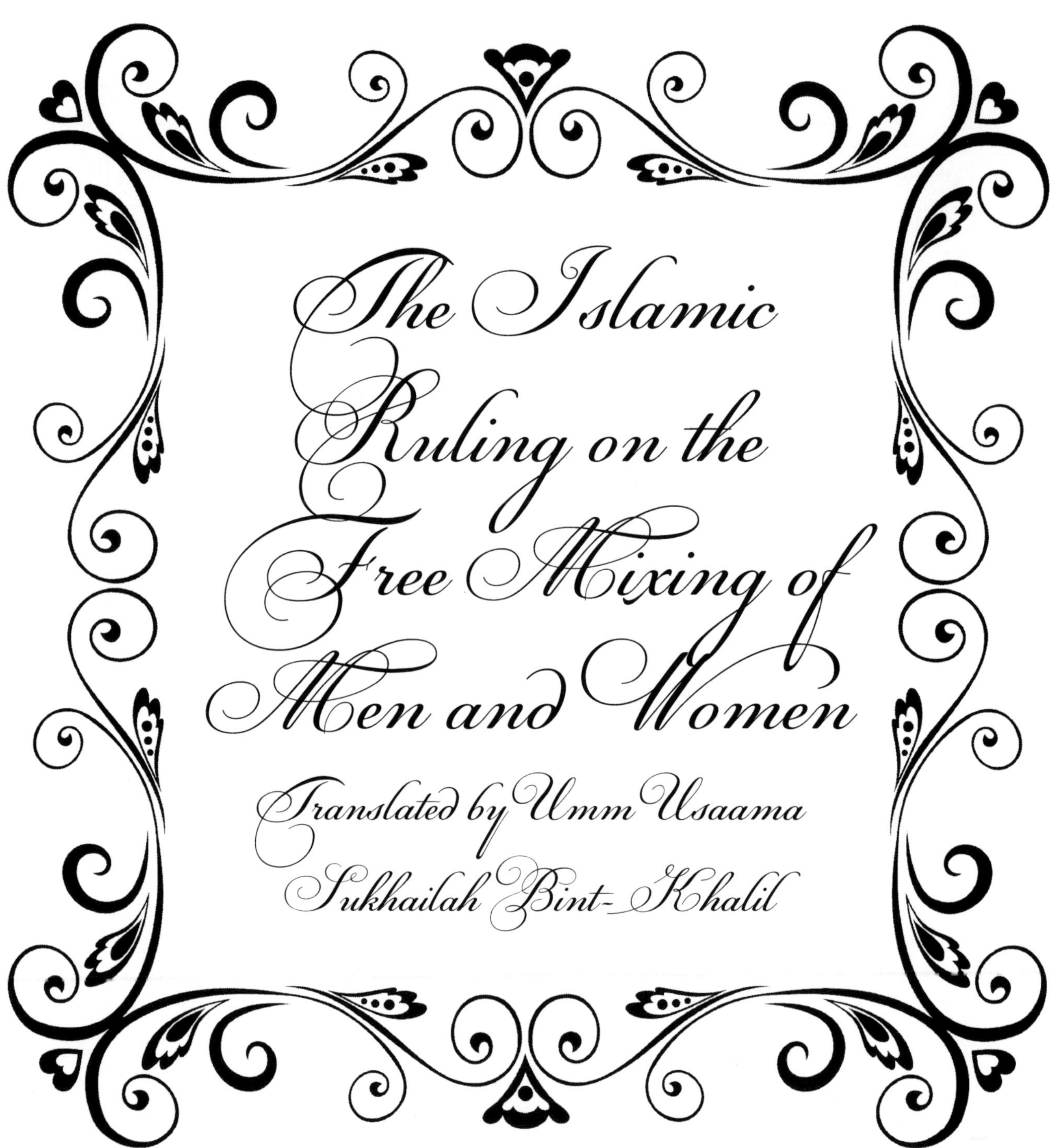

The Islamic Ruling on the Free Mixing of Men and Women

Translated by Umm Usaama Sukhailah Bint-Khalil

Question: What does Islaam say about the free mixing of men and women?

Answer from the Permanent Committee of Scholars in Saudi Arabia: The free mixing of men and women is from the most dangerous matters, and a ruling has already been issued concerning this by the Eminent *Mufti*, Sheikh Muhammad Ibn Ibrahim, may Allaah have mercy on him, and here is its text:

The free mixing of men and women is of three types:

First: The women mixing with those who are *mahram* for her, (Male relatives whom they are unable to marry), and there is no doubt that this is permissible.

Second: The women mixing with men for the purpose of evil, and there is no doubt that this is forbidden.

Third: The women mixing with men in the learning centers, shops, offices, hospitals, parties, and the like. In reality, one might first think that this does not lead to the corruption of the parties by each other, and so to expose the reality of the matter we will reply to it in two ways, one general and one specific.

As for the general, than that is that Allaah created the men with strength and an inclination towards women, and created women with an inclination towards men, as well as gentleness and weakness. Accordingly, if mixing occurs, then results come of it which lead to evil intent among the people, as the body is inclined towards evil and following its desires, and it is blinded and deafened, and the Shaytaan commands evil and wrongdoing.

As for the specific, than the Islamic legislation is built upon goals and the ways of reaching them, and the manner of reaching a goal has the same ruling as the goal itself. So as women are objects which fulfill the desires of men, then the Islamic legislation has closed the doors which lead to an attachment between individuals from the two sexes. This will be made clear by the proofs from the Book and the Sunnah which we will bring to you:

As for the proofs from the Book, then they are six

First: Allaah The Most High says, ﴾***And she, in whose house he was, sought to seduce him (to do an evil act), and she closed the doors and said: Come on, Oh you." He said: "I seek refuge in Allaah (or Allaah forbid)! Truly, he (your husband) is my master! He made my living in a great comfort! (So I will never betray him). Verily, the dhaalimun (wrong and evildoers) will never be successful.***﴿- (Surat Yusuf, Ayat 23)

The proof in this is that when mixing occurred between the wife of al-Aziz and Yusuf, may Allaah's salutations be upon him, that which was hidden in her revealed itself, and she requested him to commit adultery with her. However, Allaah had mercy on him, and made him innocent of this, as He The Most High says, ﴾***So his Lord answered his invocation and turned away from him their plot. Verily, He is the All-Hearer, the All-Knower.***﴿ Thus, if free mixing occurs between the men and the women, everyone from both sexes chooses whoever he desires from the other sex, and goes to great lengths to fulfill their desires.

Second and Third: Allaah has commanded the men and women to lower their gaze, as He says, ﴾***Tell the believing men to lower their gaze (from looking at forbidden things), and protect their private parts (from illegal sexual acts). That is purer for them. Verily, Allaah is All-Acquainted with what they do. And tell the believing women to lower their gaze (from looking at forbidden things),***﴿-(Surat an-Noor, Ayats 30-31)

The proof in these two verses is that he ordered the believing men and women to lower their gaze, and His command brings obligation. Then He The Most High makes it clear that this is more righteous and pure; and He did not exempt the streets from this ruling, except for an accidental glance. al-Haakim narrated, in *al-Mustadrak*, On the authority of 'Ali, May Allaah be pleased with him, that the Prophet, May Allaah's Praise and salutations be upon him, said to him ***{Oh 'Ali, Do not follow one glance with another, for indeed the first one is for you, but not the second one.}*** al-Haakim said after he mentioned it "It is authentic according to the conditions of Muslim, but they did not narrate it" And adh-Dhahabee agreed with him in meaning, and there are many ahadeeth which carry the same meaning.

Allaah did not command the lowering of the gaze except because looking at one who is not *mahram* (a relative who is forbidden for marriage) is fornication, as Abu Hurairah narrated that the Prophet, may Allaah's praise and salutations be upon him, said ***{The fornication of the eyes is by looking, the fornication of the ears is by listening, the fornication of the tongue is by speaking, the fornication of the hands is by reaching, and the fornication of the leg is by walking.}*** Agreed upon, and the wording is in Muslim.

And this is fornication only because it is taking pleasure from looking at the beauty of the woman, and it leads to her entering into the heart of the one who is looking, so that he goes toward committing evil acts with her. And, if the legislation forbids looking at her because of the evil which that leads to, then that is also true of the free mixing, and that is also forbidden because it leads to that which has unpraiseworthy effects, from taking pleasure in looking and going on to that which is eviler than that.

Fourth: Allaah The Most High says, ***﴾And let them not stamp their feet so as to reveal what they hide of their adornment.﴿***-(Surat an-Noor, Ayat 31)

The proof in this is that Allaah forbade the women to stamp their feet, even though it is permissible in itself, so that it does not lead to the men hearing the sound of the anklets, which might cause their desire towards the women to be aroused. Like this, free mixing is forbidden, because of what it leads to from evil.

Fifth: The saying of The Most High, ***﴾Allaah knows the fraud of the eyes, and all that the breasts conceal.﴿***- (Surat Ghaafir, Ayat 19) Ibn Abaas, may Allaah be pleased with him, and other than him, explained this to mean: It is the man who enters into the house of a people, and there is a beautiful woman among them, or she passes by him, and if her people are not watching he looks at her, then when they watch him he lowers his gaze, they ignore him so he looks, then they watch him so he lowers, while indeed Allaah knows that which is in his heart, and that he would like to violate her privacy, and that if he was able, he would commit fornication with her.

The proof in this is that Allaah the Most High describes the eye that steals glances towards women whom it is not permissible for him to look at as fraudulent, so how about mixing then?!

Sixth: He commanded the women to stay in their homes, as He says, ***﴾And stay in your houses, and do not display yourselves like that of the times of ignorance﴿***- (Surat al-Ahzaab, Ayat33)

The proof in this is that Allaah the Most High commanded the pure, purified, and good wives of the Messenger of Allaah, may Allaah's praise and salutations be upon him, to stay in their homes. This speech is general, including other than them from the Muslim women, as the knowledge of principles says: Every directed speech is general, except that which is proven by the texts to be specific. There is no proof that proves that this is specific, so if the women are ordered to stay in their homes except in times of necessity, then how can it be said that the free mixing of men and women is permissible?! In these times of ours, it has become rampant for the women to overstep the boundaries, remove the covering of shyness, go out beautified among strange men, and remove their clothing in front of them, and those who are responsible for them, from husbands and other than them, do not do anything.

As for the proofs from the Sunnah, then we will suffice with mentioning ten of them:

First: Imaam Ahmad narrated in his *Musnad* with a chain of narration on Umm Hameed, the wife of Abu Hameed as-Saa'idee, that she went to the Prophet, may praise and salutations, and said, "Oh Messenger of Allaah, indeed I love the prayer with you," He said ***{I know that you love the prayer with me, and your prayer in your inner room is better than your prayer in your outer room, and your prayer in your outer room is better than your prayer in your house, and your prayer in your house is better than your prayer in the masjid of your people, and you prayer in the masjid of your people is better than your prayer in my masjid.}*** So she ordered a place of prayer to be built in the darkest and most inner part of her house, and she, by Allaah, used to pray in it until she died.

And Ibn Khuzaymah narrated in his Saheeh, on Abdullah Ibn Mas'ood, that the Prophet may Allaah's praise and salutations be upon him, said, ***{Indeed the woman's prayer which is most beloved to Allaah is in the darkest place of her house.}*** And there are many ahaadeeth with the same meaning, which prove that the prayer of a woman in her house is better than her prayer in the *masjid.*

The proof in this is that if it is legislated for her to pray in her house, and this is better than even the prayer in the *masjid* of the Messenger, may Allaah's praise and salutations be upon him, and with him, then to forbid free mixing is even more necessary.

Second: That which was narrated by Muslim and at-Tirmidhi, and other than them, on the authority of Abi Hurairah, may Allaah be pleased with him, that the Messenger of Allaah, may Allaah's praise and salutations be upon him, said, ***{The best rows for the men are the first rows, and the worst rows are the last rows, and the best rows for the women are the last rows, and the worst rows are the first rows.}*** At-Tirmidhi said after he mentioned it, "A *saheeh* hadeeth."

The proof is that the Messenger of Allaah, may Allaah's praise and salutations be upon him, legislated for the women that if they come to the *masjid*, then they should be separated from the male worshippers, and he described the first of their rows as bad, and the last as good. That is only because of the distance of the women in the back row from the men, and from mixing with them and seeing them, and from their hearts becoming attached to the men by seeing their movements and hearing their speech, and he dispraised the first rows because of the occurrence of the opposite. Likewise, he described the last of the rows of the men as bad if there are women present in the masjid, because these men miss drawing close and nearness to the *Imaam*, and because of the nearness to the women who will occupy the brain, and perhaps ruin the act of worship, and mix up the intentions and the concentration in the prayer. So if the legislation expects this to happen in places of worship, even though there is no mixing, only nearness, then how about if mixing occurred?

Third: Muslim narrated in his *"Saheeh"*, on the authority of Zainab, the wife of Abdul-laah Ibn Mas'ood, she said: the Messenger of Allaah, may Allaah's praise and salutations be upon him, said to us, ***{If one of you attends the masjid then she should not touch perfume.}*** "

And Abu Daawud narrated in his "*Sunan*", and Imaam Ahmad and Ash-Shaafi'ee in their *Musnads*, along with the *isnaad* (chain of narration) on Abi Hurairah, that the Messenger of Allaah, may Allaah's praise and salutations be upon him, said, ***{Do not forbid the female slaves of Allaah the masjid, but they should go out while they are tafilaat ,unscented.}***

Ibn Daqeeq al-Eid said, "This contains the forbiddance of scent for the one who wants to go to the *masjid*, because of what that entails from awakening the desires and inclinations of the men, and could also awaken the desire of the woman as well... And perfume is included in with those things such as beautiful clothing and jewelry which has an apparent effect, as well as a distinguished appearance." al-Haafidh Ibn Al-Hajar said, "And also the free mixing between men and women." al-Khataabi says in "*Maalim as-Suna*", "*at-tafil*: a smell which is not fragrant, and it is said: A woman is *tafilah*, if she is unscented, and the women are *tafilaat*."

Fourth: Usaamah Ibn Zayd related on the Prophet, may Allaah's praise and salutations be upon him, said, ***{I have not left behind any trial which is harder upon the men than women. }*** Collected by Bukhaari and Muslim

The proof in this is that the women were described as a trial for the men, so why would the ones who are a trial be brought together with those whom they try?!? This is impermissible.

Fifth: On Abi Sa'eed Al-Khudri, may Allaah be pleased with him, on the Messenger of Allaah, may Allaah's praise and salutations be upon him, that he said, ***{Indeed the life of this world is sweet and green, and Allaah has placed you into it to see what you will do, so beware of this world, and beware of women, for indeed the first trial of Bani Israa'eel was with women.}*** (collected by Muslim)

The proof in this is that the Prophet, may Allaah's praise and salutations be upon him, ordered us to beware of women, and this order consists of obligation, so how can we be obeying this if the men and women mix? It is impossible, so free mixing is impermissible.

Sixth: Narrated by Abu Daawud in his "*Sunan*", and al-Bukhaari in "*Al-Kunaa*", with their chains of narration, on the authority of Hamzah Ibn Abi Usayd, on his father, that he heard the messenger of Allaah, may Allaah's praise and salutations be upon him, saying to the women, as he went out of the *masjid* and saw the men and women mixing in the path, ***{Stay back, for indeed it is not for you women to have the right of the path, stay to the sides of the path.}*** And the women would stay close to the walls, until her clothes would catch on the wall because of her closeness to it. This wording is from Abu Daawud.

Ibn Atheer said in "*Ghareeb Al-Hadeeth*", "Have the right of the path means to have the right to the middle of the path."

The proof in this is that the Messenger of Allaah, may Allaah's praise and salutations be upon him, forbade them from mixing together in the path, because that leads to trials, so how can it be said that it is permissible in other situations?!

Seventh: Narrated Abu Daawud at-Tayaalisi in his *Sunan*, as well as other than him, on the authority of Naafi', on Umar, may Allaah be pleased with him, that when the Messenger of Allaah, may Allaah's praise and salutations be upon him, built the *masjid*, he made a door for the women, and he said, ***{No one from the men should enter through this door. }***

And al-Bukhaari narrated in "*At-Taareekh Al-Kabeer*", on the authority of Ibn Umar, on Umar, may Allaah be pleased with them both, on the Messenger of Allaah, may Allaah's praise and salutations be upon him, that he said, ***{Do not enter the masjid from the women's door.}***

The proof in this is that the Messenger of Allaah, may Allaah;s praise and salutations be upon him, forbade the men and women to mix in the doors of the *masjid*, entering or leaving, and he prevented them from sharing the same doors in the *masjid*, as a precaution against mixing. So if he prevented mixing under these circumstances, then in circumstances other than that it is more important to prevent this.

Eighth: Narrated al-Bukhaari in his *Saheeh*, on the authority of Umm Salamah, may Allaah be pleased with her, she said, ***{When the Messenger of Allaah, may Allaah's praise and salutations be upon him, made the final salutations in his prayer, the women would stand when he finished, and he would sit in his place for a while." And in another narration," he would make the final salutation, and the women would leave and enter their houses, before the Messenger of Allaah would stand up.} And in a third narration: {If the women finished the prescribed prayer, then they would stand up, and the Messenger of Allaah, may Allaah's praise and salutations be upon him, would sit still, along with the men who had prayed, for as long as Allaah willed, then when the Messenger of Allaah stood, the men would also stand.}***

The proof in this is that the Messenger of Allaah prevented the mixing by this action, and this clarifies the impermissibility of mixing in other than this situation as well.

Ninth: At-Tabarani narrated in "*al-Mu'jam Al-Kabeer*", on the authority of Ma'qal Ibn Yasaar, that the Messenger of Allaah, may Allaah's praise and salutations be upon him, said, ***{For one of you to be stabbed in the head with an iron needle is better for him than that he should touch a woman who is impermissible for him.}***

al-Haythami said in "*Majma' az-Zawaa'id*", "The narrators are from those in the *Saheeh*." And al-Mundhiri said in "*at-Targheeb wa at-Tarheeb*", "It's narrators are trustworthy."

Tenth: Also narrated by at-Tabarani from the hadeeth of Abu Umaamah, that the Prophet, may Allaah's praise and salutations be upon him, said, ***{For a man to crowd against a pig covered in mud and slime is better for him than for his shoulder to crowd against the shoulder of a woman who is impermissible for him.}***

The proof in these two hadeeth is that he, may Allaah's praise and salutations be upon him, forbade a man from touching a woman, whether there is a covering between them or not, if he is not her *mahram*. This is because of what this entails of evil effects, and the free mixing of men and women is forbidden for the same reason.

So it will become clear to whoever considers the proofs which we have brought, that:
The saying that free mixing will not lead to trials, is only the result of some people's imagination, for in reality, it leads to trials, and because of this the Islamic legislation forbids it to prevent evil. However, that which is necessary and extremely important does not enter into this, for example in places of worship such as the *Haram* in Makkah and Madinah.

We ask Allaah the Most High to guide those from the Muslims who are misguided, and to grant those who are guided more guidance, and that he guides their rulers to good deed, and the leaving off of evil deeds, and that they take hold of the hands of those who are foolish, as indeed he is All hearing, and Near, and the Answerer of supplication.

Review and Discussion Questions

Questions for The Islamic Ruling on the Free Mixing

Review:

1. Who is the scholar quoted by the Permanent Committee to answer this question concerning free mixing? (Top half of Page 375)
2. What are the three categories of mixing between the men and the women? (Page 375, Top Half)
3. List three proofs from the Qur'aan that free mixing between the sexes is prohibited. Briefly explain each proof you bring in your own words. (Pages 375- Page 377)
4. List five of the proofs concerning the forbiddance of free mixing from the Sunnah. Briefly explain each one in your own words. (Pages 377-379)

Discussion & Consideration:

5. List some modern day situations in which there is free mixing that could be avoided or their evil of them lessened?

Appendix 3:

The Family & Principles of Familial Conduct

From "al-Asaalah" magazine by:

Dr. Marwaan al-Qaisee

Part One

The family is the foundational stone of society, and it is made up of individuals who maintain a constant relationship between them, which are likely the most important human relationships. Because of this, it is necessary for principles of behavior which govern and organize these relationships, so that they will fulfill the best of their wishes, and bear fruit. To fulfill this, the family life should be colored with harmony, agreement and safety. And the family's relationship is partly a relationship between husband and wife, and partly a relationship between parents and children, and the third part is the relationship between the children themselves.

The conduct of the husband:

1. It is not shameful- rather it is from good behavior- that the husband should share in taking care of his private affairs, such as caring for his clothes.
2. It is not proper for the man to stay aloof from serving himself, because the wife carries out numerous household duties; so it is from good manners that the husband lend a helping hand to his wife in the house, when it is necessary, such as when she is ill or has given birth or the like.
3. The perfect husband is one who cooperates with his wife with good treatment and manners, fulfilling all the meaning in those two words. Indeed, the best of husbands towards their wives are the best of people in the sight of Islaam. And this good treatment must be a significant characteristic of married life, even in divorce.
4. It is necessary to beware of infusing the relationship between husband and wife with excessive seriousness, as if the family life is characterized by seriousness like army life, then this is one of the reasons for failure, and is a bad sign.
5. It is from gentleness and good manners on the part of the husband that he accede to his wife's requests if they are not forbidden by the Islamic legislation, knowing that excessiveness in food and drink is one of the foremost forbidden things in Islaam.
6. It is recommended that the husband set aside a time for amusement and entertainment with his wife.
7. The relationship between the husband and wife should have a specific color, and that cannot be except if both of the spouses work to destroy the barriers between them. For example, a man should not dislike drinking from a glass which his wife has drunk from.
8. There are no perfect people; so the husband might see in his wife some things which do not appeal to his nature and ways. If these things do not go against the Islamic legislation or obedience to the husband and his rights, then he should not try to change her personality to complement his nature. He must always remember that each of the two spouses has a personality which differs from the personality of the other. He must also keep in mind that even if his wife has some characteristics which he dislikes, then there must also be other characteristics which he likes.
9. Ramadhaan should not prevent him from showing affection to his wife, by kissing her or the like, but only if he is sure of himself, for these are not forbidden in Ramadhaan.
10. Do not count the mistakes of your wife, for excessive blame and scolding ruins the relationship between you and is destructive to married life. So, ignore the

small mistakes and errors of your wife.

11. If you are able to clothe and feed your wife well, then do not refuse, and be generous in providing for her as much as you can.

12. Don't be afraid to set a specific punishment for any acts which go against the Islamic legislation which your wife commits within the house or outside of it. And this is an important reason for you to become angry but do not do it for just any reason.

13. Matters should not run to excessive leniency- so whenever you see that you might be too lenient in a matter, then weigh this with some kind of seriousness and gravity, but without excessive harshness and toughness.

14. The woman is the mistress and supervisor of the house, so do not try to enter into matters that are not within your sphere of activity such as the food or the organizing of the house.

15. Beware of finding fault with your wife in an area in which she is mistaken in front of others, even if they are your children- as that is a matter which goes against good manners and civility and leads to a hardening of hearts.

16. If you are compelled to punish your wife, then that should be by abandoning her, and that should only be in the house. Avoid cursing her, beating her or describing her as ugly. Those are things which a successful husband does not do.

17. Jealousy concerning your wife is a praiseworthy matter, and shows your love for her, but with the condition that you are not excessively jealous. If this occurs, then it changes into a blameworthy matter.

18. When entering the house, do not surprise your family at night; and enter upon them when they are expecting you. Give them *salaams* (the Islamic greeting) and ask about them and their condition. Do not forget to remember Allaah, Glorified and Exalted, when you enter the house.

19. Do not spread your secrets, as that is a matter which is warned about and prohibited.

20. Guard the cleanliness of your mouth and its pleasant scent, always.

21. Do not abuse the fact that Allaah has given you authority over your wife, so that you harm her or oppress her.

22. Respect and good treatment of your wife's family is respect and good treatment or her as well, even after her death. This is with the condition that that is not accompanied by anything which the Islamic legislation warns against, such as the mixing of men and women, or the men and women being alone together.

23. Excessive joking leads to a lowering of one's dignity and respect, so do not joke excessively with your wife.

24. Remember that fulfilling the conditions that you promised your wife in the marriage contract is a matter of extreme importance- so do not ignore that after you are married.

25. If you address your wife, or talk with her or scold her, then choose the best and most gentle of words and speech, and do not scold her in front of others or her children.

26. It is not for you to ask your wife to work outside the home or to provide for you

from her money.

27. Do not give your wife duties that she is not able to fulfill, and take into consideration the way she was raised; for the way in which a Bedouin would do a thing is different from the way in which a city dweller would do the same thing. And the way a strong woman can do something is not the same as a weak woman would do it.

28. In the obligation for the woman to serve her husband there is no contradiction in the husband sharing in this as well if he has free time. And indeed that is from the good treatment between the husband and wife.

(Vol. 2, 15 Jumaada al-Akhira 1413, Pages 67-70)

Part Two

The family is the foundational stone of society, and it is made up of individuals who maintain a constant relationship between them, which are likely the most important human relationships. Because of this, it is necessary for principles of behavior which govern and organize these relationships, so that they will fulfill the best of their wishes, and bear fruit. To fulfill this, the family life should be colored with harmony, agreement and safety. And the family's relationship is partly a relationship between husband and wife, and partly a relationship between parents and children, and the third part is the relationship between the children themselves.

We have already mentioned this in the last issue of the magazine, concerning the conduct of the husband. Today we will speak about:

The conduct of the wife:

1. It is impossible for the marital relationship to be successful if the wife does not perform her role, no matter how perfect and admirable the husband is. So pay attention, Oh Righteous Wife, to this matter, and shoulder your responsibilities; for upon you rests the success of the family or its failure.

2. If you wish to fast the voluntary fasts, then do not do so before you ask the permission of your husband; and if he does not permit you, then it is not your right to fast.

3. If your husband does not wish that one of his relatives, or your relatives, or the neighbors, or other than them to enter the house, then do not permit that person to enter.

4. Every time you take care of your husband and serve him, then you come closer to his heart; as most husbands see in their wife's serving of them a display of love. So do not be careless of your obligations towards him and be diligent concerning that which he asks of you.

5. Know that your husband's ability to earn money has limits; so be contented with a little and do not ask from him that which he cannot give by demanding that which is above his ability. As by that you will cause him and the entire family to fall into debt. And even if your husband is from the wealthiest of people- then excessiveness in clothing and furnishings is a disliked and hated matter which it is not proper for a sensible woman to enter into. And the only people who want to buy everything they want are the children.

6. Meet your husband when he returns from work smiling and beautified in your hair, clothing, appearance and scent. And if he is carrying some purchases then take them from him and help him.
7. Do not immediately inform him of your problems and the children's problems or begin by complaining; for the worries of his work that he is exposed to all day are enough for him. So if you come and add onto those things which worry him, then it is only you who will have to bear the results if he is angered. Because of this, it is upon you to bring about the atmosphere which is needed by a man who works for an extended time in a society full of problems, contradictions and surprises such as our society.
8. Discuss your problems with your husband alone, without the presence of any of the children or family or friends.
9. Your respect and good treatment towards your husband's family is respect and good treatment of your husband.
10. Always guard the cleanliness of your teeth and the pleasant scent of your mouth, and always pay attention to it.
11. You are the mistress of the house and its caretaker, so shoulder your responsibilities in a trustworthy manner, and take care of the furnishings of the house and its contents without being excessive in spending in this regard, or being miserly concerning it.
12. Indeed the right of the husband having a degree over you is a right given to him by Allaah. So do not demand equality like the Western woman. Rather, demand fair treatment and that you are given your rights which Allaah has granted you.
13. Do not leave the house often, and do not leave it when your husband does not wish that you do so.
14. Do not speak with a strange man or one who is not one of your *mahram*, except if your husband gives permission to you and you fulfill the conditions of the Islamic legislation which are well known.
15. If you go out with your husband to the market or to visit, then do not walk in front of him.
16. Do not spread the secrets of that which happens (in the household), as that is a great sin.
17. Do not speak with your husband or discuss matters with him if he does not want to talk, and beware of talking back to him in a disrespectful manner, for that is an evil custom.
18. If your husband speaks, then listen well to him.
19. When your husband is absent, then guard his wealth, children and house, as well as yourself.
20. Try not to let your husband see you except when you have a beautiful appearance and clean clothes, and are beautified.
21. Do not shy away from showing your husband your love for him, for this is from that which will bring him closer to you and the house and the family, in a time when affairs outside of the house are common.
22. Accept that which your husband provides for you and for the household with thankfulness and gratitude, not with ungratefulness and disdain.

23. If one of your husband's friends asks you about him, then do not lengthen your speech with him, and only answer that which is necessary from his questions.

24. Do not lend anyone anything from the house except with the agreement of your husband.

25. If your husband swears that you will do something, then it is not legislated that you do anything except fulfill his oath.

26. Do not abandon your husband's bed no matter what the reason is which makes you wish to do this.

These are general principles which are built upon many evidences from the Book and the Sunnah. If the man and woman carry them out, then that is a way for them to build the righteous family whose pillars are love and whose foundation is happiness.

(Vol. 3, 15 Sha'baan, 1413, Pages 44-46)

Review and Discussion Questions

Discussion & Consideration:

1. List five things that your husband does that help to make your marriage a successful one.
2. List five things that you do to help make your marriage a successful one.
3. List five things that you would recommend that your husband do to make the marriage more successful.
4. List five things that you could do to make your marriage more successful.
5. What are ten ways that the husband and wife can work together to have a happy home and family life, and to make their homes those in which Islaam is both learned, and lived every day? Mark two of these to begin working on immediately.

Nakhlah
EDUCATIONAL SERIES™

Publishers Addendum:

The Nakhlah Educational Series: Mission and Methodology

Mission

The Purpose of the 'Nakhlah Educational Series' is to contribute to the present knowledge based efforts which enable Muslim individuals, families, and communities to understand and learn Islaam and then to develop within and truly live Islaam. Our commitment and goal is to contribute beneficial publications and works that:

Firstly, reflect the priority, message and methodology of all the prophets and messengers sent to humanity, meaning that single revealed message which embodies the very purpose of life, and of human creation. As Allaah the Most High has said,

﴿ ***We sent a Messenger to every nation ordering them that they should worship Allaah alone, obey Him and make their worship purely for Him, and that they should avoid everything worshipped besides Allaah. So from them there were those whom Allaah guided to His religion, and there were those who were unbelievers for whom misguidance was ordained. So travel through the land and see the destruction that befell those who denied the Messengers and disbelieved.*** ﴾–(Surah an-Nahl: 36)

Sheikh Rabee'a ibn Haadee al-Madkhalee in his work entitled, '*The Methodology of the Prophets in Calling to Allaah, That is the Way of Wisdom and Intelligence.*' explains the essential, enduring message of all the prophets:

"So what was the message which these noble, chosen men, may Allaah's praises and salutations of peace be upon them all, brought to their people? Indeed their mission encompassed every matter of good and distanced and restrained every matter of evil. They brought forth to mankind everything needed for their well-being and happiness in this world and the Hereafter. There is nothing good except that they guided the people towards it, and nothing evil except that they warned the people against it. ...

This was the message found with all of the Messengers; that they should guide to every good and warn against every evil. However where did they start, what did they begin with and what did they concentrate upon? There are a number of essentials, basic principles, and fundamentals which all their calls were founded upon, and which were the starting point for calling the people to Allaah. These fundamental points and principles are: 1. The worship of Allaah alone without any associates 2. The sending of prophets to guide creation 3. The belief in the resurrection and the life of the Hereafter

These three principles are the area of commonality and unity within their calls, and stand as the fundamental principles which they were established upon. These principles are given the greatest importance in the Qur'an and are fully explained in it. They are also its most important purpose upon which it centers and which it continually mentions. It further quotes intellectual and observable proofs for them in all its chapters as well as within most of its accounts of previous nations and given examples. This is known to those who have full understanding, and are able to consider carefully and comprehend well. All the Books revealed by Allaah have given great importance to these points and all of the various revealed laws of guidance are agreed upon them. And the most important and sublime of these three principles, and the most fundamental of them all is directing one's worship only towards Allaah alone, the Blessed and the Most High."

Today one finds that there are indeed many paths, groups, and organizations apparently presenting themselves as representing Islaam, which struggle to put forth an outwardly pleasing appearance to the general Muslims; but when their methods are placed upon the precise scale of conforming to priorities and methodology of the message of the prophets sent by Allaah, they can only be recognized as deficient paths- not simply in practice but in principle- leading not to success but rather only to inevitable failure. As Sheikh Saaleh al-Fauzaan, may Allaah preserve him, states in his introduction to the same above mentioned work on the methodology of all the prophets,

"So whichever call is not built upon these foundations, and whatever methodology is not from the methodology of the Messengers - then it will be frustrated and fail, and it will be effort and toil without any benefit. The clearest proofs of this are those present day groups and organizations which set out a methodology and program for themselves and their efforts of calling the people to Islaam which is different from the methodology of the Messengers. These groups have neglected the importance of the people having the correct belief and creed - except for a very few of them - and instead call for the correction of side-issues."

There can be no true success in any form for us as individuals, families, or larger communities without making the encompassing worship of Allaah alone, with no partners or associates, the very and only foundation of our lives. It is necessary that each individual knowingly choose to base his life upon that same foundation taught by all the prophets and messengers sent by the Lord of all the worlds, rather than simply delving into the assorted secondary concerns and issues invited to by the various numerous parties, innovated movements, and groups. Indeed Sheikh al-Albaanee, may Allaah have mercy upon him, stated:

"... We unreservedly combat against this way of having various different parties and groups. As this false way- of group or organizational allegiances - conforms to the statement of Allaah the Most High, ﴿ ***But they have broken their religion among them into sects, each group rejoicing in what is with it as its beliefs. And every party is pleased with whatever they stand with.*** ﴾*–(Surah al-Mu'minoon: 53) And in truth they are no separate groups and parties in Islaam itself. There is only one true party, as is stated in a verse in the Qur'an, "*﴿ ***Verily, it is the party of Allaah that will be the successful.*** ﴾*–(Surah al-Mujadilaah: 58). The party of Allaah are those people who stand with the Messenger of Allaah, may Allaah's praise and salutations be upon him, meaning that an individual proceeds upon the methodology of the Companions of the Messenger. Due to this we call for having sound knowledge of the Book and the Sunnah."*

(Knowledge Based Issues & Sharee'ah Rulings: The Rulings of The Guiding Scholar Sheikh Muhammad Naasiruddeen al-Albaanee Made in the City of Medina & In the Emirates – [Emiratee Fatwa no 114. P.30])

Two Essential Foundations

Secondly, building upon the above foundation, our commitment is to contributing publications and works which reflect the inherited message and methodology of the acknowledged scholars of the many various branches of Sharee'ah knowledge who stood upon the straight path of preserved guidance in every century and time since the time of our Messenger, may Allaah's praise and salutations be upon him. These people of knowledge, who are the inheritors of the Final Messenger, have always adhered closely to the two revealed sources of guidance: the Book of Allaah and the Sunnah of the Messenger of Allaah- may Allaah's praise and salutations be upon him, upon the united consensus, standing with the body of guided Muslims in every century - preserving and transmitting the true religion generation after generation. Indeed the Messenger of Allaah, may Allaah's praise and salutations be upon him, informed us that,

{ A group of people amongst my Ummah will remain obedient to Allaah's orders. They will not be harmed by those who leave them nor by those who oppose them, until Allaah's command for the Last Day comes upon them while they remain on the right path. } (Authentically narrated in Saheeh al-Bukhaaree).

We live in an age in which the question frequently asked is, "*How do we make Islaam a reality?*" and perhaps the related and more fundamental question is, "*What is Islaam?*", such that innumerable different voices quickly stand to offer countless different conflicting answers through books, lectures, and every available form of modern media. Yet the only true course of properly understanding this question and its answer- for ourselves and our families -is to return to the criterion given to us by our beloved Messenger, may Allaah's praise and salutations be upon him. Indeed the Messenger of Allaah, may Allaah's praise and salutations be upon him, indicated in an authentic narration, clarifying the matter beyond doubt, that the only "Islaam" which enables one to be truly successful and saved in this world and the next is as he said, ***{...that which I am upon and my Companions are upon today.}*** (authentically narrated in Jaam'ca at-Tirmidhee) referring to that Islaam which was stands upon unchanging revealed knowledge. While every other changed and altered form of Islaam, whether through some form of extremism or negligence, or through the addition or removal of something, regardless of whether that came from a good intention or an evil one- is not the religion that Allaah informed us about of when He revealed, ﴾ ***This day, those who disbelieved have given up all hope of your religion; so fear them not, but fear Me. This day, I have perfected your religion for you, completed My Favor upon you, and have chosen for you Islaam as your religion.*** ﴿– (Surah al-Maa'edah: 3)

The guiding scholar Sheikh al-Albaanee, may have mercy upon him, said,

"...And specifically mentioning those among the callers who have taken upon themselves the guiding of the young Muslim generation upon Islaam, working to educate them with its education, and to socialize them with its culture. Yet they themselves have generally not attempted to unify their understanding of those matters about Islaam regarding which the people of Islaam today differ about so severely. And the situation is certainly not as is falsely supposed by some individuals from among them who are heedless or negligent - that the differences that exist among them are only in secondary matters without entering into or affecting the fundamental issues or principles of the religion; and the examples to prove that this is not true are numerous and recognized by those who have studied the books of the many differing groups and sects, or by the one who has knowledge of the various differing concepts and beliefs held by the Muslims today."

(Mukhtasir al-'Uloo Lil'Alee al-Ghafaar, page 55)

Similarly he, may Allaah have mercy upon him, explained:

"Indeed, Islaam is the only solution, and this statement is something which the various different Islamic groups, organizations, and movements could never disagree about. And this is something which is from the blessings of Allaah upon the Muslims. However there are significant differences between the different Islamic groups, organizations, and movements that are present today regarding that domain which working within will bring about our rectification. What is that area of work to endeavor within, striving to restore a way of life truly reflecting Islaam, renewing that system of living which comes from Islaam, and in order to establish the Islamic government? The groups and movements significantly differ upon this issue or point. Yet we hold that it is required to begin with the matters of tasfeeyah –clarification, and tarbeeyah -education and cultivation, with both of them being undertaken together.

As if we were to start with the issue of governing and politics, then it has been seen that those who occupy themselves with this focus firstly posses beliefs which are clearly corrupted and ruined, and secondly that their personal behavior, from the aspect of conforming to Islaam, is very far from conforming to the actual guidance of the Shareeʾah. While those who first concern themselves with working just to unite the people and gather the masses together under a broad banner of the general term "Islaam", then it is seen that within the minds of those speakers who raise such calls -in reality there is fact no actual clear understanding of what Islaam is. Moreover, the understanding they have of Islaam has no significant impact in starting to change and reform their own lives. Due to this reason you find that many such individuals from here and there, who hold this perspective, are unable to truly realize or reflect Islaam even in areas of their own personal lives in matters which it is in fact easily possible for them to implement. As he holds that no one - regardless of whether it is because of his arrogance or pridefulness - can enter into directing him in an area of his personal life!

Yet at the same time these same individuals are raising their voices saying, "Judgment is only for Allaah!" and "It is required that judgment of affairs be according to what Allaah revealed." And this is indeed a true statement. But the one who does not possess something certainly cannot give or offer it to others. The majority of Muslims today have not established the judgment of Allaah fully upon themselves, yet they still seek from others to establish the judgment of Allaah within their governments...

...And I understand that this issue or subject is not immune from there being those who oppose our methodology of tasfeeyah and tarbeeyah. As there is the one who would say, "But establishing this tasfeeyah and tarbeeyah is a matter which requires many long years!" So, I respond by saying, this is not an important consideration in this matter, what is important is that we carry out what we have been commanded to do within our religion and by our Mighty Lord. What is important is that we begin by properly understanding our religion first and foremost. After this is accomplished then it will not be important whether the road itself is long or short.

And indeed I direct this statement of mine towards those men who are callers to the religion among the Muslims, and towards the scholars and those who direct our affairs. I call for them to stand upon complete knowledge of true Islaam, and to fight against every form of negligence and heedlessness regarding the religion, and against differing and disputes, as Allaah has said, ﴾***...and do not dispute with one another for fear that you lose courage and your strength departs***﴿*–(Surah Al-Anfaal: 46).*

(Quoted from the work, 'The Life of Sheikh al-Albaanee, His Influence in Present Day Fields of Shareeʾah Knowledge, & the Praise of the Scholars for Him.' volume 1 page 380-385)

The guiding scholar Sheikh Zayd al-Madkhalee, may Allaah protect him, stated in his writing, 'The Well Established Principles of the Way of the First Generations of Muslims: It's Enduring & Excellent Distinct Characteristics' that,

"From among these principles and characteristics is that the methodology of tasfeeyah -or clarification, and tarbeeyah -or education and cultivation- is clearly affirmed and established as a true way coming from the first three generations of Islaam, and is something well known to the people of true merit from among them, as is concluded by considering all the related evidence. What is intended by tasfeeyah, when referring to it generally, is clarifying that which is the truth from that which is falsehood, what is goodness from that which is harmful and corrupt, and when referring to its specific meanings it is distinguishing the noble Sunnah of the Prophet and the people of the Sunnah from those innovated matters brought into the religion and the people who are supporters of such innovations.

As for what is intended by tarbeeyah, it is calling all of the creation to take on the manners and embrace the excellent character invited to by that guidance revealed to them by their Lord through His worshiper and Messenger Muhammad, may Allaah's praise and salutations be upon him; so that they might have good character, manners, and behavior. As without this they cannot have a good life, nor can they put right their present condition or their final destination. And we seek refuge in Allaah from the evil of not being able to achieve that rectification."

Thus the methodology of the people of standing upon the Prophet's Sunnah, and proceeding upon the 'way of the believers' in every century is reflected in a focus and concern with these two essential matters: tasfeeyah or clarification of what is original, revealed message from the Lord of all the worlds, and tarbeeyah or education and raising of ourselves, our families, and our communities, and our lands upon what has been distinguished to be that true message and path.

Methodology:

The Roles of the Scholars & General Muslims In Raising the New Generation

The priority and focus of the 'Nakhlah Educational Series' is reflected within in the following statements of Sheikh al-Albaanee, may Allaah have mercy upon him:

"As for the other obligation, then I intend by this the education of the young generation upon Islaam purified from all of those impurities we have mentioned, giving them a correct Islamic education from their very earliest years, without any influence of a foreign, disbelieving education."

(Silsilat al-Hadeeth ad-Da'eefah, Introduction page 2.)

"...And since the Messenger of Allaah, may Allaah's praise and salutations be upon him, has indicated that the only cure to remove this state of humiliation that we find ourselves entrenched within, is truly returning back to the religion. Then it is clearly obligatory upon us - through the people of knowledge- to correctly and properly understand the religion in a way that conforms to the sources of the Book of Allaah and the Sunnah, and that we educate and raise a new virtuous, righteous generation upon this."

(Clarification and Cultivation and the Need of the Muslims for Them)

It is essential in discussing our perspective upon this obligation of raising the new generation of Muslims, that we highlight and bring attention to a required pillar of these efforts as indicated by Sheikh al-Albaanee, may Allaah have mercy upon him, and others- in the golden words, "*through the people of knowledge*". Since something we commonly experience today is that many people have various incorrect understandings of the role that the scholars should have in the life of a Muslim, failing to understand the way in which they fulfill their position as the inheritors of the Messenger of Allaah, may Allaah's praise and salutations be upon him, and stand as those who preserve and enable us to practice the guidance of Islaam. Indeed, the noble Imaam Sheikh as-Sa'dee, may Allaah have mercy upon him, in his work, *"A Definitive and Clear Explanation of the Work 'A Triumph for the Saved Sect'"* pages 237-240, has explained this crucial issue with an extraordinary explanation full of remarkable benefits:

"Section: Explaining the Conditions for These Two Source Texts to Suffice You -or the Finding of Sufficiency in these Two Sources of Revelation.

Overall the conditions needed to achieve this and bring it about return to two matters:

Firstly, the presence of the requirements necessary for achieving this; meaning a complete devotion to the Book and the Sunnah, and the putting forth of efforts both in seeking to understand their intended meanings, as well as in striving to be guided by them. What is required secondly is the pushing away of everything which prevents achieving this finding of sufficiency in them.

This is through having a firm determination to distance yourself from everything which contradicts these two source texts in what comes from the historical schools of jurisprudence, assorted various statements, differing principles and their resulting conclusions which the majority of people proceed upon. These matters which contradict the two sources of revelation include many affairs which, when the worshiper of Allaah repels them from himself and stands against them, the realm of his knowledge, understanding, and deeds then expands greatly. Through a devotion to them and a complete dedication towards these two sources of revelation, proceeding upon every path which assists one's understanding them, and receiving enlightenment from the light of the scholars and being guided by the guidance that they possess- you will achieve that complete sufficiency in them. And surely, in the positions they take towards the leading people of knowledge and the scholars, the people are three types of individuals:

The first of them is the one who goes to extremes in his attachment to the scholars. He makes their statements something which are infallible as if their words held the same position as those of the statements of the Messenger of Allaah, may Allaah's praise and salutations be upon him, as well as giving those scholars' statements precedence and predominance over the Book of Allaah and the Sunnah. This is despite the fact that every leading scholar who has been accepted by this Ummah was one who promoted and encouraged the following of the Book and the Sunnah, commanding the people not to follow their own statements nor their school of thought in anything which stood in opposition to the Book of Allaah and the Sunnah.

The second type is the one who generally rejects and invalidates the statements of the scholars and forbids the referring to the statements of the leading scholars of guidance and those people of knowledge who stand as brilliant lamps in the darkness. This type of person neither relies upon the light of discernment with the scholars, nor utilizes their stores of knowledge. Or even if perhaps they do so, they do not direct thanks towards them for this. And this manner and way prohibits them from tremendous good. Furthermore, that which motivates such individuals to proceed in this way is their falsely supposing that the obligation to follow the Messenger of Allaah, may Allaah's praise and salutations be upon him, and the giving of precedence to his statements over the statements of anyone else, requires that they do without any reliance upon the statements of the Companions, or those who followed them in goodness, or those leading scholars of guidance within the Ummah. And this is a glaring and extraordinary mistake.

As indeed the Companions and the people of knowledge are the means and the agency between the Messenger of Allaah, may Allaah's praise and salutations be upon him, and his Ummah- in the transmission and spreading his Sunnah in regard to both its wording and texts as well as its meanings and understanding. Therefore the one who follows them in what they convey in this is guided through their understandings, receives knowledge from the light they possess, benefits from the conclusions they have derived from these sources -of beneficial meanings and explanations, as well as in relation to subtle matters which scarcely occur to the minds of some of the other people of knowledge, or barely comes to be discerned by their minds. Consequently, from the blessing of Allaah upon this Ummah is that He has given them these guiding scholars who cultivate and educate them upon two clear types of excellent cultivation.

The first category is education from the direction of ones knowledge and understanding. They educate the Ummah upon the more essential and fundamental matters before the more complex affairs. They convey the meanings of the Book and the Sunnah to the minds and intellects of the people through efforts of teaching which rectifies, and through composing various beneficial books of knowledge which a worshiper doesn't even have the ability to adequately describe what is encompassed within them of aspects of knowledge and benefits. Works which reflect the presence of a clear white hand in deriving guidance from the Book of Allaah and the Sunnah, and through the arrangement, detailed clarification, division and explanation, through the gathering together of explanations, comparisons, conditions, pillars, and explanations about that which prevents the fulfillment of matters, as well as distinguishing between differing meanings and categorizing various knowledge based benefits.

The second category is education from the direction of ones conduct and actions. They cultivate the peoples characters encouraging them towards every praiseworthy aspect of good character, through explaining its ruling and high status, and what benefits comes to be realized from it, clarifying the reasons and paths which enable one to attain it, as well as those affairs which prevent, delay or hinder someone becoming one distinguished and characterized by it. Because they, in reality, are those who bring nourishment to the hearts and the souls; they are the doctors who treat the diseases of the heart and its defects. As such they educate the people through their statements, actions as well as their general guided way. Therefore the scholars have a tremendous right over this Ummah. The portion of love and esteem, respect and honor, and thanks due to them because their merits and their various good efforts stand above every other right after establishing the right of Allaah, and the right of His Messenger, may Allaah's praise and salutations be upon him.

Because of this, the third group of individuals in respect to the scholars are those who have been guided to understand their true role and position, and establish their rights, thanking them for their virtues and merits, benefiting by taking from the knowledge they have, while acknowledging their rank and status. They understand that the scholars are not infallible and that their statements must stand in conformance to the statements of the Messenger of Allaah, may Allaah's praise and salutations be upon him. And that each one from among them has that which is from guidance, knowledge, and correctness in his statements taken and benefited from, while turning away from whatever in mistaken within it.

Yet such a scholar is not to be belittled for his mistake, as he stands as one who strove to reach the truth; therefore his mistake will be forgiven, and he should be thanked for his efforts. One clarifies what was stated by of any one of these leaders from among men, when it is recognizes that it has some weakness or conflict to an evidence of the Sharee'ah, by explaining its weakness and the level of that weakness, without speaking evilly of the intention of those people of knowledge and religion, nor defaming them due to that error. Rather we say, as it is obligatory to say, "And those who came after them say: ﴿ ***Our Lord! forgive us and our brethren who have preceded us in faith, and put not in our hearts any hatred against those who have believed. Our Lord! You are indeed full of kindness, Most Merciful.*** ﴾ *-(Surah al-Hashr: 10).*

Accordingly, individuals of this third type are those who fulfill two different matters. They join together on one hand between giving precedence to the Book and the Sunnah over everything else, and, on the other hand, between comprehending the level and position of the scholars and the leading people of knowledge and guidance, and establishing this even if it is only done in regard to some of their rights upon us. So we ask Allaah to bless us to be from this type, and to make us from among the people of this third type, and to make us from those who love Him and love those who love Him, and those who love every action which brings us closer to everything He loves."

Upon this clarity regarding the proper understanding of our balanced position towards our guided Muslim scholars, consider the following words about the realm of work of the general people of faith, which explains our area of efforts and struggle as Muslim parents, found in the following statement by Sheikh Saaleh Fauzaan al-Fauzaan, may Allaah preserve him.

"Question: Some people mistakenly believe that calling to Allaah is a matter not to be undertaken by anyone else other than the scholars without exception, and that it is not something required for other than the scholars according to that which they have knowledge of -to undertake any efforts of calling the people to Allaah. So what is your esteemed guidance regarding this?" The Sheikh responded by saying:

"This is not a misconception, but is in fact a reality. The call to Allaah cannot be established except through those who are scholars. And I state this. Yet, certainly there are clear issues which every person understands. As such, every individual should enjoin the good and forbid wrongdoing according to the level of his understanding. Such that he instructs and orders the members of his household to perform the ritual daily prayers and other matters that are clear and well known.

Undertaking this is something mandatory and required even upon the common people, such that they must command their children to perform their prayers in the masjid. The Messenger of Allaah, may Allaah praise and salutations be upon him, said, **{ Command you children to pray at seven, and beat them due to its negligence at ten.}** *(Authentic narration found in Sunan Abu Dawood). And the Messenger of Allaah, may Allaah praise and salutations be upon him, said,* **{ Each one of you is a guardian or a shepherd, and each of you is responsible for those under his guardianship....}** *(Authentic narration found in Saheeh al-Bukhaaree). So this is called guardianship, and this is also called enjoining the good and forbidding wrongdoing. The Messenger of Allaah, may Allaah praise and salutations be upon him, said,* **{ The one from among you who sees a wrong should change it with his hand, and if he is unable to do so, then with his tongue, and if he is not able to do this, then with his heart. }** *(Authentic narration found in Saheeh Muslim).*

So in relation to the common person, that which it is required from him to endeavor upon is that he commands the members of his household-as well as others -with the proper performance of the ritual prayers, the obligatory charity, with generally striving to obey Allaah, and to stay away from sins and transgressions, and that he purify and cleanse his home from disobedience, and that he educate and cultivate his children upon the obedience of Allaah's commands. This is what is required from him, even if he is a general person. As these types of matters are from that which is understood by every single person. This is something which is clear and apparent.

But as for the matters of putting forth rulings and judgments regarding matters in the religion, or entering into clarifying issues of what is permissible and what is forbidden, or explaining what is considered associating others in the worship due to Allaah and what is properly worshiping Him alone without any partner- then indeed these are matters which cannot be established except by the scholars"

(Beneficial Responses to Questions About Modern Methodologies, Question 15, page 22)

Similarly the guiding scholar Sheikh 'Abdul-'Azeez Ibn Baaz, may Allaah have mercy upon him, also emphasized this same overall responsibility:

"...It is also upon a Muslim that he struggles diligently in that which will place his worldly affairs in a good state, just as he must also strive in the correcting of his religious affairs and the affairs of his own family. As the people of his household have a significant right over him that he strive diligently in rectifying their affair and guiding them towards goodness, due to the statement of Allaah, the Most Exalted, ﴾ **Oh you who believe! Save yourselves and your families Hellfire whose fuel is men and stones** ﴿ *-(Surah at-Tahreem: 6)*

So it is upon you to strive to correct the affairs of the members of your family. This includes your wife, your children- both male and female- and such as your own brothers. This concerns all of the people in your family, meaning you should strive to teach them the religion, guiding and directing them, and warning them from those matters Allaah has prohibited for us. Because you are the one who is responsible for them as shown in the statement of the Prophet, may Allaah's praise and salutations be upon him, ***{ Every one of you is a guardian, and responsible for what is in his custody. The ruler is a guardian of his subjects and responsible for them; a husband is a guardian of his family and is responsible for it; a lady is a guardian of her husband's house and is responsible for it, and a servant is a guardian of his master's property and is responsible for it....}*** *Then the Messenger of Allaah, may Allaah's praise and salutations be upon him, continued to say,* ***{...so all of you are guardians and are responsible for those under your authority.}*** *(Authentically narrated in Saheeh al-Bukhaaree & Muslim)*

It is upon us to strive diligently in correcting the affairs of the members of our families, from the aspect of purifying their sincerity of intention for Allaah's sake alone in all of their deeds, and ensuring that they truthfully believe in and follow the Messenger of Allaah, may Allaah's praise and salutations be upon him, their fulfilling the prayer and the other obligations which Allaah the Most Exalted has commanded for us, as well as from the direction of distancing them from everything which Allaah has prohibited.

It is upon every single man and women to give advice to their families about the fulfillment of what is obligatory upon them. Certainly, it is upon the woman as well as upon the man to perform this. In this way our homes become corrected and rectified in regard to the most important and essential matters. Allaah said to His Prophet, may Allaah's praise and salutations be upon him, ﴾ **And enjoin the ritual prayers on your family...** ﴿ *(Surah Taha: 132) Similarly, Allaah the Most Exalted said to His prophet Ismaa'aeel,* ﴾ **And mention in the Book, Ismaa'aeel. Verily, he was true to what he promised, and he was a Messenger, and a Prophet. And he used to enjoin on his family and his people the ritual prayers and the obligatory charity, and his Lord was pleased with him.** ﴿ *-(Surah Maryam: 54-55)*

As such, it is only proper that we model ourselves after the prophets and the best of people, and be concerned with the state of the members of our households. Do not be neglectful of them, oh worshipper of Allaah! Regardless of whether it is concerning your wife, your mother, father, grandfather, grandmother, your brothers, or your children; it is upon you to strive diligently in correcting their state and condition..."

(Collection of Various Rulings and Statements- Sheikh 'Abdul-'Azeez Ibn 'Abdullah Ibn Baaz, Vol. 6, page 47)

Content & Structure:

We hope to contribute works which enable every striving Muslim who acknowledges the proper position of the scholars, to fulfill the recognized duty and obligation which lays upon each one of us to bring the light of Islaam into our own lives as individuals as well as into our homes and among our families. Towards this goal we are committed to developing educational publications and comprehensive educational curriculums -through cooperation with and based upon the works of the scholars of Islaam and the students of knowledge. Works which, with the assistance of Allaah, the Most High, we can utilize to educate and instruct ourselves, our families and our communities upon Islaam in both principle and practice. The publications and works of the Nakhlah Educational Series are divided into the following categories:

Basic: Ages 4- 6

Elementary: Ages 6-11

Secondary: Ages 11-14

High School: Ages 14- Young Adult

General: Young Adult –Adult

Supplementary: All Ages

Publications and works within these stated levels will, with the permission of Allaah, encompass different beneficial areas and subjects, and will be offered in every permissible form of media and medium. As certainly, as the guiding scholar Sheikh Saaleh Fauzaan al-Fauzaan, may Allaah preserve him, has stated,

"Beneficial knowledge is itself divided into two categories. Firstly is that knowledge which is tremendous in its benefit, as it benefits in this world and continues to benefit in the Hereafter. This is religious Sharee'ah knowledge. And secondly, that which is limited and restricted to matters related to the life of this world, such as learning the processes of manufacturing various goods. This is a category of knowledge related specifically to worldly affairs.

...As for the learning of worldly knowledge, such as knowledge of manufacturing, then it is legislated upon us collectively to learn whatever the Muslims have a need for. Yet If they do not have a need for this knowledge, then learning it is a neutral matter upon the condition that it does not compete with or displace any areas of Sharee'ah knowledge..."

("Explanations of the Mistakes of Some Writers", Pages 10-12)

So we strive always to remind ourselves and our brothers of this crucial point also indicated by Sheikh Sadeeq Ibn Hasan al-Qanoojee, may Allaah have mercy upon him, in: '*Abjad al-'Uloom*', (page 89)

"... What is intended by knowledge in the mentioned hadeeth is knowledge of the religion and the distinctive Sharee'ah, knowledge of the Noble Book and the Pure Sunnah, of which there is no third along with them. But what is not meant in this narration are those invented areas of knowledge, whether they emerged in previous ages or today's world, which the people in these present times have devoted themselves to. They have specifically dedicated themselves to them in a manner which prevents them from looking towards those areas of knowledge related to faith, and in a way which has preoccupied them from occupying themselves from what is actually wanted or desired by Allaah, the Most High, and His Messenger, who is the leader of men and Jinn. Such that the knowledge in the Qur'an has become something abandoned and the sciences of hadeeth have become obscure. While these new areas of knowledge related to manufacturing and production continually emerge from the nations of disbelief and apostasy, and they are called, "sciences", "arts", and "ideal development". And this sad state increases every day, indeed from Allaah we came and to Him shall we return....

...Additionally, although the various areas of beneficial knowledge all share some level of value, they all have differing importance and ranks. Among them is that which is to be considered according to its subject, such as medicine, and its subject is the human body. Or such as the sciences of 'tafseer' and its subject is the explanation of the words of Allaah, the Most Exalted and Most High, and the value of these two areas is not in any way unrecognized.

And from among the various areas there are those areas which are considered according to their objective, such as knowledge of upright character, and its goal is understanding the beneficial merits that an individual can come to possess. And from among them there are those areas which are considered according to the people's need for them, such as 'fiqh' which the need for it is urgent and essential. And from among them there are those areas which are considered according to their apparent strength, such as knowledge of physical sports and exercise, as it is something openly demonstrated.

And from the areas of knowledge are those areas which rise in their position of importance through their combining all these different matters within them, or the majority of them. Such as revealed religious knowledge, as its subject is indeed esteemed, its objective one of true merit, and its need is undeniably felt. Likewise one area of knowledge may be considered of superior rank than another in consideration of the results that it brings forth, or the strength of its outward manifestation, or due to the essentialness of its objective. Similarly the result that an area produces is certainly of higher estimation and significance in appraisal than the outward or apparent significance of some other areas of knowledge.

For that reason the highest ranking and most valuable area of knowledge is that of knowledge of Allaah the Most Perfect and the Most High, of His angels, and messengers, and all the particulars of these beliefs, as its result is that of eternal and continuing happiness."

We ask Allaah, the most High to bless us with success in contributing to the many efforts of our Muslim brothers and sisters committed to raising themselves as individuals and the next generation of our children upon that Islaam which Allaah has perfected and chosen for us, and which He has enabled the guided Muslims to proceed upon in each and every century. We ask him to forgive us, and forgive the Muslim men and the Muslim women, and to guide all the believers to everything He loves and is pleased with. The success is from Allaah, The Most High The Most Exalted, alone and all praise is due to Him.

Abu Sukhailah Khalil Ibn-Abelahyi
Taalib al-Ilm Educational Resources

Fundamentals of Arabic Class for Women Only

An Online Class for Muslim Women Taught by a Muslim Woman

Developed and Taught by Umm Mujaahid Khadijah Bint Lacina al-Amreekiyyah

[Available: **TBA**¦ Schedule: **Live Class Three times Weekly** ¦ price: **$60 Monthly** USD]

Course Includes All Materials In EBook Format

Course Features:

* Four Levels of Study & Supplementary Courses
* Limited class size
* Class meets online three times a week with the teacher
* Class moves at a moderate pace to ensure understanding of the concepts presented
* Begins with a short review of the Arabic alphabet, stressing correct pronunciation
* Grammar, morphology, and writing fundamentals
* Focus on understanding what is read and spoken
* Encompasses both speech and understanding
* Numerous exercises, both in class and out, to increase understanding and ability
* Practice in taking notes from Arabic lectures and simple translation
* Additional Out of class assignments and group projects
* Comprehensive reviews
* Periodic quizzes and tests
* End of class test will determine if one can advance to the next class
* Textbooks, dictionaries, and supplementary materials provided as ebooks
* Use of hadeeth texts and other Islamic material for reading, understanding and translation exercises
* Class forum to make asking questions and doing group assignments easier
* The teacher will be available through email to answer course questions and assist the students regularly

For more information about availability please visit

arabicforwomen.taalib.com

Please visit ***study.taalib.com*** *for information concerning other free and fee-based courses.*